W9-ARZ-589

THE SYNERGISM HYPOTHESIS

THE SYNERGISM HYPOTHESIS

A Theory of Progressive Evolution

PETER A. CORNING

McGraw-Hill Book Company
New York/St. Louis/San Francisco/Auckland/Bogotá/Guatemala/
Hamburg/Johannesburg/Lisbon/London/Madrid/Mexico/
Montreal/New Delhi/Panama/Paris/San Juan/São Paulo/
Singapore/Sydney/Tokyo/Toronto

First McGraw-Hill Paperback edition, 1983

1 2 3 4 5 6 7 8 9 DOCDOC 0 8 7 6 5 4 3

ISBN 0-07-013166-X {H.C.}
0-07-013172-4 {PBK.}

LIBRARY OF CONGRESS CATALOGING IN PUBLICATION DATA
Corning, Peter A., 1935–
The synergism hypothesis.
Includes bibliographical references and index.
1. Social evolution. 2. Sociobiology.
3. Political science. I. Title.
JC336.C85 1983 306 82-4643
ISBN 0-07-013166-X
ISBN 0-07-013172-4 (pbk.)

Book design by Grace Markman

For Susan
Who knows the price
and fully shared it

Contents

The truth has long been known,
and has been the bond of the wisest spirits.
This old truth—reach for it.

Goethe

Preface

> Anyone whose disposition leads him to attach more weight to unexplained difficulties than to the explanation of a certain number of facts will certainly reject my theory. *Charles Darwin*

Darwin was candid about the limitations of his theory. Indeed he characterized *The Origin of Species* as an abstract, a synopsis of an anticipated larger work that he never got around to writing. (Following the appearance of the book, however, he published five revisions and a number of related works.) I would like to be granted some of the same license. This book represents a progress report on an organic process of intellectual development which began, for me, more than ten years ago. As President Franklin Roosevelt said of the U.S. Social Security system when he signed the original bill into law in 1935, the present work constitutes the scaffolding of a structure that is by no means complete; further development is already in progress.*

My decision to go ahead with publication at this stage is based on the belief that the essential elements of the theory I have developed—the explanatory framework and certain logical deductions (or predictions) that flow from it—are essentially complete and can benefit from being subjected to the discipline of a formal synthesis and published exposition.

However, as was true of Darwin's theory of natural selection, further elucidation of the precise mechanisms underlying this theory will require many more years of research in a number of different disciplines. I believe that

* In fact, the original manuscript for the present work was approximately twice the size of what appears in print. Though the final result is much more readable, many topics are treated in less detail—and with less documentation—than was originally planned. It is anticipated that this material will form part of a subsequent two-volume work. It should also be noted that due to an unexpectedly long period between completion and publication, some sections may already seem somewhat dated.

the theory has been pushed as far as it can legitimately go at this point. I have found that, in pursuing the "deep structure" of human existence, one ultimately becomes entangled in some of the unresolved mysteries that surround the inner core of human nature, the nature of biological purposiveness, the proximate "causes" of human behavior, and the nature of life itself. These are questions that cannot now be answered definitively by scientists, and perhaps they never will be, though we can certainly hope for further progress.

This work is ultimately about the origin and nature of human societies and how they have evolved in the course of what Darwin called the "descent of man" (or what various nineteenth- and twentieth-century writers have perhaps more felicitously characterized as the "ascent of man"). I seek to explain, in accordance with the "rules of the game" of modern science, the significance of social life in general and politics in particular, as well as the process by which sociopolitical forms and practices have developed.

This is no small task. Some social scientists maintain that no general explanatory theory of social life is possible. Robert Nisbet, for one, is vehement on the subject. I believe that it is possible to erect such a theory but that it must necessarily be derived from an integration and synthesis of various partial understandings that exist in both the life sciences and the social sciences. In a way that I did not fully appreciate when I began this adventure but can now see much more clearly, an undertaking such as this must be pandisciplinary. As I have tried to understand and account for the dynamics of sociocultural evolution, I have been led by turns into evolutionary biology, ethology, anthropology, sociology, psychology, ecology, economics, history, and classical social and political thought. (The emergence of sociobiology in the past several years has only expanded an already long shopping list.)

Accordingly, the overall trend of my work has been in the direction of a more inclusive, complex, and interactive view of social causation. The culmination of this growth process is the Interactional Paradigm, which I offer as an analytical framework. This framework will be described in due course, but it is important to emphasize at the outset that one cannot understand culture or its evolution through time without adopting a multidimensional perspective. Crude reductionism and single-factor causal theories are insufficient. As anthropologist Kent Flannery has written, "Civilization is a complex process; single-cause theories, no matter how attractive, are inadequate to explain it."[1]

Nevertheless, the practice continues. Despite a growing body of evidence that simplistic assumptions about the wellsprings of human motivation and action will not suffice to anchor important theoretical structures, no matter how methodologically rigorous they may be, many economists, including even Marxist economists viewing capitalist societies, are still reluctant to abandon the sacred premise of Economic Man, while, at the other extreme, some sociobiologists cling to crudely deterministic models of altruistic and selfish genes. Furthermore, each discipline continues to assert its uniqueness and its own claim to be queen of the social sciences—or, in the case of biology, the claim to have displaced physics as the queen of all the sciences. (One might think that such rhetoric reflects a small symbolic concession to the women's movement, were it not for the fact that the custom dates at least to Aristotle, who first claimed the queenship for politics.)

On the other hand, the past decade has been a time of profound and exciting change in many of the frontier areas of the human sciences. Old paradigms have come under attack and, as many of these older approaches have exhausted their potential for enlightenment, new cross-disciplinary linkages have been made. Some forms of fusion have been easier to make than others: for instance, the growth of evolutionism in anthropology, the rapid development of ecological anthropology, the marriage between political science and economics (political economy), and the even more recent merger of political science and psychology (political psychology).

In the social sciences generally there has also been a salutary pendulum's swing away from the emphasis on macro-level social and economic forces and toward a micro-level focus on the individual and individual choice. I shall argue that it is critically important to stop the pendulum in the middle, to focus on the interaction between micro-level and macro-level causal factors. In fact, one of my central themes is that many of the dualities and paradoxes we observe in social life are in reality inescapable; they are a reflection of contradictory forces inherent in human nature and human existence, and they are capable of being accounted for in a logically consistent way.

Perhaps the most important aspect of the current intellectual climate, though, is a gradual implosion toward an integration among the social and behavioral sciences, even as new specialties continue to proliferate (another duality that is only an apparent contradiction). More exciting still, there is movement toward an integration between the social/behavioral sciences and the biological sciences. As primatologist Vernon Reynolds has observed, "Unfortunately, there is still much competition for 'rightness' of paradigm; one is surrounded by it. But not everyone can have a monopoly of it, and one sees the edges of the old monolithic explanations blur before they crumble."[2]

It is my hope that this book will contribute to the demolition process, not simply in the interest of a reconciliation among academicians, but because of the promise of a theoretically productive synthesis. Thus my primary objective has been to achieve an integration of paradigms, concepts, and data across a number of disciplinary lines. In the process, I have tried to be sensitive to the full richness of human nature and human existence. Though I have ventured, albeit with trepidation, into some arcane and highly specialized research areas and cannot pretend to have mastered the literature completely, I have sought to grasp the essentials and the larger significance of each area for the particular problems with which I am concerned. And I have tried to avoid dilettantism; I have striven to be judicious in making interpretations and sensitive to the uncertainties and controversies that abound in even the most productive research areas. Doubtless there will still be errors of fact or interpretation, but a conscientious effort has been made to minimize such inaccuracies.

Because my approach, in the end, involves some rather different ways of looking at familiar things and seeks to integrate theory and concepts in a manner that may be alien to some of the researchers on whose territory I may tread, I will probably add to the controversy. Yet I have chosen to take the risk of doing some violence to sacred dogmas in the belief that a more coherent and comprehensive framework for understanding humanity and society might thereby result. As George Homans has pointed out, calculated risks are an integral part of scientific progress.

My efforts have culminated in an explicit theory, one which asserts that there is an underlying patterning and logic to societal continuity and change (and to political continuity and change). This theory is at once analogous to the Darwinian theory of biological evolution (properly understood), and it interpenetrates and interacts with that theory. I attempt to develop here a case for this theory, and I propose what I believe are critical areas for further research and testing—thus conforming to Karl Popper's dictum that a scientific theory must be capable of being "falsified."

Accordingly, this work is as much an agenda and a work program as it is a provisional synthesis. There remain many gaps in our knowledge; in some research areas the state of the art is still too primitive to provide us with anything better than informed speculation. There are also many problems of conflicting data and hidden observer biases in the field research on which some theorizing is based. Moreover, many of the relevant research areas are dynamic and likely to continue developing rapidly.

Yet I do not believe that the synthesis attempted here is premature. The distinguished population ecologist Robert H. MacArthur often observed that scientists do not trust theory unconfirmed by facts, but on the other hand they also tend to distrust facts until they are explained by theory. Furthermore, it is generally recognized that, in the words of sociologist Otis Dudley Duncan, "all science proceeds by a selective ordering of data by means of conceptual schemes. Although [their] formulation and application . . . are recognized to entail, at some stage of inquiry, more or less arbitrary choices on the part of the theorist or investigator, we all acknowledge . . . that the nature of the 'real world' exercises strong constraints on the development of [such] schemes in science."[3] The test is whether or not the theory is fruitful, or productive of new understanding.

As a social scientist, I am acutely aware of the potential normative implications of this work; it would be disingenuous to claim otherwise. If nothing else, the reception accorded E. O. Wilson's *Sociobiology* is a reminder of how something done in the spirit of science may nonetheless have deeply threatening ideological and political implications. Darwin himself spoke wistfully of his "fiery ordeal." In this work I address some of the most sensitive issues in political theory: the relationship between social (including altruistic) and egoistic aspects of human behavior, the role of co-operative versus competitive behavior, and the significance of politics in human evolution and contemporary society.

For the record, I have tried to proceed in a spirit of nondogmatic and self-critical eclecticism. As a result, I have come to an understanding of the social and political realm that is, I think, disinterested. I see politics as being full of paradoxes and inescapable contradictions (trade-offs, if you will) which in a given case can be made better or worse—more equitable or more exploitative—but which cannot be eliminated from any form of socially organized society, whether it be a commune or a nation-state; the inevitability of politics (as here defined) is one of the most unequivocal conclusions of this work.

Finally, I see in the present trend of events the hope of a reconciliation and synthesis between reductionist and holistic views of life, between scientific and humanistic ways of understanding "man" (which I use here in the generic sense) and society, and between those who are rightly appalled by some contemporary manifestations of politics and those who would like to believe in the creative potential of politics.

Every writer has some audience in mind, even if only vaguely or subconsciously, as he or she begins to commit words to paper. However, the audience I have tried to address seems to me more than usually amorphous because of the scope of this work and the abandon with which I have crossed the Maginot Lines of the traditional disciplines. In addition, I am conscious of the fact that science can no longer be treated chauvinistically as a predominately American enterprise (if indeed it was ever justified to think so). Thus I have felt as though I were confronted simultaneously with many different kinds of linguistic and cultural barriers (in C. P. Snow's sense of the word).[4]

My response has been to homogenize my audience. In effect, I have attempted as best I could to write a work that would be accessible to a knowledgeable layman, at the risk of trying the patience of those who might already be familiar with most of the concepts and the relevant research literature. More important, I have been guided by the desire to be intelligible rather than obscurantist; I have been mindful of Voltaire's apothegm, "It is with books as with men. A very small number play a great part; the rest are lost in the multitude."

To those who over the years have encouraged and facilitated my pursuit of this work, I offer my intense and lasting gratitude. I am also indebted to the skeptics who have questioned this approach and challenged the assumptions on which it is based. These critics deserve much of the credit, though they may not wish for it, for what I hope will be a more satisfactory synthesis than might have been the case a few years ago. To take some poetic license with a famous bit of Churchillian rhetoric: Seldom in the field of scholarship have so few owed so much to so many.

I would like to single out some of these friends and constructive critics, with my apologies to any who would prefer not to be given credit. (Any blame is mine, of course.) In particular, I would like to thank: Christopher Boehm, Donald Campbell, Robert Carneiro, Kenneth Cooper, James C. Davies, Karl Deutsch, Theodosius Dobzhansky, David Easton, Heiner Flohr, Michael Ghiselin, David Hamburg, Samuel Hines, Ralph Hummel, Nannerl Keohane, Fred Kort, Robert Lane, I. Michael Lerner, Roger Masters, Ernst Mayr, Alan Mazur, S. N. Salthe, Glendon Schubert, John Paul Scott, George Gaylord Simpson, Lionel Tiger, John Wahlke, Elliott White, Thomas Wiegele, Fred Willhoite, Edward O. Wilson, and Sewall Wright. I would like to express special thanks to my one-time mentor and now friend, James C. Crown, whose support for my unconventional intellectual interests literally made it all possible. Financial support and valuable intellectual nurturance were also provided along the way by Gerald McClearn and the staff of the Institute for Behavioral Genetics, by David Hamburg, Donald Kennedy and others (then) of the Human Biology Program at Stanford, by Heinz Eulau, Alexander George, and Robert North of Stanford's Political Science Department, and by the late Bill Linvill, founder and chairman of Stanford's Engineering-Economic Systems Department. The continued support of the new chairman, Dave Luenberger, and the departmental staff over the past two years has been more than generous. A Peace Fellowship from the Hoover Institution at Stanford is also gratefully acknowledged as a valuable source of support at a critical juncture. Several able research assistants have helped materially over the years, including Kate Weber Cook, Anne DeLong, John Hansen, Joe Hardegree, Kathy Hess, Joe Saunders, Jiri Weiss, and Anne Corning. In addition, I owe a special debt to one of the world's great library systems. The wide-ranging support I received from an ever-helpful Stanford Library staff was indispensable and far beyond the call of duty. The patience, good humor, consummate editorial and political skills and, above all, unwavering faith on the part of my editor, Cynthia Merman, also played a vital role, as did the painstaking and meticulous copy editing of Vernon Nahrgang. Most important was the support of my wife, whose many contributions are inadequately acknowledged in the dedication.

I

Introduction: Quo Vadimus?*

Relentlessly accumulating evidence suggests that human life on the planet is headed for a catastrophe. *Charles E. Lindblom*

As our century enters its final quarter, I am not persuaded, despite the signs, that the end is necessarily doom. The doomsayers work by extrapolation; they take a trend and extend it, forgetting that the doom factor sooner or later generates a coping mechanism. . . . History, that is, the human narrative, never follows, and will always fool, the scientific curve. I cannot tell you what twists it will take, but I expect that, like our ancestors, we, too, will muddle through. *Barbara Tuchman*

Politics and Progress

The future remains, as always, problematical and debatable. Yet our current predicament underscores an ancient truth. All humankind and all living species are fellow participants in a three-billion-year-old adventure: the challenge of, and at times the struggle for, survival and the continuity of life.

* The title of my introduction is a play on an academic affectation. Although the practice has recently fallen out of favor, for many years it was customary at academic conferences for the chair, or some other designated person, to present a final summation under the heading, *Quo Vadimus?* (Where do we go from here?). Considering the scope (and the bulk) of this volume, it seemed to me that this might be a good way to begin our journey.

This evolutionary *problèmatique* is the central organizing principle underlying all biological and societal systems—our perceptions, illusions, and aspirations to the contrary notwithstanding—and it is, or it should be, the paradigmatic problem of our social sciences. An organized society is a *collective survival enterprise;* by and large, we are dependent on one another in a myriad of ways, which we often take for granted. Moreover, our evolutionary future always has been, and may always continue to be, contingent; it is not vouchsafed by any law of nature.

In an earlier and more optimistic era, the conventional wisdom of Western society, though never monolithic, was tilted sharply toward the view that material growth and civilizational progress were inherent trends in societal evolution. Indeed, it was a commonplace affectation among nineteenth-century social theorists to posit a universal law of progress; the dogma of progress was the one article of faith on which socialists such as Karl Marx and "liberals" (conservatives) such as Herbert Spencer could all agree. Progress for whom and how best to get there were questions that were hotly disputed.

In the past decade, though, there has emerged a new conventional wisdom, one which asserts that our species is in grave peril. The prophets of this dour vision have become legion, some of the most articulate and effective being scientists who, fired by a sense of urgency, have volunteered to become front-line combatants in the political wars.

Few if any of the scholars who have joined this rising chorus of Cassandras have actually abandoned hope, though some have come close.[1] To the contrary, most of these alarmists believe that their efforts might help induce disaster-averting political and social change. For instance, Charles Lindblom, a longtime exponent of the "muddling through" image employed by Barbara Tuchman, flatly asserts that the outcome of our "survival crisis" is not predetermined and that politics does matter, perhaps decisively so.[2] Nevertheless we have of late become preoccupied with our present peril.

This book runs against the grain. It is a book about evolutionary progress, but it is not about a "law" of progress.* Rather, it is about the causes of progress, both in nature and in human societies. Thus it is also a book about politics, and about the relationship between politics and survival. I shall argue that, for better or worse, politics is central to the survival strategies and actions—or inactions—of organized societies: we are dependent on our political systems. And just as political actions and decisions lay behind such historical landmarks as the Russian Revolution, the New Deal, World War II, and the moon program, so too what might be called the antimatter of politics consists of what we fail to do when both the need and the capabilities exist.

* The term "progress" will be used here in a very special sense.

Nor is the centrality of politics a recent development. As I will use the term, politics is as characteristically a part of the human repertoire as are language and our bipedal gait. What is more, it may be traceable in human evolution to a time long before the emergence of formal, specialized institutions of government. I will even argue that political behaviors are not derivative but may have been a major preadaptation and precipitant for the evolution of language and the explosive flowering of modern cultures, rather than the other way around. In any case, politics has been an integral part of the "progressive" evolution of human societies; it is not even uniquely human.

Although few would contest the obvious importance of politics in contemporary society, it is currently unfashionable to be an unabashed believer. People commonly despair of politics; in addition to the hordes who are politically apathetic, activists of the political left and right alike range in attitude from shrugging off politics as a necessary evil to excoriating it as unmitigated evil. The reasons for this are not hard to find. Everywhere—certainly in Western industrial societies—political systems are hamstrung by obstinate economic and political cleavages, choked by byzantine bureaucracies, and corroded by chronic and seemingly ineradicable corruption. At times our leadership seems only marginally competent, and we have become all but inured to successive revelations of bribery and various more subtle forms of venality. Instances of the rapid and inexplicable acquisition of a presidential or regal fortune now fail even to surprise us. Worse, we seem only faintly embarrassed by the hypocrisy of a nation that espouses human rights (or the welfare of the "proletariat") while covertly and overtly embracing brutal, repressive, and self-serving regimes in the name of the higher morality of national self-interest.

Even if we cannot give most political regimes very high marks, it seems important, in view of the ubiquity and the impact of politics on all our lives, to attempt to gain a better understanding of the nature of politics and its relationship to the evolution of man and society. Furthermore, I believe that if politics is properly defined and interpreted, a more measured and more balanced view is justified; it should be possible to discern in the political sphere a set of trade-offs that involve both inherent costs and offsetting benefits. These costs and benefits are not fixed. Not only do they vary from one regime to another, from one historical era to another, even from one citizen to another, but they can be manipulated within limits to improve (or worsen) the benefit-cost ratio.

Equally important, politics is where the power is; the potential is always there for people to use politics as a tool either for constructive change or for wreaking carnage and destruction, and in this duality lies the supreme incarnation of humankind's collective capacity to exercise social choices and assert political control, for better or worse, over ourselves and our environment. For this reason alone it behooves us to improve our understanding of the inner workings of politics and its relationship to the fate of our species.

Objectives of the Work

My primary concern, however, has to do with making a contribution to three overlapping and ultimately connected domains of science: (1) evolutionary biology in general and sociobiology in particular; (2) social science as a corporate entity (especially cultural evolution theory); and (3) political science.

With regard to biology and sociobiology, I will advance a theory that addresses two major unresolved issues in evolutionary theory, namely, the causes of the emergence of complex biological systems generally and the emergence of social systems in particular. It has long been dogma among biologists that evolution is a nonteleological process that is governed essentially by the canalization that natural selection imposes on random micro-level genetic changes. Yet it has been known since Darwin's day that behavioral changes often precede and precipitate changes in biological structures and the underlying genetic substrate. At the turn of the century this insight was elevated into a body of writings known as Organic Selection Theory (though it might better have been called Behavioral Selection Theory). The argument was advanced that behavioral changes should be viewed as a major cause of evolutionary change because they are often the most immediate, proximate cause of changes in the all-important relationship between an organism and its environment.

The events that resulted in the eclipse of Organic Selection Theory will be recounted in due course; here I would only point out that the role of behavior in evolutionary change remains underrated to this day. The idea needs to be revitalized and given a more central place in evolutionary theory. I also intend to carry the argument a step further, to show how the evolutionary process has been partially purposive (teleonomic) in nature, albeit in a manner consistent with Darwinian theory. That is, one of the most significant trends in evolution has been an increase in the capacity for internally controlled purposive, or goal-directed behavioral changes (I call it "teleonomic selection"), which has in turn played an increasingly important role as a causal agent in the overall course of evolution. The human species is not *sui generis;* it has merely culminated (and greatly amplified) this trend. How this trend has occurred, and its relationship to the emergence of politics (as I define it), will be a significant aspect of this work.

Natural selection and teleonomic selection have also played a central role in the progressive evolutionary trend toward more complex, hierarchically organized systems. But the key to this trend has been *functional synergism*—combinatorial or co-operative effects that have had positive consequences in relation to various aspects of the problem of survival and reproduction. For example, the light metal sodium and chlorine gas are substances that in themselves are poisonous to humans, but when they are combined, they form a substance that is positively beneficial (in moderate amounts)—ordinary table salt. NaCl has functional synergism in relation to a specific human need. Likewise, the ability of humans to lift and lower various objects with their hands and forearms depends on the coordinated efforts of both the biceps muscle (on the forward part of the upper arm) and the triceps (on the back of the upper arm). The two muscles together achieve effects that would not be possible if they acted alone.

I call this formulation the *synergism hypothesis,* and I believe that it provides a framework for a general theory of progressive evolution. Let me state the hypothesis: *It is the selective advantages arising from various synergistic effects that constitute the underlying cause of the apparently orthogenetic (or directional) aspect of evolutionary history, that is, the progressive emergence of complex, hierarchically organized systems.*

The second domain with which this book is concerned is the evolution of man and society. In essence, the synergism hypothesis also provides the basis for a theory of human evolution. Man's development as a species—from our earliest small-brained, bipedal ancestors to the most advanced modern nation-states—is quintessentially a special case of my more general theory of progressive evolution. The directional trend in our evolutionary history toward more complex social organization is also attributable to functional synergism.

Finally, I shall cap these theoretical foundations with a general theory of politics. My proposition is that there are fundamentally important commonalities that are shared by such seemingly disparate social entities as families, football teams, corporations, armies, and legislatures, and that it may be possible to reduce certain aspects of family life, team sports, commerce, war, and what is conventionally called politics to a unifying model and causal principle—the so-called cybernetic model and the principle of functional synergism. While there are obviously unique properties and unique causal forces associated with each of these very different types of social processes, synergistic effects of various kinds have nevertheless played a decisive (that is, necessary but not sufficient) role in their emergence and persistence.

A few words of explanation are in order. While the term *cybernetics* has become familiar in recent years, it is still not well understood. Cybernetics derives from the Greek word *kybernetes,* meaning helmsman or steersman, and our words *government* and *governor* (as in statesman and the old-fashioned automobile carburetor) are among its descendants. As currently employed, *cybernetics* denotes (1) a science that dates back to the pioneering work of Norbert Wiener and others on the problems of antiaircraft fire control in World War II, and (2) a set of analytical concepts (and models) that have come to be widely employed in various scientific problem areas.

As the word implies, a cybernetic system, whether in the biological realm or in human organizations, involves a dynamic set of processes organized and internally directed toward certain goals or end states. The key elements or aspects of a cybernetic system include (a) the setting of goals (and perhaps subgoals) that are instrumental to higher level goals; (b) the implementation of actions designed to coordinate the behavior of the system and its parts toward goal attainment; and, in furtherance of these activities, processes of (c) communication and (d) control. In order to carry out these functions, cybernetic systems must necessarily be processors of information, energy, and often material substances.

The cybernetic system par excellence is of course the human being. So also, in a very imperfect way, is a wolf pack, and so is the U.S. government. However, not all cybernetic systems are political systems. As I use the term, political systems include the subset of all imaginable cybernetic systems that are social organizations of some sort. Thus politics is not at heart a separate and specialized sphere of social life; it is an aspect or dimension of all organized social life.

For this one occasion, I will use the controversial organismic analogy to underscore the point. Just as the brain, the neuroendocrine system, and the sense organs together comprise the cybernetic subsystem of a human body, so social organizations require similar subsystems—political systems—to effectuate the cybernation of their behavior.*

In these terms, political processes may be highly consensual or highly coercive, highly participatory or highly authoritarian, highly formalized or highly informal, highly advantageous to participants or highly exploitative, just as our common sense and our political history tell us is the case. But whatever the properties from the viewpoint of the participant (or the moralist), the outside observer will always find implicit or explicit goals, activities oriented toward those goals, and flows of information (including feedback), energy (human or exogenous), and probably material substances of various kinds.

* The logical structure of this theory can be arrayed as follows:

(1) *Goal-oriented social systems have powerful inherent potential for improving the benefit-cost ratios* (*or "economizing"*) *on various aspects of the problems of living;*

(2) *However, this synergistic potential can be realized only if such systems are able to function with a reasonable degree of efficiency* (*so that the desired goals can be attained and the associated costs do not outweigh the benefits*);

(3) *In order for such purposive systems to function efficiently, internal processes of decision making, communication, and coordination* (*control*) *are required;*

(4) *Therefore, cybernetic* (*political*) *control processes, or subsystems, are a necessary concomitant of* (*and often a precondition for*) *achieving the synergistic potential of social organizations.*

My colleagues in the social sciences will immediately recognize that this approach, this vision of the political realm, is not an original one; in recent years a number of social scientists have espoused a similar viewpoint. Yet there is an important distinction. Others have proposed the use of the cybernetic framework as a set of analytical and taxonomic concepts for the study of contemporary social and political life. However, they did not seek to explain *why* social organizations have cybernetic properties, that is, how these properties have come to exist and why they have evolved over time. Why, indeed, is it the case that humans are so readily, so naturally able to create social systems that manifest these properties? From the larger evolutionary perspective, this is unprecedented; it is one of the most distinctive aspects of our survival strategy as a species. Man is the quintessential cybernetic animal (or political animal in a larger sense even than Aristotle meant), with a remarkable ability, unmatched in any other species, for inventing new social goals and organizing (cybernating) collective behavior toward their realization.

If this view is correct, politics is not an epiphenomenon, not a distillate of economic activities, or of the class struggle, or of the machinations of ambitious leaders. Politics is a natural and necessary process of social life, a process that occurs whenever two or more individuals come together to work out a shared problem or to coordinate their efforts toward some shared goal, such as raising children or making war. It is also a process that, as the human species evolved and as cultural life evolved in tandem with it, became specialized and institutionalized in various, increasingly distinct spheres of social life.

Furthermore, this theory of politics is as applicable to other social species as it is to human beings; human politics is but a special case (albeit a very special case) of a class of phenomena that have deep roots in the larger process of biological evolution. When we speak of the politics of, say, *Apis mellifera* (the true honeybee) or *Canus lupus* (the European wolf), it is more than a facile metaphor in the tradition of Bernard Mandeville's infamous allegory *The Fable of the Bees* (1714).[3] Strictly analogous functional processes are involved. Political systems are at bottom an emergent level of biological organization, even when they may be products of human artifice as well. Accordingly, this theory of politics is also a sociobiological theory.

Some skeptics have claimed that no such grand theory is possible. It has been said that the subject matter is inherently too refractory and that the aspiration for a bona fide scientific theory of social and political life should be written off as "a complete failure."[4] It has also been said that a theory that purports to explain everything would be able to explain nothing. But general theories are not about everything; they are theories about a problem or property shared by all the members of a particular class of phenomena.

Thus, for example, "natural selection" refers to a theory about the history of life on earth, the "descent with modification," in Darwin's phrase, of living forms and the pervasiveness of functional design in nature. However, natural selection is not a deterministic, controlling mechanism or agent, and nothing is ever actively "selected." In reality, natural selection is a way of characterizing an aspect of a dynamic process—in fact, a vast array of processes. Some recent definitions to the contrary notwithstanding, *natural selection refers to those functionally important factors which are responsible in a given context for causing differential survival and reproduction among genetically variant individuals in a population of organisms, as well as for absolute changes in the numbers and diversity of different populations and species over time.*

In other words, the consequences, or effects, of various functional interactions, both within an organism and between an organism and its environment, are the sources of natural selection. Natural selection is a causal theory, but the precise causal matrix within which natural selection occurs varies widely from one case to another. Only through careful empirical research can one identify those interactions which are responsible in a given instance for inducing evolutionary continuities and changes. Moreover, functional interactions are not the only factor that causes evolutionary change.

What I propose, then, is a general theory about certain directional (or progressive) trends in evolution—inclusive of what Herbert Spencer called "super-organic" evolution—which is strictly analogous to natural selection theory in its structure and which interpenetrates with that theory. The class of phenomena that I include in this theory are the biological processes, inclusive of social processes, that exhibit cybernetic properties; that is, they are cybernetic systems.

Theories of progressive evolution in this sense of the term are hardly a novelty; the venerable tradition of theorizing in this genre can be traced at least to Empedocles. Yet almost without exception these theories have been orthogenetic; they have postulated some form of superordinate teleology, guiding principle, energizing force, or mechanism that supercedes natural selection, such as Aristotle's *physis,* Jean Baptiste de Lamarck's "power of life," Herbert Spencer's Law of Evolution, Henri Bergson's *élan vital,* Hans Driesch's *Entelechie,* Pierre Teilhard de Chardin's Omega point, Pierre Grassé's *idiomorphon,* Ilya Prigogine's "order through fluctuation," and Jean Piaget's *savoir faire.*[5]

Unfortunately, such theories invariably explain away the very problem that requires explanation. They implicitly deny or downgrade the contingent nature of living systems and assume away the fundamental biological problem of survival and reproduction. But as biologist Theodosius Dobzhansky observed, "No theory of evolution which leaves the phenomenon of adaptedness an unexplained mystery can be acceptable."[6]

By contrast, the theory I advance is entirely compatible with natural selection. The synergism hypothesis involves a subsidiary aspect, or subset, of the causal influences that comprise natural selection. Likewise, in relation to sociocultural evolution, functional synergism comprises a subset of the causal influences that have been responsible for orienting teleonomic selection by individuals and organized groups toward more complex forms of social organization. In other words, the synergism hypothesis constitutes a unified explanation for both the directionality that has inspired various orthogenetic theories of biological evolution and the directionality in sociocultural evolution that has inspired various social theorists from Aristotle to Adam Smith, Spencer, and Marx; it is a functional theory of biological and social structures. Furthermore, cybernetic processes—the processes that I call political—have played an integral and necessary part in the process of sociocultural evolution, just as both analogous and homologous phenomena have played an integral part in the process of biological evolution.

Some logicians and philosophers of science may argue that this hypothesis does not constitute a bona fide scientific theory. However, I hope to show that, like Darwin's theory, it does conform to the so-called hypothetico-deductive model of science. That is, there will be logically derived, falsifiable inferences (predictions and "postdictions") that put the theory at risk. This does not necessarily imply the formulation of a nomological generalization or a law that conforms to the Newtonian and logical empiricist model of science. Though this theory may well lead to some subsidiary, contingent "laws" of social and political life, a general theory in the biosocial realm cannot confine itself to deterministic phenomena. It must be able to account for the dynamics of a historical process—for the evolution of biosocial phenomena through time—in much the same way that natural selection theory seeks to explain biological evolution. And just as there can be no overarching law of biological evolution, so can there be no law of sociopolitical evolution.

One of Darwin's greatest and least appreciated contributions to science was his recognition that a special kind of explanation is required for historical processes.[7] Biological evolution, and by extension the evolution of humankind and society, involves an inextricable combination of stochastic (chance), deterministic, and purposive factors. The biologist Francisco Ayala has said that the products of evolution are endowed with an "internal teleology"; but I shall use Colin Pittendrigh's term *teleonomy* to differentiate evolved biological purposiveness from the notion of an external design, or external teleology. Accordingly, a general theory must be able to encompass and synthesize the combined influences of "chance, necessity, and teleonomy"—to embellish the well-known slogan of the late Jacques Monod.[8]

Evolutionary biology offers a model for resolving the debate of the nineteenth-century social science pioneers about the relationship between history and a science of society. If history can be defined as a sequential series of processes and events, sociocultural evolution is the cumulative patterning and functioning of those events and processes over time in relation to the goals and functional requisites of various organized human populations that are embedded in human and natural ecosystems. These functional *interaction patterns* involve historically discrete configurations of functional relationships, and the process of evolutionary change entails systematic alterations in those configurations.

Consider one example, based on some elegant field work by the anthropologist Charles B. Drucker.[9] Drucker showed that the culture of an isolated Philippine people, the Igorot, involves an intricately interwoven network of ecological, technological, social, and political elements—a synergistic system.

The Igorot occupy a remote mountainous area of Luzon, where for centuries they have practiced irrigated rice cultivation within an awe-inspiring system of earthwork terraces, dams, and canals that were laboriously carved with simple tools out of the precipitous mountainsides. It was once thought that these massive structures, characterized by early explorers as the "eighth wonder of the world," were thousands of years old and had taken a thousand years to build. But now it appears that they are much more recent, the product of a heroic response to a rapid increase in population pressure. This was occasioned by the Spanish conquest and occupation of the choicest lowland and coastal areas in the early sixteenth century and the consequent wavelike flight of the natives into the mountainous regions. Where previously the Igorot inhabitants of some of the more remote areas had practiced a form of low-intensity, shifting cultivation called "slash-and-burn" (or swiddening), the sudden increases in population and the demand for food precipitated a radical shift in survival strategies to the present rice terrace technology.

However, the interaction among political-military, demographic, and technological factors is not sufficient to account for the success of this alternative subsistence mode. The remarkable sustained fecundity achieved by the Igorot system also depends on the constant replenishment of soil nutrients, especially nitrogen. Yet in this case the various external sources of nitrogen are not adequate to support such abundant harvests. The key factor is the presence in the rice ponds of a nitrogen-fixing blue-green algae that lives in a symbiotic relationship with the rice plants. Respiration from the root structures of the plants generates the quantities of carbon dioxide that the algae need for photosynthesis and nitrogen fixation. At the same time, leaves of the plants shade the rice terrace mud, where the algae live, keeping temperatures cool enough for the algae to become prolific nitrogen producers. This in turn stimulates the growth of the rice plants, and the result is extremely high productivity coupled with great ecological stability. It is a synergistic system, and, over a period of several centuries, it has been possible for the Igorot to grow almost enough staple food on a single hectare (2.47 acres) to feed a family of five.

Yet this is only half the story. The evolution of the Igorot's rice terrace system also depended on a radical shift of socioeconomic and political practices. Whereas the ancestral Igorot lived in small family groups that were well suited to shifting, small-scale plant cultivation, the successful adoption of the rice terrace mode of production required the coalescence of these groups into an integrated organization. Sustained co-operative efforts became necessary, first to design and build this remarkable system and then to utilize, maintain, and expand it over time, for without constant weeding and repair the physical plant would rapidly deteriorate.

Accordingly, the Igorot had to invent a political system, a set of social structures and processes for coordinating in a complex and disciplined manner the activities of many previously isolated family groups. It was by no means inevitable that the Igorot would develop appropriate institutions and forms of co-operative behavior, but they did in fact do so. As a result, they exhibit today a cultural system that would be unrecognizable to the Igorot of an earlier era.

How can we be so sure that the Igorot's survival strategy was dependent on an entire configuration of factors, on a synergistic system? To find out, all we would need to do is remove a single component—say, the blue-green algae—and observe the consequences.

One other lesson can be drawn from this example. While a high degree of cybernetic control is required in order for the Igorot subsistence strategy to function smoothly, it was not predetermined (as Marx would have it) that a particular form of ownership, or a particular kind of decision-making and governing process would flow from these economic patterns. Unlike many comparable food production systems of the past, the Igorot exhibit a relatively egalitarian and communal society. There are individual family units and individual rice terrace plots within the terrace system, but these elements are coupled to a co-operative ethic and a pattern of intensely organized co-operative work groups that also perform social, governmental, military, and even educational functions in the community. The problem of cybernating social behavior may be solved in a variety of ways, within the constraints imposed by the environment and other aspects of a society's cultural experience and survival strategies. Nevertheless the key elements in the progressive evolution of Igorot society were functional synergism coupled with cybernetic social processes.

What This Work Is Not

Having described in a very general way what this book is about, I want to say a few words regarding what this book is *not* about.

First, this is not an exercise in pop biology. The human being is more than a Naked Ape. In the 1960s some popular books equated animal and human behavior, but such ventures, on balance, were not very helpful. Human behavior differs in some very important ways from that of a stickleback fish or an Uganda kob. However, some of the most exciting recent animal research indicates that animal behavior has a far greater degree of malleability than had been supposed. Heretofore unsuspected capacities have been discovered in animals for "cultural" learning, for situational modification of behavior, for intelligent problem solving and rationalistic choice making. In essence, our superlative ability as a species to learn from experience, to set goals, to exercise self-control and control over the environment has many rudimentary parallels in the evolutionary process, as well as in our own evolutionary history. The theoretical significance of this discovery, which is only beginning to be assimilated, is of central importance to my theory.

Second, this work is not another exemplar of biological and social determinism; it is not "vulgar sociobiology," nor is it a political tract wrapped in the mantle of Science. It is not even a polemic either for or against sociobiology. Though I believe with Edward Wilson that sociobiology as the systematic study of social behavior from an evolutionary perspective is "an inevitable discipline," the sociobiologists' early theoretical formulations—in particular, the reductionist genetic models of human nature—now seem inadequate on scientific grounds. To a substantial degree, this book represents an alternative formulation.

Third, this work does not take sides on the bitterly contested nature-nurture (or heredity versus environment) issue. Nor does it avoid the issue. There is a middle ground position that may yet reconcile the two extremes. A clue to what the resolution may entail is contained in a parable that, even though it was suggested by a group of anti-sociobiologists, points the finger at both sides in the nature-nurture debate.

> Imagine yourself living at a time when the process of photosynthesis was not known. Suppose that in attempting to understand the phenomenon of plant growth, a group of scientists did numerous experiments in which plant growth rate was studied under different light regimes. From their experiments, they concluded that plant growth was caused by light. But, at the same time, another group of scientists did numerous experiments in which plant growth rate was studied under different water regimes. They concluded that plant growth was caused by water. A dialogue between these two groups could easily result in an entrenchment along the two different lines of thought rather than a synthesis of the two sets of experimental results. Arguments would be presented on either side to show how the other side was wrong, with scientists being called upon to align themselves with one group or the other. . . .
>
> The basic structure of this example is equivalent to the biological versus environmental determinist controversy. To see a question of the origin

> and maintenance of human social behavior or social institutions as merely a choice between determinisms, with the argument being only what percentage is environmental and what percentage is biological, is just as scientifically absurd as attempting to understand plant growth by assigning a certain fraction to light and another fraction to water. Just as water and light are utilized in the process of photosynthesis to drive the complicated biochemical processes that eventually result in plant growth, biological and environmental factors are intimately related in a complex network of interactions between human and environment, which result in the observed patterns of human behavior and social institutions. What then is the alternative to determinism?[10]

One alternative, which I describe in detail later on, is what I call the *Interactional Paradigm.* In the Interactional Paradigm, social causation is viewed as multileveled, configural, and interactive. It seeks to integrate deterministic, teleonomic (goal-oriented), and stochastic elements and—from a different perspective—internal (biopsychological) and external (social and ecological) elements into a dynamic, hierarchical framework. This paradigm is clearly implied by contemporary research and theoretical work in a number of disciplines. To varying degrees, it has been advocated by a number of theorists in recent years. The pieces need only be brought together in a more coherent and comprehensive manner. The Interactional Paradigm is distinctive primarily in that it utilizes a multileveled cybernetic framework, that is, a cybernetic-systems-within-ecosystems framework.

To illustrate, consider the role of fresh water in societal development. Fresh water is an absolute and incessant human need, though modern urbanites often take its presence for granted. This need is not a social fact but a biological fact, though it is of considerable social consequence. It happens that the distribution of human populations correlates highly with the geographic distribution of fresh water resources, the locations of which are evolved geological and climatological facts.

Clearly, in this instance biological facts interacted with environmental facts to shape initial human decisions about where settlements should be located and to determine (subject to some human manipulation) the ultimate capacity of these civilizational zygotes for subsequent growth. It is certainly no accident that almost all the world's major cities are located on or very near rivers or fresh water lakes. Nor is it coincidental that the earliest large-scale civilizations were located in river valleys where sophisticated water management technologies were developed. Yet any beginning student of statistics can tell us that a correlation does not prove causation; we need no statistician to tell us that fresh water supplies do not *cause* civilization. On the other hand, common sense tells us that the loss by any civilization of its water supply—

say, as the result of a climate shift—would indeed cause a rapid and catastrophic decline of that society.

A paradox, but one we do not find difficult to understand: fresh water is a necessary but not a sufficient condition for civilization, and we can make sense of its relationship to human evolution by understanding, first, the causal role of the biological need for water; second, the geographic pattern of fresh water distribution; and third, the fact that people have a configuration of simultaneous basic needs—for various nutrients, clothing, shelter, energy, raw materials, physical security, as well as some important social needs—the satisfaction of which are also causes of civilizational development and decay. These needs create the *a priori* challenge to which human societies have responded.

Thus, if we wish to explain an actual case of societal development, we must take the entire structure of human needs into account. A full explanation of how the sequential patterning of human choices, or teleonomic selections, occurs involves an examination of the dynamic interaction among a great many factors: climate, geography, resources, arable land, demography, technology, economic and sociopolitical organization, and, not least, interactions with other human populations. Of course, this is not a new idea. It was expressed in essence by Aristotle in *The Politics* and was revivified by Montesquieu in the eighteenth century in *The Spirit of the Laws.* We seem forever to be rediscovering (and then forgetting) what the ancients knew.

In addition, if we seek deeper knowledge of the more remote causes—the causes of the causes—we might want to probe the geological and ecological forces that were responsible for the precise geographical distribution of needed resources, as well as the evolutionary antecedents that produced a species with our precise set of needs and physical and mental capabilities *and,* not least, the evolved cultural preadaptations that enabled human populations ultimately to form dense civilizations based on crafts, commerce, agriculture, and pastoralism. The process of cultural evolution has been intensely *interactional.* Just as it is meaningless to ask which tumbler in the combination is responsible for opening a combination lock, it makes no sense to specify which particular cause in a complex network of causation is responsible for a specific social or political development.

Finally, this book is not a preface or a prolegomenon. It is not an exercise in laying the groundwork; it does not "point toward" anything. Rather, it attempts to make a landing in force and to establish a bridgehead. The very scope and boldness of this theory may be offputting to some; ambitious ideas invite instant antagonism, and it would be disingenuous of me to feign ignorance of the politics of science. However, there is nothing gratuitous about this supertheory, for I am addressing a fundamental aspect of a single (albeit many-faceted) historical process. Mindful of Albert Einstein's observation that "a theory is all the more impressive the greater is the simplicity of its premises, the more different are the kinds of things it relates and the more extended its range of applicability," I have come to believe that it is both possible and appropriate to reduce certain fundamental aspects of the evolutionary process, in nature and in human societies alike, to a unifying theoretical framework.

My theory is built on foundations that were laid by many other theorists, past and present. While such a disclaimer is commonplace and platitudinous, I mean this one to be taken literally. The theory I propose is my own, but it is also the explicit outgrowth of a cumulative process to which many others have contributed. I shall identify and evaluate some of these intellectual antecedents as I proceed.

Equally important, my theory has had a life of its own and no longer reflects my original aim. At the outset, more than a decade ago, the objective was to relate social processes to the biological problem of survival and reproduction. As the work proceeded, certain ideas emerged and certain connections were made. In the end, I have been impelled to follow where the theory led me. Only time will tell whether these connections are justified.

II

The Evolutionary Framework

Nothing makes sense in biology except in the light of evolution. *Theodosius Dobzhansky*

Darwinism is not a testable scientific theory but a *metaphysical research programme*. *Karl Popper*

We are survival machines—robot vehicles blindly programmed to preserve the selfish molecules known as genes. *Richard Dawkins*

The relation of the behavior of an animal to the evolutionary process is not solely that of a product. Behavior is also one of the factors which determines the magnitude and type of evolutionary pressure to which the animal will be subjected. . . . There is, I think, waiting to be developed a synthesis between evolutionary theory and a consideration of behavior. *C. H. Waddington*

My theory is intimately related to the theory of evolution first advanced by Darwin and Wallace. It applies the principle of natural selection to a central aspect of the evolutionary process while introducing and adding the concepts of functional synergism and teleonomic selection, the latter being a modernized and Darwinized version of an evolutionary principle advanced by one of Darwin's most important predecessors, Jean Baptiste de Lamarck. Darwin,

Lamarck, and their theories of evolution have been the subject of endless disputation and misrepresentation. For this reason it is important to begin at the beginning.[1]

Darwin's Logic

Part of the appeal of Darwin's concept of natural selection no doubt lies in its deceptive simplicity and generality. The basic ideas were summed up with exquisite economy in the full title, *On the Origin of Species by Means of Natural Selection, or the Preservation of Favoured Races in the Struggle for Life* (1859). An equally succinct elaboration can be found in the final recapitulation of this epochal work:

> It is interesting to contemplate an entangled bank, clothed with many plants of many kinds, with birds singing on the bushes, with various insects flitting about, and with worms crawling through the damp earth, and to reflect that these elaborately constructed forms, so different from each other, and dependent on each other in so complex a manner, have all been produced by laws acting around us. These laws, taken in the largest sense, being Growth with Reproduction; Inheritance which is almost implied by reproduction; Variability from the indirect and direct action of the external conditions of life, and from use and disuse; a Ratio of Increase so high as to lead to a Struggle for Life, and as a consequence to Natural Selection, entailing Divergence of Character and the Extinction of less improved forms.* [2]

These are of course only the bare bones of an argument that Darwin took great pains to flesh out fully, and this highly readable masterwork of the

* The phrases concerning the actions of the environment and the "use and disuse" of parts refer to the Lamarckian elements in Darwin's formulation—the thesis that experiential modifications of an organism could somehow be transmitted to the offspring. Specifically, the latter phrase refers to Lamarck's contention that the use or disuse of an organ or part could strengthen or weaken it, not only in the user but in the user's progeny.

An example Lamarck himself used—one which is frequently invoked by modern evolutionists to illustrate the difference between Lamarckism and Darwinism—involves the giraffe's neck. According to Lamarck's theory, the long necks of contemporary giraffes were caused by the behavior of ancestral giraffes, who stretched their necks through repeated efforts to reach the upper leaves of trees and who transmitted their acquired length to their progeny.

By contrast, the "classical" Darwinian view is that variation naturally occurs in every trait, including neck lengths, and that a transgenerational trend toward longer necks would occur in giraffes only if they were forced to become dependent upon tree leaves and if the individuals who could reach the higher branches were able to secure more food and were ultimately more successful in leaving progeny (see Figure I). In other words, the relative advantage of longer necks (and the disadvantage of shorter necks) was "naturally selected" as a result of historically specific interactions between organisms and their environments.

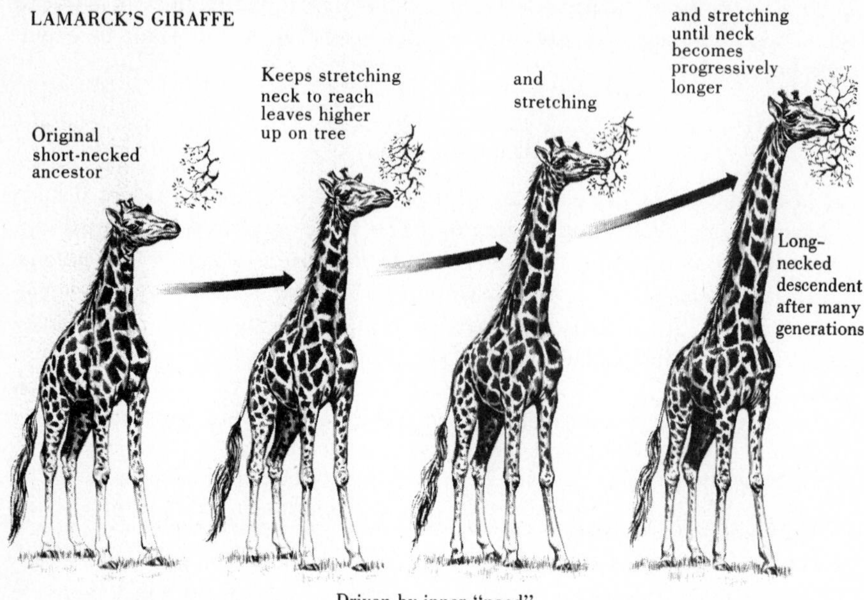
LAMARCK'S GIRAFFE
Original short-necked ancestor
Keeps stretching neck to reach leaves higher up on tree
and stretching
and stretching until neck becomes progressively longer
Long-necked descendent after many generations
Driven by inner "need"

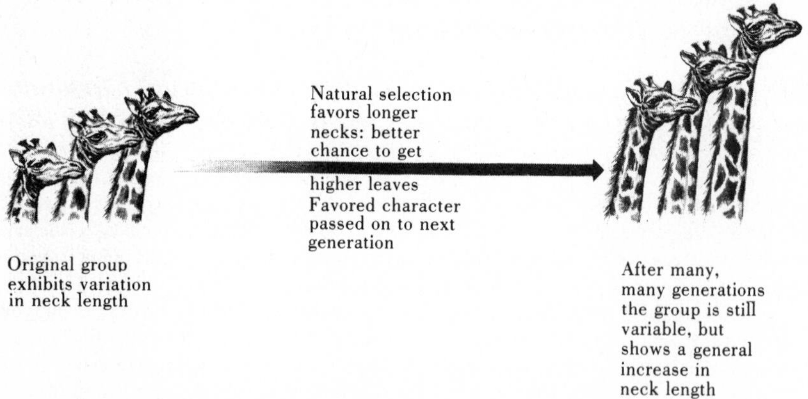
DARWIN'S GIRAFFE
Natural selection favors longer necks: better chance to get
higher leaves
Favored character passed on to next generation
Original group exhibits variation in neck length
After many, many generations the group is still variable, but shows a general increase in neck length

FIGURE I

An illustration of the difference between the Lamarckian and Darwinian theories of evolution. (From Jay M. Savage, *Evolution,* 3rd ed. [New York: Holt, Rinehart and Winston, 1977].)

scientific literature is still richly rewarding. Here we need to draw attention only to some of its more important facets.

Darwin's Vision

Darwin clearly appreciated the transgenerational nature of the evolutionary process (until late in life he preferred the phrase "transmutation of species") and thus the ultimate importance not only of individual survival but of reproductive success over time. In one of his most frequently quoted passages, Darwin says: "I should premise that I use the term Struggle for Existence in a large and metaphorical sense, including dependence of one being on another, and including (which is more important) not only the life of the individual, but success in leaving progeny."[3] By the same token, as a naturalist rather than a laboratory scientist or a mathematician, Darwin had a feeling for the intricacy and dynamic character of the living world that has sometimes been devalued by subsequent generations of academic biologists. His chapters are suffused with expressions about "the web of complex relationships" in nature, the "infinitely complex relations" among species, and the marked "interdependence" of living forms. He devoted several sections to such things as the roles in evolutionary change of climate, geographical isolation, disease patterns, and especially the interactions among different species, including what would now be called symbiosis and competitive exclusion. In his chapters on the laws of variation and "difficulties" in the theory, he recognized the influence of such factors as random drift, allometry (correlated growth), rudimentation, acclimatization, and even benefit-cost relationships.[4]

For Darwin the struggle for existence is not at all equivalent to Tennyson's "Nature, red in tooth and claw" nor to Hobbes's "war of every man against every man." Darwin was well aware of "the sometimes hostile forces of nature," but he also recognized that life is a complex enterprise, a survival enterprise in which literal struggle is an episodic aspect rather than the essence. Indeed, Darwin often spoke of the "economy of nature," by which he meant that, in the business of earning a living in the environment, every species faces a multifaceted problem (the phrase apparently traces to Linnaeus). Consider this passage:

> Two canine animals in a time of dearth, may be truly said to struggle with each other over which shall get food and live. But a plant on the edge of a desert is said to struggle for life against the drought, though more properly it should be said to be dependent on the moisture. A plant which annually produces a thousand seeds, of which on an average only one comes to maturity, may be more truly said to struggle with the plants of the same and other kinds which already clothe the ground. The missletoe is dependent on the apple and a few other trees, but can

> only in a far-fetched sense be said to struggle with these trees, for if too many of these parasites grow on the same tree, it will languish and die. But several seedling missletoes, growing close together on the same branch, may more truly be said to struggle with each other. As the missletoe is disseminated by birds, its existence depends on birds; and it may metaphorically be said to struggle with other fruit-bearing plants, in order to tempt birds to devour and thus disseminate its seeds rather than those of other plants. In these several senses, which pass into each other, I use *for convenience sake* the general term of struggle for existence [my italics].[5]

Thus Darwin was well aware of a paradox that is central to the living world: the complex interplay between competition and interdependence. The role of co-operation did not escape his notice. Nor did he have any *a priori* preconceptions or pat answers concerning what was advantageous for survival and reproduction. "It is good thus to try in our imagination to give any form some advantage over another. Probably in no single instance should we know what to do, so as to succeed. It will convince us of our ignorance on the mutual relations of all organic beings; a conviction as necessary, as it seems to be difficult to acquire."[6]

Darwin also grasped the fact that evolution involves a dualistic admixture of continuity and change, which he summed up in the winged phrase "descent with modification." Since his basic objective was to account for the origin and extinction of species and the manifest profusion of different life forms, he gave much less attention to the cumulative aspects of the process, what he referred to as "unity of descent." For instance, he did not employ the modern distinction between disruptive, normalizing, and directional selection.

In the same vein, Darwin was a convinced gradualist about evolutionary change, and his viewpoint prevailed in evolutionary theory until recent developments in paleobiology (and, some claim, in politics) forcefully reopened the issue.[7] Fond of quoting the popular canon of the time, *natura non facit saltum* (nature does not make leaps), Darwin based his views both on his own observations and on the "uniformitarian" geology of one of his contemporaries and mentors, Charles Lyell (1797–1875). Thus he flatly rejected saltationism (the biological analogue of geological catastrophism—the theory of drastic, discontinuous changes).

Another important aspect of the theory, both in Darwin's formulation and today, concerns the interplay between "chance" or nondirective variations and selection for "adaptedness" (a term Darwin used sparingly but appreciated fully). "Selectionist evolution," Ernst Mayr has observed, "is neither a chance phenomenon nor a deterministic phenomenon but a two-step tandem process combining the advantages of both."[8] Similarly, Theodosius Dobzhansky has described evolution as an "anti-chance process" wherein those chance variations which are "functional" (adaptive for survival and reproduction) are positively selected and preserved.[9] Thus natural selection can be characterized as a creative mechanism that is capable of converting chance occurrences into purposive (teleonomic) systems.

Functional Design in Nature

Perhaps the single most important aspect of Darwin's theory is that, whatever else it purported to be or is represented as being, it was preeminently a naturalistic, nonteleological explanation for the progressive emergence of functional design in nature. As usual, Darwin stated the case with admirable economy.

> Naturalists continually refer to external conditions, such as climate, food, etc., as the only possible cause of variation . . . but it is preposterous to attribute to mere external conditions, the structure, for instance, of the woodpecker, with its feet, tail, beak and tongue so admirably adapted to catch insects under the bark of trees. In the case of the missletoe, which draws its nourishment from certain trees, which has seeds that must be transported by certain birds, and which has flowers with separate sexes absolutely requiring the agency of certain insects to bring pollen from one flower to the other, it is equally preposterous to account for the structure of this parasite, with its external relations to several distinct organic beings, by the effects of external conditions, or of habit, or of the volition of the plant itself. . . . I am convinced that Natural Selection has been the main but not exclusive means of modification.[10]

Equally important, the "economy of nature," insofar as it is molded by natural selection, involves as its operative principle what might be called enlightened self-interest. The fundamental premise on which natural selection is presumed to work is exactly concordant with the "soft" form of the egoistic model of behavior posited by the social contract theorists and liberal economists (but with an important qualifier regarding altruism that I shall discuss). Not only is Darwin explicit on this point, but as if to anticipate subsequent accusations that the theory is not really scientific because it cannot be tested and falsified, Darwin threw down the gauntlet and invited challenges:

> Natural selection cannot possibly produce any modification in any one species exclusively for the good of another species; though throughout nature one species incessantly takes advantage of, and profits by, the structure of another. But natural selection can and does often produce structures for the direct injury of other species, as we see in the fang of the adder, and in the ovipositor of the ichneumon, by which its eggs are deposited in the living bodies of other insects. If it could be proved

> that any part of the structure of any one species had been formed for the exclusive good of another species, it would annihilate my theory, for such could not have been produced through natural selection.[11] *

At the heart of evolutionary theory, then, lies the stark proposition that natural selection is a utilitarian agency that leads to the creation of self-serving creatures (though in a very special sense of that term, as we shall see); natural selection favors those individuals who are the most assiduous and effective in the business of earning a living and reproducing themselves. If, as Darwin maintained, it is in one sense an ennobling vision to see all living creatures as the descendants of primordial ancestors who arose more than three billion years ago, it is also somewhat unsettling to think of ourselves as the winners (for the present) of a relentless steeplechase in which more than 99 percent of the contestants are now extinct.

Progressive Evolution

Consistent with this view, Darwin rejected the Lamarckian vision of an inherent direction in the evolutionary process. "I believe in no fixed law of development," he said emphatically. "I believe . . . in no law of necessary development."[15] Whereas Lamarck had posited a trend toward increased complexity and improvement of form and function that was later to serve

* *The Origin* contains many other examples of falsifiable propositions. For instance:

> If it could be demonstrated that any complex organ existed which could not possibly have been formed by numerous successive slight modifications, my theory would absolutely break down. (p. 219)

> Natural selection will never produce in a being anything injurious to itself, for natural selection acts [*sic*] solely by and for the good of each. . . . If a fair balance be struck between the good and evil caused by each part, each will be found on the whole advantageous. (p. 229)

> Natural selection will produce nothing in one species for the exclusive good or injury of another; though it may well produce parts, organs and excretions highly useful or even indispensable, or highly injurious to another species, but in all cases at the same time useful to the owner. (p. 232)

Darwin's theory predicts explicitly that the primary selective factors involved in differential survival and reproduction will be *utilitarian* (or economic in the broadest sense). They will not be random; nor will they conform to orthogenetic laws, vitalistic forces, or God's plan. In addition, there are many other *implicit* predictions in the theory that can be put into testable form. This has been done in an abbreviated way by Kevin Connolly and much more extensively by Mary B. Williams.[12] For example, Connolly pointed out that if it could be shown that any one of Darwin's basic premises (or those of modern evolutionists) were false—say, that mutations are not random but have orthogenetic properties—then the theory could be challenged directly.

Some may argue that such predictions would be hard to falsify. How could one devise an

(Continued)

as the inspiration for Herbert Spencer's theory of societal evolution, Darwin viewed the evolutionary process as open-ended, opportunistic, and incremental in nature.

Yet he was not totally antagonistic to the idea of evolutionary progress. In the final summation of *The Origin*, in one of the few distinctly rhetorical passages of the book, he asserted: "And as natural selection works solely by and for the good of each being, all corporeal and mental endowments will tend to progress toward perfection."[16]

This passage could readily be misinterpreted, and it has been. But a careful reading of *The Origin* shows that Darwin had in mind nothing like Aristotle's finalism or even the more limited Lamarckian notion of a self-propelled trend.[17] As anthropologist Derek Freeman has pointed out, the term "perfection" was frequently employed by nineteenth-century naturalists in a sense that is akin to "functional optimization"; the term connoted improved design in specific local organism-environment relationships.[18] *

There is a subtle but important distinction between a lawlike trend or progression, a necessary concomitant of which is some deterministic causal mechanism, and a contingent, ad hoc adaptive process in which certain past trends may be discerned retrospectively. This distinction has been drawn with clarity by molecular biologist François Jacob. If one were to make a rough comparison between the workings of natural selection and those of a human actor, he suggests, the proper analogue would not be an engineer but a tinkerer. Whereas the engineer typically works from a planned design

---

appropriately rigorous test? The philosopher Anthony Flew has observed that "We must on no account overlook [the possibility] that a theory may be in practice unfalsifiable simply because it happens in fact to be true."[13] For some of us, the inability to conjure up plausible tests of the Darwinian hypothesis may be a result of the fact that we are no longer able to entertain religious or orthogenetic hypotheses, even for the sake of argument. Yet this was not always the case. Darwinism had to fight an uphill battle against theories of Special Creation, neo-Lamarckian orthogenesis, Bergsonian vitalism, saltationism, and even Mendelian genetics. Some theorists still remain unconvinced.

More important, potential falsifiers or deflators are being proposed *and tested* all the time. One major current controversy among evolutionary biologists focuses on the extent to which evolution is the result of stochastic or chance factors, as opposed to Darwinian selection. The paleontologist S. M. Stanley, for example, has proposed that random rather than Darwinian processes may play a dominant role in the evolution of "higher" taxonomic categories.[14] Similarly, a major trend in contemporary theoretical ecology involves the formulation of explicit predictions (e.g., about foraging strategies or predator-prey interactions) based on formal mathematical models that are then taken into the field to be tested with natural populations.

* There are many instances in the fossil record of progressive improvements in functional efficiency. One classic example is *Equidae*, the ancestors of modern horses, donkeys, etc., whose padded, multi-toed feet evolved over time into the single horned toe we observe in their living descendants. Darwin was also well aware of the fact that many species do not improve but instead become extinct. He specifically eschewed the popular notion of a *scala naturae*—an ascending "ladder of perfection."

with carefully assembled materials and tools to achieve a well-defined goal, the tinkerer stumbles on solutions to problems by using whatever materials are at hand and whatever tools are available with which to fashion a workable solution.[19] As Dobzhansky put it, "natural selection has no plan, no foresight, no intention."[20]

A classic example is the eye. We now know that that revered object of nineteenth-century theology was developed independently on a number of occasions in evolutionary history, with at least three distinct functional principles being utilized—the pinhole, the lens, and multiple tubes. Nor do all the eyes of similar type work in the same manner: The photoreceptor cells in vertebrate eyes point away from the light; those in mollusks point toward the light.[21] Likewise, while squids and octopods have eyes with lenses, image focusing is achieved by moving the lens forward and backward in the eye socket rather than by changing the shape of the lens.[22]

Darwin and Lamarck

Darwin's relationship to the other major facet of the Lamarckian model of evolution, the inheritance of "habits acquired by conditions," is more complex. Although Darwin had generally been scornful of the idea in his earlier years ("heaven forfend me from Lamarck's nonsense," he wrote to a friend in 1844), in *The Origin* he displayed his characteristic scientific caution by not ruling out the possibility that environmental influences and the "use and disuse of parts" could be one source of biological variation in evolution. He even cited possible evidence in its favor. However, there is no doubt that he saw this and other agencies as subordinate to and constrained by the more powerful influence of natural selection.

Thus Darwin was not in the end anti-Lamarckian, but he did have a different vision. Whereas in Darwinian theory adaptation to immediate circumstances is central and linear trends are epiphenomenal or secondary effects, in Lamarckian theory the notion of a linear trend is central and the evident branchings, regressions, and changes of direction in nature are merely anomalous deviations from the main course. No two conceptions of nature (or of society) could be more sharply opposed.

The Darwin of the Social Sciences

Darwin's theorizing on the subject of man and society is found primarily in the first half of *The Descent of Man* (1871). (Sexual selection is the subject of the second half.)[23] * The principal thesis of that work—and Darwin's

* In *The Expression of the Emotions in Man and Animals* (1873), Darwin also dealt in detail with the sources of individual behavior (human nature). *The Expression of the Emotions* is pathbreaking in many ways, not the least of which is that evolutionary (natural selection) theory, ethology, and psychology are treated in an integrated manner.[24]

greatest contribution to the scientific view of mankind—was that the human species had arisen through the same materialistic processes that govern the rest of the natural world and that *Homo sapiens* share a common descent with other animals, especially the higher primates. The idea was shocking in his day—and still is to some people.

Equally important, Darwin offered an explanation of human evolution in terms of natural selection theory. Specifically, he attributed our uniquely dominant position in nature and remarkable cultural attainments to evolved, naturally selected social, moral, and mental faculties, in combination with language abilities.* Though Darwin has sometimes been portrayed as an apologist for laissez-faire capitalism, in reality he placed human social and moral faculties highest among those characteristics that have contributed most to our success as a species. Following a discussion of the role of social behavior and sympathy (what contemporary sociobiologists would call altruism) in various animal species, Darwin dealt at length—though in a highly speculative fashion—with "Man as a Social Animal." Ironically, his discussion includes observations that could well have been written by one of his severest modern critics.[26] For example:

> Although man, as he now exists, has few special instincts, having lost any which his early progenitors may have possessed, this is no reason why he should not have retained from an extremely remote period some degree of instinctive love and sympathy for his fellows. . . . Although man, as just remarked, has no special instincts to tell him how to aid his fellow-men, he still has the impulse, and with his improved intellectual faculties would naturally be much guided in this respect by reason and experience.[27]

Similarly, with regard to the acquisition of moral tendencies, Darwin posited that they might have developed in Lamarckian fashion, through habits that eventually came to be inherited.

When it came to explaining sociocultural evolution, Darwin's views were sharply at odds with those of Marx, Spencer, and others who believed in various forms of orthogenesis, finalism, laws of history, or laws of evolution—just as he had opposed the Lamarckian vision of linear progress in nature.†

* On this issue Darwin differed sharply with his self-effacing co-discoverer. Wallace wished to exempt the human mind from the workings of natural selection, but Darwin obviously disagreed.[25]

† Here is Darwin in *The Descent of Man:*

> It is, however, very difficult to form any judgment why one particular tribe and not another has been successful and has risen in the scale of civilization. Many savages are in the same condition as when first discovered several centuries ago. . . . Progress seems to depend on many concurrent favorable conditions, far too complex to be followed out. . . . While observing the barbarous inhabitants of

(Continued)

Darwin advanced a dualistic, interactive explanation that foreshadowed (with important differences) such co-operation-competition theories as that of zoologist Robert Bigelow and the group-selection, kin-selection, and reciprocal altruism theories of recent years. Whatever its shortcomings, *The Descent of Man* fully qualifies as an attempt at a "scientific explanation of sociocultural phenomena."[28]

Modern social and behavioral scientists seldom accord Darwin a place in their pantheon of founding fathers. Some even suggest that Darwin got most of his ideas from such social theorists as Malthus and especially Spencer.[29] Nevertheless I submit Darwin's name as a candidate for founding fatherhood. His attempt to account for the evolution of man and society within a naturalistic framework was in itself a highly important contribution. Marx and Spencer and others did likewise, but Darwin alone among these nineteenth-century pioneers argued that the process was not orthogenetic, that it was not governed by necessary trends or historical laws. Darwin saw human evolution as an incremental and contingent process. He was unpopular among the exponents of human progress precisely because he had no perfecting principle.

Tierra del Fuego, it struck me that the possession of some property, a fixed abode, and the union of many families under a chief, were the indispensable requisites for civilization. Such habits almost necessitate the cultivation of the ground; and the first steps in cultivation would probably result, as I have elsewhere shown, from some such accident as the seeds of a fruit-tree falling on a heap of refuse, and producing an unusually fine variety. The problem, however, of the first advance of savages toward civilization is at present much too difficult to be solved.

We must remember that progress is no invariable rule. It is very difficult to say why one civilized nation rises, becomes more powerful, and spreads more widely, than another; or why the same nation progresses more quickly at one time than at another. We can only say that it depends on an increase in the actual number of the population, on the number of the men endowed with high intellectual and moral faculties, as well as on their standard of excellence. Corporeal structure appears to have little influence, except so far as vigor of body leads to vigor of mind.

It has been urged by several writers that as high intellectual powers are advantageous to a nation, the old Greeks, who stood some grades higher in intellect than any race that has ever existed, ought, if the power of natural selection were real, to have risen still higher in the scale, increased in number, and stocked the whole of Europe. Here we have the tacit assumption, so often made with respect to corporeal structures, that there is some innate tendency toward continued development in mind and body. But development of all kinds depends on many concurrent favorable circumstances. Natural selection acts only tentatively. . . . The western nations of Europe, who now so immeasurably surpass their former savage progenitors and stand at the summit of civilization, owe little or none of their superiority to direct inheritance from the old Greeks, though they owe much to the written works of that wonderful people. (pp. 150, 159–60)

More important, Darwin framed the problem of explaining the emergence of the human species in terms of the biological problem of survival and reproduction. For Darwin, the biological imperatives are what define the overarching purpose and the central organizing principle of any society. Thus he had hold of the right problem: At heart, a human society is a collective survival enterprise (see Chapter IV). Accordingly, Darwin strove to account for human evolution in a manner that was consistent with natural selection theory. One may disagree with the particulars of his explanation, but the issue cannot be dismissed. Thus Darwin posed a fundamental challenge for subsequent generations of social scientists: Any scientific theory of societal and political evolution must be compatible with natural selection theory. Should there be conflict, either the social theory is invalid or natural selection theory is falsified. (A third alternative is that cultural evolution is *sui generis* and somehow freed from the constraints of our biological heritage. We shall have to clear this roadblock as we proceed.)

Subsequent generations have found fault with some aspects of Darwin's vision: his overemphasis on Malthusian population pressures, his cautious acceptance of the Lamarckian theory of the use and disuse of parts, his misconceived theory of pangenesis, in which migrating "gemmules" were postulated as a means for transmitting information through the bloodstream to the germ plasm of an organism,[30] his dogged gradualism, and his tendency to reify and personify natural selection, thereby frequently misleading others and sometimes even himself.* The tendency to treat natural selection as an external mechanism or agency led Darwin to view sexual selection (which obviously plays a critical role in differential reproduction) as though it were distinct from natural selection rather than being one facet of it. More paradoxical still, Darwin treated environmental influences as if they too were separate mechanisms rather than one dimension of an inherently relational process. For all his sophistication about nature, Darwin never quite got into focus the deeply interactional nature of biological causation. Nor did he, or many subsequent theorists for that matter, grasp the important role of behavior

* Although Darwin recognized that he had invented a metaphor, the purpose of which was to dramatize and facilitate understanding of a complex process involving a myriad of different causal mechanisms, he and many theorists of succeeding generations found irresistible the tendency to reify the concept. Natural selection was flagrantly personified by Darwin and treated as though it were an active selecting agency or a mechanism in nature rather than a taxonomic category, a way of classifying the dynamics of a specific class of organism-environment interactions. Here is one of the more vivid examples in *The Origin:* "Natural selection is daily and hourly scrutinising throughout the world, every variation, even the slightest; rejecting that which is bad, preserving and adding up all that is good; silently and insensibly working, whenever and wherever the opportunity offers, at the improvement of each organic being in relation to its organic and inorganic conditions of life" (p. 133). (In a later edition, Darwin changed this passage, adding at the beginning of the sentence: "It may be metaphorically said. . . .")

as a direct cause of evolutionary change, not in a Lamarckian fashion but in a strictly Darwinian fashion.

Nevertheless Darwin's theoretical structure has withstood the test of time, surviving successive waves of attackers and major scientific developments that could have undermined less powerful theories. As Konrad Lorenz noted, "What is surprising is the extent to which further research, based on Darwin's hypotheses and pursuing them in every conceivable direction, has invariably proved him right on every essential point."[31]

Equally important, Darwin exercised a seminal influence on the budding social sciences and helped to stimulate a naturalistic science of man and society. His contribution to the social sciences of the nineteenth century is a matter of record.[32] Whatever its flaws, the basic elements of that paradigm are sound; it deserves to be reinstated as the basis for an integrated biosocial science.

Friedrich Engels, at the grave of his lifelong friend and collaborator, asserted that, "As Darwin discovered the law of evolution [*sic*] in organic nature, so Marx discovered the law of evolution in human history." Marvin Harris concludes that, in the final analysis, "either Marx (with Engels's help) was the Darwin of the social sciences, or nobody was."[33] I, on the other hand, support the currently unfashionable view that Darwin was the Darwin of the social sciences.

Our Current Malaise

In the 133 years since the publication of *The Origin,* there has been an overwhelming increase in our understanding of the evolutionary process. The breadth and depth of our accumulating knowledge has long since spawned whole new disciplines—systematics, population genetics, molecular genetics, paleontology, behavior genetics, ethology, theoretical ecology, and (lately) sociobiology. In the first half of this century, many of these developments were brought together into what is generally referred to as the "modern synthesis."[34] For many years this synthesis was virtually unchallenged in this country, but now it is under siege from various quarters. It is important, then, to identify some of the sources of the present discontent and to discuss briefly those issues which are particularly relevant to the theory I propose here.

Our current theoretical malaise is the product of a number of contributing factors. One factor is a disaffection from the classical population genetic models of evolution, which focus on changes in the frequencies of single genes (or the additive effects of several genes) in populations under deterministic selection regimes.[35] We have come to realize that such changes may be atypical in comparison with more intricate processes involving hierarchically organized, functionally integrated interaction systems in dynamic, often non-linear relationships with complex environments.[36] Indeed, even the genetic substrate (the genotype) appears to be a hierarchically organized system and it now seems that the genetic "program" is not fixed, that various DNA sequences are "transposable."[37] These movable elements can turn genes on and off or cause massive mutations and gene rearrangements.

A second factor is the uncertainty and division of opinion over what should be considered the most appropriate unit of selection—genes, gene complexes, molar organic or organismic processes, interbreeding populations, or entire species of organisms.[38] This is more than a levels-of-analysis problem; ultimately it concerns the question of where evolutionary *causation* is concentrated. It is increasingly apparent that evolution is a multileveled process, and one major current battleground concerns the relationship between micro-level and macro-level causation.

A third factor derives from the emergence of ethology and sociobiology. There is a widespread conviction that the modern synthesis, oriented as it is to population genetics, does not take adequate account of the role of behavior in evolution. Witness one of the architects of the modern synthesis, Ernst Mayr, who in a recent exposition characterized behavioral change as a "pace-maker" of evolution yet in the next breath described evolution as a "two-step process" involving random genetic changes and natural selection. How these two conceptions are supposed to fit together is not clear.[39]

Another disquieting factor is the debate over the relative importance of stochastic elements in evolutionary change, both at the micro level in relation to the evidence for polymorphisms[40] and genetic drift[41] and at the macro level in relation to computer models and new interpretations of the fossil record that suggest an apparently saltatory (discontinuous) aspect to the patterns of speciation and phyletic evolution.[42]

The emergence of theoretical ecology has added its share of disturbing influences. Relationships that ecologists observe between organisms and their environments simply do not fit the linear and deterministic models of population genetics, for there are altogether too many situations in nature that involve environmental gradients, threshold effects, frequency and density dependence, multivariate optimization problems, multiple adaptive peaks, and so on.[43]

Perhaps most distressing are the direct attacks on the core of Darwin's theory, the fundamental premises that the contingencies of survival and reproduction (the "struggle for existence") have played a central role in shaping the history of life on earth, and that the functional adaptation of organisms to their environments is of overriding importance (albeit not the only factor) in determining both the continuities and the changes that occur in evolution.[44]

Finally, evolutionists have been embarrassed by the accusations, mainly by philosophers of science, that contemporary definitions of natural selection are tautologous. Perhaps most visible has been Karl Popper's charge that natural selection is not an explanatory theory at all but a "*metaphysical research programme.*"[45]

The Sources of Our Discontent

Although I cannot provide a detailed discussion here, it is important to address briefly those issues which are particularly pertinent to the theory I develop in the chapters to come.

A principal source of our current discontent lies in the very concept of natural selection, at once a brilliant simplification and an endless source of confusion. Charles Darwin was well aware that he had invented a metaphor, a way of characterizing "for the sake of brevity" a nonteleological process in which the multifarious interactions between organisms and their environments can produce, without external direction, the "progressive" emergence over time of functional design in nature. The inspiration for Darwin's concept was the "artificial selection" practiced by plant and animal breeders, though in fact natural selection is not at all analogous, as critics in Darwin's day and since have noted. Whereas artificial selection is teleological—that is, it involves *external* selecting agents with purposes that are *extrinsic* to the needs and reproductive advantages of a species—Darwin's theory postulated that no such exogenous agency existed or was needed to account for the "internal teleology" (or teleonomy) that is found in nature. Nevertheless, to dramatize his concept, Darwin used flagrant personification and treated natural selection as if it were an active selecting agency out there in the environment somewhere.

The tendency to reify natural selection has persisted to the present day. George Gaylord Simpson is not alone in asserting that "The mechanism of adaptation is natural selection. . . . [It] usually operates in favor of maintained or increased adaptation to a given way of life."[46] Similarly, Ernst Mayr tells us that "Natural selection does its best to favor the production of programs guaranteeing behavior that increases fitness."[47] "Acting upon genetic novelties created by mutation," Edward O. Wilson assures us, "natural selection is the agent that molds virtually all of the characters of species."[48] Nor does it clarify matters when Mayr proposes instead to characterize natural selection as "an extrinsic ordering principle."[49]

Natural Selection Redefined

The problem is that natural selection is not a mechanism and is not something extrinsic to the relationship between specific organisms and their specific environments. Natural selection does not *do* anything; nothing is ever actively "selected." Instead, it is a way of characterizing a certain aspect of a dynamic process. Recall the definition presented in Chapter I: *Natural selection refers to those functionally important factors which are responsible in a given context for causing differential survival and reproduction among genetically variant individuals in a population of organisms, as well as absolute changes in the numbers and diversity of different populations and species over time.* *

Consider a textbook example of evolutionary change, industrial melanism. Until the Industrial Revolution, a light-colored strain of the peppered moth (*Biston betularia*) predominated in numbers in the English countryside over a darker, "melanic" form of the species (*B. carbonaria*). The latter were relatively rare. For when the moths rested on tree trunks, the light "cryptic" form was all but invisible against the lichen-encrusted trees, while the darker, melanic form stood out. As a result the light form was far less subject to predation from such insect-eating birds as wrens, great tits, and robins, and they survived and reproduced in greater numbers. Then, as industrial soot inhibited lichen growth and progressively blackened the tree trunks near factory cities such as Birmingham and Manchester, the relative visibility of the light and dark forms was altered, and in time this change brought about a reversal in the relative frequencies of the two forms: The birds began to prey more heavily on the cryptic form and the melanic form increased in frequency (or relative numbers).[50]

Where in this example is natural selection "located"? Is it embodied in the perceptual abilities and food choices of the birds that prey on *B. betularia*? in the factory soot? in the human purposes that led to the production of soot? in the moths' habit of resting on certain tree trunks? in the wing pigmentation of the moths? The answer is that natural selection is located in the *configuration* of factors that combine to influence differential survival and reproduction. In this case an alteration in the relationship between the coloration of the trees and the wing pigmentation of the moths, as a consequence of industrial pollution, was an important proximate factor. But this factor was important only because of the inflexible resting behavior of the moths and the feeding habits and perceptual abilities of the birds. Had the moths been subject to predation only from insect-eating bats that use sonar rather than a visual detection system to catch insects on the wing, the change in background coloration would have made no difference. It would have been selectively neutral.

* In this definition, I hasten to add, natural selection is as much associated with continuities as with change (maintaining or stabilizing selection) and with weeding in as well as weeding out different characters or species (directional selection). This, I believe, accords both with Darwin's original vision and the views of the modern synthesizers, though not, perhaps, with those of some recent revisionists.

Furthermore, had *B. betularia* not been endowed with a polymorphism (genetically based variability) for melanic wing coloration—in this case a single-gene trait—the outcome might have been very different.[51] Increased predation on the cryptic form might well have resulted in the eradication of *B. betularia* populations in soot-blackened areas. Thus an internal genetic factor was also involved. Under preindustrial conditions, the melanic form of *B. betularia* was less common, but when the background coloration changed, the adaptive values of the cryptic and melanic forms were reversed. In relation to soot-blackened trees, the melanic variant became adaptively superior.

One cannot, then, properly speak of "mechanisms" or "selection pressures." There are only functional interactions (ends-related processes) that go on within organisms or between organisms and their environments (inclusive of other organisms) and that have consequences for survival and reproduction. Evolutionists often focus on a particular selection pressure either within the organism or in the environment while leaving the relational aspects implicit or unappreciated. But evolutionary causation is always interactional and runs backward from our conventional notion of cause and effect. In evolution, situation-specific functional consequences—or effects—are a primary (but not exclusive) cause of both transgenerational continuities and changes. This is a crucial point. The process of evolution involves a very special form of causation.* It is analogous, though for different reasons, to the psychologist

* To underscore this key point, let me provide one more example. Many years ago the geneticist P. M. Sheppard showed that the shell-banding patterns in the English land snail (*Cepaea nemoralis*) are genetically based. Now it happens that these snails are subject to predation from thrushes, which have developed the clever habit of capturing the snails and breaking open their shells with stones. Thus a behavioral innovation has enabled the thrushes to become a "selection pressure" on *C. nemoralis,* one that will favor less conspicuous shell colors. As a result of this development, a more camouflaged variety of the snail has evolved. However, its geographic distribution and relative frequency varies considerably. Why?

An answer was suggested by a long-term study of several *C. nemoralis* populations on a sand dune at Berrow. When first observed by Cyril Diver in 1926, a relatively small proportion of the snails were of the less visible single-banded variety. Twelve snail generations later, in 1959–1960, the populations were resurveyed by Bryan Clarke and J. J. Murray, Jr., who recorded a sharp increase in the frequency of the single-banded type.[52] The apparent reason for this was that the ecology of the dune had changed markedly during the intervening period, a consequence of the invasion of a shrub (the sea buckthorn) that provided shelter for a growing population of thrushes. Thus factors in the environment influencing the distribution of thrushes also indirectly influenced natural selection in *C. nemoralis.* But there is a bottom line here, too. None of the observed evolutionary changes in *C. nemoralis* could have occurred were it not for an important internal factor. *C. nemoralis* happens to be polymorphic for differences in banding patterns, so there is genetically based variability available in the species that can be differentially favored by natural selection. Had the more conspicuous banding pattern been an invariant trait, the sand dune population at Berrow might have been wiped out.

E. L. Thorndike's famous Law of Effect, which forms the backbone of the behaviorist explanation of learning and behavior.[53] *

Differential survival and reproduction is often a sort of vector sum of a number of internal and external influences, the quantitative aspects of which require the use of Sewall Wright's path coefficients.[57] *B. betularia* is a case in point. In addition to the factors I described, recent research shows that the frequencies of each form in nature are influenced by a heterozygote advantage (and thus augmented fecundity) in the melanic form, as well as, possibly, by differential susceptibilities to variations in air temperatures and to ambient sulfur dioxide levels.[58]

Accordingly, any factor that precipitates a systematic change in functional relationships—that is, in the viability and reproductive potential of an organism or the pattern of organism-environment interactions—represents a potential cause of evolutionary change. It could be a functionally significant chance mutation, a chromosomal transposition, a change in the physical environment, a change in one species that has consequences for other species, or it could very well be a change in behavior—any behavioral change that alters functional relationships is also a direct cause of evolution. In fact, complex sequential changes often occur across several levels of causation: A climate change, say, might alter the ecology, which might induce a behavioral shift to a new environment, which might lead to changes in food habits, which might lead to changes in the interactions among different species, to morphological changes, and to speciation. Both internal and external changes may be important. Conversely, genetic changes that do not alter functional relationships are "noise" or "genetic drift," just as behavioral changes that have no consequences for differential survival might be characterized as "behavioral drift."†

* Thorndike writes: "The Law of Effect is: When a modifiable connection between a situation and a response is made and is accompanied or followed by a satisfying state of affairs, that connection's strength is increased; when made and accompanied or followed by an annoying state of affairs, its strength is decreased."[54] Actually, the Law of Effect was anticipated by Darwin: "Movements which are servicable in gratifying some desire, or in relieving some sensation, if often repeated, become so habitual that they are performed, whether or not of any service, whenever the same desire or sensation is felt, even if a very weak degree."[55] In light of 75 years of experimental psychology, Richard Herrnstein offered the following refinement, which can be stated in mathematical terms: "The proportion of responses equals the proportion of rewards."[56]

† Compare Burton's "tradition drift" and Lande's "phenotypic drift."[59] From a functional perspective, an ecological niche can be defined only in terms of the relationship between a specific organism and a specific environment. Both are necessary for niche specification, and a change in one (either an internal or an external change) can alter the niche configuration. The niche is thus a fluid and relativistic concept. Moreover, dysfunctional as well as eufunctional aspects of the organism-environment relationship may be included, which removes some of the objections raised by Lewontin.[60] By the same token, the term "empty niche" can only be hypothetical. It refers to any environmental context in which a theorist envisions the possibility that some more or less specific organism could establish a viable set of functional relationships.

Misleading Formulations

In this light, it is misleading to define natural selection as a change of gene frequencies in gene pools, as expounders of the modern synthesis have been prone to do. This converts natural selection from a large class of causal factors that can be discovered only empirically to a class of statistical artifacts relating to one transitory outcome in a multileveled, dynamic process. The illogic of a formal definition in which one outcome of the evolutionary process is also defined as the chief causal agency does not seem to bother most evolutionists. However, the confounding of cause and effect has not been excused by the logicians; this is why so many critics have charged that natural selection is a tautology, for so defined it is.[61] Natural selection cannot be an explanatory theory if it is only a statistical artifact. But this is not what Darwin had in mind.*

* The tautology charge was first raised, so far as I can determine, by Bertalanffy.[62] C. H. Waddington made a similar suggestion during the Darwin centennial symposium at the University of Chicago in 1959:

> Natural selection, which was at first considered as though it were a hypothesis that was in need of experimental or observational confirmation, turns out on closer inspection to be a tautology, a statement of an inevitable although previously unrecognized relation. It states that the fittest individuals in a population (defined as those which leave most off-spring) will leave most offspring.[63]

The most influential antagonist is philosopher of science Karl Popper, whose olympian assault has received widespread attention. Popper's critique, in an essay published in 1974, is based on his well-known view of what constitutes a proper scientific theory.[64] In his so-called hypothetico-deductive model of science, a theory must consist of a set of general propositions (laws) that can be linked together to construct deductive propositions (predictions) that are capable of being tested and falsified. For example: *If* all living species are the descendants of ancestral species, and *if* any two closely related species are descended from common ancestors, *then* it follows that two species as closely related as humans and chimpanzees should have a common ancestor. Although fossil evidence of extinct ancestral forms was unknown in Darwin's time, his theory predicted that such evidence would be found, and it has been.

However, the focus of the philosopher's attacks is not Darwin's account of *how* species evolve but his explanation of *why*—the causal theory (natural selection). According to Popper, natural selection theory is an example of "situational logic," a logic applicable only to special situations. Describing it as a "theory of trial and error elimination," he stated his understanding of Darwinism in this way:

> A. Given a world, a "framework", where life can exist;
> B. And given that living entities are produced that vary, and that some of the variants will "fit" the conditions for life (others will "clash");
> C. Then some entities produced by such variation will survive and reproduce and the others will be "eliminated." (p. 134)

Popper argues that this theory is "almost logically necessary" and is therefore a tautology. Darwinism is not testable, he maintains, because it contains no laws that can be used to predict evolution or to explain the variety of living forms. It states only that some individuals will

(Continued)

Equally misleading, in this light, are suggestions that genetic (or chromosomal) changes are raw material that are somehow distinct from natural selection. They may or may not be. Consider the "raspberry gene" in the fruit fly *Drosophila melanogaster,* a recessive mutation that in the homozygous condition (when both of the alleles at a particular gene locus are recessive) is responsible for producing both raspberry-colored eyes and a sharp decline in fecundity. In a series of experiments that pitted the homozygotes against heterozygotes (where only one of the two alleles is the recessive) and individuals without this allele, the selection coefficient for the homozygote was found to be .5. In ten generations the frequency of the homozygotes was reduced

---

survive and others will not; it does not specify which ones will be successful, except in a circular manner. "Adaptation or fitness is *defined* by modern evolutionists as survival value, and can be measured by actual success in survival: there is hardly any possibility of testing a theory as feeble as this" (p. 137; his italics). Therefore, Popper concludes, "Darwinism is not a testable scientific theory but a *metaphysical research programme*" (p. 134; his italics).

Of course this is not what the theory says; it is only the population geneticists' tautological redefinition of it. The critics' confusion is therefore understandable; they conflate Darwin's theory, Darwin's metaphor, and the modern definition. Because the criticisms have been so widespread and have generated so much misunderstanding, it is important to try to lay some of them to rest.

Many critics take for granted and assume as premises the very things that Darwin was at pains to establish and that others disputed. Sometimes they argue in such a way that they implicitly deny Darwin's core premise, that survival and reproduction is the basic problem for all life forms. In the passage quoted above, for instance, Popper's logic is curious. Given a "framework" and variable "entities," it does not necessarily follow that only some "entities" will survive while others will be "eliminated"—unless, as Popper was forced to do, one adds the qualifications that (1) only some of the variants will "fit" the "conditions" (the requisites for survival and reproduction) while others will "clash" and (2) only those that fit (i.e., are well adapted) will survive. These subsidiary elements are not merely qualifiers for the premises. They allude to the very essence of Darwin's theory, to propositions that are eminently testable.

For comparison with Popper's interpretation, let me reiterate in propositional form the version of Darwin's logic presented above, with slight modification:

A. Life is contingent; survival and reproduction is the basic problem for all living forms (the "struggle for existence");
B. Survival depends on the satisfaction of specific biological needs;
C. Functional design (teleonomy) is necessary to needs satisfaction (adaptation);
D. Differential survival and reproduction are observed to occur in nature;
E. Differential reproduction is the result (primarily) of differences (variations) in functional capacities;
F. Evolution ("descent with modification") is the result (primarily) of the differential survival and reproduction that in turn results from functional differences.

Darwin's theory, properly understood, does indeed contain falsifiable propositions (as noted above). Furthermore, the case for the theory is awesome. Any major text on the subject provides ample documentation.

There is no dearth of predictions in evolutionary biology that flow more or less directly from Darwin's basic insight. Rensch lists no less than 100 generalizations about evolutionary

(Continued)

from 50 percent to about 10 percent.[69] The specific mechanism responsible for this decline was suggested in subsequent experiments with the "yellow" mutant. It was found that this mutation is associated with subtle changes in *Drosophila*'s highly stereotyped courtship ritual, which in turn causes reduced mating success.[70] While this is an example of stabilizing selection, it shows that a genetic change can be a direct, deterministic cause of differential survival and, *a fortiori,* the instrumentality of natural selection.

At the other extreme, it is misleading to treat behavioral change as a "pacemaker" that is somehow distinct from the directive influence of natural selection. To do so is to keep the role of behavior in a subsidiary status that is somehow outside the theoretical core, when in fact behavioral change may have been one of the most important causes of evolution and therefore a major subset of the causal influences that comprise natural selection.

Lamarck Revisited

Ever since the emergence of modern genetics at the turn of the century, Lamarckism has been discredited as scientific theory and the very name of this pioneering eighteenth-century naturalist has often been treated with contempt. Insofar as Lamarckism refers to a theory of evolution via the direct inheritance of characters acquired during the lifetime of the individual, this

---

development.[65] There are also Dollo's law, which states that evolution is irreversible, and Wahlund's principle, which predicts that small populations will be more homogeneous than large ones. Cody's proposition says that natural selection will lead to optimization in the development of a trait, unless specifically constrained by past history, by chance factors, or by conflicting needs and goals.[66] Hull points out that there are literally thousands of "laws" relating to the many deterministic aspects of biological processes (e.g., in biochemistry, embryogenesis, nervous system functioning, and bioenergetics).[67]

Natural selection is the only theory that can account satisfactorily for the many observed dualities in the living world: for the "organs of extreme perfection" on the one hand and outrageously jury-rigged arrangements on the other; for convergent evolution in similar environments (such as the striking analogues among Australian marsupial mammals and old world placental mammals) and divergent evolution in different environments (such as Darwin's finches or the 350-odd species of *Drosophila* in Hawaii); for mutualistic and co-operative relationships alongside exploitative and competitive relationships; for the remarkable cases of evolutionary stability and the many instances of change, ranging from superficial to saltatory; for both "progressive" and "regressive" evolution (e.g., the inability of the human species to synthesize ascorbic acid); for man's inadvertent creation of drug-resistant viruses, some 225 species of DDT-resistant insects and other arthropods, and Warfarin-resistant strains of rats (much to our dismay); and, not least, for the origin of new species and the extinction of others. It is the only theory that is compatible with modern genetics, embryology, systematics, paleontology, ecology, and ethology.

Finally, it should be noted that Popper has recently modified his position, in response to various criticisms: "I have changed my mind about the testability and logical status of the theory of natural selection; and I am glad to have an opportunity to make a recantation."[68]

rejection is certainly legitimate, if uncharitable.* On the other hand, Lamarck deserves credit for recognizing the role of behavior in evolution, and he is seldom given his due in this regard.

To be historically accurate, it was Lamarck who first proposed that changes in habits—that is, in acquired behavior—were a major cause of evolutionary change. Like Darwin, Lamarck recognized that functional adaptation to the environment was a problem for any organism. But the environment is not fixed, Lamarck argued, and if circumstances (*circonstances*) change, an animal must somehow accommodate itself or become ill-adapted. Changes in the environment over the course of time can thus be expected to give rise to new needs (*besoins*) that in turn will stimulate the adoption of new habits. Furthermore, Lamarck held that changes in habits come first and that structural changes follow. (His famous giraffes were a case in point.) Lamarck wrote:

> It is not the organs, that is to say, the nature and shape of the parts of an animal's body, that have given rise to its special habits and faculties; but it is, on the contrary, its habits, mode of life and environment that have in the course of time controlled the shape of its body, the number and state of its organs and, lastly, the faculties which it possesses.[73]

Though Lamarck was often accused, even by Darwin, of proposing that new habits arise as a result of a spontaneous "volition" or "desire," he said no such thing. This misapprehension was the apparent result of a mistranslation of the word *besoin;* the word *volonté* was used by Lamarck only in relation to some "higher" animals.[74] In fact, Lamarck viewed behavioral changes as a matter of challenge and response, of externally stimulated creativity rather than spontaneous vitalism. Yet, this formulation was still unsatisfactory in that Lamarck viewed such functional changes as *regressive,* as interruptions of an evolutionary process that he believed was essentially orthogenetic—a view that conflicts with a strictly utilitarian conceptualization. Of course, Lamarck also guessed wrong about the means of intergenerational transmission, postulating direct inheritance rather than differential success within and among highly variable populations.

* In a classic (if gruesome) experiment, biologist August Weismann cut the tails off an experimental set of mice over 20 successive generations without, of course, producing a tailless strain.[71] Other evidence against Lamarck's thesis is found in the practices of farmers and pet breeders who routinely dock tails, notch ears, castrate males, spay females, and so on. Then there are such human customs as circumcision, pierced ears and noses, shaved heads, and various forms of deliberate mutilation, none of which is heritable.

It should also be noted that there have been many attempts to revive the Lamarckian hypothesis, most notably in the work reported in E. J. Stelle's recent book *Somatic Selection and Adaptive Evolution* (1980).[72] The empirical evidence remains overwhelmingly negative, however.

Darwin also recognized the role of behavior in evolutionary change:

> As we sometimes see individuals of a species following habits widely different from those both of their own species and of the other species of the same genus, we might expect, on my theory, that such individuals would occasionally have given rise to new species, having anomalous habits, and with their structure either slightly or considerably modified from that of their proper type. And such instances do occur in nature.[75]*

However, Darwin's view of the relative importance of behavioral change was more guarded: "it is difficult to tell, and immaterial for us, whether habits generally change first and structure afterwards; or whether slight modifications of structure lead to changed habits; both probably often change almost simultaneously."[77] Accordingly, most first-generation Darwinists tended to emphasize morphological changes. At the turn of the century, however, a movement developed concurrently among several British and American scientists that in effect Darwinized Lamarckism and assigned to behavior a more prominent role in evolution. The leaders of this effort were psychologist H. Mark Baldwin and biologists C. Lloyd Morgan and Henry Fairfield Osborn. Though their perspectives differed somewhat, their views were generally lumped together under Baldwin's term Organic Selection.[78]

Their basic argument was that in the course of evolution the first step in producing systematic biological changes might well be changes in behavior, especially among the more "plastic" species. When an animal is in some way able to modify its behavior so that it can select a new habitat, after a number of generations such a change might precipitate "congenital" changes "in the same direction" (whatever that might mean) that would underpin or perfect the behavior. This would occur not because the changes are somehow stamped into the offspring but because the new environment creates a "screen" that would selectively favor individuals with the relevant "somatic variations."

From a modern perspective, Organic Selection was a crudely formulated theory. It was worded ambiguously, it was based on a rudimentary pain-pleasure model of behavior, and it was pre-Mendelian. However, the ultimate

* As usual, Darwin was able to illustrate the point with some apposite examples:

> Can a more striking instance of adaptation be given than that of a woodpecker for climbing trees and for seizing insects in the chinks of the bark? Yet in North America there are woodpeckers which feed largely on fruit, and others with elongated wings chase insects on the wing; and on the plains of La Plata, where not a tree grows, there is a woodpecker, which in every essential part of its organisation, even in its colouring, in the harsh tone of its voice, and undulatory flight, told me plainly of its close blood-relationship to our common species; yet it is a woodpecker which never climbs a tree![76]

demise of Organic Selection was due more to external events than to any intrinsic weakness. The primary reason for its decline was the emergence of Mendelism and the mutation theory of biological change, which for a time swept aside even Darwinism. According to the Mendelians, mutations (and the consequent structural changes) come first and thus lead the evolutionary parade.

The story behind the rediscovery that behavior is an important factor in evolutionary change is long and involved;* suffice it to say that the supporting evidence is now extensive.[83] Here is Ernst Mayr, a leading authority on the subject:

> A shift into a new niche or adaptive zone requires, almost without exception, a change in behavior. In the days of mutationism (De Vries, Bateson), there was much heated argument over the question whether structure precedes habit or vice versa. The choice was strictly between saltationism and Lamarckism [*sic*]. The entire argument has become meaningless in the light of our new genetic insight. It is now quite evident that every habit and behavior has some structural basis but that the evolutionary changes that result from adaptive shifts are often initiated by a change in behavior, to be followed secondarily by a change in structure. . . . It is very often the new habit which sets up the selection pressure that shifts the mean of the curve of structural variation. Let us assume, for instance, that a population of fish acquires the habit of eating small snails. In such a population any mutation or gene combination would be advantageous that would make the teeth stronger and flatter, facilitating the crushing of snail shells. In view of the ever present genetic variation, it is virtually a foregone conclusion that the new selection pressures (owing to the changed habit) would soon have an effect on the facilitating structure.
>
> Darwin was fully aware of this sequence of events. The parasitic wasp *Polynema natans,* in the family Proctotrupidae, lays its eggs mostly in the eggs of dragonflies. Most of its life-cycle, including copulation, takes place underwater. "It often enters the water and dives about by the use not of its legs, but of its wings, and remains as long as four hours beneath the surface; yet it exhibits no modification in structure in accor-

* A modest effort to rehabilitate the concept of Organic Selection was made by Simpson, who renamed it the "Baldwin effect." However, Simpson portrayed it as a subsidiary, dependent phenomenon: "It does not, however, seem to require any modification of the opinion that the *directive force* in adaptation, by the Baldwin effect or in any other particular way, is natural selection."[79] Subsequently the concept was independently revitalized and given experimental support by C. H. Waddington, who dubbed his version "genetic assimilation."[80]

A major turning point was the set of conferences sponsored jointly by the American Psychological Association and the Society for the Study of Evolution, which led to an edited volume called *Behavior and Evolution* (1958).[81] This work, often cited as a benchmark, contains a mother-lode of tantalizing ideas: There is the suggestion that adaptive radiations, a major aspect of evolutionary change, might be "fundamentally behavioral" in nature (Simpson), that behavior

(Continued)

dance with its abnormal habits." . . . Other aquatic species of parasitic wasps have since been discovered in the families Chalcididae, Ichneumonidae, Braconidae, and Agriotypidae. As Darwin stated correctly, none of them has undergone any major structural reorganization following the shift into a new adaptive zone.

The shift from water to land, as mentioned above, was likewise made possible by a prior shift in habits, in this case, in locomotor habits. There is agreement about this between the students of vertebrates . . . and of the arthropods. . . . With habitat selection playing a major role in the shift into new adaptive zones and with habitat selection being a behavioral phenomenon, the importance of behavior in initiating new evolutionary events is self-evident. A study of behavior differences among related species and genera is apt to throw much light on the sequence of events that trigger the emergence of evolutionary novelties.

Man's civilization provides many new habitats into which numerous animals have shifted successfully. Chimney swifts (*Chaetura*) nest in chimneys instead of hollow trees; nighthawks (*Chordeiles*) on the flat roofs of homes and factories instead of on the ground; house martins (*Delichon urbica*) on house walls instead of on cliffs, to cite a few avian examples. . . .

The tentative answer to our question "What controls the emergence of evolutionary novelties" can be stated as follows: Changes of evolutionary significance are rarely, except on the cellular level, the direct results of mutation pressure. Exceptions are purely ecotypic adaptations, such as cryptic coloration. The emergence of new structures is normally due to the acquisition of a new function by an existing structure. In both cases the resulting "new" structure is merely a modification of a preceding structure. The selection pressure in favor of the structural modification is greatly increased by a shift into a new ecological niche, by the acquisition of a new habit, or by both. A shift in function exposes the fully formed "preadapted" structure to the new selection pressure. This, in most cases, explains how an incipient structure could be favored by natural selection before reaching a size and elaboration where it would be advantageous in a new role. Mutation pressure, as such, plays a negligible role in the emergence of evolutionary novelties, except possibly on the cellular level.[84]

---

might often serve as an isolating mechanism in speciation (Spieth), that all organisms, inclusive of their behavior, are teleonomic systems (Pittendrigh), and that in the process of evolutionary change, many behaviors may very well appear first and genetic changes later (Mayr).

Yet, as Waddington noted in a perceptive review the following year, somehow the point was never really brought out into the daylight that behavior might be an important *cause* of evolutionary change, not just a result, "since it is the animal's behavior which to a considerable extent determines the nature of the environment to which it will submit itself and the character of the selective forces with which it will consent to wrestle. This 'feedback' or circularity in a relation between an animal and its environment is rather generally neglected in present-day evolutionary theorizing."[82]

Darwin's Finches

Perhaps one of the most decisive examples—theoretically—concerns one of Darwin's Galapagos finches, the so-called woodpecker finch (*Camarhynchus pallidus*). Though *C. pallidus* was not actually observed by Darwin, subsequent researchers have found that among the fourteen highly unusual species of finches that have evolved in the Galapagos Islands (probably from a single immigrant species of mainland finch), the woodpecker finch occupies a niche that is normally claimed on the mainland by the South American woodpecker. Yet as most beginning biology students know, the Galapagos woodpecker finch has achieved its unique adaptation in a peculiar way. Instead of excavating trees with its beak and tongue, as the mainland woodpecker does, *C. pallidus* skillfully uses cactus spines or small twigs held lengthwise in its beak to probe beneath the bark. When it succeeds in dislodging an insect larva, it quickly drops its digging tool or deftly tucks it between its claws just long enough to devour the prey. Members of this species have also been observed carefully selecting "tools" of the right size, shape, and strength and carrying them from tree to tree.[85]

The mainland woodpecker's feeding strategy is in part dependent on the fact that its ancestors evolved an extremely long, probing tongue. But *C. pallidus* has no such morphological adaptation. In the process of speciation, *C. pallidus* evolved a behavioral adaptation in place of an otherwise necessary morphological trait; the "invention" of a digging tool enabled the woodpecker finch to bypass the structural change. Whether or not the relevant genetic raw material was available in the form of heritable variations in tongue lengths is a moot point. It was not differentially favored (positively selected) in the course of speciation, even though other characteristics (such as beak structure) were.[86] Thus it is reasonably safe to conclude that a "creative" behavioral adaptation played an important causal role in this instance, by facilitating (and perhaps initiating) a systematic change in the organism-environment relationship.

Chance, Necessity, and Teleonomy

How should we conceptualize the evolutionary process? The central precept, it seems to me, is this: Evolution can be viewed as a multileveled, dynamic process which at each level of organization combines stochastic, deterministic, and teleonomic aspects in a time-bound matrix. G. Ledyard Stebbins identifies eight levels of biological organization (macromolecules, macromolecular aggregates, organelles, cells, tissues, organs, organ systems, and individuals)[87] and at least three more levels can be added: sexually reproducing pairs, symbionts and socially organized species, and ecosystems. Moreover, the linkages and interactions between each level of organization exert causal influences (directly or indirectly) on other levels. Each level of organization represents either an inner or an outer environment (in Huxley's formulation) for the next level above or below. Causation is not a one-way street.[88] In other words, higher-level systems can become the environment that defines the selective context for the lower-level parts. Though this pattern has long been understood in organismic biology,[89] it is only beginning to affect the thinking of ethologists and sociobiologists.

The first two classes of factors noted above are uncontroversial; contrary to the views expressed by some recent critics, expounders of the modern synthesis have traditionally recognized that evolution combines chance and necessity. Chance is generally taken to mean random genetic variations (or nonpurposive variations, since mutational processes now appear to be more canalized and clocklike than was once believed). Chromosomal rearrangements and recombination in the process of sexual reproduction are also important. In view of what has been said above, chance elements (in the sense only of being unpredicted) could enter into the process at any level of causation, including the behavioral. After all, migration, hybridization, Sewall Wright's "peak shifts," Mayr's "founder principle," and other "sampling errors" that introduce stochastic elements into population structures often arise from behavioral changes. Likewise, evolution is subject to a wide range of unpredictable shifts in the physical environment, from localized perturbations that might obliterate a subspecies (a volcano eruption, a dam project, an oil spill) to such a cataclysmic worldwide event as an ice age or a meteor impact (the "punctuated equilibria" postulated by Eldredge and Gould). There may even be a greater degree of indeterminacy in ontogeny than we have heretofore appreciated.[90]

In the same manner, deterministic aspects are found at every level of biological causation, from the constraints imposed by the structure and the combinatorial properties of the four nucleotide bases that comprise DNA to the thermodynamic requirements of metabolism to the more diffuse imperatives associated with the properties of the material world and the principles of physics and engineering, as D'Arcy Thompson made abundantly clear in his classic work *On Growth and Form* (1917).[91] Bernard Rensch identified at least twenty classes of phenomena that impose lawlike constraints and requirements on the evolutionary process, among them the need for basing the process on carbon compounds and a water medium, thermal boundaries at (0°C and about 60°C), the near-universal requirement for organisms to have some sensory apparatus, and the need for locomotion in animals.[92] Such imperatives mean that evolution could successfully follow only certain channels; the number of workable alternatives that could survive and reproduce has always been strictly limited, even though the current number of species is estimated to be well over two million.

Teleonomy in Evolution

Less obvious (and probably more controversial) is the assertion that teleonomic influences are operative at every level of evolutionary causation except in the physical environment. Let me summarize the argument.[93]

The history of evolutionary thought has been marked by a long succession of proponents for various theories of oriented or directed evolution. Yet such orthogenetic and/or finalistic theories are profoundly antithetical to Darwinism and the modern synthesis. Darwin's theory is incompatible with the notion that there is some transcendant causal principle that supercedes the directive influence of natural selection (that is, the exigencies of adaptation to the immediate environment), and most evolutionists remain firmly opposed to anything that suggests an external teleology. However, in recent years evolutionists have generally come to accept the view that the products of evolution, by nature, embody an internal teleology (or teleonomy).[94] For the cornerstone of Darwin's theory is the premise that life is an emergent, unstable, and contingent phenomenon. Survival and reproductive success require that utilitarian criteria take precedence; to assert otherwise is tantamount to assuming away the survival problem, as many orthogenetic and finalistic theorists (and some radical advocates of saltatory and nonadaptive forms of evolutionary change) implicitly do.* Indeed, it is just as "Panglossian" to discount the importance of the survival problem—the problem of functional design and adaptation—as it is to assume that everything in nature is well adapted.

Darwinian teleology is not static. Because it is always the result of past successes on the part of specific organisms in specific environments, it cannot be oriented to a problematical future state. Rather, it comes and goes with the vicissitudes of organism-environment interactions and must be tested anew

* In order for Jukes to argue that genetic drift plays a "leading role" in evolution, for Ho and Saunders and S. J. Gould to argue that random, nonadaptive, or structural changes are of equivalent or greater importance in speciation than natural selection, these theorists must in effect assume away the continuing necessity for survival and reproduction—for earning a living in the environment.[95] An observation of Niko Tinbergen is relevant here: "The naturalist knows perhaps better than any other zoologist how immensely complex are the relationships between an animal and its environment, how numerous and how severe are the pressures the environment exerts, the challenges the animal has to meet in order not merely to survive, but also to contribute substantially to future generations."[96] The problem of survival entails certain inherent functional requisites, beginning with thermodynamic (energetic) requisites, that necessitate functional design and the operation of an economy principle.[97] Darwin's theory is preeminently an explanation for functional design in nature, which extends to complex, hierarchically organized "systems." Theories of drift and nonadaptive evolution, on the other hand, are inherently incapable of accounting for such phenomena.

in each succeeding generation. *B. betularia* provides a good illustration, but far more dramatic are the many examples of regressive evolution among cave dwellers and endoparasites, and the loss of biosynthetic capabilities among many animals. When the organism-environment relationship changes, formerly functional traits may be selected against, atrophy, or be sloughed off as liabilities. In extreme cases, a species may become extinct.

It might seem unnecessary to add that Darwinian teleology applies not only to isolated structures and processes but to biological systems, to the organization, structure, functioning, and life cycle of integrated organisms, inclusive of their behavior, except for the fact that there has been a sharp polarization of views on this subject. On the one hand, the reductionists reject the argument that systems represent an emergent level of biological reality (and teleonomy) that cannot be derived from the atomistic actions of individual genes and discrete traits.[98] On the other hand, the holists assert that organization is an irreducible aspect of the biological realm—that biological systems are more than fortuitous concatenations of random elements; they are "designed" for survival and reproduction and are selected as "interaction systems," in Wright's term.[99]

In recent years, though, there has been increasing acceptance of the views of biologists Ludwig von Bertalanffy, Paul Weiss, C. H. Waddington, and others that biological organization fits the model of a hierarchically organized cybernetic system.[100] That is, organisms are self-organizing, goal-directed thermodynamic systems (open systems) that process "throughputs" of matter and energy and are controlled by informational programs and processes.

No vitalistic principle need be invoked to account for this fact. As Mayr observes, a teleonomic system is simply one that owes its goal-directedness to the operation of a program; the program may be closed or it may be open to learning and/or various kinds of feedback control, but it is capable of exercising control over ends-directed processes.[101]* Although relatively little is known about precisely how biological programs operate, there is sufficient indirect evidence of their existence (notably, when the programs

* Recent writings in the brain sciences do not on the whole employ cybernetic terminology explicitly, but they support the contention that the detailed workings of the brain as a system conform to the essential characteristics of the cybernetic model; the brain operates as if it were the control center of an integrated, goal-oriented, feedback dependent system.[102] Homeostasis—the maintenance of a dynamic steady state via "negative feedback"—was the "goal" postulated in some of the early cybernetic models. More recent formulations envisage such alternatives as deviation amplifying processes via "positive feedback";[103] and "homeorhesis" (a stable developmental trajectory).[104] There are also Locker and Coulter's concept of a goal-creating, or "teleogenic" system and Mittelstaedt's concept of "feed forward," that is, anticipatory controlling information flows. An example of the latter is the body's production of adrenalin in anticipation of strenuous or even violent physical activity.

go awry or are deliberately manipulated, or when feedback control processes are observed in operation) for the basic point to be widely accepted.*

Teleonomy in Evolutionary Change: Indirect Teleonomy

It is one thing to recognize teleonomy (and its concrete manifestation in the form of cybernetic systems) as a *product* of evolution, and quite another to recognize that teleonomic factors play a *causal* role in evolutionary change.

As a first approximation, teleonomic factors can be assigned to two categories, indirect and direct. Indirect factors involve emergent *system* properties and requisites that create preadaptations and define the range of functionally necessary and/or tolerable conditions, perturbations, and alterations that may occur either within the organism itself or in the organism-environment relationship. That is, *teleonomic systems are themselves part of the selective context for genetic, ontogenetic, behavioral, and environmental changes.* Contrary to the "selfish gene" metaphor of Richard Dawkins, genetic alterations are generally selected in relation to their compatibility with the teleonomic systems of which they are a part; a criterion for their perpetuation is their effect on the system or subsystem, their ability to co-operate and to subserve higher-level systemic functions. If genes are selfish, they must also be selfish co-operators. Of course there are well-known exceptions, such as linkage effects and deleterious recessives associated with heterozygote advantage, that entail

* The assumption of teleonomy in organic systems, inclusive of their behavior, has been endorsed more or less explicitly by an illustrious group of twentieth-century life-scientists. The basic argument has been expressed most eloquently by Dobzhansky:

> Purposefulness, or teleology, does not exist in nonliving nature. It is universal in the living world. It would make no sense to talk of the purpose or adaptation of stars, mountains, or the laws of physics. Adaptedness of living beings is too obvious to be overlooked. . . .
>
> Living beings have an *internal,* or natural, teleology. Organisms, from the smallest bacterium to man, arise from similar organisms by ordered growth and development. Their internal teleology has accumulated in the evolutionary history of their lineage. On the assumption that all existing life is derived from one primordial ancestor, the internal teleology of any organism is the outcome of approximately three and a half billion years of organic evolution.
>
> The origin of organic adaptedness, or internal teleology, is a fundamental, if not the most fundamental problem of biology. There are essentially two alternative approaches to this problem. One is explicitly or implicitly vitalistic. Organic adaptedness, internal teleology, is considered an intrinsic, immanent, constitutive property of all life. However, like all vitalism, this is a pseudo-explanation; it simply takes for granted what is to be explained. The alternative approach is to regard internal teleology as a product of evolution by natural selection. Internal teleology is not a static property of life. Its advances and recessions can be observed, sometimes induced experimentally, and analyzed scientifically like other biological phenomena.[105]

benefit-cost tradeoffs. But system viability still takes precedence. As Sewall Wright observes, "evolution depends on the fitting together of a harmonious system of gene effects."[106] To the extent that a higher level of biological organization is the unit of selection—to the extent that differential survival and reproduction is dependent on co-operative interactions—the more inclusive level will predominate. Over time, natural selection can be expected to effect the subordination and integration of lower levels, and relationships that are at first facultative may become obligatory. Group selection—broadly defined—is a process that can be expected to occur at all levels of biological organization.[107]

Examples are everywhere. In sexually reproducing species, much of the selection among functional variants occurs internally during fertilization, zygote formation, and the earliest stages of embryonic development. Newly emerging systems with eufunctional innovations continue "on course" while many seriously dysfunctional variations are eliminated even before they are tested in the environment. By the same token, individual cells and tissues in multicellular organisms are clearly subordinated to higher-level teleonomic control and are regularly sacrificed for the common good. Probably the most dramatic examples are the structures that many animals and plants grow and then shed for one reason or another (epithelial layers, antlers, shells, teeth, fur, flowers, leaves). Likewise, the importance of superordinate controls becomes most apparent when they are removed or break down, as when cell cultures are allowed to grow and multiply freely, when a serious organic dysfunction occurs, and when a malignant tumor metastasizes.

Indirect teleonomy also extends to the social environment,[108] and to ecosystems. An ecosystem is in part a network of organized, functional relationships among organisms and between organisms and the physical environment. The precise configuration of these relationships and the changes that occur through time helps to shape and modify the environmental context—the opportunities, the constraints, the hazards, the competitors—that other organisms must confront. Thus the actualization of human purposes has frequently produced radical alterations in the habitats of other species, and those species have had to respond as best they could.[109]

Teleonomic Selection: Direct Teleonomy

Until now we have been considering familiar aspects of the evolutionary process, but direct forms of teleonomic causation are another matter. Many years ago, Mayr drew a distinction between "proximate" and "ultimate" causation, the former referring to the equivalent of Aristotle's "efficient" causes (structure, processes, mechanisms) and the latter referring to the Darwinian equivalent of Aristotle's "final" causes (natural selection).[110] In effect,

I have collapsed that distinction; I argued that Mayr's ultimate causes are nothing more than the functional consequences, or effects, in terms of survival and reproduction of his proximate causes. Now I shall go a step further and argue that many of the proximate causes, that is, the mechanisms that determine the relationship between an organism and its environment, are neither random nor the result of phylogenetic inertia and ecological pressures (in E. O. Wilson's formulation). Instead, they involve *teleonomic selection,* a modernized, cybernetic version of Organic Selection. This leads me back to the role of behavior in evolutionary change.

While evolutionists generally concede the "pacemaker" role of behavior, they fail to agree on a theory of behavior. Either they do not attempt to account for behavioral changes (which they merely assume as givens) or they adopt a deterministic posture and treat behavior as a dependent variable that is "induced" (E. O. Wilson's term) by external factors or by "epigenetic rules."[111] Many theoretical ecologists take the position that behavioral changes involve nothing more than the tracking of environmental changes. To an extent this is true, yet there is reason to believe that evolutionary causation is a two-way street, that an interactional, cybernetic model is more nearly correct.

The crux of the issue has to do with the sources of innovation, the factors that precipitate novel behaviors or other changes in the pattern of organism-environment relationships. How do we account for the tool-using behavior of the Galapagos woodpecker finch? or the potato washing of Japanese macaques? or the "cultural" variations and traditions that have been reported for a broad spectrum of animal species? One striking piece of statistical evidence is the finding that for 19 variables across 29 different primate population samples, less than one-half of the total variance could be ascribed to phylogeny.[112]*

Two experiments, chosen more or less at random from the large and rapidly growing literature, illustrate the point. (As it happens, both experiments appeared in a single issue of *Science.*[113]) In the first paper, a team of German scientists described a series of experiments that demonstrated that the mobbing behavior (an effective antipredator defense strategy) of European blackbirds is not directly transmitted in the genes but is learned and taught through cultural transmission. In a laboratory, blackbird "students" were successfully fooled by an ingenious apparatus into mobbing a multicolored plastic bottle, imitating what appeared to them to be the behavior of their mentors.

The second paper reported on an experiment by David Premack and his

* Though most of the evidence that is currently used to support the claims for animal intelligence comes from ethological research of recent decades, some of the most striking examples can be found among the writings of various nineteenth-century pioneers, including Darwin himself.[114]

associates with Sarah, currently one of the star performers among research chimpanzees. Sarah's latest exploit involved successful completion of a test of mental ability adapted from one that is widely administered to humans. As a representative of humankind's closest biological relatives, Sarah had no difficulty making same-similar-different judgments regarding pictures of familiar objects—pencils, apples, letters of the alphabet—and was able to use a score sheet where the answers were physically removed from the questions. Her overall grade was about a B minus.

Even the traditional behaviorist model of learning implies internal capacities on the part of an animal for learning novel behaviors and for being appropriately reinforced, and the suggestion has been made that the mechanisms of learning—in effect, the behaviorist Law of Effect—might play some role in evolutionary change.[115] Just as natural selection is a process in which functional effects are causes, so systematic behavioral changes may be caused by anticipated or realized functional effects. These effects in turn are codetermined by the organism and its environment; it is not the innovation in itself that is important, but the consequences of it in relation to the organism's internal purposes and needs (teleonomy). It is the perceived or actualized utility (and/or adaptive value) of the change that counts.

Furthermore, if the cybernetic model is accepted as an accurate representation of the essential nature of animal behavior, this implies a much more complex and active role for the organism as an agency of evolutionary change. In the cybernetic model, internal goals orient the actions and reactions of an animal; learning and innovation are highly directed processes in which goals (system needs, drives, and motivations)—together with whatever information, abilities, and skills the animal may possess—will tend to focus behavioral changes on the solution of preexisting adaptational problems. In the terminology of decision science, organisms are "value-driven decision systems," and the process of behavioral innovation can be characterized as *value-driven experimentation.* Behavioral changes, then, may be the result of a problem-solving process in which the organism and the environment (which includes other organisms) interact, with the process (and the outcomes) having a teleonomic, goal-oriented (and frequently "creative") aspect. Thus *teleonomic selection* denotes a purposive internal selective process, the second-order effects of which may be evolutionary changes via natural selection.

To reiterate, any factor that brings about a change in the organism-environment relationship in such a way as to affect differential survival and reproductive success is a cause of natural selection. If such changes are the result of behavioral changes, then short-term gratifications will also have longer-term fitness consequences. Lamarck's giraffes may be an example. When the modern giraffe's relatively short-necked ancestors adopted the habit of eating tree leaves, this change in the organism-environment relationship had the ultimate consequence of selectively favoring longer-necked individuals.* Similarly, the adoption of high-altitude habitats by various human groups has precipitated significant micro-evolutionary changes among their descendants. Indeed, as J. S. Jones has pointed out, habitat selection plays a key role in maintaining genetic variability in nature.[116] This is why it can be said that teleonomic selection interpenetrates with natural selection. In many simple organisms the behavioral program is relatively "closed," even though the most rigidly stereotyped patterns may be subject to environmental triggers (releasers), feedback controls, and practice effects. More to the point, it has been demonstrated that even primitive *E. coli* bacteria, planaria (flatworms), and insects (Drosophila flies, ants, and bees) can be conditioned: They can learn novel responses to novel situations.[117] And as more complex species have evolved, behavioral systems have become more "open": A cataract of research in recent years has greatly enriched our understanding of the pervasiveness of learning and cognitive processes across a wide range of species, showing clear evidence of "progress" (though not simple linear progression) as one ascends the hierarchy to the vertebrates, the social carnivores, and the higher primates.[118]

These capabilities go well beyond the simple reinforcement paradigms of classical and operant conditioning. They involve specific learning predispositions or biases, selective attention, stimulus filtering and selection, purposive (canalized) trial-and-error learning, observational learning, and, most significant, capabilities for benefit-cost calculation, risk assessment, and decision making. To make sense of the reproductive cycle of herring gulls, for example, an entire arsenal of concepts and analytical tools is necessary, starting with a framework of hierarchically organized goals and subgoals (templates or reference signals) and including memory and information-processing functions, learned behaviors and skills, sensory input and feedback functions, benefit-cost analysis, optimization theory, and probabilistic decision analysis.[119]† Obviously the tools that are applied by economists, systems analysts,

* We are not certain how this unique adaptation came about. Some evolutionists might argue that a biological change came first—a fortuitous macro-mutation that produced a "hopeful monster," in Goldschmidt's term. Even so, any such morphological innovation could have produced only a preadaptation, the capability for adopting a new behavior that might not have been possible otherwise. Unless one adheres to the increasingly untenable position that behavioral changes are genetically determined, the role of more proximate "psychological" mechanisms must be viewed as an independent causal factor in evolutionary change.

† Ethologist Niko Tinbergen has been credited with being the first (in 1950) to propose a hierarchical control system model of animal behavior, though Tinbergen himself traces his inspiration to a little-known 1941 article by biologist Paul Weiss.[120] The following thought experiment, which is an elaboration on one of the watershed studies of animal "instincts" by Tinbergen and Konrad Lorenz, illustrates the principle of hierarchical control.[121] Designed to demonstrate what Lorenz and Tinbergen call a "fixed action pattern," the experiments involved

(Continued)

game theorists, and decision theorists to human behavior may frequently be applied to animal behavior as well.[122] As D. J. McFarland points out: "Animals must make decisions about when to feed, when to court, when to sleep, and so on, in such a way as to maximise as far as possible their chances of survival and reproductive success. . . . In addition to its motivational state and the strengths of its various behavioural tendencies, the decisions reached [by an animal] will be heavily influenced by the decision criteria embodied in objective [benefit and cost] functions. . . . The animal can be seen as carrying out a cost-benefit analysis in making its decisions."[123]

One way of testing for creative problem-solving behavior is to present an animal with a problem that evolution could not have anticipated and then observe the animal's response.[124] Two striking examples involve a social insect, the honeybee (*Apis mellifera*). Karl von Frisch reported observations in which experienced foragers, confronted by the unique situation in which artificial food sources were systematically moved further and further from the hive, learned to anticipate such moves and began to wait for the food at presumptive new locations.[125] The second example involves the honeybee's aversion to alfalfa, whose flowers possess spring-loaded anthers that deliver a sharp blow to any bee that attempts to enter. Experienced bees normally avoid alfalfa altogether, but modern, large-scale agricultural practices sometimes leave the honeybee with the choice of alfalfa or starvation. In such situations the bees have learned to avoid being clubbed by foraging only among flowers where the anthers have already been tripped or by eating a hole in the back of the flower to reach the nectar.[126]

The assimilation and acceptance of this emerging perspective on behavior leads to the following line of argument: If genotypes and phenotypes are not tightly coupled (in more complex organisms); if much "invisible" genetic variation is stored and ready to be called forth at any time by changes at higher levels of organization; if behavioral changes synthesized at higher levels of organization represent a major source of change in organism-environment relationships; and if many behavioral changes have a goal-oriented,

---

the egg-retrieval behavior of the greylag goose (*Anser anser*). If, by chance, an egg rolls out of a prospective mother goose's nest, she normally recovers it with a highly stereotyped pattern. Standing over the errant egg with her back to the nest, she gently nudges it backward with the underside of her bill, tapping it repeatedly until she and the egg have been safely returned to the nest. During this procedure, if the egg at any time rolls sideways, the goose will also give it a gentle sideways tap, in order to reposition it under her breast. Now, what Lorenz and Tinbergen did in their experiment was to remove the egg from under the goose as soon as the behavior had been initiated. They found that the goose nonetheless completed the rolling sequence, just as if the egg were still there. Suppose, however, that when the prospective greylag mother is in the middle of her egg-retrieval sequence an experimenter hidden close by suddenly fires a gun. How likely is it that the goose will complete her supposedly inflexible behavior pattern without interruption? Not very.

cybernetic character; then it is clear that teleonomy—that is, purposive adaptation caused in part by the organisms themselves—constitutes an important factor in evolutionary change. Furthermore, the importance of teleonomic influences, relative to stochastic and necessitarian influences, has increased as organisms have developed a greater capacity for making teleonomic behavioral changes. Evolution has indeed become increasingly goal-oriented, not because of some superordinate teleological principle and not independently of the exigencies of survival and reproduction, but because of the increasing ability of evolved organisms to innovate, to exploit opportunities, and to exercise cybernetic control over the process of change. Indeed, this view dissolves the traditional distinction between natural and artificial selection, or better said, collapses artificial selection into the much broader category of teleonomic selection.

This conceptualization of the role of "mind" in evolution is not new. It was expressed eloquently by L. T. Hobhouse in 1915 in a now nearly forgotten book, *Mind in Evolution.** Today the argument is buttressed by a rapidly accumulating body of empirical evidence.[127] The cybernetic model of the brain and behavior no longer rests on imaginative speculation; it is the framework that, I contend, best fits the data. Furthermore, the products of "mind" represent one important source of creativity in evolution. For better or worse, the human species has been responsible for the overwhelming majority of such teleonomic changes in recent millennia, yet there is no absolute gulf between humankind and other species—as Darwin recognized and argued to a largely hostile audience. The audience may still be largely hostile today, but—to update the plea of the geneticist and Nobel laureate H. J. Muller during the Darwin centennial—133 years without Darwin are enough.

Saltationism

One other issue must be confronted before proceeding to the development of my theory. If some theorists have rejected Darwinism because it is suppos-

* The subject was pioneered by Herbert Spencer in *The Principles of Psychology* (1855). In the latter part of the nineteenth century the literature in comparative psychology, as it came to be called, included such classics as Romanes's *Animal Intelligence* (1882), *Mental Evolution in Animals* (1883), and *Mental Evolution in Man* (1888), as well as C. Lloyd Morgan's *Animal Life and Intelligence* (1891), *Habit and Instinct* (1896), and *Animal Behaviour* (1900). In the early part of this century, there were also E. L. Thorndike's *Animal Intelligence* (1911), William McDougall's *Psychology: The Study of Behavior* (1912), and Wolfgang Köhler's *The Mentality of Apes* (1925), which included descriptions of his classic experiments on problem solving and tool use in chimpanzees. Indeed, various writers have, over the years, viewed the entire evolutionary process as being cognitive in nature, since all organisms must be knowledge-using systems. From this point of view, the human mind can be viewed as only the latest extension of a deep-rooted evolutionary trend toward forms that are more proficient at acquiring new knowledge.

edly tautological, others have charged that natural selection, if it is defined as a process of gradual, incremental change based on the differential selection of small biological variations, is incapable of accounting for the evidence of *discontinuities* in evolution—for the (apparently) sudden appearance in the fossil record of new forms and the lack of intermediates between many sharply different yet related species—for example, chimpanzees and our own hominid ancestors. (Recall Darwin's adherence to the dictum *natura non facit saltum.*)

Thomas Henry Huxley thought natural selection theory and saltationism were quite compatible, but unfortunately a mechanism capable of inducing such gross changes eluded him. St. George Jackson Mivart, on the other hand, took Darwin at his word and used the discontinuities in the fossil evidence to oppose natural selection.[128] The obvious response of Darwin's supporters was that the fossil record was at that time too spotty and incomplete and that intermediate forms would eventually be found.

A more serious challenge to Darwinism arose, as noted above, from the rediscovery of Mendel's laws in 1900 and the formulation of our modern, genetic theory of biological inheritance. One of the co-rediscoverers, botanist Hugo de Vries, proposed a "mutation theory" of the origin of new species, as opposed to natural selection, rather than seeing mutations as a source of the variation that was required as the raw material for natural selection.[129] As it happened, de Vries's theory was based on the peculiar reproductive behavior of the evening primrose (*Oenothera lamarckiana*), which produces differentiated (tetraploid) "ovules." Though subsequent progress in genetics revealed the anomalous nature of de Vries's evidence (it didn't involve gene mutations at all but chromosomal aberrations), saltationism continued to find advocates, including J. C. Willis, O. H. Schindewolf, and most prominently, geneticist Richard Goldschmidt.[130]

Goldschmidt was particularly exercised over what he considered to be the failure of Darwinian theory: It did not account for complex adaptations, such as the compound eye. How is it possible, he asked, that an organ of such extreme sophistication could have arisen in incremental stages? "The wing shape, type of flight, and correlated structure of the lungs of a humming-bird, together with a honey-suckling bill and tongue, are a beautiful adaptation to a definite ecological niche. But could selection favour such a combination before it has reached a working capacity? . . . No!"[131]

The response among the formulators of the modern synthesis was that incrementalism is not only possible but more plausible. Most evolutionists (and most functional biologists, for that matter) consider it highly *improbable* that any complex system could have emerged full blown from some random macromutation. Furthermore, some evidence *can* be traced out. Typically, a single species may last only a few million years, but an entire lineage, an "order," may have a history forty times as long, during which time structures that are at first rudimentary do indeed become progressively improved. In the case of the compound eye, for instance, progress can be observed from single, differentiated light-sensitive cells in the survivors of primitive forms, to clusters of specialized receptors, to eyes with an optic nerve, retina, and cornea but no lens, to, finally, eyes with a complex image-focusing lens such as our own.

From the 1930s through the 1950s the predominant view was that if such macromutations as Goldschmidt postulated did occur, the overwhelming likelihood was that they would be deleterious and nonviable and that hopeful monsters would have to be generated at a prodigious rate in order to produce an occasional "winner."[132]

Systemic mutations as an unaided source of supposedly saltatory leaps in evolution were thus firmly ruled out, except possibly in the cases of some asexually reproducing species and what were presumed to be rare chromosomal aberrations. And while it is true that viable genetic anomalies do occur (mutant insects and birds with stubby, vestigial wings), such anomalies differ from Goldschmidt's systemic mutations in that they are incremental, relatively speaking, and do not radically reconstitute the genotype. More important, they are not somehow excused from being tested for Darwinian fitness. So when stubby-winged insects and birds do survive and reproduce, they do so only in favorable environments, such as windy Pacific islands that are free of natural predators, or under domestication.[133]

Neo-saltationism

This was not the end of the saltationism issue. In recent years saltationism in a "modernized" form—a form consistent with modern genetics and evolutionary theory—has been resurrected by paleontologists Niles Eldredge and Stephen Jay Gould.[134] Their argument runs briefly as follows. First, Darwin's thesis of "phyletic gradualism" does not accord with an unbiased reading of the fossil record. They assert that the persistent failure of paleontologists in the 120 years since *The Origin* was published to find many of the "missing links" in the fossil record is due to the fact that the missing links do not exist. "Morphological breaks in the stratigraphic record may be real," they claim.[135] Furthermore, most paleontologists, in orienting their research toward finding evidence of gradualistic evolutionary change, have consistently overlooked widespread evidence that relative stasis, or only mild fluctuations, may be the norm in most phyletic lines. To explain these contradictions, Eldredge and Gould propose to substitute for Darwin's gradualistic model of evolution a dualistic theory of "punctuated equilibria" in which speciation is viewed as most likely to be a rapid, disruptive event that upsets a previously stable condition. New species are likely to appear "overnight" in geological time. Though natural selection is presumed by Gould and Eldredge to play a role in such changes, their view is that speciation (especially of the kind that leads to new genera) is apt to be a much more revolutionary event than many evolutionists have assumed to be the case, and that structural changes are of paramount importance.

This line of reasoning is buttressed by several contemporary aspects of evolutionary biology and genetics. First, there is the now widely accepted realization that the most important unit of macroevolutionary change is not the individual organism and its progeny but the gene pool of an interbreeding population. Though as Darwin maintained, natural selection is expressed primarily in terms of differential survival and reproduction among individuals (and their kin, according to "inclusive fitness" theory), much individual selection is normalizing, or stabilizing and acts in a conservatizing manner, weeding out deleterious mutations and gene combinations and "readapting" a population following some disturbance. Incremental improvements (microevolution) may also be the province of classical reproductive competition, but the major *discontinuities* in evolution—such as those that lead to the emergence of novel genera—are species-wide phenomena. "The species," Mayr observes, "is the keystone of evolution."[136]*

Furthermore, the origin of new species is viewed as being, more commonly, the result of divergence, reproductive isolation, and differential success among discrete breeding populations or "demes" within a species (allopatric speciation) instead of a fissioning process within a single population (sympatric speciation).† Though various microevolutionary changes might be responsible

* A brief note on the problem of defining what a species is. The concept is slippery and some biologists have questioned whether or not it is a "real" evolutionary unit.[137] A species is commonly defined as the most inclusive population of organisms that are readily able to interbreed with one another in nature. Reproductive isolation is therefore both a real phenomenon and one with significant population genetic consequences. The problem is that many so-called species are no more than a congeries of highly differentiated populations that grade into other closely related species. Two populations at either end of a distribution (a cline) might be able to interbreed with populations located in the middle, but not with each other. Conversely, there are times when two populations presumed to be of two different species because of both geographic separation and pronounced morphological differences will readily interbreed when brought together. Sometimes, too, species that will not interbreed in nature will do so in the laboratory. Furthermore, the species is not by any means the only unit of evolutionary change. Evolution occurs on many "levels" in an ascending hierarchy of biological entities, from individual genes to entire ecological communities. In fact, there is currently much controversy over the relative importance in evolution of individuals, kinship groups, local breeding populations, (and "structured demes"), versus the species as a whole.

† There is considerable confusion over the meaning of these two terms. To some extent, the differences are matters of degree and timing. Much depends upon the degree of differentiation

in the first instance for producing barriers to continuing "gene flow" between closely related populations—ranging from behavior (such as bird song "dialects") to mechanical interference with sexual reproduction (say, the shape of the genitalia or the chemical composition of the odor-producing pheromones that may serve as sexual attractant) to temporal or seasonal separations in species with short reproductive cycles (as in the geneticists' favorite research organism, the *Drosophila* fly)—geographic separation among adjacent populations is of particular importance.[139]

Wright's Model

Geneticist Sewall Wright, one of the trio of theorists who in the 1920s and 1930s founded modern population genetics (the others were R. A. Fisher and J. B. S. Haldane),* long ago proposed a "shifting balance" theory of population structure and speciation in which the theory of Eldredge and Gould may be only a special case.[141] Because of its ultimate importance to the theory being developed here, I will describe Wright's theory.

In abbreviated form, Wright's theory proceeds from the cardinal fact that a species is usually not a homogeneous entity but is rather a mosaic of local "neighborhood" populations—numbering from less than one hundred to many tens of thousands but in most cases not more than a few hundred—that are biologically and ecologically differentiated from one another (to some extent even randomly). Furthermore, while migration between populations and occasional hybridization may help to maintain the continuity of species, there may be many "racial" differences between local populations, as a result of both genetic and environmental divergence. Indeed, there are cases where the differences between the extremes *within* a species are greater than those *between* two "sibling species"—so designated by Mayr because they are morphologically indistinguishable even though they are reproductively isolated from one another.

Most species can accordingly be visualized as being distributed among different locations on an adaptive landscape (C. H. Waddington's term)—a

---

and geographic isolation prior to speciation and upon the rapidity of the change. Some argue that the extreme cases of geographic speciation are likely to be sympatric, whereas allopatric speciation is likely to be more gradual. Mayr has observed that Darwin himself was vague and inconsistent on the subject of speciation.[138] Earlier in his career Darwin seemed to appreciate full well the significance of reproductive isolation in producing new species. But in his mature work he seemed to confuse and lump together gradual modifications within a species over time with the process of splitting and formation of distinct but related species, despite the fact that he had at hand such compelling evidence as "Darwin's finches."

* S. S. Chetverikov in Russia should also be accorded a place among the founding fathers, although his work was until recently not widely known in the West.[140]

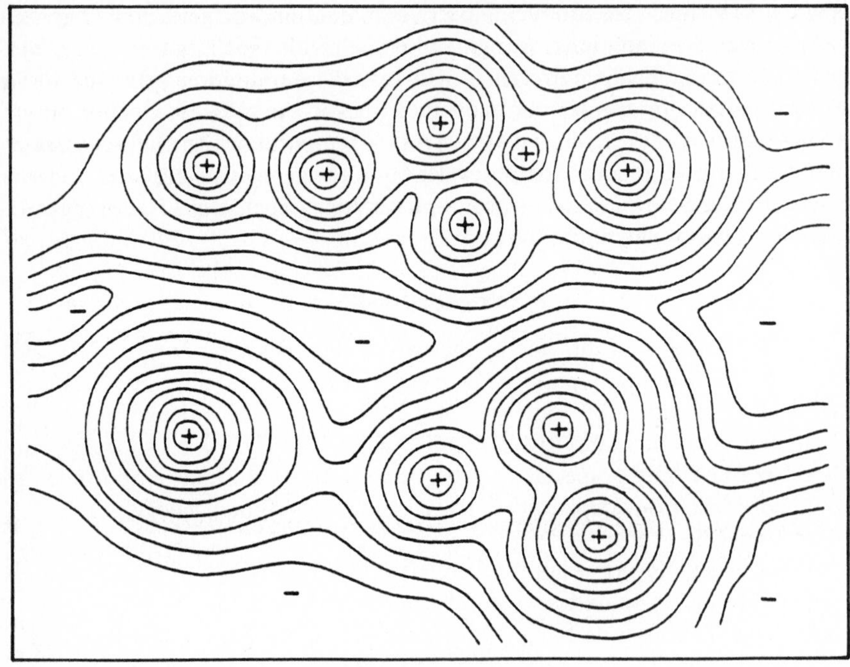

FIGURE II
Sewall Wright's adaptive landscape. (From Theodosius Dobzhansky et al., *Evolution* [San Francisco: W. H. Freeman, 1977].)

symbolic contour map (Figure II) consisting, possibly, of a large number of different adaptive peaks (+) and valleys (−), as well as various gradations in between. (Technically, Wright's landscape is a mathematical surface upon which one can represent the selective values for different gene combinations.) Thus each "selective peak" represents nothing more than a temporarily stable set of co-adapted genes, an "interaction system" that functions "cooperatively"—synergistically—to produce the various traits that are the objects of natural selection.*

Wright views a major evolutionary change, then, as a result of a "balance shift" among the many opposing pressures toward stability and change that are inherent in the genetic structure and the particular microenvironments occupied by a species. Sometimes adaptive peaks may change, possibly by

* The centrality of the entire genome (technically, a haploid set of genes) as a synergistic system has been recognized by a number of other theorists as well. Dobzhansky observed that evolution favors genes that are "good mixers," while Sandra Scarr-Salapatek characterizes an organism as a "physiological team."[142]

random diffusion of fortuitous new gene combinations, or perhaps as a consequence of an environmental change, with the result that a population previously occupying a position well down one of the slopes might find itself elevated to a selective peak. Likewise, a population may either drift or evolve in such a way that it is able to "cross a saddle" between two different peaks. Once such a "peak shift" has occurred, the favored new interaction systems may diffuse and replace less favored combinations. Such a process of differential selection among populations, as opposed to "mass selection" among individuals within a population, Wright calls "interdemic selection."*

Accordingly, what Gould and Eldredge have in mind is only one of a number of possible scenarios in Wright's model. Their scenario involves cases in which a local population is, so to speak, forced down into one of the valleys on the contour map, where the "struggle for existence" may be greatly intensified. There, the population could become extinct, or, if it succeeds in crossing the "trough" to some adjacent "fitness surface," new ecological opportunities might open up and a sharp evolutionary discontinuity occur. Not only might the new species radiate into a radically different niche, it might even reinvade its old niche and eventually displace the original parental stock.

Mayr, who dubbed this scenario a "genetic revolution," points out that any very small, inbred population derived initially from a biased sample of the parental stock (in accordance with his well-known "founder principle") and forced into a marginal or alien environment would be capable of very rapid biological change.[144] Favorable mutations would spread more quickly, other stochastic factors would have greater impact, and selection pressures would be radically altered. Though the fate of such peripheral populations is likely to be extinction, this scenario may sometimes lead to successful change and could be responsible for many of the apparently saltatory leaps in the fossil record.[145]† Indeed, this scenario may well fit the evolution of man and, in an analogous way, the evolution of complex civilizations.

* One variant of Wright's model, which involves selective forces operating on the entire genetic constitution of an organism, might be called "genome-type selection,"[143] that is, selection among differentiated interaction systems in local populations or species. It is this form of selection, Wright argues, that is largely responsible for absolute changes over time in the numbers and diversity of different populations and species. Though the more familiar term group selection is frequently used to label this conceptualization, it should not be. Group selection should refer only to selection processes that involve functionally organized social groups. This is how Darwin, who coined the concept if not the term, intended it to be used. In *The Origin,* the concept was used to account for sterile castes of bees in organized hives, and in *The Descent of Man* he applied it also to our own species.

† A similar line of argument was also developed by Haldane, while Simpson, in another version oriented specifically to the evolution of "higher taxa," employed the term "quantum evolution."[146]

So where does that leave Darwinsim—natural selection among variant individuals? While Wright's model of evolution incorporates the actions of such micro-level processes as mutation, genetic recombination, migration, hybridization, and individual selection, these processes are viewed by Wright (in contrast with some other contemporary evolutionists) as being powerfully augmented by selection among demes and among species that are in competition for the same niche (such as, to cite an example close to home, the snails, birds, rabbits, insects, and humans that compete with one another for vegetable and grain crops). In Wright's model, classical Darwinism assumes a supporting role, building preadaptations that permit adaptive radiation and the exploitation of new opportunities, as well as facilitating "post-adaptation" to newly acquired niches.

Thus, head-to-head competition among individuals who are locked into a Malthusian struggle for existence is relevant in Wright's model, but it is less important than the "selective diffusion" of co-adapted gene complexes in response to "ecological opportunities," which he calls the "greatest creative factor" in evolution. Such opportunities might occur as a result of a species having achieved an adaptive threshold where a new way of life can be developed, or by migration into new areas with unoccupied niches, or by being preadapted so as to be able to take advantage of some changing condition.[147] Classical reproductive competition is, then, only one of several levels upon which natural selection is manifested. Because genes are encased, so to speak, in a hierarchy of systems that may embrace cells, organisms, populations, species, and even multispecies "ecosystems," selection pressures can be exerted at any or all of these hierarchical levels at once, sometimes in the same direction and sometimes in opposition to one another.

A classic example is the sickle cell trait in humans. In certain African populations that live in malarial areas, there is both a strong negative selection pressure exerted at the organismic level, where individuals endowed with one alternative genotype (the homozygote) will be afflicted with the debilitating hereditary disease known as sickle-cell anemia, and a strong positive selection pressure at the ecological level favoring the heterozygote, which provides a genetic resistance to *falciparum* malaria. This is called a balanced polymorphism. Both of these selection pressures operate concurrently to keep the gene at an equilibrium frequency in those populations.[148]

Support from Genetics

Neo-saltationism has also derived some support from recent developments in genetics. Despite Wright's early recognition that evolution involves co-adapted genetic "interaction systems," the approach that dominated evolutionary biology from the 1930s to the 1960s assumed that a change in the frequency of individual genes was largely synonymous with evolution. The model that prevailed was based on simple Mendelian traits with single-gene or additive properties, and geneticists busied themselves with attempting to determine what factors—what "selection pressures"—are responsible for determining the relative frequency of different alternative genes (or "alleles"—symbolized as "A" versus "a") at any particular gene locus.

This approach was popular in part because it lent itself to a high degree of quantitative precision and controlled experimentation—an important selling point to a discipline that, in the first half of this century, was still in the shadow of physics. But it also seduced many early geneticists into drawing the incorrect conclusion that one could account for entire organisms, inclusive of their organization, their functioning, their ontogeny, and their evolution through time, simply by adding up the actions of—or upon—each of the thousands of individual genes that comprise an organism's genome. (In man, for instance, the number may be between 30,000 and 100,000.) Mayr, with his sharply honed instinct for felicitous caricatures, has called this approach "beanbag genetics."

Nevertheless, for over a generation, terms like homozygote, heterozygote, selection coefficients, dominant and recessive "alleles," and the Hardy-Weinberg equilibrium ($p^2 + 2pq + q^2 = 1$) were confidently inflicted on unsuspecting college undergraduates as if these were the total answer. A few complications were conceded—drift, linkage effects, the problem of explaining polymorphisms—but the innocent student of the 1940s, 1950s, and even the 1960s was led to believe that the basic model was essentially complete.

Two fundamental problems were downplayed or discounted. One is that the genetic program for any organism acts in an integrated manner, as Wright had recognized decades earlier, and that the relationships between (and interactions among) genes may be orders of magnitude more important than the actions of genes alone. The other problem is that changes in readily measured Mendelian traits that are assumed to be free-floating in some hypothetical model population are not typical of the processes that produce long-term, systematic evolutionary changes. Waddington summed it up in one pithy sentence: "The whole real guts of evolution—which is how do you come to have horses, and tigers and things—is outside the [textbook version of the] mathematical theory."[149] Richard Dawkins's ruling metaphor in his popularization, *The Selfish Gene* (1976), is therefore a throwback to R. A. Fisher's beanbag genetics, whereas Wright's "shifting balance" theory requires what psychologist Daniel Freedman has aptly termed a "Gestaltist" approach to genetics.[150]

Under the onslaught of both theoretical critiques and new data,[151] the importance of Wright's "interaction system" model is now more widely recognized. In the first place, the genotype must be viewed not as a beanbag but as a hierarchically organized system.[152] In fact, it is a cybernetic system.[153] Many complex interactions occur among the genes, with many genes forming functional subsystems, or "supergenes"[154] and with higher-level "regulatory gene" actions exerting overall guidance and control over the actions of the "structural genes."[155] Indeed, in the "operon" model of Jacob and Monod,[156] control over co-operating groups of genes is viewed as being exercised by "operator" and "repressor" genes. In the more general model proposed by Britten and Davidson, on the other hand, there are four kinds of genes—sensor genes, structural genes, integrator genes, and receptor genes.[157] Needless to say, changes in regulator genes can produce major structural changes in a developing organism, such as, possibly, neoteny or the fetalization of an adult form. As Stephen Jay Gould notes, such gross genetic modifications represent one concrete mechanism by which many of the apparently saltatory leaps in the fossil record could be produced.

Another recent development involves the discovery that gross chromosomal changes—transpositions—are perhaps more common than had earlier been supposed.[158] A case in point is the important work of geneticist Barbara McClintoch with maize.[159] There is also growing evidence that DNA is not static but may migrate and play a dynamic role within the genome, including (possibly) the induction of structural changes. Though some theorists imply that such changes are more important than natural selection in determining the course of evolutionary change, this conclusion implicitly downgrades the imperatives associated with the problem of survival and reproduction and the continuing necessity for adaptation.[160]*

A third development has to do with the fact that it now appears that the genotype (or genetic substrate) is not so tightly linked to the phenotype (the fully developed organism) as had once been believed. After a generation of dispute between the "classical" and "balance" schools in genetics, the recently developed technique of gel electrophoresis has established that the latter group was right and that many if not most species are characterized by a tremendous reservoir of genetic variability.[163] Data for 125 species analyzed by Selander showed that the proportion of polymorphic gene loci (loci producing more than one genotype) averaged 34.8 percent, while the number of loci that were heterozygous (or comprised of two different kinds of alleles, i.e., "Aa") averaged 9.4 percent.[164] Much of this variation, moreover, may

* Indeed, the structuralists depreciate other sources of saltatory evolutionary change. For example, Johnson and Selander discuss the rapid evolution in the North American house sparrow after its introduction onto this continent in the 1850s.[161] There is also the work of Alvarez and others suggesting an extraterrestrial (meteoric) cause for the sudden extinction of vast numbers of species at the end of the Cretaceous period.[162] But most important for the theory I am developing, functional changes (including behavioral changes) may also produce sharp discontinuities in evolution. This is clearly implied by the synergism hypothesis.

be "invisible" to natural selection and may come to the fore and be expressed only when external conditions undergo a change.

A further point is that at least some gene frequency changes may not be due to natural selection at all but to neutral, or "silent," mutations and to what is sometimes called "random walk," cases where genes may not be subject to selection pressures but may drift toward a substantial representation in the gene pool.[165]*

Finally, it has long been appreciated that organisms may have considerable developmental flexibility and "phenotypic plasticity," the capacity to modify morphology (for example, calluses or musculature), physiology (say, blood hemoglobin levels at different altitudes), or else behavior to suit environmental circumstances within some genetically predetermined "reaction range" or "norm of reaction."

All of this implies that evolutionary changes may be much less constrained than classical Mendelian genetics have led us to believe. Instead of having to await favorable mutations, the gene pool may carry a large reserve of built-in or stored-up variation that is ready to be called forth at any time. Likewise, there are many indeterminate (stochastic) influences at work, and many structural and functional changes that can produce sharp changes of course. In this revised model of evolution, furthermore, natural selection appears more like an editor than a sculptor, canalizing the overall course of evolution and occasionally producing major revisions.

Despite the arguments in its favor, neo-saltationism is controversial (as are some of the props that are helping to support it). For one thing, some of the missing links *have* been found.[167] A classic example is the early Archeopteryx, a reptile in every respect except for feathers. Indeed, we have no way of knowing to what extent even today our knowledge of prehistory remains biased and incomplete.

Another point is that both the "equilibria" and "punctuations" observed by paleontologists may be artifacts to some extent of the kind of perceptual time-scale they are using. Geological time (measured in million-year units) and fossilized bones may be too course-grained to detect what, in ecological time (measured in life-spans), are dynamic aspects of an apparent equilibrium or incremental aspects of an apparently punctuational event. As Salthe observes, the various mathematical models of macroevolution (e.g., Raup et al. and Van Valen) are only statistical artifacts based in the geological residues (or the present historical results) of the actual "functional" processes that go on at various levels of biological organization.[168] It is analogous to the

* What is now termed genetic drift was, not surprisingly, anticipated by Darwin: "Variations neither useful nor injurious would not be affected by natural selection, and would be left either a fluctuating element, as perhaps we see in certain polymorphic species, or would ultimately become fixed, owing to the nature of the organism and the nature of conditions."[166]

long-standing debate among social scientists about whether political revolutions are really discontinuities or merely incremental, threshold phenomena ("percussion caps," to borrow Lewontin's phrase) in the ongoing stream of history. Similarly, in Wright's theory, the processes that lead to the differentiation of local populations and subspecies are not different in kind but only in degree from the extreme cases where entirely new niches come to be occupied. Indeed, it may be possible to translate Wright's "shifting balances" into an economic benefit-cost calculus, in which the adoption of a new niche (as a behavioral phenomenon) can be accounted for in terms of the *relative* benefit-cost ratios for alternative choices. (I will develop this point further when I come to the subject of human evolution.)

Population biologists also tend to be wary of any attempt to fit the process of evolutionary change into a single scenario. In a recent, careful review, White identifies seven different types of speciation events and warns: "Speciation is the result of the combined action and interaction of many processes. . . . We can be confident that the diversity of living organisms is such that their evolutionary mechanisms cannot be forced into the straightjacket of any narrow, universal dogma."[169]

Finally, there remains much evidence of incrementalism in evolution—from horses to canids (the ancestors of coyotes, dogs, and wolves) to our own hominid ancestors.[170]

Despite these caveats, the neo-saltationist hypothesis remains viable and has stimulated important research. As Gould and Eldredge observe, the question ultimately may not be whether, but how often a saltatory pattern applies, under what specific circumstances, and with what proximate causal mechanisms. Perhaps the correct formulation was stated almost a century ago by C. Lloyd Morgan: "Palaeontology testifies both to evolution and revolution."[171] More important for our purposes, the synergism hypothesis posits that certain kinds of *incremental functional changes* may, via natural selection, also produce sharp *discontinuities* in the evolutionary process. This, as we shall see, is consistent with the basic framework of Darwinism, though it differs significantly in relation to the tempo and mode of evolutionary change. Indeed, one of the most outstanding examples of saltatory evolution via functional synergism may well be *Homo sapiens.* *

* Lumsden and Wilson, in their recent book on cultural evolution, posit what they call the thousand year rule. Their thesis is that 1000 years may be a reasonable time estimate for significant changes to have occurred in the gene pool of evolving hominids, given sufficiently powerful selection pressures.[172] This "rule" is conjectural, but it is supported by some indirect experimental evidence.[173]

III

A General Theory of Progressive Evolution

> From every point of view, biology is getting nearer and nearer to the molecular level. Here in the realm of heredity we now find ourselves dealing with polymers and reducing the decisive controls of life to a matter of the precise order in which monomers are arranged in a giant molecule. *Francis Crick*

> The power and majesty of nature in all its aspects is lost on one who contemplates it merely in the detail of its parts and not as a whole. *Pliny*

I come now to the general theoretical problem within which the evolution of human societies and their political systems is the special case. My theory is addressed to two intersecting theoretical issues in contemporary evolutionary biology: the explanation of biological organization (inclusive of social organization) and the nature of evolutionary "progress."

In the heyday of population genetics and molecular biology, the problem of biological organization was in effect defined out of existence or assumed away. It was widely held among biologists that organisms are aggregates of discrete traits; if one could account for individual traits in terms of the major genes or the gene combinations that code for "part," the problem of explaining the whole would essentially be solved. This aggressively reductionist viewpoint was by no means unanimous, however. As noted earlier, Sewall Wright has been insisting since the 1930s that organisms are co-operating "interaction systems," though his position and his formal models have been widely misinterpreted.

Outside the mainstream there were always theorists who insisted that the problem of organization—of biological systems—is *the* unsolved theoretical problem in evolutionary biology. Biological wholes are not simply sums of their parts; they are integrated systems with properties that require separate explanation. A landmark in this vein was the biologist Ludwig von Bertalanffy's *Problems of Life* (1949).[1] In the past decade, however, there have been dramatic changes of mind. What were once voices in the wilderness now approach the mainstream. Burgers, for one, notes with dismay the failure of biology to explain why biological structures arise and how structural innovations occur.[2] Jacob Bronowski, in one of his inimitable television performances, characterized complexity as "the central problem of evolution." John Maynard Smith likewise conceded that "there is nothing in neo-Darwinism which enables us to predict a long-term increase in complexity."[3] Pattee, emphasizing a slightly different aspect, asserts that the origin of hierarchical control is the most intractable problem in evolutionary biology.[4] Ho and Saunders, commenting on Bertalanffy's call for a general systems theory, declare that "There is, so far, no general system theory as such,"[5] while Ghiselin points out that there is no adequate explanation of the division of labor and the combining of efforts in nature.[6]

If, as George Gaylord Simpson said, there is no life without organization,[7] how can it be that there is no theory to explain biological organization? The problem is that not just any theory will do. The theory must be consistent with evolutionary theory in general and the principle of natural selection in particular. In effect, this is a problem of the relationship between parts and wholes, of *why* parts aggregate into wholes (or why wholes differentiate into parts). For it now appears that, in evolutionary history as in human history, the primordial wholes may have been built up out of formerly autonomous microorganismic parts.* So the problem of organization in biology intersects with the general problem of explaining co-operation and the more specific problem of (organized) group selection. If in nature animals are likely to be pitted in Hobbesian conflict with one another, how can organization—

* This conclusion is by no means unanimous among evolutionists. The alternative hypothesis is that the whole came first and only later differentiated into specialized parts. It is likely that both hypotheses are partially correct. The weight of the evidence seems, however, to be favoring an aggregative origin (albeit with further internal development later) for the eukaryotic (nucleated) cell, multicellular organisms, and certainly for large-scale human polities. See below.

differentiation and co-operation among the parts—come about? Dawkins and Krebs suggest that "cooperation, if it occurs, should be regarded as something surprising, demanding special explanation, rather than as something automatically to be expected."[8] Richerson claims that ideally "a general theory of ecology would be derived from the operation of natural selection at the lowest level and would be capable of explaining how successive levels of organization emerge from its operation."[9] The consensus seems to be that no totally new mechanism is needed, but some theorists believe that an as yet unappreciated principle or principles might be required. Bertalanffy, for instance, held that because of the improbabilities involved, some "organizational forces" other than random mutations would have been needed to canalize the process.[10] As will become apparent, I agree.

"Progress" in Evolution

The problem of evolutionary "progress" has a much longer history, and there has been no dearth of theories.[11]* Indeed, various theories of oriented evolution constitute one of the more enduring issues in evolutionary biology. Springing from the Aristotelian tradition, theories in this vein would superimpose on or replace natural selection with some form of intrinsic or extrinsic directionality. The basic assumption of all such theories is that evolution is ultimately directed by either a natural or a supernatural agency that transcends the mundane business of earning a living in the environment. Yet there is a basic contradiction between Darwin's vision of a struggle for existence in an open-ended, contingent "experiment," where the operative principle is trial and success, and a process in which some inherent law, trend, purpose, or end can be divined. Nevertheless, orthogenetic and finalistic theories continue to have a following.[12]

Part of the explanation no doubt lies in a psychological resistance to the vision of life as a process without an intrinsic purpose or goal. If we are so obviously goal-seeking creatures, how can the forces that gave rise to *Homo sapiens* and other species be essentially blind and indifferent? How can purposiveness have arisen in a world governed by chance and necessity? Monod called this the "anthropocentric illusion." As we shall see, there is a response to this challenge that is consistent with the Darwinian view of evolution and that may provide some solace if not inspiration.

Perhaps a more important reason for the durability of the Aristotelian model of evolution can be traced to the sort of rationale that Aristotle himself invoked. Although there are many deviations in evolutionary history, this

* The word progress is deliberately set off by quotation marks to indicate that the word is obviously value-laden. I am using it here in a strictly materialistic sense (see below).

argument says, have there not also been clear-cut evolutionary trends? Witness the profound differences between ancient pre-Cambrian prokaryotes—the ancestors of modern *E. coli* bacteria or stromatolyte communities—and the complex mammalian species that are much more recent arrivals. And Dollo's law reminds us that evolution is a cumulative, irreversible process. Does this not strongly suggest that there is some kind of unfolding or developmental aspect to evolution? If so, why is it unreasonable to postulate some kind of guiding mechanism or teleological principle at work rather than assume *a priori* that such apparently directed trends are epiphenomenal or illusory?

On the other hand, there is much evidence, both in the fossil record and among living species, of evolutionary blind alleys, regressions, and developmentally static continuities—for example, such "living fossils" as bivalve mollusks, rhinocephalian reptiles, lung fishes, certain sharks, and sclerosponges that have remained essentially unchanged for millions of years. Alongside progressive change there is evidence of much trial and error. Periods of quiescence alternate with periods of innovation and explosive radiation; mass appearances are juxtaposed with mass extinctions. How are we to interpret these dualities? Natural scientists have been arguing this issue since the time of Lamarck.[13]

According to Lamarck, the primary cause of biological evolution is a "natural tendency" toward continuous developmental progress, energized by the "power of life." Likened by Lamarck to a watchspring, the power of life was seen as a purely materialistic agency. It involved a crude notion of an inherent energy (of which Lamarck distinguished two kinds, "caloric" and "electrical") that operates within organisms through the actions of postulated inner fluids, in a sort of hydraulic manner.[14]

Lamarck's biology is obviously inadequate in light of what we know today, but the core idea of a materialistic inner source of progressive change remains an important and enduring theme in evolutionary thought.[15] In particular, the theme of increasing complexity as the standard of progress was embraced by many nineteenth-century theorists in both the life sciences and the social sciences. Embryologist Karl Ernst von Baer (1792–1857), for example, expanded his observations of functional differentiation and integration in embryos into a general "model" of biological evolution; he discerned in nature a general progression from more homogeneous to more heterogeneous forms.

Herbert Spencer

By far the most important orthogenetic theorist of the nineteenth century was Herbert Spencer (1820–1903), considered by many contemporaries to be the preeminent thinker of his age. In his so-called Synthetic Philosophy,

Spencer formulated an ambitious Universal Law of Evolution that spanned physics, biology, psychology, sociology, and ethics. In effect, he deduced society from energy by positing a sort of cosmic progression from energy (an external and universal "force") to matter, life, mind, society, and finally to complex civilizations. "From the earliest traceable cosmical changes down to the latest results of civilization," he wrote in "The Development Hypothesis," "we shall find that the transformation of the homogeneous into the heterogeneous, is that in which progress essentially consists." He defined evolution as "a change from an indefinite, incoherent homogeneity, to a definite, coherent heterogeneity through continuous differentiations [and integrations]."[16]

Many of his ideas were derived from other theorists, especially Lamarck and Baer, but Spencer turned others' sketches into an imposing intellectual structure. Spencer not only developed an all-encompassing theoretical system, he attempted to support his case with a prodigious outpouring of scholarly works that included multivolume, multiedition surveys of each of the relevant disciplines.[17]

Although his ideas had a profound impact on the nascent social sciences, Spencer's reputation ultimately went into eclipse. When Social Darwinism became an epithet, he was dismissed as a political reactionary and was treated as a parrot of the discredited Lamarck. Yet Spencer differed fundamentally from Lamarck in that he saw functional modifications as the essence of progressive evolution, not as deviations from the main course. However, he stuck doggedly to the Lamarckian doctrine of the inheritance of acquired traits as the chief mechanism of biological evolution. In this respect his position was antithetical to the core of Darwinian theory, and he suffered the fate of other so-called neo-Lamarckians.

Nevertheless, in the rubble of Spencer's theoretical edifice we find some ideas of enduring importance. At the heart of Spencer's vision was the idea that progress could be defined in functional and structural terms: He asserted a universal, self-generated progression in nature toward increased specialization and functional differentiation, together with a concomitant degree of functional integration. In itself this is only a set of descriptive abstractions, but Spencer went on to attempt to explain *why* this observed trend has occurred. In effect, he proposed that self-preservation and maintenance, or "equilibration," is a fundamental problem in any dynamic system (a premise that is not very different from Darwin's premise of a struggle for existence) and that simple, homogeneous systems are inherently less stable than those which are more differentiated and complex. While the observed progression toward more complex forms may have been energized "spontaneously," it persists ultimately because of functional superiority. More complex forms are functionally more "advantageous," though Spencer could not explain precisely why this is so. The impression he left was that evolution is somehow autocatalytic.

Darwinizing Lamarck and Spencer

Viewed in Darwinian terms, differentiated, complex biological systems may have adaptive value and be favored by natural selection under *some* circumstances, depending on the specific context. For example, many simple forms—microorganisms such as common viruses and bacteria or protozoa such as the Amoebae—have proven to be extremely durable. The key is the trade-offs involved, the relative costs and benefits associated with evolving in the direction of greater structural and functional complexity. When it is possible to achieve significant economies through synergistic effects, the benefit-cost ratios will be favorable.

Spencer might not have approved of this Darwinized (bioeconomic) version of his theory. He envisioned evolution as a unified process in which structures and functions were intimately linked, with individual cases being variations on a common theme. Nevertheless, I maintain that his perception of "progressive" evolution as a unified process was essentially correct, even though a testable explanation for it eluded him.

As we shall see, the progressive trend toward increased complexity of organization that has inspired various theories of oriented evolution can be accounted for satisfactorily without recourse to orthogenesis, within the Darwinian model, and in a way that strengthens both that theory and our overall understanding of evolutionary history. If we recognize the cumulative nature of evolution (with past "inventions" serving as facilitators, preadaptations, and components or partial determinants of new developments), and if we envision the evolutionary process as being rather like a pinball game in which certain developmental paths, when taken, yield higher "scores," then we may have a model that is compatible with natural selection theory. Creativity in evolution, then, becomes a matter not of the working of hypothetical internal forces but of organisms discovering and utilizing opportunities that are inherent in the nature of physical and biological phenomena—opportunities that are made attainable by previous evolutionary history and the particular context.

Needless to say, the triumph of Darwinism put an end to orthogenetic theorizing such as Spencer's law of evolution, at least in the natural sciences. Evolutionary laws fell victim to a new *Weltanschauung* in which there could be no preordained directionality or goals. "Progress" was necessarily both epiphenomenal and contingent. In fact, the nature of evolutionary progress was now a matter of contention. Simpson has observed that "there is no criterion of progress by which progress can be considered a *universal* phenomenon of evolution. . . . Whatever criterion you choose to adopt, you are sure to find that by it the history of life provides examples not only of progress but also of retrogression or degeneration."[18]

Ayala and Dobzhansky point out that progressive evolution in the sense only of directional change is not equivalent to evolutionary progress; the issue of progress in the sense of normative improvement or betterment (including improvements, presumably, in Darwinian "fitness") can be separated logically from the empirical determination of evolutionary trends.[19] A trend may not necessarily be for the better; it may simply reflect a response to changing environmental conditions—for example, successive co-evolutionary changes as a consequence of predator-prey interactions.[20] A directional trend might reflect nothing more than the operation of a sort of evolutionary treadmill on which a species may have to run merely to stay in place. Directional trends can also quickly reverse themselves if conditions change; the trend toward larger size in land animals, for example, was arrested and reversed with the extinction of the dinosaurs at the end of the Cretaceous.[21] However, in the oceans such reversals were far less pronounced until after the advent of humankind—a circumstance that illustrates perfectly the context-specific nature of evolution.

There has been no dearth of speculation about evolutionary trends. Some theorists have postulated global trends that, while plausible, are difficult to verify—for example, a general increase in functional efficiency[22] and a general tendency for life to expand, diversify, and fill the available niches.[23] Other postulated trends are more specific: an expansion in the total amount of energy capture and/or the efficiency of energy utilization,[24] improvements in homeostatic (or dynamically stable) control,[25] increased control over environmental contingencies,[26] and an increased adaptability or flexibility.[27] Kimura's speculation about a progressive increase in the amount of genetic information is more problematical; if it were restated to include redundant information in all the cells of an organism as well as exogenous developmental and real-time information inputs that are utilized by an animal, the case would be much stronger.[28]

As for increasing complexity, this trend may be posited in terms of the total number of parts,[29] in terms of the number of different types of parts,[30] in terms of functional interdependencies between parts,[31] in terms of the Spencerian criteria of functional differentiation and specialization (along with a correlative *structural* differentiation), in terms of greater organization over time,[32] or in terms of what Stebbins calls "relational order," that is, hierarchical structure.[33]

Many of these theorists are, of course, talking about different parts of the elephant; they focus on different aspects of what is actually an interrelated set of evolutionary trends, all of which can be subsumed in the cybernetic (open systems) model of biological organization. As C. Lloyd Morgan observed in *The Emergence of Novelty* (1933), "What we find throughout nature is advance in organization."[34] Progressive increases in energy-capturing capabilities, information content, structural and functional complexity, interdependency, order (or negative entropy), and hierarchical structuring are *all* intimately associated with the progressive evolution of biological systems. These parameters interact with and influence one another in ways that are still poorly understood. Saunders and Ho maintain that it is unlikely that there will ever be any one best, all purpose measure of organizational complexity;[35] different measures will be suited to different purposes or problems. However, this does not diminish the importance of biological organization as an existential phenomenon whose progressive development via natural selection can be traced over the entire course of evolutionary history.* The measuring rod that I favor is cybernetic; for my purpose, the most useful measure of organizational complexity is the quantity (and "power") of information utilized by a system.

Complexity in Evolution

Although it is not unanimous, there is a substantial degree of convergence among biophysicists and systems-oriented biologists to the effect that increasing organizational complexity is one of the most important progressive trends in evolution. The physicist Ilya Prigogine, for instance, maintains that "biological order is both architectural and functional, and furthermore, at the cellular and supercellular level, it manifests itself by a series of structures and coupled functions of growing complexity and hierarchical character."[38] His colleague Manfred Eigen adds that self-organization and self-reproduction *require* a functional (control) code with "legislative" and "executive"—that is, cybernetic—properties.[39]

On the other side of the fence, biologist Howard Pattee claims that "the

* Saunders and Ho hold sharply contrasting views on the subject of complexity in evolution. They claim that complexity can be detached from organization; it is complexity, not organization, that has increased over the course of time. What's more, they argue that complexity is more "fundamental" than organization. The latter arises in response to increasing complexity. Saunders and Ho also assert that the phenomenon of complexity cannot be accounted for in terms of natural selection: "No one has ever managed to show why [natural selection] should lead to an increase in complexity."[36] They go so far as to assert that a relative "lack" of natural selection may be a prerequisite for major evolutionary advances.[37] In their view, structural asymmetries are the underlying cause of evolutionary changes toward greater complexity. In my theory, on the contrary, organization is viewed as being more fundamental; the synergistic functional effects achieved by biological (or social) systems *qua* integrated, functionally ordered structures of matter, energy, and information are the key to the progressive complexification of living organisms. Furthermore, these synergistic effects are routinely filtered through the sieve of natural selection. As indicated earlier, structural constraints, imperatives, and innovations also play a causal role in evolutionary change, but they must always meet the test of fitness.

unique character of biological and social systems behavior that distinguishes them from non-living systems is their tendency to evolve greater and more significant complexity. This is true from cell to society."[40] Likewise, E. Broda writes: "The more the division of labor was developed, the more important became intercellular and interorganismal communication and control. Hence, for an understanding of more complicated systems, thermodynamics and kinetics must increasingly be supplemented by cybernetics, by applied systems analysis."[41]

By far the most compelling recent explication of the hierarchical, cybernetic model of biological organization is James G. Miller's *Living Systems* (1978), in which a general system model is applied to seven levels of organization (other theorists specify more or fewer): cells, organs, organisms, groups, organizations, societies, and supranational systems.[42] Each of these levels, Miller argues, has 19 identifiable subsystems in common, and he advances 170 cross-level hypotheses that he believes are applicable to two or more levels. Miller's encyclopedic effort is a kind of *Gray's Anatomy* of cybernetic systems. Yet it is not a general systems theory, for it does not address the questions, *why* have hierarchically organized systems evolved? and *why* do they exhibit the cybernetic properties that Miller and other theorists have so convincingly demonstrated?

Orthogenesis Through "Fluctuations"

Before proceeding to an explication of my theory, I should mention one other major contender for a general systems theory, the work of the Nobel prize–winning physicist Ilya Prigogine and his associates.

In the latter part of the nineteenth century and for the better part of this century, the combined influence of Clausius's Second Law of Thermodynamics (1850) and Darwin's theory of evolution discredited the orthogenetic viewpoint and portrayed evolution as a contingent phenomenon that could only temporarily defy the laws of nature. Evolution could not be held to have an inherent directionality, for the Second Law of Thermodynamics suggests that the inherent tendency of the physical world is toward a thermodynamic equilibrium, which entails a maximum state of entropy, or energetic *disorder* and dispersion.* If the world were in fact like a Newtonian clock-

* Entropy is a mathematical expression for the degree of thermodynamic disorder that (paradoxically) represents an equilibrium condition. Ludwig Boltzmann's famous equation for entropy is $S = K \log D$, where S is the quantity of entropy, $K \log$ is a logarithmic function, and D is the degree of atomic disorder. Organized thermodynamic systems, however, must be characterized in terms of some kind of negentropic, or disequilibrium state. This prompted Irwin Schrödinger to propose in *What Is Life* (1944) an equation that would represent the degree of order, or organization in a thermodynamic system. Schrödinger's equation for negentropy (N) is $N = K \log 1/D$. That is, the degree of order in a system is a function of the reciprocal of atomic disorder.

work, the basic tendency would be for it to wind down. In this conception, organization (biological or otherwise) is an unstable exception to the basic dynamic of the universe.

Accordingly, a thermodynamic perspective has become an important part of our vision of life and humankind.[43] Indeed, some theorists have been energetic monists. A living organism, Alfred Lotka maintained, is "primarily an energy capturing device—its other functions are undoubtedly secondary."[44] And Howard and Elizabeth Odum inform us that "everything is based on energy. Energy is the source and control of all things, all value and all actions of human beings and nature."[45]

The revival of an orthogenetic viewpoint close to that of Spencer (albeit more highly developed and different in some significant respects) is due primarily to Prigogine and his co-workers' concept of a dissipative structure.[46] A dissipative structure is an "open" thermodynamic (energy-processing) system, one that can take in energy from the environment and dissipate it to reduce entropy. In effect, an open system uses exogenous energy to reverse the tendency toward disorder and a thermodynamic equilibrium state. A dissipative structure is thus a form of thermodynamic system that maintains itself in a state of *disequilibrium* by virtue of being fed energy inputs.*

An example of a dissipative structure is the very same Newtonian clockwork that has been so influential in the development of the sciences (and so often derided). What is generally left out of the classical version of the clock metaphor is the fact that clocks can function only as long as they are in disequilibrium—as long as there are energy inputs (a human winding mechanism, a battery, or an electric current) to keep the system running. Even then the clock metaphor is incomplete because it does not explain how the clock—the dissipative structure—evolved in the first place. Moreover, the clock cannot be used as a metaphor for the universe as a whole but only for locally organized parts of it, that is, for the specific products of a larger cosmical process that has an irreversible historical character and certain stochastic properties. It is to these larger historical or evolutionary issues that the work of Prigogine and his colleagues is primarily addressed.

The key to their explanation is summed up in the phrase "order through fluctuations." Dissipative structures, Prigogine maintains, are self-organizing. They arise spontaneously as a natural response to fluctuations or perturbations in an existing thermodynamic structure. When a thermodynamic system is driven far from an equilibrium condition, nonlinear discontinuities or threshold phenomena may occur that will transform the system in the direction of more complex structural organization and greater structural stability (as

* A thermodynamic steady state is just the opposite of the conventional notion of an equilibrium. It is a stable nonequilibrium condition in terms of energetic disorder or entropy.

distinct from a thermodynamic equilibrium). This process is seen as a historically cumulative process. At each juncture or "branch point," existing structures create the context and the interactions that form the basis for new forms of order. In thermodynamic terms, a complex open system such as the human organism is "a giant fluctuation stabilized by exchanges of matter and energy."[47]

Prigogine and others offer examples to illustrate the process: When a pan of water is heated from below, the heat at first passes through the liquid by simple conduction. Then, at a well-defined critical temperature gradient, an instability occurs and the liquid molecules rapidly form into a regular pattern of convection cells. The perturbation of the fluid due to energy inputs has given rise to a new molecular order and a new pattern of heat transfer, which further energy inputs act to stabilize.

Another example involves water. When water droplets change to ice crystals or to vapor, the cause of the structural discontinuities that occur is the extraction or addition of energy. Such threshold effects also play an important role in many biological processes—for example, in synaptic transmission, in glycolysis, and in membrane permeability changes. Similarly, at higher levels of organization, living cells, Amoebae, computer-driven production processes, and *Homo sapiens* are all examples of thermodynamic systems that are far from equilibrium and are stabilized by exchanging matter and energy with the environment.

Accordingly, nonlinear, nonequilibrium structures are in no sense a deviation from the laws of nature. Just the reverse; they arise naturally as part of the ongoing process of cosmic evolution and are a consequence of properties that are inherent in the physical world.[48] Furthermore, dissipative structures involve co-operation or coordination among constituent units; the stability of a dissipative structure is a direct result of the coherent ordering of matter and energy.

Prigogine and Spencer

The foregoing vision is more reminiscent of Herbert Spencer than Prigogine and his colleagues would like to admit. Prigogine attempts to draw distinctions between himself and Spencer by suggesting that Spencer introduced some "new principle of nature,"[49] namely, an inherent "instability of the homogeneous" and the notion of a "differentiating force" (quoted from Spencer).

Spencer did suggest a universal differentiating force: energy.[50] But this understanding of nature is not fundamentally different from Prigogine's; it is only incomplete because it does not emphasize the creative role of instabilities, or fluctuations, which may also be said to involve a "new principle of nature." As for Spencer's assertions regarding the instability of the homogeneous, he was apparently half right: He correctly identified structural instability as a major factor in precipitating evolution toward more complex forms of organization. However, Prigogine and his colleagues have shown that such instabilities arise only under certain conditions. There are even parallels in the phrasing used by Spencer and Prigogine: Evolution, Spencer said, can be characterized as "a change from an indefinite, incoherent homogeneity, to a definite, coherent heterogeneity through continuous differentiations and integrations."[51] Prigogine et al. assert that "the mechanism of self-organization is 'order through fluctuation' whereby the undifferentiated uniform state becomes unstable to small deviations from uniformity [and assumes a more differentiated state]."[52]

Equally important, both Spencer and Prigogine appreciated the critical interrelationship between structure and function and, in biological systems, the important relationship between regulatory mechanisms and evolutionary change. Prigogine and his colleagues say that the likelihood that a local microstructure fluctuation will cause a change in the macrostructure is dependent on whether or not the mechanisms of internal regulation and control are *adequate.*[53] (They don't explain what they mean by "adequate.") This is the starting point for cybernetics—and for my theory.

Prigogine and his colleagues have elucidated some fundamental and pervasive properties of the physical world and have developed elegant mathematical representations. Yet however important these contributions, they do not constitute a fully articulated theory. Why do instabilities and consequent fluctuations occur? Why should the resulting fluctuations produce changes toward greater structural complexity rather than toward disaggregation, simplification, or even collapse? Why do new forms of order arise "spontaneously"? What conditions are required for their persistence? Are new forms of order a deterministic result of thermodynamic fluctuations? That is, will new stable states *necessarily* arise and be predictable once the stochastic aspects associated with the initial instabilities have been mapped? Prigogine has suggested that a process of testing might occur in the production of new forms of order and that each new form of stability is unique.* If so, what are the testing criteria? Are they functional (i.e., Darwinian)?

Thus it is claiming too much for the phenomenon of "order through fluctua-

* Prigogine says that evolution is deterministic in the neighborhood of stable regimes because small fluctuations are "damped."[54] How that happens is not clear. Near a transition threshold, evolution is stochastic because the final state depends on the pattern of fluctuations. This conclusion, so far as I can determine, is speculative. I suspect that stochastic and deterministic influences are present in both extreme cases; what differs is their magnitude and relative importance.

It should also be noted that Tregonning and Roberts have recently demonstrated mathematically that the evolution of complex systems in nature, while improbable initially, can be expected to occur in profusion over time.[55]

tion" to say, as the philosopher Erich Jantsch has done, that it is "a basic kind of mechanism for the unfolding of evolutionary processes" that seems to "govern" the evolution of physical and biological systems.[56] On the contrary, biological evolution has had many blind alleys, many examples of regression, and a preponderance of failures. Indeed, most of the life forms that have ever evolved have eventually fluctuated back toward a thermodynamic equilibrium. If there has been order through fluctuations, there has also been disorder through fluctuations. One suspects the same is true in physics. Particle physics, for instance, is rife with examples of unstable phenomena that decay, rather than the reverse. And is not the sun, the energy source that drives the evolution of our solar system (and life on Earth) evolving toward maximum entropy?

It might be profitable to Darwinize the process of cosmical evolution. The process may be viewed as being dualistic in nature; phenomena that obey the Second Law of Thermodynamics may share the stage with those that defy it, and the choice in any given instance is not predetermined but the result of a creative, trial-and-error *cum* trial-and-success process. New forms of symmetry and order must be discovered and tried out, and the nub of the theoretical problem is to account for why some new forms are successful and others are not. This is especially true for biological evolution, whatever the ultimate verdict about cosmical evolution. While Prigogine's vision may complement and enrich the Darwinian vision, it is not an alternative to it. Certainly biological evolution requires the concept of natural selection, properly understood,* and it may prove to be the case that a proper understanding of cosmical evolution requires an analogue of the concept of natural selection.[58]

Furthermore, biological systems must be able to do more than capture sufficient energy to maintain thermodynamic stability (disequilibrium). They must also solve a variety of difficult internal and external engineering problems and cybernetic problems. Most important, they must earn their livings and reproduce themselves in the economy of nature—the complex, changing, often unpredictable and sometimes hostile environment. Biological systems must be functional in ways other than the merely thermodynamic. They must be designed for survival in specific environments, and Darwin's theory of natural selection is the preeminent nonteleological explanation for the development of functional design in nature.

If we begin with the requirement that living organisms must be functionally

* Prigogine and Eigen (and others) would exclude Darwinian selection from prebiotic and early macromolecular evolution because it may not have involved competition. Like many other scientists, they have tended to interpret Darwin's principle narrowly (i.e., competition among variant individuals) rather than in engineering terms (i.e., the ability to function effectively in the environment and reproduce successfully).[57]

viable and must meet the conditions implied by the economy principle if they are to survive and reproduce themselves, we may reasonably conclude that more complex forms must also be adaptive. The other half of the remark by Simpson quoted above is: "There is no life without organization, and no organization without adaptation."[59] But this is true by definition; the question is, why are complex systems adaptive? Why do the parts participate in wholes? Or wholes into parts?

The Synergism Hypothesis

The key lies in the phenomenon of functional synergism. I call it the synergism hypothesis. One of the most ubiquitous aspects of the natural world is *synergy*—combinatorial effects that are produced by the joint action of two or more discrete elements, components, or individuals. Such combinatorial effects may be additive, multiplicative, or nonlinear, but in any event they produce discontinuities—"punctuational" or threshold effects that conform to the saltationist model, and to Sewall Wright's "peak shift" model.* In physics, for example, there are pronounced scale effects in polyatomic molecules in the 5–50 atom range and in larger molecules that consist of several hundred atoms, or more. Such co-operative groupings take on physical or chemical properties that cannot be predicted from observing the individual atoms. These new properties may produce changes in geometry, viscosity, contactility, reductions in binding energy requirements and entropy, changes in electron transfer properties, and increased stability in successive amplification processes.[60]

We are all familiar with some of the synergistic effects that arise when atoms of different elements are combined in chemical compounds. The formation of ordinary table salt was described earlier. Similarly, the combination of the gases hydrogen and oxygen in the ratio of 2:1 produces a remarkable substance with distinctive new properties: water.

Catalytic reactions of various kinds also involve synergism. A catalyst increases the rate of a chemical reaction by decreasing the activation energy

* The expression "the whole is greater than the sum of its parts" is not in reality a very satisfactory formulation. Better said, wholes have emergent, combinatorial properties that cannot be produced by the parts acting alone. Wholes are different from the sum of their parts, not necessarily greater than. The philosopher of science Ernest Nagel claims that there is no "logical necessity" for analyzing systems *qua* systems independently of their parts, or for assuming that a system cannot be explained by the actions of the parts in isolation.[61] This is untrue. If the effects produced by a system are the result of interdependent, co-operative actions of the parts, then it *is* a logical necessity for an explanation of these systemic effects to include the causal role played by the interactions among the parts (of the system as a whole, that is). It should also be noted that what constitutes a "whole" may include not only functionally integrated cybernetic systems but also "ecosystems" and economic systems.

required. For instance, if hydrogen and oxygen gases are simply mixed together nothing happens. But add a little platinum to the mixture and the explosive result will be water. Yet the platinum will remain unchanged in the process.

Synergistic effects also occur in the manufacture of such artifacts as metal alloys (stainless steel) and in technological applications of "phase transitions"—for example, in ferromagnets, when electron spins are aligned to create a magnetic field; in superconductivity, when supercooled conductors (at minus 452°F) lose their electrical resistance because of the ordering of the electrons; in lasers, when light emissions are focused and synchronized.* Our physical environment also manifests synergistic properties; the oceans, the atmosphere, and the land masses are all "media" comprised of built-up parts, aggregations of the basic elements with emergent collective properties.

Synergistic effects are fundamental to molecular biology and biochemistry. Life itself involves synergistic combinations of, primarily, carbon, oxygen, nitrogen, and energy. Synergy is also evident in the basic building blocks of living systems. While DNA consists of only four alternative nucleotide bases, the precise patterning of the bases in various stable combinations of base pairs makes possible the co-operative construction of an endless variety of organic substances. Indeed, the functional significance of DNA emerges from its combinational properties. Likewise, DNA and RNA co-operate in constructing amino acids, with DNA serving as template and RNA as a vehicle for translation.

Synergism is of central importance in the multifarious enzymatic reactions that drive the life process. In contrast with inorganic catalysis, the key to enzyme activity seems to be surface geometry, since it is the shape of an enzyme that determines its affinity for a substrate and thus the rate of reaction in producing new compounds. Synergism can be observed in epigenesis (organic development) as well. While genes can properly be considered functional units, the ontogeny of an organism involves an enormously complex network of interrelated events, with simultaneous co-operative actions occurring sequentially among many structural and regulatory genes. Most traits are polygenic, and a wide variety of gene interactions have been documented. (One of the most striking examples of genetic synergy is the phenomenon of heterosis—advantageous combinations of genes at various gene loci—and its antipode, inbreeding depression.)

Mutational synergism is another well-documented phenomenon—for exam-

* Since this work was essentially completed, a series of works by the German physicist Hermann Haken and his colleagues on what he calls "synergetics" has come to my attention.[62] Haken's work is primarily mathematical in nature, but it is compatible with my own formulation. However, the concept of synergism has not, so far, been utilized by Haken as a basis for a causal theory of progressive evolution.

ple, when gamma rays combine with certain metallic salts or ultraviolet light combines with nitrous acid to enhance mutation rates.[63]*

Synergism is also commonplace at the cellular and organismic levels. One venerable example is teeth, which Aristotle invoked as evidence for design in nature; our teeth cannot perform independently of one another or of the supporting jaw structure and musculature. Other examples are the phenomena of summation in synaptic transmission, protein-metabolite interactions in cellular coordination activities, the coordinated construction and action of bone, muscle, and neuronal complexes, and the integrated functioning of the nervous system and major organ systems (visual, auditory, respiratory, digestive, neuroendocrine).†

Synergism in Social Life

More germane to the present purpose is the growing recognition of synergism at the macro level—co-operative interactions between organisms of the same and different species which produce effects that could not otherwise be achieved. The functional significance of symbiosis is well established, and it is particularly important because it so clearly defies the "tooth and claw" model of natural selection. There are innumerable examples: the alga-fungus collaboration in lichen, where one partner specializes in photosynthesis and the other provides a secure attachment and water-retention capabilities that enable the two organisms together to occupy many otherwise uninhabitable areas;[65] endoparasite bacteria that aid the digestive processes of ruminants and termites by producing enzymes that break down cellulose;[66] the blue-

* Synergistic effects are frequently reported in physiology, endocrinology, neurochemistry, cell biology, pharmacology, food science, and soil science. A literature search for a recent three-year period produced 528 research reports with synergism as a key word. Synergism was reported for, among other things, the effects of alpha-MSH and testosterone on sebaceous gland activity, estrogen and progesterone effects in inhibiting the release of pituitary luteinizing hormone, norepinephrine and adenosine effects in cerebral cortex functioning, the effects of l-glutamate and l-aspartate on the excitatory neuromuscular junctions of crustaceans, insulin and glucagon effects in regulating liver growth, the stimulating effects of vitamin D metabolites and PTH on bone formation, and growth enhancement in rats with dietary supplements that included combinations of sodium, potassium, and chloride. There were many drug synergism studies, studies of various forms of aspirin synergism, and studies of drug-ethanol interactions. A number of different synergistic interactions were reported for various carcinogens and air pollutants. Finally, there were reports of various forms of biochemical synergy that have direct effects on behavior—for instance, norepinephrine-dopamine interactions.

† Two other striking manifestations of synergism in the biological realm are sexual reproduction and the mammalian brain. For reasons that are still not entirely clear, it happens that in a great many species individuals who are presumed to be relentlessly selfish with their genes nevertheless have found it advantageous to surrender some of their genetic autonomy and co-operate with another individual in producing offspring. One advantage of the diploid reproductive

(*Continued*)

green algae that fix nitrogen for legumes and rice plants which in return provide an anoxic environment and/or protective shade for the algae;[67] the fungus-root symbioses of mycorrhizae;[68] the Attini, several hundred ant species that maintain elaborate underground fungus "gardens";[69] ant-aphid symbioses, with the former specializing in defense and aphid nurturance and the latter in milking and processing the phloem sap of plants;[70] the fifty-odd species of cleaner fish that earn their living by removing parasites from the bodies of larger fish;[71] the bird colonies of the oropendola and cacique, who build their nests close to the nests of wasps and stingless bees, who oblige by protecting their chicks from botflies that threaten chick survival;[72] the bird species (such as cattle egrets and oxpeckers) that form attachments with large ruminants and specialize in removing ticks;[73] and the sea anemone-crab partnerships, where the former provide camouflage and protection and the latter provide legs and mobility.[74]

Perhaps the most striking examples are two colonial species that occupy a middle-ground position between symbionts and integrated organisms. One is the siphonophore *Physalia,* the Portuguese man-of-war, a floating colonial mass comprised of five different specialized polyps (a stolon plus stinging, feeding, reproductive, and protective tentacles).[75] The other is the cellular slime mold *Dictyostelium,* which functions during part of its life cycle as a congeries of fully independent Amoebae that forage for themselves and divide at frequent intervals. When food supplies diminish, the Amoebae congregate into a sausage-shaped pseudoplasmodium that migrates like a multicellular organism and, in the final stage, transforms itself into an integrated fruiting body that produces spores.[76]

Co-operative behavior is even more widespread among organisms of fully integrated species, and the range of functional interactions is diverse. They include: *co-operative hunting and foraging,* which may serve to increase capture efficiency, the size of the prey that can be pursued, or the likelihood

---

pattern is that deleterious recessive alleles can be masked and their effects damped or suppressed by more adaptive dominant alleles. Another advantage is the phenomenon of heterosis—hybrid vigor. However, the apparent paradox in sexual reproduction remains to be completely unraveled.

The functioning of the mammalian brain is also synergistic. The brain performs its routine miracles by means of a complicated set of precisely organized interactions among a multitude of morphologically and functionally specialized units.[64] The emergent products of this intricate neurological system are so impressive that over the centuries many theorists have maintained that the "mind" is a metaphysical entity that can be treated as entirely distinct from the brain. I cannot enter into the mind-brain debate here. I will only make the observation that, in my view, the mind can no more be separated from the brain than can our bodies be separated from their cells and organ systems (or an automobile from its parts, for that matter). The whole may have systemic properties and capabilities (and produce systemic effects) that cannot be accounted for by viewing the parts in isolation from one another, but the system as a whole remains a physical entity. Both atomistic and holistic viewpoints are partly correct.

of finding food patches;[77] *co-operative detection, avoidance of, and defense against predators,* the forms of which range from mobbing and other kinds of coordinated attacks to flocking, communal nesting and synchronized breeding, collective foraging and migration, and mutual augmentation of aposematism (repellent powers);[78] *co-operative competition,* particularly in relation to obtaining food, territory, social dominance, and mates;[79] *co-operative protection of food supplies,* notably among many insects and some birds that store food jointly;[80] *co-operative movement,* including formations that increase aerodynamic or hydrodynamic efficiency and reduce individual energy costs and/or facilitate navigation;[81] *co-operative reproduction,* which can include joint nest building, joint feeding, and joint protection of the young;[82] *co-operative thermoregulation,* sometimes by sharing heat and sometimes by joint cooling efforts;[83] and *co-operative environmental conditioning,* such as joint detoxification of a hypotonic solution by flatworms.[84]*

Some species derive multiple advantages from co-operative behaviors. Honeybees, for instance, benefit from co-operation in foraging, defense, protection of food supplies, reproduction, migration, nest building, and thermoregulation, all within the context of specialized castes and an elaborate division of labor.[88] Another example, in mammals, is molerats,[89] but humankind is, of course, the most outstanding example. The psychologist Donald T. Campbell coined the term *ultrasociality* to describe such complexly organized species.[90] Ultrasociality is a class that contains few members.

The Bioeconomics of Synergism

As the foregoing examples suggest, a variety of commensalistic or mutually beneficial synergistic effects exist in nature. These include economies of scale, improved benefit-cost ratios for various functions, increased efficiencies through functional specialization, the melding of functional complementarities, reduction or spreading of risks, augmentation of effects, achievement of threshold effects, and the realization of emergent new properties with significant functional consequences.

One of the most dramatic of many well-documented cases involves the

* A number of researchers have advanced the proposition that various social species besides humankind may benefit from information-sharing. In some communally nesting birds, for instance, the nest also seems to serve as an information center. When food patches are widely dispersed and of uneven quality, weaver birds (*Quelea quelea*) may forage independently until a large food source is located. Then they will pool their information and combine forces to exploit the most abundant finds.[85] Likewise, W. J. Hamilton has proposed that the many water fowl that migrate en masse may benefit from pooling information while en route.[86] And Caraco and his co-workers showed that in yellow eyed juncos (*Junco phaeonotus*), members of large flocks are able to allocate less of their time than do birds in smaller flocks to scanning for avian predators such as hawks.[87]

huddling behavior of emperor penguins. In order to survive the long and brutal antarctic winters, when temperatures can reach minus 60°F and winds can attain 100 kph, these remarkable animals congregate in the tens of thousands in tightly packed colonies for several months at a time. In so doing, each animal shares precious body heat and provides insulation while receiving body heat and insulation in return. Individual energy expenditures for thermal regulation are thus reduced by as much as 50 percent. Without the synergistic effects of this co-operative behavior, it is doubtful that any of the animals would survive the winter.[91]

Other examples include Bonner's report that the aggregates of myxobacteria which move about and feed en masse secrete digestive enzymes that enable them collectively to consume larger prey.[92] Similarly, Schaller found that the capture efficiency (captures per chase times 100) and the number of multiple kills achieved by his Serengeti lion prides increased with group size. (A later study found that these results were dependent on the size of the prey.)[93] In the highly social African wild dog (*Lycaon pictus*), overall kill probabilities in hunting forays were found to be vastly superior (between 85 and 90 percent) to those achieved by less social top carnivores.[94] Similarly, co-operative foragers among great tits locate food faster than solitary hunters.[95] Kummer found that collective defense in hamadryas baboons (*Papio hamadryas*) is highly successful and reduces the net risk to each individual troop member.[96] Ligon and Ligon analyzed the remarkable communal nesting behavior of the green wood hoopoe (*Phoeniculus purpureus*) and discovered that the extensive pattern of helping behaviors, even among unrelated individuals, markedly increased their likelihood of survival and reproductive success in the harsh Kenyan environment.[97] Partridge and his colleagues have shown that fish schooling, which may include active forms of co-operation, is highly adaptive for the individual members. For instance, evasive maneuvers practiced by dwarf-herring against predatory barracudas dramatically reduce the joint risk of being eaten. And H. O. Wagner observed that the Mexican *Leiobunum cactorum,* a species of desert spider, clusters together in the thousands during the dry season in order to avoid dehydration.[98]

In each of these cases, there are collective "economies" that could not otherwise be achieved, economies that involve functional synergism.

At this point, several comments are in order. First, the term *synergism* is a conceptual umbrella; like the term *natural selection,* synergism is not a mechanism or a controlling agency but a way of classifying an array of diverse effects in terms of a specific common property or characteristic. As noted earlier, synergism refers to co-operative effects of all kinds—effects that cannot be produced by the parts or individuals acting alone, or by any statistical summation of individual actions. Synergism refers specifically to combinatorial effects.

Functional synergism, on the other hand, denotes the subset of combinatorial (co-operative) effects that have functional significance for a living organism with respect to the biological problem of survival and reproduction. These functions are specified by and relate to biological needs and biological goals. In human societies they also relate to our culturally induced wants and our various economic and social objectives.*

It may be charged that the concept of synergism involves a tautology. Not so. Not all combinatorial phenomena are eufunctional (having "positive synergy"); there are functionally neutral phenomena and dysfunctional phenomena (they have "negative synergy" or "dysergy"). Accordingly, the functional consequences of a synergistic phenomenon are always context-specific; the consequences are always co-determined by the characteristics and functional needs of the participants and by the network of organism-environment relationships in which the phenomenon is embedded. Functional synergism involves interactional processes. Consider again the examples given above: huddling among emperor penguins would be dysfunctional during the summer feeding season; myxobacteria would find it dysfunctional to feed in large aggregations if their food sources were small and widely dispersed; lions will do better to hunt small, slow-moving prey alone; if wild dogs were ruminants, sociality might not provide any benefits; only because great tit food sources are patchy and unpredictable is coordinated foraging advantageous; in more salubrious environments, green woodhoopoes would probably not find it advantageous to feed unrelated nestings; dwarf-herring might not

* I can anticipate some objections to my use of the term synergism. One criticism might be that synergism is simply a new name for the old idea of "emergent properties" and that the phenomenon of emergence was well understood in the nineteenth century.[99] Synergism is not the same thing as emergence, and the idea that it has causal potency in evolution *is* new. Synergism refers to co-operative effects of all kinds and at all levels of the physical and organic world. Emergence refers to *any* novel effect, however it may be produced. Synergism includes additive as well as multiplicative and nonlinear phenomena. It embraces symbioses between species as well as altruism, reciprocity, commensalism, and mutualism within a species. It even includes co-operation between organic forms and inanimate objects, as in man-tool and man-machine symbioses (see below and Chapter V).

Other critics may object to a concept that lumps together so many diverse combinatorial phenomena. One reviewer of the manuscript declared flatly that salt does not provide an example of synergism. Another takes the opposite position and would limit it to what physiologists and biochemists understand the term to mean. Still another asserts that symbiosis involves something altogether different from intraspecific mutualism. My response is to point to the example provided by the concept of natural selection. It may be useful to lump many different kinds of phenomena together if they have certain common properties that can be related to a common theoretical problem. The problem in my case is to explain the evolution of complex organization in living systems *at all levels.* I believe the concept of functional synergism, representing a heterogeneous class of co-operative effects with causal potency, will prove to be very useful in that regard.

find it advantageous to school if there were no barracudas about; and desert spiders have nothing to gain by congregating in the wet season. Thus functional synergism is not a law of nature but a combinatorial effect that may arise in various specific contexts.

For this reason the Interactional Paradigm (see Chapter IV) eschews Occam's razor (the principle of parsimony) in favor of what Rubinstein and Laughlin call "the rule of minimum inclusion."[100] That is, the explanation of biological evolution, and by extension sociocultural and political evolution, requires an understanding of any and all causal influences, at any level of organization, that are "efficiently present" and capable of exerting causally relevant combinatorial effects. Indeed, it is important to recognize that a factor which may be held constant or overlooked in one context or one historical era, may become a key variable in another, and that discontinuities and threshold phenomena are endemic in the evolutionary process.

For example, energy throughputs have often been neglected by social scientists concerned with explaining human social behavior. (One exception is the anthropological tradition that relates changes in energy use to culture and cultural evolution.) Yet a substantial proportion of human activity worldwide is directly or indirectly related to the acquisition, husbanding, and consumption of energy (food, fuel, and thermoregulation). Thus thermodynamics is not at all remote from the scientific understanding of human beings, society, and politics—as our current (and anticipated) food and energy crises attest. At the same time, what one critic of energy-oriented approaches to social theory called a "calorific obsession" is not warranted either.[101] For culture cannot be *reduced* to thermodynamics. The search for a single, overarching variable, whether it be population growth,[102] energy capture,[103] or what have you, is insufficient. Such mechanistic, linear approaches are destined to be embarrassed by contradictory evidence, counterexamples, overlooked relationships, reciprocal causation, and—most important—systemic (combinatorial) influences.

The Interactional Paradigm incorporates and integrates chance, necessity, and teleonomy. The causal matrix within which evolution occurs, and within which synergistic phenomena occur, includes stochastic influences (ranging from genetic mutations to environmental perturbations), engineering constraints and imperatives, and teleonomic influences. From the perspective of the thermodynamic *cum* cybernetic framework employed here, chance and necessity enter into the evolutionary process at various levels of organization from genes to ecosystems. And the essence of the problem of goal attainment, from the perspective of any open thermodynamic/cybernetic system, is the ability to control the relationship between the system and its environment. A genome *qua* cybernetic system can be successful in constructing an organism only insofar as it is able to predict to the internal structure and external environment of the system—or to make appropriate compensations for what cannot be predicted. Likewise, the ability of an organism *qua* cybernetic system to survive and reproduce itself is a function of its ability to predict and control the functional relationship between itself and its environment—or to make appropriate compensations where necessary. This is why information and control play a crucial role in the ontogeny and operation of cybernetic systems of all kinds, from eukaryotic cells to nation-states, and why feedback (which provides an ability to compensate for uncertainty and error as well as an ability to seize opportunities) is as important to morphogenesis as it is to political change.

All these processes are time-bound. Life, society, and politics are historical processes. More precisely, they are interrelated aspects of one process, and the cumulative legacy of past events—including various "frozen historical accidents," in Pattee's phrase[104]—in part determines the structure of the present, as does the future or the anticipation of the future. In essence, complex cybernetic systems use information from the past and anticipations of future states (to borrow Alfred North Whitehead's seminal conceptualization[105]) to control the all-important relationship between themselves and their environments. To paraphrase T. S. Eliot, time future and time past are both contained in time present.

It should also be pointed out that synergistic effects are not equivalent to the economist's collective goods. The benefits (if any) of synergistic combinations are often divisible and may well be distributed unevenly. In fact, the normative implications are much more ambiguous than the terms synergism and co-operation suggest. Co-operation (hyphenated to emphasize the basic, functional connotation of the word) is not equivalent to altruism, and it is not a buzzword for "good." Although altruism and co-operation are often conflated, there can be both altruistic co-operation and egoistic co-operation.

Altruism, Co-operation, and Egoism

It is important to differentiate between altruism (self-sacrifice for another) and co-operation (operating together). *Altruism* describes a certain class of functional consequences to an individual or a group, and the concept is heavily value-laden. *Co-operation* describes a behavioral relationship in which there is coordination with respect to some goal-state, and the concept is devoid of intrinsic value. Often the twin dichotomies of egoism and altruism, on the one hand, and competition and co-operation, on the other, are treated as being equivalent when in fact they are not. Co-operative behaviors could be the result of altruism on the part of one animal toward another or toward a group; or they could be occasioned by the prospect of mutual advantage;

or they could be motivated entirely by egoistic concerns. In human societies such relationships are called markets, exchanges, co-operatives, corporations, contracts, and so on. Accordingly, to anticipate the arguments to follow, I maintain that the engine of our cultural evolution has been synergistic effects based largely on egoistic co-operation, with altruistic behaviors playing a decidedly secondary role.

The biologist Warder C. Allee, one of the most influential exponents of co-operation in evolution, illustrates perfectly the general confusion of theorists who fail to distinguish clearly between altruism and co-operation. In his classic, *The Social Life of Animals* (1951), he asserts "a general principle of automatic cooperation" as a fundamental property of the biological realm.[106] He even goes so far as to show that even "unconscious cooperation" exists at all levels of biological organization, from the constituents of individual cells to slime molds, plants, insects, and vertebrates. Of course this does not prove that co-operation is universal or automatic, but only that it does not require conscious choice. From this base, Allee is led to a conclusion that lumps co-operation and altruism together:

> We have good evidence, then, that these two types of social or subsocial interactions exist among animals: the self-centered, egoistic drives, which lead to personal advancement and self-preservation; and the group-centered, more or less altruistic drives, which lead to the preservation of the group, or of some members of it, perhaps at the sacrifice of many others. The presence of egoistic forces in animal life has long been recognized. It is not so well known that the idea of the group-centered forces of natural cooperation also has a respectable history. . . . Widely dispersed knowledge concerning the important role of basic cooperative processes in living beings may lead to the acceptance of cooperation as a guiding principle both in social theory and as a basis for human behavior.[107]

More recently, in *The Use and Abuse of Biology* (1976), Marshall Sahlins, not realizing that co-operative and even altruistic behaviors may be compatible with natural selection theory, thinks he has nailed the coonskin to the wall when he asks rhetorically, How can co-operation be explained if individuals are in competition with one another and seeking to maximize their representation in the gene pool?[108] Sahlins overlooks co-operation that adds to fitness (egoistic co-operation) and co-operation that furthers "inclusive fitness," or fitness that embraces the genes of closely related individuals.

Similarly, Donald Campbell, in "The Genetics of Altruism and Counter-Hedonic Components in Human Culture," argues that altruism (which he maintains is responsible for cementing human societies together) is the result of cultural processes and cannot be genetically based. Cultural evolution, he says, has had to counteract humankind's inherently egoistic and selfish tendencies.[109] Campbell's position is an odd one, in part because he notes the possibility of individual advantage in social life.[110] He even cites others who have made similar points.[111] Yet he fails to see the theoretical importance of the point.

Even E. O. Wilson brushed past the point without appreciating its broad application to the problem of explaining social life. Commenting on Campbell's article (his presidential address to the American Psychological Association in 1975), Wilson attempted to differentiate between what he called hard-core altruism and soft-core altruism. The former, he observed, is truly altruistic; it is unilateral, unaccompanied by expectations of repayment, and it may even be unconscious; it is likely to have evolved through kin selection. " 'Soft-core altruism,' in contrast, is really ultimately selfish; the 'altruist' expects reciprocation from society for himself or his relatives. His good behavior is calculating, often in a wholly conscious way, and it is further orchestrated by the excruciatingly intricate sanctions and demands of society."[112] So why not call it by the more familiar term, enlightened self-interest?

Some Normative Implications

The distribution of the costs and benefits associated with synergistic interactions among parts, or participants, can vary widely. Consider again the honeybee, *Apis mellifera.* We can discern among the activities and functions in the hive examples of altruism, mutualism, and collective goods with many "free riders." However, all three types of behavior can be subsumed in a model of ultimate genetic self-interest. Extreme altruism can be observed in the suicidal self-sacrifice of workers in defense of the nest and in the fact that the workers remain sterile throughout their lives and surrender their personal fitness to serve the specialized breeder commonly called the Queen. Mutualism can be observed in the worker bees' foraging behavior, which includes coordinated searches and communication by means of the famous waggle dance. And collective goods are manifest in the way the bees maintain their hives at a year-round temperature of about 35°C. This is achieved by workers who, as the season requires, either fan water droplets with their wings to cool the hive or generate heat through muscle contractions to warm the hive. Inclusive fitness theory (and the peculiar haplodiploid genetic constitution of these creatures) suggests that all these behaviors are compatible with the traditional concept of Darwinian fitness.[113]

To clarify the normative implications of synergistic co-operation, I have freely adapted a table developed originally by the ecologists Eugene and Howard Odum (Table I).[114] The signs (+), (–), and (0) indicate the potential net benefits or net costs to both the actor and the interactor in various hypo-

TABLE I

Relationship	Actor	Interactor
Competition	(+)	(–)
Parasitism	(+)	(–)
Predation	(+)	(–)
Ammensalism (mutual harm)	(–)	(–)
Co-operation		
Altruism	(–)	(+)
Commensalism	(+)	(0)
Reciprocity	(0)	(0)
Mutualism	(+)	(+)

thetical dyadic situations. Notice that synergistic co-operation can include cases in which the actor suffers net losses and the interactor net gains (altruism), cases in which the actor has net gains and the interactor is unaffected (commensalism), cases in which there are equivalent costs and benefits to both participants (reciprocity), and cases in which there are net gains to both participants (mutualism). (In all cases it is the *ratio* of benefits to costs that matters.) Synergistic effects may be involved in any one of these contexts (and in many nonco-operative contexts), but I am primarily interested in those forms which are mutually advantageous and which arise in the context of functionally integrated systems. (Note that reciprocity here is theoretically distinct from mutualism, where there are net gains for both or all participants or for the system collectively. This distinction will be important.*)

The precise degree of functional integration among co-operators can vary widely, from casual and loosely "facultative" relationships that are easily dissolved, at one extreme, to "obligative" relationships in which there is complete functional interdependency. There are also many intermediate forms in which breakdowns would be deleterious but not fatal. In the case of lichen symbiosis, for example, the constituent algae and fungi are capable of living independently and often do so, but together they are more efficient at performing complementary tasks and are therefore able to inhabit various otherwise

* Roger Masters (personal communication) would lump together mutualism and reciprocity on the one hand and sociality and altruism on the other. I prefer to keep all four separate. Reciprocity to me means strictly equivalent exchanges, while mutualism implies net gains for one or both or all parties. Mutualism may also involve collective behaviors and collective goods in contexts where the notion of reciprocity or exchanges makes no sense. One cannot, for instance, speak of reciprocity in relation to collective defense of the group, territory, or nest. By the same token, sociality should connote only a form of behavior, the functional consequences of which may be exploitative, commensalistic, mutualistic, or altruistic for one or more participants.

inhospitable environments. At the other extreme, grass-eating cattle and wood-eating termites are utterly dependent on their lignin-ingesting parasites, without which they could not break down and digest cellulose. Between the two extremes are the oxpecker birds, which feed opportunistically on various prey, only some of which are the exoparasites of their ruminant hosts.

It is also possible for synergistic relationships to arise voluntarily (nature's equivalent of democratic consent) or through coercion (as in the slave-making behaviors of various ant species).[115] However, the manner in which co-operative relationships are achieved does not necessarily map perfectly to the distribution of costs and benefits. The fungi that are carefully nurtured in underground gardens by the Attini may well be net beneficiaries in terms of their absolute Darwinian fitness, just as the dairy cattle that have been enslaved and artificially bred by human beings have at least avoided extinction at the hands of humankind (the fate of a great many other large mammals). Are we using them, or are they using us?

Another corollary is that the biological relationship among participants may vary widely, from clonally produced adjacent cells to haploid siblings, closely related diploid kin, mating pairs, unrelated individuals of the same species, and members of very different species. Indeed, the classification scheme proposed in Table I differs radically from the approaches that are conventional among biologists. For I have lumped together in a single framework both symbiotic interactions (relationships among members of different species) and co-operative interactions among conspecifics. Traditional practice has been to keep the two classes separate.[116] The rationale for the separation is that there is a fundamental difference between interspecific and intraspecific mutualism which requires different explanatory approaches and even different theoretical models. Since the rise of genetics and the modern synthesis, the primary basis for organizing data on co-operative relationships has been the genetic relationship among participants. The result is a paradoxical situation. While there is a fairly well developed literature on interspecific symbiosis, complete with formal mathematical models, relatively little attention has been given until recently to what Mary Jane West Eberhard calls "intraspecific mutualism."[117] Even West Eberhard's thoughtful and acute analysis neglected to list mutualistic behaviors that were more than incidentally mutually beneficial—that involve explicit functional integration. Likewise, Clutton-Brock and Harvey deny any adaptive significance to social organization as such: "We believe that it is important to avoid attempts to assign functions to social structures or patterns of interaction and, instead, to consider the advantages to individuals of behaving in different ways."[118] And George C. Williams has asserted that group actions are merely statistical summations of individual behaviors.[119]

Measuring Synergism

We come now to the all-important question: Can the concept of functional synergism be put to use? Can synergism be measured directly in real-world contexts? The answer was suggested in the emperor penguin study. Synergistic effects are already being measured routinely by bioeconomists, economists, human ecologists, and ecological anthropologists, using various "metrics," or quantitative measures (see Chapters IV and V).

A mathematical expression for synergistic phenomena was developed many years ago by Heinz von Foerster, who called it the "superadditive composition rule." The rule is $\phi(x,y) > \phi(x) + \phi(y)$.*[120] There have also been several recent efforts to develop formal mathematical models of mutualistic interactions between species.[121] Pianka, for example, offers the following, somewhat oversimplifying model—a modification of the Lotka-Volterra competition equations—to describe the effects of positive symbiosis on the instantaneous rate of increase $\frac{dN}{dt}$ for two cooperating species:

$$\frac{dN_1}{dt} = r_1N_1 \frac{X_1 - N_1 + \alpha_{12}N_2}{X_1}$$

$$\frac{dN_2}{dt} = r_2N_2 \frac{X_2 - N_2 + \alpha_{21}N_1}{X_2}$$

where N = the population size for each species, X = the population size in the absence of the other species, r = the instantaneous rate of increase per individual, d = the death rate, and α = the positive co-operation coefficient—a quantitative measure of the facilitative effect of one species on the other.[122]†

Boorman and Levitt's model of "reciprocity selection," concerned primarily with members of the same species, is based on the simplifying assumption of a "social gene" for commensalistic (Pareto-optimizing) or mutualistic behaviors.[124] Boorman and Levitt note that it is relatively easy to model mathematically; more to the point, their model and the restrictions they perceive are a function of their *a priori* assumption that a specific genetic

* This is only an approximation, because many synergistic effects cannot be expressed in "greater than" or "less than" terms; they may involve novel effects that are not otherwise obtainable. Also, to be more precise, the model should include a term for any associated costs (c), so that it will represent net benefits. Thus:

$$\phi(x,y) - c(x,y) > \phi(x) - c(x) + \phi(y) - c(y).$$

† In another modified version of the same basic Lotka-Volterra equation developed by Vandermeer and Boucher, both competitive and co-operative effects are included.[123]

substrate for such behaviors must arise. They must postulate a mutant gene for society that will be positively selected under specified conditions in accordance with Mendelian principles.

In contrast, I maintain that a specific genetic substrate for such behaviors may follow (or evolve in an incremental, interactive fashion) rather than precede the emergence of synergistic social behaviors. Such behaviors may lead the way and precipitate directional selection in accordance with the teleonomic selection model (the modernized version of Organic Selection Theory) posited above. The minimum requirements (preadaptations) are (1) opportunities for positive reinforcement (or positive feedback) that leads to fitness gains; (2) the reduction of direct competition among potential participants (for example, because they are close kin and/or do not prey on one another); (3) the ability to recognize co-operators; and (4) the sort of "mental powers" that would make behavioral innovations possible (and for which there is rapidly accumulating evidence). The establishment of such behaviors may be facilitated and/or accelerated by what sociobiologists call kin selection and group selection, but these factors are not essential; indeed, they are not even relevant to cases of interspecific mutualism or positive symbiosis.

Among the relevant mathematical models, the recent work of Axelrod and Axelrod and Hamilton is of particular importance.[125] So are some economic models of "collective goods."[126] In addition, there is what I call a "corporate goods" model,[127] which is based on these assumptions (among others): (1) that co-operative actions may produce many kinds of goods (or positive reinforcements or gains to reproductive fitness); (2) that the goods may or may not be divisible among the participants (that is, defense of the group is a paradigm example of a collective good while food secured by co-operating hunters may or may not be shared equitably); (3) that the goods may be more or less effectively produced, depending on each member's efforts ("free riders" or error-prone "players" may reduce or eliminate the goods produced by a system); and (4) that because co-operation normally entails costs, the key to the evolution of egoistic co-operation is net benefits to the participators.

Formal models of this kind may help to satisfy the criterion of scientific rigor and shed light on the restrictions and necessary conditions for the evolution of genetical support for such behaviors. However, the underlying functional causes—synergistic effects—can be observed and measured in various ways without recourse to these models, without the necessity for positing specifically social genes, and without regard to who benefits.* In general,

* On the other hand, these models may shed light on the specific circumstances or conditions in which synergistic effects may be attained. These models have demonstrated that interspecies mutualism is a far more robust phenomenon (in theory as well as in fact) than classical competition models suggest. In some cases, moreover, co-operator species may even dominate and drive out competitor species.[128] Such models necessarily oversimplify biological reality, but they can

(*Continued*)

any measurable function (need, want, or goal), whether it be offspring, grams of protein, calories, dollars, or widgets, can be used to measure synergistic effects. For evolutionists the primary metric is reproductive efficiency, but there are studies of energetic costs and benefits, time budgeting and risk-reward analyses, studies of prey capture efficiency and feeding efficiency, and numberless studies in the social sciences of costs and benefits in terms of dollars, francs, marks, pounds, and yen.

I want to emphasize that while synergistic effects must be viewed as macro-level phenomena, they can also be used to account for micro-level phenomena, for why individual actors might "choose" to co-operate, given the assumptions used by rational choice theorists. In a nutshell, synergistic effects of various kinds are the common denominator—the functional basis for various forms of co-operative social behavior, including symbiotic relationships between individuals of different species, various "collective goods" or "public goods" produced by the joint actions of conspecifics (whether related to one another or not), the goods produced by "coalitions," and various "corporate goods."

In essence, the synergistic effects produced by co-operative social action provide the necessary positive incentives for individual choices. The ultimate answer to the "why" question is provided by specific historical opportunities for achieving synergistic effects, while the assumptions embedded in various models of co-operative behavior specify the structural constraints and facilitators that may be present in different circumstances. At best, then, these micro-level principles and models can be only partially explanatory. They can answer only certain *co-determining* motivational questions relating to how individual actors will respond to various opportunities. The micro-level models can enable us to specify the contexts within which opportunities for realizing synergistic effects *may* be transformed into decisions and actions, into cybernetic systems. But the functional processes that create these opportunities in the first place must be separately specified. In other words, both micro- and macro-level explanations are necessary, while neither is sufficient.

Two Examples from Adam Smith

Consider now two examples of the dimensionality of functional synergism in human societies, both of which happen to be drawn from Adam Smith's

---

lead to some testable counterintuitive conclusions that buttress the functional argument for co-operative behaviors.[129] René Thom's "catastrophe" theory is of similar character, though it is not actually a theory but a set of models for different kinds of dynamic discontinuities.[130] Many people assume that these models relate only to breakdowns, but there are also constructive or "combinatorial" catastrophes, in which thresholds are crossed to achieve emergent new effects. Synergistic phenomena are catastrophes of this type, and some of the recent work in combinatorial optimization theory also holds the promise of being able to model such phenomena with quantitative precision.[131]

The Wealth of Nations (1776). The first example is a famous one. In a pin factory that Smith had personally observed, ten workers together were able to produce some 48,000 pins per day, he reckoned. They did this by dividing the production process into component tasks, each of which lent itself to specialization. If each laborer were to work alone, attempting to perform all the tasks associated with making pins, Smith thought it unlikely that on any given day they would be able to produce even one pin per man.[132]

This is the textbook example of the division of labor. However, this characterization obscures the deeper principle of functional synergism. Another way of looking at the pin factory is in terms of how various specialized skills and production operations were *combined* in an organized, goal-oriented system. The system Adam Smith described included not only the roles played by the ten workers (which had to be precisely articulated with respect to one another) but the appropriate machinery, the energy to run the machinery, sources of raw materials, a supporting transportation system, and markets in which production costs could be recovered through sales. (Adam Smith is said to have been the first academic economist to recognize that so-called economies of scale are limited by the extent of the market.) Finally, the pin factory operation was also dependent on the existence of a cybernetic (communication and control) subsystem—a "political" system—through which planning, the hiring and training of workers, production decisions and coordination, marketing, and bookkeeping could be effected. (The human being's own built-in, biologically based interpersonal communication system, which we take for granted, is still another requisite for pin factories and other forms of socioeconomic synergism.) Thus the economies (the positive synergism) realized by Adam Smith's pin factory were the result of the total organization, the total configuration of functional relationships between worker and worker, worker and machine, worker and society, and worker and environment. Remove any one of these elements and the system as a system of co-operative interactions would not work.

The second example shows how functional synergism is both systemic in nature and context-specific. Smith compared the transport of goods overland from London to Edinburgh in "broad-wheeled" wagons and the transport of goods by sailing ships between London and Leith, the seaport that serves Edinburgh. In six weeks, two men and eight horses could haul about four tons of goods to Edinburgh and back. In the same amount of time, a ship with a crew of six or eight men could carry 200 tons to Leith—an amount of freight that would require 50 wagons, 100 men, and 400 horses for overland transport.[133]

What was the critical difference here? It was not the division of labor alone; not the human skills; not the technical hardware embodied in ships as opposed to horses and wagons; not the capital needed to finance the building of ships; not the political subsystem; not the availability of markets. It was in part all these things—and more, for it included the ecological opportunity for waterborne commerce between two human settlements located (not coincidentally) near navigable waterways, and it included suitable tidal currents and prevailing winds. The total configuration of factors, human and other, in a specific historical context, was responsible for the functional synergism (the combinatorial economies) associated with shipborne commerce.

A Theory of Biological Systems

The central theoretical problem, then, is to account for the evolution of biological organization, that is, biological "systems." My hypothesis involves an analogue of Thorndike's Law of Effect. In evolution it is the functional effects or consequences of a phenomenon in terms of survival and reproduction that are central to what we call natural selection. This is as true for synergistic effects as it is for any other functional effect. The concept of functional synergism is not new, and many theorists have noted that biological systems exhibit synergistic properties, but to my knowledge, none has recognized that synergistic effects are also causal, and of central importance.

Let me state again the hypothesis: *It is the selective advantages that arise from various synergistic effects that constitute the underlying cause of the apparently orthogenetic (or directional) aspect of evolutionary history, that is, the progressive emergence of complex, hierarchically organized systems.* Synergistic effects have been the key to the emergence of all biological organization. The principle is as applicable to the evolution of the eukaryotic cell and multicellular organisms as it is to colonial organisms, endosymbionts, exosymbionts, and animal and human societies; in other words, to cellular biology, organismic biology, sociobiology, and evolutionary anthropology. Thus the synergism hypothesis involves a unifying theory; it is a functional theory of biological and social structures.*

Can this theory be tested? I have hinted at one means of doing so. If the emergence and persistence of any biological system are ultimately governed by the combinatorial effects that are achieved by the co-operative action of the system's parts in a given environment, then several predictions follow. For instance, any change in the system's environment that prevents the rele-

* An anonymous reviewer of the manuscript questioned this proposition, saying that in nature "organization is due to individual genes that have been selected to maximize their fitness." Maybe so, but this misses the point. The relevant question is: What kinds of the selective contexts (internal or external) create opportunities for individuals to enhance fitness via organized co-operation? Under what conditions will individual genes (or parts) subordinate themselves to the adaptive requirements of the system? The answer in a nutshell is that this will occur whenever there are opportunities for realizing positive synergism in such a way that the expected benefits to the parts outweigh the expected costs, by and large.

vant combinatorial effects from occurring will lead to the demise of the system. Remove horses, say, from Great Britain, and Adam Smith's pin factory, despite the presence of all other traditional factors of production, would collapse. By the same token, the removal of any major internal part would have similar consequences—if the machinery were to break down or if the workers were to engage in a boycott. (Recall also the example of the Igorot system.)

Let me illustrate the point further with a very simple thought experiment. A modern automobile consists of about 15,000 parts composed of some 60 different materials. It is manufactured through a vast division of labor that involves tens of thousands of workers; the production process entails a complex cybernetic system. Yet we need remove only a single major part from the automobile *qua* "system" to immobilize it completely—a wheel, the distributor points, the spark plugs, the battery or, for that matter, the driver. By the same token, imagine the consequences if some essential ingredient were to be removed from the external environment, say, if our elaborate and expensive network of paved roads were allowed to become filled with potholes. The reason we don't need to perform this experiment is because we already understand how (and why) such synergistic systems operate and the functional relationship between the whole automobile and its parts (and between the system and its specific environment).

One can make similar predictions about organisms. A human being is a synergistic system that, as we all know, is susceptible to a "thousand natural shocks." Deny it oxygen, water, energy, or other external nutrients, and we can predict what will happen to the system. We can also predict what will happen to the system if something goes wrong with a major piece of the internal machinery. Whole systems are dependent on the integrated functioning of their parts.

Conversely, we can predict that a synergistic system will fail to emerge and diffuse if a (known) major component is missing or if the environmental conditions are not propitious. There are specific historical reasons why the eukaryotic cell did not emerge earlier in evolution and why the automobile revolution occurred at the turn of the twentieth century and then only in certain industrialized countries.

In vivo tests of the synergism hypothesis are commonplace. Whenever an organism, or an automobile, or a society for that matter, breaks down, we can observe directly the causal relationship between parts and wholes and between the functioning of the whole and its continued persistence as a system.* Such events are familiar to us. We intuitively understand these

* The relationships between wholes and parts are routinely studied by researchers in various disciplines, ranging from functional biology to macroeconomics to systems engineering. A landmark symposium volume on the subject was Daniel Lerner's *Wholes and Parts* (1963).

relationships, yet we have not explicitly incorporated our understanding into our theoretical knowledge of the causes of progressive (and regressive) evolution.

The Eukaryotic Cell

A compelling piece of evidence for the synergism hypothesis is presented by the eukaryotic cell, a product of one of the earliest biological "revolutions" in the direction of more complex organization. While the emergence of the eukaryote, the first structurally complex, nucleated cell, involved an intricate series of steps, there is now strong support for the hypothesis that the endosymbiosis between previously independent prokaryotic bacteria, blue-green algae, and incipient or recently nucleated cells was decisive.[134] The evidence suggests that the mitochondria, chloroplasts, and perhaps other functionally specialized organelles found within eukaryotic cells had independent origins. Whether the union that led to eukaryotes was mutualistic or arose as a master-slave relationship, the result was beneficial to all parties; our cells are efficiently organized, functionally differentiated systems. (Even the simplest eukaryotic cells manifest several thousand linked chemical reactions that necessitate intricate functional organization and cybernetic regulation.)

The likely advantages associated with the evolution of eukaryotic cells are similar to those we have already identified: increased opportunities for specialization and functional differentiation, increased capability for energy capture and utilization,[135] certain economies in energy requirements, durability (the ability to replace parts and repair damage), the ability to develop specialized adaptations to suit a great variety of environmental conditions, the ability to grow larger, and perhaps most important, the ability to reproduce, diversify, and evolve more rapidly.[136] The eukaryotic cell has proven to be an essential building block for other developments in the direction of complex biological organization. Without exception, multicellular organisms are constructed of eukaryotic cells. For most of the approximately 3.5 billion years of the history of life on earth, prokaryotes were the exclusive or predominant form of living matter. The explosive proliferation of multicellular organisms (estimated by Stebbins to have occurred at least seventeen times) has been confined largely to the most recent 20 percent of this period (about 700 million years).[137] Yet of the more than two million species currently living, it is estimated that only some three thousand are prokaryotes; the prokaryotes have long since surrendered their hegemony to the latecomers. And if it is true that major ecological opportunities (e.g. an oxygen-rich environment) may have been necessary for such bursts of evolutionary change to occur, as Sewall Wright has long argued, structural preadaptations were equally important; they were part of the *configuration* of internal and external causes that are always involved in the establishment of new organism-environment relationships.

More evidence for the synergism hypothesis is found in another of the major biological revolutions, the emergence of metazoan (multicelled) creatures from single-celled protists some 600 million years ago. Biologists generally agree that multicellular organisms evolved separately in each of the three higher kingdoms of life—fungi, plants, and animals[138]—and that fungi and plants arose by the amalgamation of protist colonies. Sponges too are viewed as little more than confederations of protists. Only in the animal kingdom is the hypothesis of a symbiotic union still in question. Biologist Earl Hanson continues to defend the minority view that multicellular animals arose through internal differentiation.[139] However, laboratory techniques that are now available for comparing the DNA of different life forms may soon clarify (if not resolve) the issue. If it can be shown that the marine flatworms that Hanson believes to be unique products of evolution by differentiation are in fact regressive forms that were derived from ancestral amalgamators, then it is likely that all of the higher life forms are the products of symbiosis, of functional synergism. As Stephen Jay Gould puts it, even human beings may be the descendants of protistan colonies. Thus, from the earliest one-celled eukaryotes to the most advanced nation-states, complex biological systems may have been built up through a dual process of aggregation and progressive functional differentiation, and each major breakthrough to a more complex form of organization may have been "directed" by opportunities for realizing functional synergism.*

Hierarchy in Nature

Closely related to the problem of explaining the evolution of complex forms of organization in nature is the problem of accounting for hierarchy. Though the reasons are still imperfectly understood, there seems to be an intimate relationship between size, complexity, and hierarchy in cybernetic control systems; as organizations become larger and more complex, hierarchically ordered structures of communication and control develop. Accordingly, the synergism hypothesis is also relevant to the explanation of hierarchies.

In the first place, a hierarchy involves a partial ordering of phenomena in two dimensions, "horizontally" among components or subsystems and "vertically" between sequential levels (or between sets and supersets). The

* In an article that appeared after this work was completed, Manfred Eigen and his colleagues put forward the argument that in effect functional synergism was also involved in the emergence of the earliest prebiotic molecular assemblages. These organic building blocks, they maintain, could not have evolved via competition alone: "Certain forms of co-operation were also essential."[140] Accordingly, they postulate an "evolutionary interplay" between molecular competition and molecular co-operation.

LEVELS OF ORDER

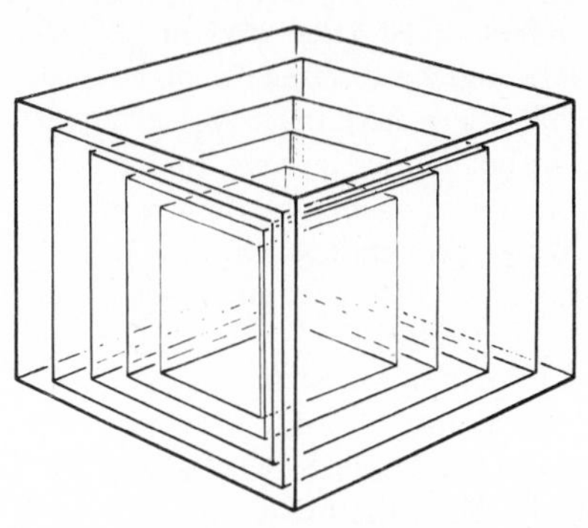

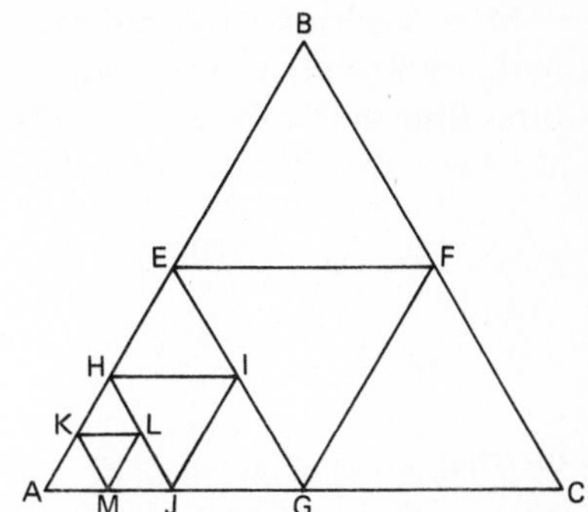

FIGURE III

Hierarchical order in Chinese boxes and subdivided triangles. Note that successively larger triangles are in each case composed of several smaller ones. (From: Clifford Grobstein, *The Strategy of Life,* 2d ed. [San Francisco: W. H. Freeman, 1974].)

simile most often invoked is a set of Chinese boxes. The biologist Clifford Grobstein also employs a figure that involves subdivided triangles (see Figure III).[141]

As noted earlier, there are two distinct kinds of hierarchies in nature, those which are "facultative" or reversible (they can be dispersed and reconstituted) and those which are "obligative" or nonreversible (when the component elements lose their autonomy). Both kinds are manifest in human organizations and often are present within the same organization—for example, unskilled laborers and highly specialized technical personnel who cannot readily transfer their skills to other employers or learn new jobs.

The existence of a hierarchy can be verified empirically in terms of the patterns of interaction. For instance, component parts of a hierarchy may or may not interact with one another, but they will generally interact with higher levels. The total number of horizontal interactions will always be far greater than the number of vertical interactions. Likewise, there tends to be an asymmetry in the exercise of control within a hierarchy. Actions at higher levels generally have greater influence over the behavior and conditions at lower levels than vice versa.

Another important characteristic of hierarchical systems is that their behavior can be viewed and interpreted differently, depending on one's perspective. The parts may be viewed alternatively as discrete units whose behavior can be examined in isolation or as units that exist as parts of a whole to the extent that their behavior is shaped and controlled by their relationship to the whole. The sociologist James S. Coleman offers an illustration:

> Once when I was sitting on the edge of a cliff, a bundle of gnats hovered in front of me, and offered a strange sight. Each gnat was flying at high speed, yet the bundle was motionless. Each gnat sped in an ellipse, spanning the diameter of the bundle, and by his frenetic flight, maintaining the bundle motionless. Suddenly, the bundle itself darted—and then hovered again. It expanded and its boundaries became diffuse; then it contracted into a tight, hard knot and darted again—all the while composed of nothing other than gnats flying their endless ellipses. It finally moved off and disappeared. Perhaps also it dissipated and ceased to exist, each gnat going his own way.
>
> Such a phenomenon offers enormous intellectual problems: how is each gnat's flight guided, when its direction bears almost no relation to the direction of the bundle? How does he maintain the path of his endless ellipse? And how does he come to change it, when the bundle moves? What is *the structure of control,* and what are the signals by which *control* is transmitted? [my italics].[142]

A number of important characteristics are associated with the properties of hierarchical organizations. One class of characteristics is *functional.* Hierarchical organizations do indeed transcend the sums of their parts—functionally. For example, hierarchical organization produces a significant simplifying and economizing of interactions among components, a phenomenon that can be demonstrated mathematically. Component parts may be freed of many constraints even as the establishment of hierarchical control imposes partial constraints (a point with which Plato was familiar). Indeed, hierarchical constraints are always highly selective; irrelevant aspects of component behavior are usually ignored. It can also be demonstrated mathematically that a system will evolve more rapidly when its component parts are organized into stable subsystems. Hierarchical organization may therefore facilitate evolutionary adaptability. Herbert Simon has invented a parable that illustrates the point perfectly:

> There once were two watchmakers, named Hora and Tempus, who manufactured very fine watches. Both of them were highly regarded, and the phones in their workshops rang frequently—new customers were constantly calling them. However, Hora prospered, while Tempus became poorer and poorer and finally lost his shop. What was the reason?
>
> The watches the men made consisted of about 1,000 parts each. Tempus had so constructed his that if he had one partly assembled and had to put it down—to answer the phone, say—it immediately fell to pieces and had to be reassembled from the elements. The better the customers liked his watches, the more they phoned him, the more difficult it became for him to find enough uninterrupted time to finish a watch.
>
> The watches that Hora made were no less complex than those of Tem-

> pus. But he had designed them so that he could put together subassemblies of about ten elements each. Ten of these subassemblies, again, could be put together into a larger subassembly; and a system of ten of the latter subassemblies constituted the whole watch. Hence, when Hora had to put down a partly assembled watch in order to answer the phone, he lost only a small part of his work, and he assembled his watches in only a fraction of the man-hours it took Tempus.[143]

The most important advantage of hierarchical organization is that it may facilitate or enhance the achievement by the component parts of systemic goals; hierarchy may lead to *functional synergy,* to combinatorial effects that are not otherwise attainable.

Recall my discussion of the Law of Effect. In the case of both natural selection and teleonomic selection, anticipated or realized functional effects are causes. The functional consequences of a phenomenon (a morphological trait, a behavior, or an invention) during one generation, or one trial, will increase or decrease the likelihood that the phenomenon will recur in subsequent iterations and be diffused through a population (or selected out). This applies just as much to hierarchical organization as to any isolated trait: *Insofar (but only insofar) as functional complexity and its concomitant, hierarchical organization, enhances the chances of survival and reproductive success, such patterns can be expected to be favored by natural selection, whether it occurs at the cellular, organismic, behavioral, or ecological level of organization. By the same token, insofar as synergistic social behaviors and processes enhance the capacity of a set of human beings to satisfy their basic needs and wants, these processes will be favored by teleonomic selection or natural selection or both.*

As for the *structural* characteristics of hierarchical organization, contrary to holistic dogma, wholes do not physically transcend the sums of their parts. Rather, they represent ordered physical arrangements and interactions among parts, which may produce many novel physical properties. Automobiles and complex organisms have emergent, systemic properties—and effects. More to the point, in hierarchically organized structures, the whole and the parts *interact.* Wholes and parts mutually constrain, impose controls, and set priorities for one another. The design of the parts of an automobile or a human body is never for long independent of the functional needs of the whole, with the exception of such nonfunctional parts as decorative paint jobs and the vermiform appendix. No automobile will run for long without lubrication, fuel, and routine maintenance; nor will a human being function for long without basic life-support activities. In a hierarchically organized system, then, the parts and the whole represent "selective environments" (inner or outer) for one another while imposing constraints and requisites.[144]

The functions of the whole specify the functional requirements and the available functional niches for the parts, and the parts in turn together specify the capabilities, limitations, and functional needs of the whole.

The precise relationships between parts and wholes can vary widely. Sometimes the relationship is confederal: The whole serves at the pleasure of the parts. Many other hierarchical systems are highly obligative. Complex organisms are unambiguous examples. If there are "selfish genes," or selfish chromosomes, selfish cells, or selfish organs, they are for the most part decisively subordinated to the common good, to the functional needs of the organism as a whole. (Is there a reductionist-oriented biologist who would claim that the functioning of an organism is only a statistical sum of the functioning of individual cells?) When I decide to go to dinner, almost every one of my roughly ten trillion cells is constrained to go with me. I may leave a few stray hairs and fingernail clippings behind, but they are the exceptions that prove the rule: For some of the parts in an obligative system, the benefit-cost trade-offs may be unfavorable.

The phenomenon of autotomy is a dramatic example of this. Some higher crustaceans and reptiles come equipped with joints that enable them to throw off an appendage, say a claw or a tail, when caught by a predator, without incurring serious damage or blood loss. Such altruistic sacrifices for the "general welfare" are commonplace. (In human societies we find not only both extremes but many intermediate kinds of relationships.)

Levels of Selection

The theoretical point behind this bit of anthropomorphism is important. *Neither natural selection nor teleonomic selection is confined to any one level of biological or social organization; functional processes go on at many interacting levels, any one or more of which may produce selective consequences. However, to the extent that the parts (lower-level structures and functions) become dependent on the whole—to the extent that the persistence of the parts depends on the persistence of the whole—the functional needs of the higher-level whole will be selectively favored, vis-à-vis the parts. By the same token, to the extent that a higher-level whole becomes the predominant unit of selection (as a function of the intensity of selection pressures at that level of organization), selection processes will favor the subordination of parts to wholes.**

* This seemingly obvious point continues to be misunderstood. Anthropologists Chagnon and Irons, in the preface to their important edited volume *Evolutionary Biology and Human Social Behavior* (1979), inform us that: "Biologists now generally agree, after much debate, that the evolved traits of organisms do not exist because they have contributed to the survival of species, breeding populations or social groups, but because they have contributed to the survival of some alleles over their alternatives" (p. xi). Contrast this with the recent observation (*Continued*)

Those formulations that portray evolution at levels other than that of individual genes as a process distinct from natural selection miss the point. Any functionally significant factor, at any level of biological organization, that affects differential survival and reproduction among genetically distinct individuals and/or differentiated groups and populations represents a direct cause of natural selection. When the unit of evolution is individuals within a local population, we speak of selection among genotypes in gene pools. When there is selection among larger aggregates, that is, when there are changes in the relative numbers of different groups (trait groups, kin groups, functionally organized groups, even species), we may speak of genome-type selection—selection among classes of genomes in genome pools. Evolution at these levels also involves natural selection as Darwin meant the term to be used.*

One way of illustrating these points is in terms of the dynamics of human organizations. To the extent that an individual is dependent on an organization (say, when jobs are scarce and there is no alternative way to obtain an income), the benefits to that person of accommodating to the functional needs of the organization may be relatively high and the costs of nonco-operation also relatively high. Accordingly, the decision matrix for that individual will be biased in favor of subordination to the welfare of the organization.

By the same token, when organizations (functional groups) are in precarious or intensely competitive environments, those that organize effectively will be selectively favored over those that do not, all other things being equal: Internal functional efficiency matters. This does not mean that a given employee will necessarily be compliant or that an organization will necessarily respond to the challenges that confront it; individuals and organizations may lack sufficient information to perceive their choices clearly, or they may not act rationally. Rational choice models are important, but they are not sufficient to account for human behavior. However, the matrix of available choices in any given context represents the selective environment within which teleonomic selection processes occur.

---

of biologist Sewall Wright: "It is fairly obvious, even on the simplistic assumption of a one-to-one relation between gene and unit character, that the selective value of any one of the unit characters will depend on the others with which it is combined."[145] The "interaction systems" of which individual genes are a part may include chromosomes, organ complexes, organisms, and "superorganisms" (in Herbert Spencer's term).

* I must disagree here with Gould's interpretation in "Darwinism and the Expansion of Evolutionary Theory" (1982). Gould claims that the classical Darwinian model of evolution was limited to individual selection processes. To the contrary, Darwin himself recognized "family" selection and group selection, as well as competition between "races" and species. Subsequent generations of Darwinians may have truncated Darwin's original vision to suit their own theoretical interests or predilections, but this should not be ascribed to the first Darwinian.

The same principle applies to other species. The emergence of functionally integrated, hierarchical forms of social organization elsewhere in nature (in wild dogs, in wolf and killer whale packs, in lion prides, in savanna baboon troops, in chimpanzee hunting parties) represents favorable responses to various ecological opportunities and constraints. However, the opportunity for functional synergism at the social level may not always be discovered and exploited.

A distinction must also be drawn between hierarchy as an aspect of a complex social organization and the ethological concept of a "dominance hierarchy." A hierarchy in the former sense denotes a structural and functional property of a goal-oriented (cybernetic) system.[146] In the latter sense, it has traditionally denoted an interpersonal relationship of dominance and subordination that arises from competitive interactions between two or more individuals and, presumably, correlates with differential access to such fitness-related items as food, mates, nesting sites, and grooming privileges.[147]

In socially organized species individual dominance may or may not coincide with the occupation of a control "role";[148] the dynamics of an organized group may not conform to any simple, linear patterns of interaction. Indeed, many contemporary ethologists express serious reservations about the very concept of dominance.[149] Dominance is not easy to define or measure empirically,* is not unambiguously related to the partitioning of resources or personal advantage, and is far more labile and context-dependent than was once thought to be the case. It is a particularly slippery concept when applied to such intensely organized social mammals as the higher primates and social carnivores.

Bernstein and Gordon, for example, found in a study of all-male rhesus monkey groups that dominance ranks were dependent on the social context. When two monkey groups were combined, the resulting patterns of dominance could not be predicted from the preexisting patterns. And when top-ranking males were transferred individually between groups they assumed a much

* One noteworthy approach to measuring dominance involves what ethologist Michael Chance has called "attention structure theory"—who pays attention to whom.[150] Unfortunately, as a theory about dominance hierarchies, attention structure theory is tautological. A dominant animal is defined as one to whom others pay attention. This is not always a valid assumption: Mothers pay close attention to their young; everyone pays close attention to a stranger; innovative or highly unusual behaviors on the part of one animal are likely to be closely observed by any others who are nearby. In short, attentional patterns can be viewed best from a cybernetic perspective. They arise from a variety of motivations and objectives on the part of both the watchers and the watched, and they have to do with information gathering and communications functions. Indeed, in a study of four different primate societies, Assumpção and Deag could find no significant relationship between male rank-orders (as determined by agonistic encounters) and patterns of visual attention.[151]

lower status. However, when these migrants were returned to their own groups, they regained their original status.[152]

Even in flocks of domestic chickens, Guhl reported the surprising result that when stable groups are dispersed and then reaggregated after a two-week period there was only a low to moderate correlation between the original status rankings and those in the reconstituted groups.[153]

Enter Sociobiology

This brings me to the question of how my theory relates to the sociocultural level of biological organization, and to the discipline of sociobiology.

Social co-operation does not occur in a vacuum; it takes place against a background of direct or indirect competition. Competition may even be a major stimulus for co-operation. Of some 2 million extant species, only about 10,000 can be considered truly eusocial.[154] Social co-operation in nature is like a chain of volcanic atolls in shark-infested waters—a few safe havens in an otherwise hostile environment. The theoretical challenge is to explain how such islands of co-operation managed to arise in the course of evolution. My approach differs sharply from that of the "classical" sociobiologists. Rather than focusing primarily on genetic relationships and altruism (and reciprocal altruism), I focus more on functional relationships and egoistic co-operation. Some historical perspective may be helpful at this point.

Edward Wilson launched his discipline-defining work *Sociobiology* (1975) with the startling assertion that altruism is "the central theoretical problem of sociobiology: how can altruism, which by definition reduces personal fitness, possibly evolve by natural selection?"[155]* The implication here is that social life is based *primarily* on altruism, and Wilson later adopts W. D. Hamilton's view that there are only three classes of social behavior: altruism (self-sacrifice for another), selfishness (raising one's own fitness at the expense of another), and spite (lowering one's own fitness in order to diminish that of another).[156]

I submit that Hamilton, Wilson, and other early sociobiologists left out of their taxonomies (and their theoretical models of social behavior) the most important category of all, egoistic co-operation, in which one's own and others' needs are simultaneously or serially satisfied by joint, coordinated, or reciprocal actions. In fact this category is not entirely excluded by Wilson; it is merely disguised and hidden in the thickets of his massive tome. He discusses mutually beneficial forms of co-operation, including many explicit

* Wilson defines *altruism* as any behavior that serves other than one's own offspring. As we shall see, this confuses the issue unless one adds the corollary, "at one's own net expense." Wilson also speaks of altruism as "self-destructive behavior," but as West Eberhard points out, it matters significantly whether the costs are great or little and whether the benefits to the recipient are great or little.

cases of synergistic behaviors, under at least four headings: (1) *adaptive advantages* of social life (described under "ecological pressures," which in Wilson's formulation are said to "induce" social life); (2) *mutualism* (positive symbiosis) between species; (3) *reciprocal altruism,* Robert Trivers's well-known though misleading term for social behaviors that may seem to provide uncompensated benefits to unrelated individuals but in fact do not; and (4) *altruistic behaviors* that can also be given a mutualistic interpretation.

How can mutualistic, synergistic forms of social behavior be included in fact but excluded in theory? In large measure, the problem stems from the failure to differentiate between altruism and co-operation. Like the rest of us, population biologists and sociobiologists frequently think they see what they are looking for and fail to see what they are not looking for. In a recent review article on the role of behavior in evolution, Maynard Smith writes: "Hamilton's work predicts that altruistic and cooperative behavior will be found more frequently in the interactions of related individuals than in the interactions of unrelated individuals."[157] This statement is true if one excludes nonaltruistic (egoistic) co-operation, which is what Maynard Smith does. But if we include egoistic co-operation, Maynard Smith's statement may be false or only marginally true. Among the many forms of co-operation among unrelated or remotely related organisms there is (1) the whole category of mutualistic symbiosis; (2) the whole category of outbreeding reproduction, in which unrelated parents co-operate to varying degrees and in various ways to produce offspring; and (3) the many cases of mutual aid and joint action among other than close kin in socially organized species.

Examples abound. *Sociobiology* contains twenty-five double-size pages on social behavior that are studded with vivid instances.[158] There are, for example, the protective advantages to the individual animal of the well-organized prairie dog towns; the benefits of flocking behavior among starlings; the so-called Fraser Darling Effect in a number of bird species, where the social context enhances individual reproductive stimulation; coalition behavior in a number of social carnivores and primates; pack hunting in killer whales and wild dogs; and the awesome defensive maneuvers of many terrestrial primates. There are many more examples in the literature, and no doubt more will come to light as further field studies delineating the biological relationships among social group members (or the lack thereof) are completed.[159]

Darwin on Social Life

To understand the theoretical consequences of this conceptual oversight, we must return to Darwin, who introduced the subject of social behavior in evolution. Darwin assumed that social behaviors posed no fundamental problem for his theory. He saw that many social behaviors clearly involve mutual advantages.

> Animals of many kinds are social; we find even distinct species living together; for example, some American monkeys; and united flocks of rooks, jackdaws and starlings. . . . We will confine our attention to the higher social animals, and pass over insects, although some of these are social, and aid one another in many important ways. The most common mutual service in the higher animals is to warn one another of danger by means of the united senses of all. . . . Wild horses and cattle do not, I believe, make any danger-signal; but the attitude of any one of them who first discovers an enemy, warns the others. Rabbits stamp loudly on the ground with their hind feet as a signal; sheep and chamois do the same with their fore feet, uttering likewise a whistle. Many birds and some mammals, post sentinels, which in the case of seals are said generally to be the females. The leader of a troop of monkeys acts as the sentinel, and utters cries expressive both of danger and of safety. Social animals perform many little services for each other; horses nibble, and cows lick each other for external parasites; and Brehm states that after a troop of the *Cercopithecus griseoriridis* has rushed through a thorny brake, each monkey stretches itself on a branch, and another monkey sitting by, "conscientiously" examines its fur, and extracts every thorn or burr.
>
> Animals also render more important services to one another; thus wolves and some other beasts of prey hunt in packs, and aid one another in attacking their victims. Pelicans fish in concert. The Hamadryas baboons turn over stones to find insects, etc.; and when they come to a large one, as many as can stand around, turn it over together and share the booty. Social animals mutually defend each other. Bull bisons in North America, when there is danger, drive the cows and calves into the middle of the herd, while they defend the outside. . . .
>
> It has often been assumed that animals were in the first place rendered social, and that they feel as a consequence uncomfortable when separated from each other, and comfortable while together; but it is a more probable view that these sensations were first developed in order that those animals which would profit by living in society should be induced to live together, in the same manner as the sense of hunger and the pleasure of eating were, no doubt, first acquired in order to induce animals to eat. The feeling of pleasure from society is probably an extension of parental or filial affections, since the social instinct seems to be developed by the young remaining for a long time with their parents; and this extension may be attributed in part to habit, but chiefly to natural selection.[160]

Some nineteenth- and early twentieth-century ideologues who wrote as though the existence of co-operation falsified Darwinian theory seem not to have read Darwin's works very carefully.[161] However, Darwin recognized that what later theorists misleadingly called altruism seemed to pose a special problem. Consider the paradigm case, the bee that sacrifices its life for the preservation of the hive: How could the gene or genes for such an apparently selfless behavior have become established in a species?

At first Darwin thought that the existence of such phenomena, and in particular the existence of sterile castes in insect societies, might be "fatal" to his theory. The solution he proposed involved the rudiments of what is now called kin selection, a term coined by Maynard Smith.[162] Darwin reasoned that natural selection could occur at the level of the family if self-sacrifice by closely related individuals for one another increased the overall reproductive potential of the family as a whole. Just as parental altruism toward offspring is commonly favored by natural selection, so might sacrifices of siblings and cousins for each other be favored. From an evolutionary perspective, such behaviors would not be altruistic at all; they would involve a form of enlightened self-interest, though in a very special sense. Hamilton called this Darwinian form of enlightened self-interest "inclusive fitness,"[163] the summed representation of one's own genes in subsequent generations via the proportion shared with offspring and/or closely related individuals and their offspring. Although Darwin had no inkling of modern genetics (his inference was drawn from routine observations by plant and animal breeders of biological resemblances within lineages), his reasoning, as E. O. Wilson noted, was impeccable.

In *The Descent of Man* Darwin carried this line of reasoning two significant steps further—and thereby helped to create the confusion between altruism and sociality. Seeking to account for the emergence of "social and moral faculties" in human beings, Darwin proposed that three distinct evolutionary "levels" were involved, necessitating a three-step solution. The steps presaged the modern theories of (1) kin selection ("family selection"); (2) selection based on what has variously been called egoistic co-operation (Corning), intraspecific mutualism (West Eberhard), reciprocant selection (Hamilton), and reciprocity selection (Boorman and Levitt); and (3) group selection. Darwin argued first that humankind's "social" traits might have arisen initially in much the same way that analogous faculties had come to exist in other species—in essence, through kin selection. But as early hominid groups began to coalesce into tribes consisting of multiple (unrelated) lineages, the further spread of group-serving behaviors could no longer be accomplished by means of kin selection. It would require a second mechanism, initially the calculus of rational self-interest:

> But it may be asked, how within the limits of the same tribe did a large number of members first become endowed with these social and

> moral qualities, and how was the standard of excellence raised? It is extremely doubtful whether the offspring of the more sympathetic and benevolent parents, or of those who were the most faithful to their comrades, would be reared in greater numbers than the children of selfish and treacherous parents belonging to the same tribe. . . . Therefore it hardly seems probable, that the number of men gifted with such virtues, or that the standard of their excellence could be increased through natural selection. . . . Although the circumstances, leading to an increase in the number of those thus endowed within the same tribe are too complex to be clearly followed out, we can trace some of the probable steps. In the first place, as the reasoning powers and foresight of the members became improved, each man would soon learn that if he aided his fellow-men he would commonly receive aid in return. From this low motive he might acquire the habit of aiding his fellows; and the habit of performing benevolent actions certainly strengthens the feeling of sympathy which gives the first impulse to benevolent actions. Habits, moreover, followed during many generations probably tend to be inherited [as Lamarck postulated]. . . . But another and much more powerful stimulus to the development of the social virtues is afforded by the praise and the blame of our fellow-men. To the instinct of sympathy, as we have already seen, it is primarily due that we habitually bestow both praise and blame on others, while we love the former and dread the latter when applied to ourselves; and this instinct no doubt was originally acquired, like all the other social instincts, through natural selection. At how early a period the progenitors of man in the course of their development became capable of feeling and being impelled by the praise or blame of their fellow-creatures we cannot of course say. (pp. 147–48)

Unfortunately, Darwin's reasoning here is less than impeccable. First he shifts his ground in mid-argument from altruism *qua* self-sacrifice to altruism *qua* mutual aid, that is, from indirectly to directly self-serving behavior. Then he invokes a Lamarckian *deus ex machina* to account for how such traits might come to be inherited. Finally, he posits the causal influence of a preexisting psychological trait, which in turn requires an explanation. Darwin also overlooked two major points. If the direct benefits of mutual aid clearly outweigh the direct costs, that is, if there is a favorable benefit-cost ratio, it may not be necessary or correct to postulate a specific biological substrate to account for the behavior, at least in *Homo sapiens.* Given Darwin's assumption (in an earlier passage) of evolved mental capacities for reasoning and for making adaptive social choices, unenlightened self-interest alone might be sufficient and a special genetic explanation is not required.

The second point that Darwin overlooked is an extension of the first. If a social species is so organized that its members are highly interdependent, that is, if there is a high degree of functional integration, every member may have a stake (a direct self-interest) in the survival and basic well-being of the larger group, whether or not its members are closely related to one another. This is not to say that the members' interests will be perfectly congruent, but there will be an area of common or complementary interests (encompassing indirect as well as direct forms of co-operation, and exchanges [reciprocities] as well as jointly produced goods). The customary dichotomy of self-serving and group-serving behaviors leaves out behaviors that may involve both. This argument is not without its problems (the cheater and the free rider, for example), but it is defensible.

The third step in Darwin's reasoning involved moving from multilineage social groups to metapopulations—large chiefdomships and states. Here Darwin prefigured the group selection hypothesis: He proposed that the spread of social traits in human beings would likely have been augmented and completed through a process of differential selection (sometimes via warfare) among different "tribes."

> Selfish and contentious people will not cohere, and without coherence nothing can be effected. A tribe rich in the above qualities would spread and be victorious over other tribes; but in the course of time it would, judging from all past history, be in its turn overcome by some other tribe still more highly endowed. Thus the social and moral qualities would tend slowly to advance and be diffused throughout the world. . . . All that we know about savages, or may infer from their traditions and from old monuments, the history of which is quite forgotten by the present inhabitants, show that from the remotest times successful tribes have supplanted other tribes. Relics of extinct or forgotten tribes have been discovered throughout the civilized regions of the earth, on the wild plains of America, and on the isolated islands in the Pacific Ocean. (pp. 146–47)

There are problems with Darwin's analysis here, especially with regard to the specifics of human evolution. Yet Darwin recognized that the evolution of social and group-serving traits might involve multiple levels.[164] Equally important, Darwin was the first to propose that what would now be called kin selection, mutualism, and group selection are not necessarily antagonistic hypotheses and could be complementary, or mutually reinforcing.

Kin Selection

When the foundations of modern population genetics were being laid in the 1930s, the problem of altruism was raised once again, and once again the solution now known as kin selection was suggested. "Insofar as it makes for the survival of one's descendants and near relations," Haldane wrote, "altruistic behavior is a kind of Darwinian fitness, and may be expected to spread as a result of natural selection."[165] However, Haldane missed other elements in Darwin's proposed solution, in particular the augmenting role of selection *between* groups, and he was unable to develop a formal quantitative genetic model to show how such behaviors might evolve in a species. In 1945, Sewall Wright independently attempted a similar explanation of altruism in terms of his "island model," though he too overlooked Darwin's tripartite solution and the role of differential survival among populations.[166] Instead his formal treatment relied on so restrictive and implausible a set of conditions that his peers were generally not persuaded.* I suspect that the group selection hypothesis was overlooked because geneticists, unlike Darwin, did not fully appreciate how group-serving behaviors are not necessarily incompatible with an increase in personal fitness. In functionally integrated groups, the effectiveness of the group as a whole may have synergistic consequences for each member, depending on the particular circumstances. Geneticists then and now have tended to assume that individual advantage and group advantage are necessarily incompatible.

During the postwar period the terms altruism, co-operation, and group life came to be taken as virtually synonymous, so it seemed necessary to have a special explanation to account for social organization. Once the semantic confusion had set in, a theoretical polarization soon occurred between advocates of a pure group selection hypothesis and those who espoused individual or kin selection. At one extreme was V. C. Wynne-Edwards, whose *Animal Dispersion in Relation to Social Behaviour* (1962) became, in E. O. Wilson's words, a stalking horse. Wynne-Edwards has since abandoned his thesis,[170] but his original arguments continue to be reprinted in sociobiology anthologies as if they were his current views.

Wynne-Edwards asserted that group-living animals regularly display behavior that involves curtailing their own personal fitness for the benefit of the group (for example, "conventional" controls over reproduction that serve to limit population densities and prevent the Malthusian dynamic). "The greatest benefit of sociality," he claimed, "arises from its capacity to override the advantage of the individual members in the interests of the survival of the group as a whole." In order for such group-serving behaviors to evolve, natural selection must occur between social groups "as evolutionary units in their own right," favoring those with the most groupish tendency.[171]

* Wright imagined many small, nearly isolated groups with "altruistic" genes arising fortuitously in certain groups and then being diffused by emigration into other groups at a rate sufficient to offset counteracting "selfish" selection, so that the gene might drift to fixation and altruistic, group-serving behaviors could eventually become established. Sir Arthur Keith subsequently applied the group selection hypothesis to the explanation of human evolution, as Darwin had done, with the emphasis on intergroup warfare.[167] A similar argument was later made independently by Bigelow, Alexander and Tinkle, and E. O. Wilson.[168] In his recently completed four-volume treatise, Wright adopts a position similar to that of Darwin.[169]

At the other extreme was George C. Williams. Williams argued that the postulate of autonomous group benefits was based on a misinterpretation and that levels of selection higher than the individual and its offspring are "impotent" and "not an appreciable factor in evolution." So-called group-serving adaptations, he claimed, can be explained as (1) misinterpretations of what are really individual adaptations, (2) fortuitous effects rather than functional design, (3) statistical artifacts, or (4) the necessary result of the operation of physical laws. For instance, we now recognize that many apparently group-serving restraints on reproduction are in fact density-dependent responses that are fully consistent with individual selection; a group selection hypothesis is not required.

The *reductio ad absurdum* of Williams's line of argument was his suggestion that there was probably no such thing in nature as an organized group: The very concept of functional organization, he said, may be a product of "romantic imagination." "A wolf can live on elk only when it [coincidentally] attacks its prey in the company of other wolves with similar dietary tendencies. I am not aware, however, of any evidence of functional organization of wolf packs." Williams even suggested that the advanced mental capabilities of human beings are not the product of natural selection but are only "an incidental effect" of selection for the ability to communicate verbally.[172]

The reestablishment of a middle-ground position began with W. D. Hamilton's important paper, "The Genetical Evolution of Social Behavior" (1964). While Hamilton reinforced the tendency to equate altruism with pro-social behavior and "selfishness" with antisocial behavior, he formalized kin selection (inclusive fitness theory) in a quantitative model that has proven to have considerable heuristic value. The key to Hamilton's argument is the coefficient of relationship (r) between two individuals. According to the conventional wisdom of population genetics, two siblings have half their genes in common; thus their coefficient of relationship is $r = 1/2$. Two first cousins have one-eighth of their genes in common: $r = 1/8$. Assuming for the moment that there is such a thing as an altruist gene, it could spread in a population via Darwinian selection, according to the model, if the increases in the summed fitnesses of close relatives due to self-sacrifices by altruistic relatives more than offset the relatives' own loss of fitness. In formal terms, the gain-loss ratio (k) must exceed the reciprocal of the average coefficient of relationship, or $k > 1/\bar{r}$. Legend has it that Haldane anticipated the argument with some barroom bravado: "I would gladly give up my life for two brothers or eight cousins."

Reciprocal Altruism

The second major theoretical step, corresponding in modernized form to Darwin's explanation for the spread of "social and moral" behaviors between unrelated lineages, was Robert Trivers's "reciprocal altruism."[173] Here we confront a theoretical tangle; the underlying problem may not exist, and if it does, a special genetic explanation may not be needed to account for it.

Trivers begins with the familiar assumption that behaviors which benefit an unrelated animal at some cost to the benefactor are by definition altruistic. Therefore they violate the logic of classical Darwinian theory and require a special explanation. But do they? Darwin had suggested a conventional Darwinian explanation: In an animal capable of reason and of calculating self-interest, aiding behaviors among unrelated individuals might arise through cultural processes, as long as the ultimate benefits outweighed the costs. In Trivers's paradigm example of a man who rescues a drowning nonrelative at small risk to himself, as long as there is a high likelihood that the shoe would eventually be on the other foot and the nonrelative would reciprocate, such an action need not be considered altruistic at all; it would in fact be egoistic co-operation with a long memory and a delayed repayment schedule. (Indeed, Trivers concedes as much.) Likewise, when an individual contributes capital or labor to a business venture with the expectation of future profit, it is gilding the nettle to call this reciprocal altruism. Although psychological motivations might ultimately evolve to help reinforce such a behavior, Darwin did not see such motivations as a necessary precondition.

Reciprocal altruism, then, is neither strictly reciprocal (as in Table I) nor altruistic. It is a subset of the broader category of egoistic co-operation, a category that embraces any co-operative behavior in which the net benefits to each participant outweigh the costs.* Perhaps the way to clarify the matter is to view parental altruism, kin selection, reciprocal altruism, mutualism, and egoistic co-operation from the common perspective of benefit-cost analysis. In general, any form of behavior is consistent with Darwinian theory when there is a *net* contribution to individual reproductive fitness, that is, when the fitness benefits outweigh the costs. When the costs extracted from an individual are compensated for by benefits to one's offspring, the behavior is parental altruism; when the benefits go to close relatives, it is kin selection; when the benefits go to an unrelated individual and the costs are somehow repaid later, it has been dubbed reciprocal altruism; and when the costs are offset by mutual or reciprocal benefits, either immediately or later, it is mutualism or reciprocity.

These four categories have in common the properties of (1) being "selfish" in terms of Darwinian fitness, (2) involving both costs and benefits, and

* There may be cases where there are net gains for only one participant, while others suffer net costs. Such "altruistic" situations may nevertheless involve synergy if there are net gains when the costs and benefits are summed across all participants. Much exploitative behavior takes this form. Egoistic co-operation, by contrast, is an umbrella term that applies to any social situation in which the gains to each participant outweigh the costs.

(3) having the potential for favorable benefit-cost ratios to at least some participants. The terminological differences among these forms of social behavior, burdened as they are with anthropomorphic value connotations and physiological undertones, obscure the important commonalities. All may be special cases of the broader category of behaviors that I would call egoistic co-operation; all may involve synergistic effects that result in net gains (collectively); and most do not require such improbable conditions as Trivers postulated.

If this analysis satisfies the question of *ultimate* (evolutionary) causation, it leaves unresolved the question of *proximate* causation. How are such behaviors motivated and maintained within a species? Do we need a special genetic model for reciprocal altruism, or for egoistic co-operation? It could be argued that there must be genes for such behaviors and that they could not be the result of more general social and mental abilities. Trivers obviously thought so. Trivers's paradigm example involves human beings. But this example is not representative of a class of evolutionary phenomena; rather, it is a contrived case that has been loaded with dubious assumptions and lifted out of nature and the evolutionary context. Trivers assumes that two isolated human beings (strangers) are placed in a situation where one is dependent on the other's help (no kin are nearby). The prospective beneficiary has fallen into a body of water and may drown (a 50 percent probability). The model assumes that there is also substantial risk to the prospective benefactor (a 5 percent chance of drowning), that the benefactor will at some future time be in the same predicament, and therefore that it is in the benefactor's self-interest to extend aid. "If we assume that the entire population is sooner or later exposed to the same risk of drowning," Trivers posits, "the two individuals who risk their lives to save each other will be selected over those who face drowning on their own."[174] Out of such incidents, repeated many times (and presumably including many drownings), a fortuitous rescuer gene might arise and spread through a species.*

But what if we alter somewhat the assumptions in this model? (The reader may decide whether the following amendments make the model more or less plausible.) Suppose the victim is not a stranger but a member of the same functionally integrated band that shares in hunting, defense against predators (and neighboring human groups), exchanges of mates, and other collaborative behaviors (as would be far more likely in the context of human evolution). Good Samaritan behavior would then be a straightforward exten-

* Haldane presaged Trivers's arguments and even used a similar example with similar probabilities of drowning to show how altruistic behaviors might evolve among close relatives through kin selection.[175] However, he did not suggest the idea of altruism among non-kin, perhaps (as we shall see) for good reason.

sion to a novel situation of a well-established pattern of self-serving mutual aid that had long since evolved in an established social network through learning and cultural tradition. Suppose also that opportunities for reciprocal altruism among strangers occur at minuscule frequencies.

In such a model, a rescuer gene would not be required or likely. If aiding behaviors provide net benefits—an economist would speak of profits on invested capital or labor—why not assume that such patterns could be learned, as Darwin posited? As for the free rider and cheater problems, instead of postulating genes to prevent unearned benefits, why not postulate ethical norms, rules, and methods of punishing cheaters and free riders? Indeed, if *Homo sapiens* has genes that act to stimulate mutual aid and/or to prevent exploitative behaviors, they certainly work imperfectly. The alternative model does not depend on the fortuitous emergence and fitness-enhancing effects of a helping gene or a social gene; it suggests that such behaviors could emerge from a network of economic and social interdependencies in which each individual has a stake in maintaining good personal standing and in helping to ensure the functional integrity and effectiveness of the group. The accompanying feelings of sympathy and concern toward unrelated individuals would not involve a radical departure but an extension to a more inclusive community of capacities for social and psychological bonds that evolved in the more primitive context of socially organized family groups (kin selection) and simple networks of cultural exchange.

In sum, if the behaviors that are called reciprocal altruism conform to a genetic model, they also conform to a cultural exchange model or a rational choice economic model.[176] The anthropologist Sherwood Washburn calls the invocation of simplistic genetic models "genitis," the genetic disease. "Sociobiologists postulate genes for altruism and others for cheating, but it would be far more adaptive to possess genes for intelligence and be able to cheat or be altruistic as occasion demanded."[177] Perhaps the truth will ultimately be found to lie in some middle ground, but so far sociobiologists have not demonstrated the theoretical necessity for altruistic genes in social life.

Of course, it could be argued that for those species which are not endowed with human social and mental capacities, a genetic model might be more parsimonious. Examples of reciprocal altruism that conform to Trivers's model have been observed among some higher primates and such tightly integrated social carnivores as dolphins, wild dogs, and wolves.[178] Far from demanding a genetic model, however, these examples may well add support to a nongenetic, teleonomic selection model, especially in light of our increasing appreciation of learning and cultural traditions in other social species.[179]*

* Two other sources of evidence invoked by Trivers in his original paper are similarly doubtful. One source involved interspecies symbiosis. Trivers alludes vaguely to altruism among sym-

(Continued)

Reciprocal altruism is a concept that may depend very much on the eye—and the interpretation—of the beholder. For example, Packer reported data on coalition behavior in baboons (*Papio anubis*), which he interpreted as lending support to the concept of reciprocal altruism.[181] Unrelated adult males often join forces—a "helper" assists a "solicitor"—in efforts to displace forcibly another male who has established a consort relationship with an estrous female. For this action the helper is generally later "repaid." However, the degree of altruism involved in such behavior is debatable. Injuries occur in fights among baboon males, but Packer's study does not report the proportion of the documented injuries that involved helpers in coalition fights. Thus Packer does not show that there is a significant risk of serious injury. It is possible that reciprocal altruists run very little risk and that one advantage of forming a coalition is precisely the (synergistic) reduction of risk. Even if Packer were able to establish that there is significant risk, this would not show that the behavior evolved through natural selection; it would suggest only that the cost side of the benefit-cost ratio is higher. It is significant that coalitions in *P. anubis* also occur in many clearly nonaltruistic situations, as we would expect in an egoistic co-operation model, and that such coalitions apparently occur only among members of the same troop.

In sum, if reciprocal altruism is not altruistic and is instead a special case of the multifaceted class of phenomena I call egoistic co-operation, and if there is no need for a special genetic model to account for such behaviors, then perhaps we do not really need the concept. It is really enlightened self-interest.

Kin Group Selection

We come now to E. O. Wilson's effort to bridge the gap between kin selection and group selection. Noting that two well-known attempts to develop formal dynamic models of evolution—the Levins model[182] and the Boorman-Levitt model[183]—indicated that the evolution of altruism via "pure" interdemic selection would require a very narrow "window" and was therefore "an improbable event," Wilson speculated that interdemic selection might nonetheless be a factor where it was a special case of kin selection.[184] Following Kalela,[185] Wilson observed that if group selection occurred among expanded family groups, it could effectively reinforce and help to spread evolutionary

---

bionts—the hosts of cleaner fish, for example—but his interpretation is questionable, and it has not to my knowledge been verified experimentally. A careful benefit-cost analysis might well reveal that as a rule there are strong *net* advantages to both hosts and cleaners. Similarly, Trivers's alarm-calling behaviors have subsequently become the subject of much research and considerable controversy; alternative models plausibly suggest net individual or inclusive fitness explanations.[180]

changes that had arisen initially as a result of kin selection—just as Darwin had posited for human evolution.[186]

Kalela reported on a particularly striking case, that of the subarctic vole. In an environment marked by alternating periods of feast and famine, this animal exercises great reproductive restraint, usually staying well below the carrying capacity. Kalela reasoned that vole groups possessing genes that potentiated reproductive self-control would have been favored over groups which were periodically decimated or even extinguished as a result of alternating booms and crashes. In such circumstances, it would not take long for genes that appeared in one or a few family groups to be diffused by interdemic selection to the entire metapopulation, as in Wright's model. Both Jerram Brown and William P. Hamilton have suggested that such kin *cum* group selection patterns be given the label "kin group selection."[187]

Some Conclusions About "Classical" Sociobiology

One problem with this framework arises from its focus on altruism, its exclusion of reciprocity and mutualism (co-operation broadly defined), and inclusion of reciprocal altruism. Stated baldly, altruism is too narrow and reciprocal altruism is too weak to support a theory of social life, while the most important category (one that does not require a special genetic model or reductionist explanation) is downplayed.

To the extent that social life is positively advantageous (both phenotypically and genetically) to the individuals involved, no exceptional condition or improbable circumstance is necessary to account for their emergence. The basic requirement is that the fitness benefits must outweigh the fitness costs. Just as reciprocal altruism can be reduced to examples of favorable benefit-cost ratios, so many cases of altruism and self-restraint for the supposed good of the group can be reduced to cases of net benefits to individuals that simultaneously benefit other group members as well. Collective defense on the part of adult male baboons is not at all altruistic when for each member the net probability of deterring a potential predator is increased over the alternative of going it alone, and when the risk of injury or death is correspondingly reduced. In such cases, collective defense is really an example of synergy, of joint effects that could not have been achieved by individuals acting separately. They involve corporate goods. Others have made similar points, though no one has focused on synergy and the role of functional organization.[188]

In assuming that social life is based mainly on altruism rather than on egoistic co-operation, Wilson burdened sociobiology with an unnecessarily restrictive set of theoretical requirements. Wilson was forced to conclude, erroneously, that the more complex forms of social behavior must be based on kinship.[189] Thus the concept of inclusive fitness represents a genetic boundary with limited scope for co-operation. In contrast, the concept of egoistic co-operation, coupled with the principle of functional synergism, provides a broad theoretical basis for integration and interdependency in social life, ranging from simple symbiosis to the international economic and political spheres in human societies.

If suicidal self-sacrifices on the part of worker bees represent one extreme on a continuum of social behaviors that ranges from the completely self-abnegating to the completely self-serving (phenotypically), as Darwin appreciated, then kin selection becomes a less important mechanism and individual selection and functional group selection both play relatively larger roles. Indeed, none of the "classical" sociobiological models is relevant to an explanation of the genetics of positive symbiosis between species. These models do not even address such phenomena.

A corollary of this point is that group selection assumes greater theoretical importance once the distinction is drawn sharply between groups that are merely reproductive demes, or differentiated trait groups, and groups that are functionally integrated (cybernated) survival enterprises, "economies" consisting of self-serving yet interdependent individuals whose behaviors are constrained by collective purposes and actions. In such species the fitness gains derived from co-operation may involve trade-offs; individual fitnesses may to a degree become interdependent with others and with the group as an organized bioeconomic system.* This is the approach I pursue in the chapters to follow.

Recent Developments

Since the publication of *Sociobiology* there have been a number of significant theoretical developments: (1) the completion of Sewall Wright's compelling four-volume treatise, in which his interdemic selection model receives exten-

* Wilson fails to appreciate fully the significance of functional integration in many socially organized species. Consider his differing treatment of castes and roles. Castes in insect societies entail functionally differentiated roles even though these roles are accompanied by a form of genetic differentiation that is not found in the higher mammals. Nevertheless, in relation to the economics (and ergonomics) of social life, caste and role are functionally equivalent terms. However, Wilson defines them in different ways. In order to avoid the "quasi-mystical vision" of Durkheim and Wheeler that society is some sort of "superorganism," Wilson shuns the idea that a role might be defined in terms of a functionally integrated social system.[190] For Wilson there are no social systems outside insect societies. In wild dogs, wolf packs, baboon troops, and human beings, there are only individual behaviors that directly or indirectly influence other individuals.[191] Other students of animal behavior would sharply disagree with this view.[192] Alexander and Borgia are exceptional in recognizing noninsect social groups as potentially functional units in evolution. (However, their appreciation of this fact is limited by a narrow vision of the precise functions that social groups might serve).[193]

sive treatment; (2) Alexander and Borgia's perceptive analysis of evolution as a multileveled process;[194] (3) Boorman and Levitt's exploration, following Darwin, of three possibly interrelated modes through which sociality might evolve;[195] and (4) David Sloan Wilson's volume on trait group selection in structured demes, which owes much to Sewall Wright but employs systems dynamics models to go a significant step or two further.[196]

D. S. Wilson's work is of particular importance, his objective being to break through the "whole" versus "parts" argument among evolutionists. Wilson focuses on two related concepts. The first, adapted from Sewall Wright (though perhaps developed independently), is a conceptualization of reproductive populations, not as pools of randomly mating individuals but as highly structured communities that often consist of many small, ethnically varied "neighborhoods" that are much more intensely interactive internally than they are with the larger metapopulation.

The second concept is that of ecological communities as superorganisms, a revival of W. C. Allee's views of fifty years ago.[197] Although for some years evolutionists have treated the superorganism concept as something to be written off as evidence of the softheaded thinking of an earlier generation, Wilson argues that the term provides a label for a valid and frequently discounted parameter of the evolutionary process.* Ecological communities are not simply gladiatorial fields dominated by deadly competition; they are networks of complex interactions, *of interdependent self-interests* (as Darwin insisted) that require mutual adjustment and accommodation with respect to both the other cohabitants and the dynamics of the local ecosystem. The necessity for competition is one half of a duality, the other half of which includes many opportunities for mutually beneficial co-operation, including many tacit arrangements that amount to an ecological division of labor and specialization of systemic functions. Again, I am speaking not about altruism but about enlightened (or embedded) self-interest.

Wilson argues that the classical population genetic models are unsatisfactory when it comes to describing such interactions. His own simulations involve systems dynamics models that include many interlocking relationships. Wilson found in his simulations that mutualism (egoistic co-operation)

* I will confine the use of the term *superorganism* strictly to organized cybernetic social systems (I believe this conforms to Spencer's original intent). Therefore I disagree with those who, like Allee and D. S. Wilson, would apply the term to ecosystems in which functional integration is epiphenomenal rather than being a manifestation of a unified purposive system. (The parallel distinction in economic theory is between firms and markets.) Likewise, human societies as wholes can qualify for the superorganism label only to the degree that they entail functions that are integrated by a unifying cybernetic (governmental) system. As political scientists know full well, the scope and degree of political integration in a society can range from minimal to totalitarian (see Chapter IV).

is a surprisingly robust phenomenon, that when ecological specialists were pitted against generalists, the former generally dominated and in time replaced the latter. In effect, these results suggest that the operation of the economy principle in ecosystems may bias ecosystem evolution (where conditions permit) toward the creation of networks of functionally interdependent specializers. This in turn imposes *indirect* restraining pressures on the behavior of the participants. Thus these interrelationships create interdependent units of selection, what Boorman and Levitt call "fitness interlocks," that may augment or counteract selection at the individual and family levels. (These models overlap with, or reformulate, some of the models for cross-species symbioses mentioned above.)

D. S. Wilson's models are by his own admission relatively primitive. The significance of Wilson's work is that it has introduced into the argument explicit models of some real-world interdependencies—constraints on competition and opportunities for functional synergism—that are excluded from the essentially atomistic competition models in the tradition of classical population genetics. Wilson's models intimate how much more scope there may be in nature for mutualism that still accords with strict Darwinian, natural selection theory than many first-generation sociobiologists believed was the case.

Like Darwin, Wright, Boorman and Levitt, and others, Wilson recognized the potentiality of a threefold (individual *cum* kin *cum* group) selection model to explain the evolution of sociality in more complex social species. Equally important, Wilson offers pertinent observations on the free rider or cheater problem. Taking some liberties with Wilson's reasoning and adding reasoning of my own, the argument says that when organisms are embedded in interdependent ecosystems (or socioeconomic systems), three classes of (possibly) mutually reinforcing mechanisms may serve to counteract cheating: (1) direct face-to-face transactions in which the benefits may be indivisible but are dependent on each member's doing his or her part (that is, the "goods" may be less good if someone shirks); (2) auxiliary structures of exogenous rewards and punishments, which may include evolved psychological components (superego, interpersonal bonding, sympathy) and/or artificially imposed cultural incentives; and (3) structures of ecological interdependency (structured demes) that indirectly create "selection pressures" favoring individual behavioral constraints. Garrett Hardin's "Tragedy of the Commons" (1968) is a paradigm human case.[198] In nature there are many threshold phenomena where nature rewards those individual organisms that exercise prudence. This does not require group selection in the classical sense but only a more structured form of individual selection.

Finally, Wilson's conclusions should be juxtaposed with those of sociologists Boorman and Levitt.[199] The latter point out that the path to "true sociality" cannot be blocked by severe genetic restrictions, any more than there can be severe ecological barriers. The behavioral substrate of an organism must permit, if not positively direct, the more or less intricately orchestrated relationships that are implied in co-operative behaviors. It is biologically naive to suppose that it could be otherwise.

However, the degree of restriction and the prerequisites that must be satisfied at the genetic level are matters that, at this point, do not go much beyond speculation. Boorman and Levitt (and others) make strict and arguable assumptions, with the result that for them the width of the bottleneck leading to sociality is very narrow indeed. They assume that there must be a specific social gene or genes that must actively compete with asocial (or antisocial) alleles, and that sociality is a limited, direct, dyadic affair (or some empirical analogue). They define sociality narrowly, so as to exclude such things as interspecific mutualism (where the very act of establishing a symbiotic relationship may remove an organism from competition with its asocial conspecifics and vault it into a different ecological niche) and reproductive co-operation among mating pairs, which can extend even to what S. A. Barnett labels "docent" behaviors.[200] Boorman and Levitt thus exclude by fiat many of the synergistic relationships I listed above.

Even more alien to Boorman and Levitt are Wilson's expansive notions about indirect ecological interdependencies, constraints, reciprocities, and specializations. (Their notion of "fitness interlocks" is more narrowly defined.) But what if nature is in fact like Darwin's "entangled bank," a complex network of relationships wherein adaptation to other organisms in both competitive and co-operative ways is a routine part of the process of adaptation to the total environment? What if the postulate of a social gene must be replaced, at least in higher mammals, by a model in which there is a field of interconnected preadaptations that may have evolved under the much less prohibitive conditions of sociality between parents and slow maturing offspring, between siblings, or between tolerant noncompetitive species?

I maintain that the existence of such primitive forms of sociality might well be sufficient as preconditions, provided that they are coupled with the assumption of intelligence, in accordance with the cybernetic and teleonomic selection model. If the phenomenon of teleonomic selection leads the way in many adaptive innovations, that is, if functionally significant social behaviors may be learned without the prior appearance of a mutant gene, then there is no theoretical or logical obstacle in the way of the proposition that synergistic social adaptations, either within or between species, can arise in the first instance through the Law of Effect and the process of teleonomic selection. This in turn may introduce selection pressures that will positively favor biological changes that serve to underpin such behaviors (changes in the ability to recognize co-operators, buffers to inhibit fearful or antagonistic reactions in the context of these relationships, increased ability to communicate and coordinate behavior, and even modifications in morphology). Sewall Wright's models involving saddle-crossing phenomena, or peak shifts in genetic "interaction systems," provide perhaps the most applicable population genetic approach here, and the results may also conform to a "punctuated equilibrium" model of evolutionary change. The models developed by Boorman and Levitt may therefore be more applicable to the social insects (social Hymenoptera and Isoptera) than to human evolution, though we should not underestimate the learning abilities of insects.

A Postscript

There have been several other developments since this book was completed. I will briefly discuss four: Plotkin and Odling-Smee's multiple-level model of evolution; Axelrod and Hamilton's approach to modeling co-operative behaviors; Cavalli-Sforza and Feldman's volume on cultural transmission and evolution; and Lumsden and Wilson's new volume on gene-culture coevolution.[201]

Plotkin and Odling-Smee's multiple-level model of evolution is based on the view that biological evolution cannot be described adequately merely in terms of selection among alternative alleles in a kind of free-floating gene pool; a hierarchy of selection processes operates at different levels of biological organization, and these processes entail very different selective mechanisms and units of selection. Arguing that adaptation is quintessentially a knowledge-gaining process, Plotkin and Odling-Smee use as a "defining feature" for each level of evolution various distinct processes of information transmission and the associated storage sites. Accordingly, they posit four levels of adaptation and evolution: (1) *genes* (in gene pools); (2) *epigenesis,* the developmental process in which information from the genes is combined with information from the environment during ontogeny; (3) individual *learning,* or the behavioral programming of the central nervous system; and (4) *sociocultural* transmission via interpersonal communications and storage in "cultural pools." Further, Plotkin and Odling-Smee insist that the genetic level must be at the top of the hierarchy, that all other levels are subordinate to and constrained by the ultimate controlling influence of the genes. They liken that process to the workings of a computer algorithm, in which the main program is equipped to write various subroutines as needed to handle unpredictable, variable, or fine-grained details.

Several criticisms leveled at Plotkin and Odling-Smee are pertinent. First, an approach that views evolution primarily as an information-gathering, storage, and transmission process is not new; more important, it distorts and even inverts the underlying structure of causal relationships and functional processes. Biological evolution has to do with changes over time in functionally organized thermodynamic systems—cybernetic systems—and natural selection entails the differential survival and reproduction among these systems. The levels upon which natural selection is manifested are levels of biological organization, not the sites of information storage and transmission. Information entails the capacity to exercise cybernetic control over the capture, distribution, and flows of matter-energy; thus informational processes are subsidiary to the purposive production and reproduction of organic (and superorganic) systems.[202]

Second, Plotkin and Odling-Smee have confused such mathematical reifications as gene pools and cultural pools with concrete "structures" of information transmission and storage. Several critics observed that Plotkin and Odling-Smee were not able to identify (and specify) the supposed storage sites at each level in such a way that it would be possible to show exactly how they are subject to natural selection.

Finally, critics noted that Plotkin and Odling-Smee left themselves open to the charge that they had adopted a biological determinist position. Because they were interested primarily in identifying levels of information processing rather than levels of purposive (teleonomic) organization and cybernetic control, they were unable to address the phenomenon of emergent (partially independent) causation, that is, of selectively significant functional changes that arise at each new level of biological organization (including social organization). This point is essential to a satisfactory model of evolution as a multileveled process. A proper understanding of the dynamics of natural selection in the evolution of a socially organized species such as humankind requires the recognition of a reciprocal, interactive relationship between the political level of organization and the genomes of its constituent individuals (not to mention the other levels in between).[203]

Two of the other recent developments can be disposed of quickly. Axelrod and Hamilton apply the classical "prisoner's dilemma" from game theory to the problem of accounting for co-operative behaviors. The virtue of this approach is that it identifies and formalizes a range of hypothetical situations in which two players, when given the option of co-operating or "defecting," will find it more advantageous to co-operate. In the kind of situations Axelrod and Hamilton posit: (1) each player will be most advantaged by defecting and exploiting the co-operative efforts of the other; (2) both players will lose if both defect; and (3) the game is iterative, that is, the players have to engage in a succession of tournament rounds. Axelrod and Hamilton were able to show that even under such conditions the most effective strategy for each player is tit for tat, with the best opening move being to co-operate.

The implication is that conditions for co-operation among strict egoists might be much more favorable in nature than classical sociobiologists supposed. This is a valuable theoretical contribution, but it has some limitations. One is that Axelrod and Hamilton's assumptions are too narrow to encompass many real-world contexts. In the real world it is equally likely that the payoffs from co-operation will depend heavily on everyone doing his or her share; the goods will be less good if someone defects. Thus any defections will penalize the system and reduce its potential for realizing functional synergism. This is the kind of situation that is addressed in the corporate goods model, but it may apply to various collective goods as well. Another limitation involves Axelrod and Hamilton's assumption that the players have foreknowledge of the fact that the game will be iterative. In a corporate goods situation, on the other hand, immediate positive reinforcements (and feedback) may be sufficient to induce the repetition and spread of a co-operative behavior, even in the absence of contextual foreknowledge.

In *Cultural Transmission and Evolution* (1981) Cavalli-Sforza and Feldman's approach is both compatible with and complementary to my own. As these writers point out, theories of cultural evolution and theories relating to the transmission of innovations by cultural means can be developed independently of one another, though a complete theory must address both types of issues. I am concerned here mainly with the former issue, with a theory of progressive sociocultural evolution toward more complex forms of social organization. Cavalli-Sforza and Feldman, on the other hand, are primarily concerned with the mechanisms and process of cultural transmission and diffusion. Moreover, they direct their attention largely to the spread of discrete cultural "traits" among individuals. As far as they go, their formalizations are elegant and highly sophisticated. But Cavalli-Sforza and Feldman pointedly steer clear of questions concerning *why* social organization arises and evolves. They treat the issue as a sand trap that they would like to avoid. But a satisfactory theory must go beyond the dynamics of cultural transmission—the *how* question—and address the *why* question as well.

Finally, there is Lumsden and Wilson's pioneering effort to develop mathematical models to describe the interconnections between genes and culture. Responding to the criticism that sociobiology lacked a theory of the mind as the organ of behavior and ultimately of sociocultural evolution, Lumsden and Wilson developed what they characterize as a theory of "gene-culture co-evolution."

The idea of a co-evolutionary process in which behavioral and biological changes interact is not new. What Lumsden and Wilson attempt is to specify with quantitative precision the exact relationship between genes, mind, and culture and how they evolve together over time.

Lumsden and Wilson write that "the pivot of gene-culture theory is epigenesis,"[204] the process by which genetic instructions are translated into the morphology and behavior of the individual. The basis of their model is what they call "epigenetic rules," genetically determined procedures which direct the assembly of the mind and bias the individual's choices among various "culturgens" (their neologism for cultural traits and artifacts). Lumsden and Wilson do not deny the role of downward causation in changing the genetic constitution of successive generations of individuals, but their primary emphasis—indeed, their mission—is to replace the *tabula rasa* view of human nature with one in which genetic influences closely constrain and mold our perceptions and our responses to the environment. They hold that an "oracle" resides within the epigenetic rules that will not be challenged.[205]

Cultural evolution, then, is the result of the interaction—which they attempt to describe in complex equations borrowed from physics—between epigenetic rules (as embodied in specific brain structures and neuronal processes) and the pattern of culturgens, or the culturgen pool, in the cultural environment. It is, they admit, an atomistic theory of culture. Rejecting out of hand the "organicist conception of many social scientists, which views culture as a virtually independent entity," they offer the view that "culture is in fact the product of vast numbers of choices by individual members of the society."[206]

As ever, the truth will be found to lie in the middle. The proposition that our behavior is biologically molded and constrained in various ways becomes increasingly irresistible (see Chapter IV). But Lumsden and Wilson's particular approach to modeling and explaining the mind and culture is flawed and incomplete. While their models are mathematically sophisticated, they are psychologically and culturally naive. The mind is a complex integrated *system,* a cybernetic system whose actions are the product of synergistic interactions that have emergent, partially autonomous properties. The mind cannot be likened to a disconnected set of decision rules, like so many pickup sticks. Despite their claims to the contrary, Lumsden and Wilson have no theory of the mind *qua* system. As Gertude Stein said of Oakland, there's no there there.

By the same token, they have no theory of human societies *qua* systems. Although they do not use the term cultural pool, their models depict culturgens as distributions of particulate units that "colonize" different minds, like so many islands of an archipelago. This imaginative application of ecological theory (for which Wilson is justly famous) is misplaced. In the case of human societies, the "islands" engage in complex functional interactions with one another and with the archipelago as a whole. Lumsden and Wilson are correct in saying that choices (teleonomic selections) are the pivot of sociocultural evolution, but these choices take place in structured cultural environments, in social systems. Our choices are not free, and we are constrained by the choices made by others. Until the sociobiologists give more weight to emergent, *co-determining* "psychological" and social processes, a reconciliation with the social sciences will remain elusive.

A Summary and Prolegomenon

I have attempted to show that my theory is clearly applicable to the molecular, cellular, and metazoan levels of evolution, and I have attempted to lay the groundwork for applying my theory to sociobiology and sociocultural evolution. This I propose to do in detail in the chapters to follow.

In contrast with various sociobiologically oriented theories (or proto-theories) of human evolution, my approach is functional. My theory proceeds from the vision that the process has been deeply interactional but that the leading edge has been "downward causation"—teleonomic selection at the behavioral level, involving novel forms of functional synergism (both technological and social) that have served to canalize our biological and sociocultural evolution. To characterize the emergence of humankind as an autocatalytic process[207] or as a kind of hypertrophy,[208] like the runaway growth of an organ, is to reduce the dynamics of a complex set of functional transformations to a mechanistic caricature.

Our biological needs and biologically based capabilities have defined the underlying survival challenge and have provided the necessary behavioral preadaptations at every stage of what has been a definite progression, but the primary locus of evolutionary creativity in humankind has not been genetic change but our ideas, our inventions, our solutions to the problems of living, our entrepreneurship, our ever-expanding array of co-operative activities, and our capacity for transmitting learned behaviors to subsequent generations. It was not primarily fortuitous mutant genes but both fortuitous and purposeful behavioral changes—new adaptive strategies—that have given directionality to human evolution. On the evidence to date, many of our unique biological characteristics may have followed rather than preceded major cultural changes. The changes have been incremental but the consequences have been saltatory. Accordingly, the behavioral and social levels of biological organization in protohominids and humankind must be viewed as emergent and partially independent sources of evolutionary causation. In a far more important sense than V. Gordon Childe had in mind in his famous book on the rise of civilization, mankind has "made" itself.

IV

The Interactional Paradigm

Every time that a social phenomenon is directly explained by a psychological phenomenon, we may be sure that the explanation is false.

Emile Durkheim

The development of fundamental theory in sociology must await the full neuronal explanation of the brain. *Edward O. Wilson*

The solution to great arguments is usually close to the golden mean.

Stephen Jay Gould

Interactionism is not new. It has been in the air, off and on, for two thousand years. The cornerstone of the Platonic/Aristotelian paradigm, after all, was based on the idea that a human society involves a set of dualities, an interplay between rational and "appetitive" tendencies in human nature, between nature and nurture, and between the individual and the social order. Accordingly, for Plato and Aristotle the central problem was how to achieve a harmonious set of relationships (a dynamic stability) for both individuals and societies. Similarly, major nineteenth-century social theorists such as Darwin, Spencer, Weber, Mill, and Marshall adopted explicitly interactional perspectives toward their various subjects, though their followers often did not. In the early decades of this century, a variety of forces (both theoretical and institutional) shifted the balance in the nascent social sciences toward narrowly deterministic and one-leveled theoretical perspectives. Over the past fifteen years, however, a sea change has taken place. Now multivariate, multileveled, and multidisciplinary approaches are commonplace. Interactionism has become a byword.

Interactionism

Not all who profess the faith of interactionism do so unreservedly. The ethologist Irenäus Eibl-Eibesfeldt, in a recent overview of human ethology, dutifully genuflected toward interactionism but devoted little of his attention to cultural variables. He was mainly concerned with arguing the case for applying classical Lorenzian concepts to human behavior: "fixed action patterns," "innate releasing mechanisms," and so forth.[1] At the other pole, anthropologist Marvin Harris espouses a "demo-techno-econo-environmental-determinism" yet studiously avoids getting inside the individual.

On close inspection it is clear that interactionism means different things to different people. For the participants in a symposium on genetics and social behavior in 1967, an "interactional" approach referred specifically to the recognition of genetic as well as environmental influences on behavior and behavioral causation.[2] For Jean Piaget it involved an epigenetic view of child development,[3] while for neurobiologist Paul Weiss it referred to causal influences at various levels of hierarchically organized biological systems.[4] The political scientist Elliott White used the term to draw attention to genetic diversity as a variable in sociopolitical behavior.[5] The anthropologist Lewis Binford used it with reference to ecological, technological, and economic interactions in different human cultures.[6] Talcott Parsons's "interactions" are focused on person-system relationships, but for Karl Popper the focus is mind-brain interactions.[7]*

As these strikingly varied uses of the term suggest, there are sharp differences on fundamental theoretical issues among those who profess to be interactionists. Four issues are relevant here.

1. *Nature versus nurture* in social causation, to borrow Sir Francis Galton's catchy phrase. Witness interactionist Marvin Harris, who opposes sociobiologists even as he embraces a rococo extrapolation from Marxian materialism.

* Interactionism of one sort or another is implicit or explicit in some very different contemporary social science paradigms and theoretical approaches: ecological anthropology, symbolic interactionism, biogenetic structuralism, biocultural ecology, ecodynamics, environmental psychology, cultural materialism, biosociology, and of course biopolitics.

Biopolitics is more than a paradigm, or theoretical approach. Rather, it is a movement with various foci and substantive research interests, ranging from basic behavioral science to evolutionism and public policy. Now more than a decade old, the biopolitics movement has enlisted a large number of contributors over the years and has amassed several hundred published articles, books, and reports.[8]

2. *External determinism versus internal goals.* The positivist tradition still thrives, and many behavioral scientists resist as metaphysical various unproven assertions of internal biopsychological "causes" that cannot be seen and measured directly, much less causes that are "emergent."

3. *Holism versus reductionism.* Notwithstanding his later clarifications, Edward Wilson's initial position on the role of the mind in evolution was that it was an epiphenomenon of the neuronal organization of the brain that could be treated, in essence, as a dependent variable in sociobiological theory. Conversely, sociologists in the Durkheimian tradition insist that the biological substrate is essentially irrelevant to the explanation of social phenomena.[9]

4. *The relative importance of different variables.* Interactionists frequently differ on the weight they assign to such factors as climate, ecology, population, technology, social values and traditions, economics, patterns of social organization, and innovation.

As will shortly become apparent, my position is that a satisfactory understanding of the questions that concern the nature and purposes of society and the political order and the causes of sociopolitical evolution lies in a paradigm that can integrate and reconcile the differences on these fundamental issues. A paradigm is required that focuses explicitly on the relationships among and the interactions between nature and nurture, internal and external factors, and reductionist and emergent causes. Alongside the specialized one-dimensional analyses that are essential to a rigorous and detailed understanding of such enormously complex phenomena, we must deliberately encourage integrative, multilevel systems approaches that are concerned with relationships and interactions in a dynamic, time-bound matrix. For the *functional relationships* between these levels and variables are the key to our gaining a better purchase on the central theoretical problem: the evolution of society in general and the political order in particular. More specifically, *it is the functional consequences of the interactions among various configurations of factors, spanning various levels of organization, that constitute the underlying causal dynamic of sociopolitical evolution.* The directional aspect of this process, moreover, has been the result of *synergistic effects* of various kinds in relation to functions that are ultimately biological in origin. But, to repeat, the precise course of this trend has entailed the combined effects of "chance, necessity, and teleonomy."

Sewall Wright has suggested a metaphor for this point that I will take the liberty of embellishing.[10] In the flight of an airplane there is always a high degree of determination involved, as a consequence of physical and aerodynamic constraints, various engineering requirements, and the technological state of the art. At the same time, teleonomic elements are involved in the decision to build the plane in the first place, in the precise design of the plane, and in the specific choices regarding where, when, and how the plane will be flown. The actual flight history of the plane will also be influenced by such unpredictable (or marginally predictable) factors as weather and wind conditions, malfunctioning components, the flight plans of other aircraft owners and pilots, and even the actions of hijackers and terrorists. So what "causes" an airplane to be at a particular airway intersection at a particular altitude, time, and date? To understand truly the "behavior" of the airplane *qua* cybernetic system, one must be prepared to synthesize a complex configuration of stochastic, deterministic, and purposive elements. This may seem to be commonsense. Yet the view that various kinds and levels of causation are involved in the production of behavioral and social phenomena is still controversial and is often accepted only with major qualifications. In my view, this resistance is no longer justified. Let me explain why.

The Case for an Interactional Paradigm

What evidence is there that our genes directly influence behavior and behavioral causation? Some genetic influences are so pervasive that we take them for granted—for example, the genetic program that defines and controls the basic trajectory of the life cycle. The biological life cycle is such a "given" that social scientists sometimes overlook it. Yet it represents a fundamental parameter for each individual and for society as a whole.

The stage of physical development or decline, inclusive of genetically influenced differences among individuals, plays an important role in shaping behavior and social experience. As we age, we experience increasing (or decreasing) physical and mental powers, which in turn influence our attitudes, goals, and priorities, our ways of responding to the environment and the ways in which the environment responds to us. Likewise, our genes and our biological constitutions define a set of basic needs (for food, water, defecation, physical safety, thermoregulation, sleep, sex and reproduction, physical activity, social contacts) that determine basic behavioral priorities for us.

The power and importance of our genetic programs are perhaps most visible when something goes awry. For it is increasingly evident that genetic factors, in concert with environmental factors, are implicated in many social pathologies and problem areas (though the evidence is not conclusive in some cases). The list includes schizophrenia and the schizoid spectrum, manic depressive psychosis and various depressive disorders, alcohol addiction, autism, hyperactivity, congenital obesity problems (not all cases of obesity), aphasia (various speech disorders), alexia (reading disabilities), and possibly certain psychopathic behavioral disorders that may be associated with some patterns of "criminality."[11] However, the hypothesis of genetic influences is not equivalent to genetic determinism; genetic and environmental influences do not require mutually exclusive hypotheses.

The list above does not include the many well-documented medical syndromes with genetic (or chromosomal) bases which afflict perhaps as much as 10 percent of the population and which in many cases are associated with marked functional deficits in behavior.*[12] Indeed, it has been estimated that roughly 20 percent of this nation's annual health care bill is attributable to problems in which a genetic component is implicated.

There is also substantial (if somewhat less conclusive) evidence that genes are involved in the variations we observe in "normal" mental and personality traits. Some of the evidence comes from other species. The house mouse *Mus musculus,* because it is economical to breed and maintain, has a short reproductive cycle and is available to researchers in a variety of closely inbred strains, is perhaps the most popular animal for behavior genetics research. Among the more than 1500 references contained in a cumulative bibliography of mouse behavior genetic research through 1975, there are numerous reports of genetically based strain differences in activity (exploratory behaviors and wheel running, for instance), aggression, emotionality, feeding behaviors, learning abilities, memory functions, psychomotor functions, reproductive behaviors, social interactions, and responses to "treatments" (such as alcohol, hormones, nervous system stimulation, and pharmacological agents).[14] Similar results have been obtained in other species.

There is also direct evidence from human behavior genetics: personality factors, perceptual and cognitive abilities, psychomotor skills, and general intelligence as measured by IQ tests.[15] The latter, only one parish in behavior genetics, has attracted the most public attention and is the most controversial.[16] But, in light of the breadth of the evidence from other behaviorally relevant domains and other species, the basic hypothesis that there are individual differences in whatever abilities IQ tests measure is plausible. However, one should be agnostic about such subsidiary issues as the usefulness of a global intelligence measure, the precise relationship between IQ test scores and real-world mental abilities, the proportion of the variance that may properly be assigned the genetic differences, the relative importance of various environmental insults, therapies, or enrichments, and the inflammatory claims made with respect to racial and sex differences.

As for the controversy surrounding race and sex differences, it is likely that some statistically significant *average* differences exist between different groups. Yet this generalization requires four important qualifications:

* For example, phenylketonuria (and several other amino acidurias), hemophilia, porphyria, galactosemia, Huntington's chorea, Wilson's disease, Hartnup's disease, Tay-Sachs disease, Niemann-Pick disease, Parkinson's disease, Down syndrome, Lesch-Nyhan syndrome, maple syrup urine disease, Spielmeyer-Vogt disease, sickle-cell anemia, albinism, congenital nephrosis, cystic fibrosis, cretinism, gargoylism, achondroplasia (dwarfism) and some other forms of mental retardation, congenital bodily malformations and perceptual problems (e.g., color blindness), and such commonplace afflictions as arthritis, diabetes, mellitus, epilepsy, and many allergies.[13]

(1) by no means do all the differences flow in one direction in terms of which group, as a group, is more or less advantaged; (2) the average differences between groups are surely far less than the differences among individuals within the groups; (3) it is differences among *individuals,* regardless of race or sex, that are relevant for practical (social) purposes; and (4) culturally based sources of economic and social differentiation between groups are manifestly more important.

Child Development

Less publicized but more significant theoretically is the evidence that has accumulated in the child development field for the role of the biological substrate in shaping our acquisition of adult behaviors. Some of the work on newborns suggests the existence of individual personality differences at birth.[17] Alexander Thomas and his co-workers identified nine characteristics on which newborns differ: motor activity, rhythmicity of basic biological functions, responsiveness to novelties, adaptability to environmental change, sensitivity to various stimuli, intensity of responses, general mood or disposition, distractibility, and attention span.[18] Anneliese Korner detected differences in startle responses, smiles, oral activity, frequency and duration of crying, and responsiveness to soothing.[19] T. Berry Brazelton monitored twenty-six kinds of behaviors, including responsiveness to human voices and faces.[20] And Freedman and Keller found evidence of mental, motor, and personality differences in a sample of twenty pairs of monozygotic and dizygotic twins.[21]

Far more important than the subtle differences between individuals is the overall competence of most newborns, and the past two decades have seen a revolution in the way we view infants. The behaviorist stereotype of the newborn as a passive sponge has given way to what amounts to a cybernetic model; the newborn is now recognized to be a self-organizing, purposive system that is able and willing to take an active role in the learning process. The infant comes equipped with innate abilities for selectively controlling and organizing what it learns, for integrating experiences, for responding to and even manipulating its environment.[22] Best known is the ability of the newborn to attend selectively to movement, novelty, and visual schema resembling the human face.[23] The experiments of Ball and Tronick[24] and Bower[25] showed that (1) by the second week of life infants display defensive responses toward approaching objects with which they have had no previous experience and that (2) infants have an innate expectancy for experiencing tactile sensations in association with the objects they observe in their environment; that is, eye-to-hand sensory integration is built in. Ball and Tronick have also shown that such responses do not occur with objects that appear to be receding or on a "miss" path. A similar unity between visual and auditory modalities has been reported by Aronson and Rosenbloom.[26]

In the same vein, it is now clear that newborn infants have a prepotency for attentiveness to the human voice and innate capacities for making subtle acoustic discriminations that enable them to recognize their mothers[27] and that facilitate language development.[28] A comparable ability to make olfactory discriminations has also been reported.[29]

Most impressive, though, are the experiments of Meltzoff and Moore, which demonstrated that infants between 17 and 21 days of age can imitate both facial expressions and manual gestures.[30] Not only is the neurological equipment for organizing certain complex motor responses already in place, but the infant is both intrinsically motivated to engage in such mimicry (even with strangers) and able to equate its own unseen behaviors with those of other humans. Indeed, imitation is considered to be one of the primary human (and primate) learning modalities.[31]

Some later developments in the child's behavioral repertoire over the first several months of life are also clearly a function of underlying maturational processes. Infants quickly develop the capacity for discriminating between real faces and drawings and between familiar and strange faces, at which point they begin to orient selectively to real faces and to the mother. They also quickly begin to generalize and integrate familiar visual experiences and to orient their attention toward discrepant phenomena.

The mother-infant bonding system is another behaviorally significant domain with deep phylogenetic roots. The importance of this affective dimension of child development, which lays the foundation for the infant's later emotional and social development, is most strikingly evident in cases of severe emotional deprivation.[32] Nor is the mother-infant relationship unique to human beings. In a famous set of deprivation experiments with monkeys, psychologist Harry Harlow found that isolated infants, when given a choice, showed a definite preference for a soft, terrycloth surrogate "mother" over a wire "mother" that supplied them with milk—a contradiction of the classical conditioning paradigm.[33]*

One of the most dramatic maturational changes is the onset at about six months of a distinct apprehension toward strange faces, a behavior that incidentally manifests marked sex differences.[36] This emergent change, a clear-cut reversal of the child's earlier pattern, cannot be accounted for in terms

* As an aside with an important bearing on the subsequent discussion, John Bowlby, in his study of attachment, separation, and loss, adopted a cybernetic framework for viewing the mother-infant dyad, which after all involves reciprocal communication and control.[34] See also Norbert Bischof's modification of Bowlby's model in which a generalized "appetence" for security is postulated that embraces both attachment and fear behaviors.[35]

of any known environmental alteration. Gordon Bronson provides a plausible evolutionary-adaptive explanation, however, and Norbert Bischof provides substantiating data from animal experiments.[37]

Conversely, one of the major factors contributing to the infant's learning process is the infant's own internal "arousal system," centered in though not exclusive to the reticular formation of the brain stem, and an intrinsic (self-reinforcing) motivational structure, apparently centered in the hippocampus, that stimulates curiosity and active exploratory behaviors in human beings and other animals.[38] In his classic experiments with maze-running rats, psychologist D. O. Hebb showed that novelty itself can be "rewarding" to an animal.[39] And D. Singh has shown that given the choice, both rats and human children may prefer working for rewards rather than freeloading.[40] In human psychology, the same phenomenon comes under the heading of a "competence" or "effectance" motivation.[41]

With regard to later development, Jean Piaget's four-stage theory of cognitive development in children (sensorimotor, pre-operational, concrete operational, and formal operational) is well known,[42] and most developmental psychologists are now inclined to accept the broad outline of an epigenetic viewpoint. However, current thinking holds that the process is more complex and multifaceted—and perhaps less divisible into discrete stages—than Piaget's schema allows.[43]* Equally important, the infant seems to be more precocious in some respects than Piaget imagined. For instance, Kagan reports that the capacity for hypothesis formation and evaluation of novel experiences emerges at about nine months of age.[46] It is in fact a prelinguistic mental skill, one that we share with other primates.[47]

Omenn and Motulsky and Scarr-Salapatek make convincing arguments for the hypothesis that sensorimotor intelligence is not only biologically more primitive (having evolved long before the emergence of man), but is largely independent of the higher cortical and linguistic abilities that are more recent in evolutionary time.[48] Evidence for this hypothesis includes the fact that children with severe motor impairments may still be able to develop normal symbolic and intellectual functions.[49] Conversely, individuals with congenital language impairments may be able to function well with respect to sensorimotor skills. Higher primates and human infants also display a remarkable degree of similarity in sensorimotor development over the first 18 months of life. Moreover, regardless of culture or home environment, only functionally impaired children fail to achieve criterion levels of performance for various

* By the same token, while Scott's concept of "critical periods" in behavioral development[44] has withstood the test of subsequent research, it is now seen as perhaps less sharply defined in some cases, with any early deprivations being more remediable than was once thought to be the case.[45]

motor skills, though acquisition rates may differ. As Scarr-Salapatak points out: "This is not a trivial observation. . . . One cannot say that all nondefec-human beings develop formal operational logic, learn a second language, are attracted to the opposite sex, or have musical talent. There is a fundamental difference between these two sets of observations: in the first case, everyone does it; in the second case, only some do."[50] The universality of walking as compared to literacy or swimming skills (at which many other animals are more proficient than human beings)[51] is *prima facie* evidence for the prepotent (canalized) nature of the developmental process.

The case is buttressed by the evidence from infant mental tests. Population genetics theory predicts that biologically important traits with high fitness values should manifest little genetically based variation (heritability). Some recent behavior genetic studies of infant abilities at first seemed to suggest that, to the contrary, there are genetically based differences.[52] But when the data were carefully reanalyzed, the results failed to reveal significant heritabilities.[53] This result contrasts dramatically with the striking evidence of gradually increasing heritability in later childhood and adulthood for performances on tests that emphasize higher cortical as opposed to sensorimotor operations.[54]

Language Development

The matter of language development in children is one of the most important theoretical issues for the present work. Verbal language, a singularly human achievement, has long been recognized to have played a crucial role in the emergence of human cultures. And the more systematic the research that has been devoted to the subject, the more complex the phenomenon of human language appears to be.

Language, or more broadly, communication, is also central to the model and theory to be developed here. A communication subsystem is essential to any cybernetic system, and all socially organized (cybernated) species utilize one or more modes of social communication—chemical, visual, auditory, tactile, electrical.[55] The most celebrated example is the dance-language of honeybees.[56] The bee language employs symbols with conventional rules, and the rules can vary between bee societies.[57] Nor are bees unique in being able to communicate by symbolic means.[58]

More relevant to the linguistic behavior of humans, though, are the rich repertoires of calls, ritualized gestures, and other prelinguistic social cues that various primate species routinely employ.[59] In some instances chimpanzees have demonstrated the ability to convey among themselves information about the existence (and properties) of objects that are not physically present.[60] The most publicized feats of primate communication have occurred in the context of various language-training projects, but these have recently come under severe criticism.[61]*

Is language biologically based? The theorist who comes closest to the middle-ground position is Eric Lenneberg.[73] Rather than deducing an underlying biological structure from the surface characteristics of language, as Chomsky did, Lenneberg assembled the evidence from various domains and levels of analysis, which he then used to draw a set of cautious inferences. On the basic proposition that language is potentiated by specific biological capabilities, Lenneberg noted that:

1. All human societies have language.
2. Every normal human being acquires language, and all languages have structural universals, as well as many idiosyncracies.
3. Language is easily learned, sometimes learned several times over, and even relearned after traumatic language loss.

* Early reports suggested that chimpanzees, using signs, lexigrams, or plastic chips, were able to perform in ways that satisfied many of the criteria of human language: the use of symbols for "naming" and to communicate intentions, goals, desires; the use of syntax, or mastery of the rules for comprehending and using structured chains of symbols (sentences); and the "creative" use of symbols in meaningful ways to produce novel chains. Washoe, the original "talking" chimp, reportedly developed a vocabulary of 132 signs.

Recently this research has been subjected to strong criticism and self-criticism.[62] In the most sweeping and vociferous attack, the Sebeoks charged that virtually all the chimpanzee language feats are cases of the "clever Hans" effect, the inadvertent cueing by experimenters or trainers, (named after a famous turn-of-the-century performing horse). Terrace and his co-workers reanalyzed their own and others' films of chimpanzee utterances and concluded that there was indeed a great deal of cueing and that the evidence is insufficient to support the claim that chimpanzees have mastered syntax and sentence structure.[63] Likewise, Savage-Rumbaugh and her colleagues maintain that certain underlying assumptions about ape communications abilities have not been tested properly.[64] They find no definite evidence that various talking apes (Washoe, Sarah, Lana, Koko, Nim) understand clearly the use of symbols to represent objects that are not physically present. (More recently they report an effort to do so.[65]) Limber points out that chimpanzees have yet to equal the performance of the average three-year-old human being.[66] Even with intensive training, chimpanzees have not been able to move beyond indicating in general ways their desires or the actions that they would like others to perform. Yet by any reasonable standard, chimpanzees have achieved *rudimentary* language capabilities—syntax, intentionality, representational capacity, and certain related cognitive abilities: causal inference, inductive reasoning, memory, and linkages between different sensory modalities.[67]

If the standard used for the acquisition of language ability, that is, the definition of language, is success in equaling the human performance, then in all likelihood no other species will ever be able to demonstrate mastery of language. But that standard may amount to loading the dice, for it is increasingly evident that human language capabilities are intimately linked to, and utilize, a much broader set of underlying cognitive abilities. In one of his early articles, David Premack stated what may well be the ultimate disposition of this line of research: "The

(Continued)

4. Language learning follows a regular pattern of development; there is an underlying synchrony to language development patterns even when the rate is slowed by retardation.

5. There is no evidence that the language learning process in young children can be accelerated; language learning is interlocked with other developmental milestones.

6. Language learning appears to be a process that involves not only the acquisition of symbols and their meanings but the induction, testing, application of underlying principles (a procedure analogous to scientific investigation).

7. Following puberty, a marked decline occurs in the ability to learn a new language or to relearn a language after an aphasia (speech loss) resulting from brain damage.*

8. There is evidence that certain congenital defects may permanently impede or prevent language acquisition.

---

ape, when properly trained, emerges as the unclear middle case [in terms of language capabilities]: Neither wholly comparable to man (the clear positive case) nor to the parrot (the clear negative). . . ."[68] Indeed, the limitations observed in talking chimpanzees strengthen the argument for the once highly controversial hypothesis that the human facility for language depends on a specific set of biologically based capabilities.

There are at least four discernible "camps" on this issue. The first, and the dominant American view for many years, is that language is a learned behavior conforming to the universal "laws" of the behaviorist paradigm. In this view, language can be explained in terms of the principles of reinforcement conditioning.[69] Human beings can be taught to "emit" language in much the same way that pigeons in Skinner boxes supposedly learn to peck for food rewards.[70] The second position is associated with Noam Chomsky's hypothesis that verbal language is a biologically based, species-specific capacity involving a "universal grammar" with three component elements:[71] *phonological* (the rules of sound production); *semantic* (rules relating to meanings, concepts, etc.); and *syntactic* (rules that link meanings with sounds). In line with this construct, Chomsky postulates the existence of biologically based "deep structures" that correspond to the semantic element, "surface structures" that correspond to the phonological element, and a universal "generative grammar" by means of which deep structures and surface structures interact with each other and with the cultural milieu to produce various specific language patterns.

Jean Piaget rejected the idea of a specific *faculté de langage.* Instead, he maintained, language skills are a special case of semiotic (symbolic) capabilities that have their origins in various aspects of sensorimotor development ("action schema" and "induction") and the mechanisms of general intelligence.[72] David Premack holds a similar view; he considers language capabilities to be the product of the "mapping" of a symbol system onto underlying mental abilities.

* The case of Genie, a modern-day "wild child," sheds additional light on this issue. Genie was deprived of all verbal communication from the age of twenty months to the age of thirteen. With extensive subsequent remedial treatment, she gained limited verbal capabilities, but the results supported the Lenneberg hypothesis of a "critical period" for language learning.[74]

9. Evidence from research on aphasics suggests that general intelligence and language capabilities are distinct, though by no means totally independent of one another, just as sensorimotor skills appear to be separate.

10. Evidence from anatomy and neuroanatomy indicates that human beings possess specialized anatomical and neurological features that participate ("collaborate" might be a better word) in the production of language.*

Other evidence could be adduced: prelinguistic intentional communication in infants before the onset of language learning;[76] the spontaneous invention of a personal sign language among deaf children;[77] the occasional invention of a personal language between twins; cases of amnesia, where memory is lost but not language skill; and the extraordinary range of deficits associated with lesions and other forms of brain damage, from transient difficulties with specific language components to virtually complete loss of speaking ability but not of comprehension, or loss of comprehension and coherence but not of speaking ability.

The most remarkable and thought-provoking piece of evidence, perhaps, is the case of Helen Keller, who, though blind, deaf, and mute, achieved the functional equivalent of language through tactile communication, first with hand signs and later with Braille. Keller's mastery of the rudiments of language, at the age of eight, occurred over a period of less than two months, and the detailed account by her teacher, Anne Sullivan, provides priceless insight into how children in effect employ the scientific method to induce and test the principles of language.[78]†

How do these pieces fit together? Lenneberg's conclusions were, in effect,

* Norman Geschwind has suggested a tentative neurobiological model inspired by the original formulation of the nineteenth-century neurologist Karl Wernicke.[75] It is based on evidence from various kinds of aphasias that involve four areas of the neo-cortex: Broca's area (where vocal production is centered), Wernicke's area (where speech comprehension is centered), the angular gyrus (where cross-modal associations and transfers occur between auditory, visual, and tactile inputs and "memories"), and the *arcuate fasciculus,* an interconnecting nerve bundle. Lenneberg, who was cautious about this hypothesis, pointed out that there are enough ambiguities and inconsistencies to suggest that, while a degree of specialization may occur during ontogeny, the brain is a very plastic organ and there may be redundancies or backup systems that are as yet poorly understood. Moreover, the brain is an integrated, interactive system.

† Some theorists have argued that language determines our thought processes.[79] An observation by Anne Sullivan contradicts this view: "It seems strange that people should marvel at what is really so simple; why, it is as easy to teach the name of an idea, if it is clearly formulated in the child's mind, as to teach the name of an object. It would indeed be a herculean task to teach the words if the ideas did not already exist in the child's mind."[80] Lorenz uses the Helen Keller story to support Chomsky's innate grammar hypothesis. I draw a different inference. Instead of having inborn grammatical representations, children come equipped with general puzzle-solving capacities (capacities for decoding the principles underlying various phenomena, including language) and a prepotency for learning patterned sounds and associating sound patterns first with objects and later with ideas.

that language is a *synergistic* phenomenon (my term): It combines basic human perceptual and cognitive abilities that we employ in many contexts (science, engineering, music, art, and the daily routine of living), along with (a) evolved, specialized capabilities for speech recognition, mimicry, retention, and production[81] and (b) an appropriate environment in which these latent capabilities can develop ("resonate," in Lenneberg's term). Thus Lenneberg occupied a middle ground between Noam Chomsky and Jean Piaget.[82] Our latent language structures are neither as language-specific as Chomsky would have it nor as derivative as Piaget maintained.

To this increasingly favored position, I would add two points. First, reinforcement learning may not be irrelevant to language learning,[83] though it is likely to play a subsidiary role (children learn to say "please" because it is reinforced by parents). Second, it may ultimately prove fruitful to adopt a cybernetic framework for understanding language and its development—as the editors and some of the contributors to a recent Lenneberg memorial volume suggest. That is, language facilitates the achievement of human goals and purposes; it is preeminently a means. As such, it emerges from (and interfaces with) underlying motivational and cognitive processes (cybernetic processes) that are not yet completely understood. In summing up a volume on language as a *functional process,* Jerome Bruner writes: "Language proper is an instrument for fulfilling various communicative functions. And communicative functions themselves exist as constituents in still broader patterns of social interaction."[84]

The Biological Substrate

The network of disciplines that includes psychobiology, biopsychology, psychopharmacology, psychophysiology, endocrinology, and the neurosciences constitutes another level of causation in human behavior, or perhaps several levels. While this research enterprise encompasses many specialties, the common denominator is a focus on elucidating the specific biological mechanisms (structures and processes) through which our genetic programs exert their influence on development and the life cycle—and, conversely, what effect environmental influences and behaviors have on biological processes. Some highlights include:

1. Research on the physiological and biochemical bases of emotions.[85]

2. The work pioneered by James Olds on the internal reward system of the brain.[86]*

* Olds (initially with Milner) conditioned laboratory rats more powerfully than ever before by using endogenous reinforcements. He implanted electrodes in the medial forebrain bundle

(Continued)

3. The rapidly growing literature on the neurotransmitter and neuromodulator substances, such as the so-called biogenic amines (epinephrine, norepinephrine, dopamine, acetylcholine, reserpine, serotonin) and the peptides, including the much-publicized endorphins (because of their opiatelike properties).[88]

4. The closely related literature on hormones and behavior, the range of which includes prenatal sex differentiation, postnatal maturation processes, processes of aging, personality characteristics, motivation, emotion, and such specific behaviors as feeding, sexual behaviors, maternal behaviors, responses to stress, social dominance, and aggression.[89]

5. The increasing volume of research in psychophysiology, that is, neurological and autonomic measures (EEG, heart rate, blood pressure, galvanic skin resistance, etc.) that have been shown to correlate with emotional, cognitive, and behavioral differences, some of which are biologically based.*

Psychologist H. J. Eysenck's theory of personality deserves special note. Eysenck has proposed that individual personalities may be ranged along two orthogonal (causally distinct) continua, one for extraversion versus introversion and the other for stability versus neuroticism.[93]

Eysenck's version of the theory commands respect for a number of reasons. First, it is based on a specific hypothesis about the properties of (and the variations in) the underlying neurological substrate, particularly the reticular activating system (RAS) or sometimes reticular formation (RF). Second, Eysenck and many other researchers over the past twenty years have amassed an impressive body of research in support of the theory, including behavior genetic, neurological, psychophysiological, psychomotor, perceptual, conditioning, and cognitive studies.[94] Eysenck's theory is also unusual in psychology

---

of the rats' hypothalamus; then, having placed the rats in a Skinner Box apparatus, he induced them to press the bar nearly continuously, for days on end, while neglecting food, water, and sleep, for the "reward" of triggering an electrical stimulus from the electrode. Subsequent work has indicated that this intrinsic "satiety" system, though probably centered in the hypothalamus, has outposts in other regions of the brain (including, significantly, those associated with curiosity, exploration, and memory formation) and that this system plays a vital role in motivating and guiding behavior.[87]

* One focal point of this research, the Lacey Hypothesis, posits markedly different arousal patterns and correlated autonomic responses for different individuals and different behavioral contexts.[90] In addition, many studies focus on such phenomena as stress, arousal, emotions, psychophysiological correlates of personality differences, and various mental disabilities and psychopathologies.[91]

One notable area of research involves biorhythms, the now well-established periodicity in the physiological and behavioral functioning of human beings, whether asleep or awake. Performance oscillations of 90 to 100 minutes have been documented for a variety of measures including oral behavior, heart rate, vigilance performance, and scores on verbal and spatial matching tasks.[92]

in that the proposed linkages between the biological substrate and behavior permit specific predictions that have been tested successfully. Eysenck and others have used the theory to account for a number of apparent paradoxes in our behavior (for example, the reactivity, sensitivity to conditioning, and high levels of cortical activity in social introverts), and they have related the extremes of the two personality continua to extreme, even pathological social behaviors.[95]* Thus Eysenck and others have built a substantial case for the argument that biological factors play a direct, multifaceted causal role in shaping individual personalities, behaviors, and social interactions.

The Behaviorist Redoubt

Evidence for the influence of biological variables in human behavior is also accumulating in that bastion of American psychology, behaviorist learning theory—or more precisely, in the work of some of its more or less friendly critics.

In a recent critique of behaviorism, psychologist Richard Herrnstein noted the paradox that the influence of Skinnerian learning principles seems to be simultaneously waxing and waning.[98] The past decade has seen an ever-increasing volume of research on behavior modification, and applications to various social problem areas have expanded apace. At the same time, Skinnerism has been attacked from many quarters as an outdated and simplistic approach to understanding behavior.[99]

The explanation for this paradox is that, like other important theoretical advances, behaviorism has illuminated a significant dimension of behavioral causation even as it has failed in its original aspiration (and formulation). It is clearly not a universal, all-purpose theory of behavior; it turns out to be only a part of the explanation, one facet of a larger causal matrix. What is relevant here is the case against radical behaviorism—or what amounts to the same thing, the case for treating the organism as an independent variable in behavioral causation. This issue bears directly on my theory.

Two basic mechanisms are postulated in behaviorist theory. In the classical (Pavlovian) conditioning paradigm, animals learn to make an association between an unconditioned stimulus (say, food) and a conditioned stimulus (say, a bell tone or a light signal) such that ultimately the animal will respond to the conditioned stimulus with behaviors appropriate to the unconditioned

* Eysenck's theories relating to criminality are among the most contentious and disputed aspects of his work.[96] Criticisms include the charge that Eysenck is too sweeping and global in his approach, the argument that psychopathology is a culturally defined entity, and the argument that there are environmental influences that are independent of personality. Eysenck has acknowledged these criticisms and has responded with modifications and efforts to circumscribe his theory.[97]

stimulus (such as salivating whenever the bell rings). In "operant" conditioning, however, an animal is selectively "reinforced" (with rewards or punishments or both) when it engages in whatever behavior the experimenter chooses. (In nature it is the environment that provides the reinforcers.) Thus Thorndike's Law of Effect states, in essence, that the effects or consequences of a behavior (positive or negative) will increase or decrease the likelihood of its reoccurrence, as the case may be.[100]

Certain auxiliary assumptions are generally included in this model: (1) The underlying relationship between stimuli, responses, and reinforcers is essentially arbitrary; it does not matter which stimulus is paired with which response or which reinforcer. Initially, all combinations are equipotential. (Skinner never specifically advocated equipotentiality, but he never qualified his "laws" of learning either. (2) All species are pretty much alike in their basic learning abilities, so the "laws" of learning are essentially universal in their application. There are only differences of degree, or differences in the precise parameter values. (3) The properties of the organism are relatively unimportant compared to the properties of the environment (external stimuli, specific reinforcers, the schedules and rates of reinforcement). (4) An animal's behavioral repertoire amounts to an externally conditioned elaboration on various primitive, nonspecific drives (hunger, thirst, sex). However, Skinner was never very enlightening about these drives, or their number. He was not much interested in them, and neither were most American psychologists of the behaviorist persuasion from the 1930s through the 1950s.

The first major challenge to this paradigm came from the European ethologists, who postulated instinctive "fixed action patterns," learning prepotencies (such as "imprinting"), and species differences in learning abilities. This was paralleled by naturalistic (as opposed to laboratory based) animal behavior research in this country.[101] John Paul Scott's work on "critical periods" in development was of particular importance.[102] Contrary evidence was also produced by psychologist D. O. Hebb, whose experiments in the 1940s with maze-running rats suggested the concept of latent learning, or learning that arose from intrinsic motivations and internal reinforcers (what is now called autoshaping).[103] Harry Harlow's rhesus monkeys, likewise, seemed willing to work hard for the reward of novelty itself, or for social contacts with other animals.[104]

Another crack in the wall appeared in 1961, when two Skinner-trained psychologists, Keller and Marian Breland, published their paper "The Misbehavior of Organisms."[105] For more than ten years the Brelands had been training animals for television, the movies, circuses, and carnivals—in all, some 6000 animals of 38 different species. In their experience, behaviorist theory worked only after a fashion; they had almost as many failures as successes, and they found that animals had minds of their own. Conditioning techniques seemed to work best when an animal could be reinforced for behavior that it was predisposed to do spontaneously.

During the next decade the crack became a chasm. A turning point was the landmark paper by John Garcia and Robert Koelling.[106] Using the classical conditioning paradigm, Garcia and Koelling exposed rats to both a taste stimulus (flavored water) and an audiovisual stimulus (a 5-watt lamp and a clicking relay), which they coupled with X-ray radiation in sufficient dosages to induce gastrointestinal illness. As any nonbehaviorist might expect, the animals subsequently associated the sickness with the flavored water and not with the light/sound stimulus. For comparison purposes, the experimenters ran a follow-up experiment in which rats were exposed to the same two unconditioned stimuli, this time coupled with foot-shock through a grid in the floor of their cages. Now the animals associated their aversive experiences with the audiovisual stimulus, not with the flavored water.

Garcia and Koelling had demonstrated what innumerable experiments have subsequently confirmed, that animals do not respond arbitrarily and equally to all stimuli.[107] There is an inner (evolutionary) logic to their responses; they are more or less "prepared" or "contraprepared" to make various associations, respond to various stimuli, and perform various behaviors. Rats will readily learn to run away to avoid foot-shock, but they are not easily taught to avoid foot-shock by running in circles or pressing a key.[108] And pigeons will happily peck at keys for food rewards but will not press keys to avoid foot-shock.[109] In fact, the classical Skinnerian pecking response is an innate food-pecking behavior in pigeons that can be elicited spontaneously, even without food rewards.[110] Moreover, Williams and Williams found that it is hard to extinguish the key pecking response in pigeons even when it is counterproductive (when it eliminates food reinforcements).[111]

In a similar vein, Moore and Stuttard reexamined the classical puzzle-box experiments of Guthrie and Horton, in which domestic cats were supposedly taught to rub their bodies against a vertical bar inside their cages in order to obtain food or to open an escape door. Moore and Stuttard found that such rewards are unnecessary; the earlier experimenters had apparently succeeded in eliciting the cat's innate greeting display, which requires only the presence of an experimenter outside the animal's cage.[112]

The phenomenon of contrapreparedness in dogs has been demonstrated by Konorsky, who found that dogs resist learning to associate food rewards with yawning and sneezing, and they yawn in a very different way when they emit true yawns.[113] Dogs can also learn to move different paws to obtain food rewards when the stimuli are sounds coming from different directions, but they cannot learn to respond differentially to different types of sound.

Both positive and negative preparedness have been demonstrated in connection with food preferences. Beginning with the pioneering work of Harris et al. and Richter, a large volume of research has shown that animals are selective about what they eat and that their selectivity is related to dietary needs.[114] For instance, when a rat becomes deficient in a particular nutrient, it develops a "specific hunger"; it will abandon its existing diet and shift its consumption pattern to foods that are rich in the missing nutrient.[115]

Animals are also highly prepared to learn an aversion to poisonous foods.[116] Indeed, food aversions violate many of the axioms of learning theory: They are often learned after only one trial; learning occurs even though the stimulus (the food) and the reinforcer (the illness) occur several hours apart; a specific cause (the food) is selected from among many possible stimuli (other foods consumed, the locality, other animals present); the aversion may prove to be extremely durable and hard to extinguish, despite subsequent nonreinforcement; and, more astonishing, such aversions can be learned by an animal even when it is under an anesthetic.[117] Indeed, an animal need not experience the taste subsequently to elicit an avoidance response; the animal can use "cues" in the environment.[118] In effect, it is an example of one-trial classical conditioning.

The preparedness principle can even help to explain an ancient behavioral quirk (and a psychiatric conundrum since Freud's day)—phobias. Seligman found that, like food aversions, phobias violate the laws of learning. They are limited and selective in nature, are often acquired after only one trial, and are extremely resistant to change or extinction. Most important, they do not appear to be irrational and inexplicable from an evolutionary perspective.[119]

Finally, consider preparedness in the monarch butterfly. As is the case with many migratory species, young monarchs routinely learn in their first migratory season the precise route they must follow over thousands of miles (down to a specific patch of trees) in subsequent seasons, when they will no longer be under parental guidance. Not only are such feats of one-trial learning without peer, but they fall completely outside the reinforcement paradigm: If anything, the ordeal of migration is negatively reinforced, in behaviorist terms, though obviously it is "reinforced" by natural selection. This is one of many cases where the conditioning paradigm and the evolutionary-adaptive paradigm are at odds with each other.

What is true of animal behavior is true also of human behavior. Preparedness in humans has been observed for food preferences, food aversions, and phobias. I have alluded to the evidence for preparedness in child development; human children are prepared to learn to walk, mostly without instruction and despite considerable negative reinforcement in the early stages (when falls are common), but they are unprepared, and perhaps in some cases they are contraprepared, to learn to swim. Painstaking instruction is usually required. Similarly, human children readily learn to talk, mainly through exposure and imitation, but must struggle, with varying degrees of success, to learn to read and write. It is also plausible that we are endowed with a readiness to learn sexual, aggressive, competitive, and co-operative social behaviors. As David Hamburg has observed, the way in which our genes are most likely to influence our behavior is via learning biases and selective responsiveness (emotional and behavioral) to environmental vicissitudes.[120] We are likely to display a readiness to learn behaviors that have had adaptive value in the past, whether or not they still do.

It is not enough, however, to recognize various constraints or prepotencies in learning; nor is it enough to "botanize" the concept of drives in order to accommodate a more complex model of the motivational substrate, as Herrnstein proposes. An entirely different model will be required, one that is more consonant with the tradition of Edward Tolman's "purposive behaviorism" and with recent attempts to reinterpret learning in terms of a cybernetic model.[121]

Downward Causation

Does all this mean that our genes determine our behavior? Yes and no. Our genes co-determine our behavior, in co-operation with many other influences. Our genomes produce human beings, not horses, dogs, or chickens, but the life trajectory of each person involves an enormously complex set of dynamic, time-bound interactions between the individual and his or her cultural environment.

Consider Donald Campbell's useful concept of downward causation, or behavioral and environmental influences that affect internal biological functioning.[122] The evidence includes: the health consequences of diet, exercise, and personal habits; the health and behavioral effects of various forms of stress; the consequences for human functioning of sensory deprivation; the many-sided influence of various environmental disturbances and insults; the growing list of "external" influences on developing fetuses;* and the research literature behind the technology of biofeedback.

There are also many examples of how broad cultural patterns—social customs—have downward effects. One familiar example is that of kuru, a wasting and ultimately fatal neurological disease that has long afflicted the Foré tribe of New Guinea. Because this disease clusters within particular family lineages, it was originally assumed to be hereditary. But later it was learned that

* As if to mimic the Lamarckian inheritance of acquired characters, maternal experiences and behaviors of various kinds can be transmitted more or less directly through the placenta to the developing fetus. Such influences include exogenous hormones, drugs, caffeine, cigarette smoke, alcohol, maternal nutrition, and, in mice and rats but not as yet confirmed in human beings, prenatal maternal stress.

kuru is caused by a virus that is communicated by the Foré's ritual eating of the brains of deceased relatives.[123]

Somewhat the converse situation applies to favism, an acute hemolytic anemia for which there is a hereditary predisposition. The incidence of favism is substantial in some countries and negligible in others, including the United States, not because the gene is missing from the gene pools of some populations but because the disease is co-determined by the *interaction* of a genetic susceptibility and the consumption of fava beans (or the inhalation of the plant pollen). Because fava beans are grown and consumed primarily in the countries that rim the Mediterranean basin, the disease is concentrated in that part of the world.

Less dramatic, but theoretically more important, are cases in which human cultural adaptations have precipitated microevolutionary biological changes, in accordance with the teleonomic selection model proposed in Chapter II. One classic example involves milk drinking. Prehistoric human populations that adopted milk as a part of the postweaning and adult diet set up selection pressures for a genetically based lactose tolerance that is not shared by the descendants of non milk-drinking populations (such as African blacks).

In the same vein, human populations that have lived in extreme environments for long periods of time generally exhibit subtle variations in morphology and physiology that correlate with the environmental conditions to which they have been exposed. For example, Eskimos tend to have short, chunky builds and relatively large amounts of subcutaneous fatty tissue; this minimizes the ratio of surface area to body mass and reduces heat loss. In contrast, some inhabitants of extremely hot regions, such as the equatorial Batutsi, are long and lean and have extremely high surface area to body mass ratios, and this facilitates the dissipation of excess body heat.

The most extensive adaptations to an extreme environment involve people living at high altitudes (of which there may be some 15 million worldwide). Biological studies of high-altitude peoples, pioneered by anthropologist Paul Baker in 1978, are still far from exhaustive, but the evidence to date indicates that some high-altitude peoples have genetic adaptations for producing infants with lower optimum birth weights, enlarged chests and lung capacities, higher basal metabolic rates, alterations in blood chemistry, greater heat flow to the extremities, and, like the Eskimos, reduced surface area to body mass ratios.[124]

And then there is the case of the mass suicides at Jonestown in 1978. That stunning example of the potential power of downward causation in human societies flies in the face of any argument for genetic, or even epigenetic, determinism. The degrees of freedom in the human biogram may under some circumstances permit human beings to violate the most elemental biological norms. (The ancient Japanese custom of hara-kiri is another example.)

Equally important are the many ways in which social organization and group dynamics in human societies can influence individual behavior and even the survival chances of the individual. One set of examples collected by Hampton et al. provides a compelling illustration.[125] These examples have to do with the striking behavioral differences among American servicemen held captive by the Nazis in World War II, by the Chinese in the Korean War, and by the North Vietnamese during the conflict in Vietnam.

World War II prisoners were maintained in organized groups under the command of their own officers. Although living conditions were poor and interrogation and torture were not uncommon, the prisoners maintained high morale, gave little information to their captors, had a low incidence of illness and death, and engineered many escapes. American prisoners of the Chinese were kept in isolation or in groups that were constantly broken up, and they were subjected to many socially divisive stratagems. As a result morale was low, the death rate was high, escapes were few, and compromising information was given more freely, despite the fact that relatively little coercion was used. Of course there were significant differences in the nature of the two wars and in the cultures of the captors. However, the hypothesis that group dynamics itself played a major role is supported by the vivid account of the treatment and conduct of Vietnam era prisoners by Commander Robert J. Naughton. Consistent with the earlier POW experiences, there were dramatic differences in behavior between captives kept in isolation and captives kept in groups that were able to organize and maintain internal order, discipline, common purpose, and mutual support. As a result of his prison camp experiences, Commander Naughton has become a believer in small group theory.[126]

What applies to the dynamics of small groups applies also to larger organizations. If Durkheimian structural functionists err in attempting to locate the causes of social behavior exclusively in macro-level social facts, atomistic, individual choice theorists are equally guilty of discounting the degree to which social systems exercise partially autonomous downward causation over the behavior of their individual members. Systems have requisites, though they may or may not fit comfortably into Talcott Parsons's rarefied categories of "pattern maintenance" and "adaptation". Anyone who works for a large organization is constrained constantly by the demands that the "whole" imposes on the parts, some of it necessary and some of it perhaps not. There used to be a saying among naval aviators that when the weight of the paperwork equals the weight of the aircraft, the mission is accomplished.

Yet these examples are trivial in comparison with the much wider (one is tempted to say traumatic) downward impact of humankind on the biosphere. For several thousand years, socially organized human groups have been cutting a swath through the world, altering local climates, radically redirecting the evolutionary course of countless species (through predation, hunting for sport, artificial selection, and pest control practices), and inadvertently polluting one ecosystem after another while radically transforming still others. (Consider the human impact on an originally pristine Los Angeles basin in less than one hundred years.) For better or worse, man has become the single most pervasive downward influence on the course of the evolutionary experiment—and possibly its nemesis.

On the other hand, we should not discount the multifarious and ultimately decisive ways in which the dynamics of the natural environment—diurnal and seasonal changes, episodic environmental disturbances, long-term environmental shifts—also exert downward causation. A striking example is "the year without a summer." When Mount Tambora in Indonesia erupted in 1815, so much volcanic dust was spewed into the upper atmosphere that it lowered ambient air temperatures in the middle latitudes during the following summer by an average of one degree Centigrade (and much more in some places). New England had snow in June and periodic frosts throughout the summer, as did Northern Ireland and Wales; crop shortfalls were so severe that there were food riots in some areas.[127] Some scientists believe the recent eruption in Mexico may have produced similar effects.

Interactional Causation

If we have good evidence of both upward and downward causation in human affairs, we must also recognize its predominantly configural and *interactional* nature. The wing coloration of *Biston betularia* was selectively important because of the background coloration, the resting patterns of the moths, and the perceptual abilities and food-getting strategies of various avian predators. By the same token, neither a genetic susceptibility nor fava beans alone causes favism, any more than kuru is caused by a virus or a bizarre cultural practice alone (a biological vulnerability to the kuru virus is a third, usually unstated cause).

Sometimes the relationship between nature and nurture, or between internal and external sources of causation, is additive or multiplicative; most often the relationship is more complex. Consider an experiment with deer mice that involved the interaction between two genotypes (a laboratory stock and a strain accustomed to life in the open field) and two habitats (field and woodland). In order to determine the habitat preferences of the two strains, Wecker built a set of connected enclosures that spanned the border between a wooded area and an open field. Given the choice, adults from the field stock showed a marked preference for the field enclosure while the laboratory stock preferred the wooded enclosure. However, when Wecker sought to determine the influence of the animals' rearing environment on their adult preferences, a strange thing happened. Field mice raised in the woods showed an adult preference for the open field, but the laboratory strain, when reared in the field, switched its adult preference to the field environment. Thus the genetic bias of the field strain could not be overridden by environmental influences, while the preferences of the laboratory stock were more labile and were susceptible to environmental influences.[128]

The same interactional framework applies to human behavior. Alice and Peter Rossi found that two very different variables, one biological and one social, appear to contribute to the normal peaks and valleys of the female mood pattern. One variable is the menstrual cycle and the other is the weekend. Sometimes the two variables act independently of one another, sometimes they reinforce one another, and sometimes they counteract one another.[129]

Research on the subject of human handedness supports the traditional view that hand preference is the result of a biological predisposition that can be reinforced or countervailed by social customs and/or brain damage.[130] The same is true for walking and talking; while there is evidence of biological programming, we must "learn" to walk and talk. Indeed, we may continue to refine and improve our locomotory and linguistic abilities over much of our lives, as some middle-aged runners and late-blooming writers can attest.

The behavioral consequences of birth order and spacing involve similar interactional influences. Although there is uncertainty about the specific mechanisms involved, it is becoming clear that both internal influences (the prenatal environment) and external (social) factors exert an influence on the well-documented variations among siblings.[131]

Other examples involve health, intelligence, race, and sex. Lynton Caldwell recently observed that "Many interactions between behavior, health, and environment have been observed by people unassisted by science."[132] Quarantine and isolation of the sick, removal of body parasites, bathing, and avoidance of stagnant ponds for drinking water are familiar instances, but recent research in the biomedical sciences has buttressed the conventional wisdom. Aging, for example, is no longer viewed as an exclusively biological process; even some of the diseases of old age, such as atherosclerosis, are now seen to involve a complex interplay between heredity, diet, and various risk factors such as smoking, stress, and physical activity levels.

Another example from the health field—exercise—illustrates the interplay among biological causes, scientific knowledge (or any source of authoritative information), social communications processes, and individual motivations and actions. The relationship between physical (especially cardiovascular) conditioning, health, and longevity has always existed, but the recent publicity given the subject has precipitated a major cultural shift in this country as millions of people have taken up jogging and other forms of vigorous activity.

As for the race issue, behavioral differences between races are influenced by obvious cultural differences.[133] However, the most decisive evidence, perhaps, that such differences are not *wholly* cultural artifacts is the extensive research by psychologist Daniel G. Freedman and his Chinese-American wife on the subject of race differences in newborns. Freedman, who pioneered epigenetic research on newborns with his study of smiling in blind infants, demonstrated clear-cut differences between Chinese and Caucasian infants across various measures of personality and psychomotor abilities (emotionality, responsiveness to stimuli, motor precocity), and these differences conform to observed "cultural" differences among older children.[134]

Despite the evidence of subtle temperamental differences (on average) between Caucasian and Japanese newborns, Caudill and Frost found that the offspring of second-generation Japanese-Americans were achieving behavioral norms close to those of Caucasian-American children in terms of relative placidity and ease of quieting. However, the Japanese-American mothers were stimulating their children about twice as much as do Caucasian mothers; thus the convergence of phenotypes was the result of a combination of a different genotype *and* a different environment.[135]

An interactional phenomenon of particular interest to political scientists involves leadership. While it can hardly be said that we have arrived at a definitive causal model, we do know that many interrelated factors can enter into the determination of which individual may occupy a leadership position in a given situation. There is good evidence that leadership can be in part a function of a particular group's task(s) or goal(s), the size, structure, membership, and other properties of the group (including its past history), and its external environment (including other groups and organizations). All these factors can have an effect on leadership selection.[136] At the same time, there is general agreement that individual personality factors—including temperament, mental abilities, knowledge, values, and leadership skills—constitute an important set of "internal" variables in leadership selection.[137]

Human adaptations to high altitude provide another striking example. Among the Quechua Indians of the Peruvian altiplano, a set of extreme environmental conditions—low oxygen density, cold, rough terrain, and a relative scarcity of energy (food and fuel)—has led to an interrelated combination of genetic, physiological, and behavioral adaptations. In addition to the biological changes noted above, R. B. Thomas found that the Quechua have developed a set of specialized cultural adaptations designed to economize on their energy requirements.[138] They exploit energy-efficient crops and animals, trade with low-altitude communities for high-energy foods, and curtail personal activity levels as much as possible. They make heavy use of animal dung for fertilizer and fuel and design their homes and clothes for maximum thermal efficiency, given the raw materials they have to work with.[139] Finally, the established cultural practice of coca chewing may have positive psychophysiological effects by providing an internal warming sensation and possibly by dulling the individual's awareness of the cold (researchers are less certain about the adaptive value here).

Lumsden and Wilson cite another example of this interaction process. Anthropologists agree that the adoption of maize cultivation was a major breakthrough in the cultural evolution of New World civilizations. (Maize was the only indigenous cereal crop in the New World until the arrival of Europeans.) Among fifty-one societies in North, Central, and South America, Katz and his colleagues found a high correlation between the intensity of maize cultivation and both population density and the complexity of social organization. Maize cultivation was clearly a necessary enabler even though it was not a sufficient cause of cultural progress.[140]

The importance of maize lies in the fact that it is relatively high in lysine, an amino acid that is an essential dietary need. Human beings must obtain lysine externally because, unlike many other animals, we cannot synthesize it internally. However, about two-thirds of the lysine in maize is bound into a fraction of the kernel that is indigestible when eaten raw. Not until alkali cooking was invented did it become possible for human beings to bypass this biological constraint and release the sequestered lysine. Thus the success of maize cultivation depended on technologies that enabled New World populations to manipulate both the macro (ecological) level and the micro level of their environment.

Finally, consider a familiar Western cultural pattern that has significant biological (health) consequences: cigarette smoking. The cigarette habit afflicts some 60 million Americans. Those who smoke are far more vulnerable to coronary heart disease, lung cancer and other forms of cancer, and stomach and intestinal ulcers. The life expectancy of smokers is lower than that of nonsmokers by an average of six to seven years, and women who smoke during pregnancy are more likely to have stillbirths, premature births, and crib deaths. Smokers experience more difficulties in sleeping, and they frequently expose nonsmokers to similar risks.[141]

How did this dangerous habit, which is only one hundred years old, emerge and become entrenched in this country? The answer involves a configuration of factors. Nicotine, a biologically active ingredient of tobacco, is mildly addictive physiologically without causing mental and behavioral aberrations, as do more potent drugs. (It is a mild stimulant.) Then there is the psychological benefit of oral gratification, for we are, as Freud pointed out, an oral species. Because cigarette smoke is extremely mild, it can readily be inhaled, allowing nicotine to pass in undiluted small doses through the lungs and into the bloodstream, so that it reaches the target areas of the brain within several seconds. This uniquely reinforcing property in cigarette smoke is actually the result of a technological innovation in the curing of tobacco leaves (a safe form of flue curing) that made the resulting smoke more acid and therefore easily inhaled. A favorable social and economic environment also helped; ours was a relatively liberal, affluent, free enterprise society with a large surplus of agricultural land. Another decisive factor was technoeconomic: After James Bonsack patented his cigarette-rolling machine in 1880, manufacturers produced cigarettes more than one hundred times faster than by hand rolling (4200 per minute versus about 40 per minute at best). The rest was informational—a matter of packaging, marketing, and promotion on the one hand and a lack of knowledge about the ultimate health consequences on the other.

Like cigarette smoking, many cultural patterns cannot be explained without reference to a configuration of causes operating at several levels of biological organization. The causal significance of any one factor, whether it be technological or physiological, is a function of its relationship to other relevant factors. The addictive nature of nicotine, for instance, is necessary but not sufficient to account for the high incidence of smoking in the United States; presumably it is no less addictive in societies where smoking is not common. Those who would argue that such a physiological factor can be treated as a constant and disregarded for analytical purposes overlook three important points. First, physiological susceptibility to the smoking habit has to be recognized as causal because it creates a prepotency to addiction. Second, this prepotency may well vary among individuals, as a function of both constitutional and environmental influences. Third, an appreciation of the full configuration of causes is essential when it comes to addressing such practical problems as how to induce a change in smoking habits.

In sum, the evidence is overwhelming that the dynamics of social life are the product of a complex interplay between nature and nurture, internal and external variables, micro-level genetic and organismic phenomena, and macro-level cultural, historical, ecological, and even geophysical phenomena. Some biologically conditioned (and constraining) social facts are obvious: our basic needs for food, water, defecation, sleep, thermoregulation, physical safety, sex and reproduction, physical activity, social contacts, and information. The lives of most human beings throughout most of our history have been preoccupied with meeting these needs. Other biological influences are more subtle: for example, the fact that patterns of smoking behavior correlate with blood levels of nicotine, which in turn are a function of the time lapse between smokes and certain other physiological influences. It is not merely social convention that induces smokers to light up with special relish after periods of deprivation, after meals, and during periods of stress. By the same token, the current revolution in genetic engineering testifies to the fact that environmental and cultural influences are penetrating ever more deeply into the micro level of causation. It is a two-way street.

The Interactional Paradigm

It is increasingly evident that the life sciences and the social sciences must converge on an Interactional Paradigm. Although I shall advance the hypothesis that the progressive aspect of sociocultural evolution has involved a unifying principle or common denominator, that is, the principle of functional synergism, I am equally convinced that the search for a single overarching causal variable, be it population growth, energy capture, or whatever, is insufficient. Such linear, deterministic approaches are destined to be embarrassed by contradictory evidence, counterexamples, overlooked relationships, reciprocal causation, threshold effects, and systemic (combinatorial) influences. Theorists such as Marshall Sahlins, who continues to insist on the "autonomy of culture," have a point—but only that. It would have been better had he said *partial* autonomy, for the cultural superstructure is built on a biological and physical base. Whatever the illusions or the aspirations of our intellectuals may be, culture is designed primarily to serve biological ends (though we may strive for much more when there is a margin of profit). A society is basically a collective survival enterprise, and the deliberate exclusion by social scientists of the constraints, imperatives, and often unpredictable forces of the natural world cannot be justified on scientific grounds. It can be justified only on political, ideological, or other antiscientific grounds.*

Whatever the phenomenological biases and "emic" interpretations of the nineteenth-century Irish, a severe potato blight caused mass starvation and radical cultural changes. Likewise, when the bubonic plague decimated the populations of Europe in the fourteenth century, equally profound cultural changes ensued. And when the ancient Mesopotamian peoples experienced declining yields due to waterlogging and salt buildup in irrigated soils, entire civilizations may have collapsed.[143]

The heart and soul of the Darwinian paradigm—and by extension that of the Interactional Paradigm—is the premise that survival and reproduction through time is the fundamental problem for all life forms. It is continuing, inescapable, often multifaceted, and unsolvable in any permanent sense. In this view, alternative visions of immortality, or utopian surcease (at least in this world), are wishful thinking. To be sure, Darwin's "struggle for existence" may exaggerate the severity of the problem in some instances. Some

* As Mary Midgely has pointed out, it is the environmentalists who hold the more radical position, because they would deny the role of biological influences in human behavior *a priori.* For this reason, they ought to assume the burden of proof.

The term *collective survival enterprise* is meant to denote the fact that survival is the basic vocation of organized societies and that many (but not all) aspects of the survival problem are pursued through organized, interdependent social systems. It does not deny the ubiquity of self-interest or imply a norm of radical equality. It is a descriptive and functional term.[142]

species have long enjoyed a stable relationship with their environments; others inhabiting relatively salubrious environments, or empty niches, may experience rapid growth. As Sewall Wright emphasized, "opportunities" have played a major role in evolutionary change. Moreover, in humankind evolution has become conscious of itself, as Pierre Teilhard de Chardin observed. Humans alone can aspire to improve the conditions of existence, to steer the course of evolution in directions of our own choosing, thereby greatly augmenting the role of teleonomic selection. Nevertheless every species, man included, must actively seek to survive; survival must necessarily be the fundamental purpose and vocation of living systems. In thermodynamic terms alone, the maintenance of life requires constant "inputs"; that we may have been programmed by natural selection to enjoy survival-related activities—the pleasures of eating, sex, and achievement—is a subsidiary factor.

The survival enterprise need not involve direct competition; various forms of mutualism have also been selectively favored and have played a directive role in evolutionary change. Survival may best be viewed as primarily an economic and engineering problem. That is, survival is an enterprise in which scarce means must be utilized to satisfy an array of structural and functional problems, or survival needs. And because there is no free lunch in nature any more than there is in human societies, the process of biological adaptation necessarily involves a special form of economic benefit-cost analysis that might be called bioeconomics.*

Accordingly, the current advocates of the primacy of orthogenesis (thermodynamic or otherwise)[144] or the equivalent importance of structural and non-adaptive forms of evolutionary change[145] err in essentially the same way. They implicitly assume away or largely discount the survival problem; they depreciate the continuing necessity for adaptation, for earning a living in the environment. To repeat, it is just as Panglossian to assume away the survival problem as it is to hold that everything in nature is well adapted.

By contrast, in the Darwinian paradigm (and in the Interactional Paradigm) various "frozen historical accidents,"[146] various engineering constraints and imperatives,[147] various "progressive" changes, and various stochastic influences (from genetic mutations to environmental perturbations) must all be subsumed and contained within what Gould and Lewontin derogate by calling an "adaptationist programme."[148]† All such changes, however they may arise,

* A version of this argument limited to energy trade-offs has been worked out by Bock and Wahlert (1965). Their so-called "economy principle" states that an organism will invest only as much energy in an activity as it gets back. Of course this excludes maladaptive characters and sacrifices for offspring.

† There have been some curious antiselectionist arguments of late. S. J. Gould would introduce structural integration as a principle independent of natural selection,[149] and Ho and Saunders argue that because major evolutionary changes are not directional, natural selection must "relax" in order for macroevolution to occur.[150] In effect, such arguments assume away the problem of survival. One cannot simply exempt by fiat various aspects of the evolutionary process from

(Continued)

are strictly edited by natural selection. And natural selection, it will be recalled, is not a mechanism or an agent somewhere in the environment; it is a way of characterizing an aspect of the functional interactions between living organisms and their environments. *Natural selection refers to those functionally important factors which are responsible in a given context for causing differential survival and reproduction among genetically variant individuals in a population of organisms, as well as for absolute changes in the numbers and diversity of different populations and species over time.* Natural selection is as much associated with functional continuities as it is with functional changes. What is more, it is as much associated with weeding in as with weeding out functionally significant traits *and* structures (*baupläne,* as Gould and Lewontin would have it). And when one population or species is growing rapidly, either in absolute terms or relative to other biological forms, even though there may be no change in gene frequencies within the group, natural selection is still going on.

Thus it is not correct to assert that natural selection has slowed or virtually stopped operating in humankind.[152] Considering the explosive growth of *Homo sapiens* in historical times, the correlative declines in and extinctions of many other species, and changes within species in the numbers of different "stock," it is clear that natural selection has been accelerating in recent millennia.[153] There have been substantial changes in the genome pool (the relative numbers of different species), and human culture *qua* functional adaptation is in large measure responsible. Therefore culture is not something disconnected from the workings of natural selection or something related to natural selection only through feedback.* Culture is a subset of the behavioral influences that have always played a direct causal role in producing changes in the functional relationships between organisms and their environments—i.e., "teleonomic selection."†

---

the overriding requirements for mechanical and energetic efficiency and for adaptation to the environment. Such requirements are always operative.[151]

* Dobzhansky may have introduced the notion that biological and cultural evolution are separate but connected by a "feedback reciprocal relation." In any event, a number of anthropologists have subsequently expressed the same idea.[154] Technically, feedback means information that controls the real-time behavior of a dynamic, goal-oriented system. What Dobzhansky apparently meant was that biology and culture influence one another, that they mutually shape and modify functional relationships across different levels of biological organization. Introducing the term "feedback" to describe these interactions is misleading, for it implies only a tenuous connection between biology and culture. Changes in the informational systems through which biological structures and cultures are transmitted do not occur primarily through feedback processes; rather, the causal interactions are direct.

† Consider a catastrophic nuclear war in which the populations of all the developed and developing countries are killed, leaving as survivors only such stone-age peoples as the Tasaday, the Australian aborigines, the !Kung San, the Yanomamö, and the Chukchi. Not only would this nuclear Armageddon result in an instant cultural regression, it would represent an important saltatory "event" in human evolution.

The evolution of humankind is a process that has involved reciprocal and systemic forms of causation. If biological preadaptations helped to make possible the evolution of culture, the reverse has been no less true.[155] One cannot make sense of the emergence of the human capacity for language, for example, without the corollary of politics *qua* cybernetic social processes—that is, a cultural context in which verbal communication behaviors would have been advantageous to survival and reproduction. Nor is culture, by any reasonable definition, uniquely human—as biologist John Tyler Bonner has shown so persuasively.[156]

Conversely, it is hardly sufficient to characterize culture as nothing more than the topmost level in a hierarchy of biological systems designed to "track" environmental changes of varying durations, as Wilson did in *Sociobiology* (following suggestions by Pringle, Bateson, Skinner, Levins, Kummer, Manning, and Slobodkin and Rapoport).[157] Wilson fully appreciates the phenomenon of emergence, and in more recent writings he seems to have partially exempted humankind from his conclusion that such higher-level systems are "only" sets of adaptations and are "not fundamental properties of organisms around which the species must shape its biology.[158]* Likewise, it is inaccurate to assert, as Ulla Olin does, that "in its simplest form . . . all our behavior is ultimately aimed at survival."[160]†

There is much contemporary evidence of partially autonomous and sometimes maladaptive cultural phenomena. Ritual suicide has been mentioned; consider also the case of the Shakers, whose distinctive furniture (their contribution to our culture) is still made in this country but whose celibacy rule led ultimately to their virtual extinction. A more commonplace example is our fondness for eating sweets, a positively reinforced behavior that sometimes crosses the border into addiction, with negative consequences. (In effect, this

* In his chapter on man, Wilson declares that "the genes have given away most of their sovereignty." He suggests that genes retain their influence mainly through biological variations underlying behavioral variations between cultures.[159] For someone who is portrayed as a biological determinist, this hardly fits the mold. Indeed, it concedes too much. Our genes also have a great deal of say in determining our biological structures, needs, drives, and capabilities.

† The biologist Richard Alexander writes: "Unless Darwin was wrong, we have evolved to maximize the reproduction of our own genetic materials, and to do nothing else."[161] In response, anthropologist Jerome Barkow, in "Culture and Sociobiology," asks: "Are you reading this article in order to maximize your inclusive fitness? Is human behavior reducible to nothing but an endless struggle to maximize one's genetic representation in the next generation?"[162] Alexander understands full well the hierarchical nature of biological organization.[163] I assume that he also recognizes the phenomenon of emergence. But apparently he does not accept the idea that purposes can be emergent. Organisms as wholes have purposes that transcend and frequently subordinate the purposes of individual genes. The genes that control the production of our baby teeth produce structures that are soon sacrificed for the common good. The same phenomenon occurs in superorganisms.

is the converse of the monarch butterfly example; both cases testify to the fact of a partial discordance between the behaviorist conditioning paradigm and the evolutionary-adaptive paradigm.)

By the same token, it is a fundamental contradiction of evolutionary theory to assert, as Eigen and Schuster apparently have done, that evolution was inevitable once certain thermodynamic and prebiotic conditions had occurred;[164] or, as J. N. Hill claims, that sociocultural evolution was "inevitable . . . when organic evolution had produced a brain and pharynx of sufficient complexity to permit the evolution of language."[165] Such viewpoints necessarily take the ongoing survival problem for granted: They ignore all the contingent aspects of the struggle for existence and treat evolution as if it were the result of the action of a single causal variable rather than the combined influence of a complex configuration of dynamically evolving functional relationships.

Unlike other approaches and paradigms, the Interactional Paradigm does not start with a set of causal variables or analytical concepts such as "neurognostic structures" (Laughlin and d'Aquili), the "integry" (Boulding), or even "culture" itself (a concept that anthropologists frequently reify). It starts with the ongoing problem of survival and reproduction, and it is concerned with the concrete interactions among the many factors that can be assigned variously to the natural environment, our biological constitutions, and sociocultural processes.

This is not to say that everything is related to the survival problem or that the functional (adaptive) significance of a particular phenomenon exhausts the explanation of how it came to be. The biologist Benson Ginsburg has noted that "many variations are not necessarily more or less adaptive—just different. It is not necessary for all variations to be adaptive in order to persist."[166] But it does assume that adaptive consequences are of primary importance and are more pervasive and unremitting in their influence (sometimes in ways we tend not to appreciate) than many social theorists, especially those whose world views have been shaped by the experience of Western industrial societies, have been prone to believe. Thus the survival relevance of a phenomenon or a cultural practice may have more to do with ultimate causation, with how it came to be, than we realize.*

* Many social scientists have uncritically adopted Durkheim's position in *The Rules of Sociological Method* that an organ—or a social fact—is independent of the function or end it serves.[167] This is a partial truth that, unless carefully qualified, can lead to erroneous conclusions. Functional effects, or consequences, are of fundamental importance in explaining both biological and cultural evolution, but functional consequences alone do not explain these phenomena, nor are all phenomena functional in nature. Not only are chance and necessity involved, but causal-functional connections may exist at many different levels of organization. The problem of survival and its expression in and through the needs, motivations, and capabilities of human actors is itself

(Continued)

On the Concept of Adaptation

Theodosius Dobzhansky was fond of characterizing the evolutionary process as a grand experiment in adaptation, and Julian Huxley, in *Evolution: The Modern Synthesis* (1942), defined adaptation as "nothing else than arrangements subserving specialized functions, adjusted to the needs and the mode of life of the species or type. . . . Adaptation cannot but be universal among organisms, and every organism cannot be other than a bundle of adaptations, more or less detailed and efficient, coordinated in greater or lesser degree."[168]

Adaptations are means to an end; they serve a purpose; they are teleonomic in nature. In George C. Williams's phrase, an adaptation is a "design for survival." Not everything is adaptive, of course. If functional adaptation is the predominant influence in evolution, it is not omnipotent; Darwin never took the position that everything in nature is useful, as Gould and Lewontin have reminded us. There are also many fortuitous effects, some of which involve nothing more than the laws of nature. To use one of Williams's illustrations, when a flying fish leaps out of the water, that may well be the result of an adaptation, but its fall back into the water is not. On the other hand, what may be a fortuitous effect initially may well become an adaptation, should it persist and enhance the survival chances of the bearer and its progeny—if it is positively selected. Melanic wing coloration in the peppered moth *Biston betularia* may well be an example; so might neoteny (fetalization of the offspring) in human evolution.[169]

The assumption of a need for adaptation, then, is nothing more or less than a logical deduction from the core premise that survival is a problem and that organisms must actively seek to survive. Richard Lewontin has written that "The modern view of adaptation is that the external world sets certain 'problems' that organisms need to 'solve,' and that evolution by means of natural selection is the mechanism [*sic*] for creating these solutions."[170] The problem with this definition is that it is one-sided. The nature of life

---

part of the causal matrix that has shaped human biological and cultural evolution, as we shall see. If survival is indeed the paradigm problem for man and society, how can we measure it? How can we measure adaptation in ways that do not involve either tautologies (whatever survives is adaptive, and vice versa) or ad hoc interpretations—what are disparagingly called Just So Stories after Rudyard Kipling's children's tales (such as "How the Camel Got Its Hump")? If evolutionists have not yet developed satisfactory tools or provided satisfactory answers, this does not entitle critics to discount the importance of the survival problem and its imperatives. The shortcomings lie in our analytical powers, not in our conceptualization of the problem. Indeed, the rules of the game of science require us to ignore what the person in the street may sometimes know from common sense about adaptation. After all, our ancestors have been adapting for millions of years, and if it turns out that there is a "human nature," perhaps it will have given us better intuitive guidance than the positivist-oriented, behaviorist model of humankind has led us to believe.

itself and the evolved internal needs and characteristics of an organism also set problems that must be solved. More important, the very definition of what constitutes a problem often has a relational aspect. For example, most plants do not have the "problem" of locomotion or the need to obtain energy by exploiting other plants and animals, though they share with all other species the need for energy. Conversely, fish and people have very different sorts of problems in and out of water. Adaptation is also a two-way street; an organism must adapt to its environments (living and nonliving), and in the process environments are often modified, perhaps in ways that in turn influence the organism. Ehrlich and Raven use the term *co-evolution* to describe such dynamic interactions, citing as a rather dramatic example the stepwise directional evolution of predator and prey species via successive incremental adaptations to one another.[171]

There has been much sloppy theorizing about adaptation. Evolutionists often engage in *a priori* reasoning to the effect that there must be an adaptive (functional) explanation for every trait and, conversely, that natural selection can be invoked as an explanation for every biological phenomenon. However, John Maynard Smith points out that *a priori* reasoning is not necessarily wrong and may well be the most efficient way to proceed.[172] Unless one is ready to set aside the core premise that survival and reproduction is the basic problem and to discount the necessity for adaptation (something a field-trained naturalist would view as ivory tower theorizing), then most traits probably evolved in relation to the problems of earning a living, even though they may not currently be optimal or in any way adaptive. For example, the number of known or presumed nonfunctional aspects of human morphology is exceedingly small.

Maynard Smith notes that it may not be necessary (and might even be considered foolish) to devise ways of testing the obvious—why animals have teeth, or why horses have legs. In such cases we can legitimately reason from a necessary function to be performed to appropriate structures for fulfilling that function, given the core premise. But when there is reason to be suspicious of the obvious explanation, when drift or allometry might be plausible alternatives, or when the function of a trait or an organ is obscure to us and subject to debate, then experimental tests or evidence should be demanded and ad hoc explanations challenged.[173]

Frequently supporting evidence can be found to buttress *a priori* functionalism. For instance, waterbugs are normally dark-colored on top and have light-colored bellies—as protection against predation from above or below, according to the adaptationist explanation. The exceptions are those waterbugs that swim on their backs; as an adaptationist would "predict," their color patterns are reversed.[174]

Another example involves behavior. Black-headed gulls (*Larus ridibundus*) roost on open beaches except when they are reproducing, at which time they move inland. The hypothesis that the beaches are safer was confirmed by Kruuk and by Tinbergen,[175] whose data showed that the number of gulls killed by foxes was much greater in the breeding areas than on the beaches. Why then do the gulls move inland to reproduce? Because there the eggs and young nestlings are less visible to potential avian predators.

Lamarck's famous giraffes present a paradigm case of adaptationist theorizing that need not rest on *a priori* reasoning alone. In what is now called Zaire, there still exists a short-necked species of *Giraffidae* called the okapi (*Okapia johnstoni*). Significantly, the okapi occupy a very different kind of environment from that of the prototypical giraffe, and they employ a very different feeding strategy. Of course this does not rule out the alternative hypotheses that either drift or orthogenesis is responsible. But the drift argument would carry more weight if the okapi occupied the same niche as their long-necked cousins, and the orthogenetic argument would carry more weight if all *Giraffidae* had long necks, even in different environments. Among the three alternatives, the adaptationist (natural selection) hypothesis best fits the data.

Accordingly, Huxley suggested that there are three basic kinds of adaptations: An organism must be adapted to the inorganic environment, the organic environment, and its own internal environment, so to speak.[176] At the time Huxley wrote, no one seems to have objected to the fact that he did not include a fourth category for the sociocultural environment, that is, socially constructed behavioral constraints, opportunities, tools, information, and other resources (including other group members) that are part of the total adaptive environment for any organism that lives in a functionally interdependent group. In the 1940s the consensus was that culture is a uniquely human "invention" that sets humankind apart absolutely from other species. However, this was an extreme reaction against the nineteenth-century social Darwinists and simplistic advocates of biological determinism. Darwin did not accept either extreme separatism or extreme biologism, and he chided his co-discoverer, Alfred Russel Wallace, for exempting the evolution of the human brain from natural selection. Nevertheless radical separatism came to dominate the social sciences in the immediate post-Social Darwinist era.

The pendulum now rests much nearer the middle; many contemporary theorists take their cues from Roe and Simpson's *Behavior and Evolution* (1958) and Dobzhansky's *Mankind Evolving* (1962), which stressed the mutual interdependence of human nature and culture. It is obvious that there are unique aspects to human cultures, but there are also important analogues with other social species. Some theorists still stress the distinctions. Marshall Sahlins speaks of the "autonomy" of culture; Richard Dawkins declares that human cultural evolution through the mechanism of memes (units of cultural transmission) is "unique"; David Barash characterizes cultural and biological evolution as two "autonomous" processes; Kenneth Boulding claims that cultural evolution is a consequence of the "noogenetic factor" (a term for culturally transmitted information borrowed from Teilhard de Chardin); and Paul Diener asserts that culture is "the *only* communication/behavior system in the animal world capable of evolution independent of genetic change." Perhaps most extreme are the views of Richerson and Boyd, who not only declare that our genes have yielded their hegemony to culture but that culture and genes may be viewed as being in competition with each other for control over our behavior.[177]

In contrast, I maintain that the sociocultural category of adaptation is not unique to humankind, is not independent of biological evolution, is not unconstrained by biological imperatives, and should properly be added to Huxley's list as a class of biological adaptations.[178] First, many species have the rudiments of culture, at least according to Bonner's quite reasonable definition (the transfer of information by behavioral means, especially via social learning and teaching).[179] Second, the functional products of culture—patterned networks of behavioral and physical structures and processes—have survival relevance and may therefore be instrumentalities of natural selection (properly understood). As Bonner writes, culture is "as biological as any other function of an organism, for instance respiration or locomotion."[180] Finally, the ongoing cultural evolution of *Homo sapiens* is radically altering the course of biological evolution. Recall that natural selection consists of continuities and/or changes in the functional relationships between organisms and their environments that affect either gene frequencies within a population *or* the numbers and diversity of different populations and species—what I call genome types. Cultural evolution in humankind has resulted in ever-intensifying genomic selection.*

* What do I mean by "changes in functional relationships"? A functional relationship refers to ends-directed transactions within organized biological structures or between such structures and their environments. The ends (goals) may be self-determined (teleonomic) or imposed from without (teleological).[181] Functional processes maintain dynamic systems, meet needs, and accomplish goals, and changes in such relationships may be of three kinds. In one case, a change in a pattern of interactions may produce functionally equivalent consequences in terms of benefits, costs, and risks to the organism. Many genetic polymorphisms, such as variations in human hemoglobin, would seem to be examples of this. So too are many behavioral changes—for example, when a predator switches prey without any detectable differences in the functional consequences for the predator's survival. Such cases do not involve natural selection but are examples of what evolutionists call multiple adaptive peaks.

The second kind of change involves situations in which the same pattern of interaction produces very different consequences, for one reason or another. One example is the rapid decline of a prey species (say, anchovies) as a threshold phenomenon, so that a predator (say, human beings) must expend ever-increasing amounts of time and energy to find a meal. Such cases might

(Continued)

There is considerable confusion about the concept of function. Williams calls it an "onerous" concept because it erroneously implies an external designer and/or an unwarranted teleology.[182] Hinde suggests that functional questions should be rephrased; instead of "what is the function of a phenomenon?" the question should be "how does such and such a phenomenon influence fitness?"[183] Certainly loose use of the term may contribute to sloppy reasoning or misplaced teleology. But some objections involve either semantic quibbling or myopia. Huxley observed that function and adaptation are really two aspects of the same thing;[184] the two terms refer to different levels of analysis or different functional domains. In one sense, a function refers to an engineering problem, to what Aristotle called an "efficient" cause. It is perfectly appropriate to ask "what are the functions of, at different levels of organization, transfer RNA, the mitochondria, estrogen, the pancreas, greeting displays, and leadership?" meaning what role do these phenomena play in the operation of dynamic, goal-oriented systems? In another, distinct sense, function also refers to how a particular phenomenon relates to adaptation *qua* fitness, that is, to aspects of the problem of survival and reproduction. That the two functional domains may be distinct becomes evident when discrepancies arise, as often occurs when environmental contexts change. For example, insects frequently use odors or "vocalizations" to locate potential mates. But because human beings have learned how to mimic some of these signals for pest control purposes, the reproductive consequences for such creatures can be dysfunctional. (Of course, they are eufunctional for human survival and reproduction purposes.)[185]

The relationship between causes and functions in teleological and teleonomic systems is complex and is often misunderstood. A great deal depends on the nature of the question or how the theoretical problem is couched. If I wish to develop a theory to explain the failure of my automobile (a teleological system) to function (operate as designed), I may attribute the cause to engine failure. Because the engine plays a necessary role (function) in the operation of a motor vehicle, the failure of the engine to function is causal. Yet engine failure may be only a proximate (efficient) cause of my problem; a more remote cause may be poor design, or poor construction, a failure on the part of my local mechanic to perform properly his function (role), or all three. The same relationships between function and causation apply to biological and cultural systems.

Many social scientists have disagreed with this fundamentally biological

---

have ramifying functional consequences which qualify as sources of natural selection. Indeed, from the point of view of the prey, the predator may be the instrumentality of natural selection.

Finally, there are the more familiar cases of different interaction patterns with different functional consequences. The migration of human populations to high altitudes or to arctic regions is one specific cultural example.

view of the purpose and consequences of culture—and have opposed any biologically oriented definition of cultural adaptation and evolution. Julian Steward, a leading anthropologist of an earlier generation, declared that "culture, rather than genetic potential for adaptation, accommodation and survival, explains the nature of human societies."[186] And in 1960 Marvin Harris defined an adaptation as "a useful trait" for a sociocultural system. This was a straightforward application of the so-called structural-functionalist approach to society, whose history goes back to Radcliffe-Brown, Parsons, Durkheim, and Comte.[187] (Nowadays Harris uses the term in a way that is generally consonant with the biologists' definition.[188]) Similarly, anthropologist Yehudi Cohen, following the tradition of Leslie White, reduced the problem of adaptation to thermodynamics: "Adaptation in man is the process by which he makes effective use for productive ends of the energy potential of his habitat. . . . Thus a culture must first be defined in terms of specific sources of energy and their social correlates. Every culture can be conceptualized as a strategy of adaptation, and each represents a unique social design for extracting energy from the habitat."[189]

An even more divergent viewpoint has been espoused by anthropologist Robert Carneiro.[190] Proposing to disconnect the process of functional adaptation from the process of evolution, Carneiro defines evolution in a fundamentally different way from that of most evolutionary biologists. According to Carneiro, adaptation refers to the process Spencer called equilibration. Organisms, Carneiro asserts, must maintain what Spencer referred to as a "moving equilibrium" between themselves and their environments—a conceptualization roughly equivalent to the modern cybernetic notion of homeostasis (compare Prigogine's concept of thermodynamic "stability"). Carneiro also recognizes the criterion of adaptation *qua* Darwinian reproductive success.[191] Evolution, on the other hand, he treats as distinct and fundamentally directional; it involves a progressive increase in the complexity of structures and functions. Conversely, his concept of devolution involves structural and functional simplification.

Evolutionary biologists shy away from imposing any such *a priori* criteria on the concept of evolution; evolution is simply "descent with modification." There are various criteria by which one can measure progressive evolution, but there is no universally valid standard of progress. Yet the differences between Carneiro and the evolutionary biologists are more than semantic. For biologists, all directional changes are ultimately connected with and mediated by the process of biological adaptation (if not fully "determined" by natural selection). However, Carneiro states flatly that changes in adaptation, while perhaps incidental to evolutionary change, are not "synonymous."[192] Presumably, then, some adaptive changes have no evolutionary significance and some progressive changes (evolutionary changes in his terminology) may not be the result of changes in adaptation. If so, they arise from some mysterious source that Carneiro has not identified. But this proposition contravenes the Darwinian theory of evolution. I shall argue the converse, that it is precisely because of the adaptive advantages, as a result of functional synergism, that more complex forms have evolved.

By the same token, Carneiro maintains that his form of evolution is reversible,[193] while evolutionary biologists (and Prigogine) hold that evolution is a fundamentally irreversible process. In the limited sense that structural simplifications may occur, there may be a degree of reversibility. But in the larger sense that any organism (or society) can return to a previous pattern of adaptation and a previous set of organism-environment relationships, the hypothesis is unsupported.[194]*

I prefer to use the terms evolution and adaptation in a way that is isomorphic with contemporary evolutionary biology. Evolution is a historical process involving descent with modification. Over the course of evolutionary history there have been striking directional trends, that is, various forms of progressive evolution. There have also been striking cases of regressive evolution. All such changes have been intimately related to the process of adaptation; adaptation (biological and cultural) has been central to evolutionary change, in whatever direction (the precise causal matrix has always included a confluence of "chance, necessity, and teleonomy"). Furthermore, progressive forms of evolution are contingent phenomena that are always subject to the strict editorial supervision of natural selection. Evolutionary progress is not assured by any law of nature, but it may be striven for.

To be sure, many cultural adaptations in human societies do not involve a direct, conscious pursuit of biological ends. Such ends may be the farthest thing from our minds as we struggle with freeway traffic, income tax forms, final exams, or deadlines at work. In what might be called the fourth category

* Another terminological and conceptual variation on this issue, one that is closer to that of Spencer (and Prigogine), has been propounded by anthropologists Marshall Sahlins and Elman Service. What they call "general evolution" involves directional changes in *both* structural complexity ("higher organization") based on the number of parts, the degree of specialization, and concomitant integration *and* the amount of "energy capture" by the system: "The difference between higher and lower life forms, it seems to us, is not how effectively energy is harnessed, but how much."[195] Again, evolution is equated with a specific form of progress. In a later work, Service asserts that evolution is "sequential, directional advance in terms of some measurable criteria of progress."[196] That criterion, he says, is energetic: "Life as a whole moves in the general direction of improved energy-capture."[197]

To illustrate the problem with this approach, consider our current energy crisis. If innovations in high technology (especially electronics and superconductivity) in addition to culturally induced conservation practices (efficiencies) should permit Americans to use less total energy per capita than during the halcyon days of cheap and plentiful oil, Service would pronounce such changes devolutionary—a regression.

of adaptation (my amendment to Huxley's typology), where most of our conscious efforts are focused, biological needs and purposes are often served in oblique and roundabout ways—and are even ill-served. There is an imperfect fit between strict biological adaptation (what serves survival and reproductive needs) and human sociocultural adaptation; in other words, there are some "degrees of freedom."

An increasing number of social scientists are essentially in agreement with this biologically oriented definition of the purpose and consequences of culture—and with a fundamentally biological view of cultural adaptation and evolution—though not all would state their position quite so strongly.[198]

Measuring Adaptation

The core analytical problem is How do we measure adaptation? The ultimate and indisputable criterion of adaptation is Darwinian fitness. Traditionally, this has been defined as the ability of an individual to produce viable progeny or of an interbreeding population to reproduce itself. However, in recent years the concept of inclusive fitness (the summed proportions of one's own genes shared by close relatives as well as progeny) has been increasingly favored as a more satisfactory measure. In population biology, which dominated evolutionary theorizing during the middle years of this century, the primary tool used to measure adaptation has been the "selection coefficient," a quantitative measure of the *relative* reproductive efficacy of different genotypes in discrete breeding populations (demes). This rigorously analytical approach has been widely used in laboratory and field studies of microevolutionary change. But the problems involved in applying such an approach to the larger evolutionary process, including sociocultural evolution, are manifold. Only now is population genetics beginning to develop ways of modeling the relationship between adaptation at the micro level (individuals) and that at higher levels of organization (trait groups, functionally integrated social organizations, demes, species, ecological communities). Yet in dealing with complexly organized species such as humankind, nothing less than a multileveled approach will do. The most important unit of adaptation in human beings must often be defined in relation to units of cybernetic (political) control and to units of functional (broadly economic) interdependency that go beyond anything in the rest of nature.

These and other limitations in the classical formulation have prompted calls for a less restrictive approach to measuring adaptation in *Homo sapiens.*[199] Various candidates have been proposed. There have been (1) efforts to develop criteria for defining and measuring the "optimal" population size; (2) attempts to specify in some concrete way the property of adaptability, or flexibility; (3) efforts to measure adaptive functions directly; and (4) applications of bioeconomic analyses, that is, benefit-cost analyses that employ various criteria, or metrics.

Here I want to take a moment to discuss bioeconomic analyses in general and energetic analyses in particular. Since the time of Darwin, theorists in both economics and biology have recognized an affinity between the two disciplines.[200] The words "economics" and "ecology" are related etymologically to the Greek word *oikos,* household, and some phenomena (competition, co-operation, specialization, division of labor, economies of scale) are common to both disciplines. Indeed, while there is no universally accepted definition of economics, some of the more popular definitions could serve for both economics and ecology ("management of the household"; "allocation of scarce resources to achieve various objectives or ends"). In both ecology and economics there is a school of thought that emphasizes competition or the division of labor, or both, as the subject matter that defines the discipline.[201] However, a broader definition has the advantage of focusing more on the underlying problem of earning a living and less on how that is accomplished.*

In my definition, both economics and bioeconomics are concerned at bottom with ends-related choices, decisions, and actions. Like economists, bioeconomists employ benefit-cost analyses, and a version of the marginal utility principle, in the study of animal behavior.[206] They also employ optimization models, strategic choice models, and game-theoretic analyses, as in economics.[207] And they attempt applications of efficiency principles, such as Zipf's Law of Least Effort and Bock and Wahlert's "economy principle."[208]

Yet in one important respect bioeconomics differs radically from conventional economics. Being in effect the economic dimension of ecology, bioeconomics focuses on adaptive (Darwinian) ends, on needs that are related to

* The term bioeconomics was first used by a turn-of-the-century theorist, Hermann Reinheimer, one of whose many works was *Evolution by Co-operation: A Study in Bioeconomics* (1913). The most aggressive contemporary exponent of bioeconomics is the economist Nicholas Georgescu-Roegen. Although Georgescu-Roegen has never defined the term so far as I know, he appears to use it to suggest that economic phenomena should be viewed from an evolutionary-adaptive perspective in general and a thermodynamic perspective in particular.[202]

The biologist Michael Ghiselin and economists Gary Becker and Jack Hirschleifer have not used the term, but they enthusiastically embrace the presumed linkages between the two disciplines.[203] Unfortunately, Ghiselin and Hirschleifer have made statements about human and animal economics that are redolent of Social Darwinism. "The evolution of society fits the Darwinian paradigm in its most individualistic form," Ghiselin concludes. "Nothing in it cries out to be otherwise explained. The economy of nature is competitive from beginning to end."[204] And Hirschleifer informs us that "Competition is the all-pervasive law of natural-economy interactions. The source of competition is the limited resource base of the globe in the face of the universal Malthusian tendency to multiply."[205]

Such rhetoric is contradicted by some of their surrounding discussions; for instance, both recognize co-operative behaviors. Nevertheless they misrepresent the basic economic condition of our species. Hirschleifer also insists on certain debatable distinctions: the supposed contrast

(*Continued*)

to biological survival and reproduction through time. Thus bioeconomics is applicable to any species. In contrast, the "science of economics" has traditionally been value-relative and human-oriented; it has deliberately avoided approaches to the analysis of human behavior that involve the use of some "external" value criterion. In a tradition that dates to Adam Smith, the laws of economics have been posited in terms of the individual's value preferences, or tastes, as expressed in the marketplace. Sophisticated economists, following the lead of Marshall's *Principles of Economics* (1890), do not deny the existence of needs. However, they pointedly exclude needs from economic analyses except where they are expressed in actual economic preferences and decisions. Therefore, if there is a discrepancy between each individual's preferences and what is biologically adaptive, there will also be a discrepancy between economic and bioeconomic analyses; what may be optimal in economic terms may not be optimal in bioeconomic terms, and vice versa.

The key to bridging the gap between economics and bioeconomics lies in analyses of the relationship between human economic behavior and its adaptive consequences, just as the key to achieving more adaptive economic behavior lies in aligning it more closely with bioeconomic criteria.

Economics and bioeconomics differ in one other important respect. This has to do with the measuring rod that is used to quantify and commensurate the relative value of the economist's apples and oranges, or alternative "wants." It is fortunate that conventional economics has money to serve as a ready-made unit of value, but those who have attempted to do bioeconomic studies are not so lucky. When fitness functions can be determined, "selection coefficients" can be used. Another approach that bioeconomists have adopted bears comparison with the labor theory of value: Thermodynamic (energetic) costs and benefits are obviously important to survival and reproduction, and they represent a potentially quantifiable dimension of the problem of adaptation. Thus energetic (and/or time-budgeting) studies have become a focal point of bioeconomic analyses. The approach is not new; however, systematic discussions and analyses along these lines have waxed and waned, and now they are waxing again.[209]

Energy-oriented analyses have also been undertaken in human ecology and ecological anthropology. There are two approaches. One, following the lead of White, Sahlins, Service, and others, stresses the *amount* of energy capture in various cultures.[210] The other, which includes most of the empirical

---

between the rationality of human behavior and the behavior of other animals; the existence of law and government only to restrain competition in human societies; and the orientation of human economies toward satisfying tastes instead of survival needs. At the other extreme, Edward Wilson declares that only humankind has an economy (because, he says, only human beings engage in elaborate exchanges among non-kin). Presumably he would not endorse the term bioeconomics at all.

studies done to date, stresses the *efficiency* of energy capture (or the benefit-cost ratios).[211]

In fact, both the amount and the efficiency of energy capture have played important roles in biological and cultural evolution. Consider data derived from a study by the anthropologist Richard B. Lee and calculations by Marvin Harris.[212] A group of !Kung Bushmen (now called !Kung San), one of the few remaining hunter-gatherer societies, were found by Lee to work only about 810 hours per year on the average. For every calorie they expend in work, they extract about 9.6 calories. In contrast, Americans of the 1960s worked 1715 hours per year on the average.[213] Yet for every calorie expended, Americans received a return of 210 calories, almost twenty-two times as much as the average Bushman. And because we worked more than twice as many hours, our per capita energy extractions were more than forty-six times greater than those of the !Kung. With 6 percent of the world's population in 1970, we were responsible for 35 percent of world energy consumption.

The comparison between Americans and a primitive hunter-gatherer society is instructive in its dramatization of the vital role of energy in the material progress of culture. U.S. energy consumption increased thirtyfold between 1850 and 1970,[214] and energy throughputs provide a useful indicator of successful (current) adaptation. However, this approach can be misleading. Although we are relatively efficient in producing energy, we are notoriously inefficient in how we consume it. In 1970 we were wasting almost half of all the energy we produced.[215] More important, a high level of energy capture, when it is based on an unsustainable short-term bonanza, can be a totally unreliable indicator of future adaptation. (In essence, such energy windfalls are thermodynamically unstable.) And because our energy future is still problematical, it remains to be seen whether this component of sociocultural (adaptive) progress in Western societies can be sustained.

If energy capture were the only important adaptive problem, all our efforts should be directed toward developing new forms of it. But it is not the only problem, and some of the constraints we have encountered in energy development, especially environmental constraints, testify to the multidimensional nature of the survival problem. From a biological perspective, energy throughputs are a means to the larger end of sustaining and enhancing the life process. The anthropologists Andrew Vayda and Bonnie McKay observe that a relative scarcity of energy may be a limiting factor in societal development,[216] in conformity with Justus von Liebig's "law of the minimum." The law states that the "carrying capacity" of a particular environment is limited by whatever requisite of life is in shortest supply. Potential shortages of calories (food and fuel) are currently major hazards for perhaps one-third of humankind. But there are many other limiting factors: protein, for instance;[217] and water; and basic raw materials that have become requisites for industrial societies (what I call instrumental needs, as distinct from primary biological needs).

The converse is also true. A bountiful supply of energy resources or a technology that permits the exploitation of otherwise unusable energy sources may be an important enabler for sociocultural progress.[218] So is water an enabler, and so are raw materials, sources of protein, tools and technical skills, organization, and physical security. For adaptation is inherently a multifaceted affair. Sociocultural evolution has been the product ultimately of *synergistic* configurations of factors that together have permitted human beings to satisfy more fully, or for more people, an evolving configuration of basic needs. Moreover, these needs are variable; they are determined in part by the context, by the situation-specific interactions of the four kinds of environments (physical, biotic, internal, and sociocultural/political). Yet each adaptive context seems to be a unique variation on a common theme; underlying these particularities there is a deep structure to the process of sociocultural adaptation and evolution.

A Basic Needs Approach to Adaptation

There is a growing recognition that we need a more inclusive and multifaceted approach to measuring adaptation. The anthropologist Eugene Ruyle urges us to concentrate on the "struggle for satisfactions."[219] The psychologist Robert W. White, calling adaptation the master concept of the behavioral and social sciences, applies it to any means-ends, or goal-oriented behavior (though surely he does not mean to include actions that are biologically maladaptive).[220]

Others, especially ecological anthropologists, have adopted an explicitly biological orientation. Donald Hardesty, for example, defines adaptation as "any beneficial response to the environment,"[221] and it is clear from the context that he means *biologically* beneficial. His colleague John Bennett conceptualizes adaptation in terms of how human actors realize objectives, meet needs, and cope with conditions.[222] Bennett wishes to stress the cognitive/purposive elements in human behavior; he wishes to treat adaptation as a goal-oriented process that is embedded in a cultural milieu. But he also makes it clear that biological problems lie at the root of the process. Vayda and McKay are also concerned with the "existential game" of survival and reproduction; in an article whose objective is to identify "new directions" in ecological anthropology, they argue for an emphasis on "health" and various "hazards" and "stresses."[223]

George C. Williams has disparaged the use of such presumptively soft approaches to measuring adaptation:

> Natural selection commonly produces fitness in the vernacular sense. We ordinarily expect it to favor mechanisms leading to an increase in health and comfort and a decrease in danger to life and limb, but the theoretically important kind of fitness is that which promotes ultimate reproductive survival. Reproduction always requires some sacrifice of resources and some jeopardy of physiological well-being, and such sacrifices may be favorably selected, even though they may reduce fitness in the vernacular sense of the term.[224]

Such "vernacular" approaches need not be inconsistent with a strictly Darwinian perspective, and they need not be all that weak. The approach I have been developing involves an engineering *cum* bioeconomic strategy, the objective of which is to measure adaptation directly.[225] The evolutionary-adaptive indicators (or Survival Indicators) approach represents a contribution to the so-called social indicators movement, which has been making extensive efforts over the past fifteen years to develop more satisfactory ways of measuring the quality of life, or societal well-being.

In essence, the Survival Indicators approach is an attempt to specify as rigorously as possible the nature and extent of our basic (primary and instrumental) survival and reproductive needs, which in turn are treated as components of a holistic concept of Health. Admittedly, some trade-offs are involved; *ex post facto* certitude is exchanged for an imperfect ability to acquire predictively useful knowledge about how specific behaviors, institutions, and processes relate to adaptation (and conversely, how adaptive needs shape our cultures). This strategy is immensely complex—and tentative. Because of the limits of our knowledge about human nature and human needs, one cannot pretend to more than an approximation. But it is a fertile approach, one that is susceptible to improvements in light of future developments in the biobehavioral and social sciences. To cite a case in point, our understanding of human nutritional needs has greatly improved during the past half century. There are still many gaps, yet we are able to use what we have learned to date to specify nutritional needs with some confidence. Furthermore, we can use that knowledge to gain deeper insight into nutritional practices and their biological (functional) consequences.[226]

To my knowledge, the first social scientist to espouse in significant detail this general approach to adaptation was anthropologist Bronislaw Malinowski. For Malinowski a society is preeminently an organized system of co-operatively pursued activities. It is purposive in nature, and its purposes relate to the satisfaction of basic needs, that is, "the system of conditions in the human organism, in the cultural setting, and in the relation of both to the natural environment, which are sufficient and necessary for the survival of the group and organism."[227]

In contrast with the hyphenated functionalism of Comte, Durkheim, and their descendants, Malinowski's "pure functionalism," like Spencer's, was concerned with relating the complexities of cultural behavior to "organic processes in the human body and to those concomitant phases of behavior which we call desire or drive, emotion or physiological disturbance, and which, for one reason or another, have to be regulated and coordinated by the apparatus of culture."[228]

The structure that Malinowski developed for his essentially biological functionalism can be reproduced in synoptic form:

BASIC NEEDS	CULTURAL RESPONSES
1. Metabolism	1. Commissariat
2. Reproduction	2. Kinship
3. Bodily comforts	3. Shelter
4. Safety	4. Protection
5. Movement	5. Activities
6. Growth	6. Training
7. Health	7. Hygiene

Malinowski drafted this listing only for the sake of simplicity; his discussion provides more detailed and more sophisticated treatment. For example, his "health" need has a dual significance: In a narrow sense it refers to the absence of physical impairment or sickness, but in a broader sense it is a condition that is affected by all the other categories. Malinowski also went on to show that these primary needs give rise to a set of "derived" societal needs. (My concept of instrumental needs is somewhat different, as will become apparent.)

Some critics have charged Malinowski with biological determinism—with the view that biological needs can fully explain the origins and existence of different cultural forms. In fact, the opposite was the case:

> This is the point in which the study of human behavior takes a definite departure from mere biological determinism. We have made this clear already in pointing out that within each vital sequence the impulse is refashioned or *co-determined* [my italics] by cultural influences. As anthropologists, we are primarily interested in the manner in which, under the primary organic drive, the conditioned responses of specific taste and appetite, attraction of sex, means of enjoyment in bodily comfort, are developed. We are also interested in the way in which the various cultural responses are constructed. Here we shall see that these responses are by no means simple. In order to provide the constant flow of nutritive goods, articles, dress, building materials, structures, weapons, and tools, human cultures have not merely to produce artifacts, but have also to develop techniques, that is, regulated bodily movements, values, and forms

> of social organization. . . . The cogency of the functional approach consists in the fact that it does not pretend to forecast exactly how a problem posed for a culture will be solved. It states, however, that the problem, since it is derived from biological necessity, environmental conditions, and the nature of cultural response, is both universal and categorical.[229]

Malinowski used the fork as an example. Can anyone doubt that the function performed by forks is a significant part of the explanation for the existence and the design of this commonplace cultural artifact? Yet the fork is not a cultural universal; so more information is needed to account for why the fork was invented and diffused and why it is used in some cultures and not in others.

In light of contemporary anthropological theory, one finds many shortcomings in Malinowski's formulations.[230] One might take exception, for instance, to Malinowski's claim that his basic needs approach was the only valid set of external, or "etic," criteria for cross-cultural classification and comparisons.[231] Nevertheless his overall approach was valid, indeed essential to an anthropology (and a sociology) that are in touch with the biological realities.

Another major progenitor of my approach is the humanistic psychologist Abraham Maslow.[232] Maslow's famous hierarchy of human needs involves nothing less than a theory of human nature and motivation. According to Maslow, the human being is neither a behavioral sponge (as the behaviorists imply) nor a tormented neurotic (as some Freudians hold) but a natural innocent endowed with an array of biologically based needs that ascend hierarchically through five categories from "deficiency motivations" (which derive from such physiological needs as food, water, shelter, sleep, sex) to "being motivations," at the apex of which is self-actualization, a kind of beatific state in which one achieves the full use of one's talents and potentialities. Maslow's five categories are: physiological needs, safety needs, "belongingness" and love needs, esteem needs, and self-actualization or "growth" needs.[233]

Evil, by which Maslow meant particularly human destructiveness, is not innate in humans, as Freud postulated, but "reactive," that is, a response to frustrations. On the other hand, the more complex and constructive human motivations are authentic and innate, and only when these "higher" motivations are satisfied is the true potential for human fulfillment realized. But this cannot occur unless the "lower," more basic (and more urgent) needs are satisfied. Not all human beings may be capable of self-actualization, but the satisfaction of basic needs will at least make such a flowering possible.

It is a noble vision. Man has the innate capability to transcend the basic problem of personal survival and the power to realize the sort of cultural and personal values to which civilized human societies have always aspired. One detects in Maslow an echo of the "good life" that Aristotle posited and that one finds in the writings of Christian and Oriental mystics, Emerson, and Thoreau. There is also some scientific merit to Maslow's model; it involves a complex and multifaceted view of human motivation, one in which social-psychological needs are treated as primary causes rather than being merely derivative or artifactual. Humans are viewed as basically healthy and positive in their relationships to life. Maslow also recognized, as Freudians and classical behaviorists did not, that the individual's motivational substrate must be hierarchically organized—that certain basic biological needs must take priority.

Yet in spite of its positive aspects, Maslow's model conflicts in important respects with a rigorously evolutionary perspective. The fundamental difference is that Maslow's needs hierarchy is based not on the problem of survival and reproduction but on the problem of personal fulfillment and mental health.[234] The former is the more empirical problem in the sense that it exists whether we care about it or not; the latter is arguably the more normative and personal problem. This is not to deny that the latter is a legitimate and important problem area, but it leads to a very different perspective toward society.

The major difficulty stems from the partiality Maslow showed toward his "metamotivations." Even if for the sake of argument we allow that such motivations exist and that they are innate, the fact that they may seem to be ends in themselves to different individuals does not mean that they are not functionally significant (either adaptive or maladaptive) in relation to more basic survival and reproductive needs. But in Maslow's hierarchy there is no connection and no inner logic; the higher needs are higher only because the lower needs take precedence. For Maslow, only the deficiency needs relate to the problem of survival. The higher needs, though equally biological, are distinct and, presumably, the frosting on the cake. However, if one wishes to explain the origin and functional significance of Maslow's metamotivations, the only theoretically sensible approach must be evolutionary-adaptive. From the perspective of the priorities and the value preferences, so to speak, of natural selection, the social and psychological needs of *Homo sapiens,* or of any other group-living species, must be viewed as having arisen (evolved) because of their instrumental relationship to continued viability and reproduction, as Darwin pointed out. It is unlikely that they would have evolved in any other way.

The discordance between Maslow's hierarchy and an evolutionary perspective is most apparent in relation to his so-called B-values. In one of his last publications, Maslow listed curiosity and the need to know as "metamotivations" or B-values, associated with self-actualization (an exalted state that not everyone is capable of attaining).[235] His view flies in the face of the fact that curiosity is a widespread behavioral phenomenon in the natural world and has obvious adaptive functions. Moreover, curiosity makes its appearance in the human neonate almost immediately after birth.*

This does not mean that the higher needs are necessarily always at the service of the lower needs. It does not even contradict the view that such needs may become ends in themselves. Nevertheless the problem of survival and reproduction is inescapable. The lower needs are not met once and for all so that we can go on to higher things, as Maslow sometimes implied; we may choose not to meet our basic needs, or we may fail to do so for one reason or another. But we cannot avoid choosing whether or not we will make the attempt, and we cannot avoid the consequences. That is what an imperative means.

Despite its popularity among various psychologically oriented social scientists, Maslow's hierarchy has only marginal status among experimental psychologists because it does not have scientific support. Although it is frequently invoked to justify a particular moral position or to anchor a model of political behavior, such uses are pseudoscientific. Fitzgerald concludes: "Most psychologists regard the purely empirical study and validation of a hierarchy of needs in Maslow's sense as presenting immense and (perhaps) insurmountable problems. It is clear that insofar as a potentially verifiable aspect can be abstracted from this ambiguous amalgam, Maslow's theory of human needs has not been empirically established to any significant extent."[237] (This is not to say that the principle of hierarchical organization is totally inapposite. A different approach will be employed below.)

Social Indicators

The point of entry for my own approach is the recent work on measuring the "quality of life." Although concern with societal well-being is not new—it is, after all, embedded in the U.S. Constitution—it is relatively new as a concern of social science. One focal point has been the so-called social indicators movement. While its origins may lie with the sociologist William F. Ogburn's *Social Trends* (1929), contemporary researchers generally identify Raymond Bauer's *Social Indicators* (1966) as the catalyst for the recent activ-

* Maslow acknowledged that his hierarchy of needs was only a first approximation. One obvious omission is the need for stimulation and goal-directed activity, a need for which we now have empirical evidence.[236] A satisfactory formulation of human needs must also account for the tension, or dynamic interplay that exists among human motivations. For instance, Maslow's "safety needs" are often put in jeopardy by competitiveness and our propensity to seek out challenges to our capacities.

ity in this area. Since the publication of Bauer's book, the growth and evolution of social indicators research has been rapid.

Much of the original impetus for the creation of a distinct body of data called social indicators arose out of a reaction against our heavy dependence on economic indicators (especially the GNP) as measuring rods for societal progress or well-being. The goal of the social indicators "idealists," as they have been called, was to develop a broad definition of the "general welfare" that subsumed economic growth and accounted for diseconomies, or economic externalities.* Just as economists had been able to articulate a theory of economic life that established a framework for aggregating data on the production and consumption of goods and services, so social indicators proponents aspired to develop a coherent system of social measures. The object was not only to augment and improve an ad hoc collection of social statistics gathered for obscure or narrow purposes. The hope was that it would also be possible to create a statistical portrait, a tapestry by means of which we could view our society at once as an integrated whole and in all of its major facets.

One of the most articulate nay-sayers to this viewpoint has been Eleanor Bernert Sheldon. In an article written with Howard E. Freeman, she said:

> Evoking the economic analogy and proposing the development of social indicators that parallel economic indicators is confusing and in part fallacious. Despite its weakness and limited rigor, economic theory provides a definition and the specifications of an economic system, and the linkages are at least hypothesized, if not empirically demonstrated, between many variables in the system. . . . At least to some extent, this model has worked and economic indicators and accounts are useful policy tools. Although some social scientists have promised similar usefulness for social indicators and social accounts, this is not even a reasonable anticipation.[239]†

* Perhaps the most frequently quoted statement of this energizing vision is to be found in *Toward a Social Report* (1969), a benchmark report written principally by Mancur Olson:

> A social indicator may be defined to be a statistic of direct normative interest which facilitates concise, comprehensive and balanced judgments about the condition of major aspects of a society. It is in all cases a direct measure of welfare and is subject to the interpretation that, if it changes in the "right" direction, while other things remain equal, things have gotten better or people are "better off."[238]

† A similar view was expressed in a recent British volume on social indicators: "The Americans were rather hopeful at that stage that they could construct simple comprehensive measures of the state of health of the nation, the degree of social inequality, of its educational performance, etc. There was no comprehensive social theory adumbrated to sustain this position. The American faith, as revealed in *Toward a Social Report,* still rested heavily on the assumption of a very definite, though sometimes inarticulate, consensus on the major issues of social policy."[240]

Other attacks on such global aspirations have come from the "relativists," those scientists who claim that well-being is necessarily a personal and subjective affair. Their number includes many workers in survey research, who promote "perceptual" indicators of well-being.[241] Campbell et al., for instance, note "the obvious fact that individual needs differ greatly from one person to another and that what will satisfy one will be totally unsatisfactory to the other. Indeed, the same individual may find the same circumstances thoroughly unsatisfactory at one stage of his life but quite acceptable at a later stage."[242]

Likewise, the sociologist Erik Allardt disputes the very idea of basic needs: "A level of need satisfaction defined once and for all has hardly any specific meaning. . . . To a large extent, needs are both created by society and culturally defined, meaning that the satisfaction and frustration of needs have to be studied in a systematic context in which societal feedback processes are considered."

Finally, the writers of a synthesis volume on the quality of life, published by the Environmental Protection Agency, claim that "Quality of life means different things to different people. It can be stated that at the present no consensus exists as to what it is or what it means. . . . QOL is viewed by many as not applying to the nation as a whole. In their view, the only way QOL could be applied at the macro-level would be by homogenizing the country and forcing everyone to accept the same value standards."[243]

Basic Needs: A Survivalist Approach

The writers of the EPA report, like others, are guilty of tacitly assuming away or taking for granted the basic survival and reproduction problem, and/or conflating wants and needs, and/or equating variation with randomness. As the foregoing discussion should have made clear, (1) a survival-oriented conception of the general welfare can be anchored in the external, objective problem of survival and reproduction for individuals and socioeconomically interdependent populations; (2) the concept of basic needs is not incompatible with the fact of variation in relation to each of the four adaptive environments listed above; and (3) the concept of objective needs must be clearly differentiated from wants and aspirations, which may be more or less concordant or discordant with needs.

A basic needs approach is not so radical or theoretically murky as the relativists claim; it was even embedded in the legislative philosophy of the New Deal, as articulated by Franklin Roosevelt in one of his famous fireside chats.* Since the 1880s, this philosophy has been implemented in numerous

* "One of the duties of the State is that of caring for those of its citizens who find themselves the victims of such adverse circumstances as makes them unable to obtain even the necessities

(Continued)

pieces of social legislation, both in Europe and in the United States, which were designed to put an economic floor under basic needs. These programs include workmen's compensation, public assistance, social security, medicare, and the minimum wage.

Until very recently there has been little interest in measuring basic needs satisfaction directly. For many years governmental "poverty line" income statistics were used as a surrogate. Now this is changing. In addition to my work on measuring basic needs,[244] there has been the study by the Stanford Research Institute for EPA (1975) concerning "Quality of Life Minimums" (QOLMs), which analyzed existing political standards; the important work sponsored by the Overseas Development Council (1977) on a "Physical Quality of Life Index" (PQLI);[245] the writings on a basic needs strategy for world development emanating from the World Bank;[246] and the manifold efforts of various United Nations agencies since 1975.[247] Harlan Cleveland observes in his introduction to the McHale and McHale report:

> Basic human needs have arrived. During three years of sudden conceptual change, from 1974 to 1977, national development strategies, international negotiations and global organizations have begun to be deeply affected by the simple notion that the purpose of economic development and international cooperation is to meet the human requirements of people, and especially the minimum needs of the neediest. Combined with new attitudes toward economic growth and environmental damage, the appearance of basic human needs at center stage begins a new act in the continuing drama of world development.[248]

I would quibble only with Cleveland's assertion that it is "a new act"; it is rather the rediscovery by politicians, planners, and social scientists of the age-old "act."

In my approach, the term *basic need* is used in the strict biological sense of *a requisite for the continued functioning of an organism in a given environmental context; that is, denial of the posited need would significantly reduce the organism's ability to function and/or reduce the statistical probability of its continued survival and successful reproduction.* For heuristic purposes I distinguish between the levels of needs satisfaction required for (1) minimal life support, (2) minimal ability to sustain transgenerational continuity (meaning both successful reproduction and surpluses for nurturance of the young during the maturational process), and (3) optimal life support (meaning maximally efficient functioning and adaptability).

I also attempt to distinguish between primary needs, instrumental needs,

---

for mere existence without the aid of others. That responsibility is recognized by every civilized nation. . . . To these unfortunate citizens aid must be extended by Government—not as a matter of charity but as a matter of social duty."

dependencies, perceived needs, and wants. Much of what are sometimes called basic needs are not primary needs at all but may involve one of these other categories. Primary needs are irreducible and nonsubstitutable. Instrumental needs, on the other hand, may be reducible to primary needs (may be subsumed), may be substitutable for functional equivalents, and may vary widely depending on the context. When such a distinction is made, some theoretical confusion dissolves.

Thermoregulation, for example, may be a primary human need, but the instrumental needs for clothing, heating fuel, and thermally insulated shelter will vary from one climatic environment and culture to another. In the same vein, mobility is an irreducible primary need, but within that category there may be instrumental needs for horses, bicycles, or automobiles, depending on the context. In this vein, I argue that walking, though pancultural and biologically primordial in humankind, is not always essential (not a primary) need. There are cultural contexts in which substitutes are available, among them prosthetic devices, the services of others, and transportation and communications systems that provide functional equivalents. Walking can be viewed as a biologically evolved *capability* that is derived from a primary need, just as a compact body build or a thick layering of subcutaneous fat may represent evolved adaptations that are derived from the need for thermoregulation. Culture may have altered the fitness value of walking.

It is also important to distinguish between needs and drives, or behavioral activators. Needs are functional requisites; drives are psychobiological mechanisms. Human sexuality involves a powerful drive that we sometimes colloquially call a need, but in reality it is an evolved instrumentality for serving our reproductive needs. The empirical distinction between the two is evident both in the practice of birth control and in artificial insemination. By the same token, a person may eat more or less than is needed to satisfy the promptings of hunger.[249]

The litmus test for a *primary need,* according to this formulation, has nothing to do with whether or not the need is reflected in correlative psychobiological motivations (although most are). Nor does it matter that these needs vary. Rather, it matters how much, why, and with what consequences. Primary needs vary within a narrow range, are pancultural, cannot be substituted for one another or replaced by functional equivalents, are largely independent of our higher motivations and the specific environmental and cultural context, and may vary significantly as a result of biologically based individual differences and the environmental context.

Instrumental needs serve the primary needs. Some instrumental needs are so pervasive as to be close to primary needs in their importance: exogenous energy for cooking and heating, shelter, various utensils and tools, clothing, language skills, and walking. Such instrumental needs are in fact the focal points of recent efforts to develop basic needs indicators.[250] My intention is not to slight instrumental needs but to categorize them properly with respect to my theoretical objective, which is to define the primary functional requisites for survival and reproductive success.*

Dependencies are induced, non-survival-related needs, some of which may be destructive (heroin, alcohol, or sugar addiction; compulsive gambling; smoking). *Perceived needs* are those that the individual thinks he or she needs, regardless of the actual situation. And *wants* are the individual's motivations, goals, and aspirations for himself or herself and others, independent of biological needs.

I should also point out the distinction between my category of instrumental needs and Malinowski's "derived needs." Malinowski's concept refers to the cultural arrangements on which humans have become dependent, that is, systems of economic co-operation, systems of rules and rule enforcement, educational systems, and political systems.[254] These derived needs include Radcliffe-Brown's structural functions and Talcott Parsons's functional requisites for social systems. For me such cultural forms are a subset of a much larger class of instrumentalities, only some of which are based on the human dependence on culture.

There are several more preliminary points. First, primary needs vary, but not as much as the relativists imply. Nor are the variations a consequence of personal whim. The obvious case in point is nutritional needs, which are known to vary systematically (and to a substantial degree predictably) as a function of genetic and physical endowment, age, sex, reproductive status, and levels of physical activity. Yet nutrition still constitutes a primary need.

Second, a complex set of interrelationships exists among all the primary needs; all needs are not equally urgent at all times. This greatly affects the organization of our behavioral systems. For example, if a person's life or physical safety were suddenly threatened during a meal, it can safely be predicted that the person would stop eating. (Recall the thought experiment with Greylag geese.)

Third, there are interactions among the primary needs; they are not entirely independent of one another, even though they cannot be reduced to one another. For example, communications (information flows) are instrumental to the satisfaction of various needs—nutrition, physical safety, physical health, effective nurturance of the young, and such derived needs as economic, social,

* There is considerable overlap among recent attempts to formulate shopping lists of basic human needs. Hicks and Streeten include nutrition, education, health, sanitation, water, and housing.[251] Geist includes among his basic "normative criteria" the social milieu, education, nutrition, exercise, natural surroundings, and emotional security.[252] And Mazess, a specialist in high-altitude peoples, has a physiologically oriented list of nine "adaptive domains."[253] My list appears below.

and political activities. By the same token, the lack of proper nutrition, sleep, or satisfactory social relationships may affect a person's mental health or physical health, or both. Likewise, waste elimination is at once a physical problem and a personal health problem.

Fourth, there are potential conflicts between needs. The obvious examples are situations where physical safety might have to be jeopardized to obtain food or other necessities, or where personal nutrition, health, and safety might have to be sacrificed for the sake of the offspring. Other things being equal, however, the individuals who can best satisfy all these needs, including those of their progeny, will be better adapted and more likely to be successful in reproducing competent offspring.

Fifth, it is important to distinguish between those analytical and measurement problems associated with determining more precisely our basic needs (and their functional relationship to survival and reproduction) and the more "applied" problem of how best to measure needs satisfaction for the purposes of social intelligence. I do not wish to underestimate the problems involved in establishing precise criteria for each need. Yet it may be that such surrogate measures as personal income or the individual's personal (perceptual) assessment might suffice as an "indicator," as our research has suggested.[255] After all, even "objective" measures are only as good as the state of the art in the biobehavioral and social sciences.

Figure IV shows the thirteen primary needs domains (so called because several of them have more than one element), which represent irreducible functional components of Darwinian fitness—of biological adaptation—for the human species. To the extent that cultural practices are functionally related to the meeting of these needs, they can be viewed as instrumentalities of human adaptation—of Darwinian fitness and natural selection—whatever our perceptions or the precise confluence of causes that may have produced such practices in the first place. It follows, therefore, that the outcome state, successful adaptation, is the direct, predictable consequence of the meeting of these needs. However, these criteria do not fully determine Darwinian fitness; the relationship is probabilistic because satisfaction of these needs cannot guarantee future adaptation. Nor does it ensure relative reproductive success. In other words, the satisfaction of these needs is necessary but not sufficient. Other things being equal, however, the chances of future reproductive success should be maximized by those whose needs are satisfied.

A basic needs approach to measuring adaptation is not the same as an explanation of culture in terms of basic needs (as Malinowski also insisted). Nor does it follow that every aspect of a cultural system is adaptive. A particular item of culture may be adaptive, neutral, or maladaptive in relation to basic needs. Some items may be more or less directly related to a particular need (would anyone doubt the adaptive function of toilets?); some items

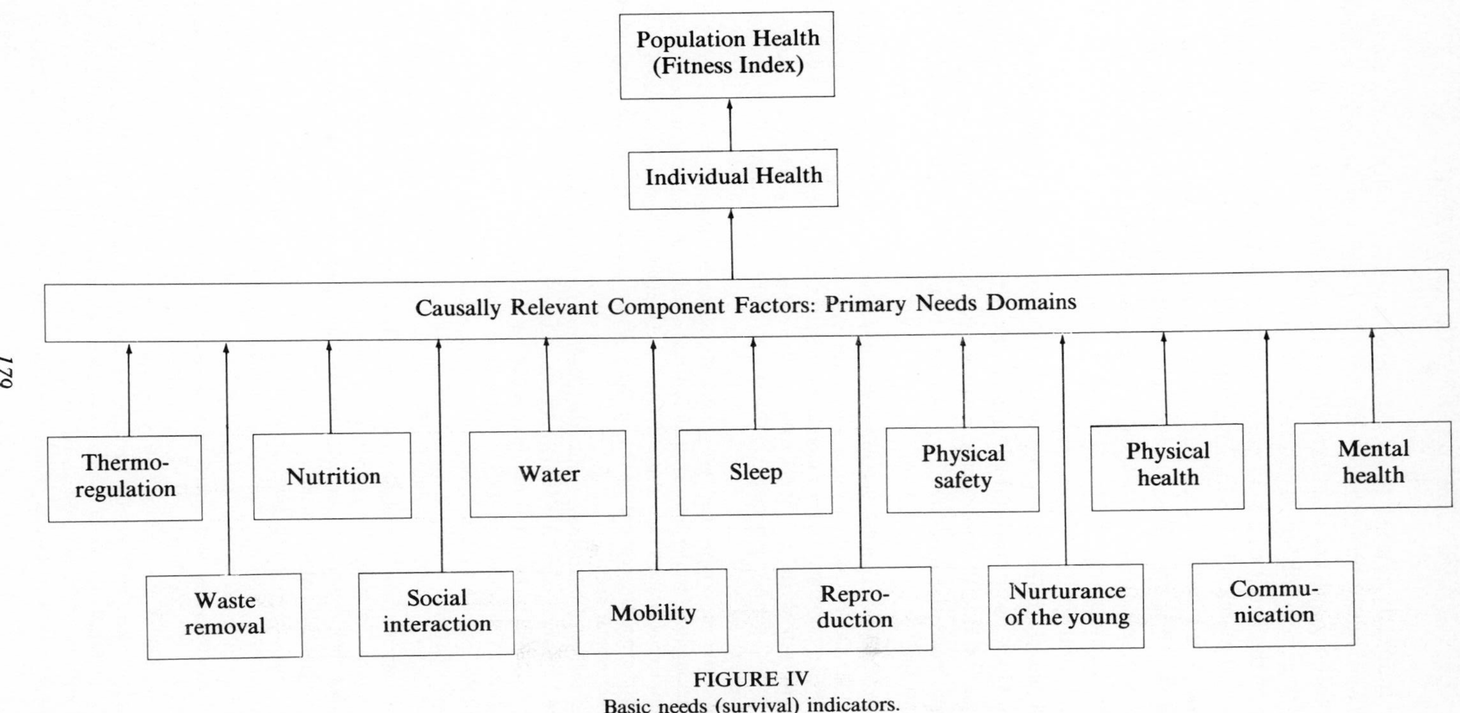

FIGURE IV
Basic needs (survival) indicators.

may be indirectly related (how do we account for sidewalks?); some items may be apparently unrelated (I would not attempt an adaptive explanation for television game shows, baseball, or amusement parks); and some items may be unequivocally maladaptive.

Some of the needs domains are self-evident and probably need no justification (the problems involved in measuring them empirically are another matter). Other needs may appear puzzling or vague and will require explanation. Physical health is defined narrowly as the absence of inborn errors of metabolism (or compensatory prosthesis), the absence of disease, parasites, or other physically debilitating conditions, and a measure of such closely related phenomena as muscle tone, cardiovascular conditioning, and personal hygiene. Physical health differs from the more inclusive and multifaceted concept of Health, which is a summary variable for adaptation itself. In this broad, holistic sense Health represents a synthesis of all the basic needs domains, and it serves as the basis for my proposed master indicator of adaptation.*

* Likewise, "mental health" is generally associated with various institutions, programs, and professional services. I use the term in a less restrictive sense, as an equivalent to the notion of psychic "tone," or "tonus"—good morale, an optimistic outlook on life and one's community, self-confidence, self-esteem, emotional stability. There is a growing scientific literature on the important relationship between mental health as a psychophysiological condition and the ability to function effectively.[256]

There is reason to believe that many cultural phenomena may be functionally related to this need, among them winter festivals, political rallies, religious rituals, charismatic leadership. And while other needs affect mental health (diet, stress, physical health, personal relationships), mental health cannot be reduced to any of them. There are even genetic influences that may directly affect mental health.

The need for social relationships and attachments is a primary need because of our lifelong dependence on others, especially for reproduction. Again, this need is related to other needs but is not reducible to any of them. Because of our emotional makeup, social relationships also constitute an important psychobiological need. Studies have shown that deficiencies in social relationships may have a significant negative effect on physical health.[257] And lack of family support has been related to mental illness, crime, and sociopathy.[258] As with the other needs listed, there are also partially substitutable instrumentalities through which our social needs can be satisfied (family, friends, work groups, church, tribal and community associations). By the same token, our motivations are here viewed as evolved internal correlates and "efficient causes" rather than as primary functional needs. Their inclusion is based on their biological, not their psychological, significance.

There are one or two conspicuous omissions that are deserving of comment. Exclusion of the need to acquire skills might raise some eyebrows. After all, learned skills are basic to the human way; no culture is without them, though the range of variations is obviously tremendous. However, I subsume this need under nurturance of the young—for reasons that I hope are self-evident.

I also leave out of my schema such biopsychological needs as the motivational complex which energizes such things as our reproductive activities and our virtually addictive way of engaging in challenging purposeful activities—games, when nothing more practical is available.

The rationale for defining physical safety as a basic need may seem obvious. There is a direct relationship between threats of injury or violent death and the problem of survival. Such

(Continued)

A Master Indicator of Adaptation

One stated objective of the social indicators "idealists" and other writers on the quality of life has been to devise some summary measure, a master indicator of societal well-being or the general welfare. As we have seen, many social scientists are skeptical of such a venture, and the problem of defining the general welfare is inherently value-laden and subject to differing opinions. Norman Hicks and Paul Streeten of the World Bank note that "systems of *social accounts,* which could integrate social indicators through some unifying concept, have not been able to overcome successfully all the difficult problems encountered."[260]

Yet the perceived need for an inclusive, integrative measure remains undiminished. There is a sense, especially among those who are concerned with the problems of Third World countries, that a baseline is needed and that some criterion or criteria of societal well-being would have practical value as a target or targets for national policy. Indeed, Streeten and Burki, and Hicks and Streeten have tentatively suggested a strategy for Third World countries that involves the aggregation of data for six basic needs.[261] Sheldon and Freeman concede that "While technical problems should not be brushed aside and the craft in the field needs improvement, it should be emphasized that the conceptual needs are the greatest—what to measure and what are valid operational measures of critical phenomena."[262]

My approach is based on the Darwinian criterion of biological adaptation;

---

threats may be associated with performing purposeful activities; accidents on the job or on the highway while traveling to or from work are examples. Other threats are purely discretionary, associated with leisure activities such as skiing or hang-gliding. Still others are pathological and without redeeming social benefit (psychopathic killings). The common denominator derives from the risks these threats pose to the individual's ability to continue functioning.

While there are data on most of these risks, at least for this country, they have not heretofore been assembled under one conceptual umbrella.[259] More important, no attempt has been made to aggregate "profiles" of physical risks for individuals in their daily lives, nor has an effort been made to develop an index for monitoring the overall degree to which a target population is at risk. Yet such a physical safety index (or physical insecurity index) is feasible.

The key to commensurating various physical risks involves two variables: (1) time, or the duration of exposure to various risks (such as the amount of time spent on the highways or on the ski slopes), and (2) the magnitude of the risk. A profile of physical safety for any individual, then, can be constructed from a knowledge of the specific environmental context and attendant risks, the daily life choices facing the individual, and the amount (percentage) of time the individual is exposed to various risks. To obtain an index number, one need only sum the risk components and divide by the amount of time involved—a day, a week, a year.

This index could be useful in providing an overall picture of the relative riskiness of different life-styles or different geographical areas. For obvious reasons, local chambers of commerce might not welcome such comparisons, but a physical safety index would provide a useful (and biologically important) addition to our stock of social indicators. (Indeed, insurance companies routinely make use of such data in establishing insurance rates, though insurors generally do so on a piecemeal basis.)

the global measure I propose is Health: *Health in a broad (adaptive) sense is the capacity to function effectively in relation to the activities that are instrumental to survival and reproduction. It involves an ability to carry on normal functioning or to engage in productive activity.* Thus Health is a measure of the ability to perform those activities that are required for survival, self-care, and the care of others, especially offspring, in a given environment. It is not an either/or variable; it is continuous and to a degree context-specific.

My use of the term Health as a synonym for "fitness" is not precisely equivalent to its conventional meanings. (But it is not antithetical to such definitions as that of the World Health Organization: "A complete state of physical, mental and social well-being, not merely the absence of disease and infirmity.") It does not necessarily involve the absence of pain. Nor can it be equated with a subjective feeling of well-being or happiness (though they are highly correlated). More important, Health as fitness is not an end in itself. It is defined functionally as a means to the end of ensuring the survival of an individual or a population. Rather than treat Health as merely one domain of social concern among others, I view it as an outcome measure (or set of measures) which summarizes the combined influence of all the other relevant quality of life domains. This global concept of Health stands in a hierarchical relationship to the thirteen domains of primary needs.

The view that a holistic concept of Health is closely associated with adaptation is shared by others. Paul Baker writes: "Few would disagree that the survival and continuity of a population is a prime indicator of that group's adaptation to an environment, and the general health of a group is also widely accepted as an overall indication of success in adjusting to a specific environment."[263] There are also the seminal writings of the ecologist Stephen Boyden[264] and the richly documented monograph by the ecologist Valerius Geist, who outlines a theory of health based on an evolutionary framework. "Health is maximized," Geist writes, "when the diagnostic features of a species are maximized phenotypically."[265] Geist details a model based on what is known about human evolution and humankind's early life-style. The essence of that life-style, he attempts to show, involves "a great amount of diverse, skillful physical activity, of intense learning of knowledge and skills, of complex interactions with nonpeers, of long-lasting intense social bonds, of developing mastery over a broad range of difficult tasks and a high level of discipline over one's intellect and emotions, and also a life filled with humor, good fellowship, a thorough exercise of bodily pleasures, and a diet both abundant and of high quality. To maximize health is to maximize humanity."[266]*

* In effect, Geist develops an argument that has been made repeatedly in recent years: that we have been tailored by natural selection for the sort of environment that existed in the late

(Continued)

Some researchers in the social indicators field have also fixed on the overriding importance of Health. Ben-Chieh Liu speaks of his search for indicators "which adequately reflect the overall 'health' of the nation and its citizens' well-being."[267] Shonfield and Shaw allude to an aspiration for measures of the "state of health" of a nation.[268] Likewise, Campbell et al. found in their survey that people rated health the single most important factor affecting their well-being.[269]

One consequence of this convergence on health has been a series of efforts to develop better measures of health status. One notable example, the Olson Indicator, "Expectation of a Healthy Life," appeared in *Toward a Social Report.* Another is the "State of Health" indicator developed by A. J. Culyer et al. A third is Martin Chen's "Population Health Index," based on mortality and disability data.[270]

The most serious problem with these research efforts concerns the conspicuous absence of a theoretical base. There is no adequate definition of good health among social scientists, much less a consensus on what aspects to measure or how to aggregate indicators. At times good health is equated with longevity or with data on life expectancy; at other times deaths are lumped together with bed disability and the subjective experience of pain. Weighting scales, when they are constructed, are marked by a high degree of arbitrary judgment. Pragmatic arguments are used to justify other approaches; that is, the appropriate measure of good health is whatever can easily be measured.

I have been pursuing a dual strategy. On the one hand, there is a long-range aspiration that for the present can be pursued only on a piecemeal basis. This involves developing empirical indicators for each of the primary needs and determining more precisely their relationship to adaptiveness. But since this framework embraces much of the combined biobehavioral and social sciences, it is a research objective that will require many years and involve a large number of specialities. My own contributions to this strategy are mainly in the area of indicators for physical safety, nutrition, and environmental health.

The short-range strategy involves an effort to develop an economical summary measure of Health that could serve as an indirect master indicator. An index of Population Health (*qua* fitness) can be developed along the

---

Paleolithic and early Neolithic eras and that a life-style approximating that context is what we are best suited for. This is a modernized version of the traditional appeal by social theorists from Plato to Marx to the "state of nature." Yet Geist's argument differs in that he attempts a systematic review of the available evidence. While I might criticize some of his interpretations and conclusions, I endorse and follow a compatible approach. The concept of global Health as defined here represents an indispensable baseline for measuring the consequences of cultural practices and policies as well as our choices for the future.

following general lines: If the basic criterion of global Health is the capacity to function productively, an appropriate "fitness unit" (let us call this unit a "Darwin") would be *one day free of restriction in the ability to function normally.*[271] "Normally" means in accordance with norms which can be specified in various ways that are not mutually exclusive: societal work and productivity standards, medical standards, specific physiological and mental tests (such as those used in military recruitment and astronaut selection), and even self-evaluations. (This approach is not entirely hypothetical; the National Center for Health Statistics routinely surveys the U.S. population and reports on the number of people whose activities have been "restricted" during the reporting year because of acute illness or various chronic conditions.) Whether the individual chooses to use his or her capacities productively, or is permitted by society to do so, is another matter.

Accordingly, the number of "Darwins" available to each individual during one year would be 365. And the maximum number of "Darwins" available to an entire population would equal the size of the population multiplied by 365. (Births during the year would add units to the total "stock," just as deaths would deplete it.) Of course, no population ever realizes its maximum potential productivity. Decrements, or losses, occur in three ways, through mortality, morbidity, and other restrictions of activity. My approach, then, has been to construct an index based on an assessment of such decrements.*

For trial purposes, consider the following example. In 1970, according to the *Statistical Abstract of the United States,* there were approximately 203,850,000 people in this country at the outset of the year and some 206,100,000 at the end of the year. Assuming an equal distribution throughout the year of births, deaths, and migrations, we can assume a net gain of some 1,125,000 person/years to the population (2.25 million divided by two). On any given day during 1970, about 2.1 million Americans were incarcerated in jails, mental hospitals, detention homes, nursing homes, and the like. In addition, some 27.1 million people suffered a physical handicap (to which I will arbitrarily assign a 20 percent average decrement in functional capacities, in the absence of specific data). Some 8 million people were in bed with

* Culyer and his colleagues used a similar measure in their composite "State of Health" index.[272] However, they proposed an arbitrary ten-point scale ranging from 0 for "normal" to 10 for "dead." My system, based on the use of a common measuring unit, allows each death to be quantified in terms of the number of days of productive activity lost during a given period. Similarly, days or fractions of days lost through morbidity and restricted activity can also be quantified. They can then be summed and subtracted from the maximum number of fitness units potentially available to the individual or to the population as a whole. When this total is divided by the theoretical maximum number, the result represents an overall measure of the efficiency, or fitness *qua* Health, of the individual or the population.

various illnesses, and perhaps as many more were walking around with illnesses that produced at least a 10 percent functional decrement. Many of those listed as chronic alcoholics and drug addicts (about 5.5 million), mental retardates (6 million), people with minimal brain dysfunction (12 million), those with congenital deformities (5 million), and those with chronic conditions such as arthritis, heart problems, and hearing, sight, speech, and reading disorders (some 25 million) overlap significantly with one another and with those in other categories. Because there is no way of eliminating this overlap on the basis of the available statistical sources, I will estimate that only one-half of these "others" had not already been counted and that each individual has on the average a 20 percent functional decrement. Finally, we must include the large number of Americans who suffer from obesity, stress, heavy smoking, and other conditions that put them at a higher illness and mortality risk and may modestly impair their functioning. This number could be nearly half the population by some estimates, but let us conservatively put the figure at about 20 million and assign them a 10 percent loss of functional efficiency. Adding up our estimates, we get a total of 24.76 million person/years of functional losses, or 12.08 percent of the potential stock of "Darwins." Thus the overall Population Health Index or fitness index for the year 1970 is estimated to have been .879 out of a possible 1.0.

I believe that this is an appropriate summary measure of any society's relative efficiency in ensuring that the basic needs of its population are met. The foregoing example is, admittedly, a crude first cut, but it can be improved. Such an index can be used in a time series to track changes through time, and it can be used to compare populations. This approach to valuing health, mortality, morbidity, and the restriction of activity is not meant to be the only way of valuing human life or human suffering; it is just one formula, designed to assess (in part) the survivability and overall fitness of a population.

A number of conceptual and methodological problems remain to be resolved before such an index could be put to use. For instance, what should be counted as productive activity? If productivity in survivalist terms is not precisely equivalent to economic productivity and gainful employment, how do we measure it empirically? How should we treat social constraints on productive activity—such as being in prison? There are many problems associated with measuring the incidence of specific causes of morbidity and activity restriction and, more important, the practical consequences in terms of functional incapacities. (How do we count the effects of a hangover? or the productivity of a bedridden individual?) Yet these problems do not appear to be insurmountable, and the basic approach seems sound.

Some critics might object that this approach embodies the fallacy of "growthmania," a bias in favor of the view that a larger population or more economic growth is necessarily better. However, the opposite may be true;

be true; additions to the population (or the GNP) add to population-level fitness only when they do not adversely affect the fitness of the other members. Only when there are net increases in the overall adaptation of the population will more be better. This may provide a solution to the vexing problem of how to define operationally the "optimum number" for a given population. As it happens, my approach coincides with what economists call Pareto optimality: *The optimum number in any given environmental and sociocultural context consists of a population size beyond which any increases will fail to improve the adaptiveness* (*the functional efficiency*) *of the aggregate.* Far from endorsing Garrett Hardin's "Tragedy of the Commons," this approach is compatible with a limits-to-growth perspective.

A corollary of this point is the charge some hard-line individual selectionists might make that this approach is unsound because it is aligned with group selectionists. Thus it may seem to some that this approach subordinates individual fitness to "the good of the species." Again, the opposite is the case. The charge confuses what is essentially an empirical analytical criterion with a normative prescription. This approach does not prescribe individual reproductive restraint; at the level of individual adaptation, my schema is neutral with respect to the issue of how many offspring an individual might have. This approach is concerned with functional adaptation, which may not equate perfectly with the population geneticist's criterion of Darwinian fitness. Functional adaptation is a necessary but not a sufficient condition for reproductive success. At the population level, fitness *qua* functional efficiency merely sums the consequences of individual actions and interactions, whatever they may be. The suggestion that individual actions might have negative systemic effects should raise no eyebrows; it is a common occurrence in nature and a well-established principle in theoretical ecology.

Basic Needs, Human Nature, and Human Behavior

How does this framework relate to the causes of human behavior and cultural evolution? The central issue is the relationship between the functional problem of adaptation (the problem of survival and reproduction) and our behavior. It is a straightforward deduction from the premise stated above: Survival is the basic problem for all life forms and the fundamental purpose (teleonomy) underlying human behavior is adaptation. Richard Dawkins claims that we are "survival machines," robot vehicles blindly programmed to preserve the selfish molecules known as genes.[273] But this is a crude and inaccurate caricature. Rather than being robotlike, we are complex, hierarchically organized systems, purposive systems with remarkable emergent (systemic) properties.

Such mechanistic images leave out the core characteristic of the human organism—that it has a mind of its own. This view is not an appeal to metaphysics but an insistence on the cardinal distinction between a machine that is nothing more than the embodiment of exogenous purposes (for Dawkins, the endogenous purposes of individual genes) and a system that has partially autonomous, systemic purposes (teleonomy).

"Human nature" has recently been revivified as a legitimate object of scientific enquiry.* This is not to say that there is agreement on the subject; as long as so much remains unknown to science, there will be room for argument. The classical Freudian model of human nature posits an interaction between innate and acquired elements—between instinctual drives (id), internalized values and norms (superego), and rational means-ends faculties (ego). The early "hydraulic" model of Konrad Lorenz combined the notion of action-specific energy with Wallace Craig's twofold model of drives (appetitive and consummatory actions) and a strongly internalist view of the mechanisms of behavior (e.g., "action patterns").

The classical Skinnerian model, by contrast, makes few concessions to the organism. To be sure, there are drives which environmental reinforcers serve to "reduce" (in a later version, "deprivations" that are "satisfied"). However, "the variables of which behavior is a function lie outside of the organism."[274] "Whatever we do, and hence however we perceive it, the fact remains that it is the environment which acts upon the perceiving person, not the perceiving person who acts upon the environment."[275] There is little need or scientific justification for looking inside the black box: "When what a person does is attributed to what is going on inside of him, investigation is brought to an end," Skinner claims, in apparent ignorance of neurobiology, psychobiology, psychophysiology, and endocrinology.[276]

At the other extreme is the humanistic model, in which our energies are directed at climbing the ladder toward the attainment of our "higher" needs. As the humanistic psychologist Carl Rogers expresses it, "Behavior is basically the goal-directed attempt of the organism to satisfy its needs as experienced, in the field as perceived."[277] The central tendency, Rogers says, is "toward fulfillment, toward actualization, toward the maintenance and enhancement of organisms."[278]

This longstanding debate over the sources of human behavior involves a nested set of issues: (1) the underlying purposes, functions, or orientation of behavior; (2) the relative importance of internal versus external sources of causation and control (nature versus nurture); (3) the relative importance of genetic, ontogenetic, and real-time mechanisms; (4) the role of the mind *qua* consciousness and rationalistic choice-making processes; and (5) the rela-

* In fact, it never disappeared completely. It was only masked by such neologisms as "drives" (Hull, Skinner, Miller), "neurognostic models" (Laughlin and D'Aquili), "biograms" (Count), "*angebornes schema*" (Lorenz), "engrams" (Lashley), "schemata" (Piaget), "pexgos" (Bindra), "plans" (Miller, Galanter and Pribram, Bowlby), "programs" (Mayr), and "cognitive maps" (Tolman, Hallowell, Barkow).

tive importance of cognitive versus affective influences. The model of behavior that I adopt, derived from cybernetics and control system theory, can at least synthesize, if not reconcile, these positions.

The Interactional Paradigm is anchored by the basic needs structure identified in Figure IV, an approach that parallels that of the humanistic psychologists but with a different orientation toward needs. Here biological needs provide the basic *raison d'être* of human behavior. At the outset, however, we need to differentiate between needs as functional requisites and the causal mechanisms that underlie behavior (motivations, urges, impulses, goals). For our conscious goals and learned behaviors may not be tightly coupled to our evolved biological needs or to strict Darwinian fitness. There is no necessary connection between functional requisites and behavioral causes—but there is a strong connection in fact. That connection has been established in the first instance by natural selection and in the second instance by teleonomic selection, behavioral choices that affect organism-environment relationships. Recall that natural selection is not an agent but an open-ended process involving functional influences and their consequences. That is, functional effects are the causes of evolutionary continuities and changes—of natural selection—insofar as evolution is governed by functional (teleonomic) processes rather than stochastic or deterministic influences. (Recall also Sewall Wright's airplane metaphor.) The quintessence of natural selection, then, is a generalized, transgenerational version of the Law of Effect.

We begin to glimpse the possibility of a theoretical synthesis between natural selection and learning theory. Natural selection involves a version of the Law of Effect in relation to transgenerational continuities and changes in genotypes, phenotypes, and genome types. That is, varying functional consequences may result in differential survival and reproduction of the mechanisms responsible for functionally consequential effects. On the other hand, the behaviorist Law of Effect reflects an analogous selective process within the lifetime of an organism, a selection process that involves behavioral alternatives. I call this process teleonomic selection because it is cybernetic and not deterministic; it involves a purposive interaction between organisms and their environments. Behaviorist theory is not wrong, it is merely incomplete because the organism is treated as an equipotential or at best as a poorly articulated "black box" that responds mechanistically to its environment. When a complex, self-organizing, goal-oriented cybernetic system is put into the black box, the Law of Effect can more accurately be seen to involve a teleonomic interaction between the organism and the environment in which the selective "effects" are co-determined by both the organism and the environment. (Haugeland calls it an "intentional black box" model.[279]) Furthermore, those teleonomic selections which differentially affect adaptation and, ultimately, reproductive success also become instrumentalities of natural selection as well. The same processes are involved. The distinction relates to different functional levels—to the difference between the immediate gratification of a motivational state versus longer-range fitness consequences ("proximate" versus "ultimate" functions).* The same event can have consequences on both levels at once.

If I should develop a smoking habit, for example, it would involve an instance of the Law of Effect (in my terms, teleonomic selection). There are immediate gratifications. But if the long-range consequence is an adverse effect on my Health (*qua* adaptation), including the number and the well-being of my offspring, my smoking habit will be maladaptive in Darwinian terms. Assuming that a differential prepotency for becoming addicted to cigarettes is heritable, which might well be so, these positive reinforcers in behaviorist terms will have negative consequences as instrumentalities of natural selection.

Perhaps the way to get a better purchase on the relationship between behavior and adaptation is to pose the question, What is it that makes a potential reinforcer reinforcing (or nonreinforcing) in specific contexts? In the past, relatively few psychologists probed the subject deeply, and even fewer fully appreciated the necessity for a dualistic, interactional view. One who did was psychologist Edward C. Tolman, whose "purposive behaviorism" was articulated in *Purposive Behavior in Animals and Men* (1932). This underrated classic is worthy of note because Tolman's formulation was superior to the crude oversimplifications that prevailed in that era and because it was fundamentally sound, whatever its shortcomings by today's standards. Only now is psychology catching up with the basic framework Tolman proposed.[280]

Tolman insisted that behavior is a "molar" phenomenon, not simply a chain of "stimuli" and mechanical "responses." Established "behavior-acts," he argued, must be viewed as "emergent" wholes that are inherently purposive, or means-ends oriented. They involve ordered "patterns" that are not haphazard, that manifest a high degree of economy or efficiency (here Tolman anticipated Zipf's Law of Least Effort and similar formulations). In addition,

* The concept of functional levels is important to an understanding of the full dynamics of biological causation, and it provides the means for reconciling such apparently antagonistic approaches to social analysis as sociobiology, "pure functionalism" (in Malinowski's term), and structural-functionalism. Contrary to the opinions of some critics, there are indeed functional requisites associated with social organizations, and these requisites may well explain certain features and behavioral properties of organizations. However, the explanation of why a particular organization evolved in the first place may involve causes that can be traced to other functional levels. By the same token, the functional requisites of an organization are not sufficient to account for the behavior of individual participants. Nor does it follow that what is functional for the organization is functional for the wants of the individual, or that what is immediately gratifying for the individual is functional for ultimate reproductive success.

behavior-acts involve "cognition," by which Tolman meant a tight linkage to the total configuration of environmental "contingencies"—not just reinforcers but the array of conditions, or "parameter values" that must remain constant across repetitions if the behavior is to be repeated without disruption. In other words, reinforcers are by no means the only environmental influence.

As an example Tolman cited his favorite experimental animal, the laboratory mouse *Mus norvegicus albinus.* Once a laboratory animal learns to run a maze, Tolman pointed out, the routine repetition of the pattern is contingent on there being no drastic change in the characteristics of the maze, the route to the goal-box, the location of the goal-box, or the reinforcement schedule. Otherwise there will be some behavioral perturbation. Today we would characterize this process in cybernetic terms: The animal is following a feedback-controlled behavioral program, and its behavior is a function of both the program and the environment in which the program occurs.

Finally, and most important, the "purposes" that Tolman imputed to behavior were in his view derived from various "in-lying drives" and initiating physiological states (both positive and "aversive") that are to be found within the organism. However, he emphasized that these internal sources alone do not cause behavior. The "initiating causes," he said, are the *combinations* of internal motivation states and external stimuli. The actual topography—the "behavioral-determinants" or efficient causes—also include the "capacities" and "cognitions" (both innate and learned) of each individual and the characteristics of the goal-objects themselves. "But surely any 'tough-minded' reader will now be up in arms," Tolman surmised. "And this surely will be offensive to any hard-headed, well-brought-up psychologist of the present day. And yet, there seems to be no other way out. Behavior . . . [as a molar phenomenon] *is* purposive and *is* cognitive."[281]

As we have seen, the radical behaviorist banner has become tattered and shot full of holes. There are one-trial learning, latent learning, autoshaping, preparedness and contrapreparedness, stimulus selectivity, innate learning predispositions, insight learning, observational learning (or modeling), nonreinforced imprinting, and what Lorenz called vacuum activity (or "appetitive" stimulus seeking by an animal). There are also James Olds's experiments with intrinsic, or self-generated psychic rewards and Kagan and Berkun's experiments with wheel-running rats, in which behaviors were conditioned without environmental reinforcers in the classical sense.[282] Even more telling are the behaviors that are performed relentlessly despite negative reinforcements. Consider the spawning salmon, the agony of the long-distance runner, and what ought to be the discouraging effects of labor pains for the reproductive preferences of the human female. This class of phenomena cries out for psychologists to learn from economists and begin using multi-valued, benefit-cost (decision-making) approaches to behavioral analysis. Sacrifices in terms of one value (say, energy or physical comfort) are frequently made to obtain other values—achievement, esteem, offspring. (A start along these lines has been made by Herrnstein with his "relative law of effect.")

There are hard-core theoretical contradictions in classical learning theory that have not to my knowledge been properly reconciled. If operant behavior is a direct "function" of the contingencies of reinforcement, why is intermittent reinforcement more potent in shaping the strength of a behavior (its resistance to extinction) than continuous reinforcement? And why does continuous reinforcement often lead not to more repetitions but to periods of satiation? Why do animals sometimes learn without reinforcements (as in "latent learning") and sometimes "habituate" and become progressively less likely to respond? Why do different species display qualitatively different learning abilities?[283] And why is there evidence that in some cases animals prefer to work for reinforcements rather than have a free lunch?

One can begin to make sense of such anomalies only by turning away from the simplistic behaviorist model and looking at the animal itself, as ethologists and physiologists have done. It is not enough to think in terms of biological boundaries to learning processes. Biological processes potentiate, motivate, canalize, and make possible the programming (learning) of various behaviors. As Tolman saw clearly, internal motivational propensities and capacities *interact* with the animal's previous experience (its "cognitive map") and real-time environmental influences to shape the precise contours of behavior. A reinforcer reinforces, then, because of the properties of both the animal and the environment *qua* systems. It is the functional relationship (the interactions) between an organism and its environment that results in hunger pangs being satisfied, anxieties being allayed, sexual appetites being sated, physical discomforts being removed, and curiosity being quenched.

Commonplace descriptions of internal psychobiological states can no longer be treated by psychologists as "mental fictions"[284] or as the unproven speculations of lay persons.* The behavioral substrate is not a black box. The internal

* There has always been in Skinner's theoretical posture a false dichotomy between the "environment" and autonomous "mental states" (or "free will").[285] He rejects the latter, of course, and he denies the causal efficacy of affective states. They are merely "collateral products" of the behavioral process. "We both strike [someone] and feel angry for a common reason, and that reason lies in the environment. . . . [Affective states] have no explanatory force."[286] Or, sex may feel good, but it is only a collateral effect (of what he does not say).[287] He denies the hypothesis that intrinsic reinforcements such as relief from pain, release from fear, dissolution of loneliness, and the "pursuit of happiness" might have causal potency. All appeals to inner sources of behavior Skinner categorizes as prescientific metaphysics.

Yet Skinner has recently acknowledged a second category of "phylogenic" (presumably he means "phylogenetic") behavior that is not based on reinforcement principles. This category, it becomes clear, is a concession to the ethologist's "fixed action patterns," "imprinting," and so forth. So it turns out that there can be inner sources of behavior after all. (Skinner does not reconcile this *ad hoc* shift with his earlier dogmatism.) Even more telling is the fact that

(Continued)

correlates and efficient causes of such potentiating states are being mapped with increasing precision and detail, and it is clear that the behaving organism is a complex dynamic system with decisively cybernetic properties.

One example relates to our nutritional needs. Food, the paradigmatic reinforcer, can have different reinforcing effects in different contexts. The reinforcing properties of food are in part a function of the individual's nutritional needs and the nutritional properties and tastes of specific foods. For a person who goes several hours without eating, the reinforcing potency of food increases. Moreover, the continued nonreinforcement of hunger can quickly become punishing (this is the negative reinforcement of noneating). For a person who is eating, it decreases. If one is then surfeited with positive reinforcements (overeats), the result may also be punishing: There may be acute discomfort. And if one should decide to diet, thereby imposing higher-level cybernetic control over one's appetite, the punishing consequences of going without food may be offset by the rewards associated with losing weight. After a short time the body undergoes changes. It begins to metabolize its own fat and produces ketones that act to suppress the appetite, thereby modifying the internal reward-punishment structure so that food becomes less positively reinforcing and the failure to eat less punishing. Finally, our behavioral systems are so constructed that we are able to learn elaborate forms of instrumental activities in anticipation of hunger, including activities that on the surface seem only remotely related to the food quest (my writing this book, for instance). The human food quest is clearly not limited to the production of "operants." It may also involve observational learning, imitation, symbolic (linguistic) learning, and what decision scientists call "value-driven experimentation," goal-oriented trial-and-error processes and innovations. The behaviorist black box model cannot even begin to make sense of all this. Nor can any other dichotomized nature-or-nurture viewpoint. Nor can an entire botanical garden full of drives. On the other hand, a biocybernetic model of behavior *can* make sense of it, I maintain.

The Cybernetic Model

Our adaptive success as a species with a heritage of more than three billion years is due to the fact that our ancestors (and ancestral species) acquired

---

while Skinner has long recognized the existence of drives (which he links to his reinforcers), he has never conceded that drives are unobservable "inner states" and that they have causal potency! Finally, although Skinner has admonished us to eschew "mentalistic" explanations of behavior, in his role as social reformer he informs us that it is possible to "design" better social practices, that a more humane and rational environment can be "explicitly designed."[288] If he is to avoid contradicting himself, Skinner must assume either that such "designs" are not the result of inner states or that they do not have causal efficacy. I say humbug.

an elaborate system of biologically based mechanisms designed to link our basic adaptive needs to appropriate environmental conditions and instrumentalities. That linkage—that set of functional relationships—is established and maintained primarily by our behavioral systems (and the morphological and neurological equipment that makes our behavior possible).

But to say that our behavior is fundamentally a biological phenomenon is not equivalent to asserting that it is instinctive, in the sense of a rigidly predetermined program. Rather, our behavior is fundamentally cybernetic in nature. The human organism, inclusive of its behavior, exhibits the properties of a complex biocybernetic system. These properties include: (1) systemic goal-directedness, including many instrumental subgoals; (2) interaction among functionally specialized components or subsystems; (3) hierarchical organization, with higher levels being more encompassing and integrative; (4) synergism (systemic properties that cannot be predicted from an understanding of the components); (5) interactions with the external environment across system boundaries (inputs and outputs); (6) internal control or self-regulation in relation to systemic goals and subgoals; (7) a complex system of learning capabilities; (8) communications processes, both within the system and between the system and its environment; (9) positive and negative feedback, a class of information inputs related specifically to controlling the behavior of the system; (10) historicity (biocybernetic systems are irreversible processes that take place through time); and (11) negentropy (cybernetic systems appear to resist the Second Law of Thermodynamics because their processes do not lead inherently to a state of maximum disorder and energy dispersal. Exactly the reverse is true; they create order and concentrate energy).[289*]

The key to understanding how a cybernetic system operates (in its simplest form) is to envision it as an integral part of a loop that includes (a) the system, (b) the system's environment, and (c) inputs from the environment, including feedback from the system's outputs into the environment (see Figure V). Unlike other models of behavior, the cybernetic model posits that the behavior of the system involves a relationship between internal goals ("reference signals") and environmental inputs ("sensor signals"). Cybernetic systems are so constructed that they act to achieve and maintain a dynamic stability (a "zero error signal") in relation to their environments.

Thus behavior is "caused" in a cybernetic system by both the internal goal structure of the system and the status of the system in relation to these goals. The desired relationship between the system and its environment is defined by a set of internal referents, and these are "compared" to the actual relationship as indicated by various external inputs (witness Tolman's maze

* I use feedback in the technical, cybernetic sense: information that regulates and/or modifies a goal-directed, dynamic process.

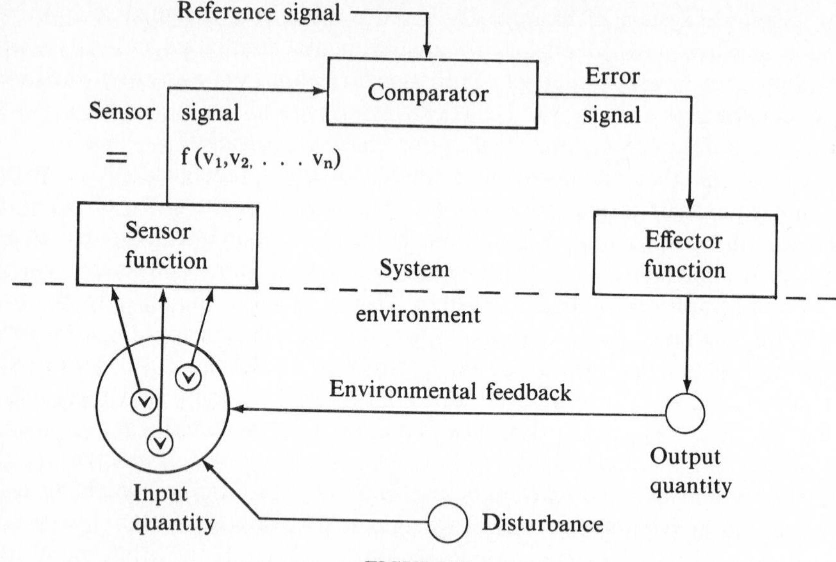

FIGURE V
A cybernetic control system. (From W. T. Powers, "Feedback: Beyond Behaviorism," *Science* 179 [1973]: 351–356.) Copyright 1973 by the American Association for the Advancement of Science. Reprinted by permission.

runners). Therefore Skinner is wrong when he asserts that environmental stimuli "exert control" over behavior.[290] The locus of control is the relationship between the sensing organism and its environment.

The systems theorist William T. Powers has shown that the behavior of such a system can be described mathematically in terms of its tendency to oppose an environmental disturbance of an internally controlled quantity. The derivation of this relationship, briefly, is as follows. Let us suppose that a controlled quantity q_c represents some function (or analog) of certain environmental variables $f\ (v_1, v_2 \ldots v_n)$, such that $q_c = 0$ when the system is in equilibrium. Disregarding signs, if a change in this controlled quantity Δq_c is equal to $g(d)$, where d is a quantitatively measurable disturbance affecting at least some of the variables and g is a function describing the relationship between the disturbance and the controlled quantity; and if h represents a function of the environmental relationship between the controlled quantity and the system's output o such that $\Delta\ q_c = h(o)$; then, assuming control is good, when $g(d) \approx -h(o)$, $\Delta q_c \approx 0$. That is to say, the system will operate in such a way that some function of its output quantities will be nearly equal and opposite to some function of a disturbance in some or all of those environmental variables that affect the controlled quantity, with the result that the controlled quantity will remain nearly at its zero point.

Consider this problem: When a rat is taught to obtain a food reward by pressing a lever in response to a light signal, the animal learns the instrumental lever-pressing behavior *and* learns to vary its behavior patterns in accordance with where it is in the cage when the light signal occurs, so that whatever the animal's starting position, the outcome is always the same. Now, how is the rat able to vary its behavior in precise, purposeful ways so as to produce a constant result? Some behaviorists have postulated environmental cues that modify the properties of the main stimulus acting on the animal and so modify the animal's behavior. But this is implausible. As Powers has pointed out, it requires the modifying cues to work with quantitative precision on the animal's nervous system; these cues are hypothetical and have never been elucidated; and most important, these cues cannot deal with novel situations in which the animal has had no opportunity to learn modifying cues. A far more parsimonious explanation is that the animal's behavior is purposive: The rat varies its behavior in response to immediate environmental feedback in order to achieve an endogenous subgoal (food), which in this case also involves a learned sub-subgoal (pressing the lever).*

The cybernetic model described above is greatly simplified and portrays only the most rudimentary example. More complex cybernetic systems are not limited to maintaining any sort of simple and eternally fixed steady state, or "homeostasis" in Cannon's durable term. In a complex system, overarching goals may be maintained by means of an array of hierarchically organized subgoals that may be pursued contemporaneously, cyclically, or seriatim; specific subgoals may be recurrent, emergent as a system develops through time, or emergent as the environment changes. On occasion the destabilizing and reorganizing of lower-level goals may serve to enhance higher-level stability or viability. Another class of cybernetic processes involves positive feedback, or "deviation amplifying feedback" in Maruyama's characterization. Positive feedback may produce processes of positive growth and development ("morphogenesis"). In other words, reference signals and feedback processes within a complex system may themselves vary in a purposeful way (as

* To my knowledge, Roger Brown and Richard Hernnstein are the first mainstream psychologists to adopt the cybernetic model of drives and motivation. While they do not explicitly identify it as cybernetic, their model incorporates the concepts of internal regulators and feedback.[291] The different reactions of Skinner and Konrad Lorenz to the cybernetic model are also revealing. Skinner acknowledges them grudgingly and claims there is nothing new in them. Such "computer metaphors," he says, involve systems that make decisions and behave; this is no different from the clay tiles of two thousand years ago.[292] In fact it is quite different. Skinner confuses record keeping with dynamic, goal-oriented behavior. More important, he fails to see that the concepts of goals and feedback control represent a fundamental challenge to the black box model. In contrast, Lorenz fully understands the implications of the cybernetic model, has abandoned his own crude hydraulic formulation, has embraced the cybernetic approach, and explores its implications at length in *Behind the Mirror* (1977).

in the nutritional example above). Some subgoals may be genetically preprogrammed, while others may be learned or unlearned, as appropriate (in human behavior, for example, the many culturally conditioned ways of satisfying our basic nutritional needs). Locker and Coulter refer to us as "teleogenic systems."

The classical Skinner box experiments with pigeons and rats and the early ethological studies of discrete traits in greylag geese and three-spined stickleback drew attention away from the question of how behavior is organized as a lifelong process. How are the elements integrated? How are the priorities set? How are time and energy budgeted in relation to the multifaceted nature of the survival problem? What are the bioeconomic strategies by which the human being (or any animal) attempts to earn a living in the economy of nature? In reality, human behavior involves not a randomly constructed chain of responses but an ordered, dynamically interrelated set of activities (and choices) that may encompass every one of the basic needs described above.

Consider data for a fairly typical American adult male (in fact a composite of eighteen individuals in various walks of life*). In the course of a 24-hour weekday this person spends about 7.75 hours sleeping, about 8.5 hours at work (producing income), 1.2 hours in transportation, 1.4 hours in activities related to satisfying nutritional needs, 1.1 hours in activities related to physical health (washing, bathing, dressing, brushing teeth, exercising), about .9 hours in activities related to reproduction and child nurturance, and 1.6 hours in acquiring information not related to work (television news, newspapers, magazines, conversations), about one-half of which is combined with other activities. In sum, about 88 percent of this person's average workday is related to "the basics." Weekend and holiday activities lower the overall daily average even though many of the basics must still be satisfied on days off. A reasonable estimate for time spent on the basics would be about 75 percent of the individual's total time budget.

Or consider how Americans allocate their incomes. On the average, a family of four with an intermediate income living in a metropolitan area in 1970 spent approximately 84 percent of its income on the basics—food, clothing, shelter, transportation, furnishings, utensils and tools, communications, medical care, insurance, and (through taxes) such public services as fire and police protection, roads, sanitation, education, and defense—according to the *Statistical Abstract of the United States.* Although many of these needs may be more than comfortably satisfied for some of us, they remain basic needs.

It can hardly be said, then, that we have been freed from the problem of adaptation, that our behavior is only loosely related to, or that it is not to

* Preliminary results of a pilot survey conducted in Santa Clara County, California, January 16–27 and July 18–22, 1981.

some degree rationally organized in relation to, our adaptive needs, even though some behavioral scientists may doggedly continue to claim otherwise.

On the contrary, behind the daily routines, the stable habit patterns, and the often marginally conscious choices and decisions that we make, both from day to day and in relation to long-range objectives, there are often implicit adaptive functions. Very often behavioral acts that seem unrelated to survival needs may in fact be linked hierarchically through elaborately organized Action Structures (as I call them). For example, while I do not think about the almost automatic act of inserting and turning the ignition key in my car, in reality this act may be part of a complex means-ends hierarchy, or goal hierarchy, that is functionally related to satisfying, say, my nutritional needs. Starting my car in order to go and purchase food is instrumental through an Action Structure that I have both learned and modified to suit the particular cultural situation to the satisfaction of a primary need. When I stop to think about it, I know this to be so. I know that I have started my car because this action is functionally related to my continued survival. And I know that this functional connection has somehow played a causal role in shaping my decisions and actions. Furthermore, while there may be many alternative ways to meet this need in our society, this particular Action Structure is the most efficient among the available alternatives that I can perceive (or cognize, as the psychologists would say).

So it is with many aspects of my life. I may do (or not do) things only because I have been taught to do so and have been reinforced (rewarded or punished) for making such choices. Or I may do things only because "everyone else" does them. I may not even be aware that such choices have adaptive consequences. Some dramatic examples have been documented by medical anthropologist Alexander Alland, who found that primitive peoples often engage in hygienically sound cultural practices (frequent bathing, removal and burial of feces, isolation of the sick) even though they have no access to Western medical knowledge.[293]

Conversely, I often do things as a result of learned responses to immediate or anticipated external conditions that have direct physiological consequences—for example, dressing warmly on a cold day. I could certainly make the connection to my basic needs, if asked to do so. Indeed, one can make a parlor game of tracing how such innocuous acts as tying a shoe or sharpening a pencil may be instrumentally related to meeting basic needs. Normally it is inefficient to think consciously about such functional connections; I for one tend to orient my thinking toward a more proximate (efficient) level of causation. Thus it is fallacious to assert that survival-related actions occur only in the context of pain, suffering, or high anxiety. Rather, my life can be characterized as first and foremost a survival enterprise. Survival-related actions are a normal part of both my daily routines and my longer-range personal and family objectives. Often these routines are designed to reduce or prevent discomfort, pain, fear, and anxiety.

To picture more clearly the concept of a goal-oriented Action Structure, consider a comparison in simplified graphic form of the nutrition-related Action Structures of two individuals living in a hunter-gatherer and an advanced industrial society (see Figure VI).

Note that each Action Structure involves a goal hierarchy. What may be viewed as an intrinsically satisfying goal at one level of analysis and/or causation (relieving discomforts, passing exams, learning a skill) can be seen as an instrumentality at a higher level. Note also that a functional (adaptive) approach to behavior turns Maslow's hierarchy more or less upside down. In this approach, Maslow's "physiological needs" are to be found near the top of the hierarchy instead of at the bottom, and they are viewed as being in turn instrumental to higher-level goals, whereas the cerebral activities that Maslow placed at the top are viewed as being lower down in this hierarchy. Some may object that my approach demeans our humanity, but this is not so. My approach is oriented to the functional problem of survival and reproduction and not to our unquestionably worthy aspirations for human betterment.

Needless to say, this conceptualization implies no *a priori* stance on the relative importance in causing behavior of physiological motivators versus learned cultural responses, personal problem solving, teleonomic choice making, and various real-time situational determinants. All are likely to be involved to some degree. For instance, depending on the day of the week, the length and the nature of my shopping list, and the nature of the errands on my list of things to do, I may "decide" to use any of three local markets for my grocery shopping. Such decisions are determined in part by my biological needs, in part by a learned, culturally molded program, and in part by situational factors.[294]

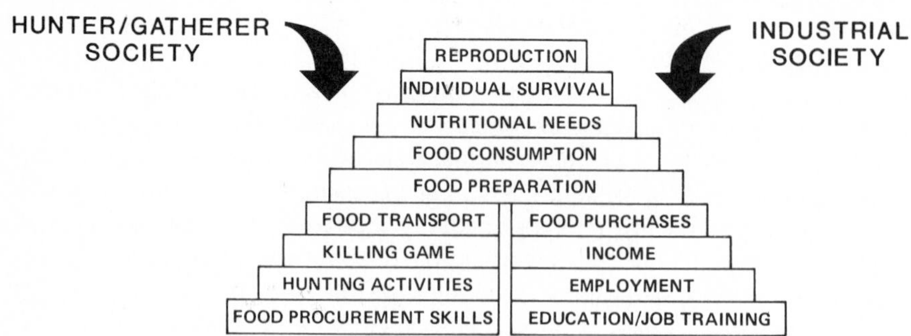

FIGURE VI

Nutrition-related action structures in primitive and modern societies. Note that at the highest levels in the hierarchy the goals are identical.

It should also be pointed out that the Action Structures for different needs overlap in such a way that many lower-level instrumentalities may serve two or more higher-level functions. Earning an income is the premier example, but not even an income is essential for all our needs. As humanistic theorists have long maintained, income may facilitate the satisfaction of our social needs, but it is neither necessary nor sufficient. On the other hand, the learning of appropriate social behaviors and modes of responding *is* necessary, if not sufficient, to the realization of satisfactory social relationships, and some individuals never master these skills.

The principle of hierarchical organization applies not only to the satisfaction of each need taken individually but to how we go about integrating the components of our overall adaptive strategies.[295] In humankind, as in other animals, coping with an immediate perceived threat to our physical safety will ordinarily displace any other activity—sleeping, eating, working, defecation, even sex. In such cases an elaborate and well-documented sequence of autonomic and biochemical responses suppresses many normal bodily functions (fatigue, hunger, digestion, peristalsis) and at the same time mobilizes the individual for emergency action (increased heart rate, increased respiration, the transfer of blood from skin and viscera to muscles and brain, the release of stored carbohydrates into the bloodstream). The only exceptions are cases that involve pathological individuals or in which the individual is prepared to trade off physical security for some predetermined goal and consequently exercises higher-level cybernetic control over what would otherwise be the normal, unmediated response propensity. The primordial examples are perhaps hunters who pursue a dangerous prey, soldiers who volunteer to go into battle, and parents who sacrifice themselves to save a child.

It is not so easy to assign fixed priorities to some of our other needs. This is because the nature and patterning of these needs fluctuate in complex ways and because degrees of freedom are involved. Some needs are fairly tightly linked to diurnal cycles (sleep, nutrition); others are emergent only under specific conditions or at a particular stage of the life cycle (thermoregulation, sex and reproduction); still others are closely keyed to our individual actions (mobility, communication). Nevertheless these needs impel us to establish both daily routines and behavioral priorities. And we are made aware of these priorities when we experience (or anticipate) disturbances or deprivations—hunger, thirst, fatigue, cold or heat, the discomfort associated with being unable to relieve oneself, emotional or psychic stresses, the pain of physical injury, the frustration of being unable to communicate, the general malaise associated with physical illness—that is, when we deviate from homeostasis, or "homeorhesis" (C. H. Waddington's term for a stable developmental pathway). Whatever the "emic" interpretations of various cultures (or cultural anthropologists), these biological priorities exert a powerful influence on the ways in which we organize (and sometimes reorganize) our behavior. Our long-range adaptive goals are fitted around and between short-term priorities for the most part and are more or less instrumental to their satisfaction.

The foregoing observations on the human condition may seem to be commonplace, yet they are very often overlooked or downgraded by social theorists who tend to fix their attention on our conscious goals and aspirations. It is myopic to suppose that as a rule we tend to maximize for any one value or need, be it energy, income, nutrition, children, or self-actualization. Normally our adaptive strategies involve efforts to strike some balance or compromise between our sometimes conflicting needs and goals. And those of us who fail to do so are sooner or later reminded of our mortality.

Conversely, both behaviorist psychology and sociobiology have downgraded a fundamental aspect of human behavior that has been well understood by perceptive observers since the time of classical Athens. Human beings have a capacity for superimposing rationalistic self-control "downward" on our impulses and sometimes on our basic biological needs. Like a muscle, that capacity may be more or less well developed. Among the more dramatic illustrations are the headline-making political protesters—self-immolating Buddhist monks, fasting political prisoners, terrorists who deliberately give their lives for a "cause." More impressive, though, are the myriad of everyday manifestations of the human capacity for the conscious self-denial of short-term "reinforcements" to achieve long-term goals. Familiar examples include the athlete who trains his or her body ruthlessly, the concert pianist who devotes many years of practice to his or her profession, and the priest who dedicates himself to celibacy and a lifetime of service.

On occasion this marvelous capacity for superordinate cybernetic control over our behavior may lead to a tragedy such as that of Jonestown or Masada. At other times the same capacity leads to our most exalted achievements, such awe-inspiring triumphs over manifest dangers or fear of the unknown as the great voyages of exploration. Indeed, we generally esteem self-control, and it colors many of our personal assessments of others, including the dieter who loses twenty pounds, the friend who stops smoking, the political leader who remains cool under pressure. On reflection it should be evident that we are surrounded by manifestations of an emergent level of cybernetic control (albeit imperfect) over our behavior as individuals (and collectively) that interacts with our more primitive, sometimes unconscious needs and urges. Because these higher-level sources of behavioral determination are excluded from the classical behaviorist and the implicit sociobiological models of behavior, such frameworks are fundamentally inadequate and are destined to be supplanted.

This is not to say that the inner workings of the remarkable organ we call the brain are now understood. While we have many insights, human behavior is organized and integrated within each individual in ways that are still imperfectly mapped. Some of the needs described above express themselves at the individual level in the form of motivational mechanisms that have been reasonably well pinpointed—for instance, the so-called deficiency motivations, such as hunger and thirst, which create internal distress and stimulate coping responses. In effect, such mechanisms involve a substrate of psychic punishments and rewards, punishments for not performing biologically necessary behaviors and rewards for doing so. Conversely, many maladaptive behaviors are discouraged by well-defined internal mechanisms that are designed to make such behaviors unpleasant, or aversive (the subjective experience of pain, various forms of discomfort, fear of the unfamiliar). Other needs, particularly those involving social, affiliative, and affectional behaviors, appear to have similar properties, but their biological substrates are less well understood.

There is also a class of emotional reactions, a set of innate "reference signals" which in effect remain at zero in a psychologically optimal environment. For instance, the "fear-fight, fear-flight" mechanism imposes on the organism a need for an unthreatening environment, and the neural substrate is so organized that it permits alternative coping responses that depend on the environmental context. Major elements of this substrate have been identified in the limbic system of the paleocortex. In a similar vein, boredom and frustration are normal responses to an environment lacking in stimulation and the opportunity for purposeful activity, and here the ascending reticular activating system in the upper brain stem is of particular importance. It is therefore safe to conclude that, in general, what we know about the neural organization of the human brain is consistent with the model I have described.

Teleonomic Selection

The process by which each person organizes and budgets his or her time and chooses among the available options and strategies for meeting needs and wants I call *teleonomic selection.* Teleonomic selection is a cybernetic process that involves a goal-directed interaction between (1) primary, biologically based needs as manifested in specific drives, motivation states, response predispositions, and capabilities; (2) culturally acquired (conditioned) instrumental needs, perceived needs, and wants; (3) learned cognitive maps, schemata, programs, instructions, or plans (depending on which of various essential similar theoretical formulations one prefers); (4) higher-level analytical and goal-setting capabilities (rationalistic decision-making functions); and (5) real-time inputs from the person's environment. In other words, teleonomic selection involves a model of behavior as a complex choice-making process that includes, but does not give an exclusive franchise to, human creativity and consciously premeditated actions.

Teleonomic selection can be viewed from at least three perspectives, or functional levels. At the *individual* level, teleonomic selection is the process by which each person (or each animal) establishes, maintains, or modifies adaptive relationships with the environment. At the *sociocultural* level, teleonomic selection is an aggregate of processes by which populations and organized groups adopt, maintain, or change cultural patterns and goal-directed social activities. At the *transgenerational* level, teleonomic selection may be an instrumentality of natural selection, insofar as there are functional consequences that affect either gene frequencies (genotypes) or the numbers and diversity of groups, populations, and species (genome types).

I chose the term teleonomic selection to reflect what I believe is an emerging model of behavioral causation that will ultimately replace the simplifying assumptions of earlier generations of social scientists (economic man). The scientific basis for this more sophisticated model, which might be called cybernetic man, has been suggested above; suffice it to say here that cybernetic man is only quasi-rational in terms of the basic assumption of the rational choice theorists. Even Herbert Simon's "bounded rationality" model, which acknowledges limitations on the information that may be available to a decision maker, is viewed here as insufficient. Cybernetic man or quasi-rational man is also constrained by a substantive *biological rationality* that interacts with considerations of efficiency in relating means to ends. This is not to say that the efficiency criterion, or the economy principle (after Bock and Wahlert), is not applicable. Rather, efficiency is constrained by other criteria and other factors, and this may result in reduced efficiency or deliberate trade-offs.

Accordingly, the matrix of causation that is necessary to account for a particular instance of teleonomic selection includes interactions among factors located in each of the four environments (internal, physical, biotic, and sociocultural). (I consider these interactions in more detail in Chapter V.) Just as natural selection refers not to the initial sources of change (say, a new mutation) but to the functional consequences of that change, so teleonomic selection refers not to cultural innovations or environmental changes *per se* but to selection based on the functional effects (or anticipated effects) of those changes in relation to the satisfaction of needs and wants. It is the perceived or actual utility, the rewarding or punishing (reinforcing) properties of the change, that count. Artifacts and behaviors that contribute to the satisfaction of needs and wants (needs and wants whose origins are, at a deep level, biological and a product of the evolutionary process) will be selectively favored, though for a variety of reasons favorable "variations" may sometimes fail to be adopted. Likewise, those that are nonrewarding, or negatively reinforcing, will be disfavored.

The vantage point that I employ for viewing the teleonomic selection process is the acting individual. However, the Interactional Paradigm is multileveled and looks both upward and downward. This framework attempts to amalgamate within a cybernetic model the perspective and theoretical work of the biological and brain sciences, classical drive-reduction theory, cognitive and Piagetian developmental psychology, learning theory, microeconomics and decision theory; human ecology and ecological anthropology, macroeconomics and structural-functionalist social science. It turns out that these are not mutually exclusive approaches but component elements or aspects of the whole. The *interactions* among these mechanisms and factors are the crucial ingredients. When linear, deterministic approaches to causation are replaced by an interactive, multileveled, cybernetic systems model, then the vexing argument over holism versus reductionism resolves itself into a one-word answer: both. It becomes possible to integrate causal influences at various levels of causation in such a way that one can observe and analyze how they interact. (Other theorists have recently made similar suggestions, though in most cases without being quite so inclusive.[296])

How do we explain a given act of food consumption—say, the dinner I am about to eat? The idea of genetic determinism is patently absurd. Yet my genes have shaped my biological constitution, in combination with various ontogenetic influences. Furthermore, the appetite that motivates me is a self-controlled physiological process that derives from a complex set of cellular, organismic, and neurological interactions; this also can be said to be partly determining. But my appetite is not a sufficient explanation. My ability to link my appetite to an appropriate set of reinforcers involves a set of cognitive representations that are in turn the result of prior learning on my part, learning shaped by my own unique cultural experience. But my cognitive map is not sufficient either; my appetite may have to wait until I finish writing this section. And instead of eating at home, I may decide to go out to dinner, thereby introducing higher-level teleonomic (cybernetic) control into the determination.

Further, the availability of food, in my refrigerator or at local restaurants, is dependent on a complex set of historically conditioned, interacting cultural, economic, ecological, and climatological causes, about which entire volumes could be written. That these "background" causes are not trivial becomes acutely obvious when the "normal" flow of foodstuffs is interrupted by a defective thermostat in my refrigerator, a trucking strike, a restaurant that goes out of business, an earthquake, an insurrection or a war, a bad harvest, or a killing frost.

In sum, there is no simple, deterministic explanation for the precise patterning of my nutritional behavior. It involves a specific, time-bound configuration of stochastic, teleonomic, and deterministic influences. However messy and complex it may be, this is the model of behavioral and social causation that must be incorporated into our thinking if we are to do justice to the subject matter.

The Interactional Paradigm is therefore antagonistic to the traditional academic disciplines as we have known them. Or better said, it is complementary. It insists on the need for giving equal status to an integrative interdiscipline, whether it be called sociobiology (in John Paul Scott's original ecumenical sense), biobehavioral science, biosocial science, or even biosocial ecology.

The notion that human behavior can be comprehended in terms of a selection process is not new. The assumption of rational choice can be found at the very roots of Western social theory, in Plato and Aristotle. From Adam Smith to the modern-day economists, economic theory has been based on the premises that economic decisions govern our actions, that our decisions are in turn governed by the criterion of self-interest, and that economic progress has been governed by improvements in our ability to satisfy our self-interests, our material needs and wants. The philosophical origins of this theme are at least as old as the Epicureans.

There has been a long (if not always illustrious) tradition of selectionism in the social sciences. The archetype was Herbert Spencer, whose "social selection" model predated *The Origin of Species.* Darwin, too, endorsed a behaviorally oriented group selectionist explanation of human evolution in *The Descent of Man.* However, these were fairly sophisticated and moderate formulations in comparison with the more one-sided and/or simplistic Social Darwinist writings that came to dominate British and American social theorizing during the late nineteenth and early twentieth centuries.[297] For most of those writers the central dynamic was competition at the institutional level. The struggle for existence was transferred without qualification to social organizations in capitalist societies, and the results were viewed in unabashedly Panglossian terms: whatever survived was the most adaptive, and vice versa. Fairly typical was the pronunciamento of anthropologist E. B. Tylor that "The institutions which can best hold their own in the world gradually supersede the less fit ones, and . . . this incessant conflict determines the general resultant course of culture."[298]*

Selectionist thinking did not die out with the demise of Social Darwinism, but it became muted. One finds less carnivorous forms of selectionism in, for example, the writings of Childe; Gerard, Kluckhohn, and Rapoport; Goldschmidt; Ginsberg; and R. Cohen.[299] The liberal economist Armen Alchain also adopted a more innocuous form of economic selectionism; he postulated that "realized positive profits," as opposed to profit maximization, is the criterion of economic survival. "Those who realize *positive profits* are the survivors; those who suffer losses disappear."[300]

Selectionism at the individual level was never entirely neglected in the

* In fact, Tylor was contradictory. On the one hand, he rejected Spencer's concept of the superorganism, declaring that collective action was never more than the result of various individual actions. On the other hand, he said that the societal evolution was concentrated in the clashes between institutions and the resulting vicissitudes.

theorizing of earlier generations. Albert Keller, a disciple and Yale colleague of the formidable Charles W. Sumner, developed a variation-and-selective-retention model in relation to Sumner's concept of "folkways" that later served as an inspiration for psychologist Donald T. Campbell.[301] In the 1950s, both systems theorist H. Ross Ashby and zoologist J. W. S. Pringle recognized an analogy between individual learning processes and natural selection. Pringle's effort was particularly notable.[302] Adopting an explicit variation-and-selection model, he identified five different types of learning, based on the typology developed by Thorpe, that he believed could serve as mechanisms of behavioral change: habituation, conditioning, trial-and-error learning, insight learning, and imprinting.

Unfortunately, Pringle's pathbreaking effort went relatively unnoticed, and selection models were generally out of favor when Campbell, in a series of at first little-noticed articles, developed a "blind variation and selective retention" model of sociocultural evolution—at both the individual and the institutional levels.[303] This model has since been criticized on several grounds, notably (1) for the premise that behavioral variations are for the most part "blind"; (2) for positing a conflict between cultural selection and natural selection with regard to altruistic traits; and most important (3) for extreme cautiousness about what the mechanisms and the selection criteria are. The latter difficulty effectively removed his framework from the category of explanatory theory; in this all-important respect, the analogy with Darwin's concept of natural selection broke down.[304]

In recent years selectionist approaches to cultural evolution have mushroomed.[305] I differ mainly in that I propose a unified, multileveled cybernetic model of the human evolutionary process (biological and cultural) that involves selection processes across various time frames and units of organization, from transgenerational genetic changes to macro-level political decisions—decisions which could conceivably alter the course of the entire evolutionary process. (The indisputable example is all-out thermonuclear war.)

Social Cybernetics

Three further points are preliminary to developing my theory of societal evolution in detail. The first has to do with the significance of hierarchical organization (and causation) in biological processes. A starting point for understanding the dynamics of life processes in general and human societies in particular is the fact that it is hierarchically organized. This is hardly news; a great many illustrious theorists have discoursed on this subject over the years.[306] Nevertheless, it is fundamental to a thorough understanding of biological causation (inclusive of behavior and social organization), and it comes closer perhaps than anything I know to being an integrative, pandisciplinary principle. Thus the causal principles elucidated in Chapter III apply also to societal evolution. That is, hierarchical social organization is quintessentially an evolved, functional phenomenon. Hierarchical social organization comes into being and persists (or fails to persist) because of its functional properties in relation to goals that are pursued by social means.

The second point has to do with the fact that cybernetic processes (communications, "steering," and control) are a necessary concomitant of any complex, goal-oriented system (not excluding one-celled organisms) and that such processes occur at both organismic and superorganismic levels of organization. The biologist Howard Pattee, a specialist in systems theory, has observed:

> It is a central lesson of biological evolution that increasing complexity of organization is always accompanied by new levels of hierarchical controls. The loss of these controls at any level is usually malignant for the organization under that level. Furthermore, our experience with many different types of complex systems, both natural and artificial, warns us that loss of hierarchical controls often results in sudden and catastrophic failure. Simple tools may wear out slowly and predictably, but as systems grow in size and complexity they reach a limit where a new level of hierarchical control is necessary if the system is to function reliably.[307]

A cybernetic superstructure is a functional requisite for any complex dynamic system. The interactions that take place within and between functional levels involve not only matter and energy but information that serves to coordinate the functioning of the parts and the whole. Thus any selective environment that favors the emergence of a complex system (any context in which there is the potential for positive synergism) will also favor the emergence of a cybernetic infrastructure (though "opportunities" are not sufficient to *determine* the course of events).

Thus informational processes play a central role in the functioning of biological systems of all kinds. However, the utility of information-oriented analyses of biological and social processes has heretofore been limited by the problem of how to measure information flows adequately. The traditional Shannon-Weaver approach has been limited to measuring only the *quantity* of information (the number of binary "bits") in information transactions. Elsewhere I propose a solution to the problem of measuring the *quality,* or "power content" of information. My strategy involves measurement of the degree of control that is exercised by a given information "bit" over the distribution and flow of matter-energy in a system. Some genes, some organic processes, and some individuals in social groups are more powerful than others; the information they purvey has greater capacity for controlling the deployment of matter-energy at various levels of organization.

I have chosen to call the class (or subset) of cybernetic infrastructures that are found without exception in socially organized species "political systems." Whether in *Apis mellifera, Canis lupus,* or in large organizations of *Homo sapiens,* cybernetic processes are a functional universal. The precise mechanisms underlying such processes vary, as do the precise functions. However, the deep functions do not. In the broadest sense, the deep functions are to coordinate the actions of the parts *and* the whole in relation to the needs (and derivative goals) of both the parts and the whole. It is not therefore a literary affectation, or misplaced anthropomorphism, or a facile use of analogies that prompts me to assert that political processes are common to honeybees, wolves, and human beings. My purpose is to establish a conceptual framework for a set of processes that are fundamentally biological in their origins and in many of their ultimate functional consequences.

My third preliminary point involves the theoretical significance of social organization. Many writers from Plato to Edward Wilson have discoursed on the advantages of social life. Among biologists, the dialogue continues under the rubric of sociobiology. Yet the sociobiologists' approach was initially inadequate.[308] In Wilson's discipline-defining volume, the problem of explaining social life was couched largely in terms of altruistic self-sacrifice for one's offspring or close kin. Following Hamilton's formulation, Wilson identified only three types of social behavior, altruism, selfishness, and spite. Accordingly, the weight of explaining social life was made to rest on the shoulders of altruism through kin selection and, as an auxiliary, an improbable set of conditions that Trivers dubbed "reciprocal altruism."

However, the dichotomy of self-serving behaviors and sacrificial group-serving behaviors leaves out the most important category of all when it comes to explaining the totality of social life. In retrospect it seems astounding that sociobiologists for the most part overlooked or downgraded mutualism (what I call egoistic co-operation, in order to differentiate the phenomenon from those forms of co-operation that connote altruism). Mutualism involves a category of behaviors that are both self-serving *and* other-serving. Some of these behaviors involve reciprocities that involve small costs and considerable benefits to the participants (heat sharing among emperor penguins). Others involve complementary functions (the sea anemone-crab partnerships). Still others involve combinatorial, or threshold phenomena (the mobbing behavior of starlings; or the synchronized breeding of ground-nesting birds that serves to reduce the likelihood of their being attacked by an avian predator). Without the category of mutualism, one cannot begin to account for the widespread incidence of symbioses between members of unrelated species, much less the enormous variety of co-operative activities among unrelated individuals in human societies. (Altruism and reciprocal altruism, however noble, are of much less importance by comparison.)

The adaptive significance of human social life is the focus of Chapter V; the issue that needs to be clarified here is how social organization is to be understood within the Interactional Paradigm. At one extreme, George C. Williams has denied the very existence of functional organization at any level higher than that of individual organisms. The hunting behavior of the wolf pack is for Williams merely a fortuitous effect of the fact that a number of wolves become hungry and coincidentally happen to hunt the same prey at the same time.[309]* At the other extreme are the theorists who enthusiastically ascribe functional significance and integration to almost any spatially contiguous population of interacting organisms. To ecologists such as Eugene and Howard Odum, for example, ecological communities must be viewed as functional wholes atop a hierarchy of lower-level wholes.[311]

The Superorganism

The issue can be framed in terms of the debate over Herbert Spencer's superorganism metaphor: To what extent is it valid? The use of an organismic analogy to characterize social life did not originate with Spencer; Plato and Aristotle used it freely, as did various Enlightenment theorists and the French physiocrats. So did Auguste Comte, Edmund Burke, Emile Durkheim, and a host of twentieth-century structural-functional theorists whose assumptions were disguised in abstract conceptual schemes. In biology the superorganism metaphor became, in Edward Wilson's words, the "dominant theme" in the scientific literature on social behavior from 1911 to about 1950.[312] However, the concept came under critical fire in the 1940s and soon fell into disfavor. The principal arguments against the term were that it had no particular heuristic value in studying social phenomena, that it often wrongly ascribed holistic properties to phenomena that do not properly qualify (that is, that the analogy was often false), and that it frequently entailed an unproven assumption that social processes are oriented toward maintaining some sort of homeostasis.[313]

A similar pattern occurred in anthropology, with a different twist. After enjoying a vogue among Social Darwinists, who parroted Spencer without showing a proper respect for his subtlety, the term was dissociated from its Spencerian heritage, laundered, and reincarnated by the anthropologist Alfred Kroeber as a device for pressing the case for an autonomous and co-equal anthropology. According to Kroeber, human societies are superorganisms and therefore cannot be explained in biological terms. "It is perhaps too

* Williams's posture involves what might be called the fallacy of misplaced parsimony. Recent research in various social species has shown convincingly that social behavior is often elaborately coordinated toward the achievement of collective ends. The hunting behavior of wolf packs is a good case in point.[310]

much to expect anyone wedded, deliberately or unknowingly, to organic explanations, to discard these wholly before such incomplete evidence as is available. . . . But it does seem justifiable to stand unhesitatingly on the proposition that civilization and heredity are two things that operate in entirely separable ways."[314] Displaying a flair for the rhetorical flourish, Kroeber defined what would become the prevailing view of culture for the next two generations of anthropologists. "The dawn of the social [realm] thus is not a link in any chain, not a step in a path, but a leap to another plane," he declared.[315]

The anthropologist Alexander Alland sharply criticized this approach and any other approach that treats culture as being radically separate from human biology and human evolution. "Analogue models of evolution applied to culture fail because they employ false analogies, ignore proper measurement, and deny continuity between biological and cultural processes, the very thing which one would expect from a more general theory of evolution."[316] More recently Alland has supplemented his earlier criticisms with the arguments that (1) the boundaries of cultures are not as definite and fixed as is the case with organisms; (2) they are not as fully integrated; (3) organisms have built-in memories in their genomes; and (4) cultures do not show an unambiguous tendency to return to an initial homeostatic condition.[317]

Alland and other critics insist that the superorganism concept is at best an analogy of limited applicability. If biologists and anthropologists had stuck to Spencer's original conceptualization, the objections to using the term might never have arisen. Spencer never equated his term with the totality of culture; he would have argued vehemently against such an idea. And he never would have asserted that organisms and societies are in any sense identical in character. In the conclusion to his section on society as an organism in *The Principles of Sociology,* he wrote:

> Here let it once more be distinctly asserted that there exist no analogies between the body politic and a living body, save those necessitated by that mutual dependence of parts which they display in common. Though, in foregoing chapters, sundry comparisons of social structures and functions to structures and functions in the human body, have been made, they have been made only because structures and functions in the human body furnish familiar illustrations of structures and functions in general. The social organism, discrete instead of concrete, asymmetrical instead of symmetrical, sensitive in all its units instead of having a single sensitive centre, is not comparable to any particular type of individual organism, animal or vegetal. All kinds of creatures are alike in so far as each exhibits co-operation among its components for the benefit of the whole; and this trait, common to them, is a trait common also to societies. Further, among individual organisms, the degree of co-operation measures

> the degree of evolution; and this general truth, too, holds among social organisms. Once more, to effect increasing co-operation, creatures of every order show us increasingly complex appliances for transfer and mutual influence; and to this general characteristic, societies of every order furnish a corresponding characteristic. These, then, are the analogies alleged: community in the fundamental principles of organization is the only community asserted.[318]

Comte, Durkheim, and the twentieth-century structural-functionalists who reified societies were guilty of treating social life generally as though it had organismic properties. But not Herbert Spencer. For Spencer, the organismic analogy referred only to organization—in modern terminology, to goal-oriented cybernetic systems with explicit systemic goals and superordinate controls.

The superorganism concept as Spencer used it includes not the whole of a culture but only those parts of it (or those aspects of the whole) which are functionally organized entities. Spencer's formulation included the assumption of equilibration (homeostasis), but this assumption is not indispensable to cybernetic models. Moreover, superorganisms are not radically separated from the organic level of biological organization any more than is culture as a whole. Rather, superorganisms are potentiated by human nature, by our evolved biological capacities for creating and sustaining cybernetic social systems. For *Homo sapiens* is the quintessential cybernetic animal, solving problems and pursuing goals collaboratively. Human beings excel at devising and playing roles in social systems, systems designed to achieve through collective efforts whatever ends we set for ourselves. And because politics (in the broad, Aristotelian sense) is the process by which we go about cybernating our behavior—the process by which we solve "public" problems, make authoritative decisions, and organize and coordinate the behavior of our fellows—man is distinctively a political animal.

In these terms, political behavior is not confined to specialized governmental institutions. It is a facet of any organized, interpersonal activity (from families to football teams to the Federal Reserve System) insofar as that activity manifests the properties of a cybernetic social system, that is, insofar as it is goal-oriented and has internal processes of communication and reciprocal control among the constituent individuals. Other species too can be said to exhibit political behaviors; however, the repertoire of such behaviors in other species is limited and by our standards often highly stereotyped. Because other species do not have language, they cannot readily adapt their social behaviors to new goals. What sets us apart and makes us a distinctively political animal is that we have learned how to elaborate upon and adapt the basic principles of cybernetic behavioral organization—the basic social building blocks—in order to encompass an extraordinary variety of goals.

Man alone is able to invent new and more intricate forms of organization, and the increasingly complex cybernation of human societies has been one of the most significant trends in cultural evolution.

We are not accustomed to treating more encompassing social levels of organization as an expression of human nature. We have been taught to think of culture as an artifact or superstructure. Yet from an evolutionary perspective, social organization is a functionally important level of biological organization. Because the human being is a social animal with a long history of "togetherness," social organization is simply an actualization of behaviors that are potentiated by our evolved biological capabilities. In an evolutionary model of human nature and society, then, various social levels of organization represent partial orderings at a more encompassing level than that of the individual organism; social organization is a natural extension of biological purposiveness. And like any other hierarchically organized cybernetic system, social systems have no existence apart from their constituent individuals yet may have collective effects that transcend what any given individual or aggregate could produce.

Accordingly, as an integral part of a system hierarchy, each individual is at once a servant of basic biological needs, a pursuer of his or her own instrumental and personal goals, and a contributor to the functioning of social, economic, and political organizations. All these levels interact with and affect one another, and all are integrally related to the enterprise of earning a living in the environment. Human society is in essence a collective survival enterprise in which various (but not necessarily all) aspects of the survival problem are dealt with collaboratively. Yet the specific organizational patterns vary widely; in every society we know, there is at least some division of labor with respect to economic tasks, and most societies deal collaboratively with certain collective problems (group defense, migration, the allocation of water rights). More complex societies divide and subdivide the survival problem into a myriad of specific functional tasks which are dealt with by various intermediate-level organizations (beginning with the nuclear family), while a number of coping and integrative functions may also be performed at the most inclusive level.

As the foregoing implies, superorganisms are also teleonomic systems. They are products of specific human (or animal) purposes, most of which have historically related (sometimes indirectly) to meeting basic needs. Thus I differ with such theorists as Williams, Ghiselin, and Richerson, who claim that teleonomic systems are not found above the level of individual organisms. (I also differ with Dunbar and D. S. Wilson in that I draw a line when it comes to characterizing ecosystems as superorganisms.)[319] Only to the extent that our cells act as though our bodies are integrated cybernetic systems can we say that we exist as organisms. (In a very real sense, it may be said that cancer involves a subversion of our cells to alien purposes.) In exactly the same way, political systems exist only to the extent that human beings (or honeybees or wolves) act as though such systems exist and coordinate their efforts toward achieving systemic goals. Unlike social theorists of subsequent generations, Spencer never lost sight of the *dualistic* nature of superorganisms. He emphasized that they are composed of "sentient" individuals yet manifest emergent teleonomic properties.

This is not to say that the stated or implicit goals of an organization are always achieved, or that organizations always pursue their purported goals, or that latent functions or dysfunctions might not also occur in the process. Nor does the goal-directedness of superorganisms necessarily imply a design for homeostasis. Superorganisms may manifest homeorhesis (a developmental trajectory), saltatory changes (political revolutions, for example), decay, decline, and "death"—just as organisms do, though for different reasons. The superorganism concept does not explain anything directly. Nor can it specify *a priori* the precise structure and functions of an organization. However, it does direct our attention to the deep principles and deep purposes of social organization and to the evolutionary origins of such phenomena. Like the concept of natural selection itself, it is not a mechanism but a heuristic tool.

In this light, there is a simple answer to the frequent charge that superorganisms *qua* social organizations are reifications—examples of Alfred North Whitehead's fallacy of misplaced concreteness. An organization exists if it produces synergistic effects (negative or positive) with respect to some specified goal—that is, effects that are attributable to "action in concert," in Talcott Parsons's phrase. Thus a baseball team between seasons, an army on paper, and a "letterhead" company are not organizations. On the other hand, if the Ayatollah Khomeini can command one million Iranians to interrupt whatever they are doing and to march together through the streets of Tehran, that is an organization. By the same token, nation-states are ontologically meaningful entities to the extent that they produce functional synergism, or act as states. Various reductionist and anti-functionalist arguments have merit insofar as they compel us to differentiate between our abstract conceptual schemata and real systems. But total rejection of holism leads to what C. F. A. Pantin called the "analytic fallacy," the view that wholes are nothing more than the sum of their parts.[320] The middle-ground view is that it should always be considered an open question whether or not in a given case a set of people and their social interactions constitute a goal-oriented system (and with what emergent, systemic consequences).

Finally, a sharp distinction must be made between superorganisms *qua* cybernetic social systems and ecosystems (either human or natural), a distinction that parallels the economist's distinction between firms and markets. The political scientist Kenneth Waltz has pointed out that a market is viewed by economic theorists as a structure or a framework of forces with emergent properties (synergistic properties) that arise from the relationships and interactions among the actors:

> The market arises out of the activities of separate units—persons and firms—whose aims and efforts are directed not toward creating an order but rather toward fulfilling their own internally defined interests by whatever means they can muster. The individual unit acts for itself. From the coaction of like units emerges a structure that affects and constrains all of them. Once formed, a market becomes a force in itself, and a force that the constitutive units acting singly or in small numbers cannot control. Instead, in lesser or greater degree as market conditions vary, the creators become the creatures of the market that their activity gave rise to. . . . [Thus] the market is a cause interposed between the economic actors and the results they produce. It conditions their calculations, their behaviors, and their interactions. It is not an agent in the sense of *A* being the agent that produces outcome *X*. Rather it is a structural cause. A market constrains the units that comprise it from taking certain actions and disposes them toward taking others.[321]

The chief difficulty with various so-called systems theories, and with various exponents of the superorganism metaphor, is that they fail to distinguish clearly between the two fundamentally different kinds of systems in social life, cybernetic systems and ecosystems.[322] Although the market model is more familiar to social scientists, the organism-ecosystem (or ecological community) model provides a far richer and more precise analogy with the dynamics of human societies, for several reasons.

First, the market model defines too narrowly the goals of the actors. Not even in the economic sector do actors single-mindedly pursue only "profits." At the minimum, they pursue organizational survival, which on reflection is not a simple goal; in addition, they may pursue a wide variety of goals that are related to such things as growth, power, and prestige. Even the profit motive turns out to be complex when one begins to probe the motivations behind it.

Second, the actors do not pursue their goals only by means of competition; they do so by a variety of means and with a variety of relationships to other actors. Besides competition, there are such ecological analogues as competitive exclusion, predation, parasitism, reciprocity, mutualistic symbiosis, niche partitioning, ecological specialization, and multifarious forms of inadvertent ecological interdependency.[323] There is even occasional altruism.*

* A classic rendering of the ecological paradigm is Darwin's description of the English countryside in the concluding passages of *The Origin of Species:* "It is interesting to contemplate an

(Continued)

Third and perhaps most important, organized social life is intimately related to the biological problem of survival and reproduction for human populations. Our social systems interact with natural ecosystems and affect them to such a degree that "ecological problems" are now a major agenda item in domestic and international politics.[324] Accordingly, the overarching paradigm of a community of goal-oriented, multileveled cybernetic systems embedded in human and natural ecosystems—what might be called *political ecology*—can encompass the full range of motives, actors, and relationships that exist in social life. Furthermore, the political ecology paradigm provides a framework for comprehending the role of functional synergism in social life, as we shall see.

Let me summarize the key characteristics of the Interactional Paradigm.

1. We have good reason for believing that both upward and downward causation play important roles in shaping social life and societal evolution; the evidence for this proposition is extensive.
2. Much social causation involves complex, dynamic interactions among functionally significant factors at and between various levels of causation.
3. The Interactional Paradigm is grounded in the premises that survival and reproduction is the paradigm problem of social life and that biological organisms are open, self-organizing thermodynamic systems. Energetic interactions between organisms and their environments represent a basic parameter.
4. Because human beings are products of the evolutionary process, they must also be products of natural selection (that is, of functional processes) in combination with chance and necessity; they are thus purposive (teleonomic).
5. Central to an understanding of the evolutionary process is the phenomenon of adaptation—design for survival. Adaptation arises from the fact that survival is a problem and that all solutions are contingent. Adaptation is as much a property of behavior and of culture as it is of morphology.
6. The classical population genetic criterion of adaptation is reproductive fitness. However, this criterion is of limited usefulness in analyzing adaptation in human societies. (The classical approach overlooks what I call genometype selection, absolute changes in the numbers and diversity of populations and species over time.) Alternative approaches to measuring adaptation in-

---

entangled bank, clothed with many plants of many kinds, with birds singing on the bushes, with various insects flitting about, and with worms crawling through the damp earth, and to reflect that these elaborately constructed forms, so different from each other, and dependent on each other in so complex a manner, have all been produced by laws acting around us. These laws, taken in the largest sense, being Growth with Reproduction; Inheritance . . . ; Variability . . . ; a Struggle for Life and . . . Natural Selection" (p. 459).

clude a class of benefit-cost analyses that can be called bioeconomic. The approach I employ is functional in nature and involves two elements: (a) a long-range effort to specify and measure postulated primary needs and (b) an effort to develop a global indicator of Population Health (or fitness in a functional sense), which is defined as the degree to which a given population approaches its maximum capacity to carry on "normal" functions. In effect, this approach inverts the basic needs hierarchy of the psychologist Abraham Maslow. Although it was developed independently, it resurrects and refines the approach originally proposed by the anthropologist Bronislaw Malinowski.

7. Our behavior as individuals is in large measure oriented toward the satisfaction of our basic (primary and instrumental) needs, even in the course of apparently routine activities. The functional organization of our behavior involves what I call Action Structures. Thus the relationship between our behavior and our needs is often indirect; sometimes our behavior may even be maladaptive or have no adaptive significance.

8. The development of our behavior as individuals and in organized groups involves *teleonomic selection,* a functional (cybernetic) process that is analogous to and interpenetrates with natural selection. That is, adaptation can be conceptualized as a functional selection process. Natural selection and teleonomic selection are explanatory principles that embody analogues of the Law of Effect. Actual or anticipated functional effects are the major cause of both functional continuities and changes in behavior.

9. The model of human nature that I adopt is that of a complex, multileveled cybernetic system. The rudiments of this approach can be found in the work of the psychologist Edward Tolman.

10. Selection processes in evolutionary change are multileveled, in conformity with the fact that biological organization is multileveled and hierarchically organized. Synergistic effects are the major underlying cause of the evolution of hierarchical organization, at both the organismic and the social levels.

11. Social organization represents an emergent level of biological organization. The term superorganism, as Herbert Spencer intended it, serves as a heuristic device. In Spencer's conceptualization, superorganisms are not equivalent to whole cultures but to specific, goal-directed (teleonomic) systems with cybernetic properties. A concomitant of this conceptualization is the proposition that a "political" superstructure is a necessary element of any organized, goal-directed social system.

12. The distinction between superorganisms (*qua* cybernetic systems) and ecosystems parallels and improves upon the economist's concepts of firms and markets. The cybernetic-systems-within-ecosystems conceptualization (political ecology) provides an appropriate framework for applying the Interactional Paradigm to sociocultural evolution.

V

A General Theory of Sociocultural Evolution

Historically, it will be recalled that biological evolution was not taken seriously until Darwin presented the first workable theory for it. . . . In short, before we can take social evolution seriously, we must have a tenable and testable theory for it. *John Paul Scott*

Sociobiology does seem to lack, however, a central image, analogous to the vision of a clockwork conjured up by the Newtonian synthesis. . . . No system with such general coherence, no such deductive testable schema based on one or a few principles can be expected to arise again in our time. *Gerald Holton*

For when a man knows not his own first principle, and when the conclusion and the intermediate steps are also constructed out of he knows not what, how can he imagine that such a fabric of convention can ever become science? *Plato*

Theories of Cultural Evolution

To a degree that is not generally appreciated (or at least acknowledged) by contemporary social theorists, both the overarching paradigms and the various proposed prime movers of sociocultural evolution that one finds in the literature today were articulated at least preliminarily well before the end of the last century. Indeed, it remains an inglorious episode in the development of the social sciences that evolutionism went into a virtual eclipse during the first third of this century. For different reasons, both Marx and Spencer were at various times consigned to the "inactive" shelves of Anglo-American libraries, while Darwin's important contributions to the development of the social sciences in general and cultural evolutionism in particular—most notably in *The Descent of Man* (1874) and *The Expression of the Emotions in Man and Animals* (1873)—remain largely unappreciated (or distorted) to this day. In communist countries, of course, almost everyone else but Marx became *persona non grata.* The result has been an extraordinary intellectual discontinuity. In the past few decades, an inordinate amount of energy and disputation have gone into rediscovering and winning acceptance for concepts that were already in the air 100 years ago.

The reasons are complex. In brief, evolutionism was the victim of a drastic sea change, a tide that was compounded partly of political ideology, disciplinary chauvinism, "scientism," and philosophical value-relativism; and injustices were done to many prominent scholars of an earlier era. Moreover, the revival occurred only with a hard, uphill struggle on many fronts. To illustrate, as late as 1969, the distinguished British sociologist J. D. Y. Peel could flatly declare that a theory of social evolution is "impossible." Evolutionism, he declared, was a product of the "infancy" of the social sciences.[1]

The revival of evolutionary theorizing began from a very narrow base. It can perhaps be dated from the appearance of the celebrated British archaeologist V. Gordon Childe's influential book *Man Makes Himself* in 1936. Compared to the grand schemes of Darwin, Spencer, and Marx, Childe's focus was limited. Childe fixed his attention primarily on the rise of "civilization"—the so-called urban revolution—and he identified surpluses (after Adam Smith) in consequence of the development of agriculture as the key determinant.

The paradox has often been noted that the title of Childe's book belied his deterministic theoretical posture, and some critics have denigrated Childe's thesis by calling it an "automatic" theory of cultural evolution. But this is not so. It was, quite simply, a theory that emphasized the primacy of economic development, especially developments in agricultural technology. But it also had a voluntaristic aspect. Implicit in Childe's thesis was the "soft" form of the social contract; the state arose initially through consent (though he also perceived class conflict and repression in its wake).

By contrast, Karl Wittfogel, in another early landmark, advanced a coercive theory of state origins that drew its inspiration partly from Marx and partly from Weber. Wittfogel's famous "hydraulic hypothesis" postulated that developments in the mode of production, namely, centralized irrigation agriculture, gave rise to coercive bureaucratic controls, political stratification, and, in time, "oriental despotism." Thus the state arose as an instrument of economic exploitation and class rule.[2]

A third important stage in the revival of evolutionary theorizing was Leslie White's effort to resurrect and elaborate on a theme that was first introduced by Lamarck and later embellished by Spencer, though White's immediate source of inspiration was the more contemporary work in various disciplines on thermodynamics.[3] White focused on the central role of energy in biological processes, advancing the thesis that energy capture has been the prime mover of cultural evolution (via technological improvements and the acquisition of information). He called it the Basic Law of Evolution: "Culture advances as the amount of energy harnessed per capita per year increases, or as the efficiency or economy of the means of controlling energy is increased, or both."[4]

White is often portrayed as an energy monist, but there was more to his evolutionism than energetics. Though he maintained that "culture thus becomes primarily a mechanism for harnessing energy,"[5] he was also a systems theorist of a sort. Inspired by Marxism, structural-functionalism, and Durkheim's reification of the social organism, White came to believe that cultural systems are independent entities that evolve as wholes and in a determinate way. It was vaguely reminiscent of the early Spencer, though (to repeat) Spencer never applied the organismic analogy to society as a whole (that posture is attributable to Durkheim [via Comte]). White also called himself a cultural determinist and argued vehemently against the "anthropocentric illusion" of free will. Culture evolves independently of our will, he claimed.[6] However, White did believe in a science of culture, what he called "culturology." "We cannot control its course," he wrote, "but we can learn to predict it."[7]

Cultural Ecology

The other major revivalist was Julian Steward. Although Steward did not differ radically from White, he shied away from White's Marxian-Spencerian determinism and from his reification of culture in favor of an approach that focused on the relationships between organized human groups and their particular environments, or their "adaptation." (Steward did not define adaptation in strictly Darwinian terms, and he included in his analyses only a limited range of "environmental" variables.) From his perspective, the actual processes of cultural evolution did not array themselves as a grand procession with unilinear properties. Cultural evolution seemed to him to be more disorderly, more locally conditioned, in a word, more multilinear.

Dubbed "cultural ecology," Steward's approach was not a theory at all but a paradigm and methodology for studying and comparing particular cultures in order to understand how their cultural systems had evolved. In fact, cultural ecology was closely related to the early work on human ecology in sociology, where the environment was not nature but the city! While Steward did believe—with Smith, Spencer, Marx, Childe, Wittfogel, and White—that the technoeconomic sphere is the engine of cultural evolution, he also saw technology as deterministically linked to the local environment. Accordingly, the political and ideological elements carried less weight in his view. At the same time he posited a general direction for evolutionary change toward more inclusive levels of sociocultural (read political) integration. The progression he perceived was from family to tribe to state. However, political organization is not the cause, it is merely the outcome. (This latter formulation became the inspiration for the more elaborate taxonomy of evolutionary stages later proposed by Elman Service—band, tribe, chiefdomship, and state.[8])

Despite the important differences between them, the first generation of twentieth-century evolutionists had in common a basically technological and economic orientation. These evolutionary revivalists (one can hardly call them pioneers) were also more linear and deterministic in their thinking than the second generation, whose works appeared mainly in the 1960s and 1970.[9]

Some of the latter have merely embellished or transmogrified the role assigned to economic advances (such as sociologist S. N. Eisenstadt's concept of "free-floating resources"[10]). Others introduced more complex, interactional perspectives. Kaplan and Manners call it "soft determinism."[11] Walter Goldschmidt, for example, posited a dual (internal and external) selection process that gave equal weight to economic and political-military factors, a formulation that is reminiscent of Spencer. Internal selection, Goldschmidt explained, involves the proposition that "those features of a culture which are more suited to maintaining the community will continue and those less suited will disappear when two or more alternative modes are available."[12] As examples he cited such "artifacts" as Pullman railway cars, battleships, and horses. (Goldschmidt also recognized the obvious complication that economic and political processes and structures may distort the selection process in various ways.) External selection, on the other hand, is of two kinds: "The direct subjugation or elimination of the weaker social entities by the stronger, and the reorganization of institutions in the face of such a manifest or potential threat."[13]

In a similar vein, Robert McC. Adams pioneered the application of modern systems theory to the process of sociocultural evolution.[14] The result was a theory of state origins that, following Mill, postulated a complex interplay between economic and political-military developments. For the first time the concepts of feedback and reciprocal causality began to creep into the cultural evolution theory, along with direct human actions—politics.[15]

Cultural Materialism

There have also been some notable hold-outs for the determinist position. Marvin Harris's important work deserves special comment in this regard. Embracing Marx as an ancestor, Harris espouses something he calls "cultural materialism."[16] What he means by this is spelled out in the introduction to his history of anthropological theory:

> My main reason for writing this book is to reassert the methodological priority of the search for laws of history in the science of man. . . . The burden of my argument is that the basic principle of a macro-theory of sociocultural evolution is already known . . . The kind of principle to which I refer . . . has its precise analogue in the doctrine of natural selection. In this analogy, the meaning of "principle" is not equivalent to the statement of the specific "laws" of evolution, but rather to the statement of a basic research strategy, from the application of which there is an expectation that a nomothetic causal understanding of sociocultural phenomena may be achieved. Darwin's contribution, which we shall have occasion to discuss later on, was to direct attention to the general conditions responsible for bio-evolution, namely differential reproductive success.[17]

Unfortunately, Harris mistates the nature of Darwin's theory and thus draws a false (that is not a "precise") analogy between what he calls the "doctrine" of natural selection and his own theoretical enterprise. We recall that Darwin's theory does not merely "direct attention" to the general conditions responsible for bio-evolution. Nor did Darwin search for any law of evolution. Darwin posited a testable hypothesis—that evolution is the result of differential reproductive success and that differential reproductive success is, in turn, the result primarily of different functional capabilities among different organisms in their environments. Darwin also derived some explicit theoretical predictions from this hypothesis.

Harris's project, on the other hand, involves something quite different. In essence, Harris advances the assertion that there is a strong correlation (or lawlike relationship) between technoeconomic change, social organization, social values, and ideology. Harris sums it up:

> I believe that the analogue of the Darwinian strategy in the realm of sociocultural phenomena is the principle of techno-environmental and

> techno-economic determinism. This principle holds that similar technologies applied to similar environments tend to produce similar arrangements of labor in production and distribution, and that these in turn call forth similar kinds of social groupings, which justify and coordinate their activities by means of similar systems of values and beliefs. Translated into a research strategy, the principle of techno-environmental, techno-economic determinism assigns priority to the study of the material conditions of sociocultural life, much as the principle of natural selection assigns priority to the study of differential reproductive success [*sic*].[18]

Harris's proposition says nothing directly about cultural evolution beyond the fact that various kinds of cultural changes are linked to one another with a certain causal priority. This begs the question: If technoeconomic change is the key to cultural evolution, what causes technoeconomic change? Harris has no causal theory of cultural evolution.

Harris traces his law to Marx. But it is a defanged version of Marxism, for Harris devotes a considerable part of his recent volume, *Cultural Materialism* (1979), to attacking the very core of Marx's theory, most notably the dialectic. The problem is that without the dialectic, Marxism can no longer sustain the claim to a theory of history. It becomes nothing more than a directive to focus on the role of the economic sphere, broadly defined. Harris's view to the contrary notwithstanding, there is nothing particularly Marxian about this directive. We do not need Marx to tell us that basic material needs are important, or that technoeconomic change has played an important role in cultural evolution. We can trace this idea to the Enlightenment, and even to Periclean Athens.

Harris embellishes his paradigm by relying on Marx's concept of the mode of production, or the technoeconomic infrastructure in Harris's term. Harris calls it "infrastructural determinism," which can range, he tells us, from virtual certainty to virtual indeterminacy.[19] He calls it "probabilistic determinism," which translated means that economic variables have at least some causal potency.

Furthermore, Harris's determinism takes two giant steps toward a tautology. To ensure that no one accuses him of oversimplifying the complexities of social life, Harris makes his infrastructure more commodius than anything Marx ever had in mind: He gives it the Teutonic label "demo-techno-econo-environmental" determinism.[20] In other words, Harris like the rest of us has been enlightened by the various crises of recent years, and so he incorporates into his paradigm some of the variables which were slighted by Marx but which were well known to Montesquieu, Malthus, Spencer, and Darwin, namely, various environmental factors, population dynamics, and reproductive needs. Indeed, insofar as Harris shifts his version of the Marxian paradigm away from material progress and toward the basic biological *problèmatique* (as he puts it, "subsistence," or "the need to eat" and "reproduction"), he covertly aligns himself with the Darwinian struggle for existence.

Harris would vehemently deny this, of course. He roundly attacks sociobiology in general and the idea of "an imaginary genetic biogram" in particular: "The most important observation that one can make about the human biogram is that it is relatively free from species-specific bio-psychological drives and predispositions."[21] Yet, hidden assumptions about basic biological needs as the underlying sources of human values, motivations, choices, and propensities for "economizing" (a tacit concession to the ghost of Adam Smith) are essential prior causes that Harris cannot avoid. In other words, Harris abjures biology in theory but includes it (loosely) in fact.

What, then, does Harris have to contribute? Other than the platitude that religion, ideology, ingrained traditions, etc., are relatively less important determinants of human behavior than bread-and-butter problems, cultural materialism is definite about one important thing: Politics is not a particularly significant "variable." In fact, the word politics is not even listed in the index of *Cultural Materialism.*

Like his nineteenth-century mentor, Harris treats politics as an epiphenomenon, an insignificant source of evolutionary change. In this sense Harris is a throwback to a viewpoint that many contemporary Marxists reject, even though it involves them in a contradiction. If we admit human purposes, goals, and goal-oriented social actions (individual or collective) as major independent variables, the very soul of the determinist position—and of the (pristine) Marxist paradigm—is fatally compromised. Harris obviously does not wish to do so. He even denigrates such approaches as muddle-headed "eclecticism." Thus, like the early Marx, Harris still adheres to a Newtonian and Comtean rather than Darwinian model of science (and history). He is the legatee of what might be called the "positivist fallacy," which can be traced from Comte to Durkheim to Skinner and beyond. The assumption that it is unscientific and unnecessary to include the mind as an independent causal agency in societal evolution is itself increasingly unscientific.

Innovation, Entrepreneurship, and Exchange

In addition to various global technoeconomic paradigms and theories, recent years have also seen an increasingly fine-grained treatment of a number of specific theoretical "subplots." One subplot involves the role of innovation in social change. The landmark work in this vein is Homer Barnett's *Innovation: The Basis of Cultural Change* (1953).[22]

Another subplot, following the lead of Max Weber, involves the creative, catalytic role of entrepreneurship. First treated in depth by Joseph Schumpeter in *The Theory of Economic Development* (1911), the subject was subsequently elaborated on by many economists, sociologists, and political scientists.[23]

A third subplot has come to be called exchange theory. This approach can probably be dated from the early recognition by Marcel Mauss that gift giving and related social transactions are a functionally important dimension of social life.[24] The literature includes, on the one hand, various frameworks for analyzing individual social behaviors and structures,[25] and on the other hand, various studies of economic transactions and economic development processes.[26] An offshoot of this work is called central place theory.

Population Pressure

In addition to these economically oriented works, two other approaches associated with nineteenth-century evolutionism have made vigorous comebacks. One is the population pressure hypothesis. Herbert Spencer saw population growth and consequent population pressures as the "proximate cause" of sociocultural progress.[27] The first generation of twentieth-century revivalists downplayed the idea,[28] but in the 1960s the population pressure hypothesis returned to the mainstream of evolutionary theorizing. Its resurrection is associated especially with three theorists: Ester Boserup, who proposed that population growth might have played a central role in the development of agricultural technologies; Don Dumond, who focused on the relationship between population growth and cultural change generally; and Michael Harner, who advanced the thesis that population pressures were the stimuli that had led to the intensification of both internal and external competition, which in turn led to social stratification and political evolution.[29]

One offshoot of this general hypothesis was a pair of population-oriented explanations for the origins of the state. One theory involved internal forces. Morton Fried, anticipating Harner's more general line of argument and his supporting data, postulated that population pressures had led, step by step, from egalitarian societies to highly stratified societies to elite class-rule in chiefdomships to coercive states.[30] The other theory was externally oriented. Robert Carneiro posited that the state arose through conquest. The impetus for such political aggrandizement was population pressure, which was itself the result of environmental (or social) "circumscription."[31] (I will address these theories in more detail below.)

Social Conflict

The other major nineteenth-century theme that has reappeared in recent years is the conflict hypothesis. Some of the theorists mentioned above can be included in this school as well (Goldschmidt, Fried, and Carneiro). Some of these theorists have fairly complex, ecologically oriented views of the underlying causal dynamics. In addition, there is a group of theorists who view warfare not primarily as a response to external pressures but as a product of aggressive or acquisitive urges and/or "positive reinforcements" (so to speak). Sir Arthur Keith was probably the first and least-known theorist of this genre, while the writings of Robert Ardrey, Konrad Lorenz and Robert Bigelow caused something of a furor in the latter 1960s.[32]

None of the recent crop of conflict theorists, it should be emphasized, condones warfare. Nor do most of them discount either external causes or political aspects of collective violence. Nobody espouses a crude biological determinism. Indeed, some hold very complex, dualistic views that assign primacy to factors other than war. (Alexander, seconded by Pitt, takes the strongest, most one-sided position.)*

Toward a Reconciliation

How do we begin to sort out all of these apparently conflicting theoretical approaches? How can we reconcile the various technoeconomic, ecological, demographic, and conflict-oriented theories? Equally important, how do we square these theories with the contradictory evidence that has been brought forth by various critics?

In the first place, technoeconomic determinism as a general methodological stance is outdated by the accumulated evidence of a more complex reality. Similar technologies do not necessarily call forth similar social organizations or similar ideologies. They may call forth alternatively an Athens or a Sparta, a Victorian England or an Imperial Germany, a United States or a Stalinist Russia. Likewise, a steel mill can be operated by a laissez-faire capitalist, a workers' collective, or a socialist state bureaucracy. The differences are significant. Furthermore, the causal arrows do not run in only one direction. The

* I should also mention the sociobiological perspective on sociocultural evolution. There are two radically different viewpoints. E. O. Wilson espouses what he calls an "autocatalytic model." He maintains that cultural evolution has been the result of the mutually reinforcing effects of the entire suite of cultural developments. While this perspective is not wrong, I believe it is insufficient. It does not move us much beyond nineteenth-century orthogenesis. Most notably, it leaves cultural selection out of the process.

Richard Alexander's approach, on the other hand, is a direct extrapolation from the Hamiltonian "inclusive fitness" paradigm (Chapter III). Alexander regards it as a "reasonable theory" that the existence, nature, and rates and direction of change in cultural evolution are due to the "cumulative effects" of fitness maximizing behavior, that is, "reproductive maximizing via all socially available descendant and non-descendant relatives."[33] It is surely the case that reproductive success is a *necessary* condition (and concomitant) for the evolution of culture. In the main, cultural evolution must be consistent with the criterion of Darwinian fitness. This is a logical and necessary deduction from Darwin's theory, and any compelling evidence to the contrary would falsify the theory. But does Alexander offer a *sufficient* theory of cultural evolution? Does this theory enlighten us about the rates and directions of cultural change? Does it explain the progressive evolution of large, complex societies? I do not think so. Nor does Alexander's theory bridge what might be called the "genetic barrier." How did it come to pass that societies evolved that are composed mainly of nonrelatives? To account for more

(Continued)

blanket assumption that technoeconomic causes will predominate over political/military causes is an assumption that has become dogma.

There is also the prior question of how a particular technology arises in the first place. Sometimes it does not. Sometimes it is merely diffused or borrowed or incorporated via symbiotic trading relationships.[34] Sometimes it is not adopted at all, such as the Amish or the !Kung San. By the same token, the vigorous development of ecological anthropology over the past decade has resulted in a greater respect for the human-environment relationship than had previously been the case.[35]

The role of various specific prime movers has also generally been found wanting. For instance, Childe's agricultural revolution thesis has been challenged as simplistic. The development of agriculture was a long and involved process, not a revolutionary event. Nor is it true that it preceded urbanization. Jane Jacobs argues that urbanization, energized by trade and the development of crafts industries, may have stimulated the technological developments that led to large-scale agriculture, rather than the reverse.[36] As noted above, R. McC. Adams takes a dynamic, interactive view of the matter and asserts that the rise of urban civilization involved multiple causes and multiple functions.[37] This thesis has been further developed by Henry T. Wright, who calls it a "synthetic" theory of the state.[38]

In the same vein, Wittfogel's so-called hydraulic hypothesis has been challenged by the evidence that in some cases political centralization occurred prior to the rise of complex irrigation systems and may have facilitated their development.[39] There is also evidence that centralized irrigation systems may sometimes have predated the state,[40] and that such systems do not by any means necessitate coercive political entities in their wake.[41] By the same token, some states, such as the Zulu, have arisen without the catalyst of irrigation agriculture. While large scale food production systems were a necessary concomitant of the development of large scale polities, in accordance with Megger's "law,"[42] their causal priority is not clearcut.

White's energy centered perspective suffers a similar fate. Energy capture has obviously been an important enabler and concomitant of societal evolution,[43] but is it really appropriate to treat energy as a prime mover? Recall that human populations also happen to be distributed geographically near fresh water supplies. Water has also been a prime mover, and so have been all of the other requisites for our survival and reproduction. If energy were our only need, then we could say it was the decisive factor. But in fact it is only a co-determinant.[44]

Similar difficulties attend the population pressure hypothesis. Populations have not grown uniformly at all times and places. The fossil record suggests

---

recent stages of sociocultural evolution, the functional synergism model is more fruitful than the inclusive fitness model.

long periods in the remote past, amounting to hundreds of thousands of years, when our hominid ancestors maintained relative population stability. In more recent millennia, population levels have grown unevenly in a series of spurts rather than in a smooth curve, as a "pressure" hypothesis might imply. In some areas population has been stable; in others it has grown rapidly after a significant breakthrough like the diffusion of plow-based agriculture or European migration to North America and Australia. In still other areas, high population densities have not been coupled with evolutionary social changes.[45]

Mark Nathan Cohen has posited a kind of automatic theory of population growth that is reminiscent of the original Malthusian thesis.[46] Contrary to Malthus's pessimistic views, there is some evidence that population levels are subject to a variety of regulative mechanisms.[47] Many primitive human societies exercise cultural controls (intentionally or not) via such practices as infanticide, delayed marriage, delay of postpartum weaning (which seems to suppress reactivation of the female cycle), and frequent, ritualistic episodes of warfare. As Flannery has observed, automatic theories of population growth beg the question *why does a population grow?* It is not inevitable.

An apparent contradiction arises when Boserup's population centered theory of technoeconomic development and Carneiro's population centered theory of war and political amalgamation are juxtaposed. To the extent that each of these hypotheses has merit, each challenges and circumscribes the other. Population pressure, it seems, might not deterministically lead either to warfare or intensification of food production. Of course, these theories need not be mutually exclusive: Both responses could occur. But in that case, population pressure is no longer a sufficient cause and other factors must be introduced to explain the outcome.

Finally, the omnipotence of the conflict hypothesis is doubtful; it cannot explain co-operation—the extensive evidence of peaceful, noncoerced exchange, mutually beneficial enterprises, and symbiotic socioeconomic integration. Spencer believed that societal evolution has been a dualistic process. More recently, sociologist Ralf Dahrendorf resurrected this theme in an effort to reconcile functionalist and conflict theories in sociology.[48] Dahrendorf sees societies as Janus-faced—admixtures of stability and change, co-operation and conflict, reciprocity and exploitation. Functionalist theorists emphasize the former aspects; conflict theorists emphasize the latter.[49] The truth involves a synthesis of both viewpoints.

Down with Prime Movers

"Down with prime-movers!" declared Elman Service in a critique of cultural evolutionism some years ago. "There is no single magical formula that will predict the evolution of every society. The actual evolution of the culture of particular societies is an adaptive process whereby the society solves problems with respect to the natural and to the social-cultural environment. These environments are so diverse, the problems so numerous, and the solutions potentially so various that no single determinant can be equally powerful for all cases."[50]

Services's views did not reflect the mainstream in anthropology until recently. In a curious sort of way, it would seem that the revitalization of cultural evolution theory in this century has reversed biologist Ernst Haeckel's famous (and now discredited) law, according to which the ontogeny of each organism recapitulated the phylogeny of the species. In the history of cultural evolution theory, phylogeny seems to have recapitulated ontogeny. Twentieth-century theorists have gradually evolved a position that resembles the mature views of such nineteenth-century thinkers as Darwin, Spencer and, somewhat more covertly, Marx; these theorists were ultimately very cautious, appreciated the complexities involved, and rejected the strident determinism that was commonplace in their youth. It appears that the twentieth century has been condemned to repeat this intellectual trajectory.

Like their progenitors, contemporary theorists retain a strong conviction that human history has involved something more than a random stream of events. There is a connectedness, an inner logic; if there is no immutable law of evolution, there has been an intelligible directionality.* Even if there has been no prime mover, there have been a number of important enablers, pressures, constraints, and imperatives that have interacted with one another to canalize societal evolution. Furthermore, the process has manifested a considerable degree of coherence. If an organized society is not exactly analogous to an organism, it does have certain superorganic properties. Robert Carneiro has developed a useful metaphor to characterize this process:

> A sociocultural system may be likened to a train of gears in which each gear represents a different sphere of culture. In the operation of this system the gears are generally in mesh. The gears differ, however. Some are larger than others, some have finer teeth, some turn faster, etc. Moreover, some are drive gears and engender motion in others, while other gears are passive and do not impart motion of their own, but merely transmit the motion they receive.
>
> The gears also vary in the closeness with which they engage one another. If the mesh between any two were perfect and continuous, then the

* The terminological preferences among various cultural evolutionists are confusing. Darwin, and most contemporary evolutionary biologists, define evolution as, simply, "descent with modification." In the interest of clarity and more effective communication, I employ the Darwinian definition.

> movement of one would automatically produce a corresponding and equivalent movement in the other. But in sociocultural systems the gears never engage perfectly *or* continuously. Now and then a gear slips out of mesh and may move forward half a turn without causing perceptible motion in the others.
>
> Yet, by and large, the train of gears moves together. A certain position of one gear is not compatible with just any position of some other gear. Thus, leaving our metaphor aside and looking at sociocultural systems directly, we cannot imagine, for example, divine kingship fitting with cave dwellings, trial by jury with percussion flaking, parliamentary procedure with human sacrifice, or cross-cousin marriage with nuclear reactors. When culture advances significantly in one sphere, other spheres do not long remain unaffected. They tend to advance with it; not always immediately or at the same rate, to be sure, but basically together, as a single coordinated system.[51]

Like all metaphors, this is an imperfect representation of a complex reality. But there is an inner logic to the process. This is what my theory tries to illuminate. What are the purposes underlying the motion of Carneiro's gear train? Why did such systems come into being in the first place? And what is the explanation for their evolution through time? The theory that I propose to explain the progressive evolution of complex organization in general can also be used to explain not just the more recent evolution of society and the state but also the emergence of animal societies and *Homo sapiens.* Though this is a bold assertion, I believe I can support it.

Synergism at Work

Functional synergism is so much a part of our daily lives that we generally take it for granted. In any complex modern society the average citizen may benefit several hundred, even several thousand times a day from applications of the synergism principle. Functional synergism is the key to understanding our biological evolution as a species and the accelerating pace of progressive cultural evolution in recent millennia, and many of its manifestations are highly fragile and contingent; history teaches us that we dare not take it for granted. Accordingly, let me begin with an overview of some of the many forms of cultural synergism.

In modern societies, functional synergism is everywhere around us. Perhaps its most visible manifestations are in the area of high technology. Take a heap of raw materials, mostly iron, bauxite, crude oil, chromium, copper, sand, and a few other minerals; add the technologies of metallurgy, glassmaking, electrical engineering, chemical engineering, textiles, plastics, electronics, and mechanical engineering; the result may still be only a heap of rusting parts in some auto wrecker's lot. However, if the thousands of parts are manufactured to precise specifications and assembled in a precise way by thousands of workers organized in a vast division of labor, and if the resulting hardware is combined with an energy source, spare parts, maintenance facilities, roads, and a skilled human controller, the result *may* be a functioning automobile. Yet even then this familiar masterwork of human inventiveness might not function. As any experienced car owner knows, the automobile is a paradigm case of the contingency of synergistic systems. Whenever the human controller is removed, the system ceases to function. Similarly, it will cease to function when the gas tank is empty, when a traffic jam immobilizes it, when roads are iced over in a blizzard, when a tire goes flat, or when the battery runs down. Surely it is an everyday miracle whenever an automobile functions as expected and does our bidding.

Even more impressive is the fact that the automobile is only one of many everyday miracles, each of which is dependent on complex supporting systems of raw materials, energy sources, manufacturing technologies, start-up capital, distribution capabilities, and consumer (or government) purchasing power. In every case these teleological systems (they are products of external, human design, and they are under external control) have capabilities that emerge from co-operation among the parts and with their human controllers. Physically these systems are no more than the sum of their parts, yet they achieve effects that could not otherwise occur.

Plato and Aristotle understood the synergism principle; so did Adam Smith:

> Observe the accommodation of the most common artificer or day-labourer in a civilized and thriving country, and you will perceive that the number of people whose industry a part, though but a small part, has been employed in procuring him this accommodation, exceeds all computation. The woolen coat, for example, which covers the day-labourer, as coarse and rough as it may appear, is the product of the joint labour of a great multitude of workmen. The shepherd, the sorter of the wool, the wool-comber or carder, the dyer, the scribbler, the spinner, the weaver, the fuller, the dresser, with many others, must all join their different arts in order to complete even this homely production. How many merchants and carriers, besides, must have been employed in transporting the materials from some of those workmen to others who often live in a very distant part of the country! How much commerce and navigation in particular, how many ship-builders, sailors, sail-makers, rope-makers, must have been employed in order to bring together the different drugs made use of by the dyer, which often come from the remotest corners of the world! What a variety of labour too is necessary in order to produce the tools of the meanest of these workmen! To say nothing of such complicated machines as the ship of the sailor, the mill of the fuller, or even the loom of the weaver. Let us consider only what a variety of labour

> is requisite in order to form that very simple machine, the shears with which the shepherd clips the wool. The miner, the builder of the furnace for smelting the ore, the feller of the timber, the burner of the charcoal to be made use of in the smelting house, the brick-maker, the bricklayer, the workmen who attended the furnace, the millwright, the forger, the smith, must all of them join their different arts to produce them. . . . If we examine, I say, all of these things, and consider what a variety of labour is employed about each of them, we shall be sensible that without the assistance and cooperation of many thousands, the very meanest person in a civilized country could not be provided, even according to, what we very falsely imagine, the easy and simple manner in which he is commonly accommodated.[52]

Of course, high technology is merely the tip of the iceberg. Consider the lowly clay brick. When bricks are combined with one another and with mortar, they can be fashioned into a variety of useful structures: houses, factories, churches, garden walls, fireplaces, defensive fortifications, canals, roads, sidewalks, watchtowers—even kilns for making more bricks.

The synergism principle is also embodied in hundreds of ordinary household implements. One way to appreciate this is to disassemble some of them in the mind's eye. Imagine a scissors with only one blade, a tweezers with one claw, a toothbrush with a single bristle, a comb with one tooth. Or imagine a disassembled wicker basket, an unraveled bath towel, a chair in pieces, a broken drinking glass, a piece of paper that has been through a paper shredder, a seesaw without a playmate, a Velcro fastener without its fuzzy partner, an electric appliance during a power outage. Only when the parts have been assembled correctly and combined with energy sources and skilled human actions do these artifacts function at all.

Language is another example of low-technology synergism. Phonemes, or letters, can be combined in precise ways to form words. A seemingly infinite variety of word combinations can then be used to convey meanings, even ideas that never existed before. Language is also dependent on the integrated functioning of the human mind (itself a complex synergistic system) and on our voice production and writing capabilities.

The same principle applies to music. My daughter recently participated in an original musical comedy at our local children's theater. In *Meemyself the Wicked Elf* one song is rendered in a quavery voice by "the only free musical note," a character named So, who has become separated from her companions Do, Re, Me, Fa, La, and Ti (they have been kidnapped). So is sad because she recognizes that she cannot make music alone; all she can do is hum. At the other extreme, Beethoven's Ninth Symphony requires that perhaps one hundred instruments (and instrumentalists) and two hundred singers combine their voices to produce an intricate and exalted patterning of sounds. Surely this is the apex of musical synergism.

Synergism is also present in the food we eat. Some of our most abundant and widely consumed foodstuffs, from corn to domesticated grains and various fruits and vegetables, are genetic hybrids that were selectively bred by humans for their combinatorial properties. Many of the plant foods we consume are heavily dependent on symbiosis between the plant roots and the microscopic bacteria and fungi that are found in almost all fertile soils.[53] For instance, the remarkable nitrogen-fixing ability of soybeans is a function of a co-operative relationship with the bacterium *Rhizobium*.[54]

We also benefit from many forms of nutritional synergism, where two and two can almost literally equal five. For example, one-half cup of beans provides the nutritional equivalent of two ounces of steak, while three cups of whole wheat flour provides the nutritional equivalent of five ounces of steak. Eaten separately, the beans and the flour provide the equivalent of seven ounces of steak. But because of the complementarity of their constituent amino acids, when the beans and the whole wheat are consumed together they provide the equivalent of nine and one-third ounces of steak, or 33 percent more usable protein.

Synergism is also an everyday aspect of the way we prepare our foods. The flavor of a lemon pie is an emergent result of the combination of lemons, butter, eggs, sugar, flour, and salt. Some of the same ingredients put together in a slightly different combination—say, egg yolks, butter, lemon juice, vinegar, salt, and pepper—and prepared in a somewhat different way produces hollandaise sauce.

Our personal health is another synergistic phenomenon. The central thesis of the so-called holistic health movement is that good health is a product of the interaction among many factors: genetic predispositions, diet, exercise, rest, environmental hazards and stresses, and social and emotional factors.*

There is also much evidence of synergism in the social science research literature on what is called collective behavior.[55] Studies of joint decision making have shown that collective decisions are often different—frequently better, sometimes worse—than the statistical aggregates of decisions made by individuals acting alone.[56] In a similar vein, Gumpert found that "teams" are more likely than individuals to be successful as entrepreneurs.[57]

Stanley Milgram's famous experiments on interpersonal aggression are another example. He found that a division (and sharing) of the responsibility for engaging in aggression served as a facilitator: When one person can make the decision and give the orders without having to carry them out, while a second person carries out the orders but is not responsible for making the decisions, the result is heightened aggression.[58] And then there is the phenome-

* The literature on mutual grooming in ethology generally interprets this behavior pattern as an example of reciprocity. In fact the behavior may be synergistic. Assuming an equal degree of diligence, the hygienic function of mutual grooming may well be performed more effectively by a third party.

non of "risky shift," the counterintuitive discovery by J. A. F. Stoner that individuals are more likely to take risks and will make more risky decisions as members of a group than when they act alone.[59]

More subtle is the influence of what the psychologist Robert Zajonc calls social facilitation.[60] It has been observed in human beings and many other animals that the mere presence of a conspecific can markedly affect the behavior of an individual: Food consumption, speed of learning, and work output may be measurably enhanced. There is also the research on mob behavior, going back to Gustav Le Bon's *The Crowd* (1896); what Le Bon called the "collective mind" is in part the mutually facilitative effect of participating in a large-scale social event, whether it be a rock concert, a political rally, or a brawl.

An entirely different aspect of the synergism principle—cost sharing and use sharing among tacitly co-operating individuals—can be found in many of the services and public facilities that we take for granted in modern societies. A parable might be useful here. There once was a fabulously wealthy sheikh who owned 10 percent of the world's oil reserves. Accordingly, he never stinted on the personal amenities, and he prided himself on being able to buy and own virtually everything he used. (While the air he breathed was not for sale, almost everything else was, including several governments, had he wanted to own them.) The sheikh's profligate possessiveness led him to acquire a vast number of properties and belongings strewn around the world: mansions, town houses, vacation retreats, hunting lodges, dude ranches, resort hotels, theaters, casinos. He also amassed a personal livery that looked like a combination of Harrah's antique auto museum and the annual automobile show, and his yachts and airplanes had their own harbors and airports. Nor did the sheikh want for the fuel to run them.

To manage all his accoutrements, the sheikh needed a large retinue of personal servants—secretaries, accountants, messengers, chauffeurs, cooks, housekeepers, tailors, launderers, mechanics, pilots, barbers, gardners, physicians, caddies, etc. In time, the sheikh found that he also needed a vast supporting infrastructure for his empire: farms and farmers, trucking companies, oil refineries, clothing manufacturers, banks, guards, a personal army and navy. Thus the sheikhdom began to take on the contours of a nation-state, all to support one man.

The lesson of this tale lies in the outcome: Because the sheikh's vast empire was used sporadically and inefficiently, his employees became the first leisured working class in history (each of them worked an average of only thirty days a year), but the sheikh wore himself to a frazzle trying to manage his domain, and he died of a heart attack while still in his prime.

Few of us are in a position to own everything we might wish to use, but we can enjoy many of the same amenities as our paradigmatic sheikh because we are willing to share the costs and to use facilities on an as-needed basis.

Although we do not ordinarily think of it in these terms, we are co-operating when we make limited use of public barbershops, restaurants, taxicabs, rental cars, hotels and motels, buses, trains, airlines, hospitals, schools, cleaning services, caterers, coin-operated laundries, parks, package travel tours, and vacation condominiums.

Consider the advantages of some principal forms of functional synergism in modern society:

- *The telephone system.* Because telephones are not linked directly with one another but pass through centralized switching systems (an electronic "commons"), each telephone set requires only one set of interconnecting lines. Because we all share the cost of keeping the entire system in operation twenty-four hours every day, we are able to make use of the system for our limited needs more or less at our convenience and to call virtually any other unit in the system.

- *Insurance.* As Winston Churchill once said, the social insurance principle brings the magic of averages to the rescue of millions. By sharing the costs and averaging the risks, we are able in most cases to protect ourselves against various hazards at a far lower cost than if each of us were self-insured.

- *Public libraries.* We share not only the cost of supporting these institutions, we share the use of the buildings, the librarians' services, and the collections of books, periodicals, and computerized data banks. There are few grandees who could afford to support single-handedly the New York Public Library.

- *Shopping centers.* Even stores that compete directly with one another may find it beneficial to co-locate; concentration has the effect of drawing more customers for everyone. And each store contributes to the support of the "commons"—the parking lots, courtyards, Christmas decorations, and media advertising. Similar co-operation among competitors can be seen in boat shows, trade fairs, and crafts fairs.

- *Multiple movie theaters.* The housing in one building of several auditoriums showing several films with a shared box office, candy stand, projection crew, administrative superstructure, and perhaps a single newspaper advertisement has the effect of reducing the overhead costs that must be borne by each movie and offers moviegoers a larger selection of films at one location.

- *Savings banks.* The cost of safekeeping is shared among many depositors, and each depositor has the opportunity to maintain liquidity while pooling small deposits in large-scale, long-term, interest yielding investments.

- *Supermarkets.* Competing food items (and brands) are co-operatively displayed and sold, and the high volume and centralized distribution of many products minimizes "unit" costs because each customer buys a larger percentage of his or her total needs. Thus the modern supermarket generally can undercut the prices of the corner grocery store *and* make higher profits.

• *Motel, hotel, restaurant, and retail store chains* have the advantages of the availability of start-up capital, economies of scale in the purchase of equipment, supplies, and merchandise, the joint use of management expertise, centralized management functions, and joint advertising.

• *Movie studios.* Once independent and fiercely competitive, the film studios have found it desirable to co-operate in the face of increased costs and greater risks. When one studio has a hot script and another has the "right" stars under contract, the two might pool their assets and even share production costs, thereby reducing their individual financial risks.

• *Management and technical consultants, temporary accountants, temporary clerical workers.* These "hired guns" provide skilled services on an as-needed basis to businesses which tacitly share the costs of supporting these workers.

• *Production sharing,* the rapidly growing phenomenon of widely dispersed international manufacturing processes. Developed countries have the technology, capital management expertise, marketing, and distribution capabilities; developing countries have surpluses of workers. Thus a pair of men's shoes may be made today of an American hide that is tanned in Brazil and shipped by a Japanese trading company to the Caribbean, where the uppers are made in the British Virgin Islands, the soles are made in Haiti, and the shoes are assembled in Puerto Rico under the U.S. tariff umbrella.[61]

• *Corporate conglomerates* may be better able to spread risks, absorb temporary losses, aggregate development capital, and achieve economies in overhead functions.

• *Architects, clothing designers, professional gardeners, interior decorators.* Their products involve emergent wholes whose "gestalt" effects arise from the way in which various elements are selected and combined.

• *Joint advertising.* A supermarket and a soft-drink maker may team up for a promotional campaign. Synergism is also involved when various companies share the cost of producing a television spectacular that will draw a vast audience (by purchasing the time slots for commercials).

Many institutions in modern societies incorporate multiple, interacting forms of functional synergism; they are synergisms of synergy. Your local restaurant, for example, involves a classic division of labor among specialized tasks (maitre d', chefs, bartenders, busboys, waiters and waitresses, dishwashers, cashiers, cleaners, bookkeepers, managers). It depends on a vast technological infrastructure of architects, construction firms, interior designers, the manufacturers of stoves, refrigerators, kitchen and dining room equipment and supplies, farmers, ranchers, fishermen, distillers, vintners, canners, bottlers, transportation and distribution systems, commercial laundries, the advertising media, and such public utilities as mail service, water supplies, electricity, and sewage and garbage disposal systems. In addition, there are the combinatorial effects associated with the dining experience: the decor, the view, the seating arrangements, the table settings, the service, the food, the wine, and the other diners.

Restaurants also enjoy economies of scale in purchasing and preparing food in large quantities. There is tacit co-operation among the patrons who share the cost of supporting a restaurant. There is nutritional synergism in the food combinations that in a well-balanced meal provide complementary sets of nutrients. When the restaurant is located in a shopping center or is part of a well-known restaurant chain, there is the advantage of being linked to external organizations. And there are the synergistic properties of verbal and written language which play an indispensable role in the enormous number of social transactions among the employees, between the restaurant and its environment, and between employees and patrons.

Another ready example of multiple synergies is book publishing. Many years of experience, years of reading and thinking, are synthesized in what I write here. As I write, I am surrounded by the technology of the modern office: word processor, copy machine, telephone and telephone answering machine, tape recorder, paper, writing implements, tables, bookshelves, files, lamps, and electric power. What I write will be processed by an editor, a copy editor, production personnel, book and book jacket designers, advertising and marketing personnel, typesetters, proofreaders, printers, binders, truck drivers, and many others. With luck, when the book appears there will be enough buyers willing to share the costs—at a relatively small incremental cost to each customer—to recover at least what was invested in its production. And if ten thousand people should read this book, what a miracle of communication that would represent. The book took about three years to produce, but if I were to try to recite it to ten thousand people, as individuals or even in small groups, that would require another lifetime of effort. Modern book publishing not only provides a means for widespread cost sharing, it enables an author to communicate with tens of thousands, even millions of people. And that is nothing compared to the tens of millions of television viewers who can be reached by a single presidential speech! How many lifetimes would it take a Ronald Reagan to perform that feat without benefit of the mass media?

Multiple, interacting forms of synergism are also found at the level of national economies. Japan understands and fully exploits the synergism principle. With a population of 115 million people living on a rocky string of islands whose total landmass is equal to about one twenty-fifth of that of the United States (an area roughly equivalent to the area of the state of Indiana), Japan has limited natural endowments. It must import about 90 percent of its energy and most of the raw materials it uses.

At the end of World War II Japan's economy was in ruins, and its cities were devastated by bombing. Yet thirty-five years later Japan had risen from the rubble to become the world's third leading economic power after the United States and Russia. It established preeminence in many areas of high technology; its overall rates of economic growth, savings, investment, and productivity improvement are the best in the industrialized world.

How did Japan do it? There have been many diagnoses recently of Japan's phenomenal success.[62] Commentators have pointed to low labor costs, government subsidies and protectionism, automation, worker productivity (especially the so-called quality circles), corporate paternalism, a low tax burden for defense, and other factors. Yet there is no key factor, no simple formula or technological gimmick that Americans could quickly adopt. Japan's success is the result of a synergistic combination of economic, social, and "political" factors. In a deep sense, Japan's success is a corporate (systemic) phenomenon: It derives from the combination of a functionally compatible set of cultural values and traditions, lessons that were derived from Japan's historical experience, advantages in the economic marketplace, and a highly intelligent set of societal development strategies that its leaders have assiduously pursued for many years.

The Japanese juggernaut is rooted in deeply ingrained cultural values: self-discipline; frugality; strong family life; individual subordination to corporate, community, and national interests; emphasis on co-operation and the conciliation of conflicts; economic and political pragmatism; a reciprocal loyalty between management and labor that can be traced to Japan's feudal past; and a co-operative relationship between government, business, and labor.

Japan's historical experience taught it the value of industrial development and the desirability of acquiring Western technology as aggressively as possible, while its extreme economic dependency created the need to compete effectively abroad. (Japan must export to survive.) In addition, Japan has followed the tried-and-true technique of nurturing and protecting infant industries, just as Western nations did in the nineteenth and early twentieth centuries. And Japan's government has taken care to avoid foreign domination of the economy and to discourage the importation of costly consumer goods produced abroad.

The result of these and other factors is an innovative, efficient, internally co-operative, externally competitive society. Japan's ascendancy has been an organic process: Growth in one sector of the economy has aided others; high-quality components have resulted in high-quality products; the relative efficiency of various parts of the system, from basic industries to public services, has meant lower costs to the whole. For the Japanese appreciate that both efficiencies and inefficiencies can have multiplier effects. When a commuter train that carries 400 passengers to work is 15 minutes late because of a malfunction that would have required one man-hour of preventive maintenance to avoid, with the result that all 400 passengers are 15 minutes late getting to work, the combinatorial effect is a net loss to society of 99 man-hours of productivity. Such slippages are examples of dysergy, or negative synergism; they are fairly common in our own society; they are fairly uncommon in Japan. Japan not only "works" better than any other industrial nation, its leadership has a more farsighted, long-range view of the nation's corporate needs and development objectives.

It has long been held that societies or civilizations experience patterns of systemic flowering—"Golden Ages" and the like. Alternatively, there are forms of decay, decline, and what Kroeber many years ago called "cultural fatigue." One of the most famous cultural climaxes was the classical age in Greece, from about 650–100 B.C., which witnessed an integrated pattern of economic and population growth, innovation and success in the military and political spheres, and breakthroughs in science, architecture, medicine, philosophy, history, literature, and the arts. Similar flowerings, or synergistic patterns, are associated with the Middle Kingdom in Egypt, the Mayans, successive Chinese dynasties (Chou, Han, and T'ang), the Romans, Elizabethan and Victorian England, and the U.S. during much of this century.

Conversely, just as low morale and poor leadership can have adverse effects on the performance of a team or a business firm, so entire societies can suffer from self-defeating moods of disillusionment and social malaise. Kroeber cites one famous example among the Polynesian Hawaiians, who in 1819, before Western colonization began, precipitously abolished an oppressive and increasingly decadent religion.[63] In more recent times one can point to French defeatism in 1940 in the face of the Nazis and the collapse of self-confidence in the post-Vietnam era United States. While such social-psychological processes are hard to measure, they seem to have measurable effects. On the other hand, societal declines are often impelled by material forces of one kind or another, such as the depletion of a critical resource or the rise of competition.

An Excursus on the Synergism Principle

It is obvious that synergism is no simple, one-dimensional phenomenon; the term denotes *combinatorial effects* of many kinds. It is not equivalent to the division of labor, to new technology, to economies of scale, or to social co-operation, though it may involve all these things. Many examples of synergism arise as a result of the coordinated action of the parts in a complex, goal-oriented (cybernetic) system. Physically such wholes are never more than the sum of their parts, but the combined efforts of the system as a whole may produce unique results that would not otherwise be possible. Joseph Schumpeter observed many years ago: "Add successively as many mail coaches as you please, you will never get a railway thereby."[64] And if you take away a major component of a teleological or teleonomic system—the engine of an automobile, the conductor of an orchestra, the brain and nervous system of a human being—you will no longer have a whole in terms of its being able to achieve the goals for which the system was designed. (If you take away a less vital part, the system may continue to function but with a diminished capacity.)

Many synergistic systems involve the production of a "new" function, but obviously this is not always the case. A system might do no more than perform an existing function more efficiently in terms of outputs and/or costs. Thus Adam Smith's pin factory was not essential to the manufacture of pins any more than a Boeing 747 differs in terms of its function from the old DC-3. Likewise, a synergistic system may achieve nothing more than an alternative means for performing an existing function when the earlier method has been ruled out. One example of this was the rapid development of synthetic rubber in the United States during World War II, when imports of natural rubber from the Far East were cut off.

Synergism may also entail threshold effects in an existing set of functional relationships. When you add another player to one side of an evenly matched tug-of-war, you tip the balance and bring the "war" closer to its end. The entry of the United States into World War I had much the same effect. When you add a 10 percent tariff to the price of an import, you effectively protect an infant domestic industry until it can achieve economies of scale. And when you add one more passenger to an airliner that has 60 percent of its seats occupied, you may make the difference between operating at a loss and breaking even. Thus synergism often involves the sort of phenomena that are expressed in the traditional economic analyses of marginal costs, marginal returns, etc., as well as in some of the mathematical models developed by the "catastrophe" theorists. The catastrophes in the models devised by René Thom and others are simply nonlinear transformations.[65] These models do not explain why such transformations occur; they merely describe them in mathematical terms. Many synergistic phenomena, to follow Thom's metaphor, are *combinatorial catastrophes:* They produce nonlinear combinatorial effects.[66]*

Not all synergistic effects occur in goal-oriented (cybernetic) systems. Many accidental or coincidental forms of synergism are not at all the result of a "design" that is shaped to some end. Anyone who has done mountain climbing understands that, while the parts were not designed for the purpose of challenging and accommodating mountain climbers (at least within the framework of scientific cosmology), the whole is nevertheless greater than the sum of its parts.

The distinction between synergism in purposive (cybernetic) systems and synergism as a result of ecological interactions is important; it intersects with the distinction between cybernetic systems and ecosystems, or between firms and markets. The participants in a natural or human ecosystem may be oblivious to overarching goals. Neither the creatures that inhabit Darwin's entangled bank nor the customers who patronize my local French restaurant can be said to be consciously playing a role in supporting these systems. On the other hand, the worker bees in Mandeville's fruitful hive and the employees of my neighborhood restaurant are definitely playing roles, and by various means their behaviors are shaped toward achieving collective ends.

To the customer, the restaurant is a part of his or her ecosystem (or marketplace). To the employee, the restaurant is a superordinate system to which his or her behavior contributes, and for which he or she is rewarded. But just as the beekeeper and the bees may have a common interest in preserving the hive, the patrons and the employees may have stakes in the well-being of the restaurant, though their stakes will be as different as the means by which their behaviors are made to subserve the goals of the system. Both are beneficiaries of the synergism produced by the restaurant. Furthermore, neither the customers nor the employees may be motivated in their behavior by the goals of the restaurant. Although higher-level systemic goals may be instrumental to their own goals as well, they may not be conscious of the fact. Yet the pursuit of their own self-interest may contribute to these higher-level goals. And the success of the restaurant in achieving the minimal goal of remaining viable contributes to the goals of the employees and the patrons. I call this phenomenon *egoistic co-operation.*

Synergistic phenomena, then, do not necessarily require (1) cybernetic systems with overarching, systemic goals; (2) human actors in social relationships; (3) a division of labor and deliberate co-operation among participants;

* A good example of a combinatorial catastrophe is love. Two individuals whose behavior patterns are independent of one another come together and, sometimes precipitously, begin to coordinate their behaviors and their personal goals in ways that may result in drastic and enduring changes of life-style.

(4) an awareness of being part of a synergistic system. (We may discover our dependency only when one of the parts goes on strike.)

The normative implications of synergistic phenomena are also more ambiguous than some moralists, who have endowed the term synergism with the properties of an intrinsic good, would lead one to believe. Some forms of synergism may well involve what the economists call collective goods (indivisible benefits to all parts or participants).[67] When the army deters an attack by another country, presumably all citizens benefit. On the other hand, synergistic effects often involve divisible goods: When a pack of wild dogs succeeds in bringing down a Thompson's gazelle, or when a skillful team of robbers makes off with the contents of your local bank's vault, the booty may or may not be shared equitably. These are what might be called corporate goods, divisible benefits produced by the actions of the whole. (This is a neglected area in economic theory.)

Not only may the benefits associated with synergistic systems be divisible but so might be the costs. Some parts of a car wear out more rapidly than others; some citizens may evade taxes or the draft while others pay more than their share or die in battle. Many forms of social co-operation are involuntary; military drafts, tax systems, legal and penal codes, and the various informal modes of coercion that are perfused throughout our political, economic, and family structures represent what might be called coerced co-operation.

Even when everyone participates willingly and shares equitably in the benefits, there is what I call the paradox of dependency. The more valuable are the benefits extracted from a synergistic system, the more costly will be the loss of that system should it fail to continue functioning. Thus a predator may become dependent on its prey (koala bears and eucalyptus trees; the Attini and their fungus gardens), just as "capitalists" are to a degree the captives of their markets and infants are captives (in a sense) of their parents.

In the 1930s, when the United States still consisted mainly of small farms widely dispersed throughout the country, a local disaster could be absorbed with minimal consequences for the country as a whole. During the famous dust bowl era, one quarter of the nation's farmland lay fallow for a time. Today we have no surplus land and our agricultural system is more concentrated, both regionally and economically. The system is much more efficient but much more vulnerable. If the so-called Medfly (the Mediterranean fruit fly) had succeeded in conquering California's Central Valley, one-half of the nation's fruit and vegetable crop might have become maggot-infested. Likewise, the entire country might someday be the captive of a California drought, should there be a more prolonged version of the one that occurred only a few years ago.

Synergistic effects may not even involve a good, in either the economic sense or the normative sense. Synergism just *is;* it is a consequential effect in the physical and social realms. It may or may not be eufunctional; that is, it may not have positive or beneficial consequences in relation to some need, want, or goal. The functional consequences of a synergistic phenomenon are always context-specific: They are co-determined by the properties of the phenomena in question and by the actors or the system whose functional requirements may be served. Thus the combinatorial properties of a mountain may be of no functional significance to human beings until someone wants to get to the other side of it or wants to use the mountain as a defensive barrier. Moreover, its functional significance may come and go. Where mountains were once formidable obstacles, various types of man-machine synergism have greatly reduced their functional significance for most of us. Rivers, another synergistic phenomenon, have also varied over the centuries in terms of their functional significance for humans. At different times and places they have been defensive barriers, transportation arteries, direct sources of food, sources of drinking water, sewers, sources of irrigation water, generators of electric power, playgrounds, an inspiration for poets, painters, and lovers, and simply landmarks.

Thus the functional significance of synergism is always *relational.* When I am hungry, an ice cream sundae may be nourishing; when I am full, it may give me indigestion. Add another player to each side in a tug-of-war and the additions may make no functional change; increase the price of aviation fuel and it may require more than one additional passenger for the airline to break even on the trip. These are the functional properties that economists and ecologists describe with their marginal cost and marginal value theorems.

The obverse of the point is that the functional consequences of a synergistic phenomenon may also depend on what alternatives are available. There may be better or worse automobiles, restaurants, and pin factories. When Henry Ford allegedly told his customers they could have any color they wanted as long as it was black, he went right on selling cars—for a while. When competitors began offering their customers a variety of colors, the Ford Motor Company almost went bankrupt before Henry, a notoriously rigid man, finally relented.

I have already suggested that there are many forms of negative synergy, or dysergy. Up to a point, an increase in the number of participants in a system may be to everyone's advantage, for there may be economies of scale, augmented effects, and threshold effects. As long as there are empty tables at the restaurant, empty seats on the bus, or unused circuits in the telephone system, an increase in utilization may ensure lower unit costs. But beyond a certain point the result may be waiting lines, traffic jams, overloaded circuits, or inflation when demand outruns supply. Similarly, drug A and drug B may be highly beneficial when taken separately, but taken together, their combined effect might be catastrophic.

Synergism, Economics, and Bioeconomics

Much of the foregoing may sound suspiciously like a restatement of elementary economics and bioeconomics in different terms. To a degree this is true, for I am concerned with the same phenomena. As I indicated in Chapter IV, my approach can claim to be more ecumenical in that it recognizes and encompasses both conventional and biologically oriented approaches. Synergistic phenomena are relevant both to the concept of utility and to the concept of adaptation. More to the point, where the economist or the theoretical ecologist is interested in quantitative measures (laws and predictive models) relative to the behavior, or choices, of individuals or firms, I am concerned with functional dynamics, with the systems of causal interactions that produce the measured effects that mold economic choices and bioeconomic outcomes. This approach involves a reconceptualization of socioeconomic processes in terms of co-operative interactions in whole systems. The approach is not opposed to the work of economists and bioeconomists; it is complementary to it.

I have said that my approach is fundamentally Darwinian and biological in the sense that the basic frame of reference for explaining the broader trends in sociocultural evolution is adaptation in relation to the biological problem of survival and reproduction. An organized society is a collective survival enterprise. The concept of adaptation is in turn specified in terms of a broad conception of basic needs, though it recognizes that social behavior is not a simple, deterministic expression of those needs. Rather, behavior is the product of a complex set of interactions among (1) bedrock needs, (2) biopsychological motivations and response propensities ("human nature"), and (3) a matrix of superorganic and ecological systems in which the individual actors develop and seek to satisfy their needs. Thus both economic and bioeconomic forms of analysis are appropriate: The former is based on the causes and consequences of behavior in relation to biological needs (adaptation), and the latter is based on culturally induced wants, tastes, or preferences (utilities). In either case the focus is on how synergistic effects interact with needs and/or wants.

To appreciate the differences between this approach and that of conventional economics or bioeconomics, consider the synergism principle in relation to concepts that one finds in standard economics texts. Can it be said that the synergism principle is equivalent to "land, labor, and capital," the division of labor,* the laws of supply and demand, marginal cost and marginal value,

* The phrase "division of labor" (or "specialization") tends to obscure the fact that there are many different kinds of co-operative behaviors involved in economic production. Adam Smith recognized three kinds, not all of which may be categorically different from each of the others. One is specialization in the production of the total mix of societal goods and services

(Continued)

utility, economies of scale, technology,* efficiency, collective goods, competition, surpluses, profits, benefit-cost ratios, or Pareto optimality? I submit that none of the concepts, nor all the concepts together, will add up to the concept of combinatorial (synergistic) effects in whole systems, to co-operative functional interactions. Synergistic effects may well have properties that can be described or measured in terms of these other concepts, but functional synergism is different: It encompasses and relates to all of them.

Synergistic effects are also measurable. In fact, they are measured routinely by economists, ecologists, business people, and military leaders, and there is no limit to the possible ways of measuring them. One can measure synergism in strictly physical terms: the number of raspberry tarts produced per hour, the number of passengers that can be flown to Bangkok on one hop, the number of customers who choose to enter your restaurant, or the number of offspring that survive to maturity (reproductive efficiency).

One can also measure synergism in terms of various economic or bioeconomic metrics, measuring rods that enable one to compare functional effects across broad categories of phenomena. These metrics include such cultural forms as dollars, yen, or marks and such thermodynamic forms as energetic benefit-cost ratios or hours of labor. For example: A farmer with a horse can plow about 2 acres per day, while a farmer with a tractor can plow about 20 acres per day. A native Amazonian using a steel ax can fell about five times as many trees in a given amount of time as could his ancestors with stone axes. One New Guinea horticulturalist can produce enough food to feed himself and about four or five other people; an American farmer can produce enough to feed him or herself and forty-five to fifty other people. In order to meet its costs, my neighborhood French restaurant must charge

---

(one person makes nails, the next makes shoes). A second kind of specialization would apply to the pin factory, where the production of pins may be divided into component tasks. The third kind involves specialization in relation to the stages in a production sequence, such as the manifold steps between the raising of sheep and the marketing of a woolen coat. Smith also appreciated how regional specialization might create opportunities for taking advantage of differences in the availability of resources, in climate, and in soil conditions. (Plato, too, emphasized the potential advantages of fitting people with different abilities to different tasks and permitting an individual to specialize in order to increase his or her skill and proficiency.)

* Some social theorists, recognizing the systemic and multifaceted nature of social change, have responded by defining technology so broadly that the definition comes close to being a tautology. If technology includes ideas, management, organization, hardware, labor, skills, information, resources, and energy, just about everything can be included. Having myself sinned in this regard, I now find it more useful to separate the components of economic life into a limited number of functionally meaningful categories. I restrict technology to hardware, software, and closely associated information. I treat the traditional "factors of production" (land, labor, and capital) as separate. I also differentiate sharply the "political" (cybernetic) aspects of the production process: goal-setting, decision making, communications, control, and feedback functions.

$11 to $13 for an entree, while a large and popular restaurant nearby serves complete dinners of comparable quality for $5 to $7 (drinks and dessert are extra).

These measurable outcomes represent more than the effects of technology or economies of scale. They measure the combined effects of the total system. When the technological hardware or the scale of an operation stands out in a theorist's mind, it is because he or she holds all other things equal or puts them into the background.*

In contrast, the synergism principle requires a systemic viewpoint. As a result, it is never embarrassed by the anomalies, exceptions, and qualifiers that arise in the real world, where all other things are seldom if ever equal. When the depletion of the soil reduces the efficiency of modern agricultural technology, it comes as no surprise. When the laws of supply and demand are warped by political incentives and constraints of various kinds, it is expected. (All economic life is political in my terms.) And when tastes change in response to new information about their bioeconomic consequences, as in smoking or the use of birth control pills, what else is new?

Because the synergism principle focuses on the functional effects produced by sociocultural systems, it offers an approach to bridging the gap between holistic systems theories and atomistic decision making, rational choice, and games theoretical approaches. The thesis is that the course of sociocultural evolution has been shaped by the synergistic effects produced in and by various superorganic and ecological systems, natural and human. These systems generate effects that are differently favored in the process of teleonomic selection, the purposive (goal-oriented) choices made by actors whose behavior conforms to a "quasirational choice" model. These synergistic effects provide the real-world quantitative values that are modeled by social scientists and behavioral biologists in their time-budgeting analyses, energetic analyses, analyses of the Law of Least Effort or the less stringent "economy principle," and analyses that utilize marginal value theorems or strategic choice and game theoretic models. Synergistic effects are particularly relevant to models of collective

* In the example of the two restaurants, one might conclude from the information that one of them seats 35 people while the other seats 250 people, which accounts for the difference in prices. It is certainly a significant factor. But there are other factors: The larger restaurant has a better location; the larger restaurant is open continuously from 8 A.M. to 10 P.M., seven days a week, while the French restaurant is open only six days a week, in the evening and for weekday lunches; and the larger restaurant has a highly efficient kitchen. In the larger restaurant the customers are served much faster and there is a faster turnover. The consequence of larger size, faster service, longer hours, high quality, and low price is that the larger restaurant has a much higher volume in relation to both its fixed costs and some semivariable costs. Indeed, there is almost always a waiting line, and few seats are unoccupied for long. (In fact, it has been so successful that it is on its way to becoming a chain.)

goods, "positive sum" games, and "prisoner's dilemma" games and "coalition theory."[68] These models collectively have demonstrated that various kinds of rational choice criteria (or efficiency in relating means to ends) are applicable, that it is often "efficient" to engage in co-operative behavior, but that an efficiency criterion is not sufficient to account for social behavior and evolution.

The Teleonomic Selection Model

Although formal models have yielded important insights into the inner logic of animal and human behavior, the teleonomic selection model provides a much broader and more inclusive framework for comprehending sociocultural evolution. It adds to the formal models a more elaborate set of assumptions about underlying sources of human values and preferences and the dynamics of behavioral and social causation.

Recall the discussion in Chapters II and IV. The notion that biological evolution is shaped in part by behavioral selection processes can be traced to Lamarck. At the turn of the century, a version of this idea that was consonant with Darwinism was articulated by the Organic Selection theorists. After many years the idea was revived and has since been espoused by numerous theorists, often independently of one another.

The idea that an analogous selection process has characterized sociocultural evolution likewise has a venerable heritage. A circumscribed version of it can be found in *The Descent of Man.* Yet the most full-throated and carnivorous of the early cultural selectionists were the Social Darwinists.[69] And after a hiatus of several decades, selectionist models are again commonplace.[70]

Processes of cultural selection do occur. One well-documented example is that of the automobile. In the late nineteenth century there were innumerable experiments with road vehicles, and at the turn of the century the large variety of motor cars on the road included Stanley Steamers, three-wheeled electric cars that resembled today's powered wheelchairs, and the Duryea and other vehicles that literally looked like horseless carriages. A major breakthrough came with the development of a practicable internal combustion engine. The basic patent was obtained by Seldon in 1879 and the first working car was produced by Daimler in 1892. Nevertheless in 1900 there were still only about 10,000 powered vehicles in the United States, versus about 25 million horses.

Then came the rapid increase in national wealth during World War I, the discovery of vast amounts of crude oil and cracking processes which lowered the price of fuel dramatically, significant improvements in the design of the automobile (such as the self-starter), and Henry Ford's mass production techniques. By 1960 (about twelve horse and automobile generations later) the horse population had declined to less than 5 million while the number of automobiles had surpassed 75 million.[71]

However, it would be wrong to characterize the evolution of the automobile as having involved blind variation, as some theorists have contended.[72] Rather, it was the result of a purposeful ("value-driven") process of experimentation and development that spanned many decades. Nor was any single factor responsible ultimately for the widespread adoption and diffusion of automobiles. The automobile revolution was the product of a synergistic combination that included a set of prior needs, appropriate cultural settings, many component technologies, and the development of a supportive infrastructure (paved roads, traffic signals, gas stations and garages, laws and traffic cops). If necessity was the mother of invention, invention was also the mother of necessity.

The selection process that led to the adoption of the automobile recurs with each generation. The recent shift in the American market to small, fuel-efficient imports illustrates the point; so does the threat of fossil fuel exhaustion, which will in time precipitate a cultural analogue of what the biologists call disruptive selection (as opposed to directional selection and normalizing or stabilizing selection).

Although we tend to be more conscious of those cultural forms which are positively selected and endure than we are of those which are rejected, the process of cultural selection and systematic change has many facets. Some cultural forms or artifacts emerge from preexisting technology (television). Others are tried, enjoy a brief popularity, and eventually fall by the wayside (stereopticons). Still others emerge to replace existing forms (electric lights versus whale oil and gas lamps) or to relegate an earlier technology to different functions (the gun versus the bow and arrow). Some innovations are retained, are modified and improved over time, and take on new functions (the automobile).

By and large, cultural evolution has involved a stringent winnowing process. We tend to forget the Rube Goldberg inventions that gather dust in attics because they do not work or because they do nothing that is particularly useful. Only about one-half of all patents granted in the United States are ever utilized; less than 10 percent of all new products are marketed successfully; and about 80 percent of new businesses eventually fail.[73] We mostly observe the winners.

Contemporary social scientists generally agree that cultural evolution can be characterized as a process of descent with modification, but the basic issue remains unresolved: How do we conceptualize and explain how and why this process has occurred? One of the earliest and best-known formulations is psychologist Donald T. Campbell's "blind variation and selective retention" model, which set the pattern of thought for a number of theorists. However, Campbell did not attempt to specify the sources of the variations or the selection criteria (or "mechanisms"), which would have qualified his model as a full-fledged theory.*[74]

Later theorists have tended to emphasize one or another aspect of the selection process. Some focus on external changes in the natural and social environments.[75] Skinner adopts a behaviorist approach.[76] Others focus on internal values or psychological processes. Alchain, for instance, offered a "positive profits" (versus profit maximization) model for economic development.[77] Boehm suggests a "rational pre-selection" framework for cultural evolution, in which a key role is assigned to decisions that derive from rational human faculties rather than to more mechanistic behavioral responses.[78]† Still other theorists posit the existence of reified cultural units analogous to genes, which are said to be the basic units of cultural evolution. These analogues have variously been called mnemotypes, ideas, idenes, instructions, sociogenes, culture types, memes, concepts, and culturgens. (For my purposes, the older concept of functionally discrete cultural traits or artifacts, still the most common in anthropology, is perfectly satisfactory.‡) The sociobiologists seem particularly prone to advancing models that parallel the established modes of conceptualizing biological evolution. Thus Mundinger offers a theory of cultural evolution based on three causal mechanisms [*sic*]: "psychological selection," "meme flow," and "memetic drift," which are said to parallel the mechanisms of biological evolution.[81]§

* Campbell's model has been criticized from various points of view. While it is of seminal importance, the model begs two key questions. One concerns the sources of the variations. That is, how can purposive, goal-directed innovations arise if the variations are blind? Some critics, myself included, have argued for a mixed model; while some variations may truly be fortunate accidents, others are the highly canalized result of a preestablished goal and purposeful trial and error. This means that some innovations may have a probability of occurrence that is far greater than random. (Campbell himself seems to have backed away from a purist position on this issue.) The second question is, what are the selection criteria by which some variations are selected and others are not? Here Campbell was tentative initially and discussed only categories, not criteria.

† Boehm differentiates between teleonomic and rational choices. I treat rationalistic choice making as a subset of a much larger category of teleonomic or purposive selection processes which includes the mechanisms of classical and operant conditioning, imitation and insight learning. This is consistent with the cybernetic model of behavior. From my perspective the distinction Boehm makes seems to imply that rational choice processes are not purposive. I believe the unified approach is superior, but we have agreed to disagree on this point (personal communication).

‡ The definitions of culture and a cultural trait refer to behaviorally relevant (that is, causally significant) information which is stored neuronally, rather than in the genome, and which is transmitted by social means rather than through biological reproduction.[79] D. L. Clarke provides a rigorously developed approach to measuring artifactual traits.[80]

§ Mundinger's analogy with natural selection, while suggestive, does not hold up well to close scrutiny. Like natural selection, we are told, psychological selection can be defined as "the differential transmission of memes." The trouble is that this parallels the defective, tautologi-

(Continued)

There are some problems with the alternative selectionist approaches that have been offered to date. One is that the sources of the variations that provide the raw material of cultural evolution must be specified more precisely, and the conflicting viewpoints on this issue need to be reconciled. Another problem is that the selective agency, the mind or brain, is generally specified only vaguely or is reduced to one of the oversimplified caricatures that have burdened social theory for generations. In effect, theorists have posited that the selecting agency is the classical economic man or rational man or behaviorist man or sociocultural man or, lately, fitness-maximizing man.[82]

A third problem is that the selection process is generally viewed in a reified way that abstracts it out of the real-world selective matrix. Items of culture are seen as randomly distributed free-floating units. Thus memes are said to be selected from meme pools, a cultural analogue of gene pools, which are themselves mathematical abstractions of limited theoretical use. In reality, both natural selection and cultural selection are more highly structured processes. Just as many population biologists have been led astray by a failure to appreciate the extent to which individual genes are embedded in—and serve as functional parts of—synergistic interaction systems (after Sewall Wright), so cultural selectionists have tended to give short shrift to the synergistic social systems in which particular cultural traits are embedded. Schumpeter, rebutting the Marxist viewpoint, had this to say on the subject: "Because of this fundamental dependence of the economic aspect of things on everything else, it is not possible to explain *economic* change by previous *economic* conditions alone. For the economic state of a people does not

---

cal definition of natural selection as the differential transmission of alternative genes, a definition which misrepresents Darwin's theory. In these terms, neither natural selection nor psychological selection can be called a mechanism or a causal theory. By contrast, the functionalist approach I employ focuses on the causes of differential success and transmission, causes that involve functional interactions in which both the organism and the environment are causally important.

A second problem has to do with the utility of inventing a reified entity called a meme or a culturgen. Geneticists have found the gene to be an analytically and theoretically useful concept. The empirical basis for the gene is the observable trait, the production of which was inferred to be the result of a basic unit of hereditary transmission and reproduction. The problem is that the meme involves an unwarranted degree of reification. There is no unitary physical vehicle of transmission and cultural causation at the social level. To suggest that this is the case, by drawing such an analogy, has the effect of reducing a complex set of mechanisms and processes for information acquisition, storage, and transmission to a single homogeneous unit and a single mechanism of causation.

I doubt that drift will be a factor of major importance in cultural evolution. Just as the drift advocates in biology discount the functional imperatives of the life process and the stringency of the economy principle, so the advocates of cultural drift tend to underrate the functional imperatives in social life.

emerge simply from the preceding economic conditions, but only from the preceding total situation."[83]

Another problem with the alternative approaches is that the fundamentally interactional nature of evolutionary causation in general and cultural evolution in particular is obscured in most frameworks. The *total* configuration of functional relationships, both within the organism and between the organism and its environment, is the agency of differential survival and reproduction. Natural selection is the outcome of an interaction between the expressed needs and capabilities of the organism on the one hand and the constraints and opportunities in its specific environment.[84] In exactly the same way, the cause of teleonomic selection—and of systematic cultural change—is the outcome of the learned behavioral interactions that occur between organisms and their cultural environments. Neither the organism nor the environment alone is responsible; the two together co-determine the outcome. Thus Thorndike's Law of Effect *approximates* the causal dynamics of sociocultural evolution: Rewards and punishments do indeed mold behavioral continuities and changes. The major shortcomings of the classical behaviorist formulation lay in its being too lawlike; it did not include a benefit-cost calculus, and it did not take sufficient account of the degree to which the organism itself generated the raw material (the variations) and specified what is rewarding and punishing—and why. Classical behaviorist psychology did not have an adequate model of the behaving organism and tended to treat reinforcements as a mechanism rather than as a loose description of a class of effects.

I call this interactional process teleonomic selection because the accumulating evidence in the behavioral and brain sciences points to a more complex model of human nature and behavioral causation than most of the classical social theorists and the classical schools of psychology were willing to recognize. The model that best fits the evidence is a purposive model; it has the properties of a multileveled cybernetic system. The inner logic of the system derives from the *a priori* challenge of survival and reproduction (and the imperatives associated with the trajectory of the biological life cycle). Some theorists have proposed that reproductive fitness (or inclusive fitness) might provide an overarching criterion that could be used to explain the process of cultural evolution.[85] While this is generally compatible with my approach, I believe that a more fine-grained set of criteria is needed.

In general, cultural evolution reflects a more proximate, partially autonomous level of causation; it is more complex than can be captured in a simple inclusive fitness model. It is absurd to argue that such systematic cultural patterns as priestly celibacy, hara-kiri, and birth control are related to maximizing the individual's inclusive fitness. Natural selection explains the origins of our mental capacities, our learning biases, and our drive states, but it does not account for how they are molded in the environment and how they operate in specific cultural contexts. Inclusive fitness theory cannot explain why Central American Indian populations adopted the cultural pattern of consuming combinations of corn and beans. Biologically, such a practice is highly adaptive, and it may well have enhanced the fitness of those populations that adopted this cultural trait, but the fitness consequences cannot account for the origin of the trait. Natural selection can explain the evolution of our taste buds and the sources of some of our underlying nutritional biases; however, reinforcement learning would seem to be the more parsimonious proximate cause in this case. Similarly, inclusive fitness theory cannot explain why the Shakers adopted a celibacy rule, but it may explain why celibacy rules tend not to diffuse very widely.

The configuration of basic needs specified in Chapter IV can be used to approximate the specifications of the survival challenge for each individual. Our ways of responding to this challenge manifest cybernetic properties. The behaving system of the individual is self-organizing. We more or less effectively use our biopsychological equipment, our previous experience, and information inputs and feedback from the cultural environment to solve problems, develop adaptive strategies, order priorities, make decisions, and take actions involving allocations of time, energy, and resources.[86] The process is not mechanistic but synthetic—synergistic. Perhaps the most economical way of elucidating an individual's game plan for adaptation is to measure how his or her time is allocated in relation to each basic need. Some preliminary data suggest that a large share of our time, even in modern industrial societies, is apportioned to meeting basic needs. For most of us most of the time, our behavior patterns are reasonably ordered.

Equally important, human nature is not simply the expression of crude physiological appetites. We have appetites that are psychological, social, and emotional. They are evolved behavioral instrumentalities that have facilitated our adaptation to both social and natural environments. Thus the well-documented needs for stimulation, achievement, and esteem, along with our curiosity and our problem-solving abilities, are also causal factors. Whatever their source, the operational goals that we pursue as individuals and organized groups provide the immediate selective focus, or screen, for the differential adoption of cultural traits. Teleonomic selection involves more than a reflexive response to reinforcers, as in the behaviorist paradigm. It involves a synergistic interplay or synthesis of motivational, affective, cognitive, and perceptual elements in a dynamically integrated goal structure. Again the concept of goals is central.[87]

Our understanding of the sources of cultural evolution will remain clouded and theoretically deficient so long as the social sciences continue to deny the indeterminate but highly purposive role of creativity, innovation, and entrepreneurship as direct causal agencies in sociocultural evolution.[88] Indeed,

Baumol's conclusion of many years ago still stands: Economists generally agree that innovation and enterprise are important aspects of economic development, yet they remain neglected subjects among academicians because they are theoretically intractable. To paraphrase Marx, economists tend to take on only those problems which can be solved (or at least modeled mathematically).*

Despite the body of rapidly accumulating data, our knowledge of human nature and human development is still imperfect. Just as in Darwin's time the science of genetics had not yet been invented, leaving obscure to Darwin and his contemporaries the precise mechanisms of biological variation, our own day awaits the developments in the behavioral and brain sciences that will give us a more precise understanding of the mechanisms of teleonomic selection.

But in general, our behavioral choices tend to conform to the economy principle. As individuals we cannot operate for very long at a deficit any more than a business firm can. We are open thermodynamic systems, yet we do not fit well into any one factor maximization model because we must strike a balance among an array of needs and wants. Thus we often satisfice, in accordance with the decision-making model pioneered by Herbert Simon.[91]

Another important aspect of the teleonomic selection model insofar as it applies to the evolution of social species is that it has more than one level. One of the most pervasive oversights of contemporary cultural selectionist models is the fact that social life is also political (in my terms). Among the social carnivores, and our close primate relatives, individuals are enmeshed in constraining cybernetic social systems. Accordingly, there is a more or less intense interplay between the processes and mechanisms of self-control for each member of the hive, troop, pack, group, or band and various forms of external (teleological) control by other members. Indeed, conflicts over the exercise of social control are ubiquitous features of animal and human societies alike. The problem is hardly unique to human beings, but we are perhaps the most contentious of social species. We also have the most complex political structures. Thus Richerson's sweeping rejection of higher-level purposiveness, which he calls the "fallacy of misplaced teleology," is too extreme and sociologically naive.[92]

* The question of how innovations occur in evolution—how the sources of variation arise—is currently being debated.[89] Many years ago, relative to a discussion of linguistic innovation, Reynolds suggested what may prove to be the ultimate middle-ground position. Novelty in language may come about by virtue of such unintentional occurrences as errors, he said, but it may also be the product of innovation by intent.[90] (Some of the neologisms to be found in this book may be examples of the latter.) When the case for a more complex model of the mind and internal causes of behavior becomes more widely accepted, this essentially subsidiary issue will, I hope, dissolve as well.

Much cultural innovation and adaptive change, especially in human societies, is collective in nature. The strategies developed by organized groups on behalf of the group, whether they be developed within the family group or larger entities, affect the choices and the behavioral patterns of the members. Many products designed for children are selected by their parents, sometimes over vehement protests; the post office may impose a new mailing system (zip plus four) on a more or less recalcitrant populace. The rice terrace adaptation of the Igorot is a paradigm case of a collective adaptation in a primitive society.

The political dimension or level of cultural evolution in human beings is of overriding importance. Our ability to coordinate behavior and to act as a group has played a decisive part in human evolution. Its role in the evolution of animal societies is more problematical, but there is evidence that political (socially organized) modes of cultural evolution are probably not uniquely human.[93]

To obtain compliance with social goals and norms, human societies erect structures of reinforcers—physical, material, and psychosocial rewards and punishments that become part of the selective environment for individual members. (Alexander Lesser called it a social field.[94]) These structures range from legal and penal systems to salaries and commissions, badges of honor and prestige, hierarchies of status and authority, classroom grades, and "objective" advancement criteria.

The social structures that we create for meeting our needs and servicing our wants have functional requisites of their own. Though social theorists of the structural-functionalist persuasion have always insisted on this point, the Durkheimian tradition has recently come under attack. The anthropologist Paul Diener could be speaking for an entire legion of anti-functionalists when he accuses Julian Steward of using "fallacious functional arguments" to explain various cultural patterns.[95]

Again the truth (or the dialectical synthesis) lies in the middle. Recall that in evolutionary processes functional requisites and functional effects are causes, albeit not the only causes. (Contrary to the argument advanced by Diener and his co-workers, functional explanations are neither identical with nor separate from evolutionary explanations.[96]) Organizations impose constraints and create imperatives for their operators that are instrumental to the survival and effective functioning of the organization. These requisites may not be sufficient to explain the origins and development of an organization; most often they are only subgoals that are instrumental to the larger goals that brought the organization into existence in the first place. But they are necessary; they are co-determinants that in part explain why a given organization exists and operates as it does or why it fails to persist. Thus organizational needs may become unavoidable (instrumental) necessities that may fuel invention and teleonomic selection. An obvious example of this is the intercom, a ubiquitous cultural artifact in modern businesses that resulted from both preexisting technologies and a specific office need.

Teleonomic selection is not a concept that lends itself exclusively to simple mathematical models and tidy theoretical analyses with aggregate statistics. The models developed by such theorists as Boorman and Levitt, Lumsden and Wilson, and Cavalli-Sforza and Feldman may shed useful light on the subject, but one also pays a price for such simplifications.[97] Over the short term the process of sociocultural evolution will remain intractable to those who aspire to develop predictive models.

In the final analysis, the processes of teleonomic selection and sociocultural evolution focus on a critical set of interactions. *Internally* there are the emergent goals of the effective unit of cybernetic choice making and control, whether it be individuals, higher-level political units, or a synthesis of the two. The basis for the revealed preferences (or operative selection criteria) is itself a synthesis of various factors. *Externally* there is the patterning of the selective field. The internal causes arise out of the cybernetic processes described earlier. The external causes arise from the synergistic effects I described.

The immediate stimulus for evolutionary changes may be "positive"—a new ecological niche, a new resource, a new technology, a new trading opportunity—or it may be "negative"—a climate shift, the exhaustion of a resource, a new threat from another human population. However, these factors alone do not cause cultural changes. They create new opportunities or needs and they change the structure of the selective field by changing the configuration or pattern of functional relationships. To attribute a cultural shift to a technological breakthrough is to ignore the matrix in which that innovation is embedded. Such breakthroughs resemble the missing pieces of a puzzle or the missing links in a chain: They complete the elements of a synergistic system, allowing it to become functional. The evolution of the automobile involved a great many causes; a reliable internal combustion engine and the self-starter were threshold developments. Similarly, Bonsack's cigarette-rolling machine was a breakthrough insofar as it greatly reduced the cost of an established cultural artifact whose prior causes were complex.

The teleonomic selection process includes both continuities (or homeostatic processes) and cultural changes. Those who have recently attacked dynamic stability models of cultural life are only half right.[98] Cultural life involves an inextricable duality, a compound of continuities and changes, and the process of teleonomic selection is central to both. Although we may assign the term "tradition" to, say, the Indian reverence for sacred cattle, and then argue about its precise causes, the custom persists because with each new encounter and each new generation the population persists in choosing the same pattern of behavior, whatever its costs and/or benefits.

B. F. Skinner has conceded that

> Something is done today which affects the behavior of an organism tomorrow. No matter how clearly that fact can be established, a step is missing, and we must wait for the physiologist to supply it. He will be able to show how an organism is changed when exposed to contingencies of reinforcement and why the changed organism then behaves in a different way, possibly at a much later date. What he discovers cannot invalidate the laws of a science of behavior but it will make the picture of human action more nearly complete.[99]

This is only part of the story. To understand human action, we must also understand the external environment, and this requires that we wait for information to be supplied by anthropologists, ecologists, economists, management scientists, political scientists, sociologists, and developmental, cognitive, and social psychologists. The subject matter of each of these domains is a part of the total fabric, the matrix within which the human organism is embedded. The Law of Effect is itself only a conceptual black box into which the many interacting real-world influences must be put if we are to explain specific historical events.

Co-operation in Social Theory

Because the objective of my theory is to explain the progressive complexification of human society, accounting for both the initial evolution of human beings and the more recent development of complex cultures which began some ten to fifteen thousand years ago, I am interested in broad evolutionary trends. This returns us to the subject of functional synergism.

Synergism, or co-operation broadly defined, is not a new theme in social theory; its centrality in social life has been appreciated since the time of classical Athens. Darwin understood the significance for biological evolution of co-operation in general and the division of labor in particular. Even that archetypical economist Adam Smith saw its importance: "In civilized society [man] stands at all times in need of the co-operation of and assistance of great multitudes. . . . In almost every other race of animals each individual, when it is grown up to maturity, is entirely independent [*sic*]. . . . But man has almost constant occasion for the help of his brethren."[100]

Darwin and Smith understood that co-operation did not necessarily cancel out competition and that it was in no way opposed to natural selection (Darwin) or to self-interest (Smith). As Smith noted, it is "in vain" for a person to hope that co-operation can be based exclusively on others' benevolence (altruism): "He will be more likely to prevail if he can interest their self-love in his favor, and show them that it is for their own advantage to do for him what he requires of them."[101] Smith thus stated the proposition that egoistic co-operation is an important facet of economic life.

The importance of co-operation in sociocultural evolution was also stated clearly by nineteenth- and early twentieth-century social evolutionists. One landmark was the widely read volume by the American economist Henry George, who formulated "the law of human progress" and of "retrogression": "Men tend to progress just as they come together closer, and by co-operation with each other increase the mental power that may be devoted to improvement, but just as conflict is provoked, or association develops inequality of condition and power, this tendency to progression is lessened, checked and finally reversed."[102*]

Herbert Spencer was the first sociologist *cum* anthropologist to emphasize the role of co-operation in societal evolution, but the theme can also be found in the works of such other early pioneers as sociologist Frank H. Giddings, publicist Henry Drummond, and the émigré Russian anarchist and naturalist Prince Pëtr Kropotkin.[103]

The most remarkable early theorist on the role of co-operation in evolution was Hermann Reinheimer, whose now all but forgotten series of books on the subject included the provocative titles *Evolution by Co-operation: A Study in Bio-economics* (1913) and *Symbiosis: A Socio-Physiological Study of Evolution* (1920). Although Reinheimer's views were frequently eccentric and his language now seems archaic, he grasped the essentially functional role of co-operation and its fundamental relationship to progressive evolution. To achieve what Reinheimer called a "rise of type," there had to be a "super-adequacy of force" (what would now be called a positive benefit-cost ratio or surpluses). "To obtain this super-adequacy of force the genius of the early organic life struck out the method of reciprocal differentiation—as a means of economising physiological labour (recognized by Darwin as of great importance) and of storing up incremental forces and qualities, which by a variety of complemental processes . . . bring about mutual enhancement."[104]

In the present century many writers have stressed the role of co-operation in biological and/or social evolution.[105] A handful of writings have even employed the specific terms synergy and synergism.[106] None, however, has fully appreciated its causal role.

* George's explanations for progress and retrogression were mentalistic and psychosocial, not strictly speaking functional. Thus his was not an economic theory of progressive evolution at all, and it saw co-operation only as an indirect means for improvement by virtue of its ability to increase the mental power devoted to improvement. The "law of human progress" amounted to a dignification of the assertion that two heads are better than one.

In recent decades the role of co-operation in evolution has generally been downplayed and underrated. Many earlier writings on the subject are now mentioned only in footnotes, and the theme has been relatively neglected among mainstream evolutionists. It is a strange state of affairs, for which no single factor seems to have been responsible. But one major cause was the semantic and conceptual confusion that clothed such terms as co-operation and synergy. Darwinists and anti-Darwinists alike have tended to identify natural selection with competition and to treat co-operation (read "altruism" or "morality") as something opposed to it.

The result was a polarization of viewpoints. Following the example set by Kropotkin, many theorists have reasoned that the existence of mutual aid either falsified the role of natural selection in evolution or, in the case of human evolution, set people apart from or above the natural world. By means of co-operation, the argument says, human beings have transcended "nature, red in tooth and claw." Ashley Montagu, for instance, wrote a diatribe against hard-line Darwinism and later advanced the "alternative" thesis that "the dominant principle of social life is not competition or the struggle for existence in the competitive sense, but is cooperation."[107] Similarly, Ruth Benedict's use of the term synergy was heavily laden with moral overtones and the implication that there must be mutual benefits to all parties: "I spoke of societies with high social synergy where their institutions insure mutual advantage from their undertakings, and societies with low social synergy where the advantage of one individual becomes a victory over another, and the majority who are not victorious must shift as they can."[108]*

This view of co-operation was reinforced by the Social Darwinists and by various liberal economists who for decades emphasized the role of competition in economic life, generally giving co-operation no more than a bit part.[109] Marxist economists have happily accepted this one-sided interpretation and turned it against the liberals. The Marxist position is that competition and social conflict are characteristic only of capitalist societies and that the transformation to socialism will bring about a co-operative society. Both viewpoints misinterpret the nature of both capitalist and extant socialist societies.

There is no inherent conflict between natural selection and co-operation, or between egoism and co-operation. Nor does co-operation necessarily require the kinds of motivations and behaviors that many social theorists equate with the term. There is not even an absolute dichotomy between competition and co-operation. Many social interactions involve co-operation in one area or with one group and competition in another.[110] Darwin himself observed

* Benedict's distinction between "high" and "low" synergy is quite useful, so long as it is employed in strictly measurable, functional terms. Thus a firm that is running at a loss and a nation in the throes of a civil war might well be characterized as low-synergy systems.

that co-operation for the purpose of engaging in competition has been a significant factor in sociocultural evolution.

I define co-operation in strictly functional terms. It is not an intrinsic good; it does not necessarily lead to positive synergism; and the costs and benefits may not be equitably distributed among the participants. Furthermore, co-operation is not confined to interactions that occur between two or more individuals; it includes human-animal, human-machine, and machine-machine symbioses. In these terms, the concept of co-operation embraces the literature on altruism and helping,[111] the literature on exchange theory,[112] and the literature on collective goods, mutualism, coalitions, and co-operative games.[113] It can also embrace the burgeoning literature on co-operation in animals, whether it be egoistic or altruistic in nature. Sociobiologists have devoted a great deal of energy to determining whether or not a particular form of social behavior can be explained as altruism toward kin (kin selection) or reciprocal altruism toward an unrelated individual. Only lately has the phenomenon of intraspecific mutualism received close attention. More to the point, both sides in the sociobiology debate have almost completely overlooked the consideration that the genetic relationship between two individuals may serve to constrain or facilitate co-operation but cannot explain it. One can do that only by invoking functional explanations.

The synergism hypothesis offers a unifying functional explanation that can embrace all forms of animal co-operation, including selfish herds, coalitions, mobbing, and the fine division of labor in our friend *Apis mellifera.* It subsumes and unites under a common functional principle the vast literatures on co-operation within a species and between individuals of different species (symbiosis). The sociobiologists' preoccupation with kin selection and altruism has narrowed their theoretical focus so that for the most part they ignore the fact that interspecies mutualism falsifies, or at least qualifies, one of the cardinal assumptions of the classical sociobiological models. Co-operation can and does frequently occur between unrelated individuals. In fact it is such a frequent occurrence that it requires a special, bioeconomic explanation: The most important requisite is that the fitness benefits outweigh the fitness costs. (This argument can also be found in *The Origin of Species.*)

Richard Alexander is one theorist associated with sociobiology who sees that it is not necessary to presuppose a genetic substrate for co-operation.[114] With certain qualifications, the mechanisms of learning could be sufficient to induce such behaviors in many cases. If this is so, it may be reasonable to suppose that co-operation might often arise through teleonomic selection and that a supportive genetic substrate often evolves to track and reinforce behavioral changes.[115]

Do we have evidence to support this once heretical and still controversial viewpoint? Man-dog symbioses are a case in point; the genome type of dogs has been altered drastically as a result of this evolutionary "marriage."[116] The fact that artificial selection may have been involved does not vitiate the point, for artificial selection is simply a subset of the larger class of evolutionary influences that can be subsumed under the heading of teleonomic selection. Nor are human beings unique in being an agency of natural selection through their behavioral choices. There are any number of examples in the ethological literature where it is probably safe to infer that one species influenced the evolutionary course of another. Recall Ehrlich and Raven's co-evolution.[117] Accordingly, I will focus on the role of behavioral change in sociocultural evolution. But, to reiterate, I define co-operation here much more broadly than in terms only of social interactions. I include man-tool, man-environment, and even machine-machine interactions.

"Progressive" Evolution and the Evolution of Culture

In a recent theoretical treatment of cultural evolution, biologist Paul Mundinger made a sharp distinction between social organization and culture (and between social evolution and cultural evolution).[118] The former refers to goal-directed social interactions of all kinds whereas the latter refers to behaviorally relevant information that is transmitted between organisms via learning. In principle, these two kinds of phenomena need not be coupled. Social insects, such as army ants or honeybees, have relatively elaborate forms of social organization but their social structures are not propagated or sustained by cultural modes of transmission. (While there is considerable evidence of learning and even, possibly, some culturally communicated "traditions" in honeybees, such artifacts are peripheral to the basic social patterns of these creatures.)

As one ascends the hierarchy (in terms of organismic complexity) to the higher mammals—especially the social carnivores and great apes—the interrelationship between sociality and culture intensifies; higher mammals have sociocultural systems. The correlation is not perfect, of course. The social organization of ungulates—from dik-dik to wildebeest to gemsbok—vary greatly in intensity. At one end of the spectrum there may be only females with offspring (e.g., duiker). At the other end one can find large herds of hundreds or even thousands of animals that may forage together, form defensive formations, and launch communal attacks against predators (e.g., buffalo). But none of these animals can be regarded as notably culture bearing.

On the other hand, the more intensely organized mammalian species, such as wolves and chimpanzees, also exhibit the most well-developed cultures. The offspring are more dependent upon the social group and they may remain with their parents long after reaching adulthood. They learn adult skills from their parents (and from one another)—mostly by observation but sometimes by instruction—and they practice adult skills, including social skills, in the context of elaborate patterns of play behavior. Not surprisingly, the range and intensity of social communications also increases proportionately.[119]

Thus we can discern a close relationship between cultural complexity and the complexity of the social system among the most highly social mammals; learning and communications capabilities go hand in hand with the elaboration of more complexly cybernated groups.[120] Indeed, there is a synergistic relationship between the two. Social organization facilitates social learning and cultural diffusion, while increased capabilities for learning, cumulation of experience, and cultural transmission facilitates the elaboration of social organization.[121] This is particularly relevant to the explanation of human evolution (see below).

The progressive evolution of sociocultural systems can be measured in several ways. Most social scientists have traditionally employed the Spencerian rubrics: size and internal complexity (structural differentiation, role specialization, and integration). These two basic dimensions are not wholly independent, but neither is one a simple function of the other as some sociologists have proposed. While increased size may precipitate increased complexity, and vice versa, the relationship of size to complexity is itself complex.

An alternative set of indicators derives from thermodynamics and cybernetics. One rubric involves the magnitude of energy flows in a sociocultural system (as noted earlier, there have been a number of analyses along these lines). The other involves the magnitude of information flows.*

My focus is synthetic. I presume that the properties of size, structural complexity, energy flows, *and* information have been interrelated in sociocultural evolution. These are merely the parameters of the process of sociocultural cybernation. The central thesis, again, is that functional synergism has been the underlying cause of the progressive evolution of sociocultural evolution in higher mammals and, especially, in the hominid line. Ecological changes may have created various stresses, challenges, or opportunities, but adaptively superior synergistic responses—among all the responses that may have been tried or could conceivably be tried—have canalized and imparted directionality to sociocultural evolution. It is safe to assume that it was at all times a trial-and-error process in which many alternatives were tried, but relatively few succeeded. By studying closely the common properties of those directional trends which were successful we can make some strong inferences. For instance, one clearcut trend has been toward greater behavioral flexibility and consequent sociocultural diversity in adapting to different natural environ-

* So far as I know, this is relatively neglected as a formal analytical approach, though the role of information in the evolution of sociocultural systems has not been unappreciated. Even more uncertain is the extent to which traditional sociological measures and thermodynamic *cum* cybernetic measures will be found to correlate with one another.

ments. This is as true of canids and chimpanzees as it is of our hominid ancestors.[122]

Sociocultural evolution is the preeminent example of the Darwinized version of Lamarckism mentioned earlier: It is becoming increasingly evident that this aspect of evolution has been driven by behavioral shifts, albeit shifts that were made attainable by previous evolutionary developments.

A case in point is the canids. As Roberta Hall points out,[123] timber wolves (*Canus lupus*), coyotes (*Canus latrans*), and the domestic dog (*Canus familiaris*) are genetically very closely related; no obvious chromosomal differences exist among the three species and viable offspring can be produced when any of them are cross-bred. Some theorists go so far as to deny that they are even separate species. Yet they are very different morphologically and behaviorally. They are also reproductively isolated from one another in nature. Moreover, this reproductive barrier is based on the behavioral differences between them and on the different ecological niches they have come to occupy. (This is not unusual; the phenomenon of speciation via behavioral divergence is widely recognized by evolutionists.)[124]

There is reason to believe that the same kind of behaviorally driven process also occurred in the hominids. Thus, mental phenomena—cognition, insight, learning, problem solving (creativity)—have played a major role in shaping the course of hominid evolution.

The archetypical example is the adoption of fire, perhaps one million years ago. The controlled use of fire had a number of important adaptive consequences and has been an important agency of natural selection. It permitted the occupation of colder regions; it became a tool that facilitated the capture of prey; it was used to condition the environment (as in slash and burn horticulture); it was probably also used for defensive purposes; and it enabled our ancestors to add to their diets many foods that are toxic if eaten raw.[125] With the acquisition of fire our ancestral niche was greatly expanded and our ability to compete with other predators (and, presumably, with nonfire-using hominids) was significantly augmented.

The Process of Cultural Evolution

I want to elaborate on six aspects of the overall process of cultural evolution: (1) innovation, (2) selective diffusion, (3) selective reproduction, (4) selective replacement, (5) selective loss, and (6) the fitness consequences of the teleonomic selection process.

Innovation has long been recognized as a major element of sociocultural evolution. In an earlier era, much emphasis was given to the role of the innovative "genius" in cultural change, that is, to the creative inspirations and actions of the Euclids, Galileos, Newtons, Pasteurs, Einsteins, and other "greats" of history. With the emergence of the social sciences in the first part of this century, the pendulum swung to a cultural determinist position. Innovation came to be portrayed as something that flowed from the cultural context, and the role of the individual was downgraded.

Many inventions were said to have resulted from accidents or impulsive changes of taste or fashion. Pasteur just happened to use a weakened culture of chicken cholera bacteria for one injection and was led thereby to the discovery of immunization via the production of antibodies. Daguerre just happened to leave an open vessel of mercury in a cupboard overnight along with some exposed bromide-coated silver plates and thus stumbled on the mercury vapor technique for developing latent photographic images. And Goodyear just happened to discover that rubber could be vulcanized with a sulfur heat treatment to prevent deterioration. It was also pointed out that many inventions and discoveries had occurred almost simultaneously to different individuals in widely separated parts of the world.

But the cultural determinist viewpoint is too pat. Pasteur was looking for ways of curing bacterial diseases; Daguerre was seeking precisely the goal of photographic image development; Goodyear was aware of the problem of rubber deterioration and had been experimenting with ways to prevent it. While serendipity may often play a role, as a rule the process of cultural innovation (I am talking about major developments, not fads or fashions) is neither the product of individual creativity alone nor the result of external, cultural factors alone; it is both together. The process normally involves an interaction between goals and problem-solving mental processes on the one hand and aspects of environment on the other. The process of innovation is co-determined by both individual minds and the particular cultural context.[126] There must be the perception of a need, the formulation of a goal, and a search for the solution. Accidents (solutions) may precede the application of an innovation to a specific problem or goal, but whatever the order of occurrence, mental processes are required to establish the appropriate means-ends connection. In some cases simple reinforcement may be involved in the discovery process, but the more complex forms of technological and organizational innovation go beyond the mechanisms of behaviorist learning theory (unless the term reinforcer is stretched far beyond its conventional usages to include goals, values, and satisfactions). Fire was a part of our ancestral environment for millions of years before someone figured out how to control it and make use of it. And as far as we know, we are the only species that has domesticated fire. More than mere accident was necessary to accomplish this; an intelligent, problem-solving mind was required.

Conversely, while necessity may often be a spur to invention, a mind or minds must perceive the problem and initiate a search for a solution. Innovation is commonly a goal-oriented process. Some necessities that stimulate innovation involve primary needs; many others involve culturally defined instrumental needs. Thus the dependence of modern societies on exogenous fossil fuels has created a need for a long-range substitute to replace our dwindling supplies, and this instrumental need has precipitated a highly goal-directed process of exploration and experimentation in many parts of the world.

Consider another energy crisis, that of sixteenth-century England. The one hundred years preceding the reign of Elizabeth I had been a time of rapid expansion, both in population and economically. The demand for wood for construction and as a fuel supply for homes and industry multiplied rapidly. At the same time, the wood supply dwindled as more land was put under cultivation. The inevitable results were shortages, soaring prices, and a search for alternatives that led ultimately to the widespread adoption of coal—the ramifications of which included the Industrial Revolution.

The history of technology is filled with examples of the cumulation of inventions, with many incremental improvements and occasional threshold changes. In the course of centuries the earliest crude mold board plow was replaced by the steel plow, which was replaced by the tractor-drawn plow, which is now being replaced in many areas by the no-tillage planting system.[127]

The cultural environment, as Kroeber argued so persuasively, affects the process of innovation in complex ways. The fact that inventions and discoveries may occur independently and nearly simultaneously supports the idea that contextual factors are important. When we say that a certain innovation was in the air, or that the time was ripe, we mean that a necessary framework of needs, technology, capital, and other cultural supports (technical education, material resources, a receptive marketplace) was present. While both Alexander Graham Bell and Elisha Gray succeeded in developing a workable telephone in the same year (1876), it is significant that these inventions occurred in an industrialized country, not among the Netsilik Eskimos or even among the Japanese of that era.

There are creative geniuses in every culture and in every age, but few cultural contexts provide the opportunities in which these abilities can be encouraged and realized. And one can be deceived by historical labels and stereotypes about the sort of cultural context in which invention may occur. The so-called Dark Ages in Europe were a time of considerable technological innovation that saw the appearance of the windmill, the stirrup, horseshoes, draft harnesses, printing, the mechanical clock, cast iron forging, cannon, spinning wheels, and sawmills.

The context-specific nature of cultural innovation can best be illustrated by noting some well-known cases of cultural obstacles to innovation. Greek astronomy, for instance, was stopped in its tracks after about 200 B.C. because the scientists of that era lacked two of the most important tools of modern astronomy, the clock and ground-lens telescopes. Similarly, Nef has noted that coal was burned for industrial purposes in China as early as the Sung era (the tenth and eleventh centuries), yet this did not precipitate an industrial revolution, for the necessary technological and cultural factors were absent.

Political constraints may also retard innovation. The first steam-driven vehicles appeared in the late 1700s, and powered stagecoaches were tried on a commercial basis in England in the mid 1800s. However, the railroad magnates of that era, and other political opponents, induced Parliament to enact a series of laws which imposed heavy road tolls on these vehicles and stipulated that they must travel at no more than 4 miles per hour. (A "flagman" also had to walk in front of them to warn horseback riders.) Neither the technology nor the road systems of that day were sufficiently well developed for steam-driven vehicles to enjoy a decisive economic advantage; nevertheless, cultural restrictions succeeded in discouraging significant improvements for several decades.

The process of major cultural innovation, then, is neither accidental nor inevitable. It is always the result of historically specific processes that include appropriate cultural antecedents or preadaptations, a favorable cultural context or opportunity, a need (a cognitively perceived goal), a creative problem-solving mind or minds, and systematic implementing actions. (Innovations do not spread when no one does anything about them.)

One hallmark of the present era is that innovation has become institutionalized; in many societies it is no longer left entirely to chance or to personal inspiration. Often it is a deliberate component of a society's adaptive strategy. Indeed, systematic technological innovation is often seen today as a strategy for dealing with pressing social problems.[128]

The interactional paradigm applies also to the process of *selective diffusion,* a complex subject with a large and growing literature. Most innovations do not diffuse at all. Many win only highly localized or temporary acceptance. Others diffuse widely and rapidly to different parts of the globe, especially those innovations that have high economic and/or military benefits and relatively low costs.[129]

The diffusion process is shaped and constrained by a number of interacting factors. In animal societies the diffusion of a new trait may be affected by such variables as age, sex, dominance relationships, and kinship status.[130] Patterns of kinship also deeply constrain the process of trait diffusion in primitive human societies.[131] In more complex societies these constraints are supplemented by many economic, social, and political factors.

The considerable research literature in this area includes studies on the diffusion of such diverse artifacts as pottery styles, contraceptive devices, water fluoridation, the city manager plan, third-party movements, innovative school programs, commercial products, medicines, children's games, and agricultural techniques. A well-known study by Bryce Ryan and Neal Gross detailed the ten-year process by which hybrid corn came to be adopted by two Iowa communities;[132] Griliches studied hybrid corn adoption in 132 crop-reporting districts across thirty-one states and found that most of the variance could be accounted for by two key variables (the percentage of each farmer's total acreage in corn prior to adoption and the date of adoption in adjacent districts);[133] a study by Coleman et al. of the adoption of a new prescription drug by doctors in four midwestern U.S. communities revealed marked differences based on the degree of integration of the doctors' social and professional relationships.[134]

A particularly striking case study of the role of political organization and political cleavages in selective diffusion is Yeracaris's account of the spread of strawberry growing (in place of tobacco) in a small Greek agricultural community.[135] The innovation was first introduced in 1950 by members of a leftist co-operative, a pacified local remnant of the National Liberation Front that had recently been defeated in the Greek guerilla war. Because the war had deeply polarized the town, the idea was at first politically tainted in the minds of many of the local conservatives. Nevertheless the innovation proved to be highly successful. By 1956, 84 percent of the co-operative's members had adopted the new crop while only 28 percent of the nonmember farmers had done so. Yet the profitability of raising strawberries was not lost on the conservatives, and in 1957 they set up their own government-backed co-operative. By 1966 some 80 percent of the local farmers had adopted strawberry cultivation.

Because selective diffusion involves the process of teleonomic selection—human choice making—it intersects with a diverse research literature that spans several disciplines and levels of analysis. The formulation of Thio is a useful point of departure.[136] In effect, Thio uses a psychological approach to diffusion processes. He advances a view of cultural diffusion that is derived from cognitive consistency theory, or cognitive balance theory.[137] There must be an overall compatibility, Thio argues, between the characteristics of a particular innovation and the psychological and social attributes, values, and relationships which the individual brings to the choice-making process; the decision each person makes normally involves a synthesis or balancing of various, possibly conflicting values and criteria.

Sociologically oriented theorists, on the other hand, naturally emphasize social factors. Davis suggested that innovations introduced by a respected or popular member of a group would be more likely to spread quickly.[138] Similarly, the better integrated the group, the faster an innovation will spread within it. Conversely, Barnett earlier argued that innovations diffuse more readily among those who are disgruntled or who are misfits in society, while Adams proposed that both types of diffusion may occur.[139]

While social and psychological factors are obviously significant, the most influential selective criteria are *functional.* An innovation must satisfy individual needs or wants, including social and psychological needs. The various mechanisms of change are: (1) independent invention, (2) selective observation and imitation, (3) selective diffusion via exchange, (4) selective diffusion via entrepreneurship, (5) selective diffusion via political action, and (6) selective diffusion via linkage effects (i.e., the coincidental effect of being associated with another trait or social process.) For example, the English language often followed the flag of Empire in the eighteenth and nineteenth centuries, as did many British customs. (Compare Cloak's concept of a "circumstantial" selective bias.[140])

The dynamics of functional (or broadly speaking economic) choice making is a complex subject. It involves the bread and butter of microeconomics, economic anthropology, and to some degree sociology, and the literature contains many excellent case studies.[141] I have already cited Salisbury's classic study of the shift from stone axes to steel axes among the Siane of New Guinea, a shift based on the clear functional superiority of the steel axe. Hames made a similar analysis of the relative hunting efficiency of the shotgun and the bow and arrow in two neotropical Indian populations of Venezuela, the Ye'Kwana and the Yanomamö. Hames concluded that the shotgun is at least two to three times more efficient. (No wonder that wherever it has been introduced the shotgun almost always rapidly replaces the bow.)[142]*

We should also take note of sociological exchange theory, which was developed independently by George C. Homans and by Jack W. Thibaut and Harold H. Kelley.[143] One significant contribution of exchange theory is that, while exchange theorists use rewards and punishments in their models of behavioral choice, they define the nature of these values broadly. Homans in particular emphasized the importance of emotional and social rewards in social life. We may adopt a particular style of dress not because it keeps us warm or because we like it but because it wins us social acceptance and approval, and these rewards may be both intrinsically (psychologically) important and instrumentally important to most of us. Homans also offered propositions concerning such things as choice making in the context of relative rewards for alternative choices and the relationship between expected and actual rewards.

These functional influences on the selective diffusion process are also affected by geographical, ecological, and climatological factors. One does not

* Even the exceptions prove the rule. Sonnefeld found that Eskimos preferred to continue using the traditional harpoon for seal hunting because a wounded seal will almost invariably escape through breathing holes in the ice—unless it has been hit by a harpoon with a retrieving line attached.

find snowmobiles in Florida or Hawaii, nor are there oceangoing yachts in Colorado. Yet consider the apparent paradox that automobiles are widely used in Alaska, where elaborate procedures are necessary to make them operable during the winter months, while they are banned from Bermuda, where the needs of the tourist industry take precedence over the personal transportation preferences of the residents and the visitors to the island.

The role of political actions in the process of selective diffusion—that is, authoritative decisions backed by sanctions (rewards and punishments) designed to elicit or proscribe appropriate behavioral choices on the part of individual citizens—is a mechanism that has been almost totally neglected of late by cultural selectionists. A notable exception is the study by Else Glahn, who found that for several thousand years all public buildings in ancient China were built in accordance with an elaborately detailed standard plan or code that, at least during the Sung period, was promulgated directly by the emperor. The design was brilliantly suited to withstanding the stresses of severe climates, windstorms, and earthquakes, and examples survive today that are more than one thousand years old. Nevertheless the imperial decree was surely responsible in part for such slavish imitations.[144]

The diffusion of specifically political or governmental innovations is marked by a similar interplay between functional and other social, psychological, and political factors, among them rivalries between local governmental elites and the properties of governmental institutions.[145] The "Australian," or secret ballot spread rapidly to democratic countries, somewhat more slowly to plebiscitarian countries, and not at all to many autocratic countries.

The process of selective diffusion *between* societies, or transcultural diffusion, is still imperfectly understood, though the literature contains innumerable case studies. Kroeber listed some of the classics: paper, printing, the alphabet, the calendar, the true arch, tobacco.[146] The most systematic analyses, however, have been done by Raoul Naroll and his colleagues. Naroll and Divale identified four ways in which a trait may spread across societies: (1) independent invention (they say it is relatively unimportant), (2) differential population growth (they say it has not received systematic attention), (3) diffusion via peaceful borrowing, and (4) migration (they say it is now almost invariably associated with coercion and warlike behaviors, though this may not have been true in the remote past).[147]

Naroll has a disconcerting tendency to argue that diffusion by any means other than independent invention involves a nonfunctional process. In criticizing some correlations among cultural traits that were reported by Lomax and Arensberg, Naroll asks, "Are these correlations indeed functional—reflecting the essential nature of human society and culture—or do they instead reflect *mere accidents of diffusion?*" (my italics)[148] While some traits may diffuse by means of the linkage effects noted above, it is also likely that a cultural trait may diffuse because it is functional. There is no evidence that cultural traits are borrowed randomly. Cross-cultural borrowing appears to be highly selective. By the same token, it is plausible that linkage effects are more often involved in diffusion by migration, but it is equally plausible, *a priori,* that successful migration is in part due to functional linkages among trait complexes. An obvious example is the combination of warm clothing, shelter, stone tools, and fire possessed by northward-migrating paleolithic hunter-gatherers. Indeed, if many traits are integral parts of functionally interdependent (synergistic) sociocultural systems, they may have both causes and effects that are inseparable from the actions performed by the group as a whole. For example, the papoose board, or cradleboard, was functionally related to (helped to make possible) the migratory patterns of certain American Plains Indians.

Naroll and Divale focused their analysis on the relative importance of borrowing versus migration in a small sample of contemporary primitive societies. They concluded that military expansion was not a significant factor in the diffusionary process. In a subsequent study, Naroll and Wirsing drew a much more elaborate sample of 78 triads (one base society, a culturally different society nearby, and a third society that had the same language but was more distant) from a pool of 852 societies. When compared for eleven cultural traits, the nearby societies resembled the base societies somewhat more than did the more distant linguistic relatives. Naroll and Wirsing concluded that the earlier study had underestimated the role of migration but that the importance of borrowing was further supported.[149]

Any analysis based on data for contemporary primitive societies is likely to underestimate the historical (evolutionary) role of migration, peaceful or otherwise. Language changes can have confounding effects on such analyses. If Latin could become Italian over a relatively short period, one must be careful about interpretations based on linguistic differences.

Three other aspects of the process of cultural evolution should be noted. *Selective reproduction,* the key to cultural continuity, is the analogue of stabilizing selection in biological evolution. It is accomplished primarily by imitation, teaching (in human and some animal societies), and selective reinforcement (broadly defined). Cultures perpetuate themselves to a considerable degree by means of social rewards and punishments that serve to canalize social behavior. Deviants may be ostracized or actively punished, and conformists will be accepted, rewarded, and selected for desired roles in the system. Such normative mechanisms are a major preoccupation of sociology. The point is that such social pressures have selective consequences for the processes of cultural continuity and change; in the absence of such constraints (and sometimes in spite of them), cultural "drift" (rapid shifts) may occur.

Selective replacement is a phenomenon that appears to have no parallel in biological evolution. Electric lights may replace such functionally inferior equivalents as oil and gas lamps; steel axes may replace stone axes; automobiles may replace horses and carriages; plastic bottles may replace glass bottles. Traits that have been "replaced" may disappear altogether from the repertoire of a culture. Only a few paleoanthropologists today are able to take a lump of obsidian and flake it into a replica of a paleolithic scraping tool; only a few antique car buffs still know how to start a Model T Ford; and spinning wool by hand is all but a lost art in industrial societies. On the other hand, the bow and arrow, the sailboat, and the horse remain a part of our culture, even though their roles have greatly changed.

Replacement is not the only means by which a trait may be selectively lost. For a variety of reasons, a particular trait may become nonfunctional or even burdensome. The medieval fortress is irrelevant in the context of modern warfare and front porches have been outmoded by such factors as air conditioners, TV, automobiles, the decline of neighborhood and family life, and building costs.

Finally, with regard to the *fitness consequences,* I want to reiterate that teleonomic selection interpenetrates with natural selection insofar as it affects reproductive fitness. I have taken the liberty of reworking one example suggested by Pulliam and Dunford.[150] Many species of wild mushrooms are poisonous to human beings. For this reason a strong cultural taboo has developed against eating wild mushrooms. No doubt the cause of the taboo was our previous cultural experience, but whatever the cause, the taboo has clear-cut fitness consequences, and any individual who violates it or who somehow fails to learn it may become a victim, thereby reinforcing the taboo among the rest of us. Even if we assume that the cause of death for a taboo violator cannot be determined, those who survive will nevertheless be taboo adherents (perhaps the survivors will be city dwellers who do not come in contact with wild mushrooms). Thus the process of sociocultural evolution cannot adequately be conceptualized in terms of a meme pool, or a concept pool. Nor will it fit into a mathematical model that involves epigenetic rules and culturgens. There are too many intervening levels of causation between genes and a specific cultural outcome to permit such reductionism.

An illustration of the interactional nature of human sociocultural evolution is sun oil.[151] Although there is evidence that American Indians had cultivated and consumed sunflower seeds for several thousand years, when the seeds were first taken to Europe in the late sixteenth century they were cultivated primarily for ornamental purposes. The oil-producing potential of one variety of the seeds was soon recognized, however, and in 1716 an English patent was granted to Arthur Bunyan for a process designed to extract sunflower oil for human consumption. But apparently there was little interest in doing this commercially, for the raising of sunflowers as a crop did not take hold until well into the nineteenth century.

The first country to grow sunflowers for human consumption was Russia, and the reason was political. The church had forbidden the eating during Lent of foods that were rich in oil, but sunflower oil, being recently introduced and not yet exploited, escaped the ban. Russian farmers took advantage of this loophole, and for many years they were virtually alone in growing sunflowers for sun oil. In the United States, peanut oil, cottonseed oil, and more recently soybean oil established preeminence. Sunflowers were not competitive with these other oil-bearing crops; their yields were not high enough, the oil content of the seeds was too low, they matured too slowly and erratically (which frustrated mechanical harvesting), and they were susceptible to rust and other plant diseases.

In the 1890s American agricultural researchers began a breeding program designed to improve the commercial potential of sunflowers. The program continued, with many false starts and setbacks, for seventy years. Finally, in the late 1960s, a hybrid was produced that had all the requisite properties: It matured rapidly, it was resistant to disease, its yields were 20 percent higher than those of nonhybrids, its seeds had an oil content that was twice that of the seeds of its ancestor, and it could readily be harvested with combines or the sheller-pickers used for corn. In addition, the residues could be used as a high-protein meal, as roughage for livestock, and as a constituent in pressed wood logs and fiberboard.

These technological breakthroughs coincided with a rapid growth in the demand for vegetable oils, first from the European market and then from a shift in U.S. consumption patterns toward polyunsaturated fats. The result of this synergistic combination has been a dramatic increase in sunflower agriculture in the United States. In the past decade, sunflower production in the United States rose from negligible levels to become the second most important oil-producing crop after soybeans. Production is predicted to increase from about 5.6 million tons in 1980 to 10 million tons within the next few years. This is a major shift in American agriculture and it cannot be modeled with Lumsden and Wilson's epigenetic rules and culturgens.

Animal Societies

One obvious testing ground for this theory is the research literature on animal societies. I discussed sociality in animals briefly in Chapter III; now I wish to emphasize the close relationship between social co-operation and functional synergism. Synergism is the unifying thread or common denominator underlying all forms of social co-operation in nature, from the altruistic sacrifices of worker bees to the patterns of reciprocity among food-sharing primates to the mutualistic hunting and feeding behaviors of social carnivores. The degree of biological relatedness (if any) between co-operators may facilitate or constrain many opportunities for achieving synergistic effects, as does the particular environmental context. However, it is the functional consequences, not the genes, that account for sociality. For almost every example of co-operation in nature a counterexample of non-co-operation can be found in a closely related species, in the same species in a different context, or even among the same individuals under different circumstances. An exhaustive survey of the literature is obviously not possible here. For those who are interested, Edward Wilson's *Sociobiology* is a good place to start. Here I will provide three representative illustrations from insect, bird, and mammal societies.

Some of the best studied and most dramatic examples of insect sociality can be found among the approximately 250 species of the subfamily *Dorylinae,* popularly known as army ants. One of entomologists' favorites is *Eciton burchelli,* a species that frequents the human forest areas of Central and South America.[152]

Eciton colonies present an awesome spectacle. Each colony consists of a single queen, whose outsized abdomen may produce 100,000 to 300,000 eggs during each reproductive cycle, plus her larvae, pupae, developing "callow" adults, and a horde of 500,000 or more anatomically specialized workers that share the tasks of colony defense, foraging for food, feeding the young, and arranging the frequent moves to new "bivouac" sites. The workers also provide shelter for *Eciton* colonies—literally. Each night they link their bodies to form a thick, interlocking fabric that coalesces into a solid mass around the queen and her brood.

Most impressive of all are these carnivorous insects' foraging and raiding behaviors. At dawn the bivouac cluster begins to dissolve as tens of thousands of workers move out in every direction in organized columns and occasional fan-shaped swarms that can attain speeds of 20 yards per hour and cover 200 yards in the course of a day. As these legions advance, they flush out a huge harvest of prey—mostly other insects, such as beetles, tarantulas, grasshoppers, and ants, but also snakes, lizards, nesting birds, and small mammals. The victims are quickly overwhelmed, stung to death, and dismembered for easy transport back to the nest site. In a single day, these raiding parties can devour more than 100,000 creatures.

Toward the end of the day the focus of *Eciton* activity may begin to shift. Since nests are changed daily during certain phases of the *Eciton* reproductive cycle, the workers may start to organize the move to a new bivouac. A site must be located, the immature young must be roused and herded to the new location, and tens of thousands of larvae must be safely transported before nightfall, when the workers will again coalesce into a cylindrical or ellipsoidal mass to protect the queen and her brood. And because these creatures are totally blind, all of their highly coordinated activities are accomplished by means only of chemical and tactile communications.

The adaptive significance of the army ant social system has been analyzed in depth by Wilson. The organized foraging behavior of a doryline species such as *Eciton* enables it to hunt larger and more diverse prey and in greater quantities than is the case with solitary foragers, such as members of the subfamily *Ponerinae.* The result is that the *Dorylinae* can attain larger colony sizes. But this is not the whole story. So efficient is the feeding behavior of a species like *Eciton* that a colony may rapidly deplete the fauna of any area in which it forages. It is for this reason that nomadism and an economical method of nest construction are also essential to the *Eciton* adaptive strategy. Wilson concludes: "The Dorylinae, then, constitute either a phyletic group of species or a conglomerate of two or more convergent phyletic groups that have triumphed as legionary ants over all their competitors. They not only outnumber other kinds of legionary ants in both species and colonies, but they tend to exclude them altogether."[153]

Sociality in birds in the form of communal breeding and helping at the nest is common to many species. One of the most striking examples is the Green Woodhoopoe (*Phoeniculus purpureus*). These tropical African birds, which have been studied extensively by David and Sandra Ligon,[154] reproduce in social units consisting of a single, monogamous breeding pair and a number of helpers that vie for the opportunity to feed, protect, groom, and vocalize with the nestlings. Most of the helpers are closely related to the breeding pairs, being younger siblings or even adult offspring of an older, established pair. But some helpers may be unrelated to the breeders and the nestlings they serve.

Why do the helpers choose to serve others, instead of striking out to establish nests and produce offspring of their own? The reasons have to do with environmental constraints. Green Woodhoopoes inhabit an open, sparsely wooded area that is relatively desiccated and subject to seasonal dry spells. Under these stringent conditions, Green Woodhoopoes must strenuously compete with one another and with other birds, mammals, and even social insects for the limited supply of suitable nesting cavities in the surrounding acacia trees. On the whole, the larger flocks are more successful in establishing and holding a breeding territory. In addition, mortality rates from various causes are extremely high (about 40 percent per year), which means that each breeding pair must attempt to produce and nurture to maturity a relatively large number of offspring. Helpers play a vital role in this effort by providing about 80 percent of the food and by aiding in the task of protecting the young from various predators.

The payoff for the helpers is that they establish social bonds with potential helpers of their own, who may in turn make it possible for them to establish a flock or to replace one of the breeders if it should fall victim to a predator. In this environment, social co-operation is so important to reproductive success that it is not limited to close kin (though such behaviors may have arisen in the first place through kin selection). The opportunity to obtain reciprocity is apparently a sufficient inducement; helping behaviors work equally well for unrelated individuals.*

Not only does the African lion provide a suitable example of a social mammal, it also sheds light on the dynamics of human evolution. Thanks to the fieldwork of George Schaller,[155] we now have a detailed and more accurate picture of the species.

The lions that inhabit open grasslands such as the Serengeti National Park in Tanzania are the most social of all the cats. But contrary to popular misconceptions, their sociality is loose knit, fluid, and situational, ranging from momentary alliances among nomad males or females to relatively stable networks (prides) of a dozen or more adults and their cubs. A cluster of closely related females (mothers and daughters, siblings, and even grandmothers and their granddaughters) usually forms the core of the pride. The females do most of the hunting and most of the child-rearing, although the males are not as parasitical as some recent commentators have suggested.† The males maintain only a loose association with the core unit; sometimes they will be in close attendance, especially when the females are in estrous, but often they go off by themselves or even occasionally shift their allegiances between prides. And because lions are polygamous, there are usually more females than males in any given pride. Proportions of two to one are not uncommon.

The pride is seldom found together in one place at one time. For the most part there are shifting subgroups that average 3.5 adults plus cubs. Because the pride's social structure is so loose and flexible, there is neither a rigid dominance hierarchy nor a well-defined leadership pattern; the lion social system might be characterized as organized anarchy. As Schaller ob-

* Ligon and Ligon suggest that the mechanism of "imprinting," by which young nestlings become "bonded" to the mature helpers, may be a key to this process. In effect, the system may work because the nestlings cannot discriminate between their relatives and unrelated helpers.

† Schaller points out that there may be good reasons why the males do not participate in hunting smaller game. The males are more conspicuous than the females and are thus more visible to potential prey, which must often be carefully stalked. Though the males commonly hang back from the pursuit of zebra, wildebeest, and gazelles, they may well be participating in a tacit division of labor by serving to protect the cubs from being preyed upon. The males also play the key role in the all-important task of patrolling and defending the pride's hunting range. Finally, several males must co-operate to hunt the most abundant source of meat on the savanna (in terms of weight)—buffalo and giraffe. These large mammals are able to put up a fierce defense and are almost never attacked by a single lion. Because less dangerous prey are relatively abundant, the Serengeti lions do not now rely for their food on these formidable beasts. They could have done so at various times and places in the past, and in that case the role of the male as provider for the pride would have been far more significant.

serves: "It is a system based on the amount of damage each animal can inflict on an aggressor; it is a system based on a balance of power, something not unknown in human affairs. A tense peace is thereby maintained and is broken only by sporadic clashes which though noisy and intimidating tend to do little damage."[156]

One of the most significant functions that are associated with this loosely co-operative system involves a phenomenon that is evident in other social carnivores. Organized co-operating groups may, in effect, lay claim to and "enclose" a particular hunting range, which they will more or less vigorously defend against other groups of the same species and/or other species. Territoriality is common in isolated animals as well, but in social species it may become a group behavior. Schaller found this the case in the Serengeti, where lion prides seek to protect their ranges from other prides, from marauding nomads, and from such competing social carnivores as hyenas. Serious fighting is infrequent, but the few violent clashes punctuate an otherwise tense peace that is marked by frequent challenges, threats, and chases.

Another function of lion sociality is to protect the cubs from other predators, a particularly serious threat when the adults are busy hunting for food. Schaller found that one-half of the cubs reared in prides survived past two years of age, while cubs reared by nomadic lionesses had a mortality rate that was greater than two-thirds.

A third important function of sociality in lions is to protect kills from being preempted by other predators; two or more lions are routinely able to drive off groups of hyenas and appropriate their kills. In effect, there is a dominance hierarchy among the top carnivores, and group size is one factor that can affect the relative status of the different species.[157]

The keys to understanding the social system of the Serengeti lion are the ecology of the area and the lion's food-getting strategy. It is not coincidental that in the lion as in other social carnivores the size of the group is generally larger in open savanna areas than in the woodlands. Not only are potential prey more plentiful and more concentrated but co-operative efforts enhance hunting efficiency in open terrain where ambushes are generally not possible. Lions are also slower than many of the animals they hunt (such as zebra, wildebeest, and Thomson's gazelle) and smaller than some others (buffalo and giraffe). Co-operative hunting increases both the probability of success and the size of the prey that can be caught.

Some quantitative evidence collected by Schaller was subsequently analyzed in detail by Thomas Caraco and Larry Wolf,[158] who found that the average size of the hunting group was also highly correlated with the type of game being pursued. An active adult lion needs about six kilograms of meat per day to survive (about five for females and seven for males). During the dry season, when the wildebeest and zebra migrate from the savanna to woodland areas, the resident prides sustain themselves primarily by hunting gazelle. Each gazelle provides about eleven kilograms of edible meat, and Schaller's data showed that lions can conveniently manage about three stalks per day. If they hunt alone they are able to make a kill about 15 percent of the time. But if they hunt in groups they can succeed 30 percent of the time.

The choice for each lion is between making a lone kill every other day that will provide enough meat for two days (if it can be defended) or making one joint kill every day and sharing it with another lion (with a higher probability of being able to defend it). On the other hand, if more than two lions team up they do not markedly increase the kill rate and at the same time they reduce the proportionate share for each individual below the critical level. Thus as expected, the prides do break up into groups of between 1.5 and 2 adult lions each during the dry season.

During the wet season, when zebra and wildebeest are plentiful, the lions generally concentrate on hunting the larger animals. A zebra carcass can provide enough meat to feed four to five lions for three days. A solitary hunter may be capable of killing a zebra, but the success rate goes up from 15 percent to over 40 percent if groups of five or more participate. More important, a solitary lion stands a good chance of losing his or her kill to hyenas. If less than four lions participate, they may expect to suffer at least a 10 percent loss. But if four or more lions co-operate, their losses will be negligible. Besides, the larger the group the easier it is to defend the hunting territory and protect the cubs. So hunting efficiency is only one of several advantages that affect the size of lion groups when meat is plentiful and easily obtained. As expected, Schaller found group sizes ranging from 3.7 to 7.3 adults.

Group life offers lions other advantages. One is a division of labor. After a successful hunt one or two lions may protect a carcass while others guard the cubs, seek a shady spot in which to feed, or engage in border patrol. Group living also may create a more effective learning environment for the young, as well as providing a form of life insurance for an animal. A sick or injured lion may be able to subsist for many months by joining others at a kill. (Lions generally share their kills, but there is also some quarrelling, occasional thefts, and even tugs-of-war over the booty.) A cub whose mother fails to produce enough milk may be suckled by other females, or if the mother dies the cub will remain with the pride.

The examples of army ants, Green Woodhoopoe, and African lions are all consistent with the hypothesis: The key to the presence of sociality is synergistic effects that confer a significant selective advantage (or advantages) that is not otherwise attainable for a given species in a given context. The theory predicts that sociality will not be the result of "drift," it will not be an end in itself, and it will not persist for very long when the costs to the participants (time, energy, reproductive efficiency) outweigh the benefits. This is fully consistent with the synthetic theory of evolution, but my theory identifies the functional effects of social co-operation as the underlying causal mechanism rather than genetic mutations, chromosomal transpositions, or what have you. Sociality in animals may occur in a variety of contexts, fit various genetic models (from altruism to inclusive fitness and mutualism among unrelated individuals), and may serve many different functions. External ecological factors will be important determinants, but each occurrence will depend also on the way in which these factors interact with the animals' "internal" needs and capabilities.

The Evolution of Humankind

The case of *Homo sapiens* is another obvious challenge for this theoretical framework. Does the theory apply to the evolution of humankind? Can it shed light on the process by which small-brained Miocene primates were transformed into large-brained, bipedal, language-using city dwellers?

The subject is endlessly fascinating because it involves our common origin as a species. It also lends itself to speculation because the evidence is still fragmentary, which allows for a generous proportion of inspired guesswork and creativity. At the same time, the gradual accumulation of new data provides new grist for the theorists' mills. Accordingly, I will propose yet another scenario.

What I call the Social Triad Scenario brings together many of the concepts developed in the preceding pages.

1. *The Interactional Paradigm,* which requires a multifaceted view of the basic survival challenge to which our evolving ancestors were exposed.

2. *The teleonomic selection model of causation,* which posits that behavioral changes are likely to have been the pacemaker; that is, the natural selection of morphological changes tracked the process of behavioral and social change (rather than vice versa).

3. *The cybernetic model of social organization,* which makes decision making, communications, and behavioral control processes (political processes) integral parts of organized (purposeful) social behavior.

4. *The synergism hypothesis,* which focuses on the functional consequences of various combinatorial processes, including social co-operation.

5. *A bioeconomic* (*benefit-cost*) *approach* to assessing the plausibility of alternative choices and strategies.

6. *A revival (with modification) of the Darwinian hypothesis* that human social evolution may have been the result of three mutually reinforcing selective processes: (a) kin selection for altruistic and group-serving behaviors among closely related individuals; (b) individual selection for mutually beneficial forms of co-operative behaviors (egoistic co-operation or enlightened self-interest); and (c) group selection among functionally interdependent groups of co-operators, which Darwin suggested would supplant one another over time for various reasons, including possibly warfare.

This scenario posits that human beings did indeed make themselves, by virtue of purposeful changes in behavior and social organization, changes which set up directional selection toward compatible improvements in morphology and in the psychological underpinnings of what has become human nature. This model can be traced from Lamarck through the Organic Selection Theorists to my concept of teleonomic selection. Earlier I said that the role of teleonomy as a cause of evolutionary change reached its apex in the evolution of humankind; now let us consider the evidence for that view.

What do we know, or what can we reasonably infer about the context of human evolution? One major factor, it is now generally agreed, was a gradual but systematic change in world ecology as a result of major climatic changes during the Miocene (from 25 million to 12 million years ago) and again during the Pliocene (from 12 million to 3 million years ago). These changes precipitated a decrease in the amount of densely forested areas and an increase in open grasslands and mixed, or mosaic, environments. This major ecological pressure (E. O. Wilson's term) created many new challenges and opportunities (in Sewall Wright's formulation), and the result was a period of intense evolutionary experimentation. Many new forms made their appearance, including primates who were adapted to living on the ground in more diversified environments. One of them was our oldest presumed hominid ancestor (who remains to be discovered).

The ancestral hominids who first began exploiting forest margins and open areas were endowed with a distinctive set of preadaptations that provided both the raw material for evolutionary change and a number of biological constraints. These preadaptations included binocular vision and an unprecedented degree of manual dexterity skill (prerequisites for a skilled toolmaker and hunter),[159] behavioral flexibility and exceptional learning capabilities,[160] some ability to stand erect (especially when manipulating objects), a high degree of sociality, and a reproductive strategy (arbitrarily termed K selection by theoretical ecologists) that involved a relatively low birth rate, a long childhood dependency, and a high level of parental investment in the young.

Much of this can be deduced from our increasing knowledge of the chimpanzee. *Pan troglodytes* is our closest primate relative, and the genetic and biochemical similarities suggest a recent divergence of the two species, the result perhaps of minor changes in regulatory genes.[161] That is, hominids have undergone extraordinarily rapid directional evolutionary change since their divergence from the chimpanzee about 5 or 6 million years ago, according to the biochemical and chromosomal evidence.[162]

The earliest known benchmark in this process of evolutionary divergence is the recent discovery of *Australopithecus afarensis,*[163] along with the corroborating bipedal footprints found at Laetolil by Mary Leakey and her coworkers.[164] We know that these early hominid ancestors were small in stature compared to modern chimpanzees and equally small brained. Yet they were fully bipedal, and they had well-developed hands that were functionally close to those of modern *Homo sapiens.* They also had a marked degree of sexual dimorphism (bodily differences between the sexes), implying a degree of functional specialization along sex lines. Most remarkable of all, these hominid ancestors lived some 3 million years ago or more.

What is the most plausible scenario that we can infer from the foregoing? Let us begin by reviewing some of the alternative hypotheses.

In general, theorists on human evolution have tended until recently to emphasize a "prime mover." One of the oldest and best known of the prime mover theories focused on tool use. Darwin singled out this development in *The Descent of Man* and argued that our increasing ability to use tools would have precipitated a reduction in our canine teeth, the emergence of a more skillful precision grip, and selection for bipedal walking in order to free the hands for other uses.

Some modern theorists have endorsed the tool use hypothesis, but recently it has found less favor.[165] There is no direct evidence of tool use among the newly discovered early hominid fossils. However, as Alexander points out, lack of evidence for a postulated trait in this domain should not be cause to rule out its existence *a priori.* Indirect evidence might even make it possible to place the burden of proof on the naysayers.

The most unequivocal evidence of tool use are the deliberately fashioned stone implements found in abundance among hominid remains of 1 to 2.5 million years ago.[166] Less direct but still plausible evidence are the collections of smashed animal bones which appear to have been broken forcefully in order to allow access to the much-prized brains and marrow. Neither kind of evidence has yet been found for our earliest known hominid ancestors, save for one battered cobble found by Louis Leakey at Fort Ternan.[167] Most likely the earliest tools were unmodified stones and/or sticks that decayed long ago, leaving no residues.

However, the indirect evidence of tool use compiled and argued by anthropologist Benjamin Beck in his *Animal Tool Behavior* (1980) is compelling.

Beck shows that tool use and tool manufacture are widespread phenomena among a vast array of species including invertebrates, fish, reptiles, birds, and many mammals. The most prolific and diverse toolmakers and users are our close primate relatives, especially the chimpanzee. *Pan troglodytes,* as Jane Goodall and her co-workers have amply demonstrated, are second only to man in using tools for digging, pounding, and prying, for display, for intimidation, and on many occasions for fighting, predation, and other aggressive purposes.[168] And much of this tool use is done in a bipedal posture.

In this light, and in light of the evidence from other species, Beck concludes that it is unlikely that our own early ancestors did not use tools. Beck believes that our shift to bipedalism was at least in part related to this technology, as Darwin supposed. When the exceptional learning and imitative abilities of the higher primates are combined with their proven manipulative skills and the multiple reinforcing (synergistic) effects of tools (such as the abilities to extend one's reach, to increase mechanical advantage, to avoid direct contact with potential hazard, and to dig up underground sources of food),[169] it would be remarkable if our ancestors did not share this commonplace primate trait. The well-developed hands of our earliest known bipedal ancestors also lend circumstantial support to this view. Indeed, Beck thinks it likely that tools have been used by our primate ancestors for 10 to 15 million years.

The fact that tool use is so common in the primates militates against its being a prime mover in human evolution (exclusive of other developments). To be sure, there is clear evidence that our ancestors became far more proficient at tool manufacture and tool use over time, but this development may have occurred later in our evolution, long after the trend leading to *Homo sapiens* was well established. It is certainly not a sufficient cause of our evolution as a species.

A second postulated prime mover is what Robert Ardrey has termed "the hunting hypothesis." The idea did not originate with him; it had occurred to Darwin, and its first contemporary appearance was in anatomist Raymond Dart's controversial paper, "The Predatory Transition from Ape to Man" (1953).[170] The anthropologist Sherwood Washburn was also an early advocate of the idea.[171] Ardrey elaborated on the thesis in his *African Genesis* (1961) and in three subsequent volumes,[172] and a number of anthropologists have since come to accept the basic elements of this scenario.[173]

In addition to the direct evidence of hunting by early hominids, there is comparative evidence from some of our primate relatives, who are now known to be at least occasional group hunters and meat eaters.[174] Equally compelling is the growing evidence from field studies of the so-called social carnivores (wolves, hyenas, wild dogs, lions), which has prompted proposals that the ecology and behavior of these animals provide the best model for understanding human evolution.[175]

The data on the social carnivores show that the hypothesis appears to be borne out: To the extent that human behavior and social organization have diverged from the characteristics of our primate relatives, they resemble more closely the patterns of pack-hunting social carnivores.[176] One particularly striking quantitative analysis was done by Philip Thompson, who compared eleven social carnivores, fourteen primate species, and *Homo sapiens* with respect to eight major behavioral variables (systematic food sharing, food storing, feeding of young, division of labor, group defense, cannibalism, surplus killing, and interspecies intolerance).[177] His major finding (which may require some modification in light of later research) was that the basic behavior mode of human hunter-gatherers is closer to the pattern found in social carnivores.* Although we are phylogenetically closer to the primates, our behavior patterns have become biased toward species that were phylogenetically very different but had similar ecological relationships and survival strategies. Human evolution appears to be another example of the fairly common phenomenon of convergent evolution.

Co-operative hunting is a prime example of functional synergism. Hunting in groups can provide significant advantages for the participants, though this is not always the case. In a detailed analysis of the economics of co-operative subsistence among contemporary hunter-gatherers, Brian Hayden notes that the relative efficiency of communal hunting in large groups depends on such variables as the size, speed, habits, and concentration of potential prey, as well as the kind of technology deployed in the hunt and the degree to which a local population must depend on meat eating.[181] A number of scholars have noted a positive relationship between group size and the density of food resources,[182] and similar relationships have been observed in other species. Paradoxically, though, a superabundance of game may not always stimulate greater co-operation. Because co-operative hunting may exact a high cost in terms of time and energy (among other things), in some resource-rich areas hunting alone or in very small groups may actually be more efficient. Hayden also points out that food sharing (or "pooling" among individuals who hunt by themselves) may provide another important impetus for group

* This is a hotly disputed issue. Recent writings emphasize that some behaviors not previously attributed to our close primate relatives (cannibalism in chimpanzees, for example) have now been observed, and that humans are biologically and psychologically more like the primates.[178] Isaac and Crader, on the other hand, argue that the evidence of much more organized, extensive, and technologically sophisticated hunting and meat-eating behaviors by both our hominid ancestors and contemporary hunter-gatherers clearly indicates an "asymmetry" that could help account for our obvious divergence from the other primates.[179] Indeed, at a very early date ancestral hominids showed evidence of being able to obtain and utilize large game animals that are, to our knowledge, well beyond the predatory capabilities of any other primate. This capability could have given our ancestors an important competitive advantage. Harding and Teleki have a point, though, that it is an exaggeration to call hunting the "master behavior pattern" of *Homo sapiens.*[180]

living. When game are widely dispersed and their locations are difficult to predict, a given hunter may find it advantageous to share his kills (if they are large enough to feed several individuals). By doing so he may be able to utilize his resources more efficiently (excess meat will not spoil or otherwise go to waste), while at the same time insuring himself against those frequent occasions when others are successful in the hunt and he is not.

In any event, our ancestors did in due course evolve into proficient group-living, food-sharing hunters and it is not difficult to conceive of a plausible context in which such behaviors would have been highly adaptive. Kortlandt found that chimpanzees that inhabit open savanna areas (an estimated 40 percent of those that survive) are on the whole more frequent hunters and meat eaters.[183] Group hunting does not require big brains or the tool kit of *Homo erectus.* Indeed, Robert Harding and Shirley Strum have demonstrated that group-living primates such as baboons can readily learn to hunt and to develop group-hunting strategies in a short period of time.[184] If *Papio anubis* can do it, there is no good reason to doubt the existence of a similar potentiality in *Australopithecus afarensis.*

For this very reason the hunting hypothesis suffers the same objections that arise with tool use. If chimpanzees and baboons can readily engage in group predation, how can the hunting hypothesis be used to account for the earliest stages in the evolution of humankind? Chimpanzees do not rely on hunting; nor is it likely that the earliest bipeds did. Again it cannot have been a sufficient cause. The current thinking is that our early ancestors (like many contemporary primates) were omnivores (generalists) and that gathering was of major importance.[185] * Furthermore, there is no direct evidence of group living, much less group hunting, among our earliest known bipedal ancestors. The question remains an open one.

Even more controversial is the warfare hypothesis, or the variant that biologist Richard Alexander calls the "balance of power hypothesis" (because, he argues, both warfare and defense against other groups would have precipitated an enlargement of human societies).[188] The idea that organized, armed fighting between groups might have played a role in human evolution can be traced back to Darwin, Spencer, and an assortment of nineteenth-century Social Darwinists. In the present century, following "the war to end all wars," the warfare hypothesis was banished for a time, but it reappeared with Sir

* Isaac and Crader point out that the term omnivore may be misleading. Actually, contemporary primates and hunter-gatherers are "eclectic."[186] That is, they tend to focus on the most abundant and easily acquired sources of food in their particular habitat. The same was likely to have been true of evolving hominids, these writers believe. Mann also notes that the lack of specialized dentition and diet—which enabled at least some of our ancestors to exploit diverse food sources in diverse environments—was likely to have provided an important adaptive advantage that was not shared by more specialized feeders.[187]

Arthur Keith's *A New Theory of Human Evolution* (1949) and Raymond Dart's controversial theory (1953), which posited that the predatory instincts, hunting skills, and weapons developed by a transitional "killer ape" would have been extended in short order to other primates and hominids. As Ardrey later wrote, the weapon was the father of the hunter, and the hunter was the father of the warrior. According to Dart, the hunting *cum* warfare hypothesis can account for many uniquely human features—our erect posture, our skill with tools, our reduced canines, our large brains, and our aggressiveness.[189] Bigelow, on the other hand, emphasizes the interplay between co-operation and intergroup conflict: "We are without doubt the most cooperative and the most ferocious animal that has ever inhabited the earth. . . . [Our] success was dependent primarily on the ability to learn social cooperation for defense and offense against threats from other human groups."[190]

Alexander's arguments for warfare as a prime mover deserve special attention because they are informed by a rigorously biological selectionist perspective and by tight reasoning.[191] Alexander points out that there are no automatic advantages to group living, that in fact there are always costs. When conspecifics cluster together, there may be increased competition for resources (food, nesting sites) and/or increased competition for mates. This may be the case especially in a polygynous species, where a dominant animal might use its power to spread its own genes at others' expense. Close contact with a conspecific may also increase the risk of acquiring disease or parasites (though social grooming can counteract some of the risk of external parasites).

Alexander discerns only three likely offsetting benefits: co-operative defense against predation, co-operation that increases the individual's ability to obtain food, and coincidental aggregation simply because some needed resource (a water hole or a nesting site) may be localized. As noted earlier, this list is too limited, especially in relation to human evolution. For instance, it is common in both social carnivore and human hunter-gatherer societies that the very process of forming tightly integrated groups precipitates an "enclosure" process in relation to needed resources and to other groups. These resources may not be especially scarce, but they come to be possessed and defended by the group. That is, a process of intergroup competition arises. The resources that may be fought over can include food and water, territory, and even mates; raiding other groups for females is a frequent cause of warfare among contemporary human hunter-gatherers.

Alexander proposes a three-stage scenario for human evolution: In stage one small polygynous multimale bands stay together for protection against large predators; in stage two small polygynous multimale bands stay together for protection against predators and/or to hunt large game animals; in stage three increasingly large polygynous multimale bands stay together "largely or entirely" because of the threat from other human groups.[192]

Well aware that a hypothesis that focuses on a single prime mover may oversimplify a more complex reality, Alexander nevertheless states his position boldly: "At some point in our history the actual function of human groups—their significance for their individual members—was protection from the predatory effects of other human groups. . . . I am suggesting that all other adaptations associated with group-living, such as cooperation in agriculture, fishing or industry, are secondary—that is, that they are *responses* to group living and neither its primary causes nor sufficient to maintain it."[193] While various economic hypotheses are neither necessary nor sufficient explanations for large-scale societies, he claims, warfare *is* both necessary and sufficient.

A number of arguments favor the view that co-operation for defensive and offensive purposes was a factor of some importance at various stages in human evolution. There is the evidence (always a very small peephole into a very large room) of intergroup hostility and occasional fighting in other primates and social carnivores.[194] There is some equivocal evidence from early fossil remains; Raymond Dart's smashed *Australopithecine* skull is controversial, and his evidence has been critiqued by Brain.[195] In an extensive review of the early evidence, Roper found that some of it could plausibly be associated with fighting.[196] There is also the more extensive and less equivocal evidence for more recent paleolithic, mesolithic, and neolithic periods. Mohr documented 158 cases of injuries to hominid skeletal remains that were most likely caused by stone axes and arrowheads.[197] Eibl-Eibesfeldt also cites indirect evidence from cave drawings and paintings and soapstone carvings that portray armed fighting among early hunter-gatherers.[198]

Ember has persuasively refuted the widely broadcast myth that contemporary hunter-gatherer peoples are generally peaceable.[199] In a systematic study of the ethnographic data for fifty hunter-gatherer societies, she found that 64 percent experienced armed fighting at least once every two years while 26 percent experienced less frequent conflicts. Only 10 percent had few or no violent confrontations. Eibl-Eibesfeldt also raises questions about possible observer biases in some earlier ethnographic studies.[200] Recent, more detailed, and longer-term studies of some supposedly peaceful peoples (such as the !Kung San) reveal higher levels of aggressive behavior than had been thought. Some ethnographers of an earlier era may have been seeing too little or seeing only what they wanted to see; as E. O. Wilson has pointed out, an episode of group selection through warfare need occur only once in a generation to influence natural selection.[201]

Judging by the historical and ethnographic records, the supposedly more peaceable hunter-gatherers represent a handful of survivors of an older mode of life that has been swamped by more expansive cultures. This residue of hunter-gatherers are most likely peoples who were pushed into marginal environments through the dynamics of population growth and pressures of various kinds from larger, more dominant groups. It could be argued that the ancestors of these marginal groups willingly chose to abandon more bountiful and less hostile environments, preferring to live in deserts, the arctic tundra, or the windswept beaches of Tierra del Fuego, but it seems more likely that they were somehow coerced into it.

Darwin's observation that the most intense competition is likely to occur within or between closely related species, or between species whose survival strategies are convergent, has been amply documented. And it is not true that top carnivores are free from predation or attack by other top carnivores;[202] certainly a group-living carnivore is much less susceptible to attack by other predators, but this situation may be due in considerable measure to the balance of power between competing species.

The latter point is important. While Alexander does not explicitly include competition between various group-living species in his balance of power scenario, it can properly be extended to such situations. I would add to the group-competition, group-selection hypothesis the corollary that direct competition between organized groups of different species can also serve as a between-species group-selection pressure that would favor the emergence of more effectively co-operating groups. Indeed, it can reinforce competition between conspecific groups. Moreover, "functional group" competition, whether within or between species, can take many forms: It can involve direct competition for scavenged or hunted game, for safe nesting sites, for water holes, or for control over a territory that contains such resources; or it can involve more effective protection against predation from other group-living species. Antipredation is one of the chief bases for social co-operation among other mammals, the degree of co-operation being generally higher in open terrain.[203] A closely co-operating group of hominids, especially when armed with sticks or similar weapons, would also be more free to explore unknown or potentially hostile environments safely.

Merely having to avoid being eaten by other group-living predators and/or having to compete with them for prey and other resources could well have stimulated a prehistoric "arms race" that was initially directed as much toward other species as to conspecifics. It is even possible that the evolution of other social carnivores was as much a response to hominid evolution as the other way around.

One need not pin this scenario entirely on undiscovered evidence of group scavenging or hunting by early hominids. If need be, it can rest on the single overriding benefit of improved defense against predation. There is some reason to believe that early hominids may have been in frequent danger from other predators.[204] Accordingly, the bioeconomic benefit-cost ratio for co-operative defense would have been extremely favorable. When this is coupled with the evidence to the effect that the higher primates are generally endowed with a relatively high degree of intelligence, learning ability, sociability, and behavioral flexibility, one can reasonably infer that such co-operative behaviors would have evolved fairly readily as the need arose. Indeed, such collective actions have frequently been observed in other primates, notably in baboons and chimpanzees. Biological changes through kin selection might have facilitated, strengthened, and otherwise helped to support the expression of these behaviors, but there is reason to suppose that social co-operation could have arisen initially by means of teleonomic selection.

There is no need to postulate a genetic mutation for such co-operative behaviors. Since there would have been immediate and powerful positive reinforcements far beyond anything B. F. Skinner had in mind, one need only assume operant conditioning and/or imitation in relation to shared goals. If the fitness value is as high as it would seem to have been, it is entirely possible for such behaviors to arise among coalitions of unrelated individuals, as in the case of baboons and chimpanzees.

A similar bioeconomic argument can be applied to scavenging and hunting. In situations where there were high potential benefits and low costs (groups of co-operators armed with crude weapons who might otherwise go hungry), it is hard to believe that such behaviors would require some mutant gene rather than teleonomic selection. Given the combination of the requisite learning abilities and positive reinforcements, scavenging and occasional group hunting would likely have coincided with, or followed at a very early date, the achievement of a fully bipedal gait and the ability to carry objects conveniently. Weapons carrying may also have played a causal role in achieving bipedalism. Some theorists maintain that these skills would have been too difficult for our earliest bipedal ancestors to learn, but the evidence from other primates makes this reasoning appear unduly pessimistic.

My scenario entails an application of the synergism principle. When the occasion warrants, co-operative defense can be a collective good; it can greatly reduce for all the co-operators the likelihood of becoming a victim of predation. Co-operative hunting, when coupled with food sharing, has similar properties; it is a corporate good, a collectively produced benefit that is divisible but can be divided so that it may be mutually beneficial to all.

Some theorists maintain that transitional bipeds were not under pressure to adopt more systematic hunting.[205] (Hunting accounts for less than 1 percent of the diet of chimpanzees and 30 percent or more of the diet of human hunter-gatherers.) That evolving hominids eventually adopted more systematic hunting behaviors is not in dispute; the question is, when did they do so? Was it causally important in shaping the course of human evolution? Or was it secondary and derivative from earlier adaptations? The argument is made that mosaic environments were not necessarily less bountiful, though there may well have been more seasonal changes. Theorists have also noted that the earliest known hominids had more generalized dentition than would be expected of a meat-getting specialist.

On the other hand, it seems unlikely that a nutritional generalist would fail to exploit a major source of food if it had the capacity and sometimes the need to do so. Not all early hominids had the need or made the appropriate adaptations, but it can be argued that those that followed this strategy had the greater versatility and survivability. They are more likely to have been our direct forebears.

One aspect of the balance of power scenario needs to be judged more critically. This is Alexander's third stage, which parallels the similar views of other theorists that warfare (or the threat of it) is the prime mover of the later phases of human evolution. Alexander claims that warfare is both a necessary and a sufficient explanation, that there is no other way to account for large scale co-operating groups, and that group hunting would not have led to this result. In support of this thesis, Pitt argues that group selection through warfare is the only mechanism that can account for the extraordinary expansion of the human brain.[206]

Possibly the dynamics of human population growth, technological innovation, political evolution, ecological constraints, and other factors interacted with conflicts between human groups to spur the progressive evolution of large-scale societies. The historical record is replete with evidence of warfare among human groups in recent millennia.[207] But warfare, or the balance of power, is not in itself a sufficient explanation. If that were all there were to it, would there not also be nation-states composed of wild dogs, wolves, or hyenas? Any prime mover argument ignores all those other needs that are also requisites for human survival, the other co-determinants that have acted together as synergistic systems to make it possible for human populations to expand while remaining organized as integrated socioeconomic systems. Populations do not grow in a vacuum; they grow in suitable environments with suitable economic and political systems, and population growth in turn creates new needs.

Without such additional determinants as the developing hominid brain, language, technology, and evolving political mechanisms and superstructures, organized warfare in human societies would never have carried us much beyond the level of the Yanomamö, or the Dugum Dani. The power in the balance of power scenario arises from the total economic and political system, as Clausewitz and many other theorists on warfare emphasize. To ignore the combinatorial, synergistic basis of progressive evolutionary change is to perpetuate an insupportable tunnel vision, for the evidence indicates that the process of cultural evolution was complex and multifaceted. Indeed, the warfare scenario begs the question of what causes such a dangerous activity as war. (I further discuss the subject below and in Chapter VII.)

If warfare and the balance of power can be called the conservative scenario, liberal scenarios have favored peaceful modes of economic adaptation and evolution. One such scenario involves what anthropologists Adrienne Zihlman and Nancy Tanner call the gathering hypothesis.[208] Zihlman and Tanner define *gathering* as the collection and transport of large quantities of food beyond personal needs for later consumption *plus* regular tool use in obtaining and preparing food *and* extensive food sharing. Many animals and birds engage in roughly analogous behaviors, and chimpanzees engage in rudimentary food sharing. But Zihlman and Tanner maintain that the adoption of a more systematic pattern among early hominids was a "critical invention" that led to the divergence of the hominid line, to bipedalism, and to extensive tool use. Moreover, this breakthrough was initiated and developed by females and their offspring as the core unit, with male and female siblings being enlisted for additional aid through strong sibling ties and the mechanism of kin selection.

Zihlman and Tanner point out that this matriarchal model is simply an extrapolation from the structure and the behavioral capabilities of chimpanzee societies. They believe that this makes more sense than seeking analogues in social carnivores, and in fact they reject the hunting hypothesis. They note the generalist character of early hominid teeth, the ambiguous meaning of early bone collections, the (limited) ability of primates to hunt without tools, and the supposed inflexibility of true carnivore societies. They also argue that scavenging and hunting with tools at that stage would have required too high a level of skill and would have entailed too high a risk and too low a reward. On the other hand, they take a rather optimistic view of the ability of hominids to scare off potential predators. Finally, they cite the work of Richard B. Lee and others on contemporary hunter-gatherers,[209] which suggests that gathering—primarily by women—plays a far more important role in the provisioning of primitive peoples than does hunting; they believe "gatherer-hunter" would better describe these societies.

There would seem to be merit in this scenario, especially in the earliest transitional stages, if we agree with the somewhat contentious proposition that contemporary chimpanzee societies can be taken as the archetype for our own ancestral patterns. But there are also problems with the scenario. The males in this feminist rendering are a curiously passive and compliant lot, selected as mates by the females on the basis of their sociability and submissiveness to the females' economic strategy. This is not an accurate portrayal of the primate model, especially in the case of the chimpanzee, and it does not account for the divergence of evolving human societies toward the social carnivore pattern and toward the patterns found in contemporary hunter-gatherers.

The scenario certainly does not account for the documented characteristics of the human male. Carol Ember found that contrary to some new myths men predominate in subsistence activities in 83 percent of her sample from the ethnographic literature from 180 such societies, while gathering contributes over half of the total dietary calories in only 10 percent of the cases (omitting the data for equestrian hunters of very recent times).[210]* Ember also found that on the whole hunter-gatherer societies are not female-centered (matrilocal) in their social organization—again, contrary to recent mythology. Some 62 percent of her sample were patrilocal (male-centered); matrilocality constituted only 16 percent and the rest were bilocal.

It is also possible, as Ardrey has argued, that the dietary patterns of our early ancestors differed of necessity from those of contemporary hunter-gatherers in one important respect: Our early ancestors did not have the use of fire for cooking.[212] Without this important technological innovation, many foods that are now routinely consumed by hunter-gatherers and modern societies alike could not have been eaten, for they are toxic when eaten raw.[213] Before the adoption (or domestication) of fire, our ancestors would have had fewer food choices; the pressure to adopt meat eating would have been somewhat greater overall than many theorists appear to believe.†

Whether our remotest bipedal ancestors were hunter-gatherers or gatherer-hunters, it is reasonable to suppose that both hunting and gathering contributed to the development of bipedalism, carrying behaviors, tool and weapon use, and co-operative behaviors. In this light the burden of proof seems to rest with those who reject the group defense/group predation scenario. To oppose that scenario, one must (a) assume away the threat of predation against early hominids; (b) downgrade the importance of meat to their sur-

* This is another area of heated debate, and Ember's analysis contradicts both an earlier study done by Lee and a more recent study done by Hayden.[211] The issue is clouded by the facts that there are too few quantitative studies of hunter-gatherer nutrition and we do not yet fully understand the relative importance of high protein foods in the subsistence strategies of primitive peoples. Hayden notes that the degree of reliance on meat among the surviving hunter-gatherer groups varies widely and that there are marked correlations with latitude; equatorial populations exhibit the least dependence on meat and populations in the extreme latitudes exhibit the most dependence. However, Hayden's estimate that meat provides on the average about 35 percent of the hunter-gatherer diet by weight is biased because many of the prehistoric hunter-gatherers of the mid-latitudes perforce could not be included in his sample; most prehistoric hunter-gatherer groups were located in areas that are now occupied by large-scale developing and industrial societies, and only a fraction of these are described in detail in the ethnographic literature. The "average" environment of our early ancestors (if one can meaningfully speak of such a thing) is also a matter of considerable debate.

† Hayden and others dispute this hypothesis, arguing that relatively few of the foods available to early hominids would have required processing in some way to remove toxins.[214] Many of the foods that we routinely cook can be eaten raw if need be. The resolution of this debate may require more detailed information concerning the diet of evolving hominids in their most probable early environments and a more thoroughgoing analysis of hunter-gatherer nutrition.

vival; (c) demean their intelligence and skills relative to their contemporary higher primates and social carnivores; (d) discount the adaptive advantage associated with being a co-operative, tool-using biped; and (e) ignore the competition that would have resulted from the adoption of such a survival strategy. I have noted that the very process of creating functionally integrated (interdependent) groups may precipitate enclosure processes and trigger competitive interactions with other groups. There is good evidence that this readily occurs in human societies.[215] But again the emphasis needs to be placed in equal measure on co-operation and competition. The threat of predation and competitive pressures created the context within which co-operation would have been advantageous. Competition through co-operation was the key to successful adaptation, whether by hunting or gathering or both.

Similar virtues and shortcomings attend anthropologist Owen Lovejoy's important "nuclear family" scenario.[216] Lovejoy begins by rejecting in turn the propositions that brain development and material culture (or tool use or hunting) were of primary importance in the earliest stages of human evolution. He uses the objections that our earliest bipedal ancestors had small brains and that small-brained primates who are not bipedal also hunt occasionally and use tools.* He also rejects the antipredator argument on similar grounds; other primates co-operate in defense against predators, so this cannot account for the differences.† Lovejoy claims that bipedalism by itself would not have been helpful in avoiding predators, but just the reverse. Beyond the big brain and language, which developed much later, what most clearly sets our species apart, Lovejoy says, is our bipedal gait, our well-developed hands, and our distinctive sexual and reproductive patterns. The latter includes a K selection reproductive strategy (relatively few offspring with long dependency and high parental investment) coupled with relatively short birth spacing (compared to chimpanzees), male provisioning of the young (as in 90 percent of bird and most canid species), marked dimorphism between

* Lovejoy claims that "contrary to popular opinion," there is no evidence that early hominids hunted and that bipedality is probably least adapted to hunting unless "sophisticated" technology is available. It is unclear whether or not Lovejoy considers unworked sticks or well-aimed stones to be sophisticated technology. While there is (currently) "no evidence" of hunting with anything as sophisticated even as sticks and stones, this cannot be ruled out. The lack of evidence may be due only to the fact that these primitive weapons would have decayed long ago, or that we would be unable to recognize them if we saw them. The postulate of bipedal hunting with weapons needs to be investigated further before any firm conclusion is drawn.

† Lovejoy brushes past the point that bipedalism combined with weapon use would provide a marked adaptive advantage against predators in any environment where the threat of predation is relatively great. Chimpanzees have been observed using sticks and stones for such purposes, but they are clumsy at it. We simply do not know whether or not our ancestors were more at risk from large carnivores than were chimpanzees.

males and females, pronounced epigamic (sex-related) display features, continuous female sexual receptivity, and monogamous pair bonding between the sexes.

Lovejoy's thesis is that the development of a relatively efficient K selection reproductive strategy, based on "co-operative parenting," was the decisive breakthrough and that it in turn led to the other early developments in the hominid line. Arguing that a K selection strategy would have been poorly suited to the relatively unstable mosaic environments in which our ancestors evolved, Lovejoy points out that the only way to reinforce and improve on a K selection strategy—as hominids obviously did—would be through co-operative parenting.

Lovejoy's scenario involves a division of labor in which females were sequestered with the young at relatively safe home bases while males foraged for food (mosaic environments would have greatly increased the search time) and then carried it back to the den by hand. Bipedalism and the development of the human hand, then, were adaptations that facilitated male provisioning of the young (this line of reasoning is similar to that of Zihlman and Tanner). And the willingness of the males to do this would have been predicated on monogamy, on knowing the paternity of one's offspring. Clearly this primeval division of labor would have been highly synergistic (my term); it would have made it feasible, as no other set of adaptations could, to meet the increased protein and calorie requirements of both mothers and offspring in a relatively less abundant environment, while at the same time increasing the amount of supervision and protection of the young required by increased numbers of offspring and lengthening periods of child dependency. This is a clear-cut case in which co-operative behaviors would have been highly functional in bioeconomic or fitness terms. (Lovejoy notes that some other primates—gibbons, siamang, and certain New World primate taxa—follow similar strategies.) Because this system would have required a high degree of behavioral coordination (cybernation), it can be viewed as the primordial hominid political system or "political economy."

Like many other prime mover theories, Lovejoy's tends to fix on a particular dimension of the total survival problem and to discount imperatives that do not fit the theory. Lovejoy does this with respect to antipredation and the relative importance of scavenging, hunting, and tool use. Yet the threat from other predators, to the young and to foraging males, would have been serious. Indeed, Lovejoy's scenario makes a case for the paradox of dependency. The fact that females and increased numbers of offspring would have become dependent on male provisioning leads to the corollary that the loss of the male provider to a predator would lower significantly the fitness of the nuclear family as a unit. A lone, unarmed father cannot afford to be caught even once by a hungry predator during many years of child rearing.

Effective antipredation would therefore have been a high priority. Even if antipredation, scavenging, and hunting activities were not sufficient to account for the early breakthrough in hominid evolution, they were likely to have been necessary.

Conversely, if monogamy and male provisioning of the young were necessary, they were insufficient by Lovejoy's arguments. Since there are nonbipedal primates who are monogamous joint providers, there is no reason to believe this pattern in and of itself would precipitate bipedalism and carrying behaviors. No doubt Lovejoy would respond that it would be likely to encourage bipedalism in some environments more than in others. Quite right; but they would have been environments in which there was a greater pressure to adopt effective antipredator strategies and to compete more effectively with other carnivores (or omnivores) for the available prey. Thus Lovejoy's scenario, like that of Zihlman and Tanner, omits or downplays important aspects of the total survival problem in our early ancestors' most probable environmental context. Lovejoy's scenario also leaves out one important facet of the human behavioral repertoire, intense co-operation among males.[217]

I believe the truth lies between the more militant and pacific scenarios, or perhaps requires a melding of the two viewpoints into what can be called a Social Triad Scenario.

The Social Triad Scenario

The Social Triad Scenario combines the strengths of the co-operative antipredation *cum* scavenging/hunting scenario and the co-operative gathering and parenting scenario. All are necessary to some degree, and only together are they sufficient. While co-operative defense and hunting by males cannot account for the nuclear family and associated biological changes, the co-operative gathering and parenting scenario cannot address other major survival challenges and other facets of our adaptive complex, especially the extensive co-operation among males in defense and food procurement. Under certain ecological conditions a three-way, multifaceted set of co-operative behaviors would have been highly adaptive, highly compatible with one another, and mutually reinforcing; they would have fit together like pieces of a puzzle.

Monogamy would have served to reduce competition among males and females for mates, and this would have facilitated co-operation. Co-operation in turn would have facilitated defense, food procurement in patchy or desiccated environments, and ultimately provisioning of the young. If the co-operating males were closely related (parent and offspring, siblings, or perhaps cousins) the mechanisms of kin selection and functional group selection would overlap with and reinforce mutualism, or egoistic co-operation; natural selection for altruism and individual sublimation to the group would complement teleonomic selection for mutually beneficial learned behaviors.[218] Co-operative behaviors could also be reinforced through socialization of the young, a process that primatologists have learned is not unique to human beings.[219]

Similarly, if food-carrying or baby-carrying behaviors would have favored the emergence of bipedalism and manual dexterity, so would the carrying of tools for various purposes including defense and in some circumstances offense. These behaviors too would have had high fitness values. A biped is not faster or more efficient at locomotion than a quadruped. Bipedalism alone would have made our hominid ancestors more vulnerable to predation, but group defense with weapons would have compensated.

To be sure, a primate that inhabits a wooded area where sticks, branches, and stones are readily at hand would have less need to carry a weapon for long distances. The preferred predator evasion strategy in such situations is more likely to be dispersal and flight. By the same token, a canid predator that pursues its prey on all fours and attacks with its long canine teeth has no reason (and no ability) to carry a weapon. The situation is different for bipeds that have small canine teeth and inhabit more open areas where weapons are not readily at hand. If carried and used co-operatively, weapons would have helped to offset the natural disadvantages associated with being a bipedal gatherer, scavenger, and hunter. Weapons would have enabled co-operating bipeds, who might have had to range widely in search of food, to venture more safely into open areas and to stand and fight (or convincingly bluff) potential predators, who would quickly learn to be careful in dealing with stick-wielding hominids.

The same kinds of advantages would have applied to the use of weapons for scavenging and hunting activities. This primeval prehuman technology would have helped to compensate in some measure for the morphological handicaps associated with being a biped with reduced dentition. Given the preadaptations described above, it is hard to believe that weapon use would not also have been favored by teleonomic selection. It is reasonable to suppose that such behaviors could have been learned readily, that they would have been rewarded, and that natural selection would have tagged along. (There would have been downward causation, in D. T. Campbell's term.)

In this vein, Robert Harding and Shirley Strum's studies of predation in olive baboons (*Papio anubus*) represent a persuasive analogy.[220] In the past these primates were not thought to be hunters or meat eaters of any consequence. However, in the course of observing a troop of forty-nine baboons over several years on a huge ranch near Nairobi, Kenya, Harding, Strum, and several other colleagues documented the emergence and spread (via teleonomic selection) of a new cultural pattern. At first it was confined almost exclusively to a few adult males who might opportunistically capture a newborn antelope or hare. It was solitary activity, and no food sharing was observed. Then, over the next several years, the pattern changed dramatically. The amount of predation increased markedly, and females and younger males began to participate. Food sharing, especially among closely related individuals, became more commonplace. Hunting skills and efficiency improved. Most important, the troop began to evolve systematic joint searches and coordinated attacks along with a greater degree of food sharing.

Harding and Strum described how this development came about.

> In one such incident, three males noticed another male chasing a gazelle and ran toward him. To get to the scene of the chase, they had to ascend a small hill that concealed their approach from both predator and prey. Just as he was about to abandon the chase, the baboon in pursuit of the gazelle suddenly found the three other males blocking the prey's escape route. The closest male then took up the effort, and when he appeared to flag, another continued it. For a moment the gazelle appeared to be outrunning its pursuers, but it changed direction in response to a similar movement from the baboon chasing it, and in so doing, ran into the third of the newly arrived males. The gazelle almost escaped when the pursuing baboon momentarily hesitated, but a quick bite to the underbelly put an end to the chase.
>
> From that point on, the male baboons gradually adopted this relay system as a regular stratagem, chasing their prey toward a nearby male instead of out on the open plain. Such joint ventures appeared to be more successful than those carried out by lone males.

Harding and Strum concluded:

> With predatory baboons now added to the equation, we can identify a primate potential for predation, one that our earliest hominid ancestors must have shared. The baboon and chimpanzee studies demonstrate how sophisticated and successful predation can be among primates without any of the unique attributes of the human hunting adaptation, such as the ability to manufacture tools.[221]

Implicit in the Social Triad Scenario is yet another set of mutually reinforcing adaptive modifications that have to do with the aspect of social behavior that I call political, or cybernetic. In order to effectuate close co-operation with respect to any social goal, processes of decision making, social communication, and behavioral coordination must be developed. A social system must come into being.[222] Political processes in socially organized species do not require large brains or language; fairly complex patterns of social co-operation have been achieved by bird, rodent, primate, and social carnivore species without such advanced behavioral tools.[223] This cultural software may be difficult to detect among animals that are long accustomed to living with one another, yet it is no less real or important than such readily measurable traits as dentition or the size of the braincase.

The development of political skills along with patterns of reciprocity (especially food sharing) and some altruism in the furtherance of inclusive fitness would have been necessary for the nuclear family scenario, the co-operative male scenario, and the co-operative female scenario. Indeed, an argument can be made that the uniqueness of *Homo sapiens,* as compared with other primates or with social carnivores, is not our intelligence *per se,* our technology, or our ability to communicate; rather, our uniqueness arises from our ability to combine these abilities in goal-oriented cybernetic social systems. All these human traits are functionally subordinate and instrumental to our evolved capacity to plan, to set social goals, and to pursue those goals by organizing ourselves into co-operative (synergistic) systems that combine individual roles with resources and technologies. We are the preeminent political animal. And if organized co-operation was the key to our evolution, politics *qua* social cybernetics was the key to the key.

Once in existence, the primordial political system became a flexible tool that could be improved on and deployed for an ever-expanding array of co-operative activities: defense against predators, exploration, gathering, scavenging, small-game hunting, intergroup fighting, migration, the forceful enclosure of resources, the acquisition of females, big-game hunting, shelter construction, and the procurement of valued resources such as water holes, firewood, and obsidian.

Finally, political organization itself was an independent causal agency in human evolution. It is now evident that social organization and culture exist in many other species and that they almost certainly appeared in evolving hominids long before the development of the big brain and our unique language capabilities.[224] As the process of cultural evolution intensified by means of teleonomic selection and natural selection for cultural abilities, the internal social environment came to play an increasing role in the evolutionary process in at least three ways. First, it created a framework for pooling and utilizing individual abilities, skills, and ideas, including the innovations of the occasional ancestral "genius," for whom ethologists have documented animal analogues. Second, it created a medium for aggregating socially accumulated knowledge, technology, and skills that could be exchanged and transmitted to successive generations. Third, the social environment itself created an internal selective screen that favored certain cultural and biological improvements. Thus the conversion of a social aggregation into a goal-directed polity required the evolution of social structures.

The structural-functionalist theorists have long maintained that social systems have structural requisites. If they are to operate efficiently, cybernetic functions must be fulfilled. In the course of human evolution, dominance hierarchies had to be converted into structures of authority that could engage in decision making, leadership functions, and control over the exercise of differentiated social roles. These adaptations could be sustained to some extent by ties of kinship, but increasingly they called forth more intricate patterns of reciprocity and/or mutualism (collective and/or corporate goods) among more distantly related individuals and even non-kin. By the same token, competition for reproductive dominance and resources had to be converted into limited competition for leadership roles.[225]

Accordingly, the social environment itself created the context within which the evolution of greater intelligence, social "instincts," communications capabilities, and self-control would have been selectively advantageous, as Darwin noted and as Reynolds has recently argued.[226] Natural selection would have favored an increasing capacity for cybernating social behavior. Moreover, these traits would have been encouraged by the paradox of dependency: As the fitness of individual members became increasingly dependent on the effective functioning and success of the co-operative system, the pressures for adherence to the "public interest" would have increased. Thus the facets of human nature that make complex goal-oriented political systems possible are both a cause and a product of progressive directional changes at the cultural level toward synergistic political systems, systems which enhance the joint fitnesses of the participating individuals.

While there is only the possibility (and hope) that the Social Triad Scenario can eventually be traced to our earliest bipedal ancestors, there is considerable evidence that it fits the later transitional groups of 2.5 to 1.5 million years ago, the Koobi Fora and Olduvai Gorge hominids that apparently engaged in systematic stone tool manufacture (at "factory" sites), shelter construction, organized meat scavenging, probably organized hunting (as evidenced by butchering sites), and the transportation of food to protected living sites. To anthropologist Glynn Isaac, an economic division of labor and food-sharing hypothesis seems the most parsimonious explanation for these fossil remains. And King argues that scavenging is very unlikely to have been the predominant mode of meat acquisition.[227] I would add only that the evidence also implies a surprisingly sophisticated political system: capabilities for planning, communications, and co-operative social organization that clearly predate the emergence of the fully developed human brain and language.

The case for the existence of politics among early hominids is buttressed by two additional items of evidence. First, the somewhat larger size and enlarged brain cases of the intermediate hominids (their precise taxonomic designations and relationship to *Homo sapiens* remain controversial) implies a greater need for food intake and greater efficiency in food acquisition techniques, of the sort that only organized food procurement could achieve in a relatively desiccated environment.[228] Second, there were at that time two and possibly four extant hominid species,[229] which suggests competition and probably some niche partitioning. Walker and Leakey believe that only one of the species, the one directly ancestral to humankind, was culture bearing. I suggest that these hominids would also have been the most closely co-operating. It is reasonable to conclude that sociocultural development helped produce our unique mental and communications skills and gave our ancestors a decisive competitive edge over other hominids, other primates, and other social carnivores.*

Can the Social Triad Scenario be tested? Not in the usual sense of the word, but one can employ a best fit approach. That is, if this scenario best fits what we know or what is most likely to have occurred in the context and sequence of human evolution, and if it leads to correct predictions regarding further, as yet undiscovered evidence, then we may provisionally adopt it. For instance, this scenario predicts that in due course evidence should be found to support the postulate that some of the bipeds of 3.5 to 4 million years ago or earlier sometimes lived in groups that transcended mating pairs and their offspring. There should also be direct evidence of systematic meat eating at an early date. Unambiguous evidence of tool use at this early date is perhaps too much to hope for, but if evidence is forthcoming that there were other group-living carnivores present in the environment (and presumably posing a threat), that evidence would provide indirect support for at least part of this scenario.

This scenario does not require that all cultural attainments and forms of co-operative behavior emerged either suddenly or full-blown. Instead it assumes that our adaptive complex evolved incrementally and haltingly over a long period of time during which there was much trial and error and many failures among the few successes.

* Stephen Jay Gould, following DeBeer, Hardy, Montagu, and others, proposed in *Ontogeny and Phylogeny* (1977) that neoteny might have played a key role in human evolution. Neoteny involves as yet poorly understood genetic changes that result in the retention through development of certain fetal or infantile characteristics, and it has often been noted that there is a closer resemblance between human infants and infant chimpanzees than between the adults of the two species. In other words, humans may have diverged from chimpanzees in part by retarding certain aspects of their development. Though there may be some truth to this argument, it does not account for many of the most important morphological differences between humans and chimpanzees—bipedalism, the human hand, reduced dentition, our big brains, and our language capabilities.

A variation on this theme has been proposed by S. M. Stanley. He holds that neoteny—perhaps due to a single regulatory gene change—may have been a major cause of bipedalism. In contrast to Lovejoy's food-carrying hypothesis, Stanley offers what might be called the baby-carrying hypothesis. Because fetalized hominid infants lost the grasping ability of their primate relatives, and because their mothers lost the body hair that primate infants readily cling to when being carried, hominid mothers would have to use their arms to carry their infants. While the phenomenon of neoteny may well have played a role, it is doubtful that it would

(Continued)

In effect, human evolution involved a mosaic pattern; there was no single breakthrough but a series of thresholds, with the final result dependent on the entire suite of progressive changes. However, male co-operation among close kin is more likely to have preceded co-operation among unrelated males; systematic co-operation in defense against predators is more likely to have preceded systematic co-operative scavenging and hunting; co-operative gathering and scavenging is more likely to have preceded co-operative hunting; the use of unmodified tools is more likely to have preceded deliberate toolmaking, and so on. However, it is probably safe to assume that the "winners" in each generation were on the whole those who developed more effective means of exploiting the inherent potentiality of social co-operation—of political organization.

What then was the cause of human evolution? There was no prime mover; our full emergence was the product of a synergistic combination, the result of the total system or adaptive complex that combined elements of our primate phylogeny, the social carnivore ecological strategy, and a high degree of functional integration and specialization of roles. This system could have arisen only through the unique combination of protohominid preadaptations and the sort of ecological pressures (according to E. O. Wilson) and ecological opportunities (Sewall Wright) that I have described, plus the unique configuration of directional biological and cultural changes that occurred subsequently. (We can assume that other, less effective adaptive changes were tried and found wanting.) The lineages that produced *Homo sapiens* required all the major factors that we have identified: bipedalism, omnivory, the dexterous hand, tools, sociality, food sharing, hunting skills, intelligence, language, cultural development, and political organization. Remove any one of these features from the equation and the result we know would not have been possible.

Other theorists have recently expressed similar thoughts about human evolution. Washburn speaks of "reciprocal feed back" processes in the dual evolution of human morphology and culture. Durham refers to the "coevolution" of human biology and culture. Tobias espouses the idea that human evolution involved an "autocatalytic system."[230]

Some theorists appear to use the term "feedback" in a loose, metaphorical sense. Technically, *feedback* is information related to controlling the behavior

---

have had priority in the causal chain. Without the prior occurrence of the necessary supportive changes in adult morphology and behavior, fetalization and drastically increased dependency would have been a very maladaptive change; it would have been selected against. It is far more likely that fetalization occurred after such necessary preadaptations as bipedalism, as the fossil record clearly indicates. Moreover, neoteny need not cause global changes in the rate of infant development. Newborn humans are still equipped with well-developed sucking reflexes, sensory equipment, digestive and cardiovascular systems, and vocalizing abilities, among other things. Indeed, newborns do have a very strong grasping reflex during the first few days of life. So there was obviously more involved in hominid evolution than neoteny.

of a goal-oriented, cybernetic system. Like the concept of "reinforcements" in learning theory, feedback involves effects that exert causal influence over the behavior of a dynamic system by "feeding back" information that serves to modify the system's actions. The difference is that reinforcements merely decrease or increase the likelihood that an operant will be repeated, while feedback is a dynamic process in which ongoing control is exercised over the relationship between internal goals (or reference signals) and the behavioral state of the system. Feedback is a communication process that enables a goal-oriented system to vary its behavior in order to achieve its goals. What some evolutionary theorists seem to mean when they speak of feedback is that evolutionary causation is reciprocal and interactive, that the functional effects or consequences of teleonomic selection and natural selection are mutually causal and constantly change the selective field for one another.

As for autocatalysis, cultural evolution is not a bit like a chemical reaction. Autocatalysis, which implies a self-sustaining (internally controlled) reaction, is a modernized form of orthogenesis, and such a notion flatly contradicts the Darwinian vision that evolution is a contingent process that is constantly constrained by the functional relationships between organisms and their environments. Autocatalysis, or any comparable formulation, assumes away the problem of adaptation; it tacitly denies the overriding importance of natural selection and teleonomic selection.

In contrast, the synergism hypothesis emphasizes specific configurations—combinations of elements, or parts, or individuals—that co-operate in relation to specific needs or goals in specific environments. In terms of human evolution, this conceptualization emphasizes the functional advantages of unique combinations of organic and cultural traits (and technology) in particular ecological settings. Thus many animals use tools, but only one animal is a biped with a large brain, complex social organization, and language. Many animals hunt in packs, but only one animal hunts bipedally, with weapons and sufficient intelligence and communications skills to progressively improve its meat-getting technology and skills. Many animals have rudimentary culture and communicate information socially, but only one animal has the unique combination of abilities that made possible a process of progressive cultural development, a process that remains at all times on trial. These adaptive combinations were mutually reinforcing to one another; evolving social relationships, technology, communications skills, and intelligence interacted with one another so as to enhance their mutual efficiency. Indeed, virtually every trait or capability possessed by *Homo sapiens* can be found in rudimentary form in one species or another. In human beings these traits have been combined and augmented to the point where differences in kind have arisen. This, it seems to me, is the broad conclusion to be drawn from the literature on animal behavior and animal skills.

The hallmark of human evolution has been an ever-widening system of synergistically interacting biological and social traits, traits that co-operated to give evolving hominids increasing power to co-operate and compete with one another in meeting survival and reproductive needs and to grow in numbers to the point where, ironically, our very success now threatens our continued survival.[231] In accordance with the evolutionary model described in Chapter III, these synergistic effects have themselves been the underlying "cause" of the progressive trend toward more elaborate and multifaceted forms of co-operative interactions among our forebears.

Man the Hunter

If my scenario can account for the appearance of lower Pleistocene *Homo erectus,* there remains the question of why this apparently well-adapted hominid underwent further evolutionary change. How do we explain the transformation of a sometime hunter that was not strikingly superior to many competitor species into a species that was clearly dominant? Why did evolving hominids ultimately come to surpass all other socially organized creatures—indeed, all other mammals? The key lay in the development and elaboration of the hominid political economy; through trial and error our direct ancestors learned how to exploit more fully the synergistic potentialities inherent in the sociocultural mode of adaption. Climatic and ecological changes may have created new pressures and opportunities for change, but they did not determine the outcome. The decisive factor was the way in which at least some of our ancestors responded; the process was interactional.

Technological innovations that entailed more elaborate forms of social organization were of prime importance. The anthropologists Richard Lee and Irven DeVore maintain that only during the last ten thousand years did human beings harness energy and improve the means of production.[232] Yet technological changes with profound adaptive consequences date to long before the emergence of humankind. Indeed, if hominid evolution constitutes a prime example of quantum evolution or a peak shift or even punctuated equilibria, it is also a prime example of an evolutionary discontinuity triggered by behavioral innovation, in accordance with the teleonomic selection model.

A *prima facie* example is the adoption of fire, which transformed our ancestors' relationship to the environment and greatly expanded the hominid niche. A number of theorists believe that the adoption of systematic big game hunting was of even greater importance.[233] C. Loring Brace writes that " 'Man the hunter' is a made-over ape, and many of the specific differences between pongids and hominids may derive from this retooling job."[234]

The payback would have been substantial. During the Pleistocene epoch there were huge herds of large herbivores in many savanna areas, and these herds represented a major ecological opportunity. In some areas large animals were probably the predominant source of meat. For example, Bourlière showed that 75 percent of the meat available to modern-day hunters in the eastern Congo in 1963 were elephant, buffalo, and hippo.[235]*

The evidence that big game hunting evolved much earlier than has been thought is indirect but highly suggestive. The fossil remains from hominid sites of 1.5 to 1 million years ago indicate that an interrelated set of life-style changes had already occurred: There had been a significant refinement in toolmaking technology and an increase in the ratio of artifacts to animal bones, and there were many more bones from large animals.[238] By the middle Pleistocene (some 700,000 years ago) the average brain size of these progenitive hunters had increased to about 1000 cc, while tooth size (a sensitive indicator of ecological shifts) had been markedly reduced.

These changes must have been accompanied by a correlative set of intellectual and political *qua* cybernetic developments. Systematic big game hunting must perforce be a highly coordinated group activity. As Laughlin observed, hunting calls forth a variety of mental, physical, and social skills, and the earliest hominid hunters had to rely on intelligence, guile, and co-operative action to offset their biological disadvantages.[239] They also had to be thoroughly familiar with every aspect of their hunting territory. Moreover, systematic hunters may have to range over several hundred square miles, whereas our primate relatives generally limit themselves to an area of ten to fifteen miles at most.[240] Coordination of search efforts and pooling of information about the unpredictable whereabouts of game concentrations would have been highly advantageous.

Arthur Jelinek has pointed out that each new technological innovation imposed new resource and planning requirements on the aboriginal hunters.[241] Stone tools and weapons created the need for mobility and the frequent movement of camp sites. The need for water was a constant preoccupation on the open savanna. Brace believes that even the rudiments of language

* Hayden disputes the large-scale communal hunting scenario, seeing relatively little advantage to the participants except under special circumstances (when large game are relatively scarce but concentrated and only in areas where meat eating is essential for survival).[236] Hayden cites various reports of seasonal fluctuations in group size that correlate with fluctuations in the concentration and location of game.[237] Noting that many contemporary hunters (even of big game) work alone or in very small co-operating groups (two to four individuals), he concludes that it is "unlikely" that prehistoric hunter-gatherers for the most part needed to form communal hunting groups. This conclusion is too strong. Hayden underestimates both the complexities and the relative advantages of larger groupings in the most probable context of human evolution, as well as the hazards and competitive pressures from other social carnivores, the influence of technology and, not least, the problem of overcoming the defenses and evasive tactics of potential prey. Since many of the social carnivores find communal hunting advantageous, it would be surprising if our early ancestors did not.

may have arisen in the context of big game hunting: "Without it, the hunting capabilities of the anatomically ill-equipped early hominids are no more believable than those of baboons or chimpanzees—sufficient to capture occasional infants and small game, but not adequate to acquire large game animals on a regular basis."[242] This opinion is a controversial one, but if Brace is correct, it may be the case that all the major components of the human mode of adaptation were present before the emergence of big-brained *Homo sapiens* some 500,000 years ago.

The crucible within which this set of developments occurred was the political system itself. Organized, cybernated social processes created a selective field that favored the further development of intelligence, social, and communications skills.[243]

Action in concert (Talcott Parsons's phrase) also requires appropriate ecological opportunities. Thus the Netsilik Eskimos co-operate in hunting seals. Because the appearance of seals at a given breathing hole in the ice is an unpredictable occurrence, a lone hunter might well go hungry on any given day. But when a group of hunters monitor a number of breathing holes, they increase the likelihood that at least one of them will be successful. Since one seal can provide enough food for several people, close co-operation and food sharing are clearly synergistic.[244] (This cultural pattern conforms to the corporate goods model described in Chapter IV.)

Similarly, as Wayne Suttles has pointed out, the relative affluence achieved by Northwest Coast American Indians was not attributable to an abundance of resources *per se,* for the resources were highly seasonal, subject to fluctuations from year to year, and in the case of such resources as salmon, not easily exploited in quantity by a lone fisherman. The key to the emergence of this archetypical affluent society were the food-getting techniques and social organization that the people deployed: salmon weirs constructed and operated jointly, co-operative boat-building and fishing expeditions, extensive food storage, elaborate patterns of food sharing and exchange, and a value system that encouraged collective effort and the accumulation of surpluses.[245]

As noted earlier, co-operation is not always advantageous. Nevertheless, evolving hominids did live in groups that may have numbered 25 to 30 persons on the average, judging by the estimates for contemporary hunter-gatherer societies. Communal hunting in large groups would have been one reason for doing so. Pooling of kills and meat sharing among irregularly successful individual hunters would have been another. In some contexts hunting together in small groups of two to four individuals, partly for protection against other predators and partly for the benefits that could be derived from coordinated efforts, would have provided still another reason. There is little evidence that gathering, mostly by women, involved direct co-operation.[246] Yet females in contemporary hunter-gatherer societies typically coordinate their individual efforts and conduct their foraging activities in groups of two or more. Though companionship may provide part of the explanation, more practical considerations, particularly protection, may also have been important. Furthermore, someone has to babysit.

One can detect a quickening in the pace of sociocultural evolution just prior to the time when the first *Homo sapiens* were making their appearance. By the lower paleolithic, some 300,000 years ago, there is evidence of larger, more widely dispersed hominid groups, from Torralba in Spain to Terra Amata on the French Riviera, Tatzhikstan in Central Asia, and Choukoutien in China. Tool kits became more diversified (cleavers, scrapers, hand axes, engravers, and borers) and more efficient. Local adaptations were more varied; more processing of food seems to have occurred and shelter construction was commonplace. There is even suggestive evidence of primitive rituals (the remains of red ochre, which is often used for body adornment).

The ability to migrate in groups and occupy remote corners of the globe was a testament to the growing importance of political organization and leadership. As the degree of functional interdependence increased, and as the technology deployed by the group as a corporate entity became increasingly important to individual survival and reproductive success, it is likely that there was increasing downward causation from the sociocultural to the biological level. That is, teleonomic selection would have been an important agency of natural selection. In accordance with the scenario first proposed by Darwin, egoistic co-operation, "family" selection and functional group selection would have augmented the directional influence of individual selection rather than working against it.

Many theorists have remarked on the extraordinary rapidity with which morphological changes occurred in human evolution. These changes seem less mysterious when one recognizes cultural innovation and egoistic co-operation (on a historical, rather than an ecological time scale) as a driving force in this process. The model of diffusion and differential group survival based on major ecological and sociocultural variations can be made to conform to Wright's "interdemic selection" model even without the assumption of direct violent conflict between human groups. Thus some of the mystery surrounding human evolution can perhaps be resolved; human beings themselves may have been partly responsible for this remarkable evolutionary sprint.[247]

The full significance of this progressive trend can best be appreciated by noting the degree to which, even among the most primitive of contemporary hunter-gatherers, organized co-operation may transcend biological kinship patterns. (The process thus conforms to the formal models of symbiosis, or egoistic co-operation, rather than kin selection). Robin Fox has noted that the patterns of co-operation and functional integration in nature (other than for symbionts) tend to be aligned with kinship patterns. Unrelated individuals do unite for mutually beneficial purposes, but in such cases the relationship transcends and may even constrain interpersonal competition in terms of "classical" Darwinian fitness.

Even in the Pleistocene epoch, then, the political unit was beginning to transcend the biological unit. In Fox's terms, the principle of alliance was moderating and would ultimately replace the principle of descent as the basis of social organization. There are many contemporary and historical examples among hunter-gatherers: The massive rabbit hunts among aggregated bands of nineteenth-century Shoshone Indians involved groups of net holders and beaters under the supervision of a "rabbit boss."[248] In the fishing activities of multifamily groups among the Ainu of Hokkaido in Japan, the leader is usually the most experienced male.[249] The seasonally varied patterns of co-operation among Netsilik Eskimo families includes collaborative seal hunting in midwinter, salmon fishing in summer, and the hunting of migrating caribou herds in late August.[250]

There is also indirect evidence from such richly documented paleoarchaeological sites as Torralba-Ambrona and Terra Amata, both of which date back 250,000 to 300,000 years. Clusters of large huts and masses of large animal bones (from elephant, deer, boar) in strategic locations attest to the fact that several bands probably came together at certain times of the year to engage in large-scale hunts, possibly using fire to stampede the animals.[251]

The early evidence of multifamily political organization, however episodic it may have been, strongly implies a high degree of political development and rudimentary government. The primordial political *cum* cybernetic problems of order, decision making, and leadership thus emerged long before the appearance of *Homo sapiens sapiens* or the neolithic revolution; moreover, they were solved to a degree that was satisfactory for the purposes at hand.

It is possible that intergroup conflict occurred episodically during this period, primarily in relation to competition for locally scarce resources. That is, there may also have been co-operation for the purpose of competing for such needed resources as animal herds, water holes, and firewood. Because frequent stochastic variations occur in the natural environment (from the point of view of an animal trying to secure a living), it is unlikely that there would always have been sufficient resources to prevent local scarcities from occurring. Indeed, the implicit or explicit assumption of universal abundance among primitive hunter-gatherers is ecologically naive.[252]

In addition, destabilizing Malthusian pressures may have been operative at various times and places. A population may expand when an opportunity presents itself. Local abundance and new developments in hunting and gathering technology (for example, the bow and arrow, mortar and pestle) could have triggered local growth processes that would in time have upset a stable relationship among contiguous populations. We do not know exactly how the process of geographical diffusion occurred among our remote hominid ancestors, but interactions among organized groups are likely to have played a role in it.

Thus it is reasonable to assume that multifunctional polities based to some degree on both descent and alliance were a prehuman development that had a role in the process of biological evolution from *Homo erectus* to the fully modern human being. These polities encompassed and integrated the synergistic combinations of biological characteristics, technology, cultural software, and communications skills that together enabled early humankind to evolve further and ultimately to gain ascendancy.

The Evolution of Complex Societies

Finally, the synergism hypothesis can be applied to the emergence of civilization—large, complex societies characterized by sedentarism, agriculture, animal husbandry, crafts specialization, urbanization, and centralized political organization (chiefdomships and states). The so-called neolithic revolution has been the subject of intensive research and theorizing over the past fifty years. As the archaeological evidence accumulated, this important cultural transition came into better focus, but there is still a tendency to fix on one or another prime mover. In the 1930s V. Gordon Childe advanced a climatic explanation. Local desiccation, he argued, forced a shift to the harvesting of cereal grains. The resulting surpluses precipitated further population growth and cultural elaboration.[253] One problem with this theory is that the neolithic transition occurred independently several times in different parts of the world. Another problem is that no such desiccating climatic change has been identified.

A variation on this theme is Binford's hypothesis that the neolithic transition was precipitated by rising sea levels at the end of the last ice age.[254] As the climate became warmer, the glaciers melted and some 20 percent of the earth's total land area, much of it lush grazing land, was inundated, with dire consequences for the herds of large mammals that inhabited these vast coastal plains (and to the hunters who depended on them for subsistence). These continental shelves are now under 250–500 feet of water.

Although it was probably a contributing factor, climate change does not account for the initial emergence of agriculture and urban civilization at only a few favored sites. Also, civilization arose much later in some areas (Northern Europe and Central America), occurred barely at all in other areas (North America prior to European colonization), and not at all in still other areas (Australia).

Another prime mover theory centers on what has been called the prehistoric overkill hypothesis. Paul S. Martin has proposed that humankind was responsible for the mass extinction of many species of large game animals at the end of the Pleistocene epoch, a traumatic evolutionary event.[255] Martin believes that a growing population of humans, supported by gradually improving group-hunting techniques, overexploited and drove to extinction the saber-toothed tigers, giant ground sloths, woolly mammoths, diprotodons, and other large mammalian species that had become man's primary food supply. The implication is that this man-made food crisis forced our ancestors to experiment with alternative means of subsistence that in due course led to agriculture.

Martin's thesis remains controversial.[256] Some theorists consider climate changes at the end of the Pleistocene to be a plausible alternative explanation, while others think that both climate changes and heavy human predation together may have contributed to this puzzling occurrence. Still others think animal diseases may have been responsible.

Population pressure has also been advanced as a prime mover. Herbert Spencer was perhaps the first social theorist to develop this idea.[257] More recently, the hypothesis has been associated with (among others) Robert Carneiro, Ester Boserup, and, lately, Mark Nathan Cohen.[258] Cohen takes the most extreme position. Calling population growth the "cause of human progress," he maintains that population pressure has been "inherent" and "continuous" in sociocultural evolution. The shift to agriculture was forced by a food crisis, to be sure, but relentless population growth was the underlying cause of the crisis.

Among Cohen's detailed and extensively documented arguments, certain points are relevant for our purposes.

- Accelerating human population growth occurred world-wide during the late paleolithic. This fact is well established. By 10,000 years ago there were an estimated 10–15 million humans, or about one per square mile. For hunter-gatherers that is a crowded environment.

- In the millennia immediately preceding the shift to agriculture and animal husbandry, there were an increasing number of indicators that human populations were experiencing some ecological stress. Many groups were occupying more marginal areas; there was a shift to hunting smaller animals; large game animals were disappearing (for whatever reasons); there was greater reliance on water-based food resources; a shift occurred to using foods that required more processing and preparation; there was greater reliance on vegetable foods; and there was a general trend toward more diversified, unspecialized diets.

- All of the major technologies associated with agriculture were known and were even utilized to a limited degree by various hunter-gatherer groups long before they were employed on a large scale as the predominant mode of subsistence.

• Agriculture was not a superior way of earning a living. It did not represent progress and was not the strategy of choice so long as there remained the alternative of hunting and gathering. Actually, the labor costs associated with food procurement were lower for hunter-gatherers.

Only the quantity of food produced per unit of space increased. "Rather than progressing, we have developed our technology as a means of approximating as closely as possible the old status quo in the face of ever-increasing numbers."[259]

Cohen's explanation is orthogenetic. Population pressure, he argues, is simply there; it is a prior cause that needs no explanation, and it was (and is) continuously operative. Cohen recognized that such pressures are a function of the particular environment and technology, but in his view sooner or later resource stresses will occur.

The most troublesome problem with Cohen's thesis is the assumption of an inherent population pressure. All species have the potential for growth and all species have ultimate limits to population growth to which they may adapt in various ways. Humans are no exception. Yet our evolutionary history differed markedly from, say, that of chimpanzees. Population pressure is not enough to account for the directional changes that occurred in human evolution. Cohen brushes aside the evidence that contemporary hunter-gatherers commonly employ various means of birth control. Though the human mode of adaptation may ensure greater reproductive potential than is the case with some of our close primate relatives (as Lovejoy has argued), this does not contradict the fact that various means of population control do exist. Nor does Cohen's argument allow for the countervailing cultural effects of communicable diseases and stress-related infertility.

More to the point, populations do not grow without the wherewithal for their support. Populations grow only when they are successful in meeting survival and reproductive needs. Was human population growth, therefore, a cause or merely an effect of sociocultural changes, including changes in subsistence technology?* A reasonable alternative hypothesis is that the causal dynamic was reciprocal; population growth was both a cause and an effect.

It is also questionable that agriculture and animal husbandry were inferior subsistence strategies. The world is not a uniform ecological surface. In many

* Some theorists maintain that increasing sedentarism among evolving paleolithic groups was itself a cause of population growth.[260] Both socioeconomic and physiological factors are said to have been involved. But as Brian Hayden has pointed out, the ethnographic evidence does not support such a contention.[261] Populations may grow or remain stable in nomadic or sedentary settings, depending on factors that are obviously extrinsic to the degree of mobility.

cases reliance on hunting and gathering may be time-consuming, hazardous, and subject to many unpredictable fluctuations. Conversely, the productivity of horticulture, agriculture, and animal husbandry can vary widely, depending on a number of factors.

Brian Hayden has recently advanced a more sophisticated "resource stress" hypothesis. Arguing that the key to understanding the process of sociocultural evolution is the relationship between a given population with its given technology and a given environmental context, Hayden postulates that the shift from big game hunting to eclecticism and ultimately to agriculture was driven by the combined influence of population growth, climatic perturbations, and technological innovations. Resource reliability not population growth, he maintains, was (is) the overarching subsistence goal, and the calculus of relative costs and benefits associated with alternative subsistence strategies would have been governed by this criterion. Resource imbalances during the Pleistocene were therefore the stimuli that triggered efforts to diversify the subsistence base and improve technology.

While Hayden's interactional perspective represents a considerable improvement over the other alternatives, it is unlikely that resource reliability, or pursuit of an ecological "equilibrium" state, would alone have determined prehistoric subsistence strategies. The basic problem was and is survival and reproduction. Resource reliability is instrumental to this goal, but so may be risk-taking and exploitation of potential opportunities for growth. Positive reinforcements play a role as well. It is also commonly the case that trade-offs are necessary; to ensure physical security in relation to other organized human groups, for instance, it may seem desirable to increase population even at some risk to economic security. Competition between human groups did not begin with urban civilization, as Hayden implies.

The problem with all prime mover theories is that they cannot deal with the historical specificity of sociocultural evolution. They remain locked into a framework of deterministic thinking that ignores the trial and error nature of evolutionary change and downgrades the role of human invention and teleonomic selection in the emergence of complex societies. Something as complex and multifaceted as the neolithic transition requires a theory that can cope with such questions as: Why did agriculture and animal husbandry arise among hominids and not among the social carnivores that were also big game hunters during the Pleistocene? Why did agriculture arise in some localities but not in others? Why did it occur in widely separated parts of the world at roughly the same time (give or take a few thousand years)? That is, why did it *not* occur after some previous (or subsequent) ice age? And why is there so much evidence of trial and error? Instead of an abrupt directional shift from big game hunting to agriculture, the archaeological record reflects a long period of experimentation and diversification. Various responses were made to ecological stresses, and a selection process was involved in the spread of agriculture, animal domestication, and urban civilization. Moreover, the death rate among early civilizations was extremely high. Progress was halting to say the least.

From the perspective of the synergism hypothesis, the emergence of civilization involved a historically unique configuration of both external and internal factors. Environmental "stresses" (after Hayden) played a role, but so also did "opportunities" and an array of previous biological and sociocultural preadaptations that were utilized in new ways or improved on as needed. Equally important, new technologies and new forms of organization were tried out. Human problem solving also played a key role. The result was an enlarging field of social co-operation in relation to various survival-related needs.

As noted earlier, the emergence of civilization had many instrumental precursors. The precise timing and characteristics of these premonitory developments differed from one region to another, but the overall pattern was strikingly similar. Sedentarism had been on the increase for several thousand years preceding the breakthrough, though the hunting and gathering lifestyle persisted in many areas. (Indeed, the hunter-gatherer way of life was replaced only gradually as agricultural civilizations arose and were imitated or diffused.) Most of the instrumental technologies had already been developed and had already been employed in various localities during the late paleolithic and transitional mesolithic. These technologies included cultivation of artificially selected grains, legumes, and pulses that were particularly well-suited to human harvesting and consumption, domestication of animals, production of artifacts, development of water control techniques, the use of symbol systems, and so forth.[262] There is also much evidence of economic exchange,[263] and some evidence of armed conflict between human groups.[264]

If the requisite technologies for civilization were all present before the fact of its appearance, how do we account for the sustained process of growth that produced the final result, the first complex "superorganisms"? Why did large urban centers arise when they did, and why did they arise specifically in the Fertile Crescent (the Tigris-Euphrates river valley), the Indus river valley, the Wei-Yellow river valley, the lowlands of Central America, the valley of Mexico, and, on a more modest scale, in the American bottom (the Mississippi flood plain).

The explanation lies in the fact that each of these "evolutionary hotspots," as Pfeiffer has called them, enjoyed a synergistic nexus of interacting factors, every one of which was essential to the outcomes that occurred. It is not coincidental that all of these pristine human civilizations were located on or near a major source of water that could be used for irrigation, transportation, human consumption, cooking, bathing, and sewers. These sources had to be sufficient to sustain a large population. River valleys (or a large lake and many underground springs, in the case of Teotihuacán) that were blessed with rich alluvial soil and a long growing season were uniquely favorable locations. However, these natural assets also had to be exploited with grains that had been discovered elsewhere and were selectively bred for their productivity, uniformity, and suitability for human harvesting techniques. Water control technology was also essential in most cases. And so was a panoply of human tools and implements, as well as the necessary raw materials: obsidian, basalt, pottery clays, reeds or other basket-making materials, firewood, and timber for construction. Where these materials were not available locally, a pattern of trade had to be developed over a period of time in which the raw materials could be brought to the emerging urban center in exchange for foodstuffs and various kinds of finished artifacts.

That is not all. Domesticated animals played a major role from an early date, as a source of nutrients that could not be obtained from cereal grains, as pack animals for traders, and as draught animals; oxen were at work in the wheat and barley fields of the Fertile Crescent at least 8,000 years ago.

The development of civilization depended on surpluses that could be used to aggregate in one place all the raw materials and artifacts necessary to sustain an evolving technological infrastructure, as well as being able to feed a growing population. Many agricultural communities made their appearance beginning around 10,000 years ago, but some communities expanded (and imploded) to become "central places" in a network of economic production and exchange that was synergistic in nature. The right set of ecological opportunities were combined with appropriate technologies and a widening pattern of economic co-operation. Surpluses begat the means to develop new technology, which begat further efficiencies and more surpluses. Among other things, bitumin came into use as a glue and a preservative; obsidian blades gave way to metal blades; wheeled vehicles made their appearance; record-keeping systems were developed; and an abstract unit of exchange (money and prices) was developed.

Food surpluses were clearly of paramount importance to the emergence of complex civilizations; they facilitated internal crafts specialization and external trade. Conversely, the ability to produce surpluses depended on various supportive technologies and on resources provided by external trade.* Jack Harlan demonstrated many years ago that a family group working in an area of average productivity with primitive obsidian-bladed sickles could easily harvest in three weeks enough grain to feed themselves for a year.[266]

* Carneiro, in his ethnographic sample of 100 communities at various stages of development, found that all but sixteen of the most primitive engaged in some external trade. Nine of these communities had less than 100 people and fewer than half of them even had a full-time political leader.[265]

Intensely irrigated and cultivated bottomland grain fields located in areas with long growing seasons may be capable of producing many times more than a family's needs. But a family that specializes in working the soil and producing cereal grains in certain favored locations must necessarily depend on a supportive economic infrastructure; the paradox of dependency comes into play. And that infrastructure, in turn, requires correlative political processes.

As centralized economies arose, so did governments that assumed certain corporate responsibilities. Although the precise mix of peak-level functions must have varied somewhat from one early civilization to the next, the overall pattern was similar. These functions generally included defense, maintenance of public order, arbitration of disputes, management of internal and external economic relations, storage and redistribution of surpluses (a prehistoric equivalent of modern welfare, social insurance, and patronage systems), and various integrative functions (ritual, religion).

Four political innovations were crucial to the growth of complex civilizations. One was the externalization of legitimate authority beyond the kin group to various larger, functionally integrated groupings—villages, supravillage communities, urban centers, and finally states. The mechanisms used for expanding political authority ranged from personal charisma to democratic consent (councils of elders and the like), religious sanction, and coercion. These sources were not mutually exclusive, of course. Some of the most successful early polities probably used combinations of these control techniques. Doubtless kinship ties were still important, but the trend was toward authority patterns based on functional relationships, or "roles."

The second major political development involved application of the division of labor and specialization to various political functions: decision making, administration, adjudication (legislative, executive, and judicial functions in the old civics textbook terminology), as well as maintenance of public order (police), external relations, defense, and social integration. Communications processes were important, and communications specialists (tablet makers, clerks, and messengers) appeared at an early date. It is hard to imagine a large, complex society functioning without such a political division of labor.

The third invention involved application of the principle of hierarchical control to social organization. Formal hierarchies arose not only among persons but also among places. By the time the first states appeared around 4000 B.C., at least four levels of authority were evident—household/family, village officials, supravillage administrators, and supreme rulers.[267] For reasons that are explored further in Chapter VI, the process of societal growth and complexification was accompanied by a flow of power to the apex of what became multi-tiered political hierarchies.

Finally, the invention of formal law and legal codes—explicit rules of social intercourse as a property or condition of life in the community—endowed evolving civilizations with a powerful and effective political tool. Impersonal rules that were made and invoked under the authority variously of the gods, the divine ruler, the council of elders, or what have you, were essential to the process of creating a social structure, that is, the process of social cybernation.

I do not deny that rulers and ruling classes were often exploitative. There was surely as much abuse of power then as there is now, and probably more. But it also is possible to differentiate between the process of social and economic stratification and the functional development of the polity as a locus of co-operative actions in relation to various collective and corporate goods. Defense against external enemies, acquisition and control over needed resources, redistribution of surpluses in times of scarcity, mobilizing labor and resources for public works (public "goods"), keeping the peace, arbitrating disputes, and engendering solidarity and patriotism among the populace were necessary functions that served and transcended the private interests of rulers and ruling classes.

Finally, a word about the relationship between warfare and the emergence of complex societies. As suggested earlier, the use of organized violence as an instrument for achieving various ends is really a subset of co-operative behaviors with potentially synergistic effects. The argument that warfare or a balance of power dynamic was *the* driving force, the prime mover, behind sociopolitical evolution overlooks the important economic and social functions of centralized politics. Equally important, the warfare hypothesis implicitly takes for granted the economic resources and economic development on which any military capabilities depended. Warfare was most likely both a cause and an effect of socioeconomic and political evolution. Just as military competition and conquest stimulated and facilitated internal growth and evolution, so internal growth and evolution precipitated external competition and armed conflicts. Moreover, the relative importance of each aspect of this reciprocally causal process varied from case to case.[268]

My argument is that one can reduce economic co-operation and co-operation in the pursuit of external military objectives, not to mention internal political co-operation (factions, parties, guilds, unions, associations, conspiracies, and revolutionary movements), to examples of functional synergism. They are all variations on the theme of social co-operation, and the unifying explanation for all of these phenomena lies in their synergistic effects in relation to various explicit or implicit goals.

Conclusion

How can we test this theory of civilization? A thought experiment with the methodology proposed earlier should be indicative. Remove any major element from the package of co-operating factors and imagine what would have been the consequences. Take away from Uruk, or Susa, or Mohenjo-daro, or Monte Alban, or Cahokia its water supply, its fertile soil, its obsidian supply, its cooking fuel, or its political order. The loss of any one of these variables would have been sufficient to bring down the system. Indeed, the many early civilizations that did in fact collapse or were overrun by larger competitors provide a rich testing ground for this theory.

In Sumer, for instance, water logging and salt build-up in the soil are strongly implicated in the decline of several urban centers. While populations expanded and material needs increased apace, agricultural yields eventually went into decline; the surpluses on which these early states were based disappeared.

In the case of Teotihuacán in the valley of Mexico, a sharp decline in annual rainfall seems to have been the most important cause. Not only were the nearby lakes and underground springs severely depleted, but deforestation occurred in the surrounding hills and soil erosion became pronounced. The population was drastically reduced, and there is evidence of dispersal away from the region. Thus weakened, this early American metropolis became vulnerable to attack. Around 750 A.D. the city center was looted and burned.[269] Many other civilizational failures, on the other hand, were attributable primarily to military conquest, subjugation, and destruction of the economy.

In sum, the functional needs of humans as biological organisms have in the course of time led, through a cumulative process of innovation and teleonomic selection, to the evolution of complex sociocultural systems. And these systems have in turn generated functional requisites for their successful operation which human actors can ignore only at their peril.

Ronald Cohen comes closest to appreciating the necessity for melding functional, systemic, and historical approaches to sociocultural evolution. Writing on the traits associated with the evolution of the state, he concludes:

> To search for specific causes among all these developments is in my view a fruitless even a spurious question. . . . Each of these features, and many more, enable the others to emerge and to select from among all possible solutions the centrally organized structure of the state. The structure requires these correlates, and the correlates enable the structure to continue, *or to emerge.* The process is systemic, and self-limiting. No matter how or where it starts, functional requirements force the development of the above correlates. . . .[270]

It might have been better to say that the functional requirements "enable" or "encourage" the development of trading systems, military specialists, law codes, record-keeping systems, and so forth. For the existence of functional requisites does not ensure that appropriate resources will be at hand and that appropriate artifacts and skills will be devised, or that they will be positively selected by the relevant human actors. All of the other enabling conditions must be included in the causal nexus. Nevertheless, it is the functional consequences or effects of various innovations as they are utilized within the systems in which they are embedded that ultimately determine which among them will be positively selected and which will fall by the wayside (or never be tried in the first place). The key to this causal dynamic has been functional synergism. However, a necessary concomitant has been the development of ever more complex and potent political *qua* cybernetic systems. This leads to my theory of politics.

VI

A General Theory of Politics

One of the functions of sociobiology, then, is to reformulate the foundations of the social sciences. *E. O. Wilson*

It may well be another decade or two before ethology and sociobiology can add significantly to our understanding of political phenomena.
Albert Somit

What needs doing is worth doing, even though *not* very well.
Abraham Maslow

Defining Politics

"Sooner or later," W. J. M. Mackenzie has written, "some attempt has to be made to define politics."[1] Whether or not Mackenzie was stating a law of nature, political science does not lack for definitions. The granddaddy of them all is the terse epigram that Harold Lasswell used as the title of his book *Politics: Who Gets What, When, How* (1936). According to Lasswell, politics is about influence and the "influentials." Hans J. Morgenthau characterized politics as "the struggle for power."[2] Robert Dahl speaks of "relationships" involving "power, rule or authority."[3] Buchanan and Tullock describe politics as a form of "exchange" between "utility maximizers," while Sheldon Wolin reaches back to Aristotle for his definition: activities relating to or affecting "the community as a whole."[4] Karl Deutsch more or less agrees with Wolin; he calls politics "the dependable coordination of human efforts and expectations for the attainment of the goals of the society."[5]

The anthropologists Lionel Tiger and Robin Fox favor an ethological definition of politics in *The Imperial Animal* (1971). For Tiger and Fox the political system is synonymous with the "dominance hierarchies" that are observed (or perceived) to exist in nonhuman species. And because dominance in most species is linked with reproductive functions, "the political system is a breeding system"; that is, politics is the "struggle for reproductive advantage."[6] (Later they back off from this definition, admitting that dominance hierarchies in human societies may have different functions and consequences.)[7]

Perhaps the definition of politics most commonly employed, at least among contemporary American political scientists, is that of David Easton: the processes through which "values are authoritatively allocated for a society."[8]

Dahl has written that a definition is in essence a "proposed treaty . . . governing the use of terms."[9] The treaty that I propose seeks to define politics as being isomorphic with social cybernetics. Politics may be seen as a "steering" process by which decisions are made with respect to public (common or intersecting) goals, as well as the processes of communication (including feedback) and control by means of which relevant goal-oriented social behaviors are implemented. In short, politics consists of goals, decisions, communications, and control.

Since this cybernetic definition can be traced to the Greek word for steersman or helmsman, the ship of state metaphor reflects both an etymological and a conceptual affinity between cybernetics and politics. Furthermore, a full century before political scientists began applying the word to political phenomena, the French scientist André Ampère took to using "cybernetics" as a synonym for political science.

I follow in that venerable tradition. At the minimum, the cybernetic definition has the virtue of embracing and incorporating most aspects of most of the definitions cited above. It includes allocations of values, relationships of influence, the deployment of power, and a focus on "public" problems. Exchanges among participants are also distinctly implied. In some instances reproductive competition might be involved, but so might reproductive co-operation. Families too have a political *qua* cybernetic aspect.

Indeed, families have patterned sets of relationships involving a hierarchy of joint, complementary, and at times conflicting goals that are effectuated by processes of decision making, control (only some of it voluntary self-control), communications, and feedback. Furthermore, many aspects of contemporary community life involve reproductive co-operation that extends beyond the individual family unit. Day-care centers, public schools, parks, children's libraries, and recreation programs are activities that are analogous to forms of reproductive co-operation in other species and in early hominids.*

Accordingly, politics *qua* social cybernetics is as much concerned with co-operative social processes as it is with competitive and conflictual social processes. For political interactions in and between complex societies almost always involve intricate combinations of co-operation and competition within and between organized, cybernated entities.

The most important difference between the cybernetic definition of politics and the other definitions given above has to do with the fact that politics *qua* cybernetics focuses on goals (whatever they may be) and the processes by which goals are established, pursued, and/or modified over time. In this light, power, the struggle for power, conflictual processes, and decision making are all subsidiary aspects of politics.[10]

If a complex society is in reality an interconnected, hierarchically arrayed set of purposive social systems (superorganisms), politics embraces not just governments but the cybernetic dimension (or subsystem) of all goal-oriented social groups, however small, however temporary, and however ephemeral they may be. Dahl writes: "Whether he likes it or not, virtually no one is completely beyond the reach of some kind of political system. A citizen encounters politics in the government of a country, town, school, church, business firm, trade union, club, political party, civic association and a host of other organizations, from the United Nations to the PTA. Politics is one of the unavoidable facts of human existence. Everyone is involved in some fashion at some time in some kind of political system."[11]

Dahl thinks in terms of his own definition, but what he says also applies to the more inclusive cybernetic definition. One diagnostic trait of a political *qua* cybernetic system is the presence of "power, rule or authority"—goal-related decision making and control over the behavior of the participants—whether in the form of consensual self-control, external coercion, or both. But a more important diagnostic trait is the presence of corporate goals. Not without reason have political theorists from Aristotle to Deutsch likened political systems to the brain and nervous system of an organism (and one might well include the sense organs, the endocrine system, and the musculature); political *qua* cybernetic systems play a functionally analogous decision-making and control role in superorganisms.

My definition of politics is imperialistic in that it suggests that there is much more to politics and political science than the workings of governments,

* From the perspective developed in Chapter IV, one could also include hospitals, roads, fire and police protection, and defense departments as forms of co-operation in human communities that are instrumentally related to survival and reproduction.

political parties, lobbyists, and voters. If contemporary economists are busying themselves with analyses of the economics of family life, higher education, voting behavior, and office seeking, the tables can be turned. Economic life from "markets" to the Common Market can be analyzed in political *qua* cybernetic terms, as many political scientists and other students of organizations are in fact doing, though not always with the cybernetic model in mind. Likewise the domains of small-group theory and formal organization theory become subspecies of a multidisciplinary political science.

There is evidence that cybernetic social processes existed well before the dawn of humankind, before the emergence of the big brain, and probably before the emergence of language. Accordingly, politics in my definition has been intimately associated with realizing the functional synergism that accounts for the directional evolution of human societies. For cybernetic social processes have been as much a cause as a necessary concomitant of the emergence of functional synergism in human societies.

This point is crucial. Absent this definition of politics and my theory of politics unravels. Yet my theory about social cybernetics as an integral part of sociocultural evolution stands; it becomes then an explanatory theory about the emergence and evolution of cybernetic processes in social life. I call such processes politics. The term is a convenient label for a class of empirical phenomena only some of which are conventionally treated by political scientists as political. For example, I consider traffic control systems (laws, police officers, road signs, traffic lights, motorists) to be political systems. To the extent that a critic may give these processes another label and/or define politics in a different way, the argument is only semantic; the theory about the relevant real-world phenomena remains intact.

The cybernetic definition of politics has the additional virtue of encompassing analogous phenomena in other socially organized species such as honeybees, wolves, chimpanzees, lions, rhesus monkeys, and baboons. Goal-oriented decision making, communications, and behavioral control processes occur in all these species and many others, and the differences among these species and between them and human beings, are highly instructive. Indeed, the universality of these processes in socially organized species, however different in terms of the precise mechanisms and functions (the proximate causes), is of enormous theoretical importance.

Equally important, my definition does not limit human politics or political science to what occurs in modern nation-states or developing countries. Politics *qua* cybernetics can be found among the most primitive band-level societies, from the Semang to the Mbuti Pygmies, and in the archaeological and paleoanthropological residues related to our remotest historical and prehistoric ancestors. Politics can be inferred even in the primeval, prehuman state of nature. The "social contract" emerged as a biological (or bioeconomic) contract among mating pairs, their offspring, and close kin. And at some unidentifiable point in the dim past, systematic, synergistic co-operation arose among unrelated individuals and groups of individuals, and this opened the door to the virtually unlimited progressive evolution of human societies.

Aspirations for a General Theory of Politics

In the late 1960s, in the wake of model-building efforts such as those of Parsons, Levy, Almond, Easton, and Deutsch and the early work in positive (rational choice) theory, there was a widespread conviction that political science was close to the development of an empirical, scientifically credible theory of politics. Ithiel de Sola Pool noted that "In large majority, [contemporary political scientists] believe they have or are on the verge of creating a modern political theory."[12] James Charlesworth concurred: "[Political scientists] see all political activity as a manifestation of a grand but as yet unrevealed design, wherein human needs and desires set in motion social and political processes called systems, and these in turn eventually bring about the creation of political laws and institutions."[13] Much has happened to political science and to the world since then, yet political scientists still do not have a fix on the "grand design."

Among the many reasons for this state of affairs, perhaps the most important has been a studied failure to frame the basic theoretical questions properly. Charlesworth suggests that a general theory of politics must be integrally related to much larger questions concerning the nature of human needs and desires and the origins and evolution of human societies. If Charlesworth's viewpoint is correct, how can a theory of politics be constructed without a deep understanding of biological evolution and sociocultural evolution? An understanding of politics must begin with the parameters of the basic biological problem of survival and reproduction and an understanding of the biopsychological roots of human nature.[14] The essence of politics can be discerned only in relation to the inescapable imperatives of the survival enterprise and the purposeful sociocultural systems through which basic needs and wants are satisfied.

Why have political phenomena arisen in the course of human evolution? Why have there been apparent directional trends in the development of political processes and institutions over the past several thousand years? What are the necessary and sufficient conditions for political systems to exist, and why do such systems persist and change? A conscientious survey of the *Handbook of Political Science* (1975), an important arbiter of what constitutes the subject matter of the discipline, reveals only oblique treatments of some of these issues and no attention whatsoever to the role of biological variables and the biological problèmatique *per se* in political life.

Consider this pronouncement by Richard Smoke: "No purpose of government is more central than the protection of its citizens' physical security. Philosophically many thinkers have held that this, in fact, is the ultimate reason why humankind form governments. Empirically, all known governments have tried to do this. . . . The idea that government exists at least to protect the security of those who create and support it has everywhere remained axiomatic."[15]

This is a veiled assertion about the fundamentally determining role of a biological function that Smoke says underpins one of the axioms of political science. But if "government" refers to something that is generic and functional rather than institutional, then our best evidence indicates that government was also associated with the most rudimentary socioeconomic behaviors in our most remote protohominid ancestors: hunting and gathering activities, care of the young, the making of primitive tools, the construction of rude shelters, the management of fire, the domestication of animals, primitive exchange patterns, migrations, and defense against predators of all kinds. Thus "government" is associated with any co-operative, survival-related social activity in human beings or animals, and it probably dates back several million years.

Does the Cybernetic Model Apply?

If there is initial agreement that a testable theory related to these questions constitutes a general theory of politics, the next issue to be confronted is this: Can the cybernetic model adequately encompass and reduce the range of phenomena that conventional political science would call political, as well as the phenomena that I maintain ought to be included?

Although there are a number of different renderings of the cybernetic model in the literature of political science, the most detailed and best-known version is that of David Easton.[16] Easton undertook to devise a fully articulated conceptual framework that would be suitable for data collection and hands-on analyses of real-world political systems. At least that was the hope, and a generation of political science students in the late 1960s and early 1970s was virtually imprinted with Eastonian concepts: inputs (demands and supports), outputs (decisions and actions), withinputs, conversion processes, feedback, stresses, etc.

Accordingly, Easton's framework became the center of gravity for systems-oriented political scientists. For example, Almond and Powell, in the second edition of *Comparative Politics* (1978), adopt and modify the Eastonian paradigm for their own purposes. By the same token, Easton has borne the brunt of the criticisms of systems approaches to political science.[17]

Because of the central importance of the cybernetic model (properly understood) to my theory, I will elaborate briefly.

Easton characterizes politics *qua* cybernetics as a "vast and perpetual conversion process" through which various inputs are transformed into outputs.[18] In essence, he says, the primary function of a political system is "authoritative allocations of values" for a society, along with the obvious corollary of enforcing its "allocations."[19] Allocations of values and the degree of public compliance are then said to be the "essential variables" of the system.[20] Accordingly, the basic problem of all political systems is to cope with the stresses that threaten to drive the essential variables beyond their "critical range" (whatever that might mean). It follows, therefore, that the primary theoretical problem to which a general theory of politics must address itself is system persistence: "How can any political system ever persist whether the world be one of stability or of change?"[21]

There are some structural inconsistencies in Easton's model. For instance, if allocations of values and compliance are the only essential variables, what happened to inputs, which Easton earlier identified (and showed in his diagrams) as an integral part of the conversion process (Figure VII)? This means, for example, that a discrepancy between demands (an input) and actions (outputs) would not constitute a stress because it does not involve essential variables.

Similarly, Easton identifies (correctly, in my view) feedback as one of the seminal ideas of the twentieth century and incorporates it into his model. He even quotes Norbert Weiner, who characterized feedback as having "the property of being able to adjust future conduct by past performances."[22] Easton then goes on to tell us that feedback enables authorities to match outputs to inputs (specifically, to demands). Yet, curiously enough, he leaves out supports, the other input variable. Presumably, then, if a government's

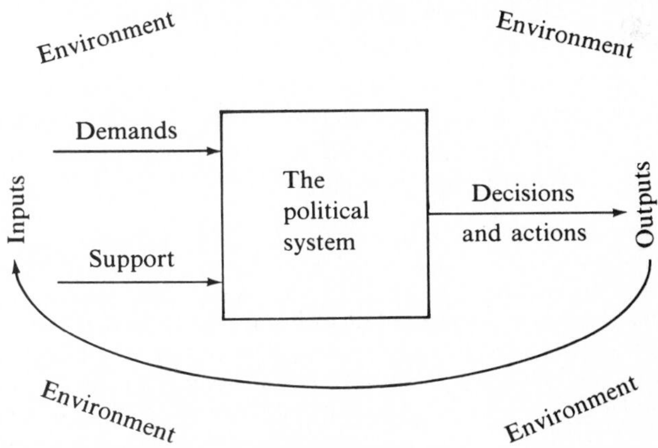

FIGURE VII
Simplified version of Easton's model. (From D. Easton, *A Systems Analysis of Political Life* [New York: John Wiley, 1965].)

tax policies resulted in a serious revenue shortfall, in Easton's political system there would be no feedback.

There are, however, more serious flaws in Easton's model. They arose, I suspect, from the combination of an irresistible tendency to confuse some of the characteristics of real-world political systems (specifically, an idealization of liberal democratic government) and a misinterpretation of cybernetic theory for which Easton was not really responsible. Indeed, misinterpretations, sometimes by the cybernetics pioneers themselves, have been so pervasive that they have retarded understanding and acceptance of cybernetics in the behavioral and social sciences.[23]

Specifically, Easton's model leaves out something important. Between the inputs and the outputs of cybernetic systems, there are goals—endogenous, in-built, or environmentally programmed purposes, behavioral templates or, in technical usage, reference signals. In Easton's model, on the other hand, the innards of the system is an empty "black box" that is no different fundamentally from the Skinnerian black box. Substitute stimuli, responses, and reinforcers, and you have the behaviorist model of an externally determined behaving system. The only endogenous goal is implicit—coping with stresses in order to keep the conversion process going. Why this should be so is not clear. Who cares? But cybernetic systems are fundamentally different; in a cybernetic system, it is the relationship and interactions between endogenous referents (goals) and the external environment that is crucial.*

Thus, Easton misstated the fundamental characteristics—and problem(s)—of cybernetic systems. The problem is not necessarily system persistence but the achievement of goals. Though system persistence can in many cases be the primary goal, it can also be secondary and instrumental to more fundamental goals. Indeed, living organisms *qua* cybernetic systems characteristically behave as if they were designed not primarily for persistence but for reproduction even at the sacrifice of persistence, in furtherance of higher-level functions (persistence of the organism's genes and of the life process itself). Lest there be any misunderstanding, I am not suggesting that Easton's analytical categories and definition of the basic problem are irrelevant, but only that they are incomplete and, perhaps, a special case.

* It is true that Easton includes what he calls withinputs, but this is strictly a subsidiary concept. Withinputs are not the heart of the system, the orienting agency. They are simply demands that are stimulated internally by actors who happen to be located within the system. This is an example of the many ad hoc modifications Easton was required to make to accommodate to real-world politics. For example, it is difficult to fit an explanation for the U.S. decision to enter the Vietnam war into a model in which external demands are the key. To make sense of Vietnam, one must begin with a hierarchy of already-existing U.S. political goals and policies and then go on to reconstruct a set of instrumental subgoals relating to that particular problem, as well as to antecedent decisions and actions by previous administrations, the decisions and actions of adversaries, and so forth.

Equally important, feedback does *not* function the way Easton portrayed it, as a linkage between outputs and inputs. Feedback links outputs to endogenous goals. In other words, behavior in a cybernetic system is controlled by the process of matching feedback (positive or negative) to reference signals. It is an informational process by which the relationship between the actual and desired state of the system is controlled.

This way of interpreting the cybernetic model fundamentally transforms the essential character of the system. If feedback is limited to matching behavior with inputs, then it becomes a teleological system that is "slaved" to external goals, as is so often the case with the systems designed and controlled by humans (thermostats, automobiles, airplanes, and, according to Marx, capitalist political systems). But if feedback is linked to endogenous goals, then the system becomes self-controlled, or teleonomic. As Deutsch recognized, in a cybernetic system the *raison d'être* is the pursuit of goals, not the conversion of inputs to outputs.[24]* Of course, the issue of how goals come to be established and "prioritized" in a system is a complex subject, as complex as the real world itself.

In this light, some of the criticisms of cybernetics are reduced to criticisms only of Easton's interpretation. Thomas Landon Thorson, for instance, discounts the cybernetic model as nothing more than another version of the Newtonian clockworks when in fact it is radically different.[26] Likewise, it is claimed that Easton's formulation of system persistence is tautological: If all viable societies must have political processes, and if political systems are co-extensive with political processes, a political system cannot fail to persist—except in the extreme cases when the entire society and its inhabitants are destroyed.

On the contrary, if political systems are defined (as they should properly be defined) as socially organized cybernetic systems, then it is possible for political systems to come into existence, to develop through time, to decay, to be transformed or replaced, to collapse or be disbanded, or perhaps to persist unchanged, as the case may be. In this formulation the basic theoretical problem becomes far more complex and multifaceted. Persistence is only one aspect of an entire suite of theoretical problems around which an even more general theory can be erected.

* This is not to say that Easton ignored goals. He discussed them in some detail in his section on feedback. But they are not explicitly incorporated into the core of his model. In contrast, John Steinbruner focuses on demonstrating the applicability of the cybernetic model to the process by which decisions are made and implemented in complex political systems.[25] Accordingly, Steinbruner emphasizes purposes or objectives and how specific decisions are fashioned and implemented. He does not attempt to fashion an explicit framework for modeling the polity as a whole, as Easton did. In effect, he concentrates on what goes on inside Easton's black box. Steinbruner thus builds a bridge between systems theorists and decision-making theorists.

Furthermore, political systems are not co-extensive with "society" (meaning some arbitrary cultural or political unit) or the "state" (meaning government institutions). Indeed, the class of social phenomena that can be modeled as political *qua* cybernetic systems and included in the theory goes well beyond those which have traditionally been allocated to political science. There is no justification in theory for excluding from the definition of political systems those cybernetic systems which have customarily been associated with social psychology, sociology, economics, and even ethology and sociobiology.[27]

Political *qua* cybernetic systems need not be viewed as tautologous abstractions. They may designate (or model) specific, real-world systems with cybernetic properties. By the same token, various more or less *ad hominem* critiques that have focused on the presumed ideological biases of functionalist and systems theories dissolve when the cybernetic model is properly understood. There is nothing inherent in the cybernetic model that implies a partiality toward conservatism or radicalism, capitalism or state socialism, totalitarianism or democracy. The precise characteristics of the model in any given application should be dictated by the characteristics of the real-world system that it is designed to idealize, and the only context in which it would be totally inapplicable is the hypothetical case of utopian, apolitical socialism or anarchism.

It is also important to reiterate the point that the best and the brightest among the theorists of the past fully appreciated that individuals are the locus of human action and that social behavior involves an interaction between individual motivations and goals on the one hand, and the constraints and opportunities (the negative and positive reinforcers) that exist in the social order on the other hand. There is a crucial distinction between what I classify as (1) *contiguity* (the physical proximity of a population in a bounded space), (2) *ecological interdependence,* by virtue of various functionally consequential interactions (the classical economic marketplace, or "ecosystems"), and (3) *organic interdependence,* by virtue of participation in a goal-directed superorganism. In such social systems it is neither the self nor the role alone that determines the behavior of the individual but the self-role interaction.

A word should also be said about the relationship between the cybernetic model (properly understood) and various Thermidorian attacks, not only against such hard science approaches but in some cases against the very aspiration for a "social science." There is the charge that the very subject matter, suffused as it is with human values, purposes, and perceptions (not to mention complex networks of time-bound causation), is not susceptible to science. It is therefore important to recognize that the cybernetic paradigm explicitly incorporates and organizes such phenomena, to the extent that they are known; cybernetic models can be used to study the joint influence of stochastic, deterministic, and teleonomic influences.

In sum, the cybernetic model, properly applied, can provide a unifying heuristic framework for political science, as well as for other disciplines that study political phenomena.[28] However, it is also important to emphasize that the model itself is not essential to my theory. It is merely a shorthand way of characterizing a functionally important aspect of all co-operative social interactions. My theory relates ultimately to the real world processes, not to the model. However, I believe that the model fits well the processes I would identify as being political.

Testing the Theory

To summarize the argument developed in the previous chapters, cybernetic processes are a necessary (functional) concomitant and co-determinant of progressive evolution. This has been as true of the eukaryotic cell as of nation-states. Politics *qua* social cybernetics has therefore been an integral part of the process of sociocultural evolution, as much a cause as an effect of other functional and nonfunctional influences.

In the sections that follow I will explore the evolution of politics in more depth. I will begin, however, by addressing the problem of how to test this theory. Earlier I proposed a simple way of testing the underlying synergism hypothesis. My approach to testing the aspect of this theory that relates to politics is more complicated. It involves the development of a series of predictions or logically derived inferences that can be related to real-world political phenomena, and to the data that have been generated by social scientists.

One set of such propositions—what might be called the Iron Laws of Organization—can be stated as follows:

1. Who says a division of labor or a combining of functions (co-operation) with respect to some goal, at any biological level, says organization.

2. Who says organization, says cybernetic control processes.

That these laws are a paraphrase of Roberto Michels's famous Iron Law of Oligarchy is no coincidence, though there are similarities and differences between his formulation and mine. Contrary to some interpretations, Michels's law, like mine, was based on an essentially functional argument. A two-page chapter in his classic *Political Parties* (1911) was devoted to the "technical" and "administrative" factors that necessitate organization. "Be the claims economic or be they political, organization appears the only means for the creation of a collective will. Organization, based as it is upon the principle of least effort, that is to say, upon the greatest possible economy of energy, is the weapon of the weak in their struggle with the strong."[29]*

Up to this point in his argument I am basically in agreement with him, and our laws might well lead to similar predictions regarding the emergence of political systems.† I go beyond Michels in focusing explicitly on cybernetic processes. My theory is concerned with cybernetic functions in relation to the production of synergistic effects; it adheres strictly to a functional perspective toward organizations and rulership, and it takes no *a priori* position on whose goals may be embodied in the system. These laws could apply equally to "rule over" as to "rule on behalf of" the parts or members.

In contrast, Michels assumed the worst and held that various inherent inequalities (inherited, experiential, and structural) coupled with "psychological factors" (especially nepotism) meant that there is a built-in tendency toward oligarchical and exploitative rulership. Of course Michels was not entirely original; similar arguments can be found in Plato, Aristotle, Machiavelli, and *The Federalist Papers.*

My theory leaves it an open question whether a given system is effectively realizing its intended goals, whatever they may be. A system may be more or less successful in attaining its goals (eufunctional or dysfunctional), and it is one of the central concerns of political science to attempt to make such determinations. By the same token, in a given system the precise functional mix of (1) the personal values, appetites, and skills of political actors, (2) the constraining or facilitating influence of the civic culture, and (3) various structural (engineering) characteristics of the system (inclusive of reciprocal feedback controls) is always an open question.

In order to get from the cybernetic model of politics to the traditional elitist model, we require some ancillary propositions concerning the ways in which power is attained and used by individuals and the ways in which wealth is distributed. These propositions may be only conditional. For political *qua* cybernetic systems come in many forms, in terms of (for example) how the steering function is attained, how the costs and benefits are distributed, and how much feedback control the members have over the steersman.

To illustrate, the cybernetic model fits well what is perhaps the best organized and most efficiently run of all extant religious sects, the communal

* Michels was not the first to note the hierarchical propensities of human societies. His was only the most vivid and unequivocal expression of a view held by many theorists, that polities are generally ruled by elites. Michels wrote, "Who says organization, says oligarchy." Mosca wrote, "The dominion of the organized minority obeying a single impulse, over the unorganized majority is inevitable."[30] Ziegler and Dye wrote, "In all societies, and under all forms of government, the few govern the many. This is true in democracies as well as in dictatorships."[31]

† Michels correctly predicted the course of events that would follow socialist revolutions. "Socialism is an administrative problem," he pointed out.

farming Hutterite Brethren. The Hutterite system has been aptly characterized as "managerial communism." By the same token, the model fits the modern armed forces, which might be characterized as "regimental socialism."

If the cybernetic model is pointedly neutral with respect to who gets what, when, and how in political systems, it is unambiguous about the organizational imperatives. If there are public goals that embrace various parts (individuals), of necessity there will be accompanying cybernetic processes that serve to coordinate the behavior of the parts toward the realization of the goals of the whole. If the individual level of biological organization consists of autonomous cybernetic systems, then superordinate communications and control processes are required to canalize (subordinate) the behavior of the constituent individuals into appropriate social "roles" designed to contribute to the realization of systemic goals. (Sociologists would speak of task-oriented groups.) Indeed, there can be no wholes without such processes, as Georg Simmel[32] and many others have pointed out. Again the mechanisms of control may be consensual or coercive; the structure of individual benefits and costs (or reinforcers) may be more or less equitable or skewed; the reinforcers may include benefits for co-operation or costs for non-co-operation or both; these costs and benefits may be internal (psychic) or external (physical and material) or both. Nevertheless, cybernetic control processes are inescapable concomitants of organization. The external goals of the whole must somehow be superimposed on or integrated with the goals of the parts.

The test of this fundamental set of theorems is falsifiability: All social organizations will manifest cybernetic processes. If any convincing exception can be found, the heart of this theory can be rejected. Although falsifiable in principle, to my knowledge these propositions cannot be falsified by any actual or hypothetical social organization, not the sexual union,* not families, not fraternal organizations, not the classical economic market, not football teams, universities, corporations, armies, or governments, not even beehives, wolf packs, lion prides, or baboon troops. Nor can it be falsified by the vast research literature in sociology and anthropology, organization theory, small-group theory, or communications theory; the literature is unequivocally supportive.

The answer to the basic "why" question arises from the fact that open thermodynamic systems must engage in purposeful transactions with their

* The sexual union has goals, not only the obvious proximate goals at the level of personal motivation but implicit superordinate goals that may be far from the participants' minds (biological reproduction). Indeed, the participants may take steps to thwart these higher-level goals, thereby superimposing conscious controls on lower-level controls. The sexual union also involves processes of communication, mutual decision making (whether voluntary or coerced), goal-oriented control over the resulting co-operative behaviors, and consummation and feedback, which ultimately terminate the system.

environments (adaptation), and this necessitates decision making, communications, and control processes. Beginning with the most basic life processes—the construction of enzymes, tissues, and organisms, cybernetic control processes have made goal-oriented biological and biosocial processes possible. There can be no thermodynamic order without organization, and organization in turn requires cybernetic processes. As each new level of biological organization evolved, there was a concomitant progressive differentiation by means of natural selection and/or teleonomic selection of specialized mechanisms of communication and control.* This has been a major aspect of the overall process of differentiation and functional specialization in evolving systems.[33]

These cybernetic mechanisms range from RNA at the microscopic level to electrochemical communications and control mechanisms at the organismal level; olfactory, tactile, visual, and auditory mechanisms linked to electrochemical mechanisms at the social level; and specialized governmental institutions at the (human) societal level. (Computer-driven and artificial control systems are only the latest innovations in an ancient lineage.)[34] The most stunning animal example is the well-documented dance-language of the honeybees, which even includes a syntax.[35] A far richer set of analogies to human communications, however, is to be found among the diverse social communications and control processes in the primates and social carnivores.[36]

The most decisive challenges to the laws stated above are probably the numerous historical and contemporary examples of human organizations based on communalistic, egalitarian, or utopian ideals. At one extreme they can be viewed as experiments that were more or less explicitly designed to falsify the Iron Laws of Organization.[37] There were, for instance, the Taoists of the fifth century B.C., the Essenes of the first century A.D., the Adamites of twelfth-century Bohemia, and the Levellers of seventeenth-century England. In eighteenth- and nineteenth-century America, utopian communities sprouted and died in profusion; once visible landmarks such as Ephrata, Plockhoy's Commonwealth, The Society of Woman in the Wilderness, the Memnonia Institute, Shalam, and the Straight-Edgers are long forgotten.

There have also been many more businesslike communal organizations, some of which have persevered and even thrived over the centuries. There are religious orders such as the Carmelites, the Jesuits, the Benedictines,

* Cybernetic systems do not evolve in a mechanistic manner; the process is not deterministic but cumulatively selective in specific contexts. With the emergence and progressive differentiation of political systems, as with cybernetic systems at lower levels, the process has entailed selective retention (D. T. Campbell's phrase) of functionally adaptive variations. Unlike the selective process at lower levels, however, teleonomic selection does not involve random variation (mutational processes are never completely random either) but more or less canalized innovation and purposive trial-and-error processes.

the Daughters of Charity, and the Sisters of Mercy; religious sects such as the Mennonites, the Amish, and the Hutterites; well-known nineteenth-century ventures such as the Oneida Community; and twentieth-century institutions such as the Israeli Kibbutzim and the collectives in various communist countries. At the most practical extreme is the diffuse phenomenon known as the co-operative movement, which had an estimated 150 million members in 57 countries at its zenith, prior to World War II.[38] Although strong on paper, this vast congeries of local groups has never moved beyond narrowly circumscribed and nominally participative modes of economic co-operation: tractor pools and community silos for farmers, co-operative grocery stores for consumers, and the like.

Certain generalizations appear to hold true for this extensive inventory of social experiments. In no case has there been an absence of decision making, communications, and regulatory processes. The greater the dependency of the members on the organization for their livelihood, the more explicitly elaborated is the cybernetic infrastructure. Similarly, the greater the size of the organization, the greater is the tendency for a controlling hierarchy to emerge. And the greater the organization's need to exercise control over its relationship to the external environment, or to obtain inputs (money, labor, or other resources) from the environment, the greater is the tendency for internal organization to become differentiated and hierarchical.

Support for these generalizations can be found in numerous case studies.[39] One striking contemporary example is the systematic study done by anthropologist Katherine Newman and her students of twelve American counterculture "collectives" established in the late 1960s. All sought at the outset to approximate the ideals of equality, collective leadership, and an informal, rotational division of labor. While each involved communal living arrangements, none was initially a source of livelihood for any of the members, who were supported by jobs in the "straight" community. In effect the members wanted to have it both ways; they would depend on the external environment for their means of support, but they would insulate the commune from the environment for domestic and social purposes.[40]

Cybernetic processes were in evidence in these "extended families" from the outset, and the burden of sustaining the governmental functions of the communes increased over time. The pattern in all cases was similar. In addition to the coordinating and performing of volunteer work in communal maintenance activities, there were frequent and time-consuming meetings (three to four times a week) and much informal discussion in between. The members began to experience time pressures in trying to manage jobs, communal responsibilities, and personal lives at the same time.

Two solutions to the problem were ultimately adopted. One involved converting the commune to a business venture such as a retail store, with capital provided by either the members or banks. The two communes that have managed to survive and retain a degree of egalitarianism and collective leadership chose this route. They are highly organized entities that are fully constrained by the realities of operating as open systems; both have had to keep the size of the operation small in order to retain its communal character.

The other solution involved strategies for bringing in enough income from government grants (CETA training programs, community service programs) to support at least some of the members, who could then devote full time to the commune. The unhappy result of this strategy was the emergence of bureaucratized organizational structures, whose staffs became more or less co-opted by the income-producing functions (by the external environment) and more or less exploitative of outside volunteer labor—with much ensuing resentment. Most of these communes did not survive, and in no case did the original ideals remain unsullied for long.

In her conclusions, Newman placed much of the blame on the rules imposed by the government agencies, but in reality these constraints were only a special case of the more general "rules of the game" for any organization that must earn its living in the ecological and/or socioeconomic environment. In these cases, as in other experiments in communal living, the ideals of the members were inevitably constrained, compromised, and sometimes thoroughly corrupted by bioeconomic realities and the Iron Laws of Organization.

Though it may only be counterintuitive to a utopian or an anarchist, it appears that a perfect correlation exists between organization and cybernetic processes in human societies. Furthermore, this correlation also exists in every other social species and at every other level of biological organization. To my mind, this represents confirmatory evidence far beyond what would be strictly required for a theory of human politics.

The Second Set of Propositions

The necessarily deterministic linkage between politics *qua* social cybernetics and social organization leads to another proposition. My argument is that political (cybernetic) processes are a requisite for the realization of functional synergism in social organizations. There can be no functional synergism without politics. Though there may be coincidental, fortuitous effects and second-order synergistic effects, there cannot be explicitly goal-related synergism without organization—and politics. (Cybernetic processes are in fact the means by which the Law of Effect operates, that is, the means by which fortuitous effects are converted to functional design.) And, if the presence of political processes is a functional requisite, then their absence or breakdown would be fatal. Accordingly we can predict that

3. Given sufficient resources or capabilities (land, money, labor, time, energy, materials, tools), any failure to achieve designed or intended synergistic effects will be due to specific failures of the relevant cybernetic communications and control (political) processes.

The historical record and the political science, sociology, economics, and management science literatures are littered with supporting evidence, case studies of political failures from lost elections to lost revolutions and lost wars, from defeated football teams to bankrupt organizations. A prime example is the recent record of Japanese and American automobile manufactures. The relative success of Japanese companies and failure of American companies has been the result primarily of political factors.[41]*

There are many apparently falsifying exceptions to this proposition, but I hold they are exceptions that prove the rule. In many cases organizational failures are the result not of a lack of adequate resources or poor organization in a structural sense but of unexpected and perhaps unpredictable factors: the wind changes that led to the defeat of the Spanish Armada, the unusually early and severe winter that stalled fatally the advance of Hitler's armies into Russia, the iceberg that sank the *Titanic,* the fire that consumed the Hindenberg, the new technologies that suddenly make an old technology obsolete.

Such manifest failures of prediction can be reduced to failures in cybernetic terms and incorporated into the scope of proposition 4. Cybernetic control is always a function not of some ideal of perfect knowledge but of whatever information happens to be available to the system (built-in information, information inputs, feedback). By definition cybernetic processes entail dynamic control of the relationship between a system and its environment. Thus insufficient information, uncertainty, and risk taking are endemic features of real-world decision making and organizational management.[42] An organizational failure due to unpredictable events is one type of control failure on the part of the system. It can properly be said that a system is poorly designed, or functionally maladaptive, when it (or its operators) is unable to predict and compensate for perturbations that result in failures to achieve the designed goals. In other words, insufficient information is a cybernetic problem. The very definitions of "information" and a "sufficiency" of information depend

* This proposition implies that many of the internal problems of organizations that are conventionally treated under separate categories (leadership, morale, management practices, communications, training) can be reduced to facets of the problem of cybernetic control. The role of management and leadership as a major factor in organizational development and success is illustrated by the Ford Motor Company's decision in the early 1970s not to develop small cars. It was this decision that led to Ford's difficulties with imports.

on the nature of the goals and the specific context; there is no information that does not actually or potentially relate to goals.*

Some of my colleagues might object to such an all embracing interpretation of what constitutes political factors. So I will restate Proposition 3 in such a way that "accidents" are excluded. Thus Proposition 4 states that if one or more examples of strictly speaking political failures can be found, this will be sufficient to confirm the validity of the restated proposition. Only if no such failures can be found would the proposition manifestly be false:

4. At least some of the failures to achieve designed or intended synergistic effect in goal-oriented social organizations will be due to specific failures of the relevant cybernetic communications and control processes. Conversely, any failure of the cybernetic (political) subsystem will be fatal for the goals of the system as a whole.

Can this proposition be tested rigorously? Obviously, when it comes to making the kinds of evaluations that are called for here, matters of judgment are involved. What are "sufficient" resources or capabilities? Yet the analytical problems may not be insurmountable.

Consider two real-world examples. The first involves data for two California hospitals. Hospital A and hospital B are so strikingly comparable that they come about as close to providing a controlled social experiment as one is likely to find, ready-made. Both hospitals are privately owned, nonprofit institutions operated by religious orders; they are in the same state and are therefore subject to the same regulatory environment; both are located in urban residential, low-income minority areas; they are of comparable size (about 180 beds and 230 beds respectively); and they have about the same mix of patients in terms of reimbursement for services.

Nevertheless hospital A produces a consistent 6 to 8 percent net return (as a percentage of gross revenues), while hospital B has averaged less than 1 percent for the past five years and in 1979 ran at a loss. As far as can be determined, the explanation does not lie in any of the externals. If anything, hospital A is at a significant disadvantage. It has an older physical plant (ten years versus two years); it has a slightly higher load of charity and low-reimbursement medical patients; it has a high volume of maternity patients (a traditional loss leader in the hospital business) while hospital B has none at all; it has 50 fewer beds; and it has double-occupancy rooms

* The basic distinction in communications theory between "information" and "noise" involves just this difference. Information is coherently organized to achieve an intended effect; noise ordinarily cannot achieve such effects and may impede the communication of information. The exception that proves the rule is noise that is deliberately used to impede communication.

while hospital B has only single-occupancy rooms, which are much easier (at least in theory) to keep full. Hospital A thus has the additional problem of matching the sex, the smoking habits, and other characteristics of its patients.

The significant differences between the two hospitals are political (cybernetic). Hospital A has a management system that is a model of how to run an institution; hospital B provides a model of how not to run an institution. The director of hospital A is open, supportive, and sensitive to his staff and the needs of the institution. He is decisive, well organized, and committed to the development of the hospital. Hospital A has a formal planning and control system that runs throughout the organization. Planning is thus an integrated, systemwide process in which each unit participates in developing the overall hospital goals. Because everyone is brought aboard, everyone works toward the same goals. Management promotes the sense of participating in a collective effort. Short-term goals and activities are developed in annual Management by Objectives plans that in turn are related to longer-range goals. Thus the hospital staff lines up behind objectives and does not sabotage them.

The external relations of the hospital are open and participatory. The board of trustees, which is not dominated by the religious order, includes members of the medical staff, the hospital staff, and the community. Members of the community also serve on every one of the hospital's boards and committees.

The result is that hospital A runs a lean, highly efficient operation with tight cost controls. Patient volume is an incredibly high 95 percent of the maximum occupancy rate for its medical and surgical services despite the double occupancy. One can even sense the difference in the hospital environment: staff morale is high, the staff is friendly and co-operative but businesslike, people are busy, no one is killing time.

The director of hospital B is young, authoritarian, and closed. He hands down orders rather than consulting. Because he is ambitious and wants to move up in the corporate hierarchy of the religious order, he calculates his actions accordingly. The hospital has no formal planning process. The board of trustees is drawn exclusively from the religious order, and all the trustees are from out of town. When it is done, planning is *ad hoc* and often at cross-purposes.

The result is that hospital B runs a very lax operation. Productivity is low; there is a chit-chat culture; there are many operating inefficiencies. Cost controls are minimal. Patient volume is only 75 to 80 percent of maximum occupancy despite the single-occupancy room arrangements. Hospital B's expenses per patient day are \$483, versus \$459 for hospital A, and the difference amounts to \$1.57 million per year more in operating expenses.

The conclusion seems well founded: Given similar resources and capabilities, the differences in performance between the two hospitals are the result of factors in their *political systems.*

My second example compares two developing countries. Country A has enjoyed several decades of political stability and sustained economic growth, despite some recent troubles. Country B has enjoyed even greater growth, but it has been coupled with increasing political turmoil and a failure to achieve modernizing objectives. The countries are Mexico and Iran, and together they illustrate well the sometimes decisive importance of politics.*

In many respects the two countries are quite comparable. Both have ancient cultures and a strong sense of national identity; both have cultures that are anchored by conservative religious institutions; both were classified as economically backward prior to World War II but emerged from the war with elites which were committed to ambitious modernizing goals; and both have been deeply enmeshed economically and politically with the United States.

In a comparison of the economic performances of the two countries, Iran appears to have had a substantial advantage in recent years (see Table II). Although Iran has a smaller land area and a smaller amount of arable land and forests, it also has a much smaller population (an estimated 34.8 million versus 63.3 million for Mexico in 1977) and a slightly smaller population growth rate. Thus Iran is endowed with significantly more land per capita. Moreover, since the Gross National Products of the two countries in 1977 were about equal ($75.3 billion versus $72.2 billion), the per capita GNP of Iran was almost twice as large as that of Mexico ($2162 versus $1160). Iran's rate of GNP growth was also much larger (9.9 percent versus 4.7 percent), thanks in considerable part to oil revenues. In recent years Iran has enjoyed a substantial trade surplus ($5 billion versus a $1.77 billion deficit for Mexico in 1977) and a far smaller burden of foreign debt repayment ($889 million versus $3.7 billion in 1977).

When we compare the two countries in terms of various social indicators, however, the picture changes dramatically. Using such time-honored measures as the number of radio receivers per capita, the number of passenger cars per capita, the percentage of dwellings having electricity, and the percentage of the Gross Domestic Product devoted to private consumption, Iran has fared much worse than Mexico. The figures for private consumption are the most startling: 41.3 percent of GDP for Iran versus 68.8 percent for Mexico.

* Numerous comparative studies have been made over the years. One of the more pertinent is the comparison of Mexico and Turkey by Huntington and Domínguez.[43] They found contrasts between the two countries that reinforce the conclusions of my Mexico-Iran comparison. We await only a comparison between Iran and Turkey to allow us a kind of triangulation, like a navigational fix.

TABLE II

Comparative demographic and economic data for Mexico and Iran. (World Bank, *World Tables,* 2d ed. [Baltimore: Johns Hopkins University Press, 1980]).

	MEXICO	IRAN
POPULATION		
Population (millions, 1977)	63.3	34.8
Population growth rate (percent, 1970–1977)	3.3	3.0
LAND		
Land area (millions of hectares)	197.2	164.8
Arable land (crops and pastures, millions of hectares)	23.2	15.9
Arable land per capita (hectares)	0.37	0.46
Forests (millions of hectares)	70.4	18.0
ECONOMY		
GNP (billions of U.S. dollars, 1977)	72.2	75.3
GNP per capita (U.S. dollars, 1977)	1160	2162
GDP by origin (as percent of total, 1970–1977)		
Agriculture	10	11.1
Mining	1.2	35.3
Manufacturing	26.5	11.8
Construction	5.9	6.5
Exports	8.9	36.6
Imports	10.5	25.3
Average annual GNP growth (percent)	4.7	9.9
Foreign debt service (millions of U.S. dollars)	3792	889.5
Balance of payments (billions of U.S. dollars)	−1.771	+5.081
SOCIAL INDICATORS		
Percent of workforce in agriculture (most recent estimates [MRE*])	34	41
Percent of income received by highest 20 percent of population (1970)	3.4	4.0
Percent of income received by highest 5 percent of population (1970)	27.9	29.7
Radio receivers (per 1,000 population, MRE*)	301	249
Passenger cars (per 1,000 population, MRE*)	41.6	18.5
Electricity (percent of dwellings, 1970)	59	25
Private consumption (percent of GDP 1970–1977)	68.8	41.3
Government expenditures by function (percent of total government expenditures, 1977)		
Defense	4.0	29.4
Education	19.5	8.6
Health	4.3	2.9
Social security and welfare	24.3	3.1

*MRE = most recent World Bank estimates as of 1979.

A much smaller proportion of Iran's governmental expenditures have been devoted to education (8.6 percent versus 19.5 percent), health (2.9 percent versus 4.3 percent) and social security and welfare (a minuscule 3.1 percent versus 24.6 percent). Iran has also been allocating a smaller proportion of its government expenditures to support agriculture (3.2 percent versus 16.6 percent) and transportation and communications systems (5 percent versus 10.6 percent). And the Iranian government was consuming almost twice the proportion of the total GDP as the Mexican government (20.4 percent versus 10.5 percent).*

Where was Iran's additional wealth going? It went to defense. By devoting about 6 percent of its total GDP to a technologically advanced (hardware intensive) defense establishment, which consumed almost 30 percent of the total government budget in 1976 (versus 4 percent for Mexico), Iran's government bore a heavy responsibility for the relative poverty of its people. The Iranian government consumed almost twice as much as it contributed to the GDP in 1976.

The international political and military ambitions of the late shah's regime, doubtless encouraged (but hardly determined) by the strategic interests of the United States, seriously distorted Iran's developmental priorities. The familiar litany of causal factors—alienation of the church, secret police repression and brutality, bureaucratic corruption—no doubt played a role, but the basic political choice with respect to the use of Iran's relatively favorable resource base was of overriding importance.* Recall Edmund Burke's warning after witnessing the carnage of the French Revolution: "A state without the means of some change is without the means of its conservation."

The foregoing examples of political success and failure illustrate the dynamic interplay between resources and capabilities on the one hand and

* Mexico's economy has recently been wounded by the so-called oil glut and consequent sharp decline in world oil prices. Whether decisive government actions, including devaluations of the peso and other reforms, will succeed in preventing a widening trade deficit anu runaway inflation remains to be seen. It is significant, though, that such actions were taken at all and that the new regime in Mexico seems to be weathering the crisis.

* We cannot explain revolutions solely in terms of a simple economic determinism. Many developing countries that are far worse off than Iran in terms of personal income have not had revolutions. Some countries (Israel, Egypt, China, Cuba) spend far more of their GNP on defense. Obviously, much depends on a set of mediating factors, what might be called the situational *gestalt.* There may be little public resentment or political opposition to large-scale military expenditures when there is widespread public perception of a serious external threat. Widespread poverty may be stoically accepted so long as it is perceived to be equitably shared and beyond the control of the people in charge. The widely shared perception that a revolution is (a) desirable, (b) likely to result in positive change if successful, and (c) likely to succeed are proximate causes of utmost significance, for these are the factors that motivate organized political action. It is only when one asks where these perceptions come from that the ultimate economic and political causes loom relatively large.

various instrumental political *qua* cybernetic processes on the other. In both pairs of case studies, the difference between success and failure was political.

Political Complexity

In contrast to the campaign rhetoric of our politicians, my theory predicts that there will always be a close functionally based relationship between the size and complexity of any synergistic system (nation-states included) and the size and complexity of its political *qua* cybernetic subsystem. That is, the greater the organizational size or complexity, the greater will be the need for commensurate mechanisms of decision-making communications and control.

This proposition also represents a functionalist challenge to the (classical) Marxist view of politics and the state. In contrast with the Marxian view that political processes and institutions are either epiphenomenal or an expression of class conflicts, this theory asserts that political processes are an integral and necessary element of any goal-oriented social organization. Whereas Marx and Engels downgraded the vital role of politics in economic enterprises and predicted the withering away of the state in due course, this theory predicts the opposite—"progressive" economic evolution will be accompanied by more, not less, politics. Let me state the proposition somewhat more formally:

5. While there may be some short-term lead or lag, in general there will always be a high degree of concordance between the size and level of complexity attained by any social system as a whole and the size and complexity of its political qua *cybernetic subsystem.*

Proposition 4 asserts that although the historical process by which organizations (or societies) and their political systems evolve is not deterministic, there is nevertheless a highly deterministic relationship between the realized size and degree of structural and functional differentiation (Spencer's term) and the size and degree of political differentiation. There will be an allometric growth of the political subsystem.[44]* In other words, if a more complex organization arises out of the historical confluence of chance, necessity, and teleonomy, it will be accompanied by a functionally equivalent degree of political development: The political structures will become larger and more elaborated, primarily for functional reasons. (The terms "lead" and "lag" refer to the role of historical contingencies, from charismatic political leadership to entrenched social classes and ossifying seniority systems.)

* The number of hierarchical levels of control will also increase, but the nature of the relationships involved is still poorly understood.

The evidence for this proposition spans at least five major social science domains that have been fraught with conceptual and methodological problems and sharp differences of opinion: formal organization theory and small group theory (sociology and management science); communications theory (engineering, sociology, management science, political science); theories of societal evolution (anthropology, sociology); and theories of political development (political science).

The Evidence in Organization Theory

We must confront first the literature in organization theory, which has been a thicket at least with respect to the issue of organizational complexity. The importance to human societies of the division of labor has been recognized since the time of Plato. It was the centerpiece of Adam Smith's vision of economic society and of Herbert Spencer's vision of cultural evolution, just as it was the target of Karl Marx's moral indignation. Although modern organization theorists studiously avoid associating their conceptualizations with Spencer (if they mention him at all), they generally adopt his formulation, that the hallmark and most important indicator of organizational development is "structural differentiation" and the concomitant of "integration."[45]

There is broad agreement that organizations can be mapped and analyzed structurally in terms of four key variables or parameters: (1) size, (2) horizontal differentiation (the specialized tasks or activities on the same organizational level), (3) vertical differentiation (the different organizational levels), and (4) the degree of spatial dispersion among the units or parts.

Disagreement begins with the problem of how to measure these parameters; they have been defined and measured in a bewildering variety of incompatible ways for the past forty years.[46] Hage would measure horizontal differentiation by using the number of occupational specialties and the duration of training and the professional requirements for each, disregarding the arbitrariness and inconsistency of training and formal requirements.[47] Similarly, Richard Hall would distinguish between differentiation based on a range of specialized but independently pursued tasks (say, various client services) and differentiation based on the component elements of a unified production operation.[48] While this distinction may well have significant organizational implications, it is hard to see in it categorically different forms of differentiation; the difference is that the division of labor is turned outward instead of inward.

A kind of theoretical tunnel vision has led to some otiose research. Herbert Spencer never lost sight of the cardinal fact that there is always an intimate relationship between structures and functions, that is, between overarching organizational goals and functionally related tasks. Organizational development, he postulated, is a historically conditioned, interactive process in which external forces and internal factors combine to shape the progressive development of various superorganisms.[49] Accordingly, all four parameters listed above are ultimately a reflection of utilitarian (functional) considerations. Organizations do not develop autonomously; for the most part they do so in consequence of specific organizational goals, functional needs, and functional transactions with specific environments (though they may be constrained by nonfunctional factors). This may seem commonsensical, but many sociologists, steeped in Durkheim's dictum that social facts should be accounted for only in terms of other social facts, have theorized about organizations as though they were disconnected from their functional (economic) bases and often from their external environments as well.[50]

As a result, an inordinate amount of time and research money has been expended in an effort to determine whether the size of an organization is the primary cause of its degree of complexity, or vice versa.[51] The star witness is Blau's theory of differentiation in organizations, which is supported by Blau and Schoenherr in a study of the fifty-three state employment security agencies (one for each state, the District of Columbia, Puerto Rico, and the Virgin Islands).[52] The authors conclude that the size of each agency (and therefore that of all organizations) is the major determinant of its degree of structural differentiation and the size of its administrative component. "Increasing size generates structural differentiation in organizations along various dimensions at decelerating rates."[53] Mileti et al. seconded this theory in a study of twenty-eight federal and state agencies in California: "The consistent findings of the two studies suggest that these are dependable generalizations in the accumulating body of organization theory."[54]

The obvious methodological objection is that fifty-three functionally identical U.S. government agencies and twenty-eight mildly diverse government bureaucracies in one state are not a random sample and are more likely to be homogeneous with respect to these variables than, say, a mixture of government bureaucracies, educational institutions, labor unions, military units, hospitals, and private industries—all of which have been the object of numerous studies.[55] Initially Blau did not reconcile his findings with the sometimes discrepant findings of others. For instance, Childers et al., in a study of thirty-seven Coast Guard operating units, noted that the necessity for continuous, twenty-four-hour operations coupled with having to be constantly ready to respond to a crisis situation imposed structural and staffing requirements on the units that many business firms and government bureaucracies do not have.[56]*

* Blau subsequently expanded his vision and acknowledged a more complex relationship between size, differentiation, and organizational functions in an article in which he reported on data collected from 416 urban government finance departments, 124 department stores, 115

(Continued)

The idea that the size of an organization or polity may have important consequences for its structure and governing functions is very old. Many theorists have recognized that size is one cause among others of organizational complexity, and that size in turn is the result of functional influences. However, latter-day sociologists have been so intent on "social facts" that they have slighted the prior question of how and *why* an organization comes into being and grows. Perhaps both bigness and complexity are correlated effects of common prior causes. Perhaps all four structural parameters are causally linked to organizational goals, functional requirements (the technological and economic imperatives), the resources available, and the synergistic effects these structures produce. If organizations are in reality open, thermodynamic *cum* cybernetic systems, they must of necessity engage in transactions with their environments. In order to survive (to support themselves and their employees), their outputs (goods and/or services) must somehow be related to obtaining sufficient inputs (money or other resources) to meet their basic needs. The underlying functional (economic) basis of an organization is inescapable, even if it is not the only important factor. In fundamental ways the structure of an organization must be functionally related to its environment (unless it is fortunate enough to be a free rider).

This is the contrasting thesis of Lawrence and Lorsch, who try to show in a study of three types of U.S. industries what probably seems obvious to most lay persons, that the degree of structural differentiation in an organization is directly related to the organization's need to adapt to its environment. Lawrence and Lorsch concluded that a high degree of structural differentiation (which for them includes behavioral and attitudinal factors in addition to work roles) is contingent on the degree of environmental differentiation and other external factors—thus the term "contingency theory," a variant (and refinement of) "open systems theory."[59]

Lawrence and Lorsch's conclusion is interesting if unsurprising. But would they have reached the same conclusion if they had been confined to using the data for employment security agencies? Conversely, what would Blau and Schoenherr have made of Lawrence and Lorsch's industry data? The problem is that these theorists have often argued from highly skewed samples, used very different measures of differentiation, and argued past one another—and sometimes past themselves. For example, Lawrence and Lorsch include in their study data relating to the internal functioning of their chosen organizations, yet the data are treated as a dependent variable. They do not explore

---

universities and colleges, and 1279 teaching hospitals.[57] Nevertheless he retained the sociological bias that size is the major causal variable in differentiation (rather than a subsidiary or second-order causal factor). Mileti et al. were more cautious about generalizing and made a concession to the possible influence of other variables—which these authors have in fact treated explicitly in subsequent writings.[58]

the possibility of an autonomous role for internal functional needs, needs imposed by the nature of the task itself, the technology, and human relations problems.*

Fortunately organization theory has seen an implosion toward a multifactorial viewpoint and away from prime-mover theories. This trend accords with my Interactional Paradigm and the open, cybernetic system model. And, just as various monochromatic theories of organization are being integrated within more inclusive frameworks, so the issue of complexity requires a more synthetic approach.[61] Organizational complexity is the result of an interacting configuration of influences that includes (1) the nature of the organization's goals and tasks, (2) internal functional considerations, (3) the available technological hardware and software, (4) external environmental influences, (5) structural requisites independent of functional considerations, and (6) idiosyncratic variables relating to the personalities, experiences, and historical context of the organization and its members. Size can be a constraining influence or a facilitator, a cause of growth or an effect of growth. Consider, for instance, the paradox that some large modern organizations—large in terms of capital, production, sales, and profits—are shrinking in terms of personnel because of automation and other technology-intensive adaptations. Or consider how data relating to ancient China's vast armies of coolie labor might refract the vision of Western sociologists.

Whatever the mix of structural, functional, and historical factors that may be responsible, organizational complexity is clearly a key variable and the overarching indicator of organizational development precisely because it reflects the combinatorial properties that are responsible for whatever forms of functional synergism an organization produces. All four complexity variables—size, horizontal differentiation, vertical differentiation, and spatial dispersion—may contribute independently to the corollary political problem of communications and control. Whatever the causes of complexity, complexity necessitates political *qua* cybernetic controls.

Measuring Complexity

The testing of the proposition that there will always be a close correlation between organizational and political size and complexity requires attention

* There are now a myriad of organizational taxonomies based on various classification criteria. No single approach is likely to be right for all purposes, but the approach that is most relevant to the theoretical issues raised here must focus on functional differentiation and integration.

Michael Crozier examined these functional factors. His study involved the French tobacco company, an industrial monopoly comprised of thirty spatially dispersed plants, each with some 350 to 400 workers. One would have expected this to be a fairly complex organization structurally. Yet because the technology was primitive by modern standards and the plants were virtual replicates of one another, there were only six relatively homogeneous categories of workers in the entire company. Structurally it was little more complex than a set of clones of Adam Smith's pin factory.[60]

to the twin problems of measuring complexity and measuring political processes. It turns out that the complexity variable is easy to measure but difficult to measure well. Countless studies have employed such indicators as the number of job categories, the number of work sites, the number of products or services rendered, and the number of horizontal and/or vertical divisions. Questions left unanswered are how well such surrogates measure functional complexity and how comparable they are to one another.

Formal organizational charts are not very reliable indicators of structural and functional complexity. Too many extraneous and arbitrary considerations and too little of the underlying network of functional interactions may be reflected in these artifacts. Indeed, vertical differentiation is likely to become an increasingly unreliable indicator in the era of matrix management, production sharing, and broker organizations. Perhaps sociologists have been getting conflicting results in part because they are measuring different parts of the elephant.

I advocate an approach that encompasses the size, differentiation, and spatial dispersion variables as well as the need to give more weight to nonhuman elements. This approach involves looking at the structure (types, total number, and hierarchical ordering) of discrete but interdependent tasks that all members of an organization perform, including tasks performed by machines under human control. For instance, a secretary may perform 50 different tasks while a trained auto mechanic, with the help of machinery, might perform more than 100 tasks—a far cry from Charlie Chaplin's legendary factory worker in the movie *Modern Times,* who performed only the one task of tightening a bolt on an assembly line.

Like most approaches to measuring social phenomena, this one involves some methodological problems. If we set about toting up the task structure for General Motors, for example, should we include the entire GM system—its suppliers, subcontractors, advertising agencies, independent dealers, government regulators, and stockholders—or only those who are formally employees? And how do we actually measure discrete tasks? For instance, do we count the process of typing, copying, collating, stapling, and distributing memos and reports as one or five or ten different tasks? (These problems might be surmounted through consistency in applying whatever criteria are adopted and through strict adherence to the desideratum of measuring all relevant combinatorial or functional elements of a complex system.*) The logistical problems involved in obtaining such measures may also be less formidable than they seem. Detailed personnel job descriptions, PERT charts, and operations flow charts are a familiar part of corporate life, and industrial

* If my purpose were to study GM as an organization, I would limit the system to formal employees and treat other actors as constraining or supporting aspects of the GM environment.

engineers, operations researchers, and organizational planners routinely work with such data in performing their functions. The major research obstacle is funding in an era of scarce resources.

While awaiting future research, it is possible to gain some purchase on the relationship between organizational structures and their political infrastructures by means of the extant research literature in sociology and the management sciences, communications theory, anthropology, and political science.

Organization theory offers an extensive literature on the relationship between size, complexity *qua* structural differentiation, and what sociologists call the administrative component of an organization. Again there are methodological problems and inconsistent results. Just as measures of complexity may be incommensurable with one another, so may be measures of administrative functions. More important, the administrative component is often measured in a too narrowly circumscribed manner. Formal administrative titles generally do not encompass the cybernetic functions in an organization; one must include administrators' secretaries, clerical staffs, receptionists, telephone operators, computer programmers and operators, security guards, messengers, and research, planning, personnel, and accounting staffs insofar as their work may relate to cybernetic functions. And what about time spent by line personnel on the telephone, in meetings, in transit, in training activities, and reading and writing memos, correspondence, and reports? To obtain an accurate measure of the cybernetic aspect of organizational life, one must engage in a far more detailed research effort than is normally the case.*

Despite the considerable shortcomings of the available indicators, the studies that attempt to correlate size, differentiation, and overhead functions are generally supportive of the hypothesis. Some of these studies have found size to be more powerfully related to the administrative component.[62] Others have found structural differentiation to be more potent.[63] Still others have found spatial dispersion to be an important factor.[64]

There is no evidence of absolute decline in the administrative component as organizations grow larger, but there is some evidence of relative decline as one or more of the complexity variables increases, in accordance with a proposition first advanced by Gaetano Mosca. That is, the ratio of administrators to the total work force may decline. This prompted Blau to posit that the overhead functions of an organization are subject to economies of scale (positive synergism). Specifically, he postulated a logarithmically declining rate of increase in the administrative component as an organization becomes more differentiated.[65]

* An alternative, cybernetic measure of organizational complexity, though relevant in theory, is probably not practicable.

Common sense, after all, tells us that the top of a pyramid remains pointed even as its base grows larger. There was only one president when the population of the United States numbered 8.6 million in 1816, and there was only one president when it recently surpassed 220 million. The ratio of presidents to citizens has declined sharply in 180 years. On the other hand, the proportionate size of the federal government as a whole has not declined, and it may be that the principle of economies of scale may need modification to accommodate specific functional contexts.

When the more stringent functional criteria proposed above are applied, any economies of scale may prove to be marginal. And those that do exist may prove to be attributable to such intervening technological variables as telephones, television, print media, and high-speed transportation—synergistic technologies that have served to increase the span of communications and control functions independently of size. Increases in size may be in part a result of such communications technologies. (Recall the reciprocal and interactive model of causation.) The total quantity of information flowing through a social system (per member, per unit of time) and the amount of time per member devoted to systemic coordination activities may remain relatively constant across each type of organization.* This prediction would be more consistent with my theory. Indeed, Theodoridis and Stark have proposed that information measured by energy flows may be used as a quantitative indicator of progressive evolution generally.[66]

The general proposition that there are correlative increases in political infrastructures as organizations grow larger is supported by the research in small-group theory. Georg Simmel was perhaps the first small-group researcher to postulate that increases in group size alone will generate structural changes toward hierarchical organization.[67] He hypothesized a series of what would now be called thresholds, structural breakpoints of the sort that can be modeled by Thom's catastrophe equations.[68] This general observation has been confirmed in numerous small-group experiments and field studies.[69] Small groups, as they grow larger and/or take on more complex tasks, quickly evolve toward specialization with respect to basic cybernetic functions. There emerge chairpersons, secretaries, committees, subcommittees, liaison persons, parliamentarians, sergeants-at-arms, and whips.

Evidence in Communications Theory

Communications theory, while providing additional support for proposition 5, is another discipline that has produced some curiously convoluted notions

* No such functionally based typology (at least not one that is wholly satisfactory) exists to my knowledge. The prediction might prove to hold true across all organizations, on a per member basis. However, it seems wise to hedge on this.

about causation. Witness Krippendorff's law of structural generation, which holds that *"any process, once initiated and maintained, leads to the genesis of social structure."*[70] Krippendorff views the hierarchical structuring of social relationships, then, as a consequence of communications. Krippendorff's law has been modeled by Mayhew et al.[71] On the theoretical premise that communications processes must (with certain exceptions) occur in serial order rather than simultaneously, because of the nature and limitations of the nervous system and our biological communications equipment,[72] Mayhew et al. proceed to define a social structure as an inequality in the sequencing of communications (a debatable definition).* Accordingly, they posit a coefficient of sequence inequality (K). Thus:

$$K = \frac{\frac{1}{2} \sum_{i=1}^{N} \sum_{j=1}^{N} |p_i - p_j|}{N - 1}, \tag{1}$$

where p_i = the proportion of instances of "system control" achieved by the ith individual of all instances in the sequence; p_j = the proportion of instances of system control achieved by the jth individual; and N = the number of individuals in the group. K is not only a measure of sequencing inequalities among participants but by definition is a measure of the power structure.

In a subsequent paper, Mayhew and Levinger extend this line of reasoning in an attempt to show that as a communications network grows in size, even under an assumption of initial random interactions, there will be an inherent tendency for the system to evolve toward a hierarchical structure.[73] The mathematical treatment of their argument, in abbreviated form, begins with a model that describes a set of random initial communications (technically, a discrete-state, discrete-time, zero-order Markov chain with stationary transition probabilities and a doubly stochastic matrix):

$$P(i_t \,|\, j_{t-1}) = 1/N, \tag{2}$$

where P = the probability operator; t = any arbitrary point in time; $i, j,$ = 1,2,3,....,N; i_t = the association of actor i with an interactive event defined as t; and j_{t-1} the association of actor j with an event defined as $t - 1$. The expected value of K (the coefficient of sequence inequality), or $E(K)$, can be described:

$$E(K) = \sum_{i=1}^{N} P(s_i) K_i, \tag{3}$$

* The authors identify music as an exception in which combinations provide meaningful patterns. Their insight could have been extended to include other forms of *gestalt* communications phenomena—art, clock faces, and verbal and written languages.

where $i = 1, 2, 3, \ldots, N$; s_i = the ith sequence; and K_i = the value of K associated with the ith sequence. It can be shown that this model predicts that the expected value of K (or the concentration of power) will increase as the group size increases. The reason for this has to do with the fact that the minimum value of K, or K_{min}, is constrained both by the size of the group (N) and by the length (L) of the communication, for any condition in which $N > 1$ and $L > 1$, with $L \leqslant N$. Thus:

$$K_{min} = \frac{N - L}{N - 1} \tag{4}$$

If L is held constant while N increases, then:

$$\lim_{N \to \infty} K_{min} = 1. \tag{5}$$

What is wrong with this line of reasoning? The problem is that these theorists, like the organization theorists, take the system and its functioning as a given. The prior causes are taken for granted. Krippendorff's law is in fact a tautology, for the existence of a purposeful communications net indicates that a structure already exists. Purposes are prior to communications; cybernetic controls must be in operation (and power must exist) in order for communications flows to occur. Communication may be linked with and instrumental to the exercise of power, but it is not the same thing. In the real world the patterns are shaped by the individual and collective purposes and instrumental actions that bring communications systems into being in the first place.

Like many elitist-oriented theorists, these theorists assume an obligative commitment by the participants, a commitment that rational choice theorists point out cannot be assumed *a priori.* Communications processes in social systems never start from randomness and never become structured by purely stochastic processes, just as economic systems never have perfect markets. At times there may be a high degree of disorder and noise in the system, but the actors are never analogous to free electrons.

Communications theory does not support the contention that hierarchical organization is a structural necessity for the communications aspect of such complex cybernetic systems as human organizations, whatever their purposes and attendant power relationships. The machinery and the physics of communications create deterministic constraints which necessitate the economies associated with a hierarchical patterning (called chunking).*

* This has been expressed mathematically by the pioneer information theorist Claude Shannon:[74] The maximum quantity of information (in "bits") that can be transmitted through a channel with band width w over time T, with a mean signal power of P and a mean noise level of N is: $w\,T\,\log_2(1 + P/N)$.

These requisites in turn create opportunities for gaining and maintaining power, as political scientists are well aware. Control over access to a communications channel or medium (a scarce resource) has been used by political operatives—dictators, revolutionaries, House Speakers—as an instrumentality for political control since time immemorial.* Yet it is not inevitable; it depends on the purposes of the actors and the operative degree of feedback control.

Macro-level Political Development

Does the linkage between organization and political complexification manifest itself in the large-scale, macro-level processes of societal development?

First let us consider the "stages" of political evolution and the basic nature of that process. As with the efforts to characterize the overall process of cultural evolution, there have been attempts to delineate a definite order or progression in the process of political development. Indeed, some theorists use a political typology as their basic rubric for differentiating among societal types. Thus Kent Flannery adopts the categories proposed by Elman Service (band, tribe, chiefdomship, and state) and attempts to show how certain kinds of institutional arrangements can be correlated with the emergence of each political type (see Figure VIII).[76]

While such taxonomic efforts can have utility, they can also be misleading. They may suggest thresholds that do not exist, or they may give too much weight to those traits which serve as basic classification criteria, while at the same time short-weighting others that are of equal or greater importance or that are causally prior. For instance, family and kinship traits remain fundamental across all four of Flannery's types, even though they have interacted with the larger polity in different ways at different levels of development. By the same token, most political scientists would find objectionable Flannery's tacit assertion that all states can be lumped together in one broad category. There is, after all, a significant difference between states ruled by hereditary monarchs, states in which power is seized and maintained by force, and states in which rulership is an office with limited tenure.

The taxonomic approach may also obscure subtle similarities across categories. For example, it is not clear how hereditary leadership in chiefdomships differs from kingship in states. Similarly, this approach may obscure significant differences within categories. The Maya can be classified as horticultural in terms of their basic food production technology, but they were highly developed in terms of crafts industries, and they were distinctive among horticultur-

* David Apter has formalized this relationship in a hypothesis to the effect that there is an inverse relationship between the degree of coerciveness of a political system and the degree to which important information about the functioning of the system is freely available.[75]

alists (though not unique) in evolving a state form of political organization.

Perhaps the most important objection is that the typological approach leads to a kind of theoretical astigmatism. Rather than focus on cultural evolution as an integrated, systemic process, various theorists have become fixated on categories and have gotten bogged down trying to explain how a society evolves from one stage to another. Some theorists have disowned this approach, but I believe it has some utility precisely because sociocultural evolution has been a systemic process.[77] But like a dangerous technology, such typologies can be useful so long as they are used carefully.

To illustrate, by putting together the economically oriented typology of Gerhard Lenski[78] and Service's politically oriented typology, one can make some useful observations. (See Figure IX.) It is apparent that there can be considerable "play" in the relationship between economic and political aspects of a society. It is also apparent that there are significant limits to the amount of "play" that is possible. Complex states do not arise on a horticultural base, and agricultural societies are never organized as simple bands. Within the range of possible economic and political types, there tends to be a clustering. In the 1966 edition of the *Ethnographic Atlas,* 90 percent of the 147 hunter-gatherer societies listed were nomadic bands, whereas only 4 percent

Type of society	Some institutions, in order of appearance	Ethnographic examples	Archeological examples
	Local group autonomy; Egalitarian status; Ephemeral leadership; Ad hoc ritual; Reciprocal economy; Unranked descent groups; Pan-tribal sodalities; Calendric ritual; Ranked descent groups; Redistributive economy; Hereditary leadership; Elite endogamy; Full time craft specialization; Stratification; Kingship; Codified law; Bureaucracy; Military draft; Taxation		
STATE		FRANCE ENGLAND INDIA U.S.A.	Classic Mesoamerica Sumer Shang China Imperial Rome
CHIEFDOM		TONGA HAWAII KWAKIUTL NOOTKA NATCHEZ	Gulf Coast Olmec of Mexico (1000 B.C.) Samarran of Near East (5300 B.C.) Mississippian of North America (1200 A.D.)
TRIBE		NEW GUINEA HIGHLANDERS SOUTHWEST PUEBLOS SIOUX	Early Formative of Inland Mexico (1500-1000 B.C.) Pre-pottery Neolithic of Near East (8000-6000 B.C.)
BAND		KALAHARI BUSHMEN AUSTRALIAN ABORIGINES ESKIMO SHOSHONE	Paleo-indian and Early Archaic of U.S. and Mexico (10,000-6000 B.C.) Late Paleolithic of Near East (10,000 B.C.)

FIGURE VIII

Flannery's sociopolitical typology, with ethnographic and archaeological examples of each. (From "The Cultural Evolution of Civilizations," *Annual Review of Ecology and Systematics* 3[1972]: 399–426.)

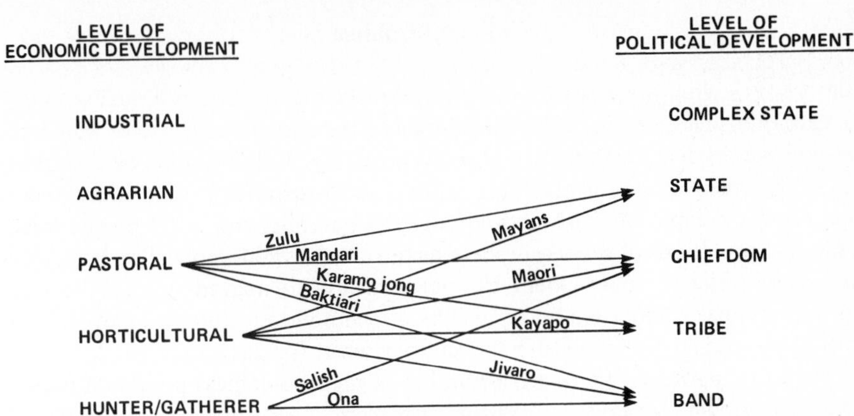

FIGURE IX
An illustration of the "play" in political evolution.

of 377 horticulturalists were nomadic. Most were quasi-sedentary tribes, villages, and chiefdomships.* Furthermore, in a preliminary analysis, Lenski determined that the median size of hunter-gatherer groups is about 40 persons (n = 62), while horticulturalist groups number about 95 persons (n = 45).[79]

The truly important progressive changes in the course of political evolution are not those that have led societies from one reified type to another. Instead they have involved specific structural and functional innovations and elaborations in political (cybernetic) superstructures. Thus it may be more fruitful to focus on the progressive cumulation of various functionally significant political traits—the nature of the changes, the order in which they appeared, and their association with other social traits—rather than on political types.†

* Some anthropologists do not believe the tribe is a meaningful functional unit. Carneiro, for one, believes the autonomous village was the true evolutionary intermediary between bands and chiefdomships (organized clusters of villages). But this ignores the archaeological and ethnographic evidence that large agglomerations of nomadic or seminomadic peoples (composed of many family units or bands) have occurred on many occasions among the hunters and netters of both large and small game animals, as well as fishermen and herdsmen. We have no way of knowing from the available evidence how many of these conglomerate bands later evolved into more sedentary villages, thus being in the line of evolutionary succession.

† In this vein, Carneiro's proposal to revitalize the Spencerian typology may be useful. Spencer differentiated among polities on the basis of their number of levels of government. He used the designations simple, compound, doubly compound, and trebly compound. Henry Wright has also been pursuing the goal of developing a law that would specify the relationship between the number of administrative levels in the political hierarchy of a society and its level of socioeconomic development. He has noted that at least three levels are found in even the most primitive states.[80]

Galton's Problem

Before reviewing the research in cultural anthropology and political science, a cautionary note is in order. While the data can be suggestive, they are not definitive. Data sources are of uneven quality. Ethnographic field studies have not been of uniformly high caliber; the researchers' informants were not always reliable, and the methodologies, data-collecting skills, perceptions, and interpretations of the researchers have varied considerably. This difficulty has been offset to some extent by recent efforts to upgrade data collecting and analytical standards and by efforts to winnow out dubious sources and otherwise screen and structure the samples used for analysis.

Equally important, there are a number of methodological pitfalls of which the best known, perhaps, is "Galton's problem." At a meeting of the Royal Anthropological Institute in 1889, the pioneer anthropologist E. B. Tylor presented a paper in which he introduced the cross-cultural survey technique. In the discussion that followed, Tylor was stopped in his tracks by Sir Francis Galton, the renaissance scientist who had pioneered in the development of statistics. Galton objected that any statistical correlation among cultural artifacts that might suggest a functional relationship between them—say, matrilocal (female-centered) residence patterns and matrilineal rules of kinship determination and descent—could be artificially inflated by nonfunctional factors, that is, patterns of cultural diffusion ("borrowing" and out-migration). The anthropologist Raoul Naroll observes: "It is the problem of dealing with the rival hypothesis that a correlation which appears to reflect a lawful tendency is merely an artifact of diffusion—a mere historical coincidence."[81]

There is reason for concern about Galton's problem, but it has been overstated; in reality it is only a special case of a more general problem associated with making statistical inferences. Galton and various statistically oriented anthropologists who followed him treated diffusion as if it were a null hypothesis, as if the diffusion of a trait through borrowing or migration is necessarily nonfunctional ("a mere historical coincidence"). But this conclusion is by no means self-evident or logically necessary. Much borrowing is likely to be functionally based; cultures do not for the most part borrow from one another at random. By the same token, the expansion of a culture by sending out migratory propagules is likely to be the result of functional (adaptive) processes. Diffusion does not occur in a vacuum or through osmosis; it occurs in the context of the struggle for existence and the operation of the economy principle. Naroll concedes that no one has yet undertaken to show that cultural diffusion processes may in fact be unrelated to functional considerations.[82] Those who assume this to be the case thus tacitly adopt the position that only if a trait is "independently invented" can it be functional.

The nub of the issue from a technical (statistical) standpoint is whether or not societies can be counted as independent cases for statistical purposes. The answer is that it depends on the kind of relationship posited between the variables. Consider an example used by Naroll to demonstrate how a discount for the effects of diffusion might reduce the size of an ethnographic sample.[83] In a study of incest taboos among 84 American Indian societies, Harold Driver discovered that by tracing the historical connections among them he was able to reduce the number of instances of independent invention of a particular kin avoidance rule to five. He concluded that a geographical-historical explanation was more potent than a psychological-functional one.[84]

In fact, kin avoidance rules are highly functional in behavioral-genetic terms, in that they serve to prevent inbreeding depression and the incidence of deleterious recessive traits. It is striking to think that the same rule for ensuring exogamy was separately invented at least five times within Driver's study area. (It is unlikely to have diffused if it were dysfunctional.)

I do not discount the more serious methodological objections—which Galton's problem merely illustrates—that statistical correlations do not necessarily reveal a functional or causal relationship between two phenomena and that there may be spurious correlations. Emile Durkheim's famous study of suicide found that the suicide rate among French army officers was relatively high, while among Catholics it was relatively low.[85] Yet with perfect Gallic logic Durkheim invoked essentially the same ad hoc causal explanation to account for both rates—the behavioral constraints associated with belonging to strict, tightly knit organizations. In the mid 1970s the suicide rate among American psychiatrists was about four times the national average. Can we assume then that there is something about psychiatry that causes suicide? Certainly not in and of itself, for the rate is still only 70 per 100,000. The vast majority of psychiatrists do not commit suicide, just as the vast majority of suicides are not psychiatrists.

Statistical correlations, even when they are not somehow biased, may or may not imply a direct causal linkage. It is more likely that they suggest functional relationships involving a number of interacting co-determinants. Or there may be co-variation as a result of common prior causes. If the males of aboriginal California tribes such as the Tolowa, the Hupa, and the Yurok wore painted deerskin capes while the women wore flat caps decorated with twined basketry overlays, we cannot say that the former caused the latter. Both traits may have had dual functions: to give protection from the elements and to symbolize a cultural identity. Moreover, their widespread local adoption may have had both historical and functional causes. The point here is that the issue cannot be resolved by statistical tests. Accordingly, the proposed "solutions" to Galton's problem are useful, but they must be applied with care lest they also introduce biases into our analyses.

The Evidence in Cultural Anthropology

Let us now consider some more recent and reliable data relating to historical and contemporary societies. These data should show that there is a complex, co-determining relationship between socioeconomic and political evolution. We should expect to find the two domains to be closely linked, whether their occurrence is due to diffusion or to independent invention. Only cases in which such couplings are not found to occur would constitute evidence against the hypothesis.

The evidence relating to primitive and certain historical societies (Rome, ancient China) strongly affirms the hypothesis. Raoul Naroll's index of societal development is a composite of three carefully constructed indicators: crafts specialization, population size (in the most populous community center), and "organizational ramifications" of the political superstructure (which he defined as stable teams of at least three persons with explicit decision-making and leadership roles in relation to various tasks). Naroll's analysis of the data for thirty ethnic units in the Human Relations Area Files produced a set of approximately linear regressions for the logarithms of (1) population versus the number of craft specialties, (2) population versus the number of team types, and (3) the number of types of craft specialties versus the number of team types (but not the total numbers). Naroll concluded: "The fact that all three regression patterns can be so closely fitted with a single formula in round numbers suggests that the underlying developmental patterns of social evolution tend, like those of biological evolution, to be allometric."[86]

Equally striking was Naroll's subsidiary analysis of contemporary data for the Los Angeles area, which did not fit the formula that had worked so well for less technologically advanced societies. Naroll found at least ten times more craft specialties than the formula would have predicted, based on the size of the population. Naroll concluded that there had been a nonallometric spurt of growth in the past two centuries.[87]

The explanation for this apparently inconsistent result is that Naroll was conflating size relationships with the relationship between size and internal differentiation, or complexity. While it may be true that there is a strong allometric linkage between the size of the whole and the size of some part, or between the complexity of the whole and the complexity of some part, the relationship between size and complexity remains somewhat problematical. For instance, had Naroll used data for Calcutta instead of Los Angeles his results would have been very different. In contrast, the synergism hypothesis predicts threshold effects, discontinuities, and step-functions in the growth and development of societies and their political systems based on the combinatorial effects of many variables, not just changes in population size. Indeed, the theory explicitly predicts that organizational development may proceed independently (to some degree) of population growth, as a function of increasing economic complexity, and this is what Naroll's data in effect showed to be the case.

On the other hand, the argument that there may also be a significant relationship between size and complexity was supported in an analysis by Carneiro.[88] Carneiro first developed a list of 354 societal traits, ranging from crafts specialization to social stratification, markets, and governing councils, that could be expected to show cumulation historically. The list was then reduced to the 205 traits that in Carneiro's judgment reflected best a society's organizational properties. From a list of 100 carefully screened societies, Carneiro extracted a subset of 46 societies that consisted of a single community. Analyzing this subset, Carneiro found that the number of societal traits approximated the square root of the population. The resulting regression line, fitted by eye, is shown in Figure X.

Carneiro noted that his preliminary analysis of the multicommunity data showed societal complexity increasing more slowly overall than population. However, this should not necessarily be construed as evidence in support of Blau's economies of scale hypothesis. Blau was referring to a relative reduction in the administrative component of a single organization (the political component narrowly defined); Carneiro was referring to the number of functionally distinct types of parts (not even the total number) in multicommunity societies. As Carneiro noted, the most logical explanation for his finding is that the communities are not functionally differentiated entities but partial replicates—aggregations of perhaps complementary but also fairly comparable economic enterprises.

Nor is the latter finding by Carneiro at odds with Naroll's Los Angeles data. Apart from the fact that Carneiro was comparing a sample of technologically primitive societies (relatively speaking), his observation was based on a comparison of single community and multicommunity societies. If Naroll's data on the number of craft specializations were extended to the entire U.S. population, doubtless there would be a comparable reduction in the ratio of craft specializations to population. It is not surprising that there remains even in modern societies a relationship between the size of the population center and the number of occupational specializations, as posited by Zipf.[89]

Elsewhere Carneiro produced a more elaborate analysis involving all 100 of his societies, in which he attempted to correlate each of the categories on his list of 354 cultural traits with 33 selected traits relating to the degree of macro-level political organization. The 33 traits ranged from the presence of a permanent headman of some sort (81 of the 100 societies had one) to the presence of a professional civil service (only four societies had one).[90] The results are summarized in Table III. Each cell in the table shows the rank-order correlation coefficient between all 100 societies for the two cultural

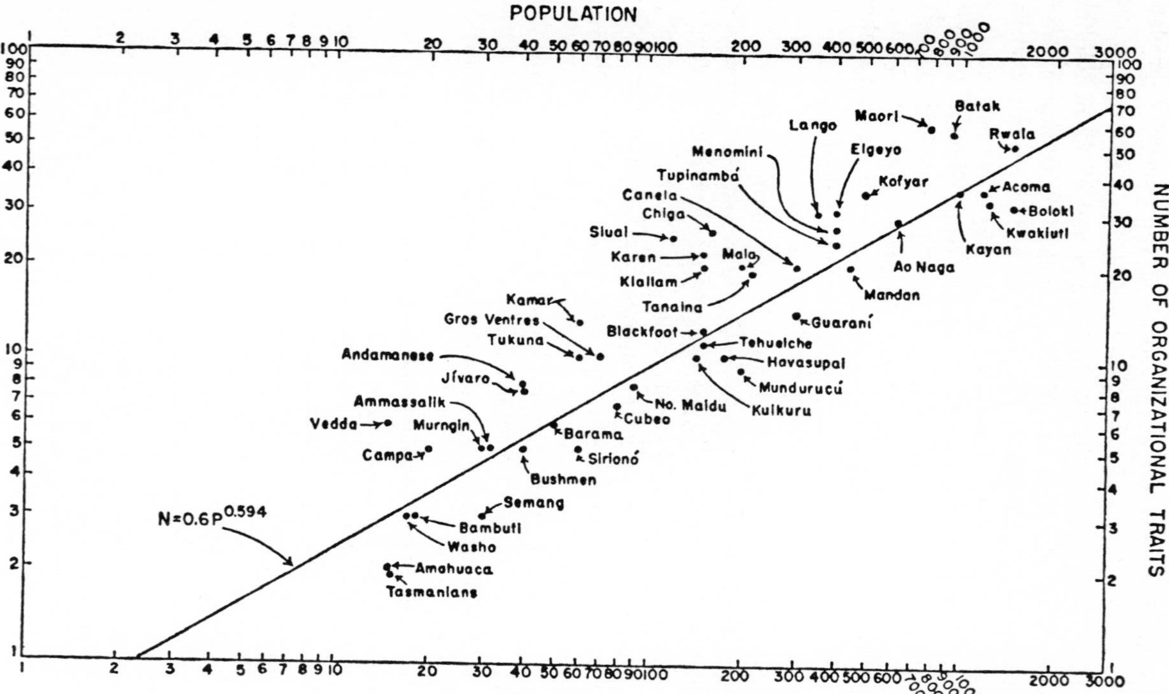

FIGURE X

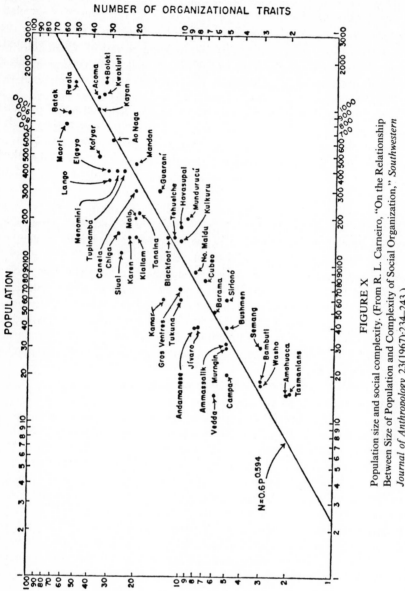

Population size and social complexity. (From R. L. Carneiro, "On the Relationship Between Size of Population and Complexity of Social Organization," *Southwestern Journal of Anthropology* 23(1967):234–243.)

categories that intersect at that cell. The table reveals that political organization traits (legal system traits were measured independently) correlate strongly with each of the other cultural categories. Indeed, all the categories correlate extraordinarily well with one another (all are statistically significant at the $p < .001$ level or better). Sociocultural evolution is clearly an integrated, systematic process, with mutually reinforcing forms of functional synergism and with closely intercorrelated processes of political differentiation, as the theory predicts.

What about the flipside of political integration, the concomitant of political differentiation? Some evidence was obtained by performing a secondary analysis of a set of societal development scales devised by Murdock and Provost from data compiled for the *Ethnographic Atlas.* Murdock and Provost ranked a carefully selected sample of 186 societies worldwide from the Hadza to the Russians on a set of five-point scales for ten measures of societal complexity: (1) writing and written records, (2) fixity of residence, (3) agricultural development, (4) urbanization, (5) technological specialization, (6) land transportation methods, (7) money, (8) population density, (9) level of political integration, and (10) social stratification. In the rankings on the political integration scale, "0" indicated political authority dispersed among house-

	Economics	Social Organization and Stratification	Political Organization	Law and Judicial Process	Warfare	Religion
Warfare						.713
Law and Judicial Process					.804	.735
Political Organization				.875	.834	.708
Social Organization and Stratification			.804	.803	.826	.648
Economics		.813	.791	.815	.751	.721
Subsistence	.773	.707	.737	.787	.764	.673

TABLE III

Correlations between seven categories of culture (n = 100). (From R. L. Carneiro, "Scale Analysis, Evolutionary Sequences and the Rating of Cultures," in R. Naroll and R. Cohen, eds., *A Handbook of Method in Cultural Anthropology* [Garden City, N.Y.: Natural History Press, 1970].)

holds or analogous units, "1" indicated politically organized local communities (as in clans or tribes), "2" indicated one administrative level above the local community (as in chiefdomships and small states), "3" indicated two administrative levels above the local community (as in regionalized small states), and "4" indicated societies with three or more superordinate administrative levels.

Using Murdock and Provost's raw data, I performed a series of Spearman rank-order correlations between the political integration scale and each of the other scales. The lowest correlation coefficient was $r_s = .347$ (land transportation) and the highest was $r_s = .699$ (social stratification). The combined coefficient, when the nine other scale rankings were aggregated and their mean values correlated with the rankings on the political integration scale, was $r_s = .512$. (All correlations were statistically significant at the $p < .001$ level.) Thus the data indicate that there is a strong but by no means perfect correlation between societal complexity and the degree of macro-level political integration.

Rolf Wirsing's study of political power (control over decisions in five public domains) across a sample of 25 preindustrial societies was also highly supportive.[91] Wirsing developed a set of scales for decisions regarding (1) the initiation or prevention of warfare, (2) adjudication of disputes, (3) appointments to lower offices, (4) allocations of wealth, and (5) assignments to involuntary labor. He found that the degree of political power was functionally related to the number of organizational levels on which politically relevant information was stored and retrieved. Equally important, Wirsing found that power distributions were much less closely related to population size *per se*. In effect, Wirsing's results supported the hypothesis that political power is strongly associated with the ability to control access to and the distribution of information, and that hierarchical organization fosters power concentration.

Similarly, in a factor analysis of 89 selected cultures, McNett found extremely high correlations between his rank-order scale of settlement pattern types and the characteristics of a society's economic, political, and religious institutions.[92] Various kinship, household, and other social traits were not significantly correlated. McNett concluded that his data strongly support the functionalist view that there is a close relationship between the areal distribution of human populations and basic, pansocietal institutions.

Perhaps the single most compelling cross-cultural study is the highly innovative multifactor analysis by Alan Lomax and Norman Berkowitz which involved a pair of new methodologies called cantometrics and choreometrics—the quantitative analysis of song and dance styles and performance patterns.[93] Because these expressive and communicative aspects of cultural evolution have been shown to correlate highly with evolutionary changes in economic and political systems, and because song and dance patterns are functionally related to the reinforcement of societal cohesion and organization, Lomax found that cantometric and choreometric "profiles" can serve as sensitive indicators of cultural patterns in general and communications patterns in particular. Using a factor analysis for 71 variables (including many conventional economic and political measures) across 148 of the cultures listed in the *Ethnographic Atlas,* Lomax was able to "reduce" the central characteristics of cultural evolution to a single global attribute—increasing organizational capabilities for controlling and manipulating the relationship to the environment. This "grand scheme" in turn was found to involve a complex interplay between two "deep attributes," differentiation and integration.

A number of studies show parallel trends within major political subsystems (legal, administrative, military, etc.). Carneiro's findings noted above regarding the correlation between legal complexity and other cultural categories were buttressed by the studies undertaken by Schwartz and Miller and by Wimberly, in which legal complexity scales were developed in relation to the progressive evolution of such specialized legal roles as mediator, court, police, and counselor or advocate.[94]

To test these relationships further, I undertook (with the assistance of Jiri Weiss) a series of rank correlation studies in which cultural traits were correlated with the population estimates found in various ethnographic sources. One involved data from the *Ethnographic Atlas:* correlation of Tuden and Marshall's political organization scales with the scale for "typical community size."[95] The highest correlations were between community size and (1) "specialization and institutionalization of police functions" ($r_s = .492$, $p < .001$, $n = 181$); (2) "administrative hierarchy," that is, the number of levels of control and the degree of centralization ($r_s = .358$, $p < .001$, $n = 183$); (3) the degree of judicial complexity ($r_s = .334$, $p < .001$, $n = 182$); and (4) the degree of centralization of executive power ($r_s = .302$, $p < .001$, $n = 183$). Using data provided by Carneiro (personal communication), we were also able to correlate the population levels in Carneiro's ethnographic sample with the number of traits in his scale of legal and judicial complexity ($r_s = .817$, $p < .001$, $n = 51$).[96]

Another subsystem in which the patterning of political evolution can be clearly perceived involves military organization and warfare. The relationship between warfare and political development has been examined by many writers, but my concern here is with military capabilities and organization as a functionally significant dimension of the political structure of a society. The best early study of this subject was Stanislav Andreski's *Military Organization and Society* (1954), which is richly laced with suggestive hypotheses and historical illustrations. A key source of empirical evidence is anthropologist Keith Otterbein's cross-cultural study of warfare patterns among a representative sample of 50 primitive cultures selected from the *Ethnographic Atlas.*[97]

Only four societies in Otterbein's sample had no military organization at all. In every case they were primitive bands such as the Copper Eskimos, which are isolated from other human populations and which appear to have been driven into the marginal environments they now occupy. Otterbein was also able to confirm a series of theoretical propositions about his sample: (1) the higher the level of political centralization (using Service's classification scheme), the more likely that its military organization will consist of specialized "professionals" (phi = .59, $p < .001$); (2) the greater the percentage of professionals in a society's military organization, the more hierarchically organized it will be (phi = .48, $p < .01$); (3) the higher the level of political centralization, the less likely that wars will be initiated by anyone other than an authorized official (phi = .59, $p < .001$).

Somewhat weaker correlations were found for such things as the degree of formality with which wars were initiated, conducted, and terminated; the kinds of tactics, weapons, and armor employed; and the utilization of cavalry, defensive fortifications, and siege operations. Combining all these traits in an 11-point "military sophistication" scale, however, Otterbein found that the overall level of military sophistication was strongly correlated with the degree of political centralization (phi = .68, $p < .001$). Finally, Otterbein found that the more centralized a society was politically, the more "advanced" (complex and numerous) were the reasons given for entering wars. Clearly there is a close relationship between progressive political evolution generally and the evolution of that dimension of political organization which relates to warfare.

In a major review of 150 cross-cultural studies, Raoul Naroll lists as "historically valid" in "broad outline" the following findings regarding cultural evolution: (1) there has been a clear-cut, allometric trend toward greater occupational specialization (except for a major spurt since the Industrial Revolution); (2) a corollary has been a trend toward an ever greater accumulation of information and informational technology; (3) a similar trend can be observed in the evolution of more diverse and complex task-oriented organizational or "team" types; (4) several factor analyses have been consistent in showing a pronounced historical trend in political system complexity and authority patterns—from egalitarian, informal, noncoercive, and of limited scope (functionally and structurally) to hierarchical, formalized, coercive (via both rewards and sanctions), and multifunctional in scope. The progressive evolution of political systems has thus been an integral part of the larger systemic process by which culture has evolved.[98]

The Evidence in Political Science

Do the same relationships hold for the developing and developed countries that are the special province of political science? While the data are not precisely comparable, they are consistent. Bruce Russett ranked 107 countries in relation to five development stages: (1) traditional primitive, (2) traditional, (3) transitional, (4) industrializing, and (5) high mass consumption. Russett found significant mean differences across such categories as GNP per capita, degree of urbanization, and central government revenues as a percentage of GNP, which can arguably be used as an indirect measure of the overall degree of political integration.[99]

An analysis by Almond and Powell provides further insight. They found that government expenditures as a percentage of Gross Domestic Product for a selection of 21 countries in 1965 ranged from a low of 10 percent for Nigeria to 41 percent for the most expansive of the noncommunist welfare states (Sweden) to 77 percent for Czechoslovakia, one of four communist states listed.[100]

Such wide differences present a challenge to my theory. To be sure, some of the variation observed by Almond and Powell reflects differences (in effect) in accounting methods between communist and capitalist countries. (From a cybernetic perspective, the differences between a private business concern and a state-run concern may be only marginal.) Differences in the levels of central government transfer payments for social welfare purposes, a large component of many national budgets, can also account for a substantial part of the variation. However, there may also be a significant residue of real structural and functional differences in the scope of governmental activity that reflect differences in the way various countries have organized their economic and political systems—that is, historically conditioned differences that are independent of any structural and functional imperatives.

Some of the "real" differences in the scope and/or distribution of governmental activities may be a reflection of the "play" in the process of societal evolution that was noted in Carneiro's data above. The contingent influence of classes, ruling elites, or individual political entrepreneurs may account for some of this play. Short-term differences in the specific functional roles assumed by different governments will also affect the size and scope of governmental activity. (For example, the United States lagged significantly behind European nations in developing various social welfare programs.) Governments also tend to grow much larger during wartime. However, my theory predicts longer term convergence toward analogous (not necessarily homologous) structural and functional arrangements, given the adoption of similar functional roles (a condition that is clearly affected by the perceptions, goals, and actions of various political actors). If there is not a high degree of structural and functional convergence over time among governments of comparable size, complexity, and functional roles, this would effectively falsify the theory.

One striking source of evidence in this regard is the elegant albeit limited study by David Cameron of the dramatic increase in public (i.e., governmental) economic activities in eighteen developed capitalist countries from 1960 to 1975, in contradiction to their capitalist ideological commitments. Cameron examined five explanations for this phenomenon and determined that expansion of the public economy was not significantly related to overall economic growth, nor was it facilitated by tax concealment. The previously existing degree of political centralization was an important factor, and so were the partisan commitments and political goals of the ruling elites. However, by far the most important factor was the relative openness of the society economically, that is, its economic interdependence with other nations and its vulnerability to the vicissitudes of international economic and political pressures. In other words, functional imperatives proved to be the overriding cause of this trend.[101]

To explore this issue further, I undertook a correlation study with some more recent (and extensive) data from the Inter-University Consortium for Political and Social Research. Specifically, I examined the relationship in 145 countries between central government expenditures and the number of government employees on the one hand, and (1) population size, (2) GNP, (3) GNP/capita, (4) total land area, (5) urbanization, and (6) military expenditures on the other. (Although results for other years were comparable, only the data for 1976, the most recent year available, are reported here.)

The results are summarized in Table IV: Government expenditures were almost perfectly correlated with total GNP (Pearson's $r = .977$); and there were also robust correlations with the total land area (.664) and population size (.433). The correlation with GNP/capita, while significant, was much weaker (3.18) and so was the correlation with urbanization (.237). Contrary to the conventional wisdom, in other words, the absolute levels of government spending are far more closely associated with the basic economic, demographic, and geographical parameters of a society than with such traditional measures of modernity as per capita wealth or urban development *per se,* as my theory predicts.

Needless to say, this does not mean that GNP, land area, or population levels cause government spending in any direct sense. Rather, such variables as GNP and government expenditures are summary measures that reflect complex, systemic processes in which a vast number of interacting factors are involved. What is significant about these relationships is that the variables are so highly intercorrelated, not that one variable can be said to cause another.

The same kind of results were obtained for government employment. The highest correlation was with population size, though the correlations with GNP and land area were almost as high. On the other hand, the number of government employees was only weakly associated with urbanization and not at all correlated with per capita wealth. Again, the level of government employment appears to bear a close, functional relationship to the underlying societal system (one should be cautious about interpreting these results, considering the small, unrepresentative sample involved).

One of the most surprising findings was that government expenditures as a percent of GNP were not correlated with any of the major variables except (very weakly) GNP/capita (.253). Yet, at the same time, the amount of variation in government spending as a percent of GNP was very wide. While the mean value was .28, the standard deviation was .16 and the range was from 2 percent to 78 percent. The implication is that government spending as a share of GNP is not significantly affected by the basic parameters that were used in this study. Other factors are more significant. The relative affluence of a society may be one preconditioning factor, but it is hardly the whole story. Another clue to what may be the cause of these variations is

	Urbinazation	Population	GNP/Cap	GNP	Military Expenditures	Government Expenditures	Number of Government Employees
Government Expenditures							.98
Military Expenditures						.91	.97
GNP					.88	.98	.96
GNP/Cap				.30	.20	.32	.06*
Population			−.02*	.38	.42	.44	.98
Urbinazation		−.06*	.52	.21	.14*	.24	.30
Land Area	.09*	.50	.12*	.64	.81	.66	.93

TABLE IV

Some correlates of central government expenditures (145 countries) and government employment (13 countries). (From Inter-University Consortium for Political and Social Research, *World Military Expenditures,* 1968–1977. [Ann Arbor: ICPSR, 1978.] Employment figures from "Employment in General Government, Industrial Market Countries," *Economic Bulletin for Europe* 30, 2 [1979].)

Note: Correlations were calculated using Pearson's *r*. *N*'s ranged from 122 to 145, depending on the number of missing values. Correlations marked * were not significant. All other correlations were significant at the $p < .01$ level or well beyond, except GNP/capita and military expenditures ($p < .02$).

the correlation obtained between government spending as a percent of GNP and military spending as a percent of GNP (.612). Another clue was provided by Cameron's results cited above, namely, that economic functions assumed by the central government for whatever reason may significantly affect its share of total consumption.

These counterintuitive results lead to the conclusion that the absolute level of government spending and employment is closely associated with the overall "bulk" of a society. The relationship is allometric. On the other hand, spending as a *proportion* of GNP is a variable that may be influenced by a variety of historical, ideological, and functional considerations. Though preliminary, these results seem to accord with my hypothesis: The cybernetic aspect of an organization or a society increases in a proportionate or scalar fashion as the system as a whole grows larger and/or more differentiated internally, and/or as the functional role of its government expands. (These results were also supported in a series of multiple regression analyses.)

One other source of evidence should be noted here—a time-series analysis for the United States from 1800 to 1980. I tried to correlate the growth over time of central government functions (using as indicators the number of federal civilian employees and central government revenues in constant dollars) with a variety of indicators of societal growth and differentiation: (1) population, (2) GNP in constant dollars (from 1869), (3) the percentage of non–farm employment (from 1870), (4) the percentage of the population living in urban areas, and (5) the total amount of energy consumed.

Again, the results were striking (see Table V). In a nutshell, the correlation coefficients were all highly significant and several were nearly perfect. The table speaks for itself. The process of societal evolution in the United States from 1800 to the present day was clearly systemic in nature, while the growth of the central government was equally clearly allometric, as my theory predicts.

I should also briefly note Donald Black's exploration of complexity in the legal subsystem of contemporary states, using the quantity of law (the number and scope of explicit obligations and prohibitions, plus the amount of legislation, rule making, and adjudication) as an indicator of the degree of governmental social control.[102] Although he was not rigorously quantitative in his approach, Black made a fairly extensive secondary survey of the research literature in anthropology and sociology, and this led him to the conclusion that the quantity of law is greater in societies that are larger, more dense, more differentiated, more complexly organized, more stratified, and have fewer informal social controls.

Finally, in their *Size and Democracy* (1973), Dahl and Tufte concluded that there appears to be a set of historically conditioned relationships in contemporary societies between size (area or population), sociocultural diver-

	GNP/Cap[1]	GNP[1,2]	Percent Nonfarm Employment[3]	Percent Urban Population	Population	Federal Government Employment	Federal Government Receipts[1]
Federal Government Employment							.51
Population						.88	.58
Percent Urban Population					.98	.91	.45
Percent Nonfarm Employment[3]				.99	.98	.92	.56
GNP[1,2]			.57	.51	.64	.51	.99
GNP/Cap[1]		.99	.59	.53	.66	.52	.99
Energy Consumption[4]	.82	.80	.94	.91	.97	.84	.80

TABLE V

Some correlates of federal government receipts and employment, 1800–1970. (From U.S. Department of Commerce, Bureau of the Census, *Historical Statistics of the United States* [Washington, D.C.: G.P.O., 1975] and Bureau of the Census, *Statistical Abstract of the United States: 1981* [Washington, D.C.: GPO, 1981]).

Note: Five-year intervals were used. However, *n*'s vary from 14 to 37, depending on the initial year in the time-series for each variable. Pearson's *r*'s were used throughout. In two cases, $p < .04$, due largely to the small *n*'s (16). All others were $p < .01$ or beyond.

[1] Constant 1967 dollars were used for GNP, GNP/capita, and Federal Government receipts. The latter figures do not include Social Security receipts.

[2] GNP time-series begin in 1870. Data points prior to 1885 were estimated from ten-year averages.

[3] Percent nonfarm employment is based on the total labor force minus the unemployed.

[4] Energy consumption figures include all sources.

sity, economic "modernization," and the size and differentiation of the political superstructure. They summed up with a conjectural proposition: "Other things being equal—particularly the socioeconomic level of a country—the larger a country, the greater the number of organizations and subunits it will contain, the more governmental subunits it will contain, and the greater the number of organized interests or interest groups it will contain."[103] My analysis has shown that other things need not be equal. Beyond that, however, their proposition is generally consistent with my results and with my theory.

Politics Versus Economics

A sixth proposition merely makes explicit what is implicit in the discussion above. It concerns the issue of causation in sociocultural evolution. Whereas many theorists past and present have assigned priority to material (or, broadly, economic) factors in sociocultural evolution, my theory is dualistic. Politics is not epiphenomenal. Political and economic factors are of equal importance; though there may be some short-term lead or lag, longer-term progressive evolutionary changes are co-determined by functional synergism and correlative cybernetic processes of decision making, communications, and control in conjunction with historically and situationally conditioned deterministic and stochastic factors. To state the proposition explicitly:

6. With the exception of short-term lead and lag phenomena, stable progressive forms of sociocultural evolution will always exhibit both positive synergism in relation to the satisfaction of specific social goals and correlative political qua *cybernetic changes.*

This proposition applies equally to business firms and the political superstructures of nation-states, but I will concentrate here on macro-level changes.

Neither economic evolution broadly defined nor political evolution as defined here can occur in isolation from one another. The forces of production do not determine political changes unless the term "forces of production" is so broadly defined that it includes almost everything. Furthermore, the causal dynamics are not primarily dialectical in nature. Dialectical "contradictions" (whatever that Marxian buzzword means) may be one catalyst for change, but they are secondary to positive reinforcements and positive feedback, adaptations that lead to the production of novel synergistic effects. Indeed, social conflict often stands in the way of realizing the inherent synergistic potentialities of a situation. The primary engine of sociocultural evolution has been configural, (co-operative) patterns of ecological, historical, socioeconomic, and political factors that yield synergistic effects.

If any example of a durable progressive political development can be found in which the net costs outweigh the net benefits, then the prediction and the proposition from which it was derived can be falsified. This is theoretically analogous to Darwin's prediction that natural selection would be falsified if any example were found of an adaptation that was solely of benefit to another species. However, the assertion here is that because cybernetic social systems exact overhead costs and impose constraints on the parts or members, they will not persist unless there are positive net benefits overall.

This is not to say that any given system is optimally designed—the best possible set of political arrangements. Nor does the proposition say anything about distributive equity; the theory is just as applicable to slavery or any other parasitical system as it is to those that are mutualistic.* The capitalist system may or may not benefit capitalists disproportionately, but it is more than coincidental that both capitalist and socialist states, despite their very different origins and aims, often end up looking like varieties of the same species. For capitalists and socialists alike the machinery of the state remains functional at the margin, and so long as this is true, it can be predicted that the state will not wither away. The gravitational forces that underlie political evolution will counteract the ideological helium that sends utopian revolutionaries aloft. Functional synergism is one cause of this process, but the dynamics associated with directional evolutionary changes also involve decisions and actions (teleonomic selection) and attendant processes of steering, communication, and control.

Proposition 6 amounts to viewing my theory of sociocultural evolution as if in a mirror. The same phenomena are involved, but we view them now from a political perspective. Goals derived from needs, wants, or preferences, plus synergism and correlative cybernetic processes are all integral (necessary) elements of stable social systems. Again, political evolution is co-determined by configural patterns of ecological, historical, economic, and political variables.

Does this require us to reduce political evolution to history, to an unstructured and theoretically amorphous stream of events? Is it impossible to say anything meaningful about the causal role of political innovation independently of economics or ecology? Historical processes involve unique concatenations of influences which together determine the directional patterns that we discern after the fact or that may be anticipated to some degree before the fact. And political innovations are co-determinants of these directional changes, necessary variables without which many potential evolutionary changes would not occur. There are many examples of potentially synergistic political changes that "might have been" save for the failure to seize political opportunities. Conversely, many an idealist or revolutionary has had his or her hopes dashed by the brutal reality that the historical context was not "right" for some dreamed-of political development. We need only think of such quixotic efforts as the Kellogg-Briand treaty of the 1920s, which sought to make governments everywhere renounce war, or Clarence Streit's vision of an Atlantic Union, or the abortive Spanish coup of February 1981.

* Contrary to Marxian mythology, the agricultural slave system in ancient Rome collapsed of its own accord long before the demise of the empire, without any documented revolution. The system simply did not work well; it was inefficient and it proved to be unprofitable. Although historians are not unanimous in their views, there is also evidence that American slavery was in decline in the years preceding the Civil War.

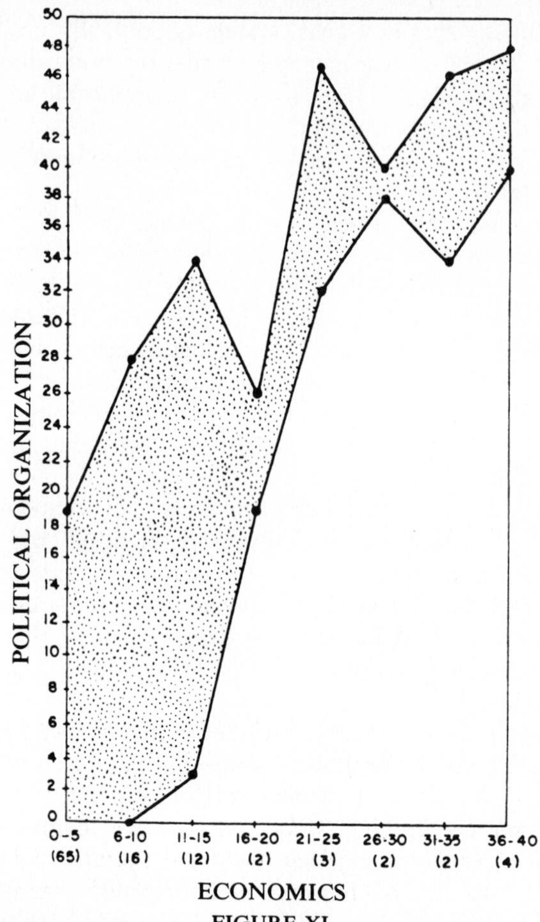

FIGURE XI

Economics versus political organization. (From R. L. Carneiro, "The Four Faces of Evolution," in J. J. Honigmann, ed. *Handbook of Social and Cultural Anthropology* [Boston: Houghton Mifflin, 1973].) Reprinted by permission of the publisher.

The causal dynamics involved in societal evolution are frequently disjointed, reciprocal, and interactive. Just as new forms of functional synergism may serve as precipitators or catalysts for correlative political changes, so too political development can either lead the way to economic changes or lag behind. Recall the data showing that there is some "play" in the relationship between sociocultural and political evolution. This is illustrated further in a figure developed by Carneiro in which 50 political (governmental) organization traits for 106 societies were plotted against 40 economic traits grouped into five-trait class intervals (Figure XI). The range between the lowest and highest numbers of political organization traits (the distance between the data points on the bottom and top lines) is indicative of the amount of "play" that may exist in the coupling of the economic and governmental spheres. The Inca, for example, ranked third in Carneiro's scale of political development and tenth in his scale of economic development.

The catalyzing events in which political scientists are most intensely interested—the political entrepreneurship of a Napoleon, a Bismarck, an Ataturk, a Cárdenas, or a Nyerere or the wrenching dialectical processes by which atrophied or dysfunctional political orders are forcibly "revitalized" (Anthony Wallace's characterization)—are neither epiphenomenal nor autonomous. There would not have been a New Deal without a President Roosevelt. And there would not have been a New Deal, and perhaps not a President Roosevelt, without a depression.*

A simile that comes to mind is the popular office toy, a variant of the Newtonian pendulum, consisting of two steel balls suspended by strings from a wooden framework. When one ball is pulled outward and released, it returns to slam into the second ball, which arcs outward until its energy is counteracted by gravity, at which point it returns to knock the first ball outward until it too is pulled back by gravity to reciprocate. This "system" involves two "actors" that reciprocally affect one another's behavior.

The Historical Evidence

We should expect to find in the historical record instances in which political forces were precipitants for closely linked synergistic functional consequences, just as functional synergism often creates a combinatorial framework for correlative political developments—though many historical changes involve both elements simultaneously.

The rise of the Zulu nation in the nineteenth century provides an instructive example.[105] Until the early 1800s, the people of Bantu origin (for the most part) who had come to inhabit what came to be known as Zululand (a region of the South African province of Natal) consisted of a disorderly patchwork of cattle-herding and minimally horticultural clans that frequently warred on one another. The most common *casus belli* were disputes over cattle, rights to grazing lands, and water rights. The ensuing combat was usually brief, for the most part involving prearranged pitched battles at a respectable distance between small groups of warriors armed with assegai (a lightweight, six-foot throwing spear) and oval cowhide shields. Injuries and fatalities were relatively low.

As the human and cattle populations increased over time, owing to what Carneiro calls "environmental circumscription,"[106] there was a corresponding

* This applies to economic processes as well. See Joseph Schumpeter's classic study *The Theory of Economic Development* (1911) and the study by a Manchester University team which concluded that the single most important factor in the success of industrial innovations is the presence of "an outstanding person in authority."[104]

increase in the frequency and intensity of warfare among the clans until a radical discontinuity occurred in 1816, when a 29-year-old warrior named Shaka took charge of the Zulu clan. Shaka had a plan. He immediately set about transforming the pattern of Natalese warfare by introducing a new military technology involving disciplined phalanxes of shield-bearing troops armed with short hooking and jabbing spears designed for combat at close quarters. Shaka's innovation was as great a revolution in that environment as the introduction of the stirrup or gunpowder into European warfare. After ruthlessly training his ragtag army of some 350 men, Shaka set out on a pattern of conquests and forced alliances that quickly became a juggernaut. Within three years Shaka had forged a nation of a quarter of a million, including a formidable and fanatically disciplined army of about 20,000 men and a domain that had increased from about 100 square miles to 11,500 square miles. There was not a tribe in all of black Africa that could oppose the new Zulu kingdom, and in short order Shaka began to expand his nation beyond the borders of his peoples' traditional lands.

The further evolution and ultimate downfall of the Zulu nation at the hands of the Europeans in the latter part of the century is another story. What is significant here is that profound structural and functional changes—changes that involved the superposition of an integrated political system—occurred among the Zulu by virtue of decisive political entrepreneurship coupled with synergistic changes in military techniques and organization. We can denounce such a brutal method of political development, but the model of cybernetic social processes coupled to functional synergism is as applicable here as it is to more benign forms of political development. Indeed, it is a paradigm example of a class of such entrepreneurial ventures. We need only invoke such names as Alexander the Great, Caesar, Charlemagne, Gengis Khan, Napoleon, Hitler; Clausewitz's *On War* (1832) makes the classic statement of this point. I am not offering here a complete theory of war and its correlates; I am making an assertion about the sometime role of warfare in political evolution.

Robert A. Hackenburg's comparison of the divergent adaptive strategies of the Pima and Papago Indians of the American southwest offers an example of a more benign pattern of political evolution.[107] In the years before the introduction of wheat cultivation by the Spaniards, these two contiguous groups had pursued different cultural patterns. The Papago remained nomadic hunters and gatherers who had incorporated in their diet relatively little in the way of domesticated foods. The Pima had evolved toward a more sedentary life-style, one that relied heavily on domesticates, and they had formed into a network of permanently settled villages that were marked by a substantial degree of intercommunity co-operation and a well-articulated political structure.

When wheat cultivars were introduced to them, the Pima were ready to exploit this important opportunity to expand their food production. In order to obtain sufficient water for growing wheat, they agreed to consolidate their scarce water supplies and to construct an intervillage water system under a centralized management structure. The Papago were unable to do the same, and many of them were ultimately reduced to becoming hired labor for the Pima. Thus political preadaptations that from the beginning were tightly linked to existing economic adaptations provided the framework within which further economic *cum* political development could occur.

The research literature in anthropology, history, economic history, and political science is rich with comparable case studies. Nevertheless certain general characteristics of this model of macro-level political evolution should be underscored. Political evolution is a cumulative process; past and present developments create the preadaptations (political inventions, structures, and processes) that are prerequisites for further development. Through selective imitation some societies may leapfrog the evolutionary sequence, but they cannot do without previously evolved instrumentalities or their functional equivalents. As students of comparative politics well know, evolutionary changes in a polity will be marked by both continuities and discontinuities. The continuities encompass existing forms of functional synergism, and the discontinuities are associated with novel forms of synergism—or with political regression.

Political evolution is not a homogeneous process; some political innovations are highly facultative and even ephemeral or episodic. The bison hunters of the North American plains in the nineteenth century adopted annual patterns of political amalgamation and dispersion that paralleled precisely the seasonal patterns of the animals they hunted.[108] Similarly, the Great Basin Shoshone, which normally subsisted in nomadic family groups, would come together periodically to participate in massive co-operative tribal hunts that involved the use of huge nets, whenever the game were plentiful enough to make the co-operative effort worthwhile. On such occasions, one man would initiate the hunt and serve as exclusive leader. Steward reported that the number of animals captured in these co-operative efforts far exceeded the total that could be obtained with each family hunting alone.[109] These co-operative hunts produced functional synergism.

On the other hand, many political innovations of a more permanent character are obligative. Fully integrated modern nation-states are so structured that the benefits for participation and compliance are generally high (one's basic needs are involved), while the costs of nonparticipation and noncompliance may also be high. (Presumably the prison or work camp populations in both noncommunist and communist countries are indicators of the degree of noncompliance.) There are many cases of durable facultative systems where self-selection is the rule, where mutual advantage is the main incentive for participation, and where the costs of nonparticipation may be low. I suppose the paradigm example is the United Nations and its clutch of international agencies.

There are also political changes that are at once episodic or historically bounded yet highly obligative—for example, the massive growth of what had been a skeleton U.S. military establishment prior to and during World War II and its precipitate dismemberment after V-J Day.

To repeat, the causal matrix within which evolutionary changes occur cannot be modeled in terms of simple linear equations or monolithic prime movers. It requires dynamic systems models that can incorporate the relationships between situation-specific configurations of variables—the local ecological context (inclusive of relationships with other human groups), the structure of human needs, wants, and revealed preferences, and the patterns of socioeconomic activities, as well as cybernetic processes, innovations, goal setting, decision making (teleonomic selection), political entrepreneurship, and so forth. The specific content and precise relationships among the variables will be unique to each historical situation. On the other hand, the basic structure of the process will remain the same—there will always be a coupling of cybernetic social processes and functional synergism.

The Evolution of the State

We can appreciate the full significance of this view of political evolution by considering how it applies to a specific case—the evolution of civilization and the state. Speculation about this issue can be traced back to classical Athens, and it has challenged social scientists for more than a century.[110]

Following the classification scheme proposed by anthropologists Ronald Cohen and Elman Service, we can identify two sharply opposed classes of theories.[111] One class emphasizes conflict, coercion, and exploitation, and the other emphasizes integration, co-operation, and various positive public goods. Theorists of the former persuasion see the state as a product of force, while those who adhere to the latter point of view see mutual advantage as the most important catalyst.

One variant of the conflict school is focused on the role of internal cleavages. Thomas Hobbes was perhaps the first modern theorist to posit that the prime function of "sovereign" power is to act as a bulwark against the natural tendency of humankind in the "state of nature" to engage in a "warre of each against all."[112] In contrast, anthropologist Lewis Morgan developed the argument that the rise of private property, growing disparities in material wealth, and consequent social stratification were the catalysts for state formation.[113] Much impressed with Morgan's argument, Marx and Engels subsequently portrayed the state as a "handmaiden" of the bourgeoisie and as an instrument of class oppression. The anthropologist Morton Fried has been the most visible exponent of this viewpoint in recent years.[114]

The other variant of the conflict school sees the state as a product of external conquest. This viewpoint traces to Ibn Khaldun, Nicolo Machiavelli, Jean Bodin, and a passel of nineteenth-century Social Darwinists (Gumplowicz, Oppenheimer, Small, Ward, Bagehot) who saw competition between societies, warfare, and conquest as the precipitators of state formation. In Spencer's well-known phrase, the state emerged from the struggle for "survival of the fittest."*

By far the most sophisticated modern version of the conflict hypothesis is Robert Carneiro's ecological theory of the state (which he defines as a multicommunity polity with a centralized government that is able to pass and enforce laws, collect taxes, and draft manpower for work or war.)[117]

Carneiro begins by rejecting such integrationist theories as that of V. Gordon Childe, who ascribed the emergence of the state to an organic process of occupational differentiation, fostered by food surpluses and coupled with peaceful integration.[118] Carneiro also rejects Karl Wittfogel's hydraulic hypothesis, which refers to the causal role Wittfogel assigned in his *Oriental Despotism* (1957) to large-scale irrigation systems. In effect, Wittfogel postulated a narrowly cybernetic theory, holding that the necessity for control over vast public works precipitated the emergence of coercive political machinery which in time became despotic. Carneiro points out that there is evidence that some of the states on which Wittfogel based his theory may have emerged before the appearance of such massive, centralized irrigation works and that the state may well have facilitated their construction and operation, rather than the reverse.[119] Similarly, there is considerable evidence that less centralized irrigation systems often predated the emergence of the state and that these systems can and do emerge through voluntaristic action.[120] †

Carneiro argues that "force, and not enlightened self-interest, is the mechanism by which political evolution has led, step by step, from autonomous villages to the state."[122] Although the state was "invented" independently many times and in many parts of the world, from Mesoamerica to Mesopotamia and from China to Colombia, Carneiro maintains that in every case warfare was the prime mover, the underlying mechanism. This mechanism was in turn a response to a specific configuration of ecological pressures that he characterizes as "environmental circumscription," that is, mountains,

* The closest contemporary approximation of this theoretical position can be found among those who espouse what might be called the sociobiological theory of the state.[115] To theorists of this persuasion, reproductive competition in general and warfare in particular was the "motor" of the state formation process. As political scientist Fred Willhoite puts it, "the ultimate 'why,' I suggest, was the natural process of reproductive competition, for which there is substantial evidence at every stage of human evolution."[116]

† Gernet reports that the emergence of the state in China was a necessary political preadaptation for its legendary irrigation projects, and Lattimore viewed the pre-state development of China's irrigation systems as initially an aggregative process involving a high degree of local control.[121]

seas, deserts, extreme resource concentration, and/or what Napoleon Chagnon calls "social circumscription" (contiguous human populations) that serve to block further population growth or dispersion. In such environmental contexts, Carneiro reasons, warfare and conquest became the only alternative to starvation once the Malthusian dynamic had run its course and population levels had reached the locally sustainable limit.

The consequent coercive processes of political amalgamation, Carneiro insists, were not rectilinear but halting and incremental. Autonomous villages in time fused to become chiefdomships, which despite occasional regressions were consolidated into kingdoms, which in time became empires. Carneiro considers the first supravillage chiefdomships to have been the decisive step; once autonomous villages were merged into larger entities, the rest of the process was incremental. Carneiro holds that processes of internal political development (legal systems, taxes, corvée labor) were not preadaptations but after-the-fact responses designed to consolidate this forceful fusion process.

The example of the Zulu kingdom mentioned above seems to offer a paradigm case, for the Zulu were hemmed in by the Indian Ocean to the east, the Drakensburg range to the west, and marshy and uninhabitable areas and/or other human populations to the north and south. The Zulu case would seem to have been more precipitate and less incremental than most such fusion processes; Shaka's military conquests, his alliances, and his use of intimidation were indisputably of decisive importance.

Carneiro's theory has much to recommend it. Functional synergism in the form of disciplined military organization combined with military technology has probably been a factor at every stage of political evolution. Large, well-organized, and technologically sophisticated groups have always had the advantage over small, poorly organized, and technologically unsophisticated groups. In a recent compendium that included 21 case studies of state development, ranging in time from about 3000 B.C. to the nineteenth century A.D., coercive force was a factor in every case. Outright conquest was implicated in about half of the cases.[123]

Yet Carneiro's theory is incomplete and one-sided. His theory is based not on direct evidence but on a plausibility argument, an imaginative and highly speculative reconstruction from circumstantial evidence. For instance, ecological limits frequently impose thresholds that lead to evolutionary discontinuities. But how constricting (and how unique) were the ecological limits confronted by the human populations that evolved into states? All habitats are ultimately circumscribed, and historically many human populations have adapted to local Malthusian limits by curtailing population growth and/or developing intensifying technologies.[124] The same dynamic that Carneiro postulates for military conquest may be used to account for various peaceful developments in subsistence patterns, as Mark Nathan Cohen in fact did with agriculture.

Carneiro does not show that in the many cases where the state did not arise "deterministically," the local populations were free of such circumspection. In the case of the Iroquois confederacy, for instance, a form of constriction occurred because of the five tribes' dependency on the fur trade and pressure from European colonists.[125] Yet despite an extensive network of tribal alliances and protracted military campaigns, a coercive state conforming to Carneiro's specifications did not arise. Therefore an iron determinism is not involved in the linkage between Malthusian limits, warfare, conquest, and political aggregation.

In a similar vein, Carneiro cites extensive archaeological evidence of warfare in association with those societies where states later arose. But again a heavy dose of supposition is required to make the assertion that these patterns were the most important, much less the exclusive cause of political integration. The data do not permit Carneiro to reject the null hypothesis that many instances of political integration were facultative responses to external threats or to protracted and self-destructive internecine warfare, instead of being a direct result of warfare. In some cases there is evidence that population pressures were an effect rather than the cause of the evolution of the state.[126]

Carneiro concedes that the emergence of chiefdomships, not the state, was the decisive political step, for this involved the first stage of intervillage integration.[127] Yet the literature in anthropology contains examples of chiefdomships (or their functional equivalents) that emerged and were sustained primarily by mutualism—by forms of enlightened self-interest.[128] (I have already cited the example of the Pima Indians.)

Carneiro's theory and its historical antecedents are incomplete. The process of state building, rather than being associated exclusively with conquest and/or defense, involved an admixture of conflict and mutualism, coercive and voluntaristic co-operation, and ecological and economic pressures *and* opportunities. Competition may have been one stimulus, but the important thing was the co-operative responses. A more balanced, dualistic scenario is required to capture the dynamics of this process.

This returns us to the perspective of the integration school, or what might also be called the functionalist school. Beginning with Plato and Aristotle (who attributed the rise of the polis to the economic and cultural advantages that the citizens enjoyed), functionalists have always stressed the role of the state as a coordinator, keeper of the peace, organizer of public works, and defender of the community against external enemies. To the integrationists, stratification is a side-effect of the development of state institutions, rather than the cause. Contrary to Carneiro's argument, they point out that institutional development may precede stratification and the state. Coercive force may also be employed, but the integrationist view is that such measures are secondary effects; they arise in relation to the functional needs of the community.

The most persuasive modern advocate of this position is Elman Service. Not only is internal conflict and warfare insufficient to account for many of the historical cases, Service notes, but emergent states were themselves a cause of stratification and external conflict.[129] Far from being based on oppression and exploitation, early states generally received widespread popular allegiance and support. They created a mechanism for new forms of organized co-operation. That is, the benefits outweighed the costs.*

Both the conflict theorists and the integrationists tacitly posit that organized, cybernated co-operation was the key to the emergence of the state. Both schools also posit that *net* benefits are important, though they differ over who benefits, and at whose expense. They differ in part because the evidence is ambiguous in many cases and subject to differing interpretations. But much of their disagreement arises from the existence of contradictory cases. In short, both schools are partly correct, or sometimes correct.

Between these two polar positions lies what has been called the synthetic theory of the state. The first expression of this view can be traced to the writings of archaeologist Robert McC. Adams, who postulated an interactive paradigm that combined military and socioeconomic developments.[133] More recently this approach has been elaborated on by archaeologist Henry Wright and anthropologist Ronald Cohen.[134] The causal matrix is now recognized to include geographic, ecological, and demographic factors, as well as internal technoeconomic development, local and long distance trade, competition with other evolving human societies (warfare and defense), and actions to protect and enhance personal privileges. As Cohen expresses it:

> In my view the process is systemic and multi-causal. Each set of factors, or any particular factor, once it develops, stimulates and feeds back onto others which are then made to change in the general direction of statehood. Although its roots may be multiple, once a society or group of them start developing toward early statehood the end result is remarkably similar no matter where it occurs.[135]

The questions that are begged, though, are how exactly did all of these factors fit together, and what energized the resulting directional changes? Granted that all of these variables may have been involved, but they had to fit together in very specific ways, so that the entire array of basic needs

* The social contract thesis finds some support in the literature on pre-state development and in some pristine states, especially Egypt, the Indus River valley, and in black Africa.[130] The process of urbanization, which was of central importance, served multiple, interacting functions of a ceremonial, marketing, redistributive, administrative, and defensive character.[131] Sanders and Price hold that the political superstructure of the state emerged from the increasing physical mass of urbanized societies, while Service argues the reverse, that political hierarchies made such urban agglomerations possible.[132]

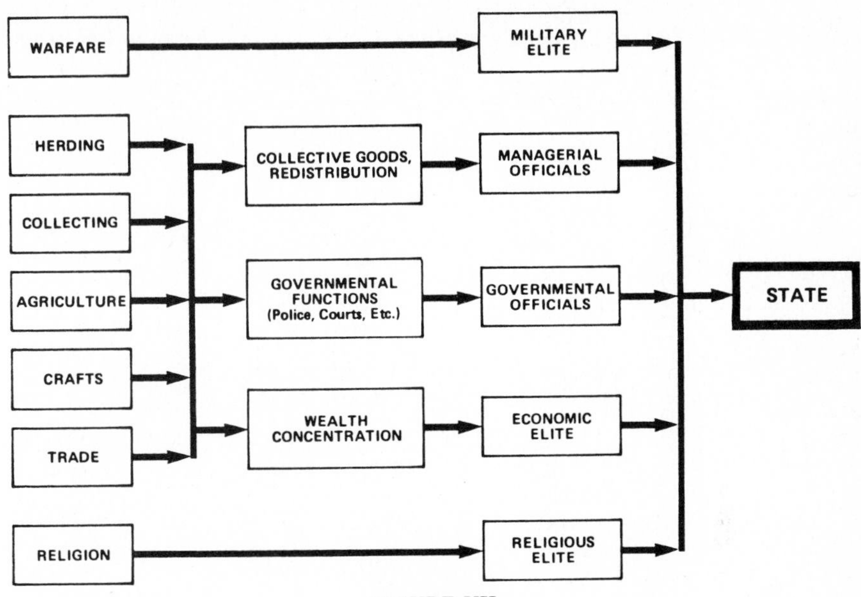

FIGURE XII
A synthetic view of state origins.

listed in Chapter IV could be satisfied. Only certain configurations or combinations were viable. The evidence suggests that there was no uniform progression and no universally consistent pattern of state building. In each case a trial-and-error process was at work, one which varied from place to place depending on numerous idiosyncratic (historically specific) circumstances.

Not all chiefdomships evolved into states; there were many failures among the few successes. Moreover, some polities that did reach statehood were extremely unstable and short-lived. In some cases, states were precipitated by internal military and political innovations and entrepreneurship (the Zulu), while in other cases they were catalyzed by military innovations introduced from outside (Hawaii). Still other states apparently grew organically out of an enlarging economic base (Teotihuacán, the Old Kingdom in Egypt and, possibly, the Mayans). By the same token, some states arose before there were sharp disparities in commodity wealth, while others arose afterward. Some emerged long after systematic patterns of external warfare were evident, while others developed to provide defense against nomadic raiders. Still others seem to have been stimulated by purely internal economic problems.[136]

Yet the results for those polities which did achieve and sustain the statehood level of political evolution were strikingly convergent. In Service's term, an "evolutionary potential" had to exist in order for such changes to occur. However, appropriate institutional innovations had to occur as well. The reason we can discern certain convergent trends is because only certain patterns—within a few degrees of freedom—were functionally efficient. The process of state building was systemic precisely because the outcome depended on systemic effects. And it was the results—the combinatorial effects in terms of the range of human needs and instrumental goals—that were responsible for the directional trends that occurred.

The common characteristics of all such developmental patterns, whether warlike or economically symbiotic, coercive or voluntary, included functional synergism and cybernetic social processes. Rather than conflicting with or excluding one another, *all* these developments tended to impose on the process of societal evolution a directionality toward more complex organization. In a great many cases, economic development, military development, and political development were likely to have been mutually reinforcing and reciprocally causal.* Synergism begat more synergism as populations learned how to create and sustain within stable political systems new forms of organized co-operative activity. The precise scenario, as the conflicting archaeological and ethnographic case studies demonstrate, varied from one context to another, but the deep structure and the underlying causal principle were the same in every case.

Not everyone agrees with this systemic view of sociocultural evolution. In a recent article on chiefdomships, Carneiro declares: "I do not share this prejudice. There is nothing wrong with a monocausal theory if it works." In opposition to those who, he claims, espouse a "democracy of causes," Carneiro defends his conflict theory: "The mechanism that brought about chiefdomships is, in my opinion, the same one that brought about states, namely, war."[137]

To the contrary, I maintain that such monocausal theories are invariably insufficient. While I do not suggest that all causes are created equal, any theory that fixes on a single predominant cause or proximate mechanism must take for granted many other factors that are also necessary. To illustrate, Carneiro recognizes "environmental circumscription" as a prior cause of warfare; chiefdomships and states arose where there were physical and/or social constraints on further expansion, outmigration, and retreat for defeated enemies. But this begs the questions. Why were human populations concentrated? and Why were they expanding in such a way that they experienced circumscription? Human populations do not grow in a vacuum. One cannot simply

* Consider one of Otterbein's key findings in his study of the evolution of warfare in primitive societies: "The more evolved the manner of waging war [i.e., the greater the degree of military sophistication], the more likely that political communities of a cultural unit will be militarily successful" (phi = .40, $p < .02$; $rpb = .44$, $p < .01$, $n = 50$). When it is recalled that military sophistication is highly correlated with the level of political centralization, the interconnection becomes evident (*The Evolution of War,* p. 106).

assume population growth as a given. Populations grow only when there exists a salubrious combination of ecological, technoeconomic, and political factors. And it is not coincidental that evolving neolithic populations tended to concentrate in and compete for fertile river valleys with abundant supplies of rich soil, fresh water, firewood, and other needed resources, resources that enabled human populations to become more sedentary and, at the same time, to support increasing numbers. Equally important, we must consider what factors enabled some human groups to prevail over others. The many factors that contribute to military success also played a role. Thus, subsistence activities and political activities—the interactions between the basic biological needs and capabilities of the human actors and their social and natural environments—represented important co-determinants. If warfare was a significant factor in the process of sociocultural evolution, it was neither necessary nor sufficient.

How can this theory of the state be tested? Again, we need only remove one major variable from any viable state system and observe the predictable consequences. Take away rainfall from Teotihuacán, or the military hegemony of the Aztecs, or energy resources from modern America, or raw materials imports from Japan. By the same token, take away a viable political order and observe the consequences: Take away political autonomy from Lebanon, or coercive force (the police and the military) from the Shah's Iran.*

Political Regression

My theory is, of course, applicable to much more than the emergence of the state. It applies to every step in the process of political evolution as to the progressive innovations that have occurred since the emergence of the state. It applies also to the numerous cases of regressive political evolution, which brings me to the next proposition.

7. Political regression—the simplification, dismemberment, or collapse of cybernetic social processes—is always associated with a decline or loss of functional synergism.

This is the obverse of proposition 6. The loss of functional synergism may not be a bad thing, for political systems are often deliberately and will-

* As our Founding Fathers appreciated, a system that is based on force must be maintained by force. Under Shaka's rule by terror, the Zulu nation remained highly unstable; only after his assassination in 1828 did true (noncoerced) political integration begin to occur.

ingly disbanded. This occurs when the goals of the participants or the controllers have been achieved—when the hunt has been completed and the catch divided, when the whistle announces the end of the game, when the last bars of the symphony have died away and the orchestra packs up its instruments, when the last hurrahs have been sounded and the candidates retire to await the returns, or when Johnny comes marching home again. Of course we do not always dismember an organization whose task has been completed. Consider those obscure government commissions that continue to live on as middle-class make-work, or perhaps to satisfy some latent function (after Robert Merton), say as a lightning rod in case of trouble.

The cases in which we are most interested, those that are the most challenging theoretically, involve systems whose goals are ongoing or yet to be attained, systems in which regressive changes are imposed on the system. When a family undergoes a divorce, when a company goes bankrupt (in the old days, before the new bankruptcy laws), or when an empire declines and falls, its political system disintegrates. Sometimes such changes involve analogues of what biologists call adaptive simplification, that is, changes that are beneficial for the goals of the system. When a system is restructured to eliminate deadwood, to remove operating inefficiencies, or otherwise to improve its capacity to perform its mission, regression may have positive functional consequences. This is not inconsistent with proposition 7. When more inclusive systems no longer produce positive synergism (when the costs outweigh the benefits, or there is dysergy), disaggregation may enable the system or some of its parts to continue operating profitably. The Chrysler Corporation of the early 1980s provides an example of adaptive simplification. At this writing the outcome is still in doubt, but there is certainly no question about the intention behind Chrysler's corporate weight-reduction program.

Adaptive simplification can also involve a fissioning among incompatible parts whose combinatorial interactions are unprofitable, on balance. (These are dialectical processes that do not lead to new syntheses; they fall completely outside the Marxian paradigm.) The Stanford Research Institute, for example, was founded and grew up within Stanford University; in time the different missions of the university and what is now known as SRI International became increasingly inharmonious, and the institute was spun off as a separate entity.

There are also many cases of political regression at the macro level. The premier modern examples are various nineteenth-century European empires; there are also numerous historical cases[138] and countless cases in the archaeological literature. So far as I know, there is not a single extant case of an autonomous state-level political system with an unbroken history going back more than a few hundred years—a long time for anyone who has lived through the convulsive events of the last hundred years but a very short time in evolutionary terms. Both historic and prehistoric states have frequently been subject to regression or absorption into more inclusive entities.

The Roman Empire

The most fascinating historical illustration of proposition 7 is the Roman empire. Recent scholarship has shed additional light on the relationship between the Roman economy and its political fortunes, and it is now more apparent than ever that there was at all times an intimate relationship between functional synergism (economic and military) and the fortunes of the Roman polity, both in the ascendancy and in decline. The lessons of Rome are also pertinent to our present historical circumstances.[139]

The rise of Rome to political preeminence in the ancient Mediterranean world was a systematic and mutually synergistic process composed of military successes, important political and administrative (cybernetic) innovations that enabled the Roman hub to extend effective political control over a vast domain, and an organic process of economic growth that, during Rome's growth phase, was highly symbiotic. Rome in the early days was essentially a yeoman economy consisting primarily of small farmers and urban craftsmen, an economy with agricultural self-sufficiency, a vigorous and technically superior crafts industry, and an expanding network of mutually advantageous foreign trade relationships. These relationships were based in part on a regionalization of resources (metals, wood, grain, hemp, wool), in part on a regionalization of technology and skills, and in part on relatively cheap water transportation. (In those days overland transport doubled the value added to an item about every hundred miles.) Thus Rome's maritime location gave it a competitive edge, allowing it to create a vast common market from Britain to Egypt.

As Rome grew, its political hegemony increased apace by virtue of a succession of military triumphs on the part of its disciplined and technologically superior legions plus a large navy that in time gained control of the Mediterranean. The Roman empire was built by winning wars, but the victories were made possible by a strong and dynamically developing economy at home. Nor were the wars always provoked by the Romans. The growth of the empire followed no agenda. Relatively little of Rome's accumulating wealth consisted of booty from successful military campaigns, or captured gold and silver mines, or tribute paid by its provinces. While the Roman treasury grew fat in the third and second centuries B.C., no taxes were paid into Roman coffers from abroad during the latter part of the period.

The Roman provinces may not have been thrilled to be under Roman rule, but there were trade-offs. In addition to a symbiotic and orderly set of trade relations within a unified, protected, and legally regulated trading system, the provinces benefited from having a stable internal order and protection by the Roman legions against competitors and "barbarians" living beyond the periphery of Roman hegemony. If physical security is one of the fundamental functions of government, it may also be one of the fundamental and highly valued functions of empires—assuming that the costs are not too great.

Unfortunately, the costs of being a Roman province increased over time. Rome's decline as a superorganism began even before it had reached the apogee of its political power. The erosion process seems to have been the result of interacting factors. One was population growth. The Italian peninsula experienced a rapid increase from about 150,000 adult male citizens in 400 B.C. to 250,000 in 325 B.C., with perhaps an additional 3 million women and children, slaves, and freedmen. By 70 B.C. metropolitan Rome alone had 500,000 citizens and perhaps an equal number of slaves and freedmen. Another census in 28 B.C. suggests that a further doubling of the population had occurred; there were now more than 4 million Roman citizens in all. While some scholars believe that at least half the official citizens of Rome lived in the provinces (much colonizing was going on at this time), the population of metropolitan Rome was put at well over 1 million inhabitants of all classes.

While this population explosion was going on, the agricultural base of the Italian peninsula also underwent a transformation. In some areas the soil had been badly depleted and was only marginally productive at best. Other vital resources, such as timber, had long been overexploited, and Rome came to depend on foreign sources. The agricultural production system also underwent a drastic change from small farms to vast landholdings called *Latifundia* that were worked inefficiently by slave labor, principally for profitable cash crops such as wine and olive oil. Rome was thus required to import increasing quantities of grain from its provinces in Sicily, Egypt, and elsewhere to feed its growing population, while small farmers, displaced from the land, went to the cities to find work.

Meanwhile, the economic base of metropolitan Rome had begun to decay. The once flourishing crafts industries and ancillary commercial activities were gradually undercut by the rise of competing industries at the periphery of the empire through a process of "import replacement." Even though locally produced artifacts might not have been of the same quality as those produced in Rome, they were much cheaper, and in time they undermined Rome's export markets. Rome's wealth began to be exported for investment abroad; the rents and taxes extracted from the peasants frequently reduced them to starvation and drove marginal (though productive) lands out of cultivation.

In effect metropolitan Rome was becoming a parasite on its provinces. The treasury was depleted by increasingly heavy foreign grain purchases needed to feed a growing population of indigents (thus the famous "bread and circuses" policy), and by Caesar's time some 350,000 people in the city of Rome were on the dole, perhaps one-fourth of the entire population. By then food prices had multiplied many times as inflation took hold, and this increased the demands on the treasury. Of necessity the Roman government began to impose burdensome taxes on the provinces, first to feed its domestic population and then to support the increased military expenditures necessitated by the resulting political instabilities. Rome was caught in a vicious circle—a dysergistic nexus.

When one adds to this the growing concentration of wealth in the hands of a politically dominant rentier class (a substantial proportion of which came to include the hierarchy of the early Christian church) and an increasing burden of fees, commissions, and kickbacks to an entrenched bureaucracy, the result was a vast parasitical superstructure on a shrinking economic base. The stage had been set for Julius Caesar and an increasingly turbulent and strife-torn Imperium, for frequent revolts and civil wars, administrative and military decay and corruption, and greater extremes of wealth and poverty. For an increasing number of its inhabitants, the perceived costs of the empire came to outweigh the benefits, and in due course there was no one left who was willing to defend it.* Some data collected by Sorokin reveal the magnitude of the changes. During the period 425–201 B.C. only four major incidents of internal strife were reported. Thereafter the figures were: 200 B.C. to 25 A.D., 41; A.D. 25–250, 49; A.D. 250–475, 61.[140] (The first century B.C. was the most disorderly of all.)

Although today one might place somewhat more emphasis on the role of demographic and economic factors, the general conclusion of the historian A. H. M. Jones remains valid:

> I have outlined what seem to me to be the principal causes of the empire's decline, and of its collapse in the West. It would be difficult, and probably profitless, to attempt to weigh their relative importance, for they interacted upon one another so as to form a single complex. The strategic vulnerability of the west [after losing the eastern half of the empire] not only exposed it to severe military pressure, but diminished

* A further comment is in order regarding Roman agriculture versus the Marxian interpretation of history. Roman food production in the early days was based on the small family farm—call it petty capitalism. In time it evolved into a system of vast *Latifundia.* But this aggregation process was not an "organic" development based on developments in the "mode of production"; it was a by-product of Rome's success in foreign wars and the practice of taking captives and turning them into slaves. It was cheap labor, not some progressive new technology, that made the slave system possible. Moreover, it evolved in a distinctly nondialectical way, through the process of teleonomic selection based initially on its competitive economic advantages. Finally, the system collapsed long before the political superstructure of Rome collapsed, again without the sort of dialectical transformation that the Marxists impute to history.

> the economic resources on which its defence was based, while its economic disequilibrium reduced its military manpower. The decline of public spirit led to the growth of the bureaucracy, and the weight of bureaucratic control crushed public spirit, while the heavy financial burden it entailed doubtless contributed to the general apathy of the population. Other-worldliness weakened the economic and military resources of the empire, and the resulting distress and defeats made men turn away from this world and set their hopes on another. The decline and fall of the Roman empire was the result of a complex of interacting causes which the historian disentangles at his peril.[141] *

Economic and Political Causes of Regression

The Roman case is not unique historically. It is only better documented than countless other examples where for one reason or another progressive political evolution was followed by regression. Often the explanation for a historical cycle remains shrouded amid the potsherds and obsidian blades that are the stock-in-trade of archaeology. In other cases plausible inferences are possible. Recent ecological research strongly suggests that in some early civilizations environmental factors—that is, instabilities in the underlying man-environment relationship—were decisive. Sometimes natural climatic events may have been involved, but there is also evidence of long-term lag effects due to changes that man has made in the environment.† The seeds of eventual destruction may in some cases have been laid at the very beginning of the historical cycle. This seems likely to have been so with the Inca and with various Mesopotamian civilizations, especially the Sumerians. At first the agricultural systems on which these civilizations were built proved to be highly synergistic; when irrigation water was first combined with a rich alluvial soil, a hot, dry climate, domesticated grains, and human organization and technology, the yields were phenomenal. Over time, however, there was gradual waterlogging and salt buildup in the soil, the consequence

* Some theorists place more emphasis on military factors.[142] They note the period of civil wars following the final defeat of Carthage, which led to the division of the empire and the consequent loss of the superior economic resources of the eastern half of the empire. More important, they note that Rome began to lose its military edge as the Teutonic warlords learned to emulate the synergistic combination of factors that had enabled Rome to establish its far-flung hegemony. These factors included superior organization, tactics (such as the famed phalanx), advanced technology (iron swords, shields, helmets, body armor, massive siege weapons, mounted cavalry), and superior means of transportation and communications. There were also morale and motivation problems and failures of leadership. This accords with Doran and Parsons's "relative capability" concept,[143] though the components of relative military capabilities are more complex than they imagine.

† A recent study correlated climate changes with periods of political crisis in Athens from 632 to 510 B.C. through the technique of tree-ring dating (dendrochronology).

of inadequate drainage. The result was a sharp decline in productivity that in many once fertile areas has not been reversed to this day.[144] On the reasonable assumption that the population had by that time grown far beyond what an impoverished agricultural base could support, it is not hard to imagine the effects on the economy and the political system.

In other cases political factors may have played a more central role in political regression; there is ample historical evidence of political fissioning, disaggregation, absorption, or destruction through the dynamics of internal civil wars and external conquests. Scratch an empire and you find within it many once and perhaps future autonomous polities. There has been speculation about the causes of such political upheavals since Periclean Athens, and recent research and theoretical work in political science has shed more light on the subject. (The research on violence-related causes of political evolution intersects with research on the causes of war, research on the causes of civil strife, and research on the role of warfare in cultural evolution.)

When we stop to think about it, it becomes apparent that political violence is Janus-faced. A war that may be part of a growth process for one polity may be the instrumentality of dismemberment for another. Civil strife may be instrumental to keeping order, or it may be an instrumentality for revitalization, or it may even be the unintended instrumentality of political self-immolation. Whether or not one is an aficionado of political violence, the statistics are impressive. The historian Quincy Wright concluded that between 1500 and 1942 there were more than 500 armed clashes per year worldwide, with formal wars averaging about one per year. According to Sorokin, over a 2500-year period eleven European states and empires averaged one year of violent conflict in every five. Between 1900 and 1965 there were some 350 violent revolutions worldwide, an average of more than five per year. Calvert counted 363 "forceful" changes of government between 1901 and 1960, while Gurr determined that for 91 nominally different nation-states (336 polities in all) during the nineteenth and twentieth centuries, the average life span was only 32 years. (Not all the changes documented by Gurr were associated with civil violence, but a depressingly large percentage of them were).[145]

The twin research and theoretical literatures relating to the causes of war and civil strife are extensive.[146] Perhaps the single most important (and reasonably safe) generalization that emerges is that the incidence and patterning of political violence generally involve a combination of external factors in the physical and material environments, structural factors in the socioeconomic and political systems, and internal political factors that include the perceptions, goals, decisions, and actions of organized political entities and their leaders.

One of the most confident conclusions that can be drawn from this research is that the decisions and actions of regimes, alliances, parties, dissident movements, rebel groups, and covert conspiracies constitute a major variable or set of variables in political violence, with consequences that may be progressive, stabilizing, revitalizing, regressive, or mutually destructive, depending on the context and outcome. Thus deterministic theories are bound to be embarrassed when a Marxist revolution occurs in a "backward" country such as Russia or China or when the Iranian mullahs lead a successful, largely nonviolent revolution from the right against a repressive modernizing regime. No doubt political scientists can refine our ability to assess the objective conditions that may contribute to revolution and war, but our predictions must always entail an assessment of the political actors themselves. Who among the theorists on war or the experts on Middle Eastern affairs could have fathomed beforehand the logic behind the late Anwar el Sadat's actions? Egypt, he said, had recovered its manhood in the Yom Kippur war, so he was free to negotiate with Israel.

Modeling Political Systems

One other major facet of this theory remains to be discussed. It has long been customary for social scientists to focus their efforts either on the micro or the macro level and to make little or no effort to relate their work to the concerns of theorists working at other levels. Indeed, many theorists take the position that micro- and macro-level theories are mutually exclusive and necessarily in competition with one another. Thus, for instance, Riker and Ordeshook deny the need for considering the properties of any collectivity independently of the actions of its parts: "We reject the necessity for organic concepts. . . ." While they concede that the properties of water are different from those of its constituent atoms, they claim that "to utter general [theoretical] sentences about the chemical properties of this compound . . . requires only that we know that it is composed of two parts hydrogen and one part oxygen."[147] This is a serious misconception. Water has an array of emergent combinatorial (synergistic) properties that cannot be derived from an understanding of the constituent elements alone. These properties can be understood only by studying the interactions among the parts and whole—water itself. And if, as I argue, such wholes have independent causal potency, then they require their own theoretical sentences. An understanding of the parts may not tell us why the whole exists.

Though there have been many recent calls for the development of a multileveled perspective, there has not been any explicit effort, to my knowledge, to develop a theory that could bridge the gap by being able to account satisfactorily for *both* systemic phenomena and the choices and actions of individual actors. However, a fully satisfactory theory of sociocultural and political evolution must be able to do just that; it must speak to the different kinds of "why" questions that concern both micro- and macro-level theorists.

Up to this point in the discussion I have been focusing mainly on systemic issues, on the functional effects produced by complex systems and how these have shaped the course of progressive evolution. Such systemic relationships between parts and wholes can, of course, be modeled with the multifactorial equations that are employed by systems theorists. Now, however, I wish to focus on the problem of accounting for political systems in terms of individual choices, or, to be more specific, in terms of the rationality assumption of positive theory. My theory seeks to illuminate the role of combinatorial (synergistic) effects in sociocultural evolution, but in order to do so I must link them to the process of teleonomic selection, to the preferences and decisions of the individual actors who create, maintain, or alter various social entities.

In a nutshell, my argument is that synergistic effects of various kinds are the common denominator, the functional basis for various forms of co-operative social behavior, including symbiotic relationships between individuals of different species, various "collective goods" or "public goods" produced by the joint actions of conspecifics (whether or not related to one another), the goods produced by political coalitions, and what I have been referring to as "corporate goods."

In essence, the synergistic effects that are produced by co-operative social action provide the necessary positive incentives for individual choices. The ultimate answer to the "why" question is provided by specific historical opportunities for achieving synergistic effects, while the assumptions embedded in various models of co-operative behavior specify the structural constraints and facilitators that may be present in different circumstances. At best, then, these micro-level principles and models can be only partially explanatory. They can answer only certain co-determining motivational questions relating to how different individual actors will respond to various opportunities. The micro-level models can enable us to specify the contexts within which opportunities for realizing synergistic effects *may* be transformed into decisions and actions. But the functional processes that create these opportunities in the first place must be specified separately. In other words, both micro- and macro-level explanations are necessary, but neither is sufficient.

It should go without saying that there already exists in the scientific literature a large number of formal models that are derived either explicitly or implicitly from the assumption that the superadditive composition rule is operative. The rule states:

$$\phi(x,y) - c(x,y) > \phi(x) - c(x) + \phi(y) - c(y) \tag{5}$$

What these models do not specify is how likely such co-operative interactions are, the contexts in which they are likely to occur, and how stable they may be once initiated. They leave out or take for granted the motivations of the participants and any attendant costs. That these motivations and costs cannot be taken for granted was underscored in an analysis by Goh, who showed that mathematically the likelihood of being able to initiate and sustain a competitive interaction is much greater than is the case for mutualism.[148] The latter are not only less likely but less stable. In other words, the greater than expected abundance of mutualism in nature can be accounted for only by the powerful functional advantages and net benefits that may be realized. But we must also analyze the logic of the decision-making process itself.

One set of structural constraints is associated with the subset of synergistic effects that are referred to as collective goods or public goods. Contrary to the widespread expectation that individuals will co-operate whenever some collective benefit can be produced by collective action, Mancur Olson argued that there are many social contexts in which "rational" individuals might not participate.[149] These are contexts involving an indivisible good, a good from which no member of the group or society can be excluded. National defense is one oft-cited example. The principal problem addressed by collective goods theory has to do with the "free rider" problem: If everyone benefits equally from a co-operatively produced good, what is to prevent certain individuals from cheating, from enjoying the good without contributing his or her fair share of the costs? The general answer is, of course, either coercive enforcement measures or additional positive inducements, which accounts for why both types of measures are in fact freely utilized in human societies. Though the point is not well developed, Olson also mentions situations in which the level of individual participation may affect the outcome, that is, the goods produced may not be quite so good when people are not sufficiently well organized, or when not enough people participate, or when someone does not contribute his or her fair share. To avoid confusion, such goods should not be called collective or public at all. They belong in a category that I refer to as corporate goods.

Two-person and n-person "games," such as the prisoner's dilemma, are designed to explore another set of structural constraints. In this class of models, the basic assumption is that each of the actors is directly affected by his decision whether or not to participate. Likewise, it is assumed that the goods that are produced are conditioned by what the other actors choose to do; their actions are interdependent. Various assumptions are then made about the costs and benefits (or payoffs) that may be associated with the strategic decision either to co-operate or "defect" from the game. Many of the early prisoner's dilemma games (so called because the paradigm examples involved fellow prisoners who were kept in ignorance of one another's actions) were unfortunately highly artificial and bore little relationship to real world situations, but some of the more recent theorizing in this vein has moved closer to the problems encountered in the actual context of biological and sociocultural evolution.

Perhaps the most notable example is the recent effort by Axelrod and Hamilton.[150] These authors begin by introducing some novel assumptions, namely, that the potential co-operators are in an "iterative" game—they are likely to meet again—and that the costs and benefits relate to reproductive fitness. The game is then defined as follows: $T > R > P > S$, and $R > (S + T)/2$, where T = the temptation to defect, R = the reward for mutual co-operation, P = the punishment for mutual defection and, S = the "sucker's" payoff (when one player co-operates and the other defects). Specifying the following values in their "payoff matrix" ($T = 5$, $R = 3$, $P = 1$, and $S = 0$), Axelrod and Hamilton then proceeded to conduct a tournament in which various game theorists were invited to submit strategies. Out of some seventy-six entries in two different rounds, the winning strategy was the simplest: tit for tat. That is, the most effective strategy was to co-operate on the initial move and then do whatever the other player did on subsequent moves. Axelrod and Hamilton concluded that "cooperation based on reciprocity is a robust strategy that can thrive in a variegated environment."

Of course, this result required the precise quantitative distribution of payoff values that these theorists specified. But more important, it also assumed that the payoffs to the players will be structured in such a way that there is a built-in incentive for defecting. In the real world, however, many co-operative interactions do not operate under these conditions. The players are not ignorant of one another's actions; they occur in a dynamic fashion over time and are at all times feedback dependent. Also, there may be built-in disincentives or sanctions for nonparticipation. In many cases, the goods may not be produced at all if anyone defects, for the outcomes may be dependent on combinatorial (synergistic) effects. Furthermore, unlike collective goods, many co-operatively produced goods are divisible and may be distributed only to active participants (and/or objects of "altruism" such as close kin). Defectors and free riders can thus be excluded altogether from the game. This suggests additional constraints on cheating and additional internal means for achieving stability in co-operative interactions that are not appreciated in "classical" collective goods and prisoner's dilemma models.

Indeed, the distinction between "public" and so-called "private" goods is not always clearcut. The concept of public goods assumes the existence of the group and the right of everyone to participate. But many putatively public goods can be excluded simply by excluding a person from the group, or by punishing him or her in some low-cost way (say, social ostracism) for not contributing. By the same token, many putatively private goods (goods that are divisible and excludable) may nevertheless have a public goods aspect. All the employees of a company (say, Chrysler Corporation) may actually have a stake in the viability of the firm, whether they recognize it or not, because their salaries are all equally dependent on the continued ability of the company to produce and sell its "goods." The basic viability of the firm as a whole is indivisible, even though its income may be divided unequally. Likewise, many fringe benefits enjoyed by all employees may be treated by the firm as public goods.

Such additional assumptions and refinements can be lumped together under the heading of "corporate goods"—co-operatively produced goods that are not so good if everyone does not do his or her part (or does a poor job) and goods that may be divided among the co-operators in accordance with any one of various distribution criteria (e.g., capitalist, socialist or perhaps some concept of fair shares).

The closest approximation of this approach can be found in the literature on "coalition theory." As the term implies, coalition theory is concerned with the problem of how to aggregate a sufficient number of individual co-operators, each of whose participation is contingent on how much he or she will receive of the payoffs (or of various "side payments"), to achieve a desired outcome. Thus the twin assumptions of contingent participation and strategically divisible benefits are introduced into the game. Though many of the applications of coalition theory are focused on such subjects as voting behavior, it can also be extended to more durable interaction patterns, such as organized groups. The basic requirement that is imposed on the game is in effect an inversion of the superadditive composition rule. That is, it must *not* be true that:

$$\phi(X,Y) < \phi(X) + \phi(Y) \tag{6}$$

The concept of corporate goods is an extension of this framework. In a sense, it adds an organismic perspective to the game—it refers to goods that are produced by an organized set of specialized activities and roles; realization of the corporate goal(s) is affected by whether everyone does his or her job; the rewards may be distributed in various ways; and there may be a strong linkage between individual performance, the success of the venture, and the internal distribution of costs and benefits. Efforts to formalize and apply this model are currently in progress. However, it should be clear enough from my brief description that this model greatly strengthens the linkage between individual choices and actions and the production of synergistic effects. It should also be obvious that this model applies to many real world contexts, including some that are sometimes erroneously assumed to involve collective goods. Examples range from large corporations to the defense establishments that, in reality, provide their supposedly collective goods more or less effectively, depending on how effectively a given society organizes and prepares itself militarily.

Some Lessons of History

There are many lessons to be drawn from surveying the historical cycles of political growth, transformation, and decay.

The causes of directional trends in biological evolution and in sociocultural evolution are always relational and systemic; they involve changes in the necessarily complex and many-faceted relationships through which synergistic patterns or combinations are achieved. Functional synergism (positive or negative) is always a consequence of the precise configuration of and the interactions among the parts of hierarchically organized systems, and between these systems and their environments. A change in any major aspect of these patterns may therefore have drastic functional consequences (positive or negative) for the system as a whole. The change might involve a positive development: a new technology (metallurgy or the moldboard plow), a new cultural artifact (money or markets), a political innovation (record-keeping systems, formal law, representative councils, election systems). Or the change might involve a negative development: a climate change, the exhaustion of a critical nonrenewable resource, a divergence of economic interests (as in the American Civil War), the rise of a larger and more powerful political competitor, or the elimination of competitors.* These developments are important only because of their functional consequences in specific situations. While we are accustomed to fixing our attention on a particular factor or variable, the functional significance of these factors can be specified and measured only in terms of their relationship to the systems of which they are a part and their consequences for culturally mediated human needs and wants. What may be a threshold variable in one context may become a background or "control" variable in another.

With regressive changes as with progressive changes, functional synergy (or dysergy) conditions but does not wholly determine the outcome. The opportunity for realizing functional synergism creates the context within which political changes may occur; functional consequences are necessary, but they are not sufficient. They are co-determinants, along with various

* A paradox with respect to the elimination of competitors arises from the fact that the benefit-cost ratio associated with political aggregation may decline sharply, not because of a change in the polity but because its function no longer exists. While the costs remain the same, the benefits fall to zero. This is why few alliances outlast the successful prosecution of the war for which they were formed. By the same token, various writers have attributed the initial stages in the decline of the Roman empire in part to the elimination of its most threatening rivals.

political processes. Neither the political decay of the Roman empire nor structural (economic) factors alone can account for its ultimate demise.

Political systems are at all times fragile entities: they are contingent. At the micro level, approximately four of every five new business ventures in the United States fail within the first few years, often for lack of sufficient capital and equally often for political reasons—inadequate planning and management. Moreover, those businesses that survive their earliest years can expect to be winnowed by bankruptcy proceedings within the next several years.[151] Similarly, Gurr's data suggest that the "infant mortality" rate among new polities is high. Fully half the total of 336 systems that he studied underwent more or less drastic transformations before or during their twelfth year of existence.[152] (A concept of political "fitness" waits to be explored.)

Political systems generally do not long outlast their usefulness to what Marsilio of Padua, in the *Defensor pacis,* called the weightier part (*pars valentior*) of a polity. For political systems are primarily instrumentalities, not, as George Orwell feared, ends in themselves.* There are always substantial costs involved in operating a political system, costs in terms of time, energy, money, lives, and constrictions on personal freedom. Political systems are open thermodynamic systems. If its participants come to perceive a political system as unprofitable, acquiescence and co-operation will become tenuous and probably short-lived. (The economy principle applies.) The Kurds, the Basques, the French Canadians, and the contending factions in Northern Ireland live in more or less precariously balanced polities. So might Americans, if our current economic and energy crises are not solved, for they threaten the basis of the political order.

The energy crisis in the United States offers a cautionary tale on a grand scale. Our current difficulties are a result of the positive synergy associated with our adoption and exploitation of fossil fuels. Until 150 years ago, the American colonies and then the nascent United States depended almost entirely on energy from wood, water, wind, and whale blubber. Our ancestors did not need fossil fuels. The introduction of coal and then oil and natural gas energized our multiple and overlapping agricultural, industrial, and population revolutions. But there is always a Faustian bargain associated with major new forms of functional synergism; along with the benefits come dependencies and new vulnerabilities. The synergism that facilitates the creation or expansion of a political system may in time become the underlying cause of its destruction.

Sobering though not necessarily alarming evidence of regular cycles in political life can be found in data developed by Rein Taagepera.[153] He found that the area growth patterns of various historical empires (including some

* As Big Brother explains in *1984,* "The purpose of power is power."

modern nation-states, in his definition) all fit logistic growth curves. Indeed, the patterns conform to the same differential equation that is used to model growth patterns in population biology:

$$\frac{dn}{dt} = K\left(n - \frac{n^2}{N}\right) \tag{7}$$

where n = the size of the landmass or population, t = time, K = some rate constant, N = the maximum area or population value, and dn/dt = the rate of change over time. The equation predicts that any growth process which fits this model will ultimately asymptote. Indeed, political empires have generally reversed direction in time, as Taagepera documents in several subsequent papers.[154] Taagepera notes that there seems to be a mathematical relationship between the "rise time" of an empire (from 20 percent to 80 percent of its maximum size) and its duration: the faster they grow, the faster they decline. With a data base of more than fifty cases, Taagepera found that duration times have averaged about three times their respective rise times.

Taagepera cautions that such statistical patterns are only suggestive. They illuminate the fragility of large-scale polities, not the underlying causal dynamics. More important, his study involves growth in the area of political control, not the patterns of population growth or economic growth. The latter variables, Taagepera notes, are much harder to measure with accuracy. Unfortunately, this is a major theoretical drawback, one that seriously weakens the analogy he would like to draw with the biological life cycle. That the areal growth-decline curves of empires happen to parallel the body-weight to life-cycle relationships of various animals is a fortuitous coincidence; it is inconceivable to me that some common causal process exists, and Taagepera's speculations about inherent processes of internal deterioration in organisms and polities seem gratuitous and inappropriate.

On the other hand, comparisons between human *population* growth patterns and those of other species (the work of population biology and ecology) are meaningful precisely because the same variable is examined in different contexts.

An important caveat must be entered in relation to the growth-decline patterns in human polities. Over the short term, a political system—whether measured in terms of landmass or population—may asymptote or disaggregate into a smaller-scale polity. Occasionally it may even vanish. We know what happened to the Pompeiians, but we do not know where the Chaco Indians went when their civilization collapsed. Of course the Romans survived and in time became Italians—a cultural transformation that still has not been fully explored by anthropologists.

Over the long term, the process of political evolution and the larger process of sociocultural evolution assume the character of a series of experiments, a trial-and-error process that has, however haltingly, maintained a generally progressive direction. Recent fine-grained scholarship relating to economic history has given ecological factors a more prominent role and filled in many of the interstices in our understanding of economic development.[155] When we view the entire spectrum of variables, we can see continuities and discontinuities, progressive and regressive changes simultaneously. Thus the Roman polity collapsed and was replaced by the Italian city-states and later by a unified Italian state, but the population of the peninsula continued to increase (in 1975 it was about 55 million). Other forms of sociocultural progress may continue unabated. Similarly, some modern nation-states comprise landmasses that are many times larger than the total area of many early empires. As the underlying economic, political, and military conditions permitted (or impelled), new attempts were made to aggregate large-scale polities.

These generally progressive trends continue to be governed by the principles and contingencies enunciated above. Polities do not disaggregate so long as they remain functional at the margin for those who have the means to ensure their continued existence. The hallmark of most revolutions (but not of civil wars) is the fact that all antagonists generally fight to control and perhaps reshape the system, not to dismantle it. (Observe what Marxists do, not what they say.) The process is not primarily dialectical, it is cybernetic. It involves a dynamic, goal-oriented adaptation process, not the blind workings of history. It is more a steering process than a clash of "ignorant armies" held in the grip of inscrutable forces.

The Ship of State

Consider the familiar ship of state metaphor. There are times when the passengers and crew are relatively satisfied with the ship of state, its course, and the speed that the captain maintains. The ship is being operated efficiently, and while there may be several classes of passengers (morally offensive but a fact of life), everyone's basic needs are satisfied and there are no extremes of wealth and poverty. In naval parlance, it is a happy ship. All passengers benefit equally from the design, structure, and functioning of the ship itself. While each passenger pays only a share of the total cost, all passengers are able to reach their common destination safely and in good health. This is another example of functional synergism.

However, things might not go so smoothly aboard the ship of state if the ship is poorly designed and poorly maintained, if the captain charts a course through storm-tossed seas, if the crew is poorly paid, ill-trained, and demoralized, if the ship is oppressively hot or cold and the food bad. If the first-class passengers travel in gilt-edged luxury while the third-class passengers are crowded into a rat-infested hold and subsist on moldy bread and thin broth, there is likely to be trouble. Third-class passengers may steal food from first class; fights may break out between passengers and crew members; representatives of all three classes and the crew may appeal to the captain to change course; the crew may divide into two factions, "loyalists" who work on deck and serve the first-class passengers and "reformers" who work in the engine room and serve the third-class passengers. Now there is dysergy in the system.

Imagine what might happen if the hapless captain were to encounter a raging typhoon. If the ship does not sink with all hands, the most disgruntled among the passengers and crew may mutiny, aiming to overthrow the captain, jettison the most incorrigible loyalists, chart a new course, and provide more equitable accommodations for the passengers.

A General Prediction

The ship of state metaphor may not be good political science, but it is more than a metaphor; it is a fairly accurate model of what the state is all about. And it leads to a prediction: *Allowing for short-term lead and lag, over the long term the boundaries of macro-level political systems will conform to the patterns of functional synergism.*

This proposition can help us to make sense of many seemingly irrational, contradictory, and even bizarre patterns of political aggregation and disaggregation. It makes them consistent and to a limited degree predictable. Thus it is not surprising that the United States might enter the Vietnam war in part to check the "domino" effect of Chinese expansionism and then emerge from that war moving toward a tacit political alliance with the very nation that had called us a paper tiger, that we found abhorrent for its atheistic communism, and that had fought us in Korea. Indeed, the Vietnam war itself may have contributed to this meeting of minds. In the wake of the Vietnam disaster our relative losses, Russia's relative gains, and China's evident weakness combined to make an alliance seem advantageous to us. After all, it was the archideologue Mao who began the dialogue between the two nations.

This proposition also enables us to understand why the United States and Russia became allies in World War II despite our earlier intervention in their civil war and our implacable antagonism to communism, as well as why the two countries might become enemies after the war, when their common enemies had been annihilated. Had that war ended in an early armistice rather than in unconditional surrender, we might still be allied with the Russians against the "axis" powers. Similarly, the proposition explains why the British and French could fight each other for a thousand years and then abruptly join forces to fight the nascent German state in two of the greatest human slaughters of all time.

At a more mundane level, the proposition enables us to reconcile such apparent inconsistencies as why we sell grain to the Russians and then use some of the profits (via taxes) to arm ourselves against them; and why religious cleavages can be associated with bitter civil conflict in Northern Ireland (because they overlap economic and political discrimination and are fostered by its next-door neighbor) while other societies that are composites of vastly more divergent ethnic groups (Switzerland, for example) can function relatively harmoniously. It can also explain why Abraham Lincoln and the founders of the Republican Party could put together an improbable coalition of otherwise antagonistic Western farmers and Eastern bankers and industrialists; why Franklin Roosevelt could form an equally improbable coalition of Northern labor unions, minorities, middle-class liberals, and intellectuals on the one hand and Southern racists, antiunion business interests, and a conservative middle class on the other; and why multinational corporations can often flagrantly disregard the national interest of their home countries, most recently with respect to the phenomenon of production sharing.

These examples can be multiplied. For the "higher" morality of human needs (as well as more crass forms of self-interest, to be sure) fairly consistently overrides political ideology and other value orientations. When there are significant opportunities for achieving functional synergism through political aggregation, human needs may override less important sources of political cleavage. They certainly override the predictions and predilections of Marxist and capitalist ideologies alike. While we may decry this state of affairs, we can confidently predict that such supposed political contradictions will be the rule.

Can we go further? Surveying the current scene, can we venture some hard predictions? What will be the future course of political evolution? Will there be a nuclear shoot-out and a return to a stone-age culture? Will environmental deterioration lead in time to collapse? Or will organic processes of sociocultural and economic evolution lead to greater political integration, to regional polities or a world order along the lines envisioned by Richard Falk and his compatriots?

Like Darwin's theory, properly understood, my theory makes only one unequivocal prediction, that the future cannot be predicted with certainty because the process is not linear or deterministic but a highly contingent concatenation of chance, necessity, and teleonomy. The future depends on changes in our natural environment that cannot now be foretold with confidence, constraints we may not yet comprehend, ideas, inventions, and other economic developments (new forms of functional synergism) that are inherently beyond our ability to predict, and potentially decisive future political decisions and actions. Functional synergism is always relational and situation-specific; it is dependent on how all of the elements and processes fit within the system, and how the system fits within its environment(s).

Some cultural evolutionists are more sanguine about predicting the future. Naroll analyzes the historical trend in Eurasian empires toward ever larger aggregates and offers some probabilities for achieving a unified world state that range from the year 2125 (a 40 percent probability) to 2750 (a 95 percent probability) to 3750 (a 99.935 percent probability). In the meantime, Naroll believes wars between independent political units will continue to occur without significant abatement.[156] Carneiro generally concurs, though he employs a different methodology for making his prognostications. He projects the historical trend toward a decreasing number of politically autonomous units. Provided that nuclear annihilation is avoided, he says, "a world state cannot be far off"; it is a matter of centuries or even decades, not millennia.[157]

Lumsden and Wilson also wish to enter the futurist sweepstakes by extending their autocatalytic model of human evolution to the goal of predicting the future. Just as their vision of cultural processes was based on the beliefs that epigenetic rules govern the production of cultural patterns and that "postulational-deductive" covering laws could be derived to explain cultures, so these authors are optimistic about predicting the future: "The ultimate triumph of both human sociobiology and the traditional social sciences would be to correctly explain and predict trends in cultural evolution on the basis of their own axioms. . . . Will the social sciences, using all of the considerable resources at their disposal and designing ever more comprehensively multifactorial models, be able to explain history more fully and perhaps even predict with moderate accuracy? We believe that the answer is yes, at least on a very limited scale. . . . The prediction of history is a worthwhile venture."[158]

We have come full circle to Spencer's Universal Law of Evolution. Although the social sciences owe more to Spencer than is generally acknowledged, in this fundamental respect we would do better to cast our lot with Darwin. For we have just as much to learn about the future from the extinction of the dinosaurs as we do from our own history as a species. It is presumptuous of us to think that even now we have sufficient knowledge of or teleonomic control over the evolutionary process to have transcended chance and necessity, much less being able to predict future human actions.

But if we cannot make deterministic predictions, we can make conditional predictions. Modern nation-states and the relationships between them have undergone dramatic changes since World War II, and it can safely be predicted that equally dramatic or even more dramatic changes will occur in the future. After all, the nation-state is not vouchsafed by any law of nature; it is a historical artifact associated with a particular sociocultural context. It could be that the nation-state will in time be replaced by a more inclusive political entity or entities or that nation-states will devolve into less inclusive entities. It could also be that the modern state is evolving in both directions at once.

Some more inclusive integrative functions might in time be surrendered upward, either through armed conflict or through piecemeal extension of the global social contract beyond postal unions and the like to an international monetary system, trade and labor conditions, the oceans, and aspects of environmental regulation. If contemporary economic trends continue, the augury is certainly for more rather than less political integration and the emergence of a new level of hierarchical control. But in whatever way such a centripetal movement might occur, it will endure only as long as it remains functionally advantageous on balance. Conversely, if there is a significant diminution in some of the forces that were responsible in the first place for integrating the sometimes strange bedfellows that comprise modern states, it can be predicted that there will also be centrifugal tendencies. Contradictory as it must seem, both progressive and regressive evolution might occur simultaneously. Only the scenario of apolitical socialism is ruled out.

By the same token, the failure to solve what John Platt called our "crisis of crises"—the nexus of problems involving population, food, water, energy, resources, and the environment—will in the long run have degenerative or catastrophic consequences. For better or worse, we are dependent on complex systems of co-determining variables. And if the Club of Rome's famous "limits to growth" projections oversimplified the situation, nevertheless they contained an element of truth. They illustrated the paradox of dependency. If any one of the requisites to sustain the complex synergistic systems that we call nation-states are for any reason undependable, the seeds of ultimate collapse may have been sown at the outset. And, unfortunately, foresight has not been the rule, either in nature or in human societies.

But, to repeat, functional consequences do not alone determine evolutionary change. Human beings do not always seize the opportunities available to them, nor do they always act expeditiously to break up dysfunctional political systems. The patterns fit the "quasi-rational choice" model: Opportunities for functional synergism must first be discerned, discovered, or invented, then communicated. There must also be a cognitive alignment of perceptions relating to functional needs and the functional consequences of actions, an alignment that is often impeded by perceptual filters.

The dynamics of progressive and regressive political evolution resemble the classic shipboard fire-control problem of tracking a rapidly moving target (an attacking enemy aircraft) with an antiaircraft gun mounted on a moving platform. As long as the trajectories of the ship and the target remain the same, the gun will eventually lock in on the target and anticipate its position. But if either the ship or the target changes course or speed, which both may be doing rather frantically in a battle situation, the fire-control problem becomes complicated; there must be constant "lagged" responses to feedback and to new trajectory information. For human populations the target is of course survival in a complex world of co-operation and competition, but the same basic cybernetic model applies. I believe that we will find no better way of modeling and understanding political processes than in such terms.

VII

Conclusion

> We cannot *predict* history but we can *make* it; and we can *make* evolution. More: we cannot avoid making evolution. Every reform deliberately instituted in the structure of society changes both history and the selective forces that affect evolution—though evolutionary change may be the farthest thing from our minds as reformers. We are not free to avoid producing evolution: we are only free to close our eyes to what we are doing.
>
> *Garrett Hardin*

I have proposed a nested set of theories about evolution as a unified historical process. Human evolution, and the changes we have wrought among ourselves and in our environment, are, to be sure, *sui generis.* But this is a truism that can gain us very little in terms of true understanding of the evolutionary process. Every morphological and behavioral invention and every "progressive" (complexifying) development of the past 3.5 billion years has been *sui generis.* Moreover, these inventions have been cumulative, and are linked to one another through an organizational hierarchy of awesome architectural and functional complexity. At each new level of biological organization new properties and new principles have emerged. Every new level of wholeness has not only transcended but ultimately organized and integrated lower-level parts.

At every emergent level of biological organization, including human polities, this multilayered process has manifested certain common properties. Progressive evolution, whether at the microscopic level of the one-celled creature or at the macroscopic level of transnational political organizations, embodies cybernetic processes coupled with functional synergism. Human political systems are not a thing apart but a variation on one of the most primordial evolutionary themes. The purposes served by our political systems spring from our basic needs as biological creatures, and the patterns of organization that we have evolved are successful only insofar as they embody the same basic principles that govern lower levels of biological organization. Just as natural selection, through trial and success, has oriented the evolutionary process toward more progressive forms of biological organization, so teleonomic selection has oriented sociocultural evolution toward more progressive forms of political organization.

Like Darwin's theory, my theory does not attempt to account in detail for every specific historical event; the causes always involve unique sets of historical factors. Rather, the theory suggests the general form of the explanation for the progressive aspect of the evolutionary process: the operative general principles and the location of past and future progressive developments. The theory does not imply an end to the social sciences; it suggests a new beginning. It provides a unifying paradigm and a common theoretical framework for understanding the nature and the causal dynamics of human societies. It is not a sociobiological theory, an anthropological theory, a psychological theory, a sociological theory, an economic theory, or a political theory; it combines and synthesizes all these theoretical perspectives.

Does the theory tell us anything we did not already know? I believe the theory involves a new and potentially fruitful synthesis. I have attempted to dissolve some of the confusion over the concept of natural selection and the functional processes in nature to which it refers. I have introduced the concept of teleonomic selection as a way of characterizing the behavioral and social processes that have been central to sociocultural evolution. Like natural selection, teleonomic selection is not a mechanism but a way of identifying and framing an open-ended class of functional processes and their consequences. These processes are cybernetic; they involve hierarchies of cybernetic systems that embrace human nature, the dynamics of human actions, and the corporate actions of human organizations.

Within this framework, I have proposed that the concept of functional synergism is central to an understanding of the progressive aspect of evolutionary history. The concept involves a way of classifying a vast array of phenomena, and its usefulness lies in its ability to identify and isolate those interacting influences in biological and social processes which have precipitated the evolution of complex systems. As I define the term, functional synergism is equivalent to no other concept in the biological or social sciences. It is not a synonym for "emergence," though synergistic phenomena often have emergent properties. Nor is it equivalent to the economist's "utilities" (individual satisfactions based on personal tastes). Functional synergism involves combinatorial effects that may or may not relate to tastes; it may also relate to needs, or to biological adaptation and fitness.

Nor is the term functional synergism equivalent to economies of scale, the division of labor, collective goods, efficiency, technological progress, or social co-operation. It may embrace any or all of these concepts—and more.

Can I be accused of trying to explain everything? Can Darwin be accused of the same with respect to the concept of natural selection? The answer to both questions is no. The concept of functional synergism provides a framework for explaining the progressive and regressive evolution of biological and social systems. The theory specifically directs our attention away from simplistic prime mover theories, be they ecological determinism, neo-Malthusianism, dialectical materialism, capitalism, the balance of power, or demo-techno-econo-environmental determinism. Instead it directs our attention to interactional, systemic patterns of causation which combine chance, necessity, teleonomy—and history.

Is the theory tautological? What is the null hypothesis? In fact there are a number of potential null hypotheses. One is the "divine plan." Another says that the underlying cause of progressive evolution has been a self-propelled sequence of syntheses among dialectically conflicting forces. A third posits an energy-centered orthogenesis that can be traced to Lamarck and Spencer. Prigogine, if I read him correctly, espouses this hypothesis. A related hypothesis attributes sociocultural evolution to autocatalysis. Neo-Malthusian and warfare theories are enjoying a vogue among some sociocultural evolutionists. Finally, there are those who would advance the random drift argument, which has a following among biologists. The analogous sociocultural concept of "tradition drift," a term coined by E. O. Wilson, has gained some currency as a factor that might have contributed to human evolution. My theory says that the functional consequences of various synergistic (co-operative) processes have played the primary role in progressive evolution, in conjunction with stochastic and deterministic influences. It is thus a functional theory of biological and social structures.

Can the theory be tested? I have described relevant formalizations—models of collective goods, egoistic co-operation, symbiosis (or mutualism), and a new approach that I call a corporate goods model. I have also revivified and refined von Foerster's "superadditive composition rule." I have proposed specific tests and I have invoked supporting evidence in each of the relevant domains, biological evolution, sociocultural evolution, and political evolution. Finally, I offered a set of propositions in relation to sociocultural and political evolution that provide opportunities for falsification. To test them, I described a number of comparative studies, including several of my own. I hope that further propositions and tests will be forthcoming.

What can we conclude? Are we an "accident of history," as Leakey has suggested? Or are we the product of an inexorable fate, a historical imperative that is beyond our control? The truth is that we are neither the masters nor the servants of our fate. Instead, we are the emergent products of ever more complex and powerful purposive systems, cybernetic systems that embody a constrained or canalized freedom to set goals and make choices. (The neurobiologist Sir Charles Sherrington called the human mind an "enchanted loom.")

We will never be free of our biological nature or the larger environment in which we must earn our livings. Yet we may be able to enlarge upon our evolved capacity for making choices and exercising self-control, individually and collectively, over our destiny. While we are not the creators of evolutionary purposiveness, we are a transcendent culmination. As Dobzhansky once said, we alone have the ability to set evolutionary courses of our own choosing.

The irony in this state of affairs is that our power to choose is as much a threat as an opportunity. We are the only species in the entire history of life on earth that can wantonly choose self-annihilation—or worse, annihilate ourselves unwittingly by failing to exercise the power we have to curb self-destructive behaviors.

Thus more than ever we are the political animal, pursuing the survival of ourselves and our progeny through an ever-expanding network of interdependencies. This has been our evolutionary trajectory, but it is not necessarily our fate. For this theory, this vision, makes no promises for the future even as it defines the nature of the problem and the general nature of the solution. The theory views the future as one of unending challenge, of great problems but also of great opportunities. It views political processes at all levels of society as the heart and soul of the process of human adaptation both for individuals and for collectivities with shared public purposes. Politics is ultimately about our survival and the survival of our species.

The late Walter Lippmann summed up our current predicament in a rare postretirement interview with journalist Henry Brandon.

> *Lippmann:* This is not the first time that human affairs have been chaotic and seemed ungovernable. But never before, I think, have the stakes been so high. I am not talking about, nor do I expect, a catastrophe like nuclear war. What is really pressing upon us is that the number of people who need to be governed and are involved in governing threatens to exceed man's capacity to govern. This furious multiplication of the masses of mankind coincides with the ever more imminent threat that, because we are so ungoverned, we are polluting and destroying the environment in which the human race must live.
>
> *Brandon:* Where does this lead us?

> *Lippmann:* The supreme question before mankind—to which I shall not live to know the answer—is how men will be able to make themselves willing and able to save themselves.[1]

I do not know the answer either. But I share with Lippmann the convictions that we need more politics, not less of it, and that the answer, if one is to be found, lies in the end, as it did in the beginning, with politics.

Notes

Notes

[*Note:* Abbreviated citations are given for references cited previously within the same chapter. Bracketed, boldface numbers refer back to the note(s) in which full citation(s) may be found.]

Preface

1. K. Flannery, "The Cultural Evolution of Civilizations," *Annual Review of Ecology and Systematics* 3(1972): 399–426.
2. V. Reynolds, *The Biology of Human Action* (San Francisco: Freeman, 1976).
3. O. D. Duncan, "From Social System to Ecosystem," *Sociological Inquiry* 31–33(1961–1963): 140–49.
4. C. P. Snow, *The Two Cultures: and a Second Look* (Cambridge: Cambridge University Press, 1964).

I. Introduction: Quo Vadimus?

1. E.g., P. R. Ehrlich and A. H. Ehrlich, *The End of Affluence* (New York: Ballantine, 1974); R. L. Heilbroner, *An Inquiry into the Human Prospect* (New York: W. W. Norton, 1974).
2. C. E. Lindblom, "The Science of Muddling Through," *Public Administration Review* 19(1959): 79–88, and *Politics and Markets* (New York: Basic Books, 1977).
3. B. Mandeville, *The Fable of the Bees: Or, Private Vices, Publick Benefits* (London: Oxford University Press, 1924 [1705–1729]).
4. R. D. Spegele, "Deconstructing Methodological Falsification in International Relations," *American Political Science Review* 74 (1980): 104–22.
5. Aristotle, *The Physics,* trans. T. Taylor (London: Wilks); J.-B. de Lamarck, *Zoological Philosophy,* trans. H. Elliot (New York: Hafner, 1963 [1809]); H. Spencer, "Progress: Its Law and Cause," in *Essays Scientific, Political and Speculative* (New York: Appleton, 1892 [1857]); H. Bergson, *L'évolution creatrice* (Paris: Alcan, 1907); H. A. E. Driesch, *Philosophie des Organischen* (Leipzig: Engelmann, 1909); P. Teilhard de Chardin, *The Phenomenon of Man* (New York: Harper & Row, 1959); P. P. Grassé, *Evolution of Living Organisms: Evidence for a New Theory of Transformation* (New York: Academic Press, 1977 [1973]); I. Prigogine, "Order Through Fluctuation: Self-Organization and Social System," in *Evolution and Consciousness,*

ed. E. Jantsch and C. H. Waddington (Reading, Mass.: Addison-Wesley, 1976); J. Piaget, *Behavior and Evolution* (New York: Random House, 1978).

6. T. Dobzhansky, *Mankind Evolving: The Evolution of the Human Species* (New Haven: Yale University Press, 1962), p. 16.

7. For a discussion, see M. Scriven, "Explanation and Prediction in Evolutionary Theory," *Science* 130(1959): 477–82; cf. K. R. Popper, *The Logic of Scientific Discovery* (New York: Harper & Row, 1968 [1935]), and *Objective Knowledge: An Evolutionary Approach* (Oxford: Clarendon Press, 1972).

8. F. J. Ayala, "Teleological Explanations in Evolutionary Biology," *Philosophy of Science* 37(1970): 1–15; C. S. Pittendrigh, "Adaptation, Natural Selection and Behavior," in *Behavior and Evolution,* ed. A. Roe and G. G. Simpson (New Haven: Yale University Press, 1958). See also G. G. Simpson, "Behavior and Evolution," in *Behavior and Evolution;* G. C. Williams, *Adaptation and Natural Selection: A Critique of Some Current Evolutionary Thought* (Princeton: Princeton University Press, 1966); F. J. Ayala and T. Dobzhansky, eds., *Studies in the Philosophy of Biology* (Berkeley: University of California Press, 1974); E. Mayr, "Teleological and Teleonomic: A New Analysis," in *Boston Studies in the Philosophy of Science,* ed. R. S. Cohen and M. W. Wartofsky, vol. XIV (Boston: D. Reidel, 1974); W. H. Thorpe, *Purpose in a World of Chance: A Biologist's View* (Oxford: Oxford University Press, 1978); P. A. Corning, "Politics and the Evolutionary Process," in *Evolutionary Biology,* ed. T. Dobzhansky et al. (New York: Plenum, 1974), and "Human Nature *Redivivus,*" in *Human Nature in Politics* (Nomos, XVII), ed. J. R. Pennock and J. W. Chapman (New York: New York University Press, 1977); J. Monod, *Chance and Necessity,* trans. A. Wainhouse (New York: Knopf, 1971).

9. C. B. Drucker, "The Price of Progress in the Philippines," *Sierra* 63(1978): 22–26.

10. E. Allen et al., "Sociobiology: A New Biological Determinism," in *Biology as a Social Weapon,* ed. Sociobiology Study Group of Boston (Minneapolis: Burgess, 1977), pp. 151–52.

II. The Evolutionary Framework

1. Special note should be made at this point of the references that will be found in various places to "Corning (forthcoming)." The original manuscript for the present volume ran to approximately twice the length of what appears here. Many subjects dealt with in more detail in the original version have thus been excised. It is contemplated that this material will be revised, further amplified, and published elsewhere, along with more extensive documentation for each of the key theoretical chapters.

2. C. R. Darwin, *On the Origin of Species by Means of Natural Selection, or the Preservation of Favoured Races in the Struggle for Life* (Baltimore: Penguin, 1968 [1859]), p. 459.

3. Ibid., p. 116.

4. Ibid., p. 229.

5. Ibid., p. 116.

6. Ibid., p. 129.

7. N. Eldredge and S. J. Gould, "Punctuated Equilibria: An Alternative to Phyletic Gradualism," in *Models in Paleobiology,* ed. T. J. M. Schopf (San Francisco: Freeman, 1972); S. J. Gould and N. Eldredge, "Punctuated Equilibria: The Tempo and Mode of Evolution Reconsidered," *Paleobiology* 3(1977): 115–51; S. J. Gould, *Ontogeny and Phylogeny* (Cambridge, Mass.: Harvard University Press, 1977).

8. E. Mayr, "Evolution," *Scientific American* 239, 3(1978): 53.

9. F. J. Ayala and T. Dobzhansky, eds., *Studies in the Philosophy of Biology* (Berkeley: University of California Press, 1974).

10. Darwin, *Origin,* pp. 66–67. **[2]**

11. Ibid., pp. 228–29.

12. K. Connolly, "The Concept of Evolution: A Comment on Papers by Mr. Manser and Professor Flew," *Philosophy* 41(1966): 356–57; M. B. Williams, "Falsifiable Predictions of Evolutionary Theory," *Philosophy of Science* 40(1973): 518–37.

13. A. G. N. Flew, "The Concept of Evolution: A Comment," *Philosophy* 41(1966): 75.

14. S. M. Stanley, "A Theory of Evolution Above the Species Level," *Proceedings of the National Academy of Sciences* 72(1975): 646–50. But cf. S. N. Salthe, "Problems of Macroevolution (Molecular Evolution, Phenotype Definition, and Canalization) as Seen from a Hierarchical Viewpoint," *American Zoologist* 15(1975): 295–314; and S. Wright, *Evolution and the Genetics of Populations,* vol. IV (Chicago: University of Chicago Press, 1978).

15. Darwin, *Origin,* pp. 318, 348. **[2]**

16. Ibid., p. 459.

17. Ibid., pp. 217–32 passim.

18. D. Freeman, "The Evolutionary Theories of Charles Darwin and Herbert Spencer," *Current Anthropology* 15(1974): 219.

19. F. Jacob, "Evolution and Tinkering," *Science* 196(1977): 1161–66.

20. T. Dobzhansky, "Darwinian or 'Oriented' Evolution," *Evolution* 29(1975): 377.

21. G. G. Simpson, *The Meaning of Evolution,* rev. ed. (New Haven: Yale University Press, 1967), p. 173.

22. R. T. Abbott, *Seashells of North America* (New York: Golden Press, 1968), p. 27.

23. C. R. Darwin, *The Descent of Man, and Selection in Relation to Sex* (New York: A. L. Burt, 1874 [1871]).

24. C. R. Darwin, *The Expression of the Emotions in Man and Animals* (Chicago: University of Chicago Press, 1965 [1873]).

25. See A. R. Wallace, "The Origin of Human Races and the Antiquity of Man Deduced from the Theory of Natural Selection," *Journal of the Anthropological Society of London* 2(1864): 157–87, and *Contributions to the Theory of Natural Selection* (New York: Macmillan, 1870). H. L. McKinney, *Wallace and Natural Selection* (New Haven: Yale University Press, 1972).

26. Darwin, *Descent,* pp. 113–23, 123–42; Critiqued by A. Montagu, *Darwin, Competition, and Cooperation* (New York: Henry Schuman, 1952).

27. Darwin, *Descent,* pp. 123–24. Cf. A. Montagu, *Culture and the Evolution of Man* (New York: Oxford University Press, 1962), p. ix, and *Man and Aggression* (New York: Oxford University Press, 1968), p. 9. **[23]**

28. *Contra* M. Harris, *The Rise of Anthropological Theory: A History of Theories of Culture* (New York: T. Y. Crowell, 1968), p. 52.

29. Ibid.

30. C. R. Darwin, *The Variations of Animals and Plants Under Domestication* (New York: Appleton, 1890 [1868]).

31. Darwin, *Expression of Emotions,* p. xi. **[24]**

32. See especially the discussions in S. Persons, ed., *Evolutionary Thought in America* (New Haven: Yale University Press, 1950); R. Hofstadter, *Social Darwinism in American Thought,* 2d ed. (Boston: Beacon Press, 1955 [1944]); J. W. Burrow, *Evolution and Society: A Study in Victorian Social Theory* (London: Cambridge University Press, 1970); R. A. Nisbet, *Social Change and History: Aspects of Western Theory of Development* (New York: Oxford University Press, 1969); M. Ruse, *Sociobiology: Sense or Nonsense?* (Boston: D. Riedel, 1979).

33. Quoted in Harris, *Rise of Anthropological Theory,* pp. 217, 218. **[28]**

34. T. Dobzhansky, *Genetics and the Origin of Species* (New York: Columbia University Press, 1937); J. S. Huxley, *Evolution: The Modern Synthesis* (New York: Harper & Row, 1942).

35. For critical analyses, see S. Wright, *Evolution and the Genetics of Populations: A Treatise,* 4 vols. (Chicago: University of Chicago Press, 1968–1978), and "Genic and Organismic Selection," *Evolution* 34(1980): 825–43; R. C. Lewontin, *The Genetic Basis of Evolutionary Change* (New York: Columbia University Press, 1974); C. Johnson, *Introduction to Natural Selection*

(Baltimore: University Park Press, 1976); P. Nevers and H. Saedler, "Transposable Genetic Elements as Agents of Gene Instability and Chromosomal Rearrangements," *Nature* 268(1977): 109–15; S. N. Cohen and J. A. Shapiro, "Transposable Genetic Elements," *Scientific American* 242(1980): 40–49.

36. S. Wright, "Gene and Organism," *American Naturalist* 87(1953): 5–18, *Evolution*, and "Genic and Organismic Selection"; also A. B. Novikoff, "The Concept of Integrative Levels and Biology," *Science* 101(1945): 209–15, and "Creativity and Discontinuity in Evolution," *Science* 102(1945): 405–06; N. Tinbergen, *The Study of Instinct* (New York: Oxford University Press, 1951); L. von Bertalanffy, *Problems of Life: An Evaluation of Modern Biological Thought* (New York: John Wiley, 1952 [1949]); E. P. Odum and H. T. Odum, *Fundamentals of Ecology*, 3rd ed. (Philadelphia: Saunders, 1971); M. J. Dunbar, "The Evolution of Stability in Marine Environments: Natural Selection at the Level of the Ecosystem," *American Naturalist* 94(1960): 129–36; K. E. Machin, "Feedback Theory and Its Application to Biological Systems," *Symposia of the Society for Experimental Biology* 18(1964): 421–45; G. L. Stebbins, *The Basis of Progressive Evolution* (Chapel Hill: University of North Carolina Press, 1969); P. A. Weiss, "The Living System: Determinism Stratified," in *Beyond Reductionism*, ed. A. Koestler and J. R. Smythies (London: Hutchinson, 1969); G. G. Simpson, *Biology and Man* (New York: Harcourt, 1969); R. C. Lewontin, "The Units of Selection," *Annual Review of Ecology and Systematics* 1(1970): 1–18, and *Genetic Basis of Evolutionary Change;* E. H. Pattee, ed., *Hierarchy Theory* (New York: Braziller, 1973); R. D. Alexander and G. Borgia, "Group Selection, Altruism, and the Levels of Organization of Life," *Annual Review of Ecology and Systematics* 9(1978): 449–74; D. S. Wilson, *The Natural Selection of Populations and Communities* (Menlo Park, Calif.: Benjamin/Cummings, 1980). **[35]**

37. F. Jacob and J. Monod, "Genetic Regulatory Mechanisms in the Synthesis of Proteins," *Journal of Molecular Biology* 3(1961): 318–56; R. J. Britten and E. H. Davidson, "Gene Regulation for Higher Cells: A Theory," *Science* 165(1969): 349–57; E. B. Ford, *Ecological Genetics*, 3rd ed. (London: Chapman and Hall, 1971); J. Monod, *Chance and Necessity*, trans. A. Wainhouse (New York: Knopf, 1971); F. J. Ayala, ed., *Molecular Evolution* (Sunderland, Mass.: Sinauer, 1976); J. H. Miller and W. S. Reznikoff, eds., *The Operon* (Cold Spring Harbor, N.Y.: Cold Spring Harbor Laboratory, 1978); Nevers and Saedler, "Transposable Genetic Elements"; Cohen and Shapiro, "Transposable Genetic Elements." **[35]**

38. Wright, *Evolution*, and "Genic and Organismic Selection"; P. M. Sheppard, *Natural Selection and Heredity*, 4th ed. (London: Hutchinson, 1969); Ford, *Ecological Genetics;* Lewontin, *Genetic Basis of Evolutionary Change;* S. M. Stanley, "A Theory of Evolution Above the Species Level," *Proceedings of the National Academy of Sciences* 72(1975): 646–50, *Macroevolution: Pattern and Process* (San Francisco: Freeman, 1979), and *The New Evolutionary Timetable: Fossils, Genes and the Origin of Species* (New York: Basic Books, 1981); Gould and Eldredge, "Punctuated Equililibria"; Alexander and Borgia, "Group Selection"; Wilson, *Natural Selection of Populations;* H. C. Plotkin and F. J. Olding-Smee, "Multiple-Level Model of Evolution and Its Implications for Sociobiology," *The Behavioral and Brain Sciences* 4(1981): 225–68. **[7, 14, 35, 36, 37]**

39. Mayr, "Evolution." **[8]**

40. J. L. Hubby and R. C. Lewontin, "A Molecular Approach to the Study of Genic Heterozygosity in Natural Populations. I. The Number of Alleles at Different Loci in *Drosophila pseudoobscura*," *Genetics* 54(1966): 577–94; R. C. Lewontin and J. L. Hubby, "A Molecular Approach . . . II. Amount of Variation and Degree of Heterozygosity in Natural Populations of *Drosophila pseudoobscura*," *Genetics* 54(1966): 595–609; R. K. Selander, "Genic Variation in Natural Populations," in Ayala, *Molecular Evolution;* P. Singh et al., "Genetic Heterogeneity Within Electrophoretic 'Alleles' of Xanthine Dehydrogenase in *Drosophila pseudoobscura*," *Genetics* 84(1976): 609–29. **[37]**

41. J. L. King and T. H. Jukes, "Non-Darwinian Evolution," *Science* 164(1969): 788–797;

M. Nei, *Molecular Population Genetics and Evolution* (New York: Elsevier, 1975); M. Kimura, "The Neutral Theory of Molecular Evolution," *Scientific American* 241, 5(1979): 98–126; T. H. Jukes, "Silent Nucleotide Substitutions and the Molecular Evolutionary Clock," *Science* 210(1980): 973–77.

42. D. M. Raup et al., "Stochastic Models of Phylogeny and the Evolution of Diversity," *Journal of Geology* 81(1973): 525–42; D. M. Raup and S. J. Gould, "Stochastic Simulation and the Evolution of Morphology—Towards a Nomothetic Paleontology," *Systematic Zoology* 23(1974): 305–22; D. M. Raup, "Probabilistic Models in Evolutionary Paleobiology," *American Scientist* 65(1977): 50–57; S. J. Gould, "Generality and Uniqueness in the History of Life. An Exploration with Random Models," *BioScience* 28(1978): 277–81; Gould and Eldredge, "Punctuated Equilibria." **[7]**

43. Wright, *Evolution;* P. R. Ehrlich et al., "Checkerspot Butterflies: A Historical Perspective," *Science* 188(1975): 221–28; E. O. Wilson, *Sociobiology: The New Synthesis* (Cambridge, Mass.: Harvard University Press, 1975); E. R. Pianka, *Evolutionary Ecology,* 2d ed. (New York: Harper & Row, 1978). **[35]**

44. For example, in "The Spandrels of San Marco and the Panglossian Paradigm: A Critique of the Adaptationist Programme," *Proceedings of the Royal Society of London* 205(1979): 581–98, Gould and Lewontin have denounced what they term the "adaptationist programme." They charge so-called adaptationists with the "Panglossian" view that everything in nature is adaptive and natural selection is omnipotent. While they are careful to avoid denying the significance of adaptation altogether, they clearly seek to downgrade its importance relative to nonadaptive influences. See also S. J. Gould, "The Promise of Paleobiology as a Nomothetic Evolutionary Discipline," *Paleobiology* 6(1980): 96–118, and "The Evolutionary Biology of Constraint," *Daedalus* 109(1980): 39–52; M. Ho and P. Saunders, "Beyond Neo-Darwinism—An Epigenetic Approach to Evolution," *Journal of Theoretical Biology* 78(1979): 573–91.

45. K. R. Popper, "Darwinism as a Metaphysical Research Programme," in *The Philosophy of Karl Popper,* ed. P. A. Schilpp (LaSalle, Ill.: Open Court, 1974), p. 134.

46. Simpson, *Meaning of Evolution,* p. 219. **[21]**

47. E. Mayr, *Evolution and the Diversity of Life: Selected Essays* (Cambridge, Mass.: Harvard University Press, 1976), p. 365.

48. Wilson, *Sociobiology,* p. 67. **[13]**

49. Mayr, "Evolution," p. 52. **[18]**

50. H. B. D. Kettlewell, "Selection Experiments on Industrial Melanism in the *Lepidoptera,*" *Heredity* 9(1955): 323–42, "Further Selection Experiments on Industrial Melanism in the *Lepidoptera,*" *Heredity* 10(1956): 287–301, "A Survey of the Frequencies of *Biston betularia* (L.) (Lep.) and Its Melanic Forms in Great Britain," *Heredity* 12(1958): 51–72, and *The Evolution of Melanism: The Study of a Recurring Necessity* (Oxford: Clarendon Press, 1973).

51. T. Dobzhansky et al., *Evolution* (San Francisco; Freeman, 1977), p. 122.

52. B. Clarke, "The Causes of Biological Diversity," *Scientific American* 233,2(1975): 50–60.

53. E. L. Thorndike, *Animal Intelligence: Experimental Studies* (New York: Hafner, 1965 [1911]).

54. E. L. Thorndike, *Educational Psychology: The Psychology of Learning* (New York: Teachers College, 1925), II:4.

55. Quoted in D. K. Candland et al., *Emotion* (Monterey, Calif.: Brooks-Cole, 1977), p. 45.

56. R. Brown and R. J. Herrnstein, *Psychology* (Boston: Little, Brown, 1975); also R. J. Herrnstein, "On the Law of Effect," in *Festschrift for B. F. Skinner,* ed. P. B. Dews (New York: Appleton, 1970).

57. S. Wright, "The Method of Path Coefficients," *Annals of Mathematical Statistics* 5(1934): 161–215.

58. D. R. Lees and E. R. Creed, "Industrial Melanism in *Biston betularia:* The Role of Selective Predation," *Journal of Animal Ecology* 44(1975): 67–83.

59. F. D. Burton, "The Integration of Biology and Behavior in the Socialization of *Macaca Sylvana* of Gibraltar," in *Primate Socialization,* ed. F. E. Poirier (New York: Random House, 1972); R. Lande, "Natural Selection and Random Genetic Drift in Phenotypic Evolution," *Evolution* 30(1976): 314–34.

60. R. C. Lewontin, "Adaptation," *Scientific American* 239, 3(1978): 213–30.

61. See especially, G. Himmelfarb, *Darwin and the Darwinian Revolution* (New York: Doubleday, 1959); J. J. C. Smart, *Philosophy and Scientific Realism* (London: Routledge, 1963); A. R. Manser, "The Concept of Evolution," *Philosophy* 40(1965): 18–34; A. D. Barker, "An Approach to the Theory of Natural Selection," *Philosophy* 44(1969): 271–90; N. Macbeth, *Darwin Retried: An Appeal to Reason* (Boston: Gambit, 1971); M. Grene, *The Understanding of Nature: Essays in the Philosophy of Biology* (Boston: D. Reidel, 1974). Also N. I. Platnick, "Review of C. N. Slobodchikoff, *Concepts of Species,*" *Systematic Zoology* 26(1977): 96–98, and "Classifications, Historical Narratives, and Hypotheses," *Systematic Zoology* 27(1978): 365–69; N. I. Platnick and E. S. Gaffney, "Systematics: A Popperian Perspective," *Systematic Zoology* 26(1977): 360–65, "Evolutionary Biology: A Popperian Perspective," *Systematic Zoology* 27(1978): 137–41, and "Systematics and the Popperian Paradigm," *Systematic Zoology* 27(1978): 381–88; D. E. Rosen, "Darwin's Demon," *Systematic Zoology* 27(1978): 370–73.

62. Bertalanffy, *Problems of Life,* p. 89. **[36]**

63. In S. Tax, ed., *Evolution After Darwin (I): The Evolution of Life* (Chicago: University of Chicago Press, 1960), p. 385.

64. K. R. Popper, *Conjectures and Refutations: The Growth of Scientific Knowledge* (London: Routledge, 1963), and *The Logic of Scientific Discovery* (New York: Harper & Row, 1968 [1935]).

65. B. Rensch, *Biophilosophy,* trans. C. A. M. Sym (New York: Columbia University Press, 1971 [1947]).

66. M. L. Cody, "Optimization in Ecology," *Science* 183(1974): 1156–64.

67. D. L. Hull, *Philosophy of Biological Science* (Englewood Cliffs, N.J.: Prentice-Hall, 1974).

68. K. R. Popper, "Evolution," *New Scientist* 87(1980): 611.

69. D. J. Merrell, "Selective Mating in *Drosophila melanogaster,*" *Genetics* 34(1949): 370–89, and "Selective Mating as a Cause of Gene Frequency Changes in Laboratory Populations of *D. melanogaster,*" *Evolution* 7(1953): 287–96.

70. M. Bastock and A. Manning, "The Courtship of *Drosophila melanogaster,*" *Behaviour* 8(1955): 85–111; M. Bastock, "A Gene Mutation which Changes a Behavior Pattern," *Evolution* 10(1956): 421–39.

71. A. Weismann, *The Evolution Theory,* vol. 1, trans. J. A. Thomson and M. R. Thomson (London: Edward Arnold, 1904).

72. See especially, the commentary by R. B. Taylor, "Lamarckist Revival in Immunology," *Nature* 286(1980): 837–38, and the unsigned critique in *Nature,* 289(1981): 631–32.

73. J. B. Lamarck, *Zoological Philosophy,* trans. H. Elliot (New York: Hafner, 1963 [1809]), p. 114.

74. See H. G. Cannon, "What Lamarck Really Said," *Proceedings of the Linnean Society of London* 168(1955): 70–87, and *Lamarck and Modern Genetics* (Manchester: University of Manchester Press, 1959).

75. Darwin, *Origin,* p. 215. **[2]**

76. Ibid.

77. Ibid., p. 216.

78. J. M. Baldwin, *Mental Development in the Child and the Race: Methods and Processes* (New York: Macmillan, 1895), "Heredity and Instinct: Discussions (Revised) Following Professor C. Lloyd Morgan Before the New York Academy of Sciences, January 31, 1896," *Science* 3(1896): 438–41, 558–61, "On Criticisms of Organic Selection," *Science* 4(1896): 724–27, "A

New Factor in Evolution," *American Naturalist* 30(1896): 441–51, 536–53, and "Organic Selection," *Nature* 55(1897): 555–58; C. Lloyd Morgan, "On Modification and Variation," *Science* 4(1896): 733–40, and *Animal Behaviour,* 2d ed. (London: Arnold, 1908 [1900]); H. F. Osborn, "Discussion Following Presentation of Paper by A. Graf, 'The Problem of the Transmission of Acquired Characters,' " *Transactions of the New York Academy of Sciences* 15(1896): 141–43, "Ontogenetic and Phylogenetic Variation," *Science* 4(1896): 786–89, and "The Limits of Organic Selection," *American Naturalist* 31(1897): 941–51.

79. G. G. Simpson, "The Baldwin Effect," *Evolution* 7(1953): 116.

80. C. H. Waddington, *New Patterns in Genetics and Development* (New York: Columbia University Press, 1962).

81. A. Roe and G. G. Simpson, eds., *Behavior and Evolution* (New Haven: Yale University Press, 1958).

82. C. H. Waddington, *The Evolution of an Evolutionist* (Ithaca: Cornell University Press, 1975), p. 170.

83. Reviewed in Corning (forthcoming). See also Huxley, *Evolution;* W. H. Thorpe, "The Evolutionary Significance of Habitat Selection," *The Journal of Animal Ecology* 14(1945): 67–70; Roe and Simpson, *Behavior and Evolution;* R. F. Ewer, "Natural Selection and Neoteny," *Acta Biotheoretica* 13(1960): 161–84; E. Mayr, *Animal Species and Evolution* (Cambridge, Mass.: Harvard University Press, 1963), and *Populations, Species, and Evolution* (Cambridge, Mass.: Harvard University Press, 1970); C. H. Waddington, "Canalization of Development and the Inheritance of Acquired Characters," *Nature* 150(1942): 563–65, "Selection of the Genetic Basis for an Acquired Character," *Nature* 169(1952): 169–278, *The Strategy of the Genes: A Discussion of Some Aspects of Theoretical Biology* (New York: Macmillan, 1957), and *The Nature of Life* (New York: Harper & Row, 1961); A. C. Hardy, *The Living Stream: Evolution and Man* (New York: Harper & Row, 1965); L. L. Whyte, *Internal Factors in Evolution* (New York: Braziller, 1965); R. A. Hinde, *Animal Behaviour: A Synthesis of Ethology and Comparative Psychology,* 2d ed. (New York: McGraw-Hill, 1970); P. A. Corning, "Politics and the Evolutionary Process," in T. Dobzhansky et al., eds., *Evolutionary Biology,* vol. VII (New York: Plenum, 1974); Wilson, *Sociobiology;* J. Piaget, *Behavior and Evolution* (New York: Random House, 1978). **[34, 35]**

84. E. Mayr, "The Emergence of Evolutionary Novelties," in Tax, *Evolution After Darwin,* 2: 371, 377–78. **[63]**

85. D. Lack, *Darwin's Finches* (New York: Harper & Row, 1961 [1947]).

86. P. T. Boag and P. R. Grant, "Heritability of External Morphology in Darwin's Finches," *Nature* 274(1978): 793–94; B. R. Grant and P. R. Grant, "Darwin's Finches: Population Variation and Sympatric Speciation," *Proceedings of National Academy of Sciences* 76(1979): 2359–63.

87. Stebbins, *Basis of Progressive Evolution.* **[36]**

88. The hierarchical nature of biological organization has been recognized by numerous theorists (the full ramifications of the insight have yet to be explored, however). Especially good discussions can be found in B. Rensch, *Evolution Above the Species Level* (New York: Columbia University Press, 1960 [1947]); Wright, *Evolution;* Stebbins, *Basis of Progressive Evolution;* I. Franklin and R. C. Lewontin, "Is the Gene the Unit of Selection?" *Genetics* 65(1970): 707–34; J. H. Milsun, "The Hierarchical Basis for General Living Systems," in *Trends in General Systems Theory,* ed. G. J. Kliv (New York: Wiley-Interscience, 1972); Salthe, "Problems of Macroevolution"; Pattee, *Hierarchy Theory;* R. Riedl, *Order in Living Organisms: A Systems Analysis of Evolution* (New York: Wiley, 1978 [1975]); J. G. Miller, *Living Systems* (New York: McGraw-Hill, 1978). **[14, 35, 36]**

89. See D'A. W. Thompson, *On Growth and Form,* 2d ed. (Cambridge: Cambridge University Press, 1942 [1917]); R. McN. Alexander, *Animal Mechanics* (Seattle: University of Washington Press, 1968); K. S. Schmidt-Nielsen, *How Animals Work* (Cambridge: Cambridge University Press, 1972); T. McMahon, "Size and Shape in Biology," *Science* 179(1973): 1201–04.

90. J. C. Fentress, ed., *Simpler Networks and Behavior* (Sunderland, Mass.: Sinauer, 1976);

J. L. Spudich and D. E. Koshland, Jr., "Non Genetic Individuality: Chance in the Single Cell," *Nature* 262(1976): 467–71.

91. Thompson, *Growth and Form.* See also C. F. A. Pantin, "Organic Design," *The Advancement of Science* 8(1951): 138–50; Alexander, *Animal Mechanics;* Schmidt-Nielsen, *How Animals Work;* C. R. Taylor et al., "Running Up and Down Hills: Some Consequences of Size," *Science* 178(1972): 1096–97; McMahon, "Size and Shape." **[89]**

92. B. Rensch, "The Laws of Evolution," in Tax, *Evolution After Darwin.* **[63]**

93. For more detailed treatment, see Corning (forthcoming).

94. A. Rosenbluth et al., "Behavior, Purpose and Teleology," *Philosophy of Science* 10(1943): 18–24; C. S. Prittendrigh, "Adaptation, Natural Selection and Behavior," in Roe and Simpson, *Behavior and Evolution;* G. G. Simpson, "Behavior and Evolution," in Roe and Simpson, *Behavior and Evolution;* G. C. Williams, *Adaptation and Natural Selection: A Critique of Some Current Evolutionary Thought* (Princeton: Princeton University Press, 1966); C. H. Waddington, ed., *Towards a Theoretical Biology,* vol. I (Chicago: Aldine, 1968); Stebbins, *Basis of Progressive Evolution;* F. J. Ayala, "Teleological Explanations in Evolutionary Biology," *Philosophy of Science* 37(1970): 1–15; Monod, *Chance and Necessity;* Ayala and Dobzhansky, *Studies in Philosophy of Biology;* F. Jacob, *The Logic of Living Systems: A History of Heredity,* trans. B. E. Spillmann (London: Allen Lane, 1974); E. Mayr, "Teleological and Teleonomic: A New Analysis," in *Boston Studies in the Philosophy of Science,* ed. R. S. Cohen and M. W. Wartofsky, vol. XIV (Boston: D. Reidel, 1974); W. H. Thorpe, *Purpose in a World of Chance: A Biologist's View* (Oxford: Oxford University Press, 1978). **[36]**

95. Jukes, "Silent Nucleotide Substitutions"; Ho and Saunders, "Beyond neo-Darwinism"; Gould, "The Promise of Paleobiology," and "Evolutionary Biology of Restraint." **[41, 44]**

96. N. Tinbergen, *Social Behavior in Animals* (London: Methuen, 1965 [1953]), p. 522.

97. G. K. Zipf, *Human Behaviour and the Principle of Least Effort: An Introduction to Human Ecology* (Cambridge, Mass.: Addison-Wesley, 1949); W. J. Bock and G. von Wahlert, "Adaptation and the Form-Function Complex," *Evolution* 19(1965): 269–99.

98. E.g., Williams, *Adaptation;* Monod, *Chance and Necessity;* M. T. Ghiselin, *The Economy of Nature and the Evolution of Sex* (Berkeley: University of California Press, 1974); Richard Dawkins, *The Selfish Gene* (New York: Oxford University Press, 1976).

99. See also M. Polanyi, "Life's Irreducible Structure," *Science* 160(1968): 1308–12; A. Koestler and J. R. Smythies, eds., *Beyond Reductionism: New Perspectives in the Life Sciences* (London: Hutchinson, 1969); Ayala and Dobzhansky, *Studies in Philosophy of Biology.* **[9]**

100. See especially N. Wiener, *Cybernetics* (New York: Wiley, 1948), and *The Human Use of Human Beings; Cybernetics and Society* (Boston: Houghton Mifflin, 1950); W. R. Ashby, *Design for a Brain* (New York: Wiley, 1952), and *An Introduction to Cybernetics* (New York: Wiley, 1956); Bertalanffy, *Problems of Life;* D. K. Stanley-Jones, *The Kybernetics of Natural Systems: A Study in Patterns of Control* (New York: Pergamon, 1960); Waddington, *Towards a Theoretical Biology;* H. T. Milhorn, Jr., *An Application of Control Theory to Physiological Systems* (Philadelphia: Saunders, 1966); Weiss, "The Living System"; P. A. Weiss et al., *Hierarchically Organized Systems in Theory and Practice* (New York: Hafner, 1971); D. J. McFarland, *Feedback Mechanisms in Animal Behaviour* (New York: Academic Press, 1971); Pattee, *Hierarchy Theory;* W. T. Powers, "Feedback: Beyond Behaviorism," *Science* 179(1973): 351–56, *Behavior: The Control of Perception* (Chicago: Aldine, 1973), and "Quantitative Analysis of Purposive Systems: Some Spadework at the Foundations of Scientific Psychology," *Psychological Review* 85(1978): 417–35; Miller, *Living Systems;* R. Riedl, "A Systems-Analytical Approach to Macro-Evolutionary Phenomena," *Quarterly Review of Biology* 52(1977): 351–70, and *Order in Living Things;* L. Stark, *Neurological Control Systems: Studies in Bioengineering* (New York: Plenum, 1968); D. M. McKay, *Information, Mechanism and Meaning* (Cambridge, Mass.: MIT Press, 1969). See also the multivolume series *Control and Dynamic Systems* (New York: Academic Press, 1964–1981). **[36, 80, 88, 94]**

101. Mayr, "Teleological and Teleonomic." **[94]**

102. See especially M. C. Wittrock, ed., *The Brain and Psychology* (New York: Academic Press, 1980). Also see W. Penfield, *Mystery of the Mind* (Princeton: Princeton University Press, 1975); G. Globus et al., eds., *Consciousness and the Brain* (New York: Plenum, 1976); P. A. Buser and A. Rouguel-Buser, eds., *Cerebral Correlates of Conscious Experience* (New York: Elsevier, 1978); R. Restak, *Brain: The Last Frontier* (New York: Doubleday, 1979); G. Wolfstenholme and M. O'Conner, eds., *Brain and Mind,* Ciba Foundation Symposia, vol. 69 (New York: Elsevier, 1979); D. McFadden, ed., *Neural Mechanisms in Behavior: A Texas Symposium* (New York: Springer, 1980); A. Routtenberg, ed., *Biology of Facets of Brain Stimulation Reward* (New York: Academic Press, 1980); Y. Tsukada and B. W. Agranoff, eds., *Neurobiological Basis of Learning and Memory,* Second Taniguchi Symposium of Brain Sciences, Otsu, Japan, 1978 (New York: Wiley, 1980); T. S. Wallstein, ed., *Cognitive Processes in Choice and Decision Behavior* (Hillsdale, N.J.: Erlbaum, 1980).

103. M. Maruyama, "The Second Cybernetics: Deviation-Amplifying Mutual Causal Processes," *American Scientist* 51(1963): 164–79; J. Milsum, ed., *Positive Feedback; A General Systems Approach to Positive/Negative Feedback and Mutual Causality* (New York: Pergamon, 1968).

104. Waddington, *Towards Theoretical Biology.* **[94]**

105. Dobzhansky, *Evolution,* pp. 95–96. **[51]**

106. S. Wright, "Biology and the Philosophy of Science," in *Process and Divinity: The Hartshorne Festschrift,* ed. W. R. Reese and E. Freeman (LaSalle, Ill.: Open Court, 1964), p. 108.

107. Cf. Alexander and Borgia, "Group Selection"; P. J. Richerson and R. Boyd, "A Dual Inheritance Model of Human Evolutionary Process I: Basic Postulates and a Simple Model," *Journal of Social and Biological Structures* 1(1978): 127–54; Wilson, *Natural Selection of Populations;* Plotkin and Olding-Smee, "Multiple-Level Model." **[36, 38]**

108. J. P. Scott, "Social Genetics," *Behavior Genetics* 7(1977): 327–46.

109. For example, see L. Kavanagh, "Invasion of the Forest by an African Savannah Monkey," *Behaviour* 73(1980): 238–60.

110. E. Mayr, "Cause and Effect in Biology," in *Cause and Effect,* ed. D. Lerner (New York: Free Press, 1965).

111. In C. J. Lumsden and E. O. Wilson, *Genes, Mind and Culture: The Co-Evolutionary Process* (Cambridge, Mass.: Harvard University Press, 1981). However, Wilson's views have been modified.

112. W. C. McGrew et al., "Chimpanzees, Tools, and Termites: Cross-Cultural Comparisons of Senegal, Tanzania, and Rio Muni," *Man* 14(1979): 185–214; Bonner, *Evolution of Culture* (Princeton: Princeton University Press, 1980); P. C. Mundinger, "Animal Cultures and a General Theory of Cultural Evolution," *Ethology and Sociobiology* 1(1980): 183–223. J. D. Baldwin and J. I. Baldwin, *Beyond Sociobiology* (New York: Elsevier, 1981) reviews studies of cultural differences in leadership styles, intragroup aggression, group size, tool use, migration patterns, etc., in chimpanzees, langurs, spider monkeys, rhesus macaques, and baboons. L. B. Jorde and J. N. Spuhler, "A Statistical Analysis of Selected Aspects of Primate Demography, Ecology and Social Behavior," *Journal of Anthropological Research* 30(1974): 199–224.

113. E. Curio et al., "Cultural Transmission of Enemy Recognition," *Science* 202(1978): 899–901; D. Premack et al., "Paper-Marking Test for Chimpanzee," *Science* 202(1978): 903–05.

114. For early evidence of animal "intelligence," see Darwin, *Descent;* G. J. Romanes, *Mental Evolution in Animals* (London: Kegan Paul, Trench, 1883); C. Lloyd Morgan, *Animal Life and Intelligence* (Boston: Ginn, 1891), *Habit and Instinct* (London: Arnold, 1896), and *Animal Behaviour;* Thorndike, *Animal Intelligence;* W. Köhler, *The Mentality of Apes* (New York:

Harcourt, 1925); O. L. Tinklepaugh, "An Experimental Study of Representative Factors in Monkeys," *Journal of Comparative Psychology* 8(1928): 197–236; H. W. Nissen, *A Field Study of the Chimpanzee; Observations of Chimpanzee Behavior in Western French Guinea* (Baltimore: Johns Hopkins University Press, 1931), and "Primate Psychology," in *Encyclopedia of Psychology,* ed. P. L. Harriman (New York: Citadel, 1946); I. Krechevsky, " 'Hypotheses' in Rats," *Psychological Review* 39(1932): 516–32; E. C. Tolman, *Purposive Behavior in Animals and Men* (New York: Century, 1932), and "Cognitive Maps in Animals and Man," *Psychological Review* 55(1948): 189–208; R. M. Yerkes and B. W. Learned, *Chimpanzee Intelligence and Its Vocal Expression* (Baltimore: Williams & Wilkins, 1925); D. O. Hebb, *The Organization of Behavior* (New York: Wiley, 1949); I. A. Hallowell, "Self, Society, and Culture in Phylogenetic Perspective," in Tax, *Evolution After Darwin.* For more recent evidence, see W. H. Thorpe, *Learning and Instinct in Animals,* 2d ed. (Cambridge, Mass.: Harvard University Press, 1963); D. M. Rumbaugh, "Learning Skills of Anthropoids," in *Primate Behavior: Developments in Field and Laboratory Research,* ed. L. A. Rosenblum (New York: Academic Press, 1970); E. W. Menzel, Jr., "Spontaneous Invention of Ladders in a Group of Young Chimpanzees," *Folia Primatalogica* 17(1972): 87–106; D. L. Mech, *The Wolf: The Ecology and Behavior of an Endangered Species* (Garden City, N.Y.: Natural History Press,1970); B. B. Beck, "Baboons, Chimpanzees, and Tools," *Journal of Human Evolution* 3(1974): 509–16, "Primate Tool Behavior," in *Primate Socioecology and Psychology,* ed. R. H. Tuttle (The Hague: Mouton, 1975), and *Animal Tool Behavior: The Use and Manufacture of Tools by Animals* (New York: Garland, 1980); R. H. Tuttle, ed., *Primate Functional Morphology and Evolution* (The Hague: Mouton, 1975); Wilson, *Sociobiology;* D. R. Griffin, "A Possible Window on the Minds of Animals," *American Scientist* 64(1976): 530–35, *The Question of Animal Awareness: Evolutionary Continuity of Mental Experience* (New York: Rockefeller University Press, 1976), and "Prospects for a Cognitive Ethology," *Behavioral and Brain Sciences* 4(1978): 527–38; D. Premack, *Intelligence in Ape and Man* (Hillsdale, N.J.: Erlbaum, 1976), and "Language and Intelligence in Ape and Man," *American Scientist* 64(1976): 674–83; D. Premack and G. Woodruff, "Does the Chimpanzee Have a Theory of Mind?" *Behavioral and Brain Sciences* 4(1978): 515–26, and "Chimpanzee Problem-Solving: A Test for Comprehension," *Science* 202(1978): 532–35; D. Premack, "Paper-Marking Test for Chimpanzee"; Curio, "Cultural Transmission"; S. H. Hulse et al., *Cognitive Processes in Animal Behavior* (Hillsdale, N.J.: Erlbaum, 1978); W. C. McGrew and C. E. G. Tutin, "Evidence for a Social Custom in Wild Chimpanzees?" *Man* 13(1978): 234–51; J. Dalgish and S. Anderson, "A Field Experiment on Learning by Raccoons," *Journal of Mammalogy* 60(1979): 620–22; D. W. Macdonald, " 'Helpers' in Fox Society," *Nature* 282(1979): 69–71; M. Bekoff and M. C. Wells, "The Social Ecology of Coyotes," *Scientific American* 242, 4(1980): 130–48; Bonner, *Evolution of Culture;* D. J. Gillan et al., "Reasoning in the Chimpanzee: I. Analogical Reasoning," *Journal of Experimental Psychology: Animal Behavior Processes* 7(1981): 1–17. **[23, 43, 53, 63, 78, 113]**

115. Thorpe, "Evolutionary Significance of Habitat"; J. W. S. Pringle, "On the Parallel Between Learning and Evolution," *Behaviour* 3(1951): 174–215; Hinde, *Animal Behaviour;* Corning, "Politics and Evolutionary Process"; P. J. Darlington, "Group Selection, Altruism, Reinforcement, and Throwing in Human Evolution," *Proceedings of the National Academy of Sciences* 72(1975): 3748–52; Piaget, *Behavior and Evolution;* B. F. Skinner, "Selection by Consequences," *Science* 213(1981): 501–04. **[83]**

116. J. S. Jones, "Can Genes Choose Habitats?" *Nature* 286(1980): 757–58.

117. W. H. Thorpe and F. G. W. Jones, "Olfactory Conditioning in a Parasitic Insect and Its Relation to the Problem of Host Selection," *Proceedings of the Royal Society* 124(1937): 56–81; Schneirla, "Modifiability in Insect Behavior," and "Interrelationship of the 'Innate' and 'Acquired' in Instinctive Behavior," in *L'Instinct dans le Comportement des Animaux et de l'Homme,* ed. M. Autouri et al. (Paris: Masson, 1956); Menzel, "Behavioral Access to Memory

in Bees"; R. Menzel et al., "Learning and Memory in the Honeybee," in *Experimental Analysis of Insect Behavior,* ed. L. Barton-Brown (New York: Springer, 1975); Menzel and Erber, "Learning and Memory"; Bonner, *Evolution of Culture;* Jaisson, "Parental Relationships in Hymenoptera"; Acevas Piña and Quinn, "Learning in *Drosophila* Larvae."

118. Köhler, *Mentality of Apes;* Yerkes and Learned, *Chimpanzee Intelligence;* E. C. Tolman, "Cognitive Maps in Animals and Man," *Psychological Review* 55(1948): 189–208, and *Purposive Behavior;* N. R. F. Maier and T. C. Schneirla, *Principles of Animal Psychology* (New York: McGraw-Hill, 1935); M. P. Crawford, "The Coöperative Solving of Problems by Young Chimpanzees," *Comparative Psychology Monographs* (no. 68) 14, 2(1937): 1–88; Hebb, *Organization of Behavior;* J. A. Nevin, "Decision Theory in Studies of Discrimination in Animals," *Science* 150(1965): 1057; R. B. Zajonc, *Animal Social Psychology: A Reader of Experimental Studies* (New York: Wiley, 1969); McFarland, *Feedback Mechanisms;* Menzel, "Spontaneous Invention," and "Chimpanzee Spatial Memory Organization," *Science* 182(1973): 943–45; M. E. P. Seligman and J. L. Hager, eds., *Biological Boundaries of Learning* (New York: Appleton, 1972); R. A. Hinde and J. Stevenson-Hinde, eds., *Constraints on Learning: Limitations and Predispositions* (New York: Academic Press, 1973); H. J. Jerison, *The Evolution of the Brain and Intelligence* (New York: Academic Press, 1973); N. J. MacKintosh, *The Psychology of Animal Learning* (New York: Academic Press, 1974); Brown, *Evolution of Behavior;* Tuttle, *Primate Socioecology and Psychology;* Wilson, *Sociobiology;* P. P. G. Bateson and R. A. Hinde, *Growing Points in Ethology* (Cambridge: Cambridge University Press, 1976); G. Bicker and H. C. Spatz, "Maze-Learning Ability of *Drosophila melanogaster,*" *Nature* 260(1976): 371; Premack, *Intelligence in Ape and Man,* and "Language and Intelligence"; S. Chevalier-Skolnikoff and F. E. Poirier, eds., *Primate Bio-Social Development: Biological, Social, and Ecological Determinants* (New York: Garland, 1977); Griffin, "A Possible Window," and *Question of Animal Awareness;* Hulse, *Cognitive Processes;* J. R. Krebs and N. B. Davies, *Behavioral Ecology: An Evolutionary Approach* (Sunderland, Mass.: Sinauer, 1978); Premack and Woodruff, "Does the Chimpanzee Have a Theory of Mind?" (and peer commentaries); Crook, *Evolution of Human Consciousness;* B. Heinrich, *Bumble-Bee Economics* (Cambridge, Mass.: Harvard University Press, 1980); Gillan, "Reasoning in the Chimpanzee." **[43, 100, 102, 114]**

119. See G. P. Baerends, "The Functional Organization of Behaviour," *Animal Behaviour* 24(1976): 726–38.

120. See Tinbergen, *Study of Instinct,* and "The Hierarchical Organization of Nervous Mechanisms Underlying Instinctive Behaviour," *Symposia of the Society for Experimental Biology* 4(1950): 305–12. Also P. A. Weiss, "Self-Differentiation of the Basic Patterns of Coordination," *Comparative Psychological Monographs* 17(1941): 1–96. **[36]**

121. Described in Tinbergen, *Study of Instinct.* **[36]**

122. Among the numerous references, see especially J. M. Emlen, "The Role of Time and Energy in Food Preference," *American Naturalist* 100(1966): 611–17; R. H. MacArthur and E. Pianka, "On Optional Use of a Patchy Environment," *American Naturalist* 100(1966): 603–09; D. J. Rapport, "An Optimization Model of Food Selection," *American Naturalist* 105(1971): 575–87; T. W. Schoenher, "Theory of Feeding Strategies," *Annual Review of Ecology and Systematics* 2(1971): 369–404; S. A. Altmann, "Baboons; Space, Time and Energy," *American Zoologist* 14(1974): 221–48; Cody, "Optimization"; J. Maynard Smith, *Models in Ecology* (Cambridge: Cambridge University Press, 1974), "The Theory of Games and the Evolution of Animal Conflicts," *Journal of Theoretical Biology* 47(1974): 209–21, "Evolution and the Theory of Games," *American Scientist* 64(1976): 41–45, "The Evolution of Behavior," *Scientific American* 239, 3(1978): 176–92, and "Optimization Theory in Evolution," *Annual Review of Ecology and Systematics* 9(1978): 31–56; G. A. Parker, "Assessment Strategy and the Evolution of Fighting Behavior," *Journal of Theoretical Biology* 47(1974): 223–43; E. L. Charnov, "Optimal Foraging, The Marginal Value Theorem," *Theoretical Population Biology* 9(1976): 129–36; G. A. Parker and R. A. Stuart, "Animal Behaviour as a Strategy Optimizer: The Evolution of Resource Assessment

Strategies and Optimal Emigration Thresholds," *American Naturalist* 110(1976): 1055–76; R. H. McCleery, "On Satiation Curves," *Animal Behaviour* 25(1977): 1005–15; D. J. McFarland, "Decision Making in Animals," *Nature* 269(1977): 15–21; G. H. Pyke et al., "Optimal Foraging: A Selective Review of Theory and Tests," *Quarterly Review of Biology* 52(1977): 137–54; T. R. E. Southwood, "Habitat, the Templet for Ecological Strategies?" *Journal of Animal Ecology* 46(1977): 337–69; G. L. Smutz, "Interrelations Between Predators, Prey, and Their Environments," *BioScience* 28(1978): 316–20; Heinrich, *Bumble-Bee Economics.* **[66, 118]**

123. McFarland, "Decision Making in Animals." McFarland also emphasizes that not all animals carry out such analyses in a cognitive fashion. Needless to say, it is more likely to occur in higher mammals. **[122]**

124. J. L. Gould, "Behavioral Programming in Honeybees," *Behavioral and Brain Sciences* 4(1978): 572–73.

125. K. von Frisch, *The Dance Language and Orientation of Bees,* trans. L. Chadwick (Cambridge, Mass.: Harvard University Press, 1967).

126. J. F. Reinhardt, "Responses of Honeybees to Alfalfa Flowers," *American Naturalist* 86(1952): 257–75; P. Pankiw, "Studies of Honeybees on Alfalfa Flowers," *Journal of Apicultural Research* 6(1967): 105–12.

127. For example, see J. O'Keefe and L. Nadel, *The Hippocampus as a Cognitive Map* (Oxford: Clarendon Press, 1978). Especially striking is the evidence for self-awareness in primates. See G. G. Gallup, Jr., "Self-Recognition in Primates: A Comparative Approach to the Bidirectional Properties of Consciousness," *American Psychologist* 32(1977): 329–38, and "Self-Awareness in Primates," *American Scientist* 64(1979): 417–19; G. G. Gallup, Jr., et al., "A Mirror for the Mind of Man, or Will the Chimpanzee Create an Identity Crisis for *Homo sapiens?*" *Journal of Human Evolution* 6(1977): 303–13; Griffin, "A Possible Window," and *Question of Animal Awareness.* **[114]**

128. St. G. J. Mivart, *On the Genesis of Species* (New York: Appleton, 1871).

129. H. de Vries, *Mutation Theory,* 2 vols., trans. J. B. Farmer and A. D. Darbishire (Chicago: Open Court, 1909–1910 [1901–1903]).

130. J. C. Willis, *Ape and Area: A Study in Geographic Distribution and Origin of Species* (Cambridge: Cambridge University Press, 1922), and *The Course of Evolution* (Cambridge: Cambridge University Press, 1940); O. H. Schindewolf, *Grundfragen der Palaontologie* (Stuttgart: Schweizerbart, 1950); R. B. Goldschmidt, *The Material Basis of Evolution* (New Haven: Yale University Press, 1940), "Egotype, Ecospecies, and Macroevolution," *Experientia* 4(1948): 465–72, and "Evolution as Viewed by One Geneticist," *American Scientist* 40(1952): 84–98.

131. Goldschmidt, "Evolution Viewed by One Geneticist," p. 93. **[130]**

132. Mayr, *Animal Species.* For rebuttals of Goldschmidt, see T. Dobzhansky, *Genetics and the Origin of Species,* 3rd ed., rev. (New York: Columbia University Press,1951 [1937]), and *Genetics of the Evolutionary Process* (New York: Columbia University Press, 1970). **[83]**

133. Lack, *Darwin's Finches.* **[85]**

134. N. Eldredge, "The Allopatric Model and Phylogeny in Paleozoic Invertebrates," *Evolution* 25(1971): 156–67; Eldredge and Gould, "Punctuated Equilibria"; Gould and Eldredge, "Punctuated Equilibria."

135. Gould and Eldredge, "Punctuated Equilibria," p. 116. **[7]**

136. Mayr, *Animal Species,* p. 621. **[83]**

137. See ibid.; Dobzhansky, *Evolution;* E. Wiley, "The Evolutionary Species Concept Reconsidered," *Systematic Zoology* 27(1978): 17–27. **[51]**

138. Mayr, *Animal Species,* pp. 483–84. **[83]**

139. Some evolutionists, such as Mayr (*Animal Species* and *Populations, Species, and Evolution*), think geography is all-important. Others, such as Dobzhansky (*Evolution*), and Wright (*Evolution and the Genetics of Populations,* vols. 3 and 4), are more pluralistic. **[35, 51]**

140. Dobzhansky, *Evolution,* pp. 16, 37, 129. **[51]**

141. S. Wright, "Evolution in a Mendelian Population," *Anatomical Record* 44(1929): 287, "Evolution in Mendelian Populations," *Genetics* 16(1931): 97–159, "The Roles of Mutation in Breeding, Crossbreeding, and Selection in Evolution," *Proceedings of the VI International Congress on Genetics* 1(1932): 356–66, "Tempo and Mode in Evolution: A Critical Review," *Ecology* 26(1945): 415–19, and "Population Structure in Evolution," *Proceedings of the American Philosophical Society* 93(1949): 471–78.

142. Dobzhansky, *Genetics and Origin of Species;* S. Scarr-Salapatek, "An Evolutionary Perspective on Infant Intelligence: Species Patterns and Individual Variations," in *Origins of Intelligence: Infancy and Early Childhood,* ed. M. Lewis (New York: Plenum, 1976). See also Salthe, "Problems of Macroevolution"; D. Layzer, "A Macroscopic Approach to Population Genetics," *Journal of Theoretical Biology* 73(1978): 769–88. **[14, 34]**

143. Cf. Stanley's "Species selection" in "A Theory of Evolution," and *Macroevolution.* Also see E. Leigh, "How Does Selection Reconcile Individual Advantage with the Good of the Group," *Proceedings of the National Academy of Sciences* 74(1977): 4542–46; Wilson, *Natural Selection of Populations.* **[14, 38]**

144. E. Mayr, "Change of Genetic Endowment and Evolution," in *Evolution as a Process,* ed. J. S. Huxley (London: Allen and Unwin, 1975). Also *Animal Species,* and *Populations, Species, and Evolution.* **[83]**

145. Mayr, *Animal Species,* p. 530. **[83]**

146. J. B. S. Haldane, *The Causes of Evolution* (New York: Harper & Row, 1932); G. G. Simpson, *Tempo and Mode in Evolution* (New York: Columbia University Press, 1944), and *The Major Features of Evolution* (New York: Columbia University Press, 1953).

147. Wright, *Evolution and Genetics of Populations,* I: 468, II: 509. **[35]**

148. Still the classic report on this phenomenon is F. B. Livingstone, "Anthropological Implications of Sickle Cell Gene Distributed in West Africa," *American Anthropologist* 60(1958): 533–62.

149. Quoted in Rosen, "Darwin's Demon," p. 371. **[61]**

150. D. G. Freedman, *Human Sociobiology: A Holistic Approach* (New York: Free Press, 1979).

151. E.g., Lewontin, *Genetic Basis of Evolutionary Change;* Johnson, *Introduction to Natural Selection;* J. A. Endler, *Geographic Variation, Speciation, and Clines* (Princeton: Princeton University Press, 1977). **[35]**

152. Dobzhansky, *Evolution,* p. 256. **[51]**

153. This is still contentious, but see Monod, *Chance and Necessity.* **[37]**

154. Ford, *Ecological Genetics.* **[37]**

155. Wright, "Gene and Organism"; see also J. N. Thompson, Jr., "Quantitative Variation and Gene Number," *Nature* 258(1975): 665–68; A. Vetta, "Evidence for Polygenes," *Nature* 261(1976): 525–26. **[36]**

156. Jacob and Monod, "Genetic Regulatory Mechanisms." See also Miller and Reznikoff, *Operon.*

157. Britten and Davidson, "Gene Regulation," and "Repetitive and Non-Repetitive DNA Sequences and a Speculation on the Origins of Evolutionary Novelty," *Quarterly Review of Biology* 46(1971): 111–38; E. H. Davidson and R. J. Britten, "Note on the Control of Gene Expression During Development," *Journal of Theoretical Biology* 32(1971): 123–30, "Organization, Transcription and Regulation in the Animal Genome," *Quarterly Review of Biology* 48(1973): 565–613, and "Regulation of Gene Expression: Possible Role of Repetitive Sequences," *Science* 204(1979): 1052–59; E. H. Davidson et al., "Sequence Organization in Animal DNA and a Speculation on hnRNA as a Coordinate Regulatory Transcript," *Developmental Biology* 55(1977): 69–84. For specific evidence of regulator gene control, see M.-C. King and A. C. Wilson, "Evolutions at Two Levels in Humans and Chimpanzees," *Science* 188(1975): 107–16; J. W. Valentine and C. A. Campbell, "Genetic Regulation and the Fossil Record," *American Scientist* 63(1975): 673–80. **[37]**

158. See G. L. Bush, "Modes of Animal Speciation," *Annual Review of Ecology and Systematics* 6(1975): 339–64; G. L. Bush et al., "Rapid Speciation and Chromosomal Evolution in Mammals," *Proceedings of the National Academy of Sciences* 74(1977): 3942–46; Nevers and Saedler, "Transposable Genetic Elements"; M. J. D. White, *Modes of Speciation* (San Francisco: Freeman, 1941); Stanley, *Macroevolution;* G. D. Carr, "Experimental Evidence for Saltational Chromosome Evolution in *Cylacadenia pauciflora* gray (Asteraceae)," *Heredity* 45(1980): 107–12; Cohen and Shapiro, "Transposable Genetic Elements." **[35, 38]**

159. E. F. Keller, "McClintock's Maize," *Science 81* 2(1981): 54–58.

160. E.g., Gould, "Generality and Uniqueness," and "Promise of Paleobiology"; Stanley, *New Evolutionary Timetable.* **[38, 42, 44]**

161. R. F. Johnson and R. K. Selander, "House Sparrows: Rapid Evolution of Races in North America," *Science* 144(1964): 548–50. Also see J. G. Brittnacher et al., "Genetic Differentiation Between Species of the Genus Speyeria (Lepidoptera: nymphalidae)," *Evolution* 32(1978): 199–210.

162. L. W. Alvarez et al., "Extraterrestrial Cause for the Cretaceous-Tertiary Extinction," *Science* 208(1980): 1095–1107; K. J. Hsü, "Terrestrial Catastrophe Caused by Cometary Impact at the End of Cretaceous," *Nature* 285(1980): 201–03; D. A. Russell, "The Mass Extinctions of the Late Mesozoic," *Scientific American* 246, 1(1982): 58–65. See also J. Hsü et al., "Mass Mortality and Its Envirionmental and Evolutionary Consequences," *Science* 216(1982): 249–56.

163. Lewontin and Hubby, "A Molecular Approach"; Hubby and Lewontin, "A Molecular Approach."

164. R. K. Selander, "Genic Variation in Natural Populations," in *Molecular Evolution,* ed. F. J. Ayala (Sunderland, Mass.: Sinauer, 1976).

165. Nei, "Molecular Population Genetics"; Kimura, "Neutral Theory of Molecular Evolution." For a contrary view, see F. J. Ayala, "Biological Evolution," *American Scientist* 62(1974): 692–701. **[41]**

166. P. M. Sheppard, *Natural Selection and Heredity,* 4th ed. (London: Hutchinson, 1975), p. 19.

167. G. G. Simpson, *The Major Features of Evolution;* Rensch, "Evolution Above Species Level"; Mayr, *Animal Species,* and *Populations, Species, and Evolution;* R. E. Leakey and R. Lewin, *Origins* (New York: Dutton, 1977). **[83, 88, 146]**

168. Salthe, "Problems of Macroevolution."

169. White, *Modes of Speciation,* p. 349. **[158]**

170. For critiques of the punctuated equilibrium model, see J. S. Levinton and C. M. Simon, "A Critique of the Punctuated Equilibria Model and Implications for the Detection of Speciation in the Fossil Record," *Systematic Zoology* 29(1980): 130–42; G. L. Stebbins and F. J. Ayala, "Is a New Evolutionary Synthesis Necessary?" *Science* 213 (1981): 967–71. See also the evidence adduced by O. A. Schwartz and K. B. Armitage, "Genetic Variation in Social Mammals: The Marmot Model," *Science* 207 (1980): 665–67.

171. Morgan, *Animal Life,* p. 120. **[114]**

172. Lumsden and Wilson, *Genes, Mind and Culture.* **[111]**

173. E.g., J. N. Anderson, "Ecological Anthropology and Anthropological Ecology," in *Handbook of Social and Cultural Anthropology,* ed. J. J. Honigmann (Chicago: Rand McNally, 1973). See also the "raspberry gene" experiments cited above in notes 69 and 70.

III. A General Theory of Progressive Evolution

1. L. von Bertalanffy, *Problems of Life: An Evaluation of Modern Biological Thought* (New York: Wiley, 1952 [1949]), and *General Systems Theory: Foundations, Development, Application* (New York: Braziller, 1968). See E. P. Odum and H. T. Odum, *Fundamentals of Ecology,*

3rd ed. (Philadelphia: Saunders, 1971); also D. Lerner, "Toward a Communications Theory of Modernization," in *Communications and Political Development,* ed. L. W. Pye (Princeton: Princeton University Press, 1963); L. L. Whyte, *Internal Factors in Evolution* (New York: Braziller, 1965), and *Hierarchical Structures* (New York: Elsevier, 1969); C. H. Waddington, *The Evolution of an Evolutionist* (Ithaca: Cornell University Press, 1975); P. A. Weiss, "The Living System: Determinism Stratified," in *Beyond Reductionism,* ed. A. Koestler and J. R. Smythies (London: Hutchinson, 1969); E. H. Pattee, ed., *Hierarchy Theory* (New York: Braziller, 1973).

2. J. M. Burgers, "Causality and Anticipation," *Science* 189(1975): 194–98.

3. J. Maynard Smith, "The Status of Neo-Darwinism," in *Towards a Theoretical Biology,* ed. C. H. Waddington, vol. II (Chicago: Aldine, 1969), p. 88.

4. Pattee, *Hierarchy Theory,* p. 41. **[1]**

5. M. Ho and P. Saunders, "Beyond neo-Darwinism—an Epigenetic Approach to Evolution," *Journal of Theoretical Biology* 78(1979): 573–91. See also R. M. Khailor, "The Problem of Systematic Organization in Theoretical Biology," *General Systems* 9(1964): 151–57.

6. M. T. Ghiselin, "The Economy of the Body," *American Economic Review* 68 (1978): 233–37.

7. G. G. Simpson, "Behavior and Evolution," in *Behavior and Evolution,* ed. A. Roe and G. G. Simpson (New Haven: Yale University Press, 1958), p. 532.

8. J. R. Krebs and N. B. Davies, *Behavioural Ecology: An Evolutionary Approach* (Sunderland, Mass.: Sinauer, 1978), p. 289.

9. P. J. Richerson, "Ecology and Human Ecology: A Comparison of Theories in the Biological and Social Sciences," *American Ethnologist* 4(1977): 1–25.

10. Bertalanffy, *General Systems Theory.* **[1]**

11. For overviews, see especially J. B. Bury, *The Idea of Progress: An Inquiry into Its Origin and Growth* (London: Macmillan, 1928); C. J. Herrick, "Progressive Evolution," *Science* 104(1946): 469; G. G. Simpson, *The Major Features of Evolution* (New York: Columbia University Press, 1953), and *The Meaning of Evolution,* rev. ed. (New Haven: Yale University Press, 1967); F. J. Teggart, *Theory and Processes of History* (Berkeley: University of California Press, 1962); B. Mazlish, "The Idea of Progress," *Daedalus* 92(1963): 447–61; K. E. Bock, "Theories of Progress and Evolution," in *Sociology and History,* ed. W. J. Cahnman and A. Boskoff (New York: Free Press, 1964); R. A. Nisbet, *Social Change and History: Aspects of the Western Theory of Development* (New York: Oxford University Press, 1969); G. L. Stebbins, *The Basis of Progressive Evolution* (Chapel Hill: University of North Carolina Press, 1969); F. J. Ayala, "The Concept of Biological Progress," in *Studies in the Philosophy of Biology,* ed. F. J. Ayala and T. Dobzhansky (Berkeley: University of California Press, 1974).

12. For example, see P. P. Grassé, *Evolution of Living Organisms: Evidence for a New Theory of Transformation* (New York: Academic Press, 1977 [1973]); also the discussion in E. Boesiger, "Evolutionary Theories After Lamarck and Darwin," in Ayala and Dobzhansky, *Philosophy of Biology.* **[11]**

13. For full discussions of this issue, see J. S. Huxley, *Evolution: The Modern Synthesis* (New York: Harper & Row, 1942); Simpson, *Features of Evolution,* and *Meaning of Evolution;* Ayala, "Biological Progress." **[11]**

14. J.-B. de Lamarck, *Zoological Philosophy* (New York: Hafner, 1963 [1809]). Also see R. W. Burkhardt, Jr., *The Spirit of System: Lamarck and Evolutionary Biology* (Cambridge, Mass.: Harvard University Press, 1977).

15. E.g., H. F. Osborn, "Aristogenesis, The Creative Principle in the Origin of Species," *American Naturalist* 68(1934): 193–235; Waddington, *Evolution of Evolutionist;* J. Piaget, *Behavior and Evolution* (New York: Random House, 1978). **[1]**

16. H. Spencer, "The Development Hypothesis," in *Essays Scientific, Political and Speculative* (New York: Appleton, 1892 [1852]), p. 10, and *First Principles* (London: Watts, 1862), p. 216.

17. For detailed summaries and analyses, see R. L. Carneiro, ed., *The Evolution of Society* (Chicago: University of Chicago Press, 1967), and "Structure, Function, and Equilibrium in the Evolutionism of Herbert Spencer," *Journal of Anthropological Research* 29(1973): 77–95; R. M. Young, "The Development of Herbert Spencer's Concept of Evolution," *Actes du XI Congres Internationale d'Histoire des Sciences* 2(1967): 273–78; A. Andreski, ed., *Herbert Spencer: Structure, Function and Evolution* (New York: Scribner, 1971); J. D. Y. Peel, *Herbert Spencer: The Evolution of a Sociologist* (London: Heinemann, 1971); D. Freeman, "The Evolutionary Theories of Charles Darwin and Herbert Spencer," *Current Anthropology* 15(1974): 211–37; P. A. Corning, "Durkheim and Spencer," *British Journal of Sociology* 33(1982): 359–82.

18. Simpson, *Meaning of Evolution*, p. 242. **[11]**

19. Ayala and Dobzhansky, *Philosophy of Biology*. **[11]**

20. P. R. Ehrlich and P. H. Raven, "Butterflies and Plants: A Study in Coevolution," *Evolution* 18(1964): 586–608.

21. L. W. Alvarez et al., "Extraterrestrial Cause for the Cretaceous-Tertiary Extinction," *Science* 208(1980): 1095–1107; K. J. Hsü, "Terrestrial Catastrophe Caused by Cometary Impact at the End of the Cretaceous," *Nature* 285(1980): 201–03; D. A. Russell, "The Mass Extinctions of the Late Mesozoic," *Scientific American* 246, 1(1982): 58–65.

22. Huxley, *Evolution*. **[13]**

23. Simpson, *Meaning of Evolution*. **[11]**

24. A. J. Lotka, "The Law of Evolution as a Maximal Principle," *Human Biology* 17(1945): 167–94; G. K. Zipf, *Human Behaviour and the Principle of Least Effort: An Introduction to Human Ecology* (Cambridge, Mass.: Addison-Wesley, 1949); Simpson, *Meaning of Evolution*; H. J. Morowitz, *Energy Flow in Biology: Biological Organization as a Problem in Thermal Physics* (New York: Academic Press, 1968); K. S. Schmidt-Nielsen, *How Animals Work* (Cambridge: University Press, 1972). **[11]**

25. I. M. Lerner, *Genetic Homeostasis* (London: Oliver and Boyd, 1954); A. E. Emerson, "Dynamic Homeostasis: A Unifying Principle in Organic, Social, and Ethical Evolution," *Scientific Monthly* 78(1754): 67–85; L. B. Slobodkin, "The Strategy of Evolution," *American Scientist* 52(1964): 342–57; J. A. Wicken, "A Thermodynamic Theory of Evolution," *Journal of Theoretical Biology* 87(1980): 9–23.

26. Huxley, *Evolution*; Stebbins, *Progressive Evolution*. **[11, 13]**

27. Huxley, *Evolution*; J. M. Thoday, "Components of Fitness," *Symposia of the Society for Experimental Biology* 7(1953): 96–113, and "Non-Darwinian 'Evolution' and Biological Progress," *Nature* 255(1975): 675–77. **[13]**

28. M. Kimura, "Natural Selection as the Process of Accumulating Genetic Information in Adaptive Evolution," *Genetic Research* 2(1961): 127–40. See also G. C. Theodoridis and L. Stark, "Information as a Quantitative Criterion of Biospheric Evolution," *Nature* 224(1969): 860–63.

29. E.g., J. von Neuman, *The Theory of Self-Reproducing Automata* (Urbana: University of Illinois Press, 1966).

30. P. T. Saunders and M. W. Ho, "On the Increase in Complexity in Evolution," *Journal of Theoretical Biology* 63(1976): 375–84.

31. D'A. W. Thompson, *On Growth and Form*, 2d ed. (Cambridge: Cambridge University Press, 1942 [1917]); Whyte, *Internal Factors, Aspects of Form* (New York: Elsevier, 1968), and *Hierarchical Structures*; Schmidt-Nielsen, *How Animals Work*; C. R. Taylor et al., "Running Up and Down Hills: Some Consequences of Size," *Science* 178(1972): 1096–97; T. McMahon, "Size and Shape in Biology," *Science* 179(1973): 1201–04; S. J. Gould, *Ontogeny and Phylogeny* (Cambridge, Mass.: Harvard University Press, 1977).

32. H. F. Blum, *Time's Arrow and Evolution* (Princeton: Princeton University Press, 1968 [1951]); C. Grobstein, *The Strategy of Life* (San Francisco: Freeman, 1964); R. Riedl, *Order in Living Organisms: A Systems Analysis of Evolution*, trans. R. P. S. Jeffries (New York: Wiley,

1978 [1975]); F. Jacob, *The Logic of Living Systems: A History of Heredity,* trans. B. E. Spillman (London: Allen Lane, 1974).

33. Stebbins, *Progressive Evolution.* See also Riedl, *Order in Living Organisms.* **[11, 32]**

34. C. Lloyd Morgan, *The Emergence of Novelty* (London: Williams & Norgate, 1933), p. 15.

35. Saunders and Ho, "Increase in Complexity," and "On the Increase in Complexity in Evolution II. The Relativity of Complexity and the Principle of Minimum Increase," *Journal of Theoretical Biology* 90(1981): 515–30. **[30]**

36. Saunders and Ho, "Increase in Complexity," p. 376. See also Saunders and Ho, "Increase in Complexity II," p. 526. **[30, 35]**

37. Ho and Saunders, "Beyond neo-Darwinism." **[5]**

38. I. Prigogine et al., "The Evolution of Complexity and the Laws of Nature," in *Goals in a Global Society,* ed. E. Laszlo and J. Bierman (New York: Pergamon, 1977), p. 18.

39. M. Eigen, "Selforganization of Matter and the Evolution of Biological Macromolecules," *Die Naturwissenschaften* 58(1971): 465–523.

40. H. H. Pattee, "The Complementarity Principle in Biological and Social Structures," *Journal of Social and Biological Structures* 1(1978): 191–200.

41. E. Broda, *The Evolution of the Bioenergetic Processes* (New York: Pergamon, 1975).

42. J. G. Miller, *Living Systems* (New York: McGraw-Hill, 1978).

43. See especially, J. W. Gibbs, "On the Equilibrium of Heterogeneous Substances," *Transactions of the Connecticut Academy of Arts and Sciences* 3(1877): 108–248, 343–520; L. Boltzmann, "Der zweite Hapsatz der mechanischen Wärmetheorie," *Populäre Schriften* (1905): 39–40; W. K. Gregory, "The New Anthropogeny: Twenty-Five Stages of Vertebrate Evolution, from Silurian Chordate to Man," *Science* 77(1933): 30; R. W. Gerard, *Unresisting Cells* (New York: Harper & Row, 1940); R. L. Lindeman, "The Trophic-Dynamic Aspect of Ecology," *Ecology* 23(1942): 399–418; L. A. White, "Energy and the Evolution of Culture," *American Anthropologist* 45(1943): 335–56, and *The Evolution of Culture* (New York: McGraw-Hill, 1959); E. Schrödinger, *What Is Life?* (New York: Cambridge University Press, 1944); S. Brody, *Bioenergetics and Growth* (New York: Reinhold, 1945); Zipf, *Human Behaviour;* F. Cottrell, *Energy and Society: The Relation Between Energy, Social Change, and Economic Development* (New York: McGraw-Hill, 1955); M. Kleiber, *The Fire of Life: An Introduction to Animal Energetics* (New York: Wiley, 1961); D. M. Gates, *Energy Exchange in the Biosphere* (New York: Harper & Row, 1962); Odum and Odum, *Fundamentals of Ecology;* Morowitz, *Energy Flow;* N. Georgescu-Roegen, *The Entropy Law and Economic Process* (Cambridge, Mass.: Harvard University Press, 1971), "Bioeconomics: A New Look at the Nature of Economic Activity," in *The Political Economy of Food and Energy,* ed. L. Junker (Ann Arbor: University of Michigan Press, 1976), and "The Steady State and Ecological Salvation: A Thermodynamic Analysis," *Bioscience* 27 (1977): 266–70; Schmidt-Nielsen, *How Animals Work;* R. N. Adams, *Energy and Structure: A Theory of Social Power* (Austin: University of Texas Press, 1975); E. Cook, *Man, Energy, Society* (San Francisco: Freeman, 1976); J. W. Bennett, *The Ecological Transition: Cultural Anthropology and Human Adaptation* (New York: Pergamon, 1976). **[1, 24]**

44. A. J. Lotka, *Elements of Physical Biology* (Baltimore: Williams & Wilkins, 1925), p. 354.

45. H. T. Odum and E. C. Odum, *The Energy Basis for Man and Nature* (New York: McGraw-Hill, 1976), p. 1.

46. I. Prigogine and C. Nicolis, "Biological Order, Structure and Instabilities," *Quarterly Review of Biophysics* 4(1971): 107–48; I. Prigogine et al., "Thermodynamics of Evolution (I)," *Physics Today* 25(1972): 23–28, and "Thermodynamics of Evolution (II)," *Physics Today* 25(1972): 38–44, and "Evolution of Complexity"; I. Prigogine, "Order Through Fluctuation: Self-Organization and Social System," in *Evolution and Consciousness: Human Systems in Transi-*

tion, ed. E. Jantsch and C. H. Waddington (Reading, Mass.: Addison-Wesley, 1976), and "Time, Structure, and Fluctuations," *Science* 201(1978): 777–84; G. Nicolis and I. Prigogine, *Self Organization in Nonequilibrium Systems* (New York: Wiley, 1977).

47. Prigogine, "Evolution of Complexity," p. 38. **[38]**

48. For a more detailed discussion of this controversial point, see P. A. Corning, "To Be or Entropy, That Is the Question: Has Science Really Decreed Our Doom?," unpublished manuscript.

49. Prigogine, "Evolution of Complexity," p. 18. **[38]**

50. H. Spencer, "Progress: Its Law and Cause," in *Essays Scientific* . . . **[16]**

51. Ibid., p. 216.

52. Prigogine, "Evolution of Complexity," p. 38. In a recent volume Prigogine adopts a viewpoint that is even closer to Spencer's. There is, he says, an inherent instability in the physical world that makes thermodynamic processes irreversible: I. Prigogine and I. Stengers, *Dialogue with Nature* (New York: Doubleday, 1980). **[38]**

53. Prigogine, "Evolution of Complexity," p. 39. **[38]**

54. Prigogine, "Thermodynamics of Evolution (I)," p. 27. **[46]**

55. K. Tregonning and A. Roberts, "Ecosystem-like Behavior of a Random-Interaction Model I," *Bulletin of Mathematical Biology* 40(1978): 513–24, and "Complex Systems Which Evolve Towards Homeostasis," *Nature* 281(1979): 563–64.

56. E. Jantsch, *Design for Evolution* (New York: Braziller, 1975), p. xvi.

57. Eigen, "Selforganization of Matter." **[39]**

58. See Corning, "To Be or Entropy"; cf. Prigogine and Stengers, *Dialogue with Nature.* **[48, 52]**

59. Simpson, "Behavior and Evolution," p. 532. **[7]**

60. J. R. Platt, "Properties of Large Molecules That Go Beyond the Properties of Their Chemical Sub-Groups," *Journal of Theoretical Biology* 1(1961): 342–58.

61. E. Nagel, "Wholes, Sums and Organic Unities," in *Parts and Wholes,* ed. D. Lerner (New York: Free Press, 1963).

62. H. Haken, *Synergetics: An Introduction,* 2d ed. (New York: Springer, 1978), H. Haken, ed., *Cooperative Effects. Progress in Synergetics* (New York: Elsevier, 1974), and *Dynamics of Synergetic Systems* (New York: Springer, 1980).

63. T. P. Reddy and K. Vaidyanath, "Synergistic Interaction of Gamma Rays and Some Metallic Salts in the Induction of Chlorophyll Mutations in Rice," *Mutation Research* 52(1978): 361–65; H. E. Kubitschek, "Mutational Synergism of Nitrous Acid and Ultraviolet Light," *Mutation Research* 53(1978): 214–15; T. Dobzhansky et al., *Evolution* (San Francisco: Freeman, 1977).

64. See especially the discussion in Broda, *Evolution of the Bioenergetic Process.* **[41]**

65. M. E. Hale, *The Biology of Lichens* (London: Edward Arnold, 1967); D. C. Smith, *The Lichen Symbiosis* (London: Oxford, 1973).

66. R. E. Hungate, *The Rumen and Its Microbes* (New York: Academic Press, 1966); T. C. Cheng, *Symbiosis, Organisms Living Together* (New York: Pegasus, 1970).

67. G. D. Scott, *Plant Symbiosis* (New York: St. Martin's Press, 1969); P. S. Nutman, ed., *Symbiotic Nitrogen Fixation in Plants* (New York: Cambridge University Press, 1976).

68. R. Cooke, *The Biology of Symbiotic Fungi* (New York: Wiley, 1977); J. L. Ruehle and D. H. Marx, "Fiber, Food, Fuel, and Fungal Symbionts," *Science* 206(1979): 419–22.

69. E. O. Wilson, *The Insect Societies* (Cambridge, Mass.: Harvard University Press, 1971).

70. Ibid.

71. W. B. Vernberg, *Symbiosis in the Sea* (Columbia: University of South Carolina Press, 1973); G. S. Losey, Jr., "The Symbiotic Behavior of Fishes," in *Behavior of Fish and Other Aquatic Animals,* ed. D. I. Mostofsky (New York: Academic Press, 1978).

72. E. R. Pianka, *Evolutionary Ecology*, 2d ed. (New York: Harper & Row, 1978).
73. Cheng, *Symbiosis*. **[66]**
74. Vernberg, *Symbiosis*. **[71]**
75. Grobstein, *Strategy of Life*. **[32]**
76. J. T. Bonner, *The Cellular Slime Molds*, 2d ed. (Princeton: Princeton University Press, 1967).
77. W. C. Allee, *Animal Aggregations: A Study in General Sociology* (Chicago: University of Chicago Press, 1931), and *Cooperation Among Animals: With Human Implications* (revised edition of *The Social Life of Animals*) (New York: Henry Schuman, 1951 [1938]); J. H. Crook, "The Adaptive Significance of Avian Social Organizations," *Symposium of the Zoological Society of London* 14(1965): 181–218; D. L. Mech, *The Wolf: The Ecology and Behavior of an Endangered Species* (Garden City, N.Y.: Natural History Press, 1970); H. van Lawick and J. van Lawick-Goodall, *Innocent Killers* (Boston: Houghton Mifflin, 1971); G. B. Schaller, *The Serengeti Lion: A Study of Predator-Prey Relations* (Chicago: University of Chicago Press, 1972); H. Kruuk, *The Spotted Hyena: A Study of Predation and Social Behavior* (Chicago: University of Chicago Press, 1972), and "Functional Aspects of Social Hunting by Carnivores," in *Function and Evolution in Behavior*, ed. G. Baerends (Oxford: Clarendon Press, 1975); J. R. Krebs et al., "Flocking and Feeding in the Great Tit, *Parus Major:* An Experimental Study," *Ibis* 114(1972): 507–30; R. D. Alexander, "The Evolution of Social Behavior," *Annual Review of Ecology and Systematics* 5(1974): 325–83; E. O. Wilson, *Sociobiology: The New Synthesis* (Cambridge, Mass.: Harvard University Press, 1975); J. W. Burgess, "Social Spiders," *Scientific American* 234, 3(1976): 100–06; P. R. Thompson, "The Evolution of Territoriality and Society in Top Carnivores," *Social Science Information* 17(1978): 949–92.
78. N. Tinbergen, *The Study of Instinct* (New York: Oxford University Press, 1951), and *Social Behavior in Animals* (London: Methuen, 1965 [1953]); J. D. Goss-Custard, "Feeding Dispersion in Some Overwintering Wading Birds," in *Social Behaviour in Birds and Mammals*, ed. J. H. Crook (New York: Academic Press, 1970); E. A. Carl, "Population Control in Arctic Ground Squirrels," *Ecology* 52(1971): 395–413; Krebs, "Flocking and Feeding"; H. Kummer, *Primate Societies: Group Techniques of Ecological Adaptation* (Chicago: Aldine, 1971), and *Social Organization of Hamadryas Baboons; A Field Study* (New York: Karger, 1968); Kruuk, *Spotted Hyena;* W. A. Thompson et al., "The Survival Value of Flocking in Birds: A Simulation Model," *Journal of Animal Ecology* 43(1974): 785–820; Wilson, *Sociobiology;* T. Caraco et al., "Avian Flocking in the Presence of a Predator," *Nature* 285(1980): 400–01. **[77]**
79. Kruuk, *Spotted Hyena;* Wilson, *Sociobiology;* J. Lamprecht, "The Relationship Between Food Competition and Foraging Group Size in Some Larger Carnivores," *Zeitschrift für Tierpsychologie* 46(1978): 337–43; J. D. Bygott et al., "Male Lions in Large Coalitions Gain Reproductive Advantages," *Nature* 282(1979): 839–41.
80. W. E. Rutter, *The California Woodpecker and I* (Berkeley: University of California Press, 1938); J. L. Brown, "Types of Group Selection," *Nature* (London) 211(1966): 870, and *The Evolution of Behavior* (New York: W. W. Norton, 1975); Wilson, *Sociobiology*. **[77]**
81. W. Etkin, *Social Behavior from Fish to Man* (Chicago: University of Chicago Press, 1967); Wilson, *Sociobiology;* D. Weihs, "Hydromechanics of Fish Schooling," *Nature* 241(1973): 290–91, and "Some Hydrodynamical Aspects of Fish Schooling, in *Swimming and Flying in Nature*, ed. T. Y.-T. Wu et al. (New York: Plenum, 1975); but cf. B. L. Partridge et al., "The Three-Dimensional Structure of Fish Schools," *Behavioral Ecology and Sociobiology* 6(1980): 277–88.
82. Allee, *Animal Aggregations*, and *Cooperation Among Animals;* D. E. Davis, "The Phylogeny of Social Nesting Habits in the Crotophaginae," *Quarterly Review of Biology* 17(1942): 115–34; A. F. Skutch, "Helpers Among Birds," *Condor* 63(1961): 198–226; Brown, "Types of Group Selection"; M. J. West-Eberhard, *The Social Biology of Polistine Wasps* (Ann Arbor:

University of Michigan Press, 1969); E. J. Kullmann, "Evolution of Social Behavior in Spiders (araneae, eresidae and theridiidae)," *American Zoologist* 12(1972): 419–26; Wilson, *Sociobiology;* S. T. Emlen, "The Evolution of Cooperative Breeding in Birds," in *Behavioural Ecology: An Evolutionary Approach,* ed. J. R. Krebs and N. B. Davies (Sunderland, Mass.: Sinauer, 1978); J. D. Ligon and S. H. Ligon, "Communal Breeding in Green Woodhoopoes as a Case for Reciprocity," *Nature* 276(1978): 496–98, and "The Communal Social System of the Green Woodhoopoe in Kenya," in *The Living Bird,* vol. XVII, 1978 (Ithaca, N.Y.: Cornell University Laboratory of Ornithology, 1979). **[77, 80]**

83. C. D. Michener, *The Social Behavior of the Bees: A Comparative Study* (Cambridge, Mass.: Harvard University Press, 1974); I. Muul, "Behavioral and Physiological Influences in the Distribution of the Flying Squirrel, *Glaucomys jolans,*" University of Michigan Zoological Publication no. 134, 1968; Wilson, *Sociobiology;* Y. LeMaho, "The Emperor Penguin: A Strategy to Live and Breed in the Cold," *American Scientist* 65(1977): 680–93. **[77]**

84. Allee, *Animal Aggregations.* **[77]**

85. See especially P. Ward, "Feeding Ecology of the Black-Faced Dioch (*Quelea quelea*) in Nigeria," *Ibis* 107(1965): 173–214; P. Ward and W. Zahavi, "The Importance of Certain Assemblages of Birds as 'Information Centres' for Food Finding," *Ibis* 115(1973): 517–34; P. de Groot, "Information Transfer in a Socially Roosting Weaver Bird (*Quelea quelea; Ploceinae*): An Experimental Study," *Animal Behaviour* 28(1980): 1249–54.

86. W. J. Hamilton, "Social Aspects of Bird Orientation Mechanisms," in *Animal Orientation and Navigation,* ed. R. M. Storm (Corvallis: Oregon State University Press, 1969).

87. Caraco, "Avian Flocking." **[78]**

88. Michener, *Social Behavior of Bees;* Wilson, *Sociobiology;* G. F. Oster and E. O. Wilson, *Caste and Ecology in the Social Insects* (Princeton: Princeton University Press, 1978). **[77, 83]**

89. J. U. M. Jarvis, "Eusociality in a Mammal: Cooperative Breeding in Naked Mole-Rat Colonies," *Science* 212(1981): 571–73.

90. D. T. Campbell, "The Two Distinct Routes Beyond Kin Selection to Ultrasociality: Implications for the Humanities and Human Social Sciences," unpublished manuscript, 1980.

91. According to estimates based on experimental data by LeMaho ("Emperor Penguin"). See also J. Prévost, "Ecologie du Manchot empereur: *Aptenodytes forsteri* Gray," in *Expedition polaires Francaises,* Publ. No. 222 *Actual. scient. et Industr.,* no. 291 (Paris: Herman, 1961). **[83]**

92. J. T. Bonner, "The Chemical Ecology of Cells in the Soil," in *Chemical Ecology,* ed. E. Sondheimer and J. B. Simeone (New York: Academic Press, 1970).

93. Schaller, *Serengeti Lion;* T. Caraco and L. Wolf, "Ecological Determinants of Group Sizes of Foraging Lions," *American Naturalist* 109(1975): 343–52. **[77]**

94. R. D. Estes and J. Goddard, "Prey Selection and Hunting Behavior of the African Wild Dog," *Journal of Wildlife Management* 31(1967): 52–70; Schaller, *Serengeti Lion;* Kruuk, *Spotted Hyena.* **[77]**

95. Krebs, "Flocking and Feeding." **[77]**

96. Kummer, *Organization of Baboons,* and *Primate Societies.* **[78]**

97. Ligon and Ligon, "Communal Breeding of Woodhoopoes," and "Communal Social System of Woodhoopoes." **[82]**

98. H. O. von Wagner, "Massenansammlungen von Weberknechten in Mexiko," *Zeitschrift für Tierpsychologie* 11(1954): 348–52.

99. See G. H. Lewes, *Problems of Life and Mind* (Boston: J. R. Osgood, 1875).

100. R. A. Rubenstein and C. D. Laughlin, Jr., "Bridging Levels of Systemic Organization," *Current Anthropology* 18(1977): 459–81.

101. H. C. Brookfield, "Intensification and Disintensification in Pacific Agriculture: A Theoretical Approach," *Pacific Viewpoint* 13(1972): 30–48.

102. E. Boserup, *The Conditions of Agricultural Growth: The Economies of Agrarian Change Under Population Pressure* (Chicago: Aldine, 1965); B. Spooner, ed., *Population Growth: Anthropological Implications* (Cambridge, Mass.: MIT Press, 1972); M. N. Cohen, *The Food Crisis in Prehistory: Overpopulation and the Origins of Agriculture* (New Haven: Yale University Press, 1977).

103. E.g., Lotka, *Physical Biology;* White, "Energy and Evolution," *The Science of Culture: A Study of Man and Civilization* (New York: Grove Press, 1949), and *Evolution of Culture;* Cottrell, *Energy and Society;* E. R. Service, *Cultural Evolutionism: Theory in Practice* (New York: Holt, 1971); Y. A. Cohen, "Culture as Adaptation," in *Man in Adaptation: The Cultural Present,* 2d ed., ed. Y. A. Cohen (Chicago: Aldine, 1974 [1968]); Odum and Odum, *Energy Basis for Man.* **[43, 44, 45]**

104. Pattee, "Complementarity Principle," p. 194. **[40]**

105. A. N. Whitehead, *Adventures in Ideas* (New York: Macmillan, 1933), also *Science and the Modern World* (New York: Macmillan, 1925), and *Process and Reality: An Essay in Cosmology* (Cambridge, Mass.: Harvard University Press, 1929).

106. Allee, *Cooperation Among Animals,* p. 30. **[77]**

107. Ibid., pp. 212–13.

108. M. D. Sahlins, *The Use and Abuse of Biology: An Anthropological Critique of Sociobiology* (Ann Arbor: University of Michigan Press, 1976).

109. D. T. Campbell, "On the Genetics of Altruism and the Counter-Hedonic Components in Human Culture," *Journal of Social Issues* 28(1972): 21–37. For more recent statements of his views, see "On the Conflicts Between Biological and Social Evolution and Between Psychology and Moral Tradition," *American Psychologist* 30(1975): 1103–26, and "Comments on the Sociobiology of Ethics and Moralizing," *Behavioral Science* 24(1979): 37–45; see also L. G. Wispé and J. N. Thompson, Jr., "The War Between the Worlds: Biological versus Social Evolution and Some Related Issues," *American Psychologist* 31(1976): 341–347; L. G. Wispé, ed., *Altruism, Sympathy and Helping: Psychological and Sociological Principles* (New York: Academic Press, 1978).

110. Campbell, "Conflicts Between Biological and Social Evolution," p. 111. **[109]**

111. E.g., biologists G. C. Williams (*Adaptation and Natural Selection: A Critique of Some Current Evolutionary Thought* [Princeton: Princeton University Press, 1966]) and M. T. Ghiselin (*The Economy of Nature and the Evolution of Sex* [Berkeley: University of California Press, 1974]); exchange theorists J. W. Thibaut and H. H. Kelley (*The Social Psychology of Groups* [New York: Wiley, 1959]), and G. C. Homans ("Social Behavior as Exchange," *American Journal of Sociology* 62(1958): 597–606 and *Social Behavior: Its Elementary Forms* [New York: Harcourt, 1961]); psychologist R. Hogan ("Theoretical Egocentrism and the Problem of Compliance," *American Psychologist* 30(1975): 533–40 and *Personality Theory: The Personological Tradition* [Englewood Cliffs, N.J.: Prentice-Hall, 1975]).

112. E. O. Wilson, "Comment on D. T. Campbell, 'On the Conflict Between Biological and Social Evolution and Between Psychology and Moral Tradition,'" *American Psychologist* 31(1976): 370; also *On Human Nature* (Cambridge, Mass.: Harvard University Press, 1978), pp. 155–57. The tendency to confound co-operation and altruism seems to be pandisciplinary, e.g., biologists E. O. Wilson (*Sociobiology,* p. 114) and John Maynard Smith ("The Evolution of Behavior," *Scientific American* 239, 3[1978]: 176–192); psychologist Lauren Wispé (*Altruism,* p. 309); political scientist Roger Masters. Masters asks: "Are human beings by nature cooperative and altruistic or is human nature intrinsically egoistic and competitive? This fundamental issue is as old [as], or older than, the Western tradition of political theory" ("Of Marmots and Men: Animal Behavior and Human Altruism," in Wispé, *Altruism,* p. 57); see also "The Political Implications of Sociobiology," paper presented at the Second Annual Meeting, International Society of Political Psychology, 1979, p. 10. **[77, 109]**

113. See Michener, *Social Behavior of Bees;* Wilson, *Sociobiology;* Oster and Wilson, *Caste and Ecology.* **[77, 83, 88]**

114. Odum and Odum, *Fundamentals of Ecology,* p. 226. **[1]**

115. Wilson, *Insect Societies,* and *Sociobiology.* **[69, 77]**

116. E.g., see Wilson, *Sociobiology.* **[77]**

117. M. J. West Eberhard, "The Evolution of Social Behavior by Kin Selection," *Quarterly Review of Biology* 50(1975): 1–33. In addition, see Williams, *Adaptation and Natural Selection;* R. D. Alexander and G. Borgia, "Group Selection, Altruism, and the Levels of Organization of Life," *Annual Review of Ecology and Systematics* 9(1978): 449–74; T. H. Clutton-Brock and R. G. Harvey, eds., *Readings in Sociobiology* (San Francisco: Freeman, 1978); S. A. Boorman and P. R. Levitt, *The Genetics of Altruism* (New York: Academic Press, 1980); R. Axelrod and W. D. Hamilton, "The Evolution of Cooperation," *Science* 211(1981): 1390–96.

118. Clutton-Brock and Harvey, *Readings in Sociobiology,* p. 141. **[117]**

119. Williams, *Adaptation and Natural Selection,* p. 211. **[117]**

120. H. von Foerster, "Bio-Logic" in *Biological Prototypes and Synthetic Systems,* ed. E. Bernard and N. R. Kare (New York: Plenum, 1962).

121. E.g., A. Rescigno and I. W. Richardson, "The Deterministic Theory of Population Dynamics," in *Foundations of Mathematical Biology,* vol. III, ed. R. Rosen (New York: Academic Press, 1973); J. Roughgarden, "Evolution of Marine Symbiosis—a Simple Cost-Benefit Model," *Ecology* 56(1975): 1201–08; R. M. May, ed., *Theoretical Ecology: Principles and Applications* (Philadelphia: Saunders, 1976); R. E. Ricklefs, *The Economy of Nature* (Portland, Ore.: Chiron, 1976); Pianka, *Evolutionary Ecology;* J. H. Vandermeer and D. H. Boucher, "Varieties of Mutualistic Interaction in Population Models," *Journal of Theoretical Biology* 74(1978): 549–58; C. C. Travis and W. M. Post III, "Dynamics and Comparative Statics of Mutualistic Communities," *Journal of Theoretical Biology* 78(1979): 553–71; B. S. Goh, "Stability in Models of Mutualism," *American Naturalist* 113(1979): 261–75; T. G. Hallam, "Effects of Cooperation on Competitive Systems," *Journal of Theoretical Biology* 82(1980): 415–23. **[72]**

122. Pianka, *Evolutionary Ecology,* p. 228. **[72]**

123. Vandermeer and Boucher, "Varieties of Mutualistic Interaction." See also the model developed by Haken, *Synergetics.* **[61, 121]**

124. Boorman and Levitt, *Genetics of Altruism.*

125. R. Axelrod, "More Effective Choice in the Prisoner's Dilemmas," *Journal of Conflict Resolution* 24(1980): 379–403, and "The Emergence of Cooperation Among Egoists," *American Political Science Review* 75(1981): 306–18; Axelrod and Hamilton, "Evolution of Cooperation." **[117]**

126. M. Olson, Jr., *The Logic of Collective Action: Public Goods and the Theory of Groups* (Cambridge, Mass.: Harvard University Press, 1965).

127. See P. A. Corning, "Modelling Social and Biological Structures," *Journal of Social and Biological Structures* (forthcoming).

128. Hallam, "Effects of Cooperation." **[121]**

129. See especially the model and predictions for symbiosis developed by Roughgarden, "Marine Symbiosis," and the dynamic analysis of mutualistic community in Travis and Post, "Dynamics of Mutualistic Communities." **[121]**

130. R. Thom, *Structural Stability and Morphogenesis: An Outline of a General Theory of Models* (Reading, Mass.: Benjamin, 1975); E. C. Zeeman, "Catastrophe Theory," *Scientific American* 234, 4(1976): 65–83.

131. N. Christofides et al., *Combinatorial Optimization* (New York: Wiley-Interscience, 1979).

132. A. Smith, *The Wealth of Nations* (London: Dent, 1964 [1776]), p. 5.

133. Ibid., p. 16.

134. H. Ris and W. Plaut, "Ultrastructure of DNA-Containing Areas in the Chloroplast of

Chlamydomonas," *Journal of Cell Biology* 13(1962): 383–391; L. Margulis, *Origin of Eukaryotic Cells* (New Haven: Yale University Press, 1970), and *Symbiosis in Cell Evolution: Life and Its Environment on the Early Earth* (San Francisco: Freeman, 1981); Broda, *Evolution of Bioenergetic Processes.* **[41]**

135. T. R. Parsons and B. Harrison, "Energy Utilization and Evolution," *Journal of Social and Biological Structures* 4(1981): 1–5.

136. H. A. Simon, "The Architecture of Complexity," *General Systems* 10(1965): 63–76; G. G. Simpson, *This View of Life: The World of an Evolutionist* (New York: Harcourt, 1964); T. J. M. Schopf et al., "Genomic Versus Morphologic Rates of Evolution: Influence of Morphologic Complexity," *Paleobiology* 1(1975): 63–70.

137. Stebbins, *Progressive Evolution;* J. W. Schopf, "The Evolution of the Earliest Cells," *Scientific American* 239, 3(1978): 110–38. **[11]**

138. S. J. Gould, "Back to the Beginning," *New Scientist* 18(1980): 802–805.

139. E. D. Hanson, *The Origin and Early Evolution of Animals* (Middletown, Conn.: Wesleyan University Press, 1977).

140. M. Eigen et al., "The Origin of Genetic Information," *Scientific American* 224, 4(1981): 88.

141. Grobstein, *Strategy of Life.* **[32]**

142. J. S. Coleman, ed., *Educational and Political Developments* (Princeton: Princeton University Press, 1965), p. 69.

143. H. A. Simon, "Architecture of Complexity," *General Systems* 10(1965): 65–66.

144. On this point, see also Huxley, *Evolution;* Alexander and Borgia, "Group Selection"; Lerner, "Communications Theory"; R. C. Lewontin, *The Genetic Basis of Evolutionary Change* (New York: Columbia University Press, 1974); Miller, *Living Systems;* A. P. Kozlov, "Evolution of Living Organisms as a Multilevel Process," *Journal of Theoretical Biology* 81(1979): 1–17; H. C. Plotkin and F. J. Olding-Smee, "Multiple-Level Model of Evolution and Its Implications for Sociobiology," *The Behavioral and Brain Sciences* 4(1981): 225–68. For other recent discussions of hierarchical organization, see Pattee, *Hierarchy Theory;* R. Dawkins, "Hierarchical Organization: A Candidate Principal for Ethology," in *Growing Points in Ethology,* ed. P. P. G. Bateson and R. A. Hinde (Cambridge: Cambridge University Press, 1976); Riedl, *Order in Living Organisms.* **[1, 13, 42, 117]**

145. S. Wright, "Genic and Organismic Selection," *Evolution* 34(1980): 825–843.

146. Ethological discussions of the concept of "social structure" and of how it applies to animal societies can be found in J. H. Crook, "Social Organization and the Environment: Aspect of Contemporary Social Ethology," *Animal Behaviour* 18(1970): 197–209, and "Sources of Cooperation in Animals and Man," in *Man and Beast: Comparative Social Behavior,* ed. J. F. Eisenberg and W. S. Dillon (Washington, D.C.: Smithsonian Institution Press, 1971); Kummer, *Primate Societies;* J. H. Crook et al., "Mammalian Social Systems: Structure and Function," *Animal Behavior* 24(1976): 261–74; also R. A. Hinde, "The Concept of Function," in *Function and Evolution of Behaviour: Essays in Honor of Professor Niko Tinbergen,* ed. G. Baerends et al. (Oxford: Clarendon Press, 1976), "Interactions Relationships and Social Structure," *Man* (n.s.) 11(1976): 1–17, and "Dominance and Role: Two Concepts with Dual Meanings," *Journal of Social and Biological Structures* 1(1978): 27–38; D. R. Omark, "The Group: A Factor or an Epiphenomenon in Evolution," in *Dominance Relations,* ed. D. R. Omark et al. (New York: Garland, 1980). **[78]**

147. The concept of hierarchy traces to the work of T. Schjelderup-Ebbe on "peck orders" in birds, "Honsenes stemme. Bidvag til honsenes psykologi," *Naturen* 37(1913): 262–76, and "Social Behavior of Birds," in *A Handbook of Social Psychology,* ed. C. Murchison (Worcester, Mass.: Clark University Press, 1935). There is now a vast literature on the subject.

148. On the concept of "roles" in ethology, see I. S. Bernstein and L. G. Sharpe, "Social Roles in a Rhesus Monkey Group," *Behaviour* 26(1966): 91–104; Crook, "Social Organization,"

and "Sources of Cooperation"; Kummer, *Primate Societies;* Wilson, *Sociobiology;* I. S. Bernstein, "Dominance, Aggression and Reproduction in Primate Societies," *Journal of Theoretical Biology* 60(1976): 459–72; Hinde, "Interactions," and "Dominance and Role"; Omark, "The Group." **[78, 146]**

149. For a summary of the arguments see I. S. Bernstein, "Dominance: A Theoretical Perspective for Ethologists," in Omark, *Dominance Relations;* also T. E. Rowell, "The Concept of Social Dominance," *Behavioral Biology* 11(1974): 131–54; I. D. Chase, "Social Process and Hierarchy Formation in Small Groups: A Comparative Perspective," *American Sociological Review* 45(1980): 905–24.

150. M. R. A. Chance, "The Organization of Attention in Groups," in *Methods of Inference from Animal to Human Behavior,* ed. M. von Cranach (The Hague: Mouton, 1976), and "Attention Structure as the Basis of Primate Rank Orders," *Man* 2(1967): 503–18; M. R. A. Chance et al., "Attention and Avoidance in Human Groups," *Social Science Information* 12(1973): 27–44; M. R. A. Chance and R. R. Larsen, eds., *The Social Structure of Attention* (New York: Wiley, 1976); C. Barner-Barry, "The Biological Correlates of Power and Authority: Dominance and Attention Structure," paper presented at the Annual Meeting, American Political Science Association, 1978; R. D. Masters, "Attention Structures and Political Campaigns," paper prepared for the Annual Meeting, American Political Science Association, 1978.

151. C. T. de Assumpção and J. M. Deag, "Attention Structure in Monkeys: A Search for a Common Trend," *Folia Primatologica* 31(1979): 285–300.

152. I. S. Bernstein and T. P. Gordon, "The Social Component of Dominance Relationships in Rhesus Monkeys (*Macaca mulatta*)," *Animal Behavior* 28(1980): 1033–39.

153. A. M. Guhl, "Social Behavior and the Domestic Fowl," in *Social Hierarchy and Dominance,* ed. M. Schein (Stroudsburg, Pa.: Hutchinson and Ross, 1975).

154. Boorman and Levitt, *Genetics of Altruism.* Their estimate is conservative, being limited to within-species social organization. They exclude reproductive co-operation among mating pairs, indirect forms of co-operation, and symbiosis between species. **[117]**

155. Wilson, *Sociobiology,* p. 3. **[77]**

156. W. D. Hamilton, "Innate Social Aptitudes of Man: An Approach from Evolutionary Genetics," in *Biosocial Anthropology,* ed. R. Fox (London: Malaby Press, 1975), p. 117.

157. Maynard Smith, "Evolution of Behavior," p. 168. **[112]**

158. Wilson, *Sociobiology,* pp. 37–62. **[77]**

159. For examples see C. Packer, "Male Transfer in Olive Baboons," *Nature* 255(1975): 219–20, and "Reciprocal Altruism in *Papio anubis,*" *Nature* 265(1977): 441–43; B. C. R. Bertram, "Kin Selection in Lions and in Evolution," in Bateson and Hinde, *Growing Points.*

160. C. R. Darwin, *The Descent of Man, and Selection in Relation to Sex* (New York: A. L. Burt, 1874 [1871]), pp. 115–17, 119.

161. E.g., P. A. Kropotkin, *Mutual Aid: A Factor of Evolution* (New York: New York University Press, 1972 [1902]); M. F. A. Montagu, "The Origin and Nature of Social Life and the Biological Basis of Cooperation," *Journal of Social Psychology* 29(1949): 267–83, and *Darwin, Competition and Cooperation* (New York: Henry Schuman, 1952).

162. J. Maynard Smith, "Group Selection and Kin Selection: A Rejoinder," *Nature* 201 (1964): 1145–47.

163. W. D. Hamilton, "The Genetical Evolution of Social Behaviour (I and II)," *Journal of Theoretical Biology* 17(1964): 1–52.

164. This insight was revived by Jerram Brown, "Alternate Routes to Sociality in Jays—with a Theory for the Evolution of Altruism and Communal Breeding," *American Zoologist* 14(1974): 63–80. See also Boorman and Levitt, *Genetics of Altruism.* **[117]**

165. J. B. S. Haldane, *The Causes of Evolution* (New York: Harper & Row, 1932), p. 131.

166. S. Wright, "Tempo and Mode in Evolution: A Critical Review," *Ecology* 26(1945): 415–19.

167. A. Keith, *A New Theory of Human Evolution* (New York: Philosophical Library, 1949).

168. R. Bigelow, *The Dawn Warriors: Man's Evolution Toward Peace* (Boston: Little, Brown, 1969); R. D. Alexander and D. W. Tinkle, "Review of *On Aggression* by Konrad Lorenz and *The Territorial Imperative* by Robert Ardrey," *BioScience* 18(1968): 245–48 (also "The Evolution of Social Behavior," *Annual Review of Ecology and Systematics* 5(1974): 325–83, and "Search for a General Theory"); E. O. Wilson, "On the Queerness of Social Evolution," *Social Research* 40(1973): 144–52.

169. S. Wright, *Evolution and the Genetics of Populations* (Chicago: University of Chicago Press, 1977–1978), vols. 3 and 4.

170. See V. C. Wynne-Edwards, "Intrinsic Population Control: An Introduction," in *Population Control by Social Behavior,* ed. F. J. Ebling and D. M. Stoddart (London: Institute of Biology, 1978).

171. V. C. Wynne-Edwards, "Intergroup Selection in the Evolution of Social Systems," *Nature* 200(1963): 623.

172. Williams, *Adaptation and Natural Selection,* pp. 8, 220, 217–218, 14–15. **[111]**

173. R. L. Trivers, "The Evolution of Reciprocal Altruism," *Quarterly Review of Biology* 46(1971): 35–57.

174. Ibid., p. 36.

175. J. B. S. Haldane, "Population Genetics," *New Biology* 18(1955): 44.

176. See G. S. Becker, "Altruism, Egoism and Genetic Fitness: Economics and Sociobiology," *Journal of Economic Literature* 14(1976): 817–26.

177. S. L. Washburn, "Human Behavior and the Behavior of Other Animals," *American Psychologist* 33(1978): 416.

178. Wilson, *Sociobiology,* p. 120. **[77]**

179. See J. T. Bonner, *The Evolution of Culture in Animals* (Princeton: Princeton University Press, 1980); P. C. Mundinger, "Animal Cultures and a General Theory of Cultural Evolution," *Ethology and Sociobiology* 1(1980): 183–223.

180. E.g., J. Alcock, *Animal Behavior: An Evolutionary Approach* (Sunderland, Mass.: Sinauer, 1975); E. L. Charnov and J. R. Krebs, "The Evolution of Alarm Calls: Altruism or Manipulation?" *American Naturalist* 109(1975): 107–12; P. W. Sherman, "Nepotism and the Evolution of Alarm Calls," *Science* 194(1977): 1246–53. See also Wilson, *Sociobiology,* pp. 123 ff.

181. Packer, "Reciprocal Altruism." **[159]**

182. R. Levins, "Extinction," in *Some Mathematical Questions in Biology,* ed. M. Gerstenhaber (Providence, R.I.: American Mathematical Society, 1970).

183. S. A. Boorman and P. R. Levitt, "Group Selection on the Boundary of a Stable Population," *Proceedings of the National Academy of Sciences* 69(1972): 2711–13, and "A Frequency-Dependent Natural Selection Model for the Evolution of Social Cooperation Networks," *Proceedings of the National Academy of Sciences* 70(1973): 187–89.

184. Wilson, *Sociobiology,* p. 113. **[77]**

185. O. Kalela, "Über den Revierbesitz bei Vögeln und Säugetieren als population sökologischer Faktor," *Annales Zoologic: Societatis Zoologicae Botanicae Fennicae "Vanamo"* (Helsinki) 16(1954): 1–48, and "Regulation of Reproductive Rate in Subarctic Populations of the *Clethrionomys rufocanus* (Sund.)," *Annales Academiae Scientiarum Fennicae* (Suomalaisen Tiedeakatemian Toimituksia), ser. A (IV, Biologica) 43(1957): 1–60.

186. Similar views were expressed independently by R. L. Snyder, "Evolution and Integration of Mechanisms That Regulate Population Growth," *Proceedings of the National Academy of Sciences* 47(1961): 449–55; J. L. C. Brereton, "Evolved Regulatory Mechanisms of Population Control," in *The Evolution of Living Organisms,* ed. G. W. Leeper (Parkville, Australia: Melbourne University Press, 1962); P. A. Corning, "Politics and the Evolutionary Process," in T. Dobzhansky et al., eds., *Evolutionary Biology,* vol. VII (New York: Plenum, 1974).

187. Brown, "Sociality in Jays"; W. D. Hamilton, "Review of E. O. Wilson's *Sociobiology: The New Synthesis,*" *Journal of Animal Ecology* 46(1977): 975–77.

188. E.g., West Eberhard, "Evolution of Social Behavior"; Alexander and Borgia, "Group Selection."

189. Wilson, *Sociobiology,* p. 73.

190. Ibid., p. 298.

191. Ibid. Cf. George Williams.

192. See especially Crook, "Sources of Cooperation"; Crook et al., "Mammalian Social Systems."

193. Alexander and Borgia, "Group Selection." See also Alexander, "Evolution of Social Behavior"; D. S. Wilson, *The Natural Selection of Populations and Communities* (Menlo Park, Calif.: Benjamin/Cummings, 1980).

194. Alexander and Borgia, "Group Selection."

195. Boorman and Levitt, *Genetics of Altruism.*

196. Wilson, *Natural Selection of Populations.*

197. Allee, *Animal Aggregations,* and *Cooperation Among Animals.*

198. G. Hardin, "The Tragedy of the Commons," *Science* 162(1968): 1243–48.

199. Boorman and Levitt, *Genetics of Altruism.*

200. S. A. Barnett, "Homo Docens," *Journal of Biosocial Science* 5(1973): 393–403. See also Bonner, *Evolution of Culture.*

201. Plotkin and Olding-Smee, "Multiple-Level Model"; Axelrod and Hamilton, "Evolution of Cooperation"; L. L. Cavalli-Sforza and M. W. Feldman, *Cultural Transmission and Evolution: A Quantitative Approach* (Princeton: Princeton University Press, 1981); C. J. Lumsden and E. O. Wilson, *Genes, Mind and Culture: The Co-Evolutionary Process* (Cambridge, Mass.: Harvard University Press, 1981).

202. See Miller, *Living Systems.*

203. See also H. R. Pulliam and C. Dunford, *Programmed to Learn: An Essay on the Evolution of Culture* (New York: Columbia University Press, 1980); R. Boyd and P. J. Richerson, "Culture, Biology and the Evolution of Variation Between Human Groups," in *Science and the Questions of Human Equality,* ed. M. Collins et al. (Washington, D.C.: American Association for the Advancement of Science, 1981).

204. Lumsden and Wilson, *Genes, Mind and Culture,* p. 343.

205. Ibid., p. 359.

206. Ibid., p. 177.

207. Wilson, *Sociobiology,* pp. 567–75, and *On Human Nature,* p. 84; Lumsden and Wilson, *Genes, Mind and Culture,* pp. 7, 327.

208. Lumsden and Wilson, *Genes, Mind and Culture.*

IV. The Interactional Paradigm

1. I. Eibl-Eibesfeldt, "Human Ethology: Concepts and Implications for the Sciences of Man," *Behavioral and Brain Sciences* 2(1979): 1–26.

2. D. C. Glass, ed., *Environmental Influences, Biology and Behavior* Series, vol. III (New York: Rockefeller University Press, 1968).

3. J. Piaget, *The Origins of Intelligence in Children,* trans. M. Cook (New York: International Universities Press, 1952), *The Psychology of the Child* (New York: Basic Books, 1969), and *Biology and Knowledge: An Essay on the Relations Between Organic Regulations and Cognitive Processes* (Chicago: University of Chicago Press, 1971).

4. In A. Koestler and J. R. Smythies, eds., *Beyond Reductionism: New Perspectives in the Life Sciences* (London: Hutchinson, 1969).

5. E. White, "Genetic Diversity and Political Life," *Journal of Politics* 34(1972): 1203–42.

6. L. R. Binford, *Nunamiut Ethnoarchaeology* (New York: Academic Press, 1978).

7. T. Parsons, "Interaction: Social Interaction," in *International Encyclopedia of the Social Sciences,* ed. D. Sills, vol. VII (New York: The Free Press, 1968); K. R. Popper and J. C. Eccles, *The Self and Its Brain* (New York: Springer, 1977).

8. See especially the comprehensive bibliography in Somit, *Literature of Biopolitics.* See also the overviews in Corning, "Biopolitics," and "Political Science and Life Sciences"; Wiegele, *Biopolitics.*

9. P. A. Corning, "Natural Selection and Teleonomic Selection," *Journal of Social and Biological Structures* (in press).

10. S. Wright, "Biology and the Philosophy of Science," in *Process and Divinity: The Hartshorne Festschrift,* ed. W. R. Reese and E. Freeman (LaSalle, Ill.: Open Court, 1964), p. 122.

11. For schizophrenia and the schizoid spectrum, see J. Huxley et al., "Schizophrenia as a Genetic Morphism," *Nature* 204(1964): 220–21; I. I. Gottesman and J. Shields, "Schizophrenia in Twins: 16 Years' Consecutive Admissions to a Psychiatric Clinic," *Diseases of the Nervous System* 27(1966): 11–19, *Schizophrenia and Genetics: A Twin Study Vantage Point* (New York: Academic Press, 1972), "A Critical Review of Recent Adoption, Twin and Family Studies of Schizophrenia," *Schizophrenia Bulletin* 2(1976): 36–398, and "Rejoinder: Toward Optimal Arousal and Away from Original Din," *Schizophrenia Bulletin* 2(1976): 447–53; L. L. Heston, "Psychiatric Disorders in Foster-Home Reared Children of Schizophrenic Mothers," *British Journal of Psychiatry* 112(1966): 819–25, "The Genetics of Schizophrenic and Schizoid Disease," *Science* 167(1970): 249–56, and "Discussion," in L. Ehrman et al., eds., *Genetics, Environment, and Behavior: Implications for Educational Policy* (New York: Academic Press, 1972); D. Rosenthal, ed., *The Transmission of Schizophrenia: Proceedings of the Second Research Conference* (New York: Pergamon, 1968), *Genetic Theory and Abnormal Behavior* (New York: McGraw-Hill, 1970), and *Genetics of Psychopathology* (New York: McGraw-Hill, 1970); D. Rosenthal and S. S. Kety, eds., "The Transmission of Schizophrenia," *Journal of Psychiatric Research* 6, supplement 1(1968); A. H. Buss and E. H. Buss, eds., *Theories of Schizophrenia* (New York: Atherton, 1969); R. R. Grinker, "An Essay on Schizophrenia and Science," *Archives of General Psychiatry* 20(1969): 1–24; S. S. Kety et al., "Mental Illness in the Biological and Adoptive Families of Adopted Schizophrenics," *American Journal of Psychiatry* 128(1971): 82–86, "Mental Illness in the Biological and Adoptive Relatives of Adopted Individuals Who Became Schizophrenic," in *Genetic Research in Psychiatry,* ed. R. Fierie et al. (Baltimore: Johns Hopkins University Press, 1975), and "Studies Based on a Total Sample of Adopted Individuals and Their Relatives: Why They Were Necessary, What They Demonstrated and Failed to Demonstrate," *Schizophrenia Bulletin* 2(1976): 413–28; D. Rosenthal et al., "Schizophrenics' Offspring Reared in Adoption Homes," in Rosenthal and Kety, *Transmission of Schizophrenia,* "The Adopted-Away Offspring of Schizophrenics," *American Journal of Psychiatry* 128(1971): 87–91, "Assessing Degree of Psychopathology from Diagnostic Statements," *Canadian Psychiatric Association Journal* 20(1975): 35–45, and "Parent-Child Relationships and Psychopathological Disorder in the Child," *Archives of General Psychiatry* 32(1975): 446–76; G. E. McClearn and J. C. DeFries, *Introduction to Behavioral Genetics* (San Francisco: Freeman, 1973); L. Ehrman and P. A. Parsons, *The Genetics of Behavior* (Sunderland, Mass.: Sinauer, 1976); S. S. Kety and S. Matthysse, "Genetic Aspects of Schizophrenia," in *Human Diversity: Its Causes and Social Significance,* ed. B. D. Davis and P. Flaherty (Cambridge, Mass.: Ballinger, 1976); C. E. Boklage, "Schizophrenia, Brain Asymmetry Development, and Twinning," *Biological Psychiatry* 12(1977): 19–35; R. Cancro, "Genetic Evidence for the Existence of Subgroups of the Schizophrenic," *Schizophrenia Bulletin* 5(1979): 453–59; F. Schulsinger, "Biological Psychopathology," in *Annual Review of Psychology,* ed. M. R. Rozenzweig and L. W. Porter, vol. 31 (Palo Alto, Calif.: Annual Reviews, 1980). For manic depressive psychosis and various depressive disorders, see G. Winokur, "Genetic Findings and Methodological Considerations in Manic

Depressive Disease," *The British Journal of Psychiatry* 67(1970): 267–74; G. Winokur and T. Reich, "Two Genetic Factors in Manic-Depressive Disease," *Comprehensive Psychiatry* 11 (1970): 93–99; H. S. Akiskal and W. T. McKinney, Jr., "Depressive Disorders: Toward a Unified Hypothesis," *Science* 182(1973): 20–29; J. Mendlewicz and B. Shoprin, eds., *Genetic Aspects of Affective Illnesses* (New York: SP Medical and Scientific Books, 1979). For alcohol addiction, see J. Partanen et al., *Inheritance of Drinking Behavior* (Stockholm: Almqvist and Wiksell, 1966); G. Whitney et al., "Heritability of Alcohol Preference in Laboratory Mice and Rats," *Journal of Heredity* 61(1970): 165–69; M. A. Schuckit et al., "Alcoholism: The Influence of Parental Illness," *The British Journal of Psychiatry* 119(1971): 663–65, and "A Study of Alcoholism in Half Siblings," *American Journal of Psychiatry* 128(1972): 1132–36; G. E. McClearn, "Genetics as a Tool in Alcohol Research," *Annals of the New York Academy of Sciences* 197(1972): 26–31; P. H. Wolff, "Ethnic Differences in Alcohol Sensitivity," *Science* 175(1972): 449–50; D. W. Goodwin et al., "Alcohol Problems in Adoptees Raised Apart from Alcoholic Biological Parents," *Archives of General Psychiatry* 28(1973): 238–43, "Drinking Problems in Adopted and Nonadopted Sons of Alcoholics," *Archives of General Psychiatry* 31(1974): 164–69, "Alcoholism and the Hyperactive Child Syndrome," *Journal of Nervous and Mental Disease* 160(1975): 349–53, "Alcoholism and Depression in Adopted-Out Daughters of Alcoholics," *Archives of General Psychiatry* 34(1977): 751–55, and "Psychopathology in Adopted and Nonadopted Daughters of Alcoholics," *Archives of General Psychiatry* 34(1977): 1005–09; D. W. Goodwin, *Is Alcoholism Hereditary?* (New York: Oxford University Press, 1976), and "Alcoholism and Heredity," *Archives of General Psychiatry* 36(1979): 57–61; D. W. Goodwin and C. K. Erickson, eds., *Alcoholism and Affective Disorders: Clinical Genetic and Biochemical Studies* (New York: SP Medical and Scientific Books, 1979); C. V. Cavey, "Alcoholism—A Biological Approach," *Trends in Neurosciences* 2(1979): 23–25; M. A. Schuckit and V. Rayses, "Ethanol Ingestion: Differences in Blood Acetaldehyde Concentrations in Relatives of Alcoholics and Controls," *Science* 203(1979): 54–55; Schulsinger, "Biological Psychopathology." For autism, see L. Kanner, "Autistic Disturbances of Affective Contact," *Nervous Child* 2(1943): 217–50; L. Kanner and L. Eisenberg, "Notes on the Follow up Studies of Autistic Children," in P. H. Hock and J. Zubin, eds., *Psychopathology of Childhood* (New York: Grune and Stratton, 1955); L. Eisenberg and L. Kanner, "Early Infantile Autism," *American Journal of Orthopsychiatry* 26(1956): 556; B. Rimland, *Infantile Autism: The Syndrome and Its Implications for a Neural Theory of Behavior* (New York: Appleton, 1964); M. Rutter, "Concepts of Autism: A Review of Research," *Journal of Child Psychology and Psychiatry* 9(1968): 1–25; G. O'Gorman, *The Nature of Childhood Autism* (London: Butterworth, 1970); V. Reynolds, *The Biology of Human Action* (San Francisco: Freeman, 1976); J. Richer, "The Social Avoidance Behaviour of Autistic Children," *Animal Behaviour* 24(1976): 896–906; S. Folstein and M. Rutter, "Genetic Influences and Infantile Autism," *Nature* 265(1977): 726–28; D. G. Freedman, *Human Sociobiology: A Holistic Approach* (New York: Free Press, 1979). For hyperactivity, see M. A. Stewart, "Hyperactive Children," *Scientific American* 222, 4(1970): 94–98; G. Weiss and L. Hechtman, "The Hyperactive Child Syndrome," *Science* 205(1979): 1348–54. For congenital obesity, see D. L. Coleman, "Obesity Genes: Beneficial Effects in Heterozygous Mice," *Science* 203(1979): 663–65. For aphasia, see K. K. Kidd et al., "A Genetic Analysis of Stuttering Suggesting a Single Major Locus," *Genetics* 74(1973): 137; Ehrman and Parsons, *Genetics of Behavior;* H. Hécaen and M. L. Albert, *Human Neuropsychology* (New York: Wiley, 1978). For alexia, see B. Hallgren, "Specific dyslexia ('Congenital Word-Blindness'): A Clinical and Genetic Study," *Acta Psychiatrica et Neurologica,* supplement 65(1950); E. H. Lenneberg, *Biological Foundations of Language* (New York: Wiley, 1967); M. Critchley, *The Dyslexic Child* (London: Heinemann, 1970); Hécaen and Albert, *Human Neuropsychology.* For certain psychopathic behavioral disorders, see H. J. Eysenck, *Crime and Personality* (London: Routledge & Kegan Paul, 1977 [1964]); Heston, "Genetics of Schizophrenia"; Rosenthal, *Genetics of Psychopathology;* R. R. Crowe, "The

Adopted Offspring of Women Criminal Offenders: A Study of Their Arrest Records," *Archives of General Psychiatry* 27(1972): 600–03; Ehrman and Parsons, *Genetics of Behavior;* S. A. Mednick and K. O. Christiansen, eds., *Biosocial Bases of Criminal Behavior* (New York: Gardner, 1977); R. R. Monroe, *Brain Dysfunction in Aggressive Criminals* (Lexington, Mass.: D. C. Heath, 1978); C. R. Jeffrey, ed., *Biology and Crime* (Beverly Hills, Calif.: Sage, 1979). **[11]**

12. C. R. Scriver et al., "Genetics and Medicine: An Evolving Relationship," *Science* 200(1978): 946–52.

13. L. S. Penrose, *The Biology of Mental Defect,* 3rd ed. (London: Sidgwick and Jackson, 1963); S. Eiduson et al., *Biochemistry and Behavior* (Princeton: Van Nostrand, 1964); McClearn and DeFries, *Introduction to Behavioral Genetics;* Ehrman and Parsons, *Genetics of Behavior;* C. J. Epstein and M. S. Golbus, "Prenatal Diagnosis of Genetic Diseases," *American Scientist* 65(1977): 703–11. **[11]**

14. R. L. Sprott and J. Staats, "Behavioral Studies Using Genetically Defined Mice—A Bibliography," *Behavior Genetics* 5(1975): 27–82, and "Behavioral Studies Using Genetically Defined Mice—A Bibliography (July 1973–July 1976)," *Behavior Genetics* 8(1978): 183–206. There have also been numerous experiments with Drosophilia flies, bacteria, paramecia, mosquitos, wasps, bees, crickets, fish, quail, chickens, turkeys, geese, horses, dogs, and bulls.

15. For personality factors, see H. J. Eysenck and D. B. Prell, "The Inheritance of Neuroticism: An Experimental Study," *Journal of Mental Science* 97(1951): 441–65; H. J. Eysenck, "The Inheritance of Extraversion-Introversion," *Acta Psychologica* 12(1956): 95–110, *The Biological Basis of Personality* (Springfield, Ill.: Thomas, 1967), "Genetic Factors in Personality Development," in *Human Behavior Genetics,* ed. A. R. Kaplan (Springfield, Ill.: Thomas, 1976), and *Measurement of Personality* (Baltimore: University Park Press, 1976); S. G. Vandenberg, "Hereditary Factors in Normal Personality Traits (as Measured by Inventories)," in *Recent Advances in Biological Psychiatry,* ed. J. Wortis, vol. 9 (New York: Plenum, 1967), and *Progress in Human Behavior Genetics* (Baltimore: Johns Hopkins University Press, 1968); D. Rosenthal, "The Genetics of Intelligence and Personality," in *Biology and Behavior-Genetics,* ed. D. C. Glass (New York: Rockefeller University Press, 1968); R. C. Nichols, "The Resemblance of Twins in Personality and Interests," in G. Manosewitz et al., eds., *Behavioral Genetics: Method and Research* (New York: Appleton Century Crofts, 1969); J. L. Jinks and D. W. Fulker, "Comparison of the Biometrical Genetical, Mava, and Classical Approaches to the Analysis of Human Behavior," *Psychological Bulletin* 73(1970): 311–49; G. Claridge et al., eds., *Personality Differences and Biological Variations: A Study of Twins* (New York: Pergamon, 1973); L. Eaves and H. J. Eysenck, "The Nature of Extraversion: A Genetical Analysis," *Journal of Personality and Social Psychology* 32(1975): 102–12; J. C. Loehlin and R. C. Nichols, *Heredity, Environment, and Personality: A Study of 850 Sets of Twins* (Austin: University of Texas Press, 1976); A. P. Matheny, "Relations Between Twins," *Behavior Genetics* 6(1976): 343–51; L. J. Eaves, "Twins as a Basis for the Causal Analysis of Human Personality," in *Twin Research, Part A: Psychology and Methodology,* ed. W. E. Nance et al. (New York: Liss, 1978); S. G. Vandenberg and A. R. Kuse, "Temperaments in Twins," in *Twin Research,* and "Genetic Determinants of Spatial Ability," in Wittig and Peterson, *Determinants of Sex-Related Differences in Cognitive Functioning.* For perceptual and cognitive abilities, see J. N. Spuhler and G. Lindzey, "Racial Differences in Behavior," in J. Hirsch, ed., *Behavior-genetic Analysis* (New York: McGraw-Hill, 1967); R. T. Osborne and A. J. Gregor, "The Heritability of Visualization, Perceptual Speed and Spatial Orientation," *Perceptual and Motor Skills* 23(1966): 379–90; R. T. Osborne et al., "Heritability of Numerical Facility," *Perceptual and Motor Skills* 24(1967): 659–66, and *Human Variation;* R. Guttman, "Parent-Offspring Correlations in the Judgement of Visual Number," *Human Heredity* 20(1970): 57–65; Jinks and Fulker, "Comparison of Approaches"; B. J. Murawski, "Genetic Factors in Tests of Perception and the Rorschach," *The Journal of Genetic Psychology* 119(1971): 43–52; McClearn and DeFries, *Behavioral Genetics;* J. C. DeFries et al., "Parent-

Offspring Resemblance for Specific Cognitive Abilities in Two Ethnic Groups," *Nature* 261(1976): 131–33; Eysenck, *Measurement of Personality;* S. G. Vandenberg, "Genetic Factors in Human Learning," *Educational Psychology* 12(1976): 59–63; L. J. Kamin, "The Hawaii Family Study of Cognitive Abilities: A Comment," *Behavior Genetics* 8(1978): 275–79 and reply in J. C. DeFries et al., "The Hawaii Family Study of Cognition: A Reply," *Behavior Genetics* 8(1978): 281–88; J. Park et al., "Parent-Offspring Resemblance for Specific Cognitive Abilities in Korea," *Behavior Genetics* 8(1978): 43–52; S. G. Vandenberg and A. R. Kuse, "Temperaments in Twins," in Nance, *Twin Research,* and "Genetic Determinants of Spatial Ability," in *Determinants of Sex-Related Differences in Cognitive Functioning,* ed. M. C. Wittig and A. C. Peterson (New York: Academic Press, 1978); S. G. Vandenberg and K. Wilson, "Failure of the Twin Situation to Influence Twin Differences in Cognition," *Behavior Genetics* 9(1979): 55–60; R. J. Rose et al., "Twin-Family Studies of Perceptual Speed Ability," *Behavioral Genetics* 9(1979): 71–86, and "Genetic Variance in Nonverbal Intelligence: Data from the Kinships of Identical Twins," *Science* 205(1979): 1153–55; Vernon, *Intelligence;* Holden, "Identical Twins Reared Apart." For psychomotor skills, e.g., reaction times, manual dexterity, rotary pursuit, card sorting, rhythmic abilities, and athletic skills, see S. G. Vandenberg, "Contributions of Twin Research to Psychology," *Psychological Bulletin* 66(1966): 327–52, and "What Do We Know Today?"; M. B. Jones, "Individual Differences," in *The Psychomotor Domain,* ed. R. N. Singer (Philadelphia: Lea & Febiger, 1972); Loehl in, *Race Differences;* Eysenck, *Measurement of Personality;* C. E. Noble, "Age, Race, and Sex in the Learning and Performance of Psychomotor Skills," in Osborne, *Human Variation.*

16. See especially, A. R. Jensen, "How Much Can We Boost IQ and Scholastic Achievement?" *Harvard Educational Review* 39(1969): 1–123; S. Scarr-Slapatek, "Unknowns in the IQ Equation," *Science* 174(1971): 1223–28, "Race, Social Class, and I.Q.," *Science* 174(1971): 1285–95, and "An Evolutionary Perspective on Infant Intelligence: Species Patterns and Individual Variations," in *Origins of Intelligence: Infancy and Early Childhood,* ed. M. Lewis (New York: Plenum, 1976); S. G. Vandenberg, "What Do We Know Today?" in Cancro, *Intelligence;* H. J. Eysenck, *The Measurement of Intelligence* (Baltimore: Williams & Wilkins, 1973), and *Crime and Personality;* L. J. Kamin, *The Science and Politics of I.Q.* (Potomac, Md.: Erlbaum, 1974); S. H. Broman et al., *Preschool IQ: Prenatal and Early Developmental Correlates* (Hillsdale, N.J.: Erlbaum, 1975); Loehlin, *Race Differences in Intelligence;* R. C. Lewontin, "Genetic Aspects of Intelligence," *Annual Review of Genetics* 9(1975): 387–405; M. W. Feldman and Richard C. Lewontin, "The Heritability Hangup," *Science* 190(1975): 1163–68; H. Munsinger, "The Adopted Child's IQ: A Critical Review," *Psychological Bulletin* 82(1975): 623–59, and "Children's Resemblance to Thier Biological and Adopting Parents in Two Ethnic Groups," *Behavior Genetics* 5(1975): 239–54; B. Adams et al., "Evidence for a Low Upper Limit of Heritability of Mental Test Performance in a National Sample of Twins," *Nature* 263(1976): 314–16; A. Oliverio, ed., *Genetics, Environment and Intelligence* (Amsterdam: Elsevier, 1977); R. B. McCall, "Childhood IQ's as Predictors of Adult Educational and Occupational Status," *Science* 197(1977): 482–83; R. S. Wilson, "Twins and Siblings: Concordance for School-age Mental Development," *Child Development* 48(1977): 211–16; R. Lynn, "Ethnic and Racial Differences in Intelligence: International Comparisons," in *Human Variation,* ed. Osborne; M. Schiff et al., "Intellectual Status of Working-class Children Adopted Early into Upper-middle-class Families," *Science* 200(1978): 1503–04; J. M. Horn et al., "Intellectual Resemblance Among Adoptive and Biological Relatives: The Texas Adoption Project," *Behavior Genetics* 9(1979): 177–207; Vernon, *Intelligence;* Holden, "Identical Twins Reared Apart." For more detailed overviews of behavior genetics, see R. Plomin et al., *Behavioral Genetics: A Primer* (San Francisco: Freeman, 1980) and P. McBroom, *Behavioral Genetics,* National Institute of Mental Health, Science Monographs No. 2 (Washington, D.C.: Government Printing Office, 1980). **[11, 15]**

17. See the reviews in D. G. Freedman, *Human Infancy: An Evolutionary Perspective* (Hills-

dale, N.J.: Erlbaum, 1974), and *Human Sociobiology;* D. G. Freedman and M. M. DeBoer, "Biological and Cultural Differences in Early Child Development," in *Annual Review of Anthropology,* ed. B. J. Siegel, vol. 3 (Palo Alto, Calif.: Annual Reviews, 1979). **[11]**

18. A. Thomas et al., *Behavioral Individuality in Early Childhood* (New York: New York University Press, 1963), *Temperament and Behavior Disorders in Childhood* (New York: New York University Press, 1968), and "The Origin of Personality," *Scientific American* 223, 2(1970): 102–10.

19. A. F. Korner, "Neonatal Startles, Smiles, Erections, and Reflect Sucks as Related to State Sex, and Individuality," *Child Development* 40(1969): 1039–53, and "Individual Differences at Birth: Implications for Early Experience and Later Development," *American Journal of Orthopsychiatry* 41(1971): 608–19; A. Korner and R. Grobstein, "Individual Differences at Birth: Implications for Mother-Infant Relationship and Later Development," *Journal of the American Academy of Child Psychiatry* 6(1967): 676–90.

20. T. B. Brazelton, *Neonatal Behavioral Assessment Scale* (Philadelphia: Lippincott, 1976), and "The Newborn as Individual," *Harper's* 256(1978): 47–48.

21. D. G. Freedman and B. Keller, "Inheritance of Behavior in Infants," *Science* 140(1963): 196–98.

22. See L. B. Cohen and P. Salapatek, eds., *Infant Perception: Sensation to Cognition* (New York: Academic Press, 1976).

23. J. Kagan, "Attention and Psychological Change in the Young Child," *Science* 170(1970): 826–832; M. P. M. Richards, "First Steps in Becoming Social," in *The Integration of a Child into a Social World,* ed. M. P. M. Richards (Cambridge: Cambridge University Press, 1974).

24. W. Ball and E. Tronick, "Infant Responses to Impending Collision: Optical and Real," *Science* 171(1971): 818–20.

25. T. G. R. Bower, "The Object in the World of the Infant," *Scientific American* 225, 4(1971): 30–38.

26. E. Aronson and S. Rosenbloom, "Space Perception in Early Infancy," *Science* 172(1971): 1161–63. For an extended discussion of the case for the unity and interconnectedness of the senses, see L. E. Marks, *The Unity of the Senses: Interrelations Among the Modalities* (New York: Academic Press, 1978).

27. A. J. DeCasper and W. P. Fifer, "Of Human Bonding: Newborns Prefer Their Mothers' Voices," *Science* 208(1980): 1174–76.

28. P. D. Eimas et al., "Speech Perception in Infants," *Science* 171(1971): 303–06; Richards, "First Steps"; L. A. Streeter, "Language Perception of 2-Month-Old Infants Shows Effects of Both Innate Mechanisms and Experience," *Nature* 259(1976): 39–41; P. D. Eimas and J. L. Miller, "Contextual Effects in Infant Speech Perception," *Science* 209(1980): 1140–41. **[23]**

29. J. A. Macfarlane, "Olfaction in the Development of Social Preferences in the Human Neonate," in *Parent-Infant Interaction,* ed. (New York: Elsevier, 1975); M. J. Russell, "Human Olfactory Communication," *Nature* 260(1976): 520–22.

30. A. N. Meltzoff and M. K. Moore, "Imitation of Facial and Manual Gestures by Human Neonates," *Science* 198(1977): 75–78.

31. J. S. Bruner, "The Nature and Uses of Immaturity," *American Psychologist* 27(1972): 687–708.

32. R. A. Spitz, "Hospitalism: An Inquiry into the Genesis of Psychiatric Conditions in Early Childhood," *Psychoanalytic Study of the Child* 1(1945): 53–74, and "Hospitalism: A Follow-up Report," *Psychoanalytic Study of the Child* 2(1946): 113–17; H. Bakwin, "Emotional Deprivation in Infants," *Journal of Pediatrics* 35(1949): 512–24; W. Goldfarb, "Emotional and Intellectual Consequences of Psychologic Deprivation in Infancy: A Re-evaluation," in *Psychopathology of Childhood,* ed. P. H. Hoch and J. Zubin (New York: Grune & Stratton, 1955).

33. H. F. Harlow, "Love in Infant Monkeys," *Scientific American* 200, 6(1959): 68–74; H. F. Harlow and M. K. Harlow, "Social Deprivation in Monkeys," *Scientific American* 207,

5(1962): 136–46, and "The Affectional System," in *Behavior of Non-Human Primates,* ed. A. M. Schrier et al., vol. 2 (New York: Academic Press, 1965).

34. J. Bowlby, *Attachment and Loss* (New York: Basic Books, 1969–1980), vol. 1.

35. N. Bischof, "A Systems Approach Toward the Functional Connections of Attachment and Fear," *Child Development* 46(1975): 801–817.

36. G. W. Bronson, "The Fear of Novelty," *Psychological Bulletin* 69(1968): 350–58, "The Development of Fear in Man and Other Animals," *Child Development* 39(1968): 410–31, "Fear of Visual Novelty: Developmental Patterns in Males and Females," *Developmental Psychology* 2(1969): 33–40, and "Sex Differences in the Development of Fearfulness: A Replication, *Psychonomic Science* 17(1969): 367–68.

37. Bischof, "Functional Connections of Attachment and Fear." **[35]**

38. R. A. Butler, "Curiosity in Monkeys," *Scientific American* 190, 2(1954): 70–75; D. E. Berlyne, *Conflict, Arousal and Curiosity* (New York: McGraw-Hill, 1960), "Curiosity and Exploration," *Science* 153(1966): 25–33, and "Conflict and Arousal," *Scientific American* 215, 2(1966): 82–87; J. Piaget, *Play, Dreams and Imitation in Childhood* (London: Routledge & Kegan Paul, 1962); P. A. Jewell and C. Loizos, eds., *Play, Exploration and Territory in Mammals* (New York: Academic Press, 1966); A. Weisler and R. B. McCall, "Exploration and Play: Resume and Redirection," *American Psychologist* 31(1976): 492–508; J. O'Keefe and L. Nadel, *The Hippocampus as a Cognitive Map* (Oxford: Clarendon Press, 1978).

39. D. O. Hebb, *The Organization of Behavior* (New York: Wiley, 1949).

40. D. Singh, "Preference for Bar Pressing to Obtain Reward Over Freeloading in Rats and Children," *Journal of Comparative and Physiological Psychology* 73(1970): 320–27.

41. R. W. White, "Motivation Reconsidered: The Concept of Competence," *Psychological Review* 66(1959): 297–333. Although it is less firmly established than some other behavioral domains, the concept of an effectance motivation is supported by various convergent theoretical formulations, e.g., G. W. Allport, *Personality: A Psychological Interpretation* (New York: Holt, 1937); K. Goldstein, *The Organism: A Holistic Approach to Biology Derived from Pathological Data in Man* (New York: American, 1939), and *Human Nature in Light of Psychopathology* (Cambridge, Mass.: Harvard University Press, 1940); H. A. Murray and C. Kluckhohn, "Outline of a Conception of Personality," in *Personality in Nature, Society, and Culture,* ed. C. Kluckhohn et al. (New York: Knopf, 1953); S. Coopersmith, *The Antecedents of Self-Esteem* (San Francisco: Freeman, 1967); R. De Charms, *Personal Causation* (New York: Academic Press, 1968).

42. J. Piaget, *The Psychology of Intelligence* (New York: International Universities Press, 1950), *Origins of Intelligence in Children,* and *Psychology of the Child.* **[3]**

43. J. Kagan, "Emergent Themes in Human Development," *American Scientist* 64(1976): 186–96; L. S. Siegel and C. J. Brainerd, eds., *Alternatives to Piaget: Critical Essays on the Theory* (New York: Academic Press, 1978); C. J. Brainerd, *Piaget's Theory of Intelligence* (Englewood Cliffs, N.J.: Prentice-Hall, 1978), and "The Stage Question in Cognitive-Developmental Theory," *Behavioral and Brain Sciences* 1(1978): 173–213, plus commentaries in ibid. and *Behavioral and Brain Sciences* 2(1979): 137–54.

44. J. P. Scott, "Critical Periods in Behavioral Development," *Science* 138(1962): 949–58.

45. See especially, J. Kagan and R. E. Klein, "Cross-Cultural Perspectives on Early Development," *American Psychologist* 28(1973): 947–61; J. P. Scott, "What Are the Expectations Regarding the Scope and Limits of Exploring the Biological Aspects of Behavior? Considerations of Methodology," paper prepared for the annual meeting of the American Political Science Association, 1978.

46. J. Kagan, "Do Infants Think?" *Scientific American* 226, 3(1972): 74–82.

47. Scarr-Salapatek, "Evolutionary Perspective on Infant Intelligence." **[16]**

48. G. S. Omenn and A. G. Motulsky, "Pharmacogenetics and Mental Disease," *Psychological Medicine* 4(1974): 125–29; Scarr-Salapatek, "An Evolutionary Perspective." **[16]**

49. C. B. Kopp and J. Shaperman, "Cognitive Development in the Absence of Object Manipulation During Infancy," *Developmental Psychology* 9(1973): 430.

50. Scarr-Salapatek, "An Evolutionary Perspective," p. 185. **[16]**

51. J. Wind, "Human Drowning: Phylogenetic Origin," *Journal of Human Evolution* 5(1976): 349–69.

52. R. S. Wilson, "Twins: Early Mental Development," *Science* 175(1972): 914–17; R. S. Wilson and E. B. Harpring, "Mental and Motor Development in Infant Twins," *Developmental Psychology* 7(1972): 277–87; P. L. Nichols and S. H. Broman, "Familial Resemblance in Infant Mental Development," *Developmental Psychology* 10(1974): 442–46.

53. Scarr-Salapatek, "An Evolutionary Perspective"; R. B. McCall, "Toward an Epigenetic Conception of Mental Development in the First Three Years of Life," in *Origins of Intelligence: Infancy and Early Childhood,* ed. M. Lewis (New York: Plenum, 1976).

54. R. S. Wilson, "Twins and Siblings," and "Synchronies in Mental Development: An Epigenetic Perspective," *Science* 202(1978): 939–48.

55. See E. O. Wilson, *Sociobiology* (Cambridge, Mass.: Harvard University Press, 1975).

56. K. von Frisch, *The Dance Language and Orientation of Bees,* trans. L. Chadwick (Cambridge, Mass.: Harvard University Press, 1967); J. L. Gould, "Honeybee Recruitment: The Dance-Language Controversy," *Science* 189(1975): 685–93, "The Dance-Language Controversy," *Quarterly Review of Biology* 51(1976): 211–244, "Behavioral Programming in Honeybees," *Behavioral and Brain Sciences* 4(1978): 572–73, and "Sun Compensation by Bees," *Science* 207(1980): 545–47.

57. Gould, "Honeybee Recruitment"; M. L. Brines and J. L. Gould, "Bees Have Rules," *Science* 206(1979): 571–73. **[56]**

58. See E. S. Savage-Rumbaugh et al., "Symbolic Communication Between Two Chimpanzees (*Pan troglogytes*)," *Science* 201(1978): 641–44, and "Linguistically Mediated Tool Use and Exchange by Chimpanzees (*Pan troglodytes*)," *Behavioral and Brain Sciences* 4(1978): 539–54; R. Epstein et al., "Symbolic Communication Between Two Pigeons (*Columba livia domestica*)," *Science* 207(1980): 543–45.

59. For other primates, see J. Bastian, "Primate Signaling Systems and Human Languages," in *Primate Behavior: Field Studies of Monkeys and Apes,* ed. I. DeVore (New York: Holt, 1965); P. Marler, "Communications in Monkeys and Apes," in DeVore, *Primate Behavior;* J. B. Lancaster, "Primate Communication Systems and the Emergence of Human Language," in *Primates,* ed. P. C. Jay (New York: Holt, 1968); R. A. Hinde, ed., *Non-Verbal Communication* (Cambridge: Cambridge University Press, 1972), and *Biological Bases of Human Social Behavior* (New York: McGraw-Hill, 1974); Wilson, *Sociobiology;* H. Frings and M. Frings, *Animal Communication,* 2d ed. (Norman: University of Oklahoma Press, 1977 [1964]). For humans, see R. L. Birdwhistell, *Introduction to Kinesics: An Annotation System for Analysis of Body Motion and Gesture* (Louisville: University of Louisville Press, 1952); E. T. Hall, *The Silent Language* (New York: Doubleday, 1959), and *Hidden Dimension* (New York: Doubleday, 1966); M. Argyle, *The Psychology of Interpersonal Behaviour* (London: Penguin, 1967); Hinde, *Non-Verbal Communication;* D. E. Morris, *Man Watching: A Field Guide to Human Behavior* (New York: Abrams, 1977). **[55]**

60. E. W. Menzel, Jr., "Communication About the Environment in a Group of Young Chimpanzees," *Folia Primatologica* 15(1971): 220–32; E. W. Menzel, Jr. and S. Halperin, "Purposive Behavior as a Basis for Objective Communication Between Chimpanzees," *Science* 189(1975): 652–54.

61. See B. T. Gardner and R. A. Gardner, "Teaching Sign Language to a Chimpanzee," *Science* 165(1969): 664–72, "Comparing the Early Utterances of Child and Chimpanzee," in *Behavior of Nonhuman Primates,* ed. A. M. Schrier and F. Stollnitz, vol. 4 (New York: Academic Press, 1974), and "Evidence for Sentence Constituents in the Early Utterances of Child and Chimpanzee," *Journal of Experimental Psychology* 104(1975): 244–67; R. S. Fouts, "The Use

of Guidance in Teaching Sign Language to a Chimpanzee (*Pan troglodytes*)," *Journal of Comparative and Physiological Psychology* 80(1972): 515–22, "Acquisition and Testing of Gestural Signs in Four Young Chimpanzees," *Science* 180(1973): 978–80, and "Language: Origins, Definitions and Chimpanzees," *Journal of Human Evolution* 3(1974): 475–82; David Premack, "Language in Chimpanzee?" *Science* 172(1971): 808–22, *Intelligence in Ape and Man* (Hillsdale, N.J.: Erlbaum, 1976), and "Language and Intelligence in Ape and Man," *American Scientist* 64(1976): 674–83; A. J. Premack and D. Premack, "Teaching Language to an Ape," *Scientific American* 227, 4(1972): 92–99; D. M. Rumbaugh et al., "Reading and Sentence Completion by a Chimpanzee (pan)," *Science* 182(1973): 731–33, and "Language in Man, Monkeys and Machines," *Science* 185(1974): 872–73; Savage-Rumbaugh, "Symbolic Communication," and "Linguistically Mediated Tool Use." **[58]**

62. J. Limber, "Language in Child and Chimp?" *American Psychologist* 32(1977): 280–95; T. A. Sebeok and J. Umiker-Sebeok, "Performing Animals: Secrets of the Trade," *Psychology Today* 13(1979): 78–91, and *Speaking of Apes: A Critical Anthology of Two-Way Communication with Man* (New York: Plenum, 1980); H. S. Terrace, *Nim* (New York: Knopf, 1979); H. S. Terrace et al., "Can an Ape Create a Sentence?" *Science* 206(1979): 891–902; E. S. Savage-Rumbaugh et al., "Reference: The Linguistic Essential," *Science* 210(1980): 922–25, and "Do Apes Use Language?" *American Scientist* 68(1980): 49–61.

63. Terrace, "Can an Ape Create a Sentence?" **[62]**

64. Savage-Rumbaugh, "Do Apes Use Language?" **[62]**

65. Savage-Rumbaugh, "Reference." **[62]**

66. Limber, "Language in Child and Chimp?" **[62]**

67. See W. Köhler, *The Mentality of Apes* (New York: Harcourt, 1925); R. M. Yerkes and B. W. Learned, *Chimpanzee Intelligence and Its Vocal Expression* (Baltimore: Williams & Wilkins, 1925); K. J. Hayes and C. H. Nissen, "Higher Mental Functions of a Home-Raised Chimpanzee," in Schrier, *Behavior of Nonhuman Primates;* E. W. Menzel, Jr., "Chimpanzee Spatial Memory Organization," *Science* 182(1973): 943–45, and *Precultural Primate Behavior* (Basel: S. Karger, 1973); Rumbaugh, "Reading and Sentence Completion"; D. M. Rumbaugh et al., "Lana (Chimpanzee) Learning Language—Progress Report," *Brain and Language* 1(1974): 205–12; Menzel and Halperin, "Purposive Behavior"; Premack, *Intelligence in Ape and Man,* and "Language and Intelligence"; D. Premack and G. Woodruff, "Does the Chimpanzee Have a Theory of Mind?" *Behavioral and Brain Sciences* 4(1978): 515–26, and "Chimpanzee Problem-Solving: A Test for Comprehension," *Science* 202(1978): 532–35; D. Premack et al., "Paper-Marking Test for Chimpanzee: Simple Control for Social Cues," *Science* 202(1978): 903–905; K. H. Pribam, "Consciousness, Classified and Declassified," *Behavioral and Brain Sciences* 4(1978): 590–592; Savage-Rumbaugh, "Symbolic Communication," "Linguistically Mediated Tool Use," "Do Apes Use Language?" and "Reference"; G. Woodruff et al., "Conservation of Liquid and Solid Quantity by the Chimpanzee," *Science* 202(1978): 991–94. **[60, 61, 62]**

68. Premack, "Language in Chimpanzee?" p. 808. **[61]**

69. Lenneberg, *Biological Foundations of Language.* **[11]**

70. B. F. Skinner, *Verbal Behavior* (New York: Appleton Century, 1957).

71. But see the critiques in N. Chomsky, "Review of *Verbal Behavior* by B. F. Skinner," *Language* 35(1959): 26–58, and "The Case Against B. F. Skinner," *New York Review of Books* 17(1971): 18–24.

72. N. Chomsky, *Aspects of the Theory of Syntax* (Cambridge, Mass.: M.I.T. Press, 1965), *Language and Mind* (New York: Harcourt, 1972 [1968]), *Studies on Semantics in Generative Grammar* (The Hague: Mouton, 1972), and *Rules and Representations* (New York: Columbia University Press, 1980).

73. J. Piaget, *Six Psychological Studies,* trans. A. Tenzer (New York: Random House, 1967), pp. 88–98, and *Biology and Knowledge,* pp. 46–47. **[3]**

74. See V. A. Fromkin et al., "The Development of Language in Genie: A Case of Language

Acquisition Beyond the 'Critical Period,'" *Brain and Language* 1(1974): 81–107; S. Curtiss, *Genie: A Psycholinguistic Study of a Modern-Day "Wild Child"* (New York: Academic Press, 1977).

75. N. Geschwind, "The Development of the Brain and the Evolution of Language," *Monographs Series on Language and Linguistics* 17(1964): 155–69, and "Language and the Brain," *Scientific American* 226, 4(1972): 76–83.

76. R. Clark, "The Transition from Action to Gesture," in *Action, Gesture and Symbol,* ed. A. Lock (London: Academic Press).

77. S. Goldin-Meadow and H. Feldman, "The Development of Language-Like Communication Without a Language Model," *Science* 197(1977): 401–03; H. Feldman et al., "Beyond Herodotus: The Creation of Language by Linguistically Deprived Deaf Children," in *Action, Gesture and Symbol: The Emergence of Language,* ed. A. Lock (London: Academic Press, 1978).

78. A. S. Macy, *The Instruction of Helen Keller* (Rochester, N.Y.: Western New York Institution for Deaf Mutes, 1894).

79. E.g., B. L. Whorf, *Language, Thought and Reality* (New York: Wiley, 1956).

80. Quoted in K. Lorenz, *Behind the Mirror: A Search for a Natural History of Human Knowledge,* trans. R. Taylor (London: Methuen, 1977[1973]), p. 189.

81. See G. Ojemann et al., "Human Language Cortex: Localization of Memory, Syntax, and Sequential Motor-Phoneme Identification Systems," *Science* 205(1979): 1401–03; A. Lock, ed., *Action, Gesture and Symbol: The Emergence of Language* (London: Academic Press, 1978).

82. J. Bronowski and U. Bellugi, "Language, Name and Concept," *Science* 168(1970): 669–73; J. S. Bruner, "From Communication to Language: A Psychological Perspective," *Cognition* 3(1975): 255–87.

83. See Skinner, *Verbal Behavior;* Terrace, *Nim;* Epstein, "Symbolic Communication Between Two Pigeons." **[58, 62, 69]**

84. J. S. Bruner, "Foreword," in *Action, Gesture and Symbol: The Emergence of Language,* ed. A. Lock (London: Academic Press, 1978), p. vii.

85. See D. K. Candland et al., *Emotion* (Monterey, Calif.: Brooks-Cole, 1977).

86. J. Olds and P. Milner, "Positive Reinforcement Produced by Electrical Stimulation of Septal Area and Other Regions of Rat Brain," *Journal of Comparative and Physiological Psychology* 47(1954): 419–27; J. Olds, "A Preliminary Mapping of Electrical Reinforcing Effects in the Rat Brain," *Journal of Comparative and Physiological Psychology* 49(1956): 281–85, "Hypothalamic Substrates of Reward," *Physiological Review* 42(1962): 554–604, and *Drives and Reinforcements: Behavioral Studies of Hypothalamic Functions* (New York: Raven Press, 1977); also A. Routtenberg, "The Reward System of the Brain," *Scientific American* 239, 5(1978): 154–64.

87. A. Wauquier and E. T. Rolls, *Brain-Stimulation Reward: A Collection of Papers Prepared for the First Conference on Brain-Stimulation Reward* (Amsterdam: North-Holland, 1976); Olds, *Drives and Reinforcements;* S. P. Grossman, "The Biology of Motivation," *Annual Review of Psychology* 30(1979): 209–42.

88. See P. L. McGeer and E. G. McGeer, "Chemistry of Mood and Emotion," in *Annual Review of Psychology,* vol. 31, ed. M. R. Rosenzweig (Palo Alto, Calif.: Annual Reviews Inc., 1980).

89. See especially J. M. Crabtree and K. E. Moyer, *Bibliography of Aggressive Behavior: A Reader's Guide to the Research Literature* (New York: Liss, 1977).

90. J. I. Lacey, "Psychophysiological Approaches to the Evaluation of Psychotherapeutic Process and Out-come," in *Research in Psychotherapy,* ed. E. A. Rubinstein and M. B. Parloff, vol. 1 (Washington, D.C.: American Psychological Association, 1959), "Autonomic Indices of Attention, Readiness, and Rejection of the External Environment," in *Readiness to Remember,* ed. D. P. Kimble (New York: Gordon and Breach, 1969), and "Some Cardiovascular Correlates

of Sensorimotor Behavior: Examples of Visceral Afferent Feedback?" in *Limbic System Mechanisms and Autonomic Function,* ed. C. H. Hackman (Springfield, Ill.: Thomas, 1972); J. I. Lacey and B. C. Lacey, "The Relationship of Resting Autonomic Activity to Motor Impulsivity," in *The Brain and Human Behavior: Association for Research in Nervous and Mental Disease,* vol. 36 (Baltimore: Williams and Wilkins, 1958), and "Some Autonomic-Central Nervous System Interrelationships," in *Physiological Correlates of Emotion,* ed. P. Black (New York: Academic Press, 1970); W. L. Libby, Jr., et al., "Pupillary and Cardiac Activity During Visual Attention," *Psychophysiology* 10(1973): 270–94. Also see the critique in R. Elliott, "The Significance of Heart Rate for Behavior: A Critique of Lacey's Hypothesis," *Journal of Personality and Social Psychology* 22(1972): 398–409; and the rebuttal in J. I. Lacey and B. C. Lacey, "On Heart Rate Responses and Behavior: A Reply to Elliott," *Journal of Personality and Social Psychology* 30(1974): 1–18.

91. Stress: L. Levi, ed., *Emotional Stress* (New York: Elsevier, 1967), and *Society, Stress and Disease* (London: Oxford University Press, 1971); R. O. Frost et al., "Stress and EEG-Alpha," *Psychophysiology* 15(1978): 394–97; H. Ursin et al., *Psychobiology of Stress* (New York: Academic Press, 1978); R. S. Bundy and S. M. Mangan, "Electrodermal Indices of Stress," *Psychophysiology* 16(1979): 30–33; S. M. Miller, "Coping with Impending Stress," *Psychophysiology* 16(1979): 572–81; H. Selye, *The Stress of Life* (New York: McGraw-Hill, 1976 [1956]), *Stress in Health and Disease* (Boston: Butterworths, 1976), and "Stress and Disease," *Science* 122(1955): 625–31. Arousal: C. M. Miezejeski, "Relationships Between Behavioral Arousal and Some Components of Autonomic Arousal," *Psychophysiology* 15(1978): 417–21. Emotions: H. Konzett, "Cardiovascular Parameters and Methods of Measuring Emotions" and M. Lader, "Psychophysiological Parameters and Methods," both in Levi, *Emotions;* R. Klorman et al., "Individual Differences in Fear and Autonomic Reactions to Affective Stimulation," *Psychophysiology* 14(1977): 45–51. Personality differences: H. J. Eysenck, *Biological Basis of Personality, Readings in Extraversion-Introversion,* vol. 3 (London: Staples Press, 1971), and *Measurement of Personality;* A. Gale et al., "Extraversion-Introversion and the EEG," *British Journal of Psychology* 60(1969): 209–23; A. Crider and R. Lunn, "Electrodermal Lability as a Personality Dimension," *Journal of Experimental Research in Personality* 5(1971): 145–50; J. A. Gray, "The Psychophysiological Nature of Introversion-Extraversion: A Modification of Eysenck's theory," in *Biological Bases of Individual Behavior,* ed. V. D. Nebylitsyn and J. A. Gray (New York: Academic Press, 1972); R. M. Stelmack et al., "Extraversion and Individual Differences in Auditory Evoked Responses," *Psychophysiology* 14(1977): 368–74; J. J. Gange et al., "Autonomic Differences Between Extraverts and Intraverts During Vigilance," *Psychophysiology* 16(1979): 392–97; M. L. Knight and R. J. Bordon, "Autonomic and Affective Reactions of High and Low Socially-Anxious Individuals Awaiting Public Performance," *Psychophysiology* 16(1979): 209–13. Mental disabilities: R. E. Passingham, "Crime and Personality: A Review of Eysenck's Theory," in Nebylitsyn and Gray, *Biological Bases of Behavior;* K. R. Sobotka and J. G. May, "Visual Evoked Potentials and Reaction Time in Normal and Dyslexic Children," *Psychophysiology* 14(1977): 18–24; M. S. Buchsbaum, "Psychophysiology and Schizophrenia," *Schizophrenia Bulletin* 3(1977): 7–14; S. A. Mednick, "Berkson's Fallacy and High-Risk Research," in *The Nature of Schizophrenia,* ed. L. C. Wynne et al. (New York: Wiley, 1978); T. Patterson and P. H. Venables, "Bilateral Skin Conductance and Skin Potential in Schizophrenic and Normal Subjects: The Identification of the Fast Habituator Group of Schizophrenics," *Psychophysiology* 15(1978): 556–60; R. Blackburn, "Cortical and Autonomic Arousal in Primary and Secondary Psychopaths," *Psychophysiology* 16(1979): 143–50; H. E. Spohn and T. Patterson, "Recent Studies of Psychophysiology in Schizophrenia," *Schizophrenia Bulletin* 5(1979): 581–611.

92. E. Aserinsky and N. Kleitman, "Regularly Occurring Periods of Eye Motility, and Concomitant Phenomena, During Sleep," *Science* 118(1953): 273–274; N. Kleitman, *Sleep and Wake-*

fulness (Chicago: University of Chicago Press, 1963); D. Kripke, "An Ultradian Biologic Rhythm Associated with Perceptual Deprivation and REM Sleep," *Psychosomatic Medicine* 34(1972): 221–34; I. Oswald et al., "Cyclical 'On Demand' Oral Intake by Adults," *Nature* 225(1970): 959–60; W. C. Orr et al., "Ultradian Rhythms in Extended Performance," *Aerospace Medicine* 45(1975): 995–1000; R. Klein and R. Armitage, "Rhythms in Human Performance: 1½-Hour Oscillations in Cognitive Style," *Science* 204(1979): 1326–28.

93. Eysenck, *Biological Basis of Personality, Readings in Extraversion-Introversion,* "A Brief Note on Extraversion and Performance," *Journal of Abnormal Psychology* 83(1974): 308–10, *Measurement of Personality.* **[15]**

94. Collected in Eysenck, *Readings in Extraversion-Introversion* and *Measurement of Personality.* See also, J. A. Gray, "The Psychophysiological Basis of Introversion-Extraversion," *Behavior Research and Therapy* 8(1970): 249–66, and "Psychophysiological Nature of Introversion-Extraversion"; M. W. Eysenck and M. C. Eysenck, "Memory Scanning Introversion-Extraversion, and Levels of Processing," *Journal of Research in Personality* 13(1979): 305–15; Nebylitsyn and Gray, *Biological Bases of Behavior.* **[15, 91]**

95. Eysenck, *Crime and Personality.* **[11]**

96. E.g., see R. J. Smith, *The Psychopath in Society* (New York: Academic Press, 1978).

97. Eysenck, "Brief Note on Extraversion." See also Passingham, "Crime and Personality." **[91, 93]**

98. R. J. Herrnstein, "The Evolution of Behaviorism," *American Psychologist* 32(1977): 593–603, and "Doing What Comes Naturally: A Reply to Professor Skinner," *American Psychologist* 32(1977): 1013–16.

99. See M. E. P. Seligman and J. L. Hager, eds., *Biological Boundaries of Learning* (New York: Appleton Century, 1975); S. J. Shettleworth, "Constraints on Learning," in *Advances in the Study of Behavior,* ed. D. S. Lehrman et al., vol. 4 (New York: Academic Press, 1972); R. A. Hinde and J. Stevenson-Hinde, eds., *Constraints on Learning: Limitations and Predispositions* (New York: Academic Press, 1973); William T. Powers, "Feedback: Beyond Behaviorism," *Science* 179(1973): 351–56, and *Behavior: The Control of Perception* (Chicago: Aldine, 1973); M. E. Bitterman, "The Comparative Analysis of Learning," *Science* 188(1975): 699–709. See also Skinner's response to Herrnstein in "Herrnstein and the Evolution of Behaviorism," *American Psychologist* 32(1977): 1006–12 and Herrnstein's reply. **[98]**

100. E. L. Thorndike, *Animal Intelligence: Experimental Studies* (New York: Hafner, 1965 [1911]).

101. E.g., H. W. Nissen, *A Field Study of the Chimpanzee: Observations of Chimpanzee Behavior in Western French Guinea* (Baltimore: Johns Hopkins University Press, 1931); C. R. Carpenter, "A Field Study of the Behavior and Social Relations of the Howling Monkeys (*Alouatta palliata*)," *Comparative Psychology Monographs* 10(1934): 1–168, and "A Field Study in Siam of the Behavior and Social Relations of the Gibbon (*Hylobates lav*)," *Comparative Psychology Monographs* 16(1940): 1–212; W. C. Allee, *Cooperation Among Animals: With Human Implications,* revised edition of *The Social Life of Animals* (New York: Henry Schuman, 1951 [1938]); R. M. Yerkes, *Chimpanzees: A Laboratory Colony* (New Haven: Yale University Press, 1943).

102. J. P. Scott and M. Marston, "Critical Periods Affecting the Development of Norman and Mal-Adjustive Social Behavior of Puppies," *Journal of Genetic Psychology* 77(1950): 25–60; Scott, "Critical Periods." **[44]**

103. Hebb, *Organization of Behavior.* **[39]**

104. H. F. Harlow, "Learning and Satiation of Response in Intrinsically Motivated Complex Puzzle Performance in Monkeys," *Journal of Comparative and Physiological Psychology* 43(1950): 289–294, "Mice, Monkeys, Men and Motives," *Psychological Review* 60(1953): 23–32, and "Love in Infant Monkeys"; Harlow and Harlow, "Social Deprivation in Monkeys"; C. M. Locurto et al., eds., *Autoshaping and Conditioning Theory* (New York: Academic Press, 1981). **[33]**

105. K. Breland and M. Breland, "The Misbehavior of Organisms," *American Psychologist* 16(1961): 681–84.

106. J. Garcia and R. Koelling, "Relation of Cue to Consequence in Avoidance Learning," *Psychonomic Science* 4(1966): 123–24.

107. Seligman and Hager, *Biological Boundaries of Learning;* Hinde and Stevenson-Hinde, *Constraints on Learning.* **[99]**

108. R. C. Bolles, "Species-Specific Defense Reactions and Avoidance Learning, *Psychological Review* 77(1970): 32–48.

109. H. Rachlin and P. N. Hineline, "Training and Maintenance of Key-Pecking in the Pigeon by Negative Reinforcement," *Science* 157(1967): 954–55.

110. P. L. Brown and H. M. Jenkins, "Auto-Shaping of the Pigeon's Key-Peck," *Journal of the Experimental Analysis of Behavior* 11(1968): 1–8.

111. D. R. and H. Williams, "Auto-Maintenance in the Pigeon," *Journal of the Experimental Analysis of Behavior* 12(1969): 511–20. See also Locurto, *Autoshaping and Conditioning Theory;* E. Hearst and H. M. Jenkins, *Sign-Tracking, Monographs of the Psychonomic Society* 5, 104(1974).

112. B. R. Moore and S. Stuttard, "Dr. Guthrie and *felis domesticus* or: Tripping over the Cat," *Science* 205(1979): 1031–33. See E. R. Guthrie and G. P. Horton, *Cats in a Puzzle Box* (New York: Rinehart, 1946).

113. J. Konorski, *Integretive Activity of the Brain* (Chicago: University of Chicago Press, 1967).

114. L. J. Harris et al., "Appetite and Choice of Diet: The Ability of the Vitamin B Deficient Rat to Discriminate Between Diets Containing and Lacking the Vitamin," *Proceedings of the Royal Society,* London, series B 113(1933): 161–90; C. P. Richter, "Increased Salt Appetite in Adrenalectomized Rats," *American Journal of Physiology* 115(1936): 155–61, and "Total Self-Regulatory Functions in Animals and Human Beings," *Harvey Lecture Series* 38(1943): 63–103.

115. See especially P. Rozin et al., "Thiamine Specific Hunger: Vitamin in Water Versus Vitamin in Food," *Journal of Comparative and Physiological Psychology* 57(1964): 78–84; W. Rodgers and P. Rozin, "Novel Food Preferences in Thiamine-Deficient Rats," *Journal of Comparative and Physiological Psychology* 61(1966): 1–4; P. Rozin, "Thiamine Specific Hunger," in *Handbook of Physiology,* vol. I (Washington, D.C.: American Physiological Society, 1967), and "The Selection of Foods by Rats, Humans, and Other Animals," in J. S. Rosenblatt et al., eds., *Advances in the Study of Behavior,* vol. VI (New York: Academic Press, 1976); P. Rozin and J. W. Kalat, "Learning as a Situation-Specific Adaptation," in Seligman and Hager, *Biological Boundaries of Learning.* **[99]**

116. D. Chitty and H. N. Southern, *Control of Rats and Mice* (Oxford: Clarendon Press, 1954); S. A. Barnett, *The Rat: A Study in Behavior* (London: Methuen, 1963); Rozin and Kalat, "Learning as Situation-Specific Adaptation," and "Specific Hungers and Poison Avoidance as Adaptive Specializations of Learning," *Psychological Review* 78(1971): 459–86; A. W. Logue, "Taste Aversion and the Generality of the Laws of Learning," *Psychological Bulletin* 86(1979): 276–96. **[99]**

117. D. L. Roll and J. C. Smith, "Conditioned Taste Aversion in Anesthetized Rats," in Seligman and Hager, *Biological Boundaries of Learning.* **[99]**

118. J.-S. Chen and A. Amsel, "Recall (Versus Recognition) of Taste and Immunization Against Aversive Taste Anticipations Based on Illness," *Science* 209(1980): 831–33.

119. M. E. P. Seligman, "On the Generality of the Laws of Learning," *Psychological Review* 77(1970): 406–18, and "Phobias and Preparedness," *Behavior Therapy* 2(1971): 307–20.

120. D. A. Hamburg, "Emotions in the Perspective of Human Evolution," in *Expression of the Emotions in Man,* ed. P. H. Knapp (New York: International Universities Press, 1963).

121. Herrnstein, "Evolution of Behaviorism," p. 596. Powers, "Feedback," and "Behavior."

Also relevant is the learning and decision-making model in J. A. Gray, *Elements of a Two-Process Theory of Learning* (London: Academic Press, 1975), and "Neuropsychology of Anxiety," *The British Journal of Psychology* 69(1978): 417–34. **[98, 99]**

122. D. T. Campbell, " 'Downward Causation' in Hierarchically Organised Biological Systems," in T. Dobzhansky and F. J. Ayala, *Studies in the Philosophy of Biology* (London: Macmillan, 1974). The matter is reviewed in depth in Corning (forthcoming).

123. D. C. Gajdusek, "Unconventional Viruses and the Origin and Disappearance of Kuru," *Science* 197(1977): 943–60.

124. M. A. Little and J. M. Hanna, "The Responses of High-Altitude Populations to Cold and Other Stresses," in *The Biology of High-Altitude Peoples,* ed. P. T. Baker (Cambridge: Cambridge University Press, 1978).

125. D. R. Hampton, *Organizational Behavior and the Practice of Management* (Glenview, Ill.: Scott-Foresman, 1978).

126. R. J. Naughton, "Motivational Factors of American Prisoners of War," *Naval War College Review* 27(1975): 2–14.

127. R. A. Bryson and T. J. Murray, *Climates of Hunger: Mankind and the World's Changing Weather* (Madison, Wisc.: University of Wisconsin Press, 1977).

128. S. C. Wecker, "Habitat Selection," *Scientific American* 211, 4(1964): 109–16. For other relevant experiments, see R. M. Cooper and J. P. Zubek, "Effects of Enriched and Restricted Early Environments on the Learning Ability of Bright and Dull Rats," *Canadian Journal of Psychology* 12(1958): 159–64; N. D. Henderson, "Genetic Influences on the Behavior of Mice Can Be Observed by Laboratory Rearing," *Journal of Comparative Physiology and Psychology* 72(1970): 505–11; V. H. Denenberg, "Interactional Effects in Early Experience Research," in *Genetics, Environment and Intelligence,* ed. A. Oliverio (Amsterdam: Elsevier, 1977).

129. A. S. Rossi and P. E. Rossi, "Body Time and Social Time: Mood Patterns by Menstrual Cycle Phase and Day of the Week," *Social Science Research* 6(1977): 273–308.

130. R. E. Hicks and M. Kinsbourne, "Human Handedness: A Partial Cross-Fostering Study," *Science* 192(1976): 908–10; E. L. Teng et al., "Handedness in a Chinese Population: Biological, Social, and Pathological Factors," *Science* 193(1976): 1148–50; L. Carter-Saltzman, "Biological and Sociocultural Effects on Handedness: Comparison Between Biological and Adoptive Families," *Science* 209(1980): 1263–65.

131. See especially, A. Anastasi, "Intelligence and Family Size," *Psychological Bulletin* 53(1956): 187–209; W. D. Altus, "Birth Order and Its Sequence," *Science* 151(1966): 44–49; J. R. Warren, "Birth Order and Social Behavior," *Psychological Bulletin* 65(1966): 38–49; L. Belmont and F. A. Marolla, "Birth Order, Family Size and Intelligence," *Science* 182(1973): 1096–1101; L. Belmont et al., "Comparison of Associations of Birth Order with Intelligence Test Score and Height," *Nature* 255(1975): 54–56; R. B. Zajonc and G. B. Marcus, "Birth Order and Intellectual Development," *Psychological Review* 82(1975): 74–87; D. J. Davis et al., "Birth Order and Intellectual Development," *Science* 196(1977): 1470–72; J. W. Foster and S. J. Archer, "Birth Order and Intelligence—Immunological Interpretations," *Perceptual and Motor Skills* 48(1979): 79–93; E. U. Nuttall and R. L. Nuttall, "Child-Spacing Effects on Intelligence, Personality and Social Competence," *The Journal of Psychology* 102(1979): 3–12.

132. L. Caldwell, "Implications of Biopolitics: Reflections on a Politics of Survival," paper presented at the annual meeting, International Society of Political Psychology, 1979, p. 16.

133. Reviewed in Noble, "Age, Race, and Sex"; also Freedman, *Human Infancy,* and *Human Sociobiology;* Freedman and DeBoer, "Biological and Cultural Differences." **[15, 17]**

134. D. G. Freedman and N. C. Freedman, "Behavioral Differences Between Chinese-American and European-American Newborns," *Nature* 224(1969): 1227; Freedman, *Human Infancy,* and *Human Sociobiology;* Freedman and DeBoer, "Biological and Cultural Differences"; J. Kuchner, *Chinese and European-Americans: A Cross-Cultural Study of Infants and Mothers,*

unpublished Ph.D. dissertation, University of Chicago, 1979. Corroboration of the Freedmans' work has been obtained in, among others, Japanese infants: W. Caudill and H. Weinstein, "Maternal Care and Infant Behavior in Japan and America," *Psychiatry* 32(1969): 12–43; W. Caudill and F. Frost, "A Comparison of Maternal Care and Infant Behavior in Japanese-American, American, and Japanese Families," in *Influences on Human Development,* ed. U. Bronfenbrenner and M. A. Maloney (Hinsdale, Ill.: Dryden, 1975); Navajo Indians: J. S. Chisholm, *Cradleboarding Practices Among the Navajo,* unpublished Ph.D. dissertation, Rutgers University, 1977; J. K. Nisselius, *Behavioral Assessment of the Navajo Newborn,* unpublished M.A. thesis, University of Utah, 1976; Zincanteco Indians: T. B. Brazelton et al., "Infant Development in the Zincanteco Indians of Southern Mexico," *Pediatrics* 44(1969): 274–90; and (for psychomotor abilities) in African and American blacks: N. Bayley, "Comparison of Mental and Motor Test Scores for Ages 1–15 Months by Sex, Birth Order, Race, Geographical Location and Age of Parents," *Child Development* 36(1965): 379–411; N. Warren, "African Infant Precocity," *Psychological Bulletin* 78(1972): 353–67. **[17]**

135. Caudill and Frost, "Maternal Care and Infant Behavior."

136. For overviews of this extensively researched area, see especially, D. Cartwright and A. Zander, *Group Dynamics: Research and Theory,* 3rd ed. (New York: Harper & Row, 1968); G. T. Force et al., *Theory and Research in the Study of Leadership: An Annotated Bibliography* (Carbondale, Ill.: Southern Illinois University Press, 1972); G. D. Paige, ed., *Political Leadership: Readings for an Emerging Field* (New York: Free Press, 1972), and *The Scientific Study of Leadership* (New York: Free Press, 1977); E. A. Fleishman and J. G. Hunt, eds., *Current Developments in the Study of Leadership* (Carbondale, Ill.: Southern Illinois University Press, 1973); J. G. Hunt and L. Larson, *Leadership Frontiers* (Kent, Ohio: Kent State University Press, 1975); F. E. Fiedler and M. M. Chemers, *Leadership and Effective Management* (Glenview, Ill.: Scott, Foresman, 1974); R. M. Stogdill, *Handbook of Leadership: A Survey of Theory and Research* (New York: Free Press, 1974); A. P. Hare, *Handbook of Small Group Research,* 2d ed. (New York: Free Press, 1976); L. Berkowitz, ed., *Group Processes: Papers from Advances in Experimental Social Psychology* (New York: Academic Press, 1978).

137. See also, W. E. Halal, "Toward a General Theory of Leadership," *Human Relations* 27(1974): 401–16; B. Schultz, "Characteristics of Emergent Leaders of Continuing Problem-Solving Groups," *Journal of Psychology* 88(1974): 167–73; R. W. Rice and M. M. Chemers, "Personality and Situational Determinants of Leader Behavior," *Journal of Applied Psychology* 60(1975): 20–27; J. Pandey, "Effects of Leadership Style, Personality Characteristics and Method of Leader Selection on Members' and Leaders' Behavior," *European Journal of Social Psychology* 6(1976): 475–89.

138. B. Winterhalder et al., "Dung as an Essential Resource in a Highland Peruvian Community," *Human Ecology* 2(1974): 89–104; R. B. Thomas, "Human Adaptation to a High Andean Energy Flow System," *Occasional Papers in Anthropology,* no. 7 (University Park, Pa.: Pennsylvania State University Department of Anthropology, 1973).

139. Little and Hanna, "Responses of High-Altitude Populations." **[124]**

140. S. H. Katz et al., "Traditional Maize Processing Techniques in the New World," *Science* 184(1974): 765–73.

141. W. Bennett, "Cigarette Century," *Science 80* 1, 6(1980): 36–43.

142. P. A. Corning, "The Biological Bases of Behavior and Their Implications for Political Theory," paper prepared for the annual meeting of the American Political Science Association, 1969.

143. C. Woodham-Smith, *The Great Hunger* (London: Hamilton, 1962); B. W. Tuchman, *A Distant Mirror* (New York: Knopf, 1978); E. P. Eckholm, *Losing Ground* (New York: Norton, 1976).

144. E.g., P.-P. Grassé, *Evolution of Living Organisms: Evidence for a New Theory of Transfor-*

mation (New York: Academic Press, 1977 [1973]); J. Piaget, *Behavior and Evolution* (New York: Random House, 1978); M. Ho and P. Saunders, "Beyond Neo-Darwinism—An Epigenetic Approach to Evolution," *Journal of Theoretical Biology* 78(1979): 573–91.

145. S. J. Gould and R. C. Lewontin, "The Spandrels of San Marco and the Panglossian Paradigm: A Critique of the Adaptationist Programme," *Proceedings of the Royal Society of London* 205(1979): 581–98; Ho and Saunders, "Beyond Neo-Darwinism"; S. J. Gould, "The Evolutionary Biology of Constraint," *Daedalus* 108(1980): 39–52. **[144]**

146. H. H. Pattee, "The Complementarity Principle in Biological and Social Structures," *Journal of Social and Biological Structures* 1(1978): 194.

147. After D. Thompson, *On Growth and Form,* 2d ed. (Cambridge: Cambridge University Press, 1942 [1917]), and B. Rensch, *Evolution Above the Species Level* (New York: Columbia University Press, 1960 [1947]).

148. Gould and Lewontin, "Spandrels of San Marco." **[145]**

149. Gould, "Evolutionary Biology of Constraint." **[145]**

150. Ho and Saunders, "Beyond Neo-Darwinism." **[144]**

151. See especially, Thompson, *Growth and Form;* C. F. A. Pantin, "Organic Design," *The Advancement of Science* 8(1951): 138–150; Rensch, *Evolution Above Species Level.* **[147]**

152. E.g., W. H. Durham, "Adaptive Significance of Cultural Behavior," *Human Ecology* 4(1976): 89–121; J. H. Barkow, "Culture and Sociobiology," *American Anthropologist* 80(1978): 5–20; K. E. Boulding, *Ecodynamics* (Beverly Hills: Sage, 1978).

153. See M. Pettersson, "Acceleration in Evolution, Before Human Times," *Journal of Social and Biological Structures* 1(1978): 201–06.

154. E.g., A. Alland, Jr., *Evolution and Human Behavior* (New York: Natural History Press, 1967); C. Geertz, *Agricultural Innovation: Process of Ecological Change in Indonesia* (Berkeley: University of California Press, 1963); Barkow, "Culture and Sociobiology," and "Prestige and Culture: A Biosocial Interpretation," *Current Anthropology* 16(1975): 553–72; W. H. Durham, "The Adaptive Significance of Cultural Behavior."

155. J. S. Huxley, *Evolution: The Modern Synthesis* (New York: Harper & Row, 1942), p. 419.

156. J. T. Bonner, *The Evolution of Culture in Animals* (Princeton: Princeton University Press, 1980). Also see P. C. Mundinger, "Animal Cultures and a General Theory of Cultural Evolution," *Ethology and Sociobiology* 1(1980): 183–223.

157. J. W. S. Pringle, "On the Parallel Between Learning and Evolution," *Behavior* 3(1951): 174–215; G. Bateson, "The Role of Somatic Change in Evolution," *Evolution* 17(1963): 529–39; B. F. Skinner, "The Phylogeny and Ontogeny of Behavior," *Science* 153(1966): 1205–13; R. Levins, *Evolution in Changing Environments: Some Theoretical Explorations* (Princeton: Princeton University Press, 1968); H. Kummer, *Primate Societies: Group Techniques of Ecological Adaptation* (Chicago: Aldine, 1971); A. Manning, *An Introduction to Animal Behavior,* 2d ed. (Reading, Mass.: Addison-Wesley, 1972); L. B. Slobodkin and A. Rapoport, "An Optimal Strategy of Evolution," *The Quarterly Review of Biology* 49(1974): 181–200.

158. Wilson, *Sociobiology,* p. 145. **[55]**

159. Ibid., p. 550.

160. U. Olin, "The Challenge of Human Expansion," *Social Science Information* 13(1974): 48.

161. R. D. Alexander, "The Search for a General Theory of Behavior," *Behavioral Science* 20(1975): 77–100.

162. Barkow, "Culture and Sociobiology," p. 5. **[152]**

163. See R. D. Alexander and G. Borgia, "Group Selection, Altruism, and the Levels of Organization of Life," *Annual Review of Ecology and Systematics* 9(1978): 449–74.

164. Cited in E. Curio, "Towards a Methodology of Teleonomy," *Experientia* 29(1973): 1045–58.

165. J. N. Hill, "The Origin of Sociocultural Evolution," *Journal of Social and Biological Structures* 1(1978): 383.

166. B. E. Ginsburg, "Genetics of Social Behavior," in *Perspectives in Ethology,* ed. P. P. G. Bateson and P. H. Klopfer, vol. 3 (New York: Plenum, 1978), pp. 4–5.

167. E. Durkheim, *The Rules of Sociological Method,* trans. S. A. Soloway and J. H. Mueller (Chicago: University of Chicago Press, 1938 [1895]), p. 91. See also the discussion in A. Alland, Jr., "Adaptation," *Annual Review of Anthropology* 4(1975): 59–73.

168. Huxley, *Evolution,* p. 420. **[155]**

169. A. Montagu, *Culture and Evolution of Man* (New York: Oxford, 1962); S. J. Gould, *Ontogeny and Phylogeny* (Cambridge, Mass.: Harvard University Press, 1977).

170. R. C. Lewontin, "Adaptation," *Scientific American* 239, 3(1978): 213.

171. P. R. Ehrlich and P. H. Raven, "Butterflies and Plants: A Study in Coevolution," *Evolution* 18(1964): 586–608.

172. J. Maynard Smith, *The Theory of Evolution,* 3rd ed. (New York: Penguin, 1975).

173. This issue was joined in detailed critiques by R. C. Lewontin, "Adaptation," in *The Encyclopedia Einaudi* (Turin: Giulio Einaudi, 1977), and "Adaptation," and in a defense by Maynard Smith, "Optimization Theory in Evolution," *Annual Review of Ecology and Systematics* 9(1978): 31–56. For further discussions, see N. Tinbergen, *Social Behavior in Animals* (London: Methuen, 1965 [1953]); R. A. Hinde, "The Concept of Function," in *Function and Evolution in Behavior,* ed. C. Baerends et al. (Oxford: Clarendon Press, 1975); R. D. Alexander, "Natural Selection and Societal Laws," in *Morals, Science and Society,* ed. T. Englehardt and D. Callahan (Hastings-on-Hudson, N.Y.: Hastings Center, 1978).

174. Maynard Smith, *Theory of Evolution.* **[172]**

175. H. Kruuk, *Predators and Anti-Predator Behaviour of the Black-Headed Gull* (Larus Ridibundus L.), Behaviour, Supplement, vol. XI (London: Brill, 1964); Tinbergen, *Social Behavior in Animals.*

176. Huxley, *Evolution.* Cf. Alland, *Evolution and Human Behavior,* and *Adaptation in Cultural Evolution: An Approach to Medical Anthropology* (New York: Columbia University Press, 1970) and D. L. Hardesty, *Ecological Anthropology* (New York: Wiley, 1977). Following Radcliffe-Brown, identify only two kinds: internal and external.

177. M. S. Sahlins, *Use and Abuse of Biology* (Ann Arbor: University of Michigan Press, 1976); R. Dawkins, *The Selfish Gene* (New York: Oxford University Press, 1976); D. P. Barash, *Sociobiology and Behavior* (New York: Elsevier, 1977); Boulding, *Ecodynamics;* P. Diener, "On Evolution and Culture: A Reply," *Current Anthropology* 21(1980): 680; P. J. Richerson and R. Boyd, "A Dual Inheritance Model of Human Evolutionary Process I: Basic Postulates and a Simple Model," *Journal of Social and Biological Structures* 1(1978): 127–54. See also D. T. Campbell, "On the Genetics of Altruism and the Counter-Hedonic Components in Human Culture," *Journal of Social Issues* 28(1972): 21–37; F. T. Cloak, Jr., "Is a Cultural Ethology Possible?" *Human Ecology* 3(1975): 161–82, and "That a Culture and a Social Organization Mutually Shape Each Other Through a Process of Continuing Evolution," *Man-Environment Systems* 5(1975): 3–6. **[152]**

178. See also R. D. Alexander, *Darwinism and Human Affairs* (Seattle: University of Washington Press, 1979), and "Evolution and Culture," in *Evolutionary Biology and Human Social Behavior: An Anthropological Perspective,* ed. N. A. Chagnon and W. Irons (North Scituate, Mass.: Duxbury, 1979); Bonner, *Evolution of Culture in Animals;* Mundinger, "Animal Cultures"; C. J. Lumsden and E. O. Wilson, *Genes, Mind and Culture: The Co-Evolutionary Process* (Cambridge, Mass.: Harvard University Press, 1981). **[156]**

179. Bonner, *Evolution of Culture in Animals,* p. 10. **[156]**

180. Ibid., p. 11.

181. For discussions of the concept of "goals" in biological and social systems, see A. Rosenbleuth et al., "Behavior, Purpose and Teleology," *Philosophy of Science* 10(1943): 18–24; also

K. W. Deutsch, *The Nerves of Government: Models of Political Communication and Control* (New York: Free Press 1966 [1963]); H. A. Simon, "On the Concept of Organizational Goal," *Administrative Science Quarterly* 9(1964): 1–22; W. Buckley, *Sociology and Modern Systems Theory* (Englewood Cliffs, N.J.: Prentice-Hall, 1967); and *Modern Systems Research for the Behavioral Scientist: A Sourcebook* (Chicago: Aldine, 1968); A. Etzioni, *The Active Society: A Theory of Societal and Political Processes* (New York: Free Press, 1968); H. von Foerster et al., eds., *Purposive Systems: Proceedings of the First Symposium of the American Society for Cybernetics* (New York: Spartan Books, 1968); R. L. Ackoff and F. E. Emery, *On Purposeful Systems* (Chicago: Aldine, 1972); J. G. Miller, *Living Systems* (New York: McGraw-Hill, 1978); W. H. Thorpe, *Purpose in a World of Chance: A Biologist's View* (Oxford: Oxford University Press, 1978), *inter alia.*

182. G. C. Williams, *Adaptation and Natural Selection: A Critique of Some Current Evolutionary Thought* (Princeton: Princeton University Press, 1966).

183. R. A. Hinde, "The Concept of Function," in *Function and Evolution of Behaviour: Essays in Honor of Professor Niko Tinbergen,* ed. G. Baerends et al. (Oxford: Clarendon Press, 1976).

184. Huxley, *Evolution,* p. 417. **[155]**

185. The concept of "function" and of functional explanation in biological and social life has been much exercised over the years. See especially the discussions in Huxley, *Evolution;* E. Mayr, "Cause and Effect in Biology," in *Cause and Effect,* ed. D. Lerner (New York: Free Press, 1965); Tinbergen, *Social Behavior in Animals;* Williams, *Adaptation and Natural Selection;* Buckley, *Sociology and Modern Systems Theory;* Hinde, "Concept of Function"; Curio, "A Methodology of Teleonomy"; Alexander, "Natural Selection"; Miller, *Living Systems;* and the various writings collected in Buckley, *Modern Systems Research.* **[155, 164, 173, 178, 181, 182, 183]**

186. J. H. Steward, *Theory of Culture Change: The Methodology of Multilinear Evolution* (Urbana, Ill.: University of Illinois Press, 1955), p. 32.

187. A. R. Radcliffe-Brown, "The Concept of Function in Social Science," *American Anthropologist* 37(1935): 394–402; T. Parsons, *The Structure of Social Action: A Study of Social Theory with Special Reference to a Group of Recent European Writers,* 2d ed. (Glencoe, Ill.: Free Press, 1949 [1937]), and *The Social System* (Glencoe, Ill.: Free Press, 1951).

188. M. Harris, *Culture, People, Nature: An Introduction to General Anthropology,* 2d ed. (New York: T. Y. Crowell, 1975), pp. 16–18.

189. L. A. White, *The Concept of Cultural Systems: A Key to Understanding Tribes and Nations* (New York: Columbia University Press, 1975), p. 46.

190. R. L. Carneiro, "Culture: Cultural Adaptation," in *International Encyclopedia of the Social Sciences,* ed. D. Sills, vol. III (New York: Macmillan, 1968), and "The Four Faces of Evolution," in *Handbook of Social and Cultural Anthropology,* ed. J. H. Honigmann (Chicago: Rand McNally, 1973).

191. Carneiro, "Four Faces of Evolution," p. 553. **[190]**

192. Ibid.

193. Ibid., p. 91.

194. For discussions of this issue and of "Dollo's Law" of evolutionary irreversibility, see G. G. Simpson, *The Major Features of Evolution* (New York: Columbia University Press, 1953); B. Rensch, "The Laws of Evolution," in Tax, *Evolution After Darwin,* and *Evolution Above Species Level;* T. Dobzhansky, *Genetics of the Evolutionary Process* (New York: Columbia University Press, 1970). **[147]**

195. M. D. Sahlins, "Evolution: Specific and General," in *Evolution and Culture,* ed. M. D. Sahlins and E. R. Service (Ann Arbor: University of Michigan Press, 1960), pp. 20–21.

196. E. R. Service, *Cultural Evolutionism: Theory in Practice* (New York: Holt, 1971), p. 3.

197. Ibid., p. 97.

198. See especially, S. L. Washburn, "Behavior and Human Evolution," in *Classification and Human Evolution,* ed. S. L. Washburn (Chicago: Aldine, 1963), and *The Study of Human Evolution* (Eugene: University of Oregon Press, 1968); Alland, *Evolution and Human Behavior, Adaptation in Cultural Evolution,* and "Adaptation"; Vayda and Rappaport, "Ecology"; J. W. Bennett, *Northern Plainsmen: Adaptive Strategy and Agrarian Life* (Chicago: Aldine, 1969), "Anticipation," and *The Ecological Transition: Cultural Anthropology and Human Adaptation* (New York: Pergamon, 1976); A. P. Vayda, ed., *Environment and Cultural Behavior: Ecological Studies in Cultural Anthropology* (Garden City, N.Y.: Natural History Press, 1969); B. J. Meggers, *Amazonia: Man and Culture in a Counterfeit Paradise* (Chicago: Aldine, 1971); L. Tiger and R. Fox, *The Imperial Animal* (New York: Holt, 1971); E. H. Willhoite, Jr., "Ethology and the Tradition of Political Thought," *Journal of Politics* 33(1971): 615–41; A. Alland, Jr., and B. McKay, "The Concept of Adaptation in Biological and Cultural Evolution," in Honigmann, *Handbook of Social and Cultural Anthropology;* G. V. Coelho et al., eds., *Coping and Adaptation* (New York: Basic Books, 1974); Freedman, *Human Infancy,* and *Human Sociobiology;* R. Fox, ed., *Biosocial Anthropology* (London: Malaby Press, 1975); R. D. Masters, "Politics as a Biological Phenomenon," *Social Science Information* 14(1975); Vayda and McCay, "New Directions in Ecology"; Durham, "Adaptive Significance of Behavior"; R. Fox and U. Fleising, "Human Ethology," *Annual Review of Anthropology* 5(1976): 265–88; Moos, *Human Adaptation;* G. Schubert, "Politics as a Life Science: How and Why the Impact of Modern Biology Will Revolutionize the Study of Political Behavior," in *Biology and Politics,* ed. A. Somit (The Hague: Mouton, 1976); Barash, *Sociobiology and Behavior;* J. H. Barkow, "Human Ethology and Intraindividual Systems," *Social Science Information* 16(1977): 133–45, and "Culture and Sociobiology"; Hardesty, *Ecological Anthropology;* P. L. Van den Berghe, *Man in Society: A Biosocial View* (New York: Elsevier, 1975); P. T. Baker, *Biology of High-Altitude Peoples;* Chagnon and Irons, *Evolutionary Biology;* R. Chase, "Structural-Functional Dynamics in the Analysis of Socio-Economic Systems: Development of the Approach to Understanding the Processes of Systematic Change," *American Journal of Economics and Sociology* 38(1979): 293–305, and "Structural-Functional Dynamics in the Analysis of Socio-Economic Systems: Adaptation of Structural Change Processes to Biological Systems of Human Interaction," *American Journal of Economics and Sociology* 39(1980): 49–64; Wiegele, *Biopolitics;* R. E. Dunlap, "Paradigmatic Change in Social Science: The Decline of Human Exemptionalism and the Emergence of an Ecological Paradigm," *American Behavioral Scientist* 24(1980): 1–12; Peter and Petryszak, "Sociobiology Versus Biosociology." See also P. A. Corning, "The Biological Bases of Behavior and Some Implications for Political Science," *World Politics* 23(1971): 321–70, "Toward a Survival-Oriented Policy Science," in *Biology and Politics,* ed. A. Somit (The Hague: Mouton, 1975), "Human Nature *Redivivus,*" in *Human Nature in Politics,* ed. J. R. Pennock and J. W. Chapman, Nomos, XVII (New York: New York University Press, 1977), and "Biopolitics." **[8, 17, 124, 152, 176, 177, 178, 190]**

199. E.g., D. A. Hamburg et al., "Coping and Adaptation: Steps Toward a Synthesis of Biological and Social Perspectives," in *Coping and Adaptation,* ed. G. V. Coelhoe et al. (New York: Basic Books, 1974); Hardesty, *Ecological Anthropology.*

200. E.g., A. Marshall, *Principles of Economics* (London: Macmillan, 1890).

201. E.g., M. T. Ghiselin, *The Economy of Nature and the Evolution of Sex* (Berkeley: University of California Press, 1974), and "The Economy of the Body," *American Economic Review* 68(1978): 233–37; J. Hirschleifer, "Further Comments on Economics and Anthropology," *Current Anthropology* 18(1977): 133–34, and "Natural Economy Versus Political Economy," *Journal of Social and Biological Structures* 1(1978): 319–37.

202. N. Georgescu-Roegen, "Bioeconomics: A New Look at the Nature of Economic Activity," in *The Political Economy of Food and Energy,* ed. L. Junker (Ann Arbor: University of Michigan Press, 1976), "The Steady State and Ecological Salvation: A Thermodynamic Analysis," *BioScience* 27(1977): 266–70, and "A Bioeconomic Viewpoint," *Review of Social Economy* 35(1977): 361–75.

203. Ghiselin, *Economy of Nature,* and "Economy of the Body"; G. S. Becker, "Altruism, Egoism and Genetic Fitness: Economics and Sociobiology," *Journal of Economic Literature* 14(1976): 817–26; Hirschleifer, "Further Comments," and "Natural Economy." **[201]**

204. Ghiselin, *Economy of Nature,* p. 247. **[201]**

205. Hirschleifer, "Natural Economy," p. 322. **[201]**

206. E.g., D. J. Rapport, "An Optimization Model of Food Selection," *American Naturalist* 105(1971): 575–87; T. W. Schoener, "Theory of Feeding Strategies," *Annual Review of Ecology and Systematics* 2(1971): 369–404; E. L. Charnov, "Optimal Foraging, The Marginal Value Theorem," *Theoretical Population Biology* 9(1976): 129–36; G. A. Parker and R. A. Stuart, "Animal Behaviour as a Strategy Optimizer: The Evolution of Resource Assessment Strategies and Optimal Emigration Thresholds," *American Naturalist* 110(1976): 1055–76; Baker, *Evolutionary Ecology of Animal Migration.*

207. See note 206 and R. H. MacArthur and E. Pianka, "On Optimal Use of a Patchy Environment," *American Naturalist* 100(1966): 603–09; R. H. MacArthur, *Geographical Ecology: Patterns in the Distribution of Species* (New York: Harper & Row, 1972); M. L. Cody, "Optimization in Ecology," *Science* 183(1974): 1156–64; Wilson, *Sociobiology;* D. J. Rapport and J. E. Turner, "Economic Models in Ecology," *Science* 195(1977): 367–73; J. Maynard Smith, "The Evolution of Behavior," *Scientific American* 239, 3(1978): 176–92, and "Optimization Theory"; J. R. Krebs and N. B. Davies, *Behavioral Ecology: An Evolutionary Approach* (Sunderland, Mass.: Sinauer, 1978). **[55]**

208. E.g., W. W. Denham, "Energy Relations and Some Basic Properties of Primate Social Organization," *American Anthropologist* 73(1971): 77–95; Curio, "Methodology of Teleonomy"; S. A. Altmann, "Baboons; Space, Time and Energy," *American Zoologist* 14(1974): 221–48; Wilson, *Sociobiology.*

209. See S. Brody, *Bioenergetics and Growth* (New York: Reingold, 1945); G. K. Zipf, *Human Behavior and the Principle of Least Effort: An Introduction to Human Ecology* (Cambridge, Mass.: Addison-Wesley, 1949); M. Kleiber, *The Fire of Life: An Introduction to Animal Energetics* (New York: Wiley, 1961); D. M. Gates, *Energy Exchange in the Biosphere* (New York: Harper & Row, 1962); K. S. Schmidt-Nielsen, *How Animals Work* (Cambridge: Cambridge University Press, 1972); Curio, "Towards a Methodology"; J. M. Emlen, "The Role of Time and Energy in Food Preference," *The American Naturalist* 100(1966): 611–17; H. J. Morowitz, *Energy Flow in Biology: Biological Organization as a Problem in Thermal Physics* (New York: Academic Press, 1968); Schoener, "Feeding Strategies"; Cody, "Optimization in Ecology"; Rapport and Turner, "Economic Models in Ecology"; Wilson, *Sociobiology;* E. P. Odum and H. T. Odum, *Fundamentals of Ecology,* 3rd ed. (Philadelphia: Saunders, 1971); V. Geist, *Life Strategies, Human Evolution, Environmental Design: Toward a Biological Theory of Health* (New York: Springer, 1978); Maynard Smith, "Optimization Theory in Evolution." **[55, 164, 173, 206, 207]**

210. White, "Energy and Evolution of Culture," and *The Evolution of Culture* (New York: McGraw-Hill, 1959); Sahlins, "Evolution"; Service, *Cultural Evolutionism.* **[195, 196]**

211. See R. B. Lee, "What Hunters Do for a Living, or, How to Make Out on Scarce Resources," in *Man the Hunter,* ed. R. B. Lee and I. DeVore (Chicago: Aldine, 1968); R. A. Rappaport, *Pigs for the Ancestors: Ritual in the Ecology of a New Guinea People* (New Haven: Yale University Press, 1968), and "The Flow of Energy in an Agricultural Society," *Scientific American* 224, 3(1971): 116–33; Denham, "Energy Relations"; Harris, *Culture, People, Nature;* Durham, "Significance of Cultural Behavior"; Hardesty, *Ecological Anthropology.* **[152, 176, 188, 198, 208]**

212. Lee, "What Hunters Do"; Harris, *Culture, People, Nature.* **[188, 211]**

213. E. Cook, "The Flow of Energy in a Hunting Society," *Scientific American* 224, 3(1971): 134–47.

214. C. Starr, "Energy and Power," *Scientific American* 224, 3(1971): 36–49.

215. Cook, "Flow of Energy." **[213]**

216. Vayda and McCay, "New Directions in Ecology." **[198]**

217. D. R. Gross, "Protein Capture and Cultural Development in the Amazon Basin," *American Anthropologist* 77(1975): 526–49.

218. For a historical and analytical account, see F. Cottrell, *Energy and Society.* (New York: McGraw-Hill, 1955).

219. E. E. Ruyle, "Genetic and Cultural Pools: Some Suggestions for a Unified Theory of Biocultural Evolution," *Human Ecology* 1(1973): 201–15.

220. R. W. White, "Strategies of Adaptation: An Attempt at Systematic Description," in Coelho, *Coping and Adaptation.* **[198]**

221. Hardesty, *Ecological Anthropology,* p. 22. **[176]**

222. Bennett, "Anticipation," and *Ecological Transition.* **[198]**

223. Vayda and McCay, "New Directions in Ecology." **[198]**

224. Williams, *Adaptation and Natural Selection,* p. 26. **[182]**

225. P. A. Corning, "Evolutionary Indicators: Applying the Theory of Evolution to Political Science," paper prepared for the International Political Science Association meeting, 1970, "Toward a Survival-Oriented Policy Science," and *A Basic Needs Approach to Measuring the Quality of Life* (Sacramento, Calif.: State of California Department of Benefit Payments, 1978). **[143]**

226. For overviews, see S. M. Garn, "Nutrition in Physical Anthropology," *American Journal of Physical Anthropology* 24(1966): 289–92; J. Mayer, "Nutrition and Civilization," *Transactions of the New York Academy of Sciences* 2, 29(1967): 1014–32; N. S. Scrimshaw and J. E. Gordon, eds., *Malnutrition, Learning, and Behavior* (Cambridge, Mass.: MIT Press, 1968); M. S. Read, "Nutrition and Ecology: Crossroads for Research," in *Malnutrition Is a Problem of Ecology,* ed. P. György and O. L. Kline (Basel: Karger, 1970); M. T. Newman, "Nutritional Adaption in Man," in *Physiological Anthropology,* ed. A. Damon (New York: Oxford University Press, 1975).

227. B. Malinowski, *A Scientific Theory of Culture and Other Essays* (Chapel Hill: University of North Carolina Press, 1944), p. 90. I thank my colleague Robert Izaak for pointing this out to me.

228. Ibid., p. 74.

229. Ibid., pp. 94–95, 115.

230. See especially the critique in M. Harris, *The Rise of Anthropological Theory: A History of Theories of Culture* (New York: T. Y. Crowell, 1968).

231. Malinowski, *Scientific Theory of Culture,* p. 176. **[227]**

232. A. H. Maslow, *Motivation and Personality* (New York: Harper & Row, 1954), *Toward a Psychology of Being* (Princeton: Van Nostrand, 1962), and *The Farther Reaches of Human Nature* (New York: Viking, 1971).

233. Maslow, *Motivation and Personality,* pp. 80ff. The concept of self-actualization was first developed by Kurt Goldstein in *The Organism* and *Human Nature in Light of Psychopathology.* **[41, 232]**

234. For an extended discussion, see J. N. Knutson, *The Human Basis of the Polity* (Chicago: Aldine, 1972).

235. A. H. Maslow, "A Theory of Metamotivation: The Biological Rooting of the Value-Life," *Journal of Humanistic Psychology* 7(1967): 38–39, 58–61.

236. See Berlyne, *Conflict, Arousal and Curiosity,* "Conflict and Arousal," and "Curiosity and Exploration." **[38]**

237. R. Fitzgerald, ed., *Human Needs and Politics* (Rushcutters Bay, Australia: Pergamon, 1977), p. 46.

238. U.S. Department of Health, Education and Welfare, *Toward a Social Report* (Washington, D.C.: GPO, 1969), p. 97.

239. E. B. Sheldon and H. E. Freeman, "Notes on Social Indicators: Promises and Potential," *Policy Sciences* 1(1970): 102–03.

240. A. Shonfield and S. Shaw, eds., *Social Indicators and Social Policy* (London: Heinemann, 1972), p. ix.

241. E.g., A. Campbell et al., *The Quality of American Life: Perceptions, Evaluations, and Satisfactions* (New York: Russell Sage Foundation, 1976); F. M. Andrews and S. B. Withey, *Social Indicators of Well-Being: Americans' Perceptions of Life Quality* (New York: Plenum, 1976).

242. Campbell, *Quality of American Life,* p. 9. **[241]**

243. U.S. Environmental Protection Agency, *The Quality of Life Concept: A Potential New Tool for Decision-Makers* (U.S. Environmental Protection Agency, 1973), pp. 1, 11.

244. Corning, "Evolutionary Indicators," "Survival-Oriented Policy Science," and *Basic Needs Approach to Quality of Life.* **[198, 225]**

245. See M. D. Morris, *Measuring the Condition of the World's Poor: The Physical Quality of Life Index* (New York: Pergamon, 1979) and the statistical critique in D. A. Larson and W. Wilford, "The Physical Quality of Life Index: A Useful Social Indicator?" *World Development* 7(1979): 581–84.

246. E.g., P. Streeten, "Distinctive Features of a Basic Needs Approach to Development," *International Development Review* 19(1977): 8–16, and "Basic Needs: Premises and Promises," *Journal of Policy Modelling* 1(1979): 136–46; P. Streeten and S. J. Burki, "Basic Needs: Some Issues," *World Development* 6(1978): 411–21; N. Hicks and P. Streeten, "Indicators of Development: The Search for a Basic Needs Yardstick," *World Development* 7(1979): 567–580.

247. See especially the study by J. McHale and M. C. McHale, *Basic Human Needs: A Framework for Action* (New Brunswick: Transaction, 1978) for the U.N. Environmental Programme.

248. Ibid., p. 3.

249. For further discussion, see Brown and Herrnstein, *Psychology* (Boston: Little, Brown, 1975).

250. See especially, McHale and McHale, *Basic Human Needs;* Streeten and Burki, "Basic Needs"; Hicks and Streeten, "Indicators of Development." **[246]**

251. Hicks and Streeten, "Indicators of Development." **[246]**

252. Geist, *Life Strategies.* **[209]**

253. R. B. Mazess, "Human Adaptation to High Altitude," in Damon, *Physiological Anthropology* (New York: Oxford, 1975).

254. Malinowski, *Scientific Theory of Culture,* p. 125 and passim. **[227]**

255. Corning, *Basic Needs Approach to Quality of Life;* also Campbell, *Quality of American Life.* **[225, 241]**

256. See Selye, "Stress and Disease," *Stress of Life,* and *Stress in Health and Disease;* Coehlo, *Coping and Adaptation;* Dodge and Martin, *Social Stress;* Levi, *Society, Stress and Disease;* Gunderson and Rahe, *Life Stress;* Hamburg, "Coping and Adaptation"; Insel and Moos, *Health and Social Environment;* Seligman, *Helplessness;* Moos, *Human Adaptation;* Monat and Lazarus, *Stress and Coping.* To cite some "hard" evidence, it has been shown that emotional upset can have a negative impact on the body's immune system (Hinkel, "Studies of Human Ecology"; Seligman, *Helplessness*) and that stress—such as erratic sleep patterns—can accelerate the aging process (Bourlière, "Ecology of Human Senescence"; C. A. Czeisler, "Human Sleep: Its Duration and Organization Depend on Its Circadian Phase," *Science* 210[1980]: 1264–67). **[91, 198, 199]**

257. J. E. Teele, "Social Pathology and Stress," in *Social Stress,* ed. N. A. Scotch (Chicago:

Aldine, 1970); also the review in J. G. Rabkin and E. C. Streuning, "Life Events, Stress and Illness," *Science* 194(1976): 1013–20.

258. R. L. Kyllonen, "Crime Rates Versus Population Density in the United States," *Yearbook of the Society for General Systems Research* 12(1967): 137–45; O. R. Galle et al., "Population Density and Pathology: What Are the Relations for Man," *Science* 176(1972): 23–30; M. L. Belfer and B. S. Brown, "Juvenile Delinquency," in *Maternal and Child Health Practices,* ed. H. M. Wallace et al. (Springfield, Ill.: Thomas, 1973).

259. But see Corning, *Basic Needs Approach to Quality of Life,* in which survey data and objective data were compared for a sample of California welfare recipients. **[225]**

260. Hicks and Streeten, "Indicators of Development," p. 577. **[246]**

261. Streeten and Burki, "Basic Needs"; Hicks and Streeten, "Indicators of Development." **[246]**

262. Sheldon and Freeman, "Notes on Social Indicators," p. 104. **[239]**

263. Baker, *Biology of High-Altitude Peoples,* p. 317. **[124]**

264. S. V. Boyden, "Biological Determinants of Optimum Health," in *The Human Biology of Environmental Changes,* ed. D. J. M. Vorster (London: International Biological Programme, 1972), and "Evolution and Health," *Ecologist* 3(1973): 304–09.

265. Geist, *Life Strategies,* p. x. **[209]**

266. Ibid., p. 402.

267. B.-C. Liu, "Quality of Life Indicators: A Preliminary Investigation," *Social Indicators Research* 1(1974): 187.

268. Shonfield and Shaw, *Social Indicators,* p. ix. **[240]**

269. Campbell, *Quality of American Life.* **[241]**

270. A. J. Culyer et al., "Health Indicators," in Shonfield and Shaw, *Social Indicators;* M. K. Chen, "A Comprehensive Population Health Index Based on Mortality and Disability Data," *Social Indicators Research* 3(1976): 267–72. A critical review of these efforts, and an alternative approach based on the use of systems analysis, can be found in F. Fagnani and G. Dumenil, "Health Indicators or Health System Analysis? Extracts from a French Survey," *Social Indicators Research* 3(1976): 337–74. **[240]**

271. Corning, *Basic Needs Approach to Quality of Life.* **[225]**

272. Culyer, "Health Indicators." **[270]**

273. Dawkins, *Selfish Gene,* p. ix. **[177]**

274. B. F. Skinner, *Science and Human Behavior* (New York: Free Press, 1965 [1953]), p. 31.

275. B. F. Skinner, *Beyond Freedom and Dignity* (New York: Knopf, 1971), p. 188.

276. B. F. Skinner, *About Behaviorism* (New York: Knopf, 1974), p. 11.

277. C. R. Rogers, *Client-Centered Therapy: Its Current Practice, Implications and Theory* (Boston: Houghton Mifflin, 1951), p. 491.

278. C. R. Rogers, "The Actualizing Tendency in Relation to 'Motives' and to Consciousness," in *Nebraska Symposium on Motivation,* ed. M. R. Jones (Lincoln: University of Nebraska Press, 1963), p. 6.

279. J. Haugland, "The Nature and Plausibility of Cognitivism," *The Behavioral and Brain Sciences* 2(1978): 215–60.

280. E. C. Tolman, *Purposive Behavior in Animals and Men* (New York: Century, 1932). And see W. and H. N. Mischel, *Essentials of Psychology* (New York: Random House, 1977).

281. Tolman, *Purposive Behavior,* p. 12.

282. Olds and Milner, "Positive Reinforcement"; Olds, "Preliminary Mapping," "Hypothalamic Substrates," and *Drives and Reinforcements;* J. Kagan and M. Berkun, "The Reward Value of Running Activity," *Journal of Comparative and Physiological Psychology* 47(1954): 108. **[86]**

283. M. E. Bitterman, "The Evolution of Intelligence," *Scientific American* 212, 1(1965): 92–100, and "Comparative Analysis of Learning." **[99]**

284. Skinner, *About Behaviorism,* p. 12. **[276]**

285. E.g., B. F. Skinner, *Reflections on Behaviorism and Society* (Englewood Cliffs, N.J.: Prentice-Hall, 1978).

286. B. F. Skinner, "The Steep and Thorny Way to a Science of Behavior," *American Psychologist* 30(1975): 43.

287. Skinner, *Reflections on Behaviorism,* p. 53. **[285]**

288. Ibid., p. 55.

289. For a sampler of the extensive literature on control-system theory, see L. von Bertalanffy, "The Theory of Open Systems in Physics and Biology," *Science* 111(1950): 23–29, and *General Systems Theory: Foundations, Development, Application* (New York: Braziller, 1968; N. Wiener, *The Human Use of Human Beings: Cybernetics and Society* (Boston: Houghton Mifflin, 1950); W. R. Ashby, *Design for a Brain* (New York: Wiley, 1952), and *An Introduction to Cybernetics* (New York: Wiley, 1956); D. K. Stanley-Jones, *The Kybernetics of Natural Systems: A Study in Patterns of Control* (New York: Pergamon, 1960); K. E. Machin, "Feedback Theory and Its Application to Biological Systems," *Symposia of the Society for Experimental Biology* 18(1964): 421–45; K. W. Deutsch, *Nerves of Government;* H. T. Milhorn, Jr., *The Application of Control Theory to Physiological Systems* (Philadelphia: Saunders, 1966); von Foerster, *Purposive Systems;* J. Milsum, ed., *Positive Feedback: A General Systems Approach to Positive/Negative Feedback and Mutual Causality* (New York: Pergamon, 1968); J. Bowlby, "A Control Systems Approach to Attachment Behaviour," in *Attachment and Loss,* vol. 1; D. J. McFarland, *Feedback Mechanisms in Animal Behaviour* (New York: Academic Press, 1971); P. A. Weiss et al., *Hierarchically Organized Systems in Theory and Practice* (New York: Hafner, 1971); Ackoff and Emery, *Purposeful Systems;* M. A. Arbib, *The Metaphorical Brain: An Introduction to Cybernetics as Artificial Intelligence and Brain Theory* (New York: Wiley Interscience, 1972); G. Bateson, *Steps to an Ecology of Mind* (San Francisco: Chandler, 1972); M. A. Boden, *Purposive Explanation in Psychology* (Cambridge, Mass.: Harvard University Press, 1972); H. H. Pattee, ed., *Hierarchy Theory* (New York: Braziller, 1973); Powers, *Behavior;* Lorenz, *Behind the Mirror;* Miller, *Living Systems.* For critical analyses, see D. Berlinski, *On Systems Analysis: An Essay Concerning the Limitations of Some Mathematical Methods in the Social, Political, and Biological Sciences* (Cambridge, Mass.: MIT Press, 1976); R. Lilienfeld, *The Rise of Systems Theory: An Ideological Analysis* (New York: Wiley, 1978). **[34, 80, 99, 181]**

290. Skinner, *Reflections on Behaviorism,* p. 169. **[285]**

291. Brown and Herrnstein, *Psychology.* **[249]**

292. Skinner, "Steep and Thorny Way," pp. 45–46. **[286]**

293. Alland, *Adaptation in Cultural Evolution.* **[167]**

294. See Bowlby, *Attachment and Loss,* especially vol. 1, for a much more detailed application of this general approach to the domain of social needs. **[34]**

295. For earlier discussions of this principle, see S. Freud, *Collected Papers,* trans. J. Rivière (London: Hogarth Press, 1915); C. Lloyd Morgan, "Instinctual Dispositions," *Scientia* 28(1920): 269–77; W. McDougall, *An Outline of Psychology* (New York: Scribner, 1923); N. Tinbergen, "The Hierarchical Organization of Nervous Mechanisms Underlying Instinctive Behaviour," *Symposia of the Society for Experimental Biology* 4(1950): 305–12, and *The Study of Instinct* (New York: Oxford University Press, 1951); G. P. Baerends, "The Functional Organization of Behaviour," *Animal Behaviour* 24(1976): 726–738; R. Dawkins, "Hierarchical Organization: A Candidate Principal for Ethology," in Bateson and Hinde, *Growing Points in Ethology* (Cambridge: Cambridge University Press, 1976).

296. See R. J. Herrnstein, "Nature as Nurture: Behaviorism and the Instinct Doctrine," *Behaviorism* 1(1972): 23–52, and "The Evolution of Behaviorism"; Laughlin and D'Aquili,

Biogenetic Structuralism; Alland, "Adaptations"; Brown and Herrnstein, *Psychology;* A. M. Dupree, "Biological and Social Theories—A New Opportunity for a Union of Systems," in *Science and Society: Past, Present and Future,* ed. N. H. Steneck (Ann Arbor: University of Michigan Press, 1975); Bennett, "Anticipation," and *Ecological Transition;* Schubert, "Politics as a Life Science"; Mischel and Mischel, *Essentials of Psychology,* pp. 388–89; E. P. Odum, "The Emergence of Ecology as a New Integrative Discipline," *Science* 195(1977): 1289–93; R. A. Rubenstein and C. D. Laughlin, Jr., "Bridging Levels of Systemic Organization," *Current Anthropology* 18(1977): 459–81; J. H. Barkow, "Social Norms, the Self, and Sociobiology: Building on the Ideas of A. I. Hallowell," *Current Anthropology* 19(1978): 99–118, and "Culture and Sociobiology"; Petryszak, "Biosociology of Social Self." **[167, 178, 249, 280]**

297. See especially W. Bagehot, *Physics and Politics; Or Thoughts on the Application of the Principles of "Natural Selection" and "Inheritance" to Political Society* (New York: Appleton, 1872); F. H. Giddings, *The Principles of Sociology* (New York: Macmillan, 1896), and *The Elements of Sociology* (New York: Macmillan, 1898); C. H. Cooley, *Human Nature and the Social Order* (New York: Scribner, 1902), and *Social Process* (New York: Scribner, 1918); A. G. Keller, *Societal Evolution,* rev. ed. (New Haven: Yale University Press, 1931 [1915]); W. G. Sumner, *Essays of William Graham Sumner,* ed. A. G. Keller and M. R. Davie (New Haven: Yale University Press, 1934); E. B. Tylor, *Primitive Culture: Researches into the Development of Mythology, Philosophy, Religion, Art and Custom,* 2 vols. (New York: Henry Holt, 1889 [1871]).

298. Tylor, *Primitive Culture,* vol. 1, p. 62. **[297]**

299. V. G. Childe, *Social Evolution* (London: Watts, 1951); R. W. Gerard et al., "Biological and Cultural Evolution: Some Analogies and Explorations," *Behavioral Science* 1(1956): 6–34; W. Goldschmidt, *Man's Way: A Preface to the Understanding of Human Society* (New York: Holt, 1959); M. Ginsberg, "Social Evolution," in *Darwinism and the Study of Society,* ed. M. R. Banton (Chicago: Quadrangle, 1961); R. Cohen, "The Strategy of Social Evolution," *Anthropologica* 4(1962): 321–48.

300. A. A. Alchain, "Uncertainty, Evolution and Economic Theory," *Journal of Political Economy* 58(1950): 211–21. Subsequently a number of other theorists adopted what Herbert A. Simon calls a "satisficing" model of social choice (*Models of Man: Social and Rational* [New York: Wiley, 1957]). See S. Enke, "On Maximizing Profits: A Distinction Between Chamberlin and Robinson," *American Economic Review* 41(1951): 566–78; S. G. Winter, "Satisficing, Selection and the Innovating Remnant," *Quarterly Journal of Economics* 86(1971): 237–61; R. R. Nelson and S. G. Winter, "Neoclassical vs. Evolutionary Theories of Economic Growth: Critique and Prospectus," *Economic Journal* 84(1974): 886–905.

301. Keller, *Societal Evolution.* **[297]**

302. Ashby, *Design for a Brain;* Pringle, "Parallel Between Learning and Evolution." **[157, 289]**

303. D. T. Campbell, "Blind Variation and Selective Retention in Creative Thought as in Other Knowledge Processes," *Psychological Review* 67(1960): 380–400, "Variation and Selective Retention in Sociocultural Evolution, in *Social Change in Developing Areas,* ed. H. R. Barringer (Cambridge, Mass.: Shenkman, 1965), "Natural Selection as an Epistemological Model," in *A Handbook of Method in Cultural Anthropology,* ed. R. Naroll and R. Cohen (Garden City, N.Y.: Natural History Press, 1970), and "On the Conflicts Between Biological and Social Evolution."

304. For critiques, see P. A. Corning, "Politics and the Evolutionary Process," in Dobzhansky, *Evolutionary Biology,* vol. 3; and the commentaries organized by L. G. Wispé and J. N. Thompson, Jr., "The War Between the Words: Biological Versus Social Evolution and Some Related Issues," *American Psychologist* 31(1976): 341–47. Campbell has recently modified some of his views, see "Comments on the Sociobiology of Ethics and Moralizing," *Behavioral Science* 24(1979): 37–45. **[143]**

305. E.g., Cavalli-Sforza and Feldman, "Models for Cultural Inheritance," *American Journal of Human Genetics* 25(1973): 618–37, and *Cultural Transmission and Evolution: A Quantitative Approach* (Princeton: Princeton University Press, 1981); M. J. Farrell, "Some Elementary Selection Processes in Economics," *Review of Economic Studies* 37(1970): 305–19; G. E. Lenski, *Human Societies: A Macrolevel Introduction to Sociology* (New York: McGraw-Hill, 1970); F. T. Cloak, Jr., "Elementary Self-Replicating Instructions and Their Works: Toward a Radical Reconstruction of General Anthropology Through a General Theory of Natural Selection," in *Toward Naturalistic Explanations of Cultural Adaptations* ed. F. T. Cloak, Jr., (The Hague: Mouton, 1973), and "Culture and Social Organization Mutually Shape Each Other"; Ruyle, "Genetic and Cultural Pools: Some Suggestions for a Unified Theory of Biocultural Evolution," *Human Ecology* 1(1973): 201–15; Alland and McKay, "Concept of Adaptation"; Corning, "Politics and the Evolutionary Process"; Nelson and Winter, "Neoclassical vs. Evolutionary Theories"; P. Diener, "Ecology or Evolution?: The Hutterite Case," *American Ethnologist* 1(1974): 601–18, "Quantum Adjustment, Macroevolution, and the Social Field: Some Comments on Evolution and Culture," *Current Anthropology* 21(1980): 423–43, and "On Evolution and Culture"; Alland, "Adaptations"; M. W. Feldman and L. L. Cavalli-Sforza, "Models for Cultural Inheritance: A General Linear Model," *Annals of Human Biology* 2(1975): 215–26, and "Evolution of Continuous Variation: Direct Approach Through Joint Distribution of Genotypes and Phenotypes," *Proceedings of the National Academy of Sciences* 73(1976): 1689–92; Dawkins, *Selfish Gene;* W. H. Durham, "Resource Competition and Human Aggression, Part I: A Review of Primitive War," *Quarterly Review of Biology* 51(1976): 385–415, and "Toward a Coevolutionary Theory of Human Biology and Culture," in Chagnon and Irons, *Evolutionary Biology;* R. Naroll and W. T. Divale, "Natural Selection in Cultural Evolution: Warfare Versus Peaceful Diffusion," *American Ethnologist* 3(1976): 97–129; Hardesty, *Ecological Anthropology;* Barkow, "Culture and Sociobiology"; C. Boehm, "Rational Preselection from Hamadryas to *Homo sapiens:* The Place of Decisions in Adaptive Process," *American Anthropologist* 80(1978): 265–96; Richerson and Boyd, "Dual Inheritance Model"; Marion Blute, "Sociocultural Evolutionism: An Untried Theory," *Behavioral Science* 24(1979): 46–59; J. Langton, "Darwinism and the Behavioral Theory of Sociocultural Evolution: An Analysis," *American Journal of Sociology* 85(1979): 288–309; Alexander, "Evolution and Culture"; S. P. Reyna, "Social Evolution: A Learning-Theory Approach," *Journal of Anthropological Research* 35(1979): 336–49; Mundinger, "Animal Cultures"; Lumsden and Wilson, *Genes, Mind and Culture.* **[156, 167, 176, 177, 178, 190, 296, 304]**

306. The list is almost endless. In addition to such nineteenth-century luminaries as Spencer, Durkheim, Weber, Tylor, and Morgan, twentieth-century theorists include: in physics, H. Haken, *Cooperative Effects: Progress in Synergetics* (New York: Elsevier, 1974), *Synergetics: An Introduction,* 2d ed. (New York: Springer, 1978), and *Dynamics of Synergetic Systems* (New York: Springer, 1980); in biology, A. B. Novikoff, "The Concept of Integrative Levels and Biology," *Science* 101(1945): 209–15; W. C. Allee et al., *Principles of Animal Ecology* (Philadelphia: Saunders, 1949); Bertalanffy, "Theory of Open Systems"; Tinbergen, "Hierarchical Organization of Nervous Mechanisms," and *Study of Instinct;* C. H. Waddington, *The Strategy of the Genes: A Discussion of Some Aspects of Theoretical Biology* (New York: Macmillan, 1957); Odum and Odum, *Fundamentals of Ecology;* W. J. Bock, "The Role of Adaptive Mechanisms in the Higher Levels of Organization," *Systematic Zoology* 14(1965): 272–87; P. A. Weiss, *Dynamics of Development: Experiments and Inferences* (New York: Academic Press, 1968); S. Wright, *Evolution and the Genetics of Populations; A Treatise,* 4 vols. (Chicago: University of Chicago Press, 1968–1978); L. L. Whyte, *Hierarchical Structures* (New York: Elsevier, 1969); R. C. Lewontin, "The Units of Selection," *Annual Review of Ecology and Systematics* 1(1970): 1–18, and *The Genetic Basis of Evolutionary Change* (New York: Columbia University Press, 1974); Pattee, *Hierarchy Theory;* S. M. Stanley, "A Theory of Evolution Above the Species Level," *Proceedings of the National Academy of Sciences* 72(1975): 646–50, and *Macroevolution:*

Pattern and Process (San Francisco: Freeman, 1979); Dawkins, "Hierarchical Organization"; P. J. Richerson, "Ecology and Human Ecology: A Comparison of Theories in the Biological and Social Sciences," *American Ethnologist* 4(1977): 1–25; Richerson and Boyd, "Dual Inheritance Model"; Alexander and Borgia, "Group Selection"; Miller, *Living Systems;* R. Riedl, *Order in Living Organisms: A Systems Analysis of Evolution,* trans. R. P. S. Jeffries (New York: Wiley, 1978 [1975]); Scott, "Expectations of Political Behavior"; D. S. Wilson, *The Natural Selection of Populations and Communities* (Menlo Park, Calif.; Benjamin/Cummings, 1980); in the behavioral and social sciences: R. Redfield, ed., *Levels of Integration in Biological and Social Systems,* Biological Symposia, vol. 8 (Lancaster, Pa.: Jaques Cattell, 1942); G. A. Miller et al., *Plans and the Structure of Behavior* (New York: Henry Holt, 1960); Bateson, "Role of Somatic Change"; Deutsch, *Nerves of Government;* D. Lerner, "Toward a Communications Theory of Modernization," in *Communications and Political Development,* ed. L. W. Pye (Princeton: Princeton University Press, 1963); Buckley, *Modern Systems Research;* Simon, *Models of Man,* and "Architecture of Complexity"; Vayda and Rappaport, "Ecology"; Bowlby, "Control Systems Approach"; Campbell, "Genetics of Altruism," and " 'Downward Causation' "; Alland, "Adaptation"; Durham, "Adaptive Significance of Cultural Behavior." Hierarchical approaches are also being utilized extensively in such practical fields as the design of computers, production systems, and information storage systems. **[34, 122, 154, 157, 163, 167, 173, 177, 181, 209, 289, 295]**

307. Pattee, *Hierarchy Theory,* p. xi. **[289]**

308. At least this was so as of 1975. Important new books published after this work was essentially completed parallel some of my own arguments. See Wilson, *Natural Selection of Populations;* S. A. Boorman and P. R. Levitt, *The Genetics of Altruism* (New York: Academic Press, 1980); Lumsden and Wilson, *Genes, Mind and Culture.* **[178, 306]**

309. See also, Ghiselin, *Economy of Nature;* Richerson, "Ecology and Human Ecology." **[182, 201, 306]**

310. See Mech, *The Wolf* (New York: Natural History Press, 1970); E. Klinghammer, ed., *The Behavior and Ecology of Wolves* (New York: Garland, 1979); D. L. Allen, *Wolves of Minong: Their Vital Role in a Wild Community* (Boston: Houghton Mifflin, 1979).

311. Odum and Odum, *Fundamentals of Ecology;* Odum, "Emergence of Ecology," *Science* 195(1977): 1289–93. See also, Wilson, *Natural Selection of Populations.* **[209, 306]**

312. E. O. Wilson, *The Insect Societies* (Cambridge, Mass.: Harvard University Press, 1971), p. 317.

313. Ghiselin seems to have modified his views on this issue somewhat, in "Categories, Life, and Thinking," *The Behavioral and Brain Sciences* 4(1981): 269–313. But see the critique in P. A. Corning, "Rethinking Categories and Life," *The Behavioral and Brain Sciences* 4(1981): 286–288.

314. A. L. Kroeber, "The Superorganic," *American Anthropologist* 19(1917): 184.

315. Ibid., p. 209. For a similar usage of the superorganism concept, see Steward, *Theory of Culture Change.* **[186]**

316. Alland, *Evolution and Human Behavior,* p. 191. **[154]**

317. Alland, "Adaptations," p. 64. **[167]**

318. H. Spencer, *The Principles of Sociology,* 3 vols., 3rd ed. (New York: Appleton, 1897 [1874–1882]), I: 592.

319. Williams, *Adaptation and Natural Selection;* Ghiselin, *Economy of Nature;* Richerson, "Ecology and Human Ecology"; M. J. Dunbar, "The Evolution of Stability in Marine Environments: Natural Selection at the Level of the Ecosystem," *American Naturalist* 94(1960): 129–36; Wilson, *Natural Selection of Populations.* **[182, 201, 306]**

320. C. F. A. Pantin, *The Relations Between the Sciences* (Cambridge: Cambridge University Press, 1968), p. 175.

321. K. N. Waltz, *Theory of International Politics* (Reading, Mass.: Addison-Wesley, 1979), p. 90.

322. Again, see the discussion in Ghiselin, "Categories, Life, and Thinking," and the critique in Corning, "Rethinking Categories and Life." **[313]**

323. See Odum and Odum, *Fundamentals of Ecology;* E. R. Pianka, *Evolutionary Ecology,* 2d ed. (New York: Harper & Row, 1978). **[209]**

324. D. C. Pirages, *The New Context for International Relations: Global Ecopolitics* (North Scituate, Mass.: Duxbury), *inter alia.*

V. A General Theory of Sociocultural Evolution

1. J. D. Y. Peel, "Spencer and the Neo-Evolutionists," *Sociology* 3(1969): 179.

2. K. Wittfogel, *Oriental Despotism: A Comparative Study of Total Power* (New Haven: Yale University Press, 1957). See also the contributions in J. H. Steward, *Theory of Culture Change: The Methodology of Multilinear Evolution* (Urbana, Ill.: University of Illinois Press, 1955).

3. L. A. White, "Energy and the Evolution of Culture," *American Anthropologist* 45(1943): 335–56, *The Science of Culture: A Study of Man and Civilization* (New York: Grove Press, 1949), and *The Evolution of Culture* (New York: McGraw-Hill, 1959).

4. White, *Evolution of Culture,* p. 56. For other energetic approaches to cultural evolution, see F. Cottrell, *Energy and Society: The Relation Between Energy, Social Change, and Economic Development* (New York: McGraw-Hill, 1955); B. J. Meggers, "The Law of Cultural Evolution as a Practical Research Tool," in *Essays in the Science of Culture in Honor of Leslie A. White,* ed. G. Dole and R. Carneiro (New York: T. Y. Crowell, 1960); E. P. Odum and H. T. Odum, *Fundamentals of Ecology,* 3rd ed. (Philadelphia: Saunders, 1971); E. Cook, "The Flow of Energy in a Hunting Society," *Scientific American* 224, 3(1971): 134–47, and *Man, Energy, Society* (San Francisco: Freeman, 1976); R. A. Rappaport, *Pigs for the Ancestors: Ritual in the Ecology of a New Guinea People* (New Haven: Yale University Press, 1968), and "The Flow of Energy in an Agricultural Society," *Scientific American* 224, 3(1971): 116–33; W. B. Kemp, "The Flow of Energy in a Hunting Society," *Scientific American* 224, 3(1971): 104–15; Y. A. Cohen, ed., *Man in Adaptation,* 2d ed., 3 vols. (Chicago: Aldine, 1974 [1968]). **[3]**

5. White, *Study of Man,* p. 39. **[3]**

6. Ibid., pp. 330ff. **[3]**

7. Ibid., p. 335. **[3]**

8. Steward, *Culture Change;* E. R. Service, *Primitive Social Organization: An Evolutionary Perspective* (New York: Random House, 1962).

9. E.g., K. E. Boulding, *Ecodynamics: A New Theory of Societal Evolution* (Beverly Hills: Sage, 1978); M. D. Sahlins, *Stone Age Economics* (Chicago: Aldine, 1972); W. Goldschmidt, *Man's Way: A Preface to the Understanding of Human Society* (New York: Holt, 1959); C. Geertz, *Agricultural Involution: Process of Ecological Change in Indonesia* (Berkeley: University of California Press, 1963); G. E. Lenski, *Human Societies: A Macrolevel Introduction to Sociology* (New York: McGraw-Hill, 1970); Cohen, *Man in Adaptation;* T. Parsons, *Societies: Evolutionary and Comparative Perspectives* (Englewood Cliffs, N.J.: Prentice-Hall, 1966); M. Harris, *Cultural Materialism: The Struggle for a Science of Culture* (New York: Random House, 1979). **[4]**

10. S. N. Eisenstadt, "Social Change, Differentiation and Evolution," *American Sociological Review* 29(1964): 375–86.

11. D. Kaplan and R. A. Manners, *Culture Theory* (Englewood Cliffs, N.J.: Prentice-Hall, 1972), p. 100.

12. Goldschmidt, *Man's Way,* p. 119. **[9]**

13. Ibid., p. 128. **[9]**

14. R. McC. Adams, *The Evolution of Urban Society: Early Mesopotamia and Prehispanic Mexico* (Chicago: Aldine, 1966), and "Patterns of Urbanization in Early Southern Mesopotamia," in *Man, Settlement and Urbanism,* ed. P. J. Ucko et al. (London: Duckworth, 1972).

15. See also, S. R. Binford, "Early Upper Pleistocene Adaptations in Levant," *American Anthropologist* 70(1968): 707–17; K. V. Flannery, "Archaeological Systems Theory and Early Meso-America," in *Anthropological Archaeology in the Americas,* ed. B. Meggers (Washington, D.C.: Anthropological Society of Washington, 1968); M. Harris, *The Rise of Anthropological Theory: A History of Theories of Culture* (New York: T. Y. Crowell, 1968); H. T. Wright and G. A. Johnson, "Population, Exchange, and Early State Formation in Southwestern Iran," *American Anthropologist* 77(1975): 267–89; R. Cohen, "Introduction" and "State Foundations: A Controlled Comparison," and H. T. Wright, "Toward an Explanation of the Origin of the State," all in *Origins of the State: The Anthropology of Political Evolution,* ed. R. Cohen and E. R. Service (Philadelphia: ISHI, 1978).

16. Harris, *Rise of Anthropological Theory,* and *Cultural Materialism.* **[9, 15]**

17. Harris, *Rise of Anthropological Theory,* pp. 3–4. **[15]**

18. Ibid., p. 4.

19. Harris, *Cultural Materialism,* p. 74. **[9]**

20. M. Harris, "Monistic Determinism: Anti-Service," *Southwestern Journal of Anthropology* 25(1969): 199.

21. Harris, *Cultural Materialism,* p. 62. **[9]**

22. H. G. Barnett, *Innovation: The Basis of Cultural Change* (New York: McGraw-Hill, 1953). See also, E. M. Rogers's important work, *Diffusion of Innovations* (New York: Free Press, 1962), which exhaustively surveys the literature up to that time. More recent works include G. Zaltman et al., *Innovations and Organizations* (New York: Wiley, 1973); and R. Naroll and W. T. Divale, "Natural Selection in Cultural Evolution: Warfare Versus Peaceful Diffusion," *American Ethnologist* 3(1976): 97–129.

23. J. Schumpeter, *The Theory of Economic Development* (Cambridge: Harvard University Press, 1934 [1911]). For instance, see F. Barth, ed., *The Role of the Entrepreneur in the Social Change in Northern Norway* (Bergen: Scandinavian University Books, 1972 [1963]); C. S. Belshaw, *Traditional Exchange and Modern Markets* (Englewood Cliffs, N.J.: Prentice-Hall, 1965); A. Strathern, "The Entrepreneurial Model of Social Change: From Norway to New Guinea," *Ethnology* 11(1972): 368–79; R. R. Nelson and G. Winter, "Neoclassical vs. Evolutionary Theories of Economic Growth: Critique and Prospectus," *Economic Journal* 84(1974): 886–905; C. E. Lindblom, *Politics and Markets* (New York: Basic Books, 1977).

24. Marcel Mauss, *The Gift: Forms and Functions of Exchange in Archaic Societies,* trans. I. Cunnison (New York: Norton, 1967 [1925]).

25. E.g., G. C. Homans, "Social Behavior as Exchange," *American Journal of Sociology* 62(1958): 597–606, and *Social Behavior: Its Elementary Forms* (New York: Harcourt, 1961); J. W. Thibaut and H. H. Kelley, *The Social Psychology of Groups* (New York: Wiley, 1959); A. W. Gouldner, "The Norm of Reciprocity: A Preliminary Statement," *American Sociological Review* 25(1960): 161–78; P. M. Blau, *Exchange and Power in Social Life* (New York: Wiley, 1964), and "Interaction: Social Exchange," in *International Encyclopedia of the Social Sciences,* vol. 7, ed. D. E. Sills (New York: Free Press, 1968); L. Berkowitz and E. Walster, eds., *Equity Theory: Toward a General Theory of Social Interaction* (New York: Academic Press, 1976); K. J. Gergen et al., eds., *Social Exchange: Advances in Theory and Research* (New York: Plenum, 1980).

26. E.g., K. Polanyi, *The Great Transformation* (New York: Farrar and Rinehart, 1944); Belshaw, *Traditional Exchange;* Sahlins, *Stone Age Economics;* G. Dalton, *Studies in Economic Anthropology* (Washington, D.C.: American Anthropological Association, 1971), and *Economic Systems and Society* (London: Penguin, 1974); E. N. Wilmsen, ed., *Social Exchange and Interac-*

tion (Ann Arbor: University of Michigan Press, 1972); H. K. Schneider, *Economic Man: The Anthropology of Economics* (New York: Free Press, 1974); J. A. Sabloff and C. C. Lamberg-Karlovsky, *Ancient Civilization and Trade* (Albuquerque: University of New Mexico Press, 1975); T. K. Earle and J. E. Ericson, eds., *Exchange Systems in Prehistory* (New York: Academic Press, 1977). See also the review in H. Befu, "Social Exchange," *Annual Review of Anthropology* 6(1977): 255–81. **[9, 23]**

27. H. Spencer, "A Theory of Population Deduced from the General Law of Animal Fertility," *The Westminster Review* 57(1852): 468–501. See also E. B. Tylor, *Primitive Culture: Researches into the Development of Mythology, Philosophy, Religion, Art and Custom,* 2 vols. (New York: Henry Holt, 1889 [1871]), p. 267.

28. It was mentioned by Steward, *Culture Change,* and White, *Evolution of Culture.* **[2, 3]**

29. E. Boserup, *The Conditions of Agricultural Growth: The Economics of Agrarian Change Under Population Pressure* (Chicago: Aldine, 1965); D. E. Dumond, "Population Growth and Cultural Change," *Southwestern Journal of Anthropology* 21(1965): 302–24; M. J. Harner, "Population Pressure and the Social Evolution of Agriculturalists," *Southwestern Journal of Anthropology* 26(1970): 67–86. See also the important discussions in B. Spooner, ed., *Population Growth: Anthropological Implications* (Cambridge, Mass.: MIT Press, 1972); M. N. Cohen, *The Food Crisis in Prehistory: Overpopulation and the Origins of Agriculture* (New Haven: Yale University Press, 1977); J. L. Simon, *The Economics of Population Growth* (Princeton: Princeton University Press, 1977).

30. M. H. Fried, *The Evolution of Political Society* (New York: Random House, 1967).

31. R. L. Carneiro, "A Theory of the Origin of the State," *Science* 169(1970): 733–38.

32. A. Keith, *A New Theory of Human Evolution* (New York: Philosophical Library, 1949); R. Ardrey, *The Territorial Imperative* (New York: Atheneum, 1966); K. Lorenz, *On Aggression,* trans. M. K. Wilson (New York: Harcourt, 1966 [1963]); R. Bigelow, *The Dawn Warriors: Man's Evolution Toward Peace* (Boston: Little, Brown, 1969). To varying degrees these shock troops have since been reinforced, and their arguments refined, by the works of R. D. Alexander and D. W. Tinkle, "Review of *On Aggression* by Konrad Lorenz and *The Territorial Imperative* by Robert Ardrey," *BioScience* 18(1968): 245–48; R. D. Alexander, "The Search for an Evolutionary Philosophy of Man," *Proceedings of the Royal Society of Victoria* (Melbourne) 84(1971): 99–120, "The Evolution of Social Behavior," *Annual Review of Ecology and Systematics* 5(1974): 325–83, and *Darwinism and Human Affairs* (Seattle: University of Washington Press, 1979); L. Tiger and R. Fox, *The Imperial Animal* (New York: Holt, 1971); K. Otterbein, *The Evolution of War* (New Haven: HRAF Press, 1979); A. Vayda, "Warfare in Ecological Perspective," *Annual Review of Ecology and Systematics* 5(1974): 183–93; D. Webster, "Warfare and the Evolution of the State: A Reconsideration," *American Antiquity* 40(1975): 464–70; W. D. Hamilton, "Innate Social Aptitudes of Man: An Approach from Evolutionary Genetics," in *BioSocial Anthropology,* ed. R. Fox (London: Malaby Press, 1975); E. O. Wilson, "On the Queerness of Social Evolution," *Social Research* 40(1973): 144–152, and *Sociobiology: The New Synthesis* (Cambridge, Mass.: Harvard University Press, 1975); W. H. Durham, "Resource Competition and Human Aggression, Part I: A Review of Primitive War," *The Quarterly Review of Biology* 51(1976): 385–415; F. H. Willhoite, Jr., "Rank and Reciprocity: Speculations on Human Emotions and Political Life," unpublished paper; R. Pitt, "Warfare and Hominid Brain Evolution," *Journal of Theoretical Biology* 72(1978): 551–575; I. Eibl-Eibesfeldt, "Human Ethology: Concepts and Implications for the Sciences of Man," *Behavioral and Brain Sciences* 2(1979): 1–26; G. Borgia, "Human Aggression as a Biological Adaptation," in *The Evolution of Human Social Behavior,* ed. J. S. Lockard (New York: Elsevier, 1980). See also the review and middleground viewpoint espoused in P. A. Corning, "The Biological Bases of Behavior and Some Implications for Political Science," *World Politics* 23(1971): 321–70, "Human Violence: Some Causes and Implications," in *Peace and War,* ed. C. R. Beitz and T. Herman (San Francisco: Freeman,

1973), and "An Evolutionary Paradigm for the Study of Human Aggression," in *War: Its Causes and Correlates,* ed. M. Nettleship (Paris: Mouton, 1976); P. A. Corning and C. H. Corning, "Toward a General Theory of Violent Aggression," *Social Science Information* 11(1973): 7–35.

33. Alexander, *Darwinism and Human Affairs.* **[32]**

34. See A. L. Kroeber, *Anthropology: Race, Language, Culture, Psychology, Prehistory* (New York: Harcourt, 1948); H. E. Driver, "Cultural Diffusion," in *Main Currents in Cultural Anthropology,* ed. R. Naroll and F. Naroll (New York: Appleton-Century, 1973); Wilmsen, *Social Exchange;* Sabloff and Lamberg-Karlovsky, *Ancient Civilization;* Naroll and Divale, "Natural Selection in Cultural Evolution." **[2, 26]**

35. See especially, J. N. Anderson, "Ecological Anthropology and Anthropological Ecology," in *Handbook of Social and Cultural Anthropology,* ed. J. J. Honigmann (Chicago: Rand McNally, 1973); A. P. Vayda and B. J. McCay, "New Directions in Ecology and Ecological Anthropology," *Annual Review of Anthropology* (1975): 293–306; J. W. Bennett, "Anticipation, Adaptation, and the Concept of Culture in Anthropology," *Science* 192(1976): 847–53, and *The Ecological Transition: Cultural Anthropology and Human Adaptation* (New York: Pergamon, 1976); D. L. Hardesty, *Ecological Anthropology* (New York: Wiley, 1977).

36. J. Jacobs, *The Economy of Cities* (New York: Random House, 1969).

37. Adams, *Evolution of Urban Society.* **[14]**

38. H. T. Wright, "Recent Research on the Origin of the State," *Annual Review of Anthropology* 6(1977): 379–97, and "Toward an Explanation of the Origin of the State." **[15]**

39. Adams, *Evolution of Urban Society;* J. Gernet, *Ancient China, From the Beginnings to the Empire,* trans. R. Rudorff (Berkeley: University of California Press, 1968); K. V. Flannery, "The Cultural Evolution of Civilizations," *Annual Review of Ecology and Systematics* 3(1972): 399–426. **[14]**

40. Adams, *Evolution of Urban Society;* E. R. Service, *Origins of the State and Civilization: The Process of Cultural Evolution* (New York: Norton, 1975). **[14]**

41. R. B. Woodbury, "A Reappraisal of Hohokam Irrigation," *American Anthropologist* 63(1961): 550–60; E. Hunt and R. Hunt, "Irrigation, Conflict, and Politics," in *Irrigation's Impact on Society,* ed. T. E. Downing and McG. Gibson (Tucson: University of Arizona Press, 1974); R. Hunt and E. Hunt, "Canal Irrigation and Local Social Organization," *Current Anthropology* 17(1976): 389–411.

42. B. J. Meggers, "Environmental Limitation on the Development of Culture," *American Anthropologist* 56(1954): 801–24.

43. Cottrell, *Energy and Society;* C. Starr, "Energy and Power," *Scientific American* 224, 3(1971): 36–49; H. T. Odum and E. C. Odum, *The Energy Basis for Man and Nature* (New York: McGraw-Hill, 1976). **[4]**

44. See also the arguments against White's thesis by Sahlins. Adopting a Zen Buddhist view of affluence, Sahlins concludes that hunter-gatherers were the original "affluent society" (*Stone Age Economics*). **[9]**

45. H. C. Brookfield and P. Brown, *Struggle for Land: Agriculture and Group Territories Among the Chimbu of the New Guinea Highlands* (New York: Oxford University Press, 1963).

46. Cohen, *Food Crisis in Prehistory.* **[29]**

47. On this point see Wilson, *Sociobiology;* Hardesty, *Ecological Anthropology.* **[32, 35]**

48. R. Dahrendorf, *Class and Class Conflict in Industrial Society* (Stanford, Calif.: Stanford University Press, 1959).

49. See also Lenski, *Power and Privilege* (New York: McGraw-Hill, 1966).

50. E. R. Service, *Cultural Evolutionism: Theory in Practice* (New York: Holt, 1971), p. 25.

51. Carneiro, "Four Faces of Evolution," in Honigmann, *Handbook of Social and Cultural Anthropology,* p. 108.

52. A. Smith, *The Wealth of Nations,* 2 vols. (London: Dent, 1964 [1776]), pp. 10–11.

53. R. Cooke, *The Biology of Symbiotic Fungi* (New York: Wiley, 1977); J. L. Ruehle and D. H. Marx, "Fiber, Food, Fuel, and Fungal Symbionts," *Science* 206(1979): 419–22.

54. A. W. Galston, "Sex and the Soybean," *Natural History* 87(1978): 132–40.

55. See especially the review by H. Blumer, "Collective Behavior," in *Review of Sociology,* ed. J. B. Gittler (New York: Wiley, 1957); also R. H. Turner and L. M. Killian, *Collective Behavior* (Englewood Cliffs, N.J.: Prentice-Hall, 1957).

56. See A. J. Marrow et al., *Management by Participation* (New York: Harper & Row, 1967).

57. D. E. Gumpert, "Growing Concerns," *Harvard Business Review* 57(1979): 198–206.

58. S. Milgram, "Some Conditions of Obedience and Disobedience to Authority," *Human Relations* 18(1965): 57–76, and *Obedience to Authority* (New York: Harper & Row, 1973).

59. J. A. F. Stoner, "A Comparison of Individual and Group Decisions Involving Risk," unpublished master's thesis, School of Industrial Management, Massachusetts Institute of Technology, 1961. Reviewed in K. L. Dion et al., "Why Do Groups Make Riskier Decisions than Individuals?" *Advances in Experimental Social Psychology* 5(1970): 305–77.

60. R. B. Zajonc, "Social Facilitation," *Science* 149(1965): 269–74.

61. P. F. Drucker, *Managing in Turbulent Times* (New York: Harper & Row, 1980).

62. See especially M. Y. Yoshino, *Japan's Managerial System: Tradition and Innovation* (Cambridge, Mass.: MIT Press, 1968); H. Kahn, *The Emerging Japanese Superstate: Challenge and Response* (Englewood Cliffs, N.J.: Prentice-Hall, 1970); C. Nakane, *Japanese Society* (Berkeley: University of California Press, 1970); R. Clark, *The Japanese Company* (New Haven: Yale University Press, 1979); E. Vogel, *Japan as Number One: Lessons for America* (Cambridge, Mass.: Harvard University Press, 1979); W. Ouchi, *Theory Z* (Reading, Mass.: Addison-Wesley, 1981); R. T. Pascale and A. G. Athos, *The Art of Japanese Management: Applications for American Executives* (New York: Simon & Schuster, 1981).

63. Kroeber, *Anthropology,* pp. 403–05. **[34]**

64. J. A. Schumpeter, *The Theory of Economic Development,* pp. 64ff. **[23]**

65. See R. Thom, *Structural Stability and Morphogenesis: An Outline of a General Theory of Models* (Reading, Mass.: Benjamin, 1975); E. C. Zeeman, "Catastrophe Theory," *Scientific American* 234, 4(1976): 65–83, and *Catastrophe Theory, Selected Papers 1972–1977* (Reading, Mass.: Addison-Wesley, 1977); A. E. R. Woodcock and M. Davis, *Catastrophe Theory* (New York: Dutton, 1978); P. T. Saunders, *An Introduction to Catastrophe Theory* (New York: Cambridge University Press, 1980).

66. See also the important analysis in M. Granovetter, "Threshold Models of Collective Behavior," *American Journal of Sociology* 83(1978): 1420–43.

67. M. Olson, Jr., *The Logic of Collective Action: Public Goods and the Theory of Groups* (Cambridge, Mass.: Harvard University Press, 1965).

68. See J. M. Emlen, "Natural Selection and Human Behavior," *Journal of Theoretical Biology* 12(1966): 410–18; Wilson, *Sociobiology;* J. Hirshleifer, "Natural Economy Versus Political Economy," *Journal of Social and Biological Structures* 1(1978): 319–37. For energetic analyses, see Boserup, *Conditions of Agricultural Growth;* Rappaport, *Pigs for the Ancestors;* R. B. Lee, "What Hunters Do for a Living, or, How to Make out on Scarce Resources," in *Man the Hunter,* ed. R. B. Lee and I. DeVore (Chicago: Aldine, 1968); M. Harris, *Culture, People, Nature: An Introduction to General Anthropology,* 2d ed. (New York: T. Y. Crowell, 1975). For discussions of the so-called "Law of Least Effort," see G. K. Zipf, *Human Behavior and the Principle of Least Effort: An Introduction to Human Ecology* (Reading, Mass.: Addison-Wesley, 1949); V. Geist, *Life Strategies, Human Evolution, Environmental Design: Toward a Biological Theory of*

Health (New York: Springer, 1978). For discussions of the related "economy principle," see J. S. Huxley, *Evolution: The Modern Synthesis* (New York: Harper & Row, 1942); E. Curio, "Towards a Methodology of Teleonomy," *Experientia* 29(1973): 1045–58; S. A. Altmann, "Baboons, Space, Time and Energy," *American Zoologist* 14(1974): 221–48; J. M. Emlen and M. Emlen, "Optimal Choice in Diet: Test of a Hypothesis," *American Naturalist* 109(1975): 427–35; S. T. Emlen and L. W. Oring, "Ecology, Sexual Selection, and the Evolution of Mating Systems," *Science* 197(1977): 215–23. Analyses that employ bioeconomic versions of the marginal utility theory include D. J. Rapport, "An Optimization Model of Food Selection," *American Naturalist* 105(1971): 575–87; T. W. Schoener, "Theory of Feeding Strategies," *Annual Review of Ecology and Systematics* 2(1971): 369–404; E. L. Charnov, "Optimal Foraging. The Marginal Value Theorem," *Theoretical Population Biology* 9(1976): 129–36; G. A. Parker and R. A. Stuart, "Animal Behavior as a Strategy Optimizer: The Evolution of Resource Assessment Strategies and Optimal Emigration Thresholds," *American Naturalist* 110(1976): 1055–76; R. R. Baker, *The Evolutionary Ecology of Animal Migration* (London: Hodder and Stoughton, 1978). Optimization, strategic choice, and game theoretical analyses include R. H. MacArthur and E. Pianka, "On Optimal Use of a Patchy Environment," *American Naturalist* 100(1966): 603–09; R. H. MacArthur, *Geographical Ecology: Patterns in the Distribution of Species* (New York: Harper & Row, 1972); M. L. Cody, "Optimization in Ecology," *Science* 183(1974): 1156–64; E. L. Charnov and J. R. Krebs, "The Evolution of Alarm Calls: Altruism or Manipulation?" *American Naturalist* 109(1975): 107–12; G. H. Pyke et al., "Optimal Foraging: A Selective Review of Theory and Tests," *Quarterly Review of Biology* 52(1977): 137–54; D. J. Rapport and J. E. Turner, "Economic Models in Ecology," *Science* 195(1977): 367–73; J. Maynard Smith, "The Evolution of Behavior," *Scientific American* 239, 3(1978): 176–92, and "Optimization Theory in Evolution," *Annual Review of Ecology and Systematics* 9(1978): 31–56; J. R. Krebs and N. B. Davies, *Behavioural Ecology: An Evolutionary Approach* (Sunderland, Mass.: Sinauer, 1978); R. Axelrod and W. D. Hamilton, "The Evolution of Cooperation," *Science* 211(1981): 1390–96. The classic work on collective goods is Olson, *Logic of Collective Action.* **[32]**

69. See especially W. Bagehot, *Physics and Politics; Or Thoughts on the Application of the Principles of "Natural Selection" and "Inheritance" to Political Society* (New York: Appleton, 1872); A. G. Keller, *Societal Evolution,* rev. ed. (New Haven: Yale University Press, 1931 [1915]); W. G. Sumner, *Essays of William Graham Sumner,* ed. A. G. Keller and M. R. Davie (New Haven: Yale University Press, 1934). **[4, 29, 67]**

70. Those who have proposed the use of selectionist approaches in one way or another include Schumpeter, *Theory of Economic Development;* A. A. Alchain, "Uncertainty, Evolution and Economic Theory," *Journal of Political Economy* 58(1950): 211–21; J. W. S. Pringle, "On the Parallel Between Learning and Evolution," *Behaviour* 3(1951): 174–215; W. R. Ashby, *Design for a Brain* (New York: Wiley, 1952); R. W. Gerard et al., "Biological and Cultural Evolution: Some Analogies and Explanations," *Behavioral Science* 1(1956): 6–34; C. Russell and W. M. S. Russell, "An Approach to Human Ethology," *Behavioral Science* 2(1957): 169–200; Homans, "Social Behavior as Exchange," and *Social Behavior;* Goldschmidt, *Man's Way;* D. T. Campbell, "Blind Variation and Selective Retention in Creative Thought as in Other Knowledge Processes," *Psychological Review* 67(1960): 380–400, "Variation and Selective Retention in Sociocultural Evolution," in *Social Change in Developing Areas,* ed. H. R. Barringer (Cambridge, Mass.: Shenkman, 1965), "'Downward Causation' in Hierarchically Organised Biological Systems," in *Studies in the Philosophy of Biology,* ed. T. Dobzhansky and F. J. Ayala (London: Macmillan, 1974), and "On the Conflicts Between Biological and Social Evolution and Between Psychology and Moral Tradition," *American Psychologist* 30(1975): 1103–26; R. Burling, "Maximization Theories and the Study of Economic Anthropology," *American Anthropologist* 64(1962): 802–21; S. E. Toulmin, "The Evolutionary Development of Natural Science," *American Scientist*

55(1967): 456–71; M. Harris, *Rise of Anthropological Theory, Cannibals and Kings: The Origins of Cultures* (New York: Random House, 1977), and *Cultural Materialism;* Bigelow, *Dawn Warriors;* B. F. Skinner, *Contingencies of Reinforcement: A Theoretical Analysis* (New York: Appleton-Century, 1969), and "Selection by Consequences," *Science* 213(1981): 501–04; M. J. Farrell, "Some Elementary Selection Processes in Economics," *Review of Economic Studies* 37(1970): 305–19; G. E. Lenski, *Human Societies: A Macrolevel Introduction to Sociology* (New York: McGraw-Hill, 1970); S. G. Winter, "Satisficing, Selection and the Innovating Remnant," *Quarterly Journal of Economics* 86(1971): 237–61; Flannery, "Cultural Evolution of Civilization"; E. E. Ruyle, "Genetic and Cultural Pools: Some Suggestions for a Unified Theory of Biocultural Evolution," *Human Ecology* 1(1973): 201–15; A. Alland, Jr. and B. McKay, "The Concept of Adaptation in Biological and Cultural Evolution," in Honigmann, *Handbook of Anthropology;* L. L. Cavalli-Sforza and M. W. Feldman, "Models for Cultural Inheritance I. Group Mean and Within Group Variation," *Theoretical Population Biology* 4(1973): 42–55; P. A. Corning, "Politics and the Evolutionary Process," in *Evolutionary Biology,* ed. T. Dobzhansky et al., vol. VII (New York: Plenum, 1974); P. Diener, "Ecology or Evolution? The Hutterite Case," *American Ethnologist* 1(1974): 601–18; Nelson and Winter, "Neoclassical vs. Evolutionary Theories"; Schneider, *Economic Man;* F. T. Cloak, Jr., "That a Culture and Social Organization Mutually Shape Each Other Through a Process of Continuing Evolution," *Man-Environment Systems* 5(1975): 3–6; J. E. R. Staddon, "A Note on the Evolutionary Significance of 'Supernormal' Stimuli," *American Naturalist* 109(1975): 541–45; R. Dawkins, *The Selfish Gene* (New York: Oxford University Press, 1976); W. H. Durham, "The Adaptive Significance of Cultural Behavior," *Human Ecology* 4(1976): 89–121, "Resource Competition," and "Toward a Coevolutionary Theory of Human Biology and Culture," in *Evolutionary Biology and Human Social Behavior,* ed. N. A. Chagnon and W. Irons (North Scituate, Mass.: Duxbury, 1979); Naroll and Divale, "Natural Selection in Cultural Evolution"; Hardesty, *Ecological Anthropology;* J. H. Barkow, "Culture and Sociobiology," *American Anthropologist* 80(1978): 5–20; C. Boehm, "Rational Preselection from Hamadryas to *Homo sapiens:* The Place of Decisions in Adaptive Process," *American Anthropologist* 80(1978): 265–96; Boulding, *Ecodynamics;* P. J. Richerson and R. Boyd, "A Dual Inheritance Model of Human Evolutionary Process I.: Basic Postulates and a Simple Model," *Journal of Social and Biological Structures* 1(1978): 127–54; M. Blute, "Sociocultural Evolutionism: An Untried Theory," *Behavioral Science* 24(1979): 46–59; J. Langton, "Darwinism and the Behavioral Theory of Sociocultural Evolution: An Analysis," *American Journal of Sociology* 85(1979): 288–309; S. P. Reyna, "Social Evolution: A Learning-Theory Approach," *Journal of Anthropological Research* 35(1979): 336–349; P. C. Mundinger, "Animal Cultures and a General Theory of Cultural Evolution," *Ethology and Sociobiology* 1(1980): 183–223; C. J. Lumsden and E. O. Wilson, *Genes, Mind and Culture: The Co-Evolutionary Process* (Cambridge, Mass.: Harvard University Press, 1981); L. L. Cavalli-Sforza and M. W. Feldman, *Cultural Transmission and Evolution: A Quantitative Approach* (Princeton: Princeton University Press, 1981). **[9, 22, 23, 25, 26, 35, 39, 64]**

71. Kroeber, *Anthropology;* J. J. Flink, *America Adopts the Automobile, 1895–1910* (Cambridge, Mass.: MIT Press, 1970). **[34]**

72. E.g., Campbell, "Variation and Selective Retention"; Langton, "Darwinism."

73. See Barnett, *Innovation;* Blute, "Sociocultural Evolutionism." **[22, 70]**

74. See Corning, "Politics and Evolutionary Process," and the commentaries in L. G. Wispé and J. N. Thompson, Jr., "The War Between the Words: Biological Versus Social Evolution and Some Related Issues," *American Psychologist* 31(1976): 341–47 following Campbell's "Conflicts Between Biological and Social Evolution" (the published version of his presidential address to the American Psychological Association). **[70]**

75. E.g., Flannery, "Cultural Evolution of Civilizations"; Skinner, Contingencies of Reinforcement, *About Behaviorism* (New York: Knopf, 1974), and "Selection by Consequences." **[39, 70]**

76. See also Langton, "Darwinism"; Reyna, "Social Evolution." **[70]**

77. Alchain, "Uncertainty." **[70]**

78. Boehm, "Rational Preselection." **[70]**

79. Cf. Bonner, *Evolution of Culture* (Princeton: Princeton University Press, 1980).

80. D. L. Clarke, *Analytical Archaeology,* 2d ed., rev. B. Chapman (New York: Columbia University Press, 1978); see also Lumsden and Wilson, *Genes, Mind and Culture.* **[76]**

81. Mundinger, "Animal Cultures." **[70]**

82. Durham, "Adaptive Significance of Behavior," and "Toward a Coevolutionary Theory"; Alexander, *Darwinism.* Cloak's "Culture and Social Organization Mutually Shape Each Other," provides one of the best treatments of this issue to date. For similar statements by holistically oriented anthropologists, see R. Benedict, *Patterns of Culture,* 2d ed. (New York: New American Library, 1958 [1934]), pp. 52–61; E. Wolf, *Anthropology* (Englewood Cliffs, N.J.: Prentice-Hall, 1964), pp. 92–93; W. Irons, "Natural Selection, Adaptation, and Human Social Behavior," in Chagnon and Irons, *Evolutionary Biology,* pp. 32–33. **[33, 70]**

83. Schumpeter, *Theory of Economic Development,* p. 58. **[23]**

84. Cf., A. Alland, Jr., "Adaptation," *Annual Review of Anthropology* 4(1975): 59–73.

85. Irons, "Natural Selection"; Durham, "Adaptive Significance of Cultural Behavior," and "Toward a Coevolutionary Theory"; R. D. Alexander, "Evolution and Culture," in Chagnon and Irons, *Evolutionary Biology,* and *Darwinism.* **[33, 70, 82]**

86. For a classic ethnographic study, see R. F. Salisbury, *From Stone to Steel: Economic Consequences of a Technological Change in New Guinea* (Victoria: Melbourne University Press, 1962); also Lee, "What Hunters Do." **[68]**

87. For enlightening discussions of the concept of goals, see A. Rosenbleuth et al., "Behavior, Purpose and Teleology," *Philosophy of Science* 10(1943): 18–24; K. W. Deutsch, *The Nerves of Government: Models of Political Communication and Control* (New York: Free Press, 1966 [1963]); H. A. Simon, "On the Concept of Organizational Goal," *Administrative Science Quarterly* 9(1964): 1–22; W. Buckley, *Sociology and Modern Systems Theory* (Englewood Cliffs, N.J.: Prentice-Hall, 1967), and *Modern Systems Research for the Behavioral Scientist: A Sourcebook* (Chicago: Aldine, 1968); A. Etzioni, *The Active Society: A Theory of Societal and Political Processes* (New York: Free Press, 1968); H. von Foerster et al., eds., *Purposive Systems: Proceedings of the First Symposium of the American Society for Cybernetics* (New York: Spartan Books, 1968); R. L. Ackoff and F. E. Emergy, *On Purposive Systems* (Chicago: Aldine, 1972); A. Locker and N. A. Coulter, "A New Look at the Description and Prescription of Systems," *Behavioral Science* 22(1977): 197–206; J. G. Miller, *Living Systems* (New York: McGraw-Hill, 1978); W. H. Thorpe, *Purpose in a World of Chance: A Biologist's View* (Oxford: Oxford University Press, 1978).

88. For a detailed discussion of this issue, see Corning (forthcoming); also the treatments in M. Weber, *Economy and Society: An Outline of Interpretive Sociology,* trans. E. Foschoff et al. (New York: Bedminster, 1968 [1922]), and *The Theory of Social and Economic Organization,* trans. T. Parsons (New York: Free Press, 1947 [1924]); Schumpeter, *Theory of Economic Development;* Kroeber, *Anthropology;* L. H. Jenks, *Change and the Entrepreneur* (Cambridge, Mass.: Harvard University Press, 1949); Barnet, *Innovation;* F. Barth, "On the Study of Social Change," *American Anthropologist* 69(1967): 661–69; Rogers, *Diffusion of Innovation* and references therein; W. J. Baumol, "Entrepreneurship in Economic Theory," *American Economic Association Papers and Proceedings* 80(1968): 64–71; Zaltman, *Innovations and Organizations;* E. M. Rogers and F. F. Shoemaker, *Communication of Innovations: A Cross-Cultural Approach,* 2d ed. (New York: Free Press, 1971 [1962]); Nelson and Winter, "Neoclassical vs. Evolutionary Theories"; M. Zey-Farrell, *Dimensions of Organizations: Environment, Context, Structure, Process, and Performance* (Santa Monica, Calif.: Goodyear, 1979); H. Brooks, "Technology, Evolution, and Purpose," *Daedalus* 109(1980): 65–81; Lumsden and Wilson, *Genes, Mind and Culture.* **[22, 23, 70]**

89. See the discussions in Toulmin, "Evolutionary Development of Natural Science"; T. Dobzhansky, "Chance and Creativity in Evolution," in Ayala and Dobzhansky, *Philosophy of Biology;* M. Ruse, *Sociobiology: Sense or Nonsense?* (Boston: D. Riedel, 1979); Locker and Coulter, "Description and Prescription of Systems"; B. C. Goodwin, "A Cognitive View of Biological Process," *Journal of Social and Biological Structures* 1(1978): 117–25; Lumsden and Wilson, *Genes, Mind and Culture.* **[70, 87]**

90. P. C. Reynolds, "Evolution of Primate Vocal-Auditory Communication Systems," *American Anthropologist* 70(1968): 300–08.

91. H. A. Simon, *Models of Man: Social and Rational* (New York: Wiley, 1957), and *Administrative Behavior,* 3rd ed. (New York: Free Press, 1976).

92. P. H. Richerson, "Ecology and Human Ecology: A Comparison of Theories in the Biological and Social Sciences," *American Ethnologist* 4(1977): 1–25.

93. For descriptions and discussions of innovative behavior in animals, see M. P. Crawford, "The Cooperative Solving of Problems by Young Chimpanzees," *Comparative Psychology Monographs,* no. 68. 14, 2(1937): 1088; W. H. Thorpe, *Learning and Instinct in Animals,* 2d ed. (Cambridge, Mass.: Harvard University Press, 1963); E. W. Menzel, Jr., and S. Halperin, "Purposive Behavior as a Basis for Objective Communication Between Chimpanzees," *Science* 189(1975): 652–54; Wilson, *Sociobiology;* B. B. Beck, *Animal Tool Behavior: The Use and Manufacture of Tools by Animals* (New York: Garland, 1980); Bonner, *Evolution of Culture;* Mundinger, "Animal Cultures." **[32, 70]**

94. A. Lesser, "Social Fields and the Evolution of Society," *Southwestern Journal of Anthropology* 17(1961): 40–48.

95. P. Diener, "Quantum Adjustment, Macroevolution, and the Social Field: Some Comments on Evolution and Culture," *Current Anthropology* 21(1980): 439.

96. P. Diener et al., "Ecology and Evolution in Cultural Anthropology," *Man* (n.s.) 15 (1980): 1–31; C. G. Hempel, *Aspects of Scientific Explanation and Other Essays in the Philosophy of Science* (New York: Free Press, 1965).

97. S. A. Boorman and P. R. Levitt, *The Genetics of Altruism* (New York: Academic Press, 1980); Lumsden and Wilson, *Genes, Mind and Culture;* Cavalli-Sforza and Feldman, *Cultural Transmission.* **[70]**

98. Diener, "Quantum Adjustment." **[95]**

99. Skinner, *About Behaviorism,* p. 215. **[75]**

100. Smith, *Wealth of Nations,* I: 12–13. **[52]**

101. Ibid., p. 13. **[52]**

102. H. George, *Progress and Poverty: An Inquiry into the Cause of Industrial Depressions and of Increase of Want with Increase of Wealth . . . the Remedy* (New York: Robert Schalkenbach Foundation, 1955 [1879]), p. 508.

103. F. H. Giddings, *The Principles of Sociology* (New York: Macmillan, 1896); H. Drummond, *The Ascent of Man* (London: Hodder & Stoughton, 1894); P. A. Kropotkin, *Mutual Aid: A Factor of Evolution* (New York: New York University Press, 1972 [1902]).

104. H. Reinheimer, *Evolution by Co-operation: A Study in Bio-Economics* (London: Kegan, Paul, Trench, Trubner, 1913), p. vii.

105. See in particular, Benedict, *Patterns of Culture;* W. M. Wheeler, *Social Life Among the Insects* (New York: Harcourt, 1930), and *Essays in Philosophical Biology* (Cambridge, Mass.: Harvard University Press, 1939); M. Mead, *Cooperation and Competition Among Primitive Peoples* (New York: McGraw-Hill, 1937); W. C. Allee, *Cooperation Among Animals: With Human Implications,* revised edition of *The Social Life of Animals* (New York: Henry Schuman, 1951 [1938]); W. Galt, "The Principle of Co-operation in Behavior," *Quarterly Review of Biology* 15(1940): 401–10; R. Redfield, ed., *Levels of Integration in Biological and Social Systems,* Biological Symposia, vol. 8 (Lancaster, Pa.: Jaques Cattell, 1942); M. F. A. Montagu, "The Origin

and Nature of Social Life and the Biological Basis of Cooperation," *Journal of Social Psychology* 29(1949): 267–83, *Darwin, Competition and Cooperation* (New York: Henry Schuman, 1952), and *The Direction of Human Development: Biological and Social Bases* (New York: Harper & Row, 1955); Lenski, *Power and Privilege;* Henri Tajfel, "Co-operation Between Human Groups," *Eugenics Review* 58(1966): 77–84; J. H. Crook, "Cooperation in Primates," *Eugenics Review* 58(1966): 63–70, and "Sources of Cooperation in Animals and Man," in *Man and Beast: Comparative Social Behavior,* ed. J. F. Eisenberg and W. S. Dillon (Washington, D.C.: Smithsonian Institution Press, 1971); R. A. Nisbet, "Cooperation," in *International Encyclopedia of the Social Sciences,* ed. D. L. Sills, vol. 3 (New York: Free Press, 1968) and references therein; Wilson, *Sociobiology;* Boulding, *Ecodynamics.* **[9, 32, 49, 82]**

106. E.g., anthropologist Ruth Benedict, as reported in A. H. Maslow, "Synergy and the Society in the Individual," *Journal of Individual Psychology* 29(1964): 153–64, and in A. H. Maslow and J. J. Honigman, "Synergy: Some Notes of Ruth Benedict," *American Anthropologist* 72(1970): 320–33; A. Coulter, *Synergetics: An Experiment in Human Development* (Wichita, Kans.: Wichita Human Study Group, 1955); R. B. Fuller, *Synergetics: Explorations in the Geometry of Thinking* (New York: Macmillan, 1965); B. J. Grindal, "The Idea of Synergy and Its Bearing on an Anthropological Humanism," *Anthropology and Humanism Quarterly* 1(1976): 4–6; H. Haken, *Dynamics of Synergetic Systems* (New York: Springer, 1980), and *Cooperative Effects: Progress in Synergetics* (New York: Elsevier, 1974).

107. Montagu, *Darwin, Competition and Cooperation,* and *Direction of Human Development,* p. 31. **[105]**

108. Quoted in Maslow, "Synergy in the Society," p. 156. **[106]**

109. For an important exception, see A. A. Alchain and H. Demsetz, "Production, Information Costs and Economic Organization," *American Economic Review* 62(1972): 777–95; also Boulding, *Ecodynamics;* J. S. Boswell, "Social Cooperation in Economic Systems—A Business History Approach," *Review of Social Economy* 36(1980): 155–77. **[9]**

110. Cf. Lenski, *Power and Privilege.* **[49]**

111. E.g., L. G. Wispé, "Positive Forms of Social Behavior: An Overview," *Journal of Social Issues* 28(1972): 1–19, and *Altruism, Sympathy and Helping: Psychological and Sociological Principles* (New York: Academic Press, 1978); and the summary in Wilson, *Sociobiology.* **[32]**

112. E.g., Mauss, *The Gift;* Thibaut and Kelley, *Social Psychology of Groups;* Homans, "Social Behavior as Exchange," and *Social Behavior;* Blau, *Exchange and Power;* Belshaw, *Traditional Exchange;* Sahlins, *Stone Age Economics;* G. S. Becker, "A Theory of Social Institutions," *Journal of Political Economy* 82(1974): 1063–83; Schneider, *Economic Man;* Berkowitz and Walster, *Equity Theory;* Befu, "Social Exchange"; Gergen, *Social Exchange.*

113. E.g., Olson, *Logic of Collective Action;* A. Rescigno and I. W. Richardson, "The Deterministic Theory of Population Dynamics," in *Foundations of Mathematical Biology,* ed. R. Rosen, vol. III (New York: Academic Press, 1973); J. Roughgarden, "Evolution of Marine Symbiosis—A Simple Cost-Benefit Model," *Ecology* 56(1975): 1201–08; R. M. May, ed., *Theoretical Ecology: Principles and Applications* (Philadelphia: Saunders, 1976); E. R. Pianka, *Evolutionary Ecology,* 2d ed. (New York: Harper & Row, 1978); B. S. Goh, "Stability in Models of Mutualism," *American Naturalist* 113(1979): 261–75; R. Axelrod, "More Effective Choice in the Prisoner's Dilemmas," *Journal of Conflict Resolution* 24(1980): 379–403, and "The Emergence of Cooperation Among Egoists," *American Political Science Review* 75(1981): 306–18; Boorman and Levitt, *Genetics of Altruism;* Axelrod and Hamilton, "Evolution of Cooperation." **[67, 68, 97]**

114. Alexander, *Darwinism and Human Affairs.* **[33]**

115. This conclusion is supported by recent mathematical work that was published after this volume was substantially completed. Most notably, Axelrod and Hamilton, "Evolution of Cooperation"; Cavalli-Sforza and Feldman, *Cultural Transmission.* **[68, 70]**

116. See J. P. Scott and J. L. Fuller, *Genetics and the Social Behavior of the Dog* (Chicago: University of Chicago Press, 1965); K. Lorenz, *Man Meets Dog,* trans. M. Kerr (London: Methuen, 1954).

117. A good overview is Wilson's chapter on symbiosis in *Sociobiology.* **[32]**

118. Mundinger, "Animal Cultures." **[70]**

119. R. A. Hinde, ed., *Non-Verbal Communication* (London: Cambridge University Press, 1972); Wilson, *Sociobiology.* **[32]**

120. See especially the discussions in D. L. Mech, *The Wolf: The Ecology and Behavior of an Endangered Species* (Garden City, N.Y.: Natural History Press, 1970); R. H. Tuttle, ed., *Socioecology and Psychology of Primates* (The Hague: Mouton, 1975); J. van Lawick-Goodall, *In the Shadow of Man* (Boston: Houghton Mifflin, 1971); R. L. Hall and H. S. Sharp, eds., *Wolf and Man: Evolution in Parallel* (New York: Academic Press, 1978).

121. Cf. H. Kummer, *Primate Societies: Group Techniques of Ecological Adaptation* (Chicago: Aldine, 1971).

122. Ibid.; A. Suzuki, "The Origin of Hominid Hunting: A Primatological Perspective," R. Peters and L. D. Mech, "Behavioral and Intellectual Adaptations of Selected Mammalian Predators to the Problem of Hunting Large Animals," both in Tuttle, *Socioecology;* Mech, *The Wolf;* R. L. Hall, "Paleobiology and Systematics of Canids and Hominids," *Journal of Human Evolution* 6(1977): 519–31, and "Variability and Speciation in Canids and Hominids," in Hall and Sharp, *Wolf and Man.* **[120]**

123. Hall, "Variability and Speciation." **[122]**

124. See T. Dobzhansky et al., *Evolution* (San Francisco: Freeman, 1977).

125. J. E. Pfeiffer, *The Emergence of Man* (New York: Harper & Row, 1969); A. C. Leopold and R. Ardrey, "Toxic Substances in Plants and the Food Habits of Early Man," *Science* 176(1972): 512–14; H. T. Lewis, "Indian Fires of Spring," *Natural History* 89, 1(1980): 76–83.

126. See the parallel arguments in Kroeber, *Anthropology,* and Barnett, *Innovation.* **[22, 34]**

127. R. E. Phillips et al., "No-Tillage Agriculture," *Science* 208(1980): 1108–13.

128. A. Etzioni and R. Remp, "Technological 'Shortcuts' to Social Change," *Science* 175(1972): 31–38.

129. Such famous examples as gunpowder and Arabic numerals are described in Kroeber, *Anthropology.* **[34]**

130. See J. Itani, "On the Acquisition and Propagation of a New Food Habit," *Primates* 1(1958): 84–98; D. Miyadi, "On Some New Habits and Their Propagation in Japanese Monkey Groups," *Proceedings, XV International Congress of Zoology* (1959): 857–60, and "Social Life of Japanese Monkeys," *Science* 143(1964): 783–86; S. A. Altmann, "Sociobiology of Rhesus Monkeys: III, The Basic Communication Network," *Behaviour* 32(1968): 17–32; J. Itani and A. Nishimura, "The Study of Infrahuman Culture in Japan," *Symposium of the Fourth International Congress of Primatology,* vol. 1 (Basel: Karger, 1973); Wilson, *Sociobiology.*

131. T. R. Williams, "The Socialization Process: A Theoretical Perspective," in *Primate Socialization,* ed. F. E. Poirier (New York: Random House, 1972).

132. B. Ryan and N. C. Gross, "The Diffusion of Hybrid Seed Corn in Two Iowa Communities," *Rural Sociology* 8(1945): 15–24.

133. Z. Griliches, "Hybrid Corn: An Exploration of the Economics of Technological Change," *Econometrica* 25(1957): 501–22.

134. J. S. Coleman et al., "The Diffusion of an Innovation Among Physicians," *Sociometry* 20(1957): 253–70.

135. C. A. Yeracaris, "Political Conflict and the Diffusion of Innovations," *Rural Sociology* 35(1970): 488–99.

136. A. O. Thio, "A Reconsideration of the Concept of Adopter-Innovation Compatibility in Diffusion Research," *Sociological Quarterly* 12(1971): 56–68.

137. See R. P. Abelson et al., eds., *Theories of Cognitive Consistency: A Sourcebook* (Chicago: Rand McNally, 1968); F. Heider, *The Psychology of Interpersonal Relations* (New York: Wiley, 1958).

138. J. A. Davis, "Structural Balance, Mechanical Solidarity, and Interpersonal Relations," *American Journal of Sociology* 68(1963): 444–62.

139. R. N. Adams, "Personnel in Culture Change: A Test of a Hypothesis," *Social Forces* 30(1951): 185–89; also Rogers and Shoemaker, *Communication of Innovations.* **[88]**

140. F. T. Cloak, Jr., "Comment on The Adaptive Significance of Cultural Behavior," *Human Ecology* 5(1977): 49–52.

141. See especially the reviews by R. F. Salisbury, "Economic Anthropology," *Annual Review of Anthropology* 2(1973): 85–94 and Befu, "Social Exchange"; also Dalton, *Studies in Economic Anthropology,* and *Economic Systems;* H. K. Schneider, "Economic Development," *Annual Review of Anthropology* 4(1975): 271–92, and "Recent Contributions," *Current Anthropology* 16(1975): 427–42. **[26]**

142. J. Sonnefeld, "Changes in Eskimo Hunting Technology, and Introduction to Implement Geography," *Association of American Geographers, Annals* 50(1960): 172–86.

143. Homans, "Social Behavior as Exchange," and *Social Behavior;* Thibaut and Kelley, *Social Psychology of Groups.* See also Gouldner, "Norm of Reciprocity"; Blau, *Exchange and Power;* Berkowitz and Walster, *Equity Theory;* Gergen, *Social Exchange.* **[25]**

144. E. Glahn, "Chinese Building Standards in the 12th Century," *Scientific American* 244, 10(1981): 162–65.

145. See J. L. Walker, "The Diffusion of Innovations Among American States," *American Political Science Review* 63(1969): 880–99; V. Gray, "Innovation in the States: A Diffusion Study," *American Political Science Review* 67(1973): 1174–85; R. Eyestone, "Confusion, Diffusion, and Innovation," *American Political Science Review* 71(1977): 441–47; D. Klingman, "Temporal and Spatial Diffusion in the Comparative Analysis of Social Change," *American Political Science Review* 74(1980): 123–37.

146. Kroeber, *Anthropology.* **[34]**

147. Naroll and Divale, "Natural Selection in Cultural Evolution." **[22]**

148. A. Lomax and C. M. Arensberg, "A Worldwide Evolutionary Classification of Cultures by Subsistence Systems," *Current Anthropology* 18(1977): 659–708.

149. R. Naroll and R. Wirsing, "Borrowing Versus Migration as Selection Factors in Cultural Evolution," *Journal of Conflict Resolution* 20(1976): 187–212.

150. H. R. Pulliam and C. Dunford, *Programmed to Learn: An Essay on the Evolution of Culture* (New York: Columbia University Press, 1980), pp. 79–80.

151. B. H. Beard, "Sunflower Crop," *Scientific American* 244, 5(1981): 150–61.

152. See T. C. Schneirla and G. Piel, "The Army Ant," *Scientific American* 178, 6(1948): 16–23.

153. Wilson, *Sociobiology,* p. 428.

154. J. D. Ligon and S. H. Ligon, "Communal Breeding in Green Woodhoopoes as a Case for Reciprocity," *Nature* 276(1978): 496–98.

155. G. B. Schaller, *The Serengeti Lion: A Study of Predator-Prey Relations* (Chicago: University of Chicago Press, 1972).

156. Ibid., p. 136.

157. G. B. Schaller and G. R. Lowther, "The Relevance of Carnivore Behavior to the Study of Early Hominids," *Southwestern Journal of Anthropology* 25(1969): 307–41.

158. T. Caraco and L. L. Wolf, "Ecological Determinants of Group Sizes of Foraging Lions," *American Naturalist* 109(1975): 343–52.

159. Beck, *Animal Tool Behavior;* G. E. King, "Alternative Uses of Primates and Carnivores in the Reconstruction of Early Hominid Behavior," *Ethology and Sociobiology* 1(1980): 99–109. **[93]**

160. C. E. Parker, "Opportunism and the Rise of Intelligence," *Journal of Human Evolution* 7(1978): 597–608.

161. See M.-C. King and A. C. Wilson, "Evolution at Two Levels in Humans and Chimpanzees," *Science* 188(1975): 107–16; L. M. Cherry et al., "Frog Perspective on the Morphological Difference Between Humans and Chimpanzees," *Science* 200(1978): 209–10; E. J. Bruce and F. J. Ayala, "Humans and Apes are Genetically Very Similar," *Nature* 276(1978): 264–65; J. J. Yunis et al., "The Striking Resemblance of High-Resolution G-Banded Chromosomes of Man and Chimpanzee," *Science* 208(1980): 1145–48.

162. V. W. Sarich and A. C. Wilson, "Immunological Time Scale for Hominid Evolution," *Science* 158(1967): 1200–1203; V. M. Sarich, "The Origin of the Hominids: An Immunological Approach," in *Perspectives on Human Evolution,* ed. S. L. Washburn and P. C. Jay (New York: Holt, 1968); A. C. Wilson and V. W. Sarich, "A Molecular Time Scale for Human Evolution," *Proceedings of the National Academy of Sciences* 63(1969): 1088–93; King and Wilson, "Evolutions at Two Levels"; Cherry, "Frog Perspective"; J. J. Yunis and O. Prakash, "The Origin of Man: A Chromosomal Pictorial Legacy," *Science* 215(1982): 1525–30. **[161]**

163. D. C. Johanson and T. D. White, "A Systematic Assessment of Early African Hominids," *Science* 203(1979): 321–30; D. C. Johanson and M. A. Edey, *Lucy: The Beginnings of Humankind* (New York: Simon and Schuster, 1981).

164. M. D. Leakey et al., "Fossil Hominids from the Laetolil Beds," *Nature* 262(1976): 460–66; T. D. White, "Evolutionary Implications of Pliocene Hominid Footprints," *Science* 208(1980): 175–176.

165. E.g., S. L. Washburn and V. Avis, "Evolution of Human Behavior," in *Behavior and Evolution,* ed. A. Roe and G. G. Simpson (New Haven: Yale University Press, 1958); S. L. Washburn, "Behavior and Human Evolution," in *Classification and Human Evolution,* ed. S. L. Washburn (Chicago: Aldine, 1963); *The Study of Human Evolution* (Eugene: University of Oregon Press, 1968), and "Human Evolution," in Dobzhansky, *Evolutionary Biology.*

166. G. L. Isaac, "The Activities of Early African Hominids: A Review of Archaeological Evidence from the Time Span Two and a Half to One Million Years Ago," in *Human Origins: Louis Leakey and the East African Evidence,* ed. G. L. Isaac and E. R. McCown (Menlo Park, Calif.: Benjamin, 1976), and "The Food-Sharing Behavior of Protohuman Hominids," *Scientific American* 238, 4(1978): 90–108; S. L. Washburn and R. Moore, *Ape to Man: A Study of Human Evolution* (Boston: Little, Brown, 1974); S. L. Washburn, "Animal Behavior and Social Anthropology," in *Sociobiology and Human Nature: An Interdisciplinary Critique and Defense,* ed. M. S. Gregory et al. (San Francisco: Jossey-Bass, 1978), and "The Evolution of Man," *Scientific American* 239, 3(1978): 194–208.

167. R. E. Leakey and R. Lewin, *Origins* (London: Macdonald and Jane's, 1977).

168. van Lawick-Goodall, *Shadow of Man.* See especially the review in Beck, *Animal Tool Behavior,* pp. 82–125. **[93, 122]**

169. D. G. Coursey, "Hominid Evolution and Hypogeous Plant Foods," *Man* 8(1973): 634–35.

170. See also R. A. Dart, *Adventures with the Missing Link* (New York: Viking, 1959).

171. Washburn and Avis, "Evolution of Human Behavior." **[165]**

172. Ardrey, *Territorial Imperative, The Social Contract: A Personal Inquiry into the Evolutionary Sources of Order and Disorder* (New York: Delta, 1970), *African Genesis,* and *Hunting Hypothesis.*

173. See Lee and DeVore, *Man the Hunter,* especially the articles by Laughlin, Washburn, and Lancaster; also L. Tiger, *Men in Groups* (New York: Random House, 1969); D. R. Pilbeam, *The Evolution of Man* (New York: Funk and Wagnalls, 1970); Tiger and Fox, *Imperial Animal;* B. Campbell, *Human Evolution,* 2d ed. (Chicago: Aldine, 1974); B. M. Fagan, *Men of the Earth: An Introduction to World Prehistory* (Boston: Little, Brown, 1974); J. Z. Young, *An*

Introduction to the Study of Man (New York: Oxford, 1974); Washburn and Moore, *Ape to Man;* Washburn, "Animal Behavior," and "Evolution of Man."

174. van Lawick-Goodall, *Shadow of Man;* R. S. O. Harding, "Predation by a Troop of Olive Baboons (*Papio anubis*)," *American Journal of Physical Anthropology* 38(1973): 587–92; R. A. Dart, "The Carnivorous Propensity of Baboons," *Symposia of the Zoological Society of London* 10(1963): 49–56; G. Teleki, *The Predatory Behavior of Wild Chimpanzees* (Cranberry, N.J.: Associated University Presses, 1973), "Chimpanzee Subsistence as Technology: Materials and Skills," *Journal of Human Evolution* 3(1974): 575–94, and "Primate Subsistence Patterns: Collector-Predators and Gatherer-Hunters," *Journal of Human Evolution* 4(1975): 125–84; S. C. Strum, "Primate Predation: Interim Report on the Development of a Tradition in a Troop of Olive Baboons," *Science* 187(1975): 755–57, and "Life with the Pumphouse Gang," *National Geographic* 147(1975): 687–91; Suzuki, "Origin of Hominid Hunting"; R. S. O. Harding and S. C. Strum, "Predatory Baboons of Kekopey," *Natural History* 85(1976): 46–53; V. Reynolds, *The Biology of Human Action* (San Francisco: Freeman, 1976); S. J. C. Gaulin and J. A. Kurland, "Primate Predation and Bioenergetics," *Science* 191(1976): 314–15; G. Hausfater, "Predatory Behavior of Yellow Baboons," *Behaviour* 56(1976): 45–68; R. S. O. Harding and G. Teleki, eds., *Omnivorous Primates* (New York: Columbia University Press, 1981). **[120]**

175. In addition to Schaller and Lowther, "Relevance of Carnivore Behavior," see Mech, *The Wolf;* Hall and Sharp, *Wolf and Man;* E. Klinghammer, ed., *The Behavior and Ecology of Wolves* (New York: Garland, 1979); J. van Lawick-Goodall and H. van Lawick, *Innocent Killers* (Boston: Houghton Mifflin, 1971); Schaller, *Serengeti Lion;* H. Kruuk, *The Spotted Hyena: A Study of Predation and Social Behavior* (Chicago: University of Chicago Press, 1972). **[120, 155, 157]**

176. See the comparative analyses by G. E. King, "Socioterritorial Units Among Carnivores and Early Hominids," *Journal of Anthropological Research* 31(1975): 69–87, "Society and Territory in Human Evolution," *Journal of Human Evolution* 5(1976): 323–32, "Socioterritorial Units and Interspecific Competition: Modern Carnivores and Early Hominids," *Journal of Anthropological Research* 32(1976): 276–84, and "Alternative Uses of Primates"; P. R. Thompson, "A Behavior Model for *Australopithecus africanus,*" *Journal of Human Evolution* 5(1976): 547–58, "A Cross-Species Analysis of Carnivore, Primate, and Hominid Behavior," *Journal of Human Evolution* 4(1975): 113–124, and "The Evolution of Territoriality and Society in Top Carnivores," *Social Science Information* 17(1978): 949–92; Hall and Sharp, *Wolf and Man;* Peters and Mech, "Behavior of Mammalian Predators." **[120, 122]**

177. Thompson, "Cross-Species Analysis." **[176]**

178. G. Teleki, "Primate Subsistence Patterns," and "The Omnivorous Diet and Eclectic Feeding Habits of Chimpanzees in Gombe National Park, Tanzania," in Harding and Teleki, *Omnivorous Primates.* **[174]**

179. G. L. Isaac and D. C. Crader, "To What Extent Were Early Hominids Carnivorous? An Archaeological Perspective," in Harding and Teleki, *Omnivorous Primates.* **[174]**

180. Harding and Teleki, *Omnivorous Primates,* p. 7. **[174]**

181. B. Hayden, "Subsistence and Ecological Adaptations of Modern Hunter/Gatherers," in ibid.

182. P. V. Tobias, "Bushman Hunter-Gatherers: A Study in Human Ecology," in *Ecological Studies in Southern Africa,* ed. D. H. S. Davis (The Hague: W. Junk, 1964); R. A. Gould, "Living Archaeology: The Ngatatjara of Western Australia," *Southwestern Journal of Anthropology* 24(1968): 101–22; B. C. Campbell, "Ecological Factors and Social Organization in Human Evolution," in *Primate Ecology and Human Origins: Ecological Influences on Social Organizations,* ed. I. S. Bernstein and E. O. Smith (New York: Garland, 1979).

183. A. Kortlandt, *New Perspectives on Ape and Human Evolution* (Amsterdam: Stichting

Voor Psychobiologie, 1972), and "Chimpanzees in the Wild," *Scientific American* 206(1962): 128–38.

184. Harding, "Predation by Olive Baboons"; Strum, "Primate Predation"; Harding and Strum, "Predatory Baboons"; S. C. Strum, "Processes and Products of Change: Baboon Predatory Behavior at Gilgil, Kenya," in Harding and Teleki, *Omnivorous Primates.*

185. Lee and DeVore, *Man the Hunter;* A. L. Zihlman and N. Tanner, "Gathering and the Hominid Adaptation," in *Female Hierarchies,* ed. L. Tiger and H. Fowler (Chicago: AVC, 1978); Harding and Teleki, *Omnivorous Primates,* especially the chapters by Mann, Harding, and Teleki. **[68, 174]**

186. Isaac and Crader, "Were Early Hominids Carnivorous?" See also R. S. O. Harding, "An Order of Omnivores: Nonhuman Primate Diets in the Wild," and A. E. Mann, "Diet and Human Evolution," both in Harding and Teleki, *Omnivorous Primates;* Teleki, "Omnivorous Diet of Chimpanzees." **[174, 178, 179]**

187. Mann, "Diet and Human Evolution." **[186]**

188. Alexander, *Darwinism.* **[33]**

189. Keith, "A New Theory"; R. A. Dart, "The Predatory Transition from Ape to Man." With some modifications, this general thesis was later picked up and developed by Robert Ardrey, *African Genesis;* Alexander and Tinkle, "Review of *On Aggression* and *Territorial Imperative*"; Bigelow, *Dawn Warriors;* Wilson, "Queerness of Social Evolution," and *Sociobiology;* Pitt, "Warfare and Brain Evolution"; Alexander, *Darwinism;* J. M. Strate, "The Sovereign as Protector: The Functional Priority of Defense," prepared for the Annual Meeting, American Political Science Association, 1981. See also the discussions in Corning, "Biological Bases of Behavior," "Human Violence," and "Evolutionary Paradigm"; Corning and Corning, "General Theory of Violent Aggression." **[32, 33, 170, 172]**

190. Bigelow, *Dawn Warriors,* pp. 3, 7. **[32]**

191. Alexander, *Darwinism.* **[33]**

192. Ibid., p. 223.

193. Ibid., pp. 222, 223.

194. Mech, *The Wolf;* Kummer, *Primate Societies;* Schaller, *Serengeti Lion;* Kruuk, *Spotted Hyena;* van Lawick-Goodall and van-Lawick, *Innocent Killers;* King, "Alternative Uses of Primates." **[120, 121, 155, 159, 175]**

195. R. A. Dart, "The Osteodontokeratic Culture of *Australopithecus prometheus,*" *Transvaal Museum Memoir* 10(1957): 1–105, and "The Bone Tool-Manufacturing Ability of *Australopithecus prometheus,*" *American Anthropologist* 62(1960): 134–43; C. K. Brain, "Some Principles in the Interpretation of Bone Accumulations Associated with Man," in Isaac and McCown, *Human Origins.* **[166]**

196. M. K. Roper, "A Survey of Evidence for Intrahuman Killing in the Pleistocene," *Current Anthropology* 10(1969): 427–59.

197. Cited in I. Eibl-Eibesfeldt, *The Biology of Peace and War: Men, Animals, and Aggression* (New York: Viking Press, 1979 [1975]).

198. Ibid.

199. C. R. Ember, "Myths About Hunter-Gatherers," *Ethnology* 17(1978): 439–48.

200. Eibl-Eibesfeldt, "Human Ethology." **[32]**

201. Wilson, "Queerness of Social Evolution." See also Lumsden and Wilson, *Genes, Mind and Culture.* **[32, 70]**

202. See Schaller and Lowther, "Relevance of Carnivore Behavior"; C. K. Brain, "New Finds at the Swartkrans Australopithecine Site," *Nature* 225(1970): 1112–119; Schaller, *Serengeti Lion;* Kruuk, *Spotted Hyena.* **[155, 157]**

203. Kortlandt, *New Perspectives on Evolution;* Thompson, "Evolution of Territoriality." **[176, 183]**

204. H. B. S. Cooke, "Pleistocene Mammal Faunas of Africa, with Particular Reference to Southern Africa," in *African Ecology and Human Evolution,* ed. F. C. Howell and F. Bourlière (Chicago: Aldine, 1963); Brain, "New Finds at Swartkrans," and *The Hunters or the Hunted?* **[202]**

205. Suzuki, "Origin of Hominid Hunting"; Zihlman and Tanner, "Gathering and Hominid Adaptation"; Campbell, "Ecological Factors and Social Organization"; C. O. Lovejoy, "The Origin of Man," *Science* 211(1981): 341–50. **[174, 185]**

206. Pitt, "Warfare and Brain Evolution." **[32]**

207. Q. Wright, *A Study of War,* 2d ed. (Chicago: University of Chicago Press, 1965 [1942]); L. Richardson, *Statistics of Deadly Quarrels* (Pittsburgh: Boxwood, 1960).

208. Zihlman and Tanner, "Gathering and Hominid Adaptation." See also N. Tanner and A. Zihlman, "Women and Evolution, Part I: Innovation and Selection in Human Origins," *Signs* 1(1976): 585–608; A. L. Zihlman, "Women in Evolution, Part II: Subsistence and Social Organization Among Early Hominids," *Signs* 4(1978): 4–20. **[185]**

209. Lee, "What Hunters Do"; Hayden, "Subsistence Adaptations of Hunter/Gatherers"; Mann, "Diet and Human Evolution." **[68, 186]**

210. Ember, "Myths About Hunter-Gatherers." **[199]**

211. Lee, "What Hunters Do"; Hayden 1981. **[68]**

212. Ardrey, *Hunting Hypothesis.* **[172]**

213. Leopold and Ardrey, "Toxic Substances." **[125]**

214. Hayden, "Subsistence Adaptations of Hunter/Gatherers," p. 34.

215. L. A. Coser, *The Functions of Social Conflict* (New York: Free Press, 1956); H. Tajfel, "Experiments in Intergroup Discrimination," *Scientific American* 223, 11(1970): 96–102; King, "Alternative Uses of Primates." **[159]**

216. Lovejoy, "Origin of Man." **[205]**

217. Tiger, *Men in Groups.* **[173]**

218. Cf. King, "Alternative Uses of Primates." **[159]**

219. See especially F. E. Poirier, ed., *Primate Socialization* (New York: Random House, 1972); S. Chevalier-Skolnikoff and F. E. Poirier, eds., *Primate Bio-Social Development: Biological, Social, and Ecological Determinants* (New York: Garland, 1977).

220. Strum, "Primate Predation," "Life with Pumphouse Gang," and "Processes and Products of Change"; Harding, "Predation by Olive Baboons"; Harding and Strum, "Predatory Baboons of Kekopey." **[174, 184]**

221. Harding and Strum, "Predatory Baboons of Kekopey," pp. 51, 53. **[174]**

222. See the discussions in R. A. Hinde, "Interactions, Relationships and Social Structure," *Man* (n.s.) 11(1976): 1–17, "The Nature of Social Structure," in *The Great Apes,* ed. D. A. Hamburg and E. R. McCown (Menlo Park, Calif.: Benjamin/Cummings, 1979), and "Dominance and Role: Two Concepts with Dual Meanings," *Journal of Social and Biological Structures* 1(1978): 27–38; U. Nagel, "On Describing Primate Groups as Systems: The Concept of Ecosocial Behavior," in Bernstein and Smith, *Primate Ecology.* **[185]**

223. See especially, Kummer, *Primate Societies;* and the experiments and discussions in E. W. Menzel, Jr., "Communication About the Environment in a Group of Young Chimpanzees," *Folia Primatologica* 15(1971): 220–32, "Natural Language of Young Chimpanzees," *New Scientist* 65(1975): 127–30, and "Communication of Object-Locations in a Group of Young Chimpanzees," in Hamburg and McCown, *The Great Apes;* Menzel and Halperin, "Purposive Behavior." **[93, 121, 222]**

224. See, for examples, R. Fox, "In the Beginning: Aspects of Hominid Behavioral Evolution, *Man* 2(1967): 415–33; J. B. Lancaster, *Primate Behavior and the Emergence of Human Culture* (New York: Holt, 1975); S. L. Gabow, "Population Structure and the Rate of Hominid Brain Evolution," *Journal of Human Evolution* 6(1977): 643–65; Leakey and Lewin, *Origins;* Pfeiffer,

Emergence of Society (New York: McGraw-Hill, 1977); Isaac, "Food-Sharing Behavior"; Thompson, "Evolution of Territoriality"; Bonner, *Evolution of Culture;* Lovejoy, "Origin of Man"; Lumsden and Wilson, *Genes, Mind and Culture.* **[70, 166, 167, 176, 205]**

225. See especially the discussions in Tiger and Fox, *Imperial Animal;* Corning, "Politics and Evolutionary Process"; Hinde, "Interactions, Relationships and Social Structure"; F. H. Willhoite, Jr., "Reciprocity, Political Origins, and Legitimacy," prepared for the International Meeting of the Conference for the Study of Political Thought, 1978.

226. P. Reynolds, *On the Evolution of Human Behavior* (Berkeley: University of California Press, 1981).

227. F. C. Howell, "The Hominization Process," in *Horizons of Anthropology,* ed. S. Tax and L. G. Freeman, 2d ed. (Chicago: Aldine, 1977); Isaac, "Food-Sharing Behavior"; King, "Alternative Uses of Primates"; Isaac and Crader, "Were Early Hominids Carnivorous?" Cf. Peters and Mech, "Adaptations of Mammalian Predators"; C. E. Read-Martin and D. W. Read, "Australopithecine Scavenging and Human Evolution: An Approach from Faunal Analysis," *Current Anthropology* 16(1975): 359–68; F. S. Szalay, "Hunting-Scavenging Protohominids: A Model for Hominid Origins," *Man* 10(1975): 420–29. **[59, 122, 159, 166, 179]**

228. C. L. Hamilton, "Long Term Control of Food Intake in the Monkey," *Physiology and Behavior* 9(1972): 1–6.

229. A. Walker and A. E. F. Leakey, "The Hominids of East Turkana," *Scientific American* 239, 2(1980): 54–66.

230. Washburn, "Evolution of Man"; Durham, "Adaptive Significance of Cultural Behavior," and "Toward an Evolutionary Theory"; reported in G. L. Isaac, "The Emergence of Man," *Nature* 285(1980): 72. The term autocatalysis may have originated with Wilson, *Sociobiology.* **[32, 70, 166]**

231. Cf. Isaac and Crader, "Were Early Hominids Carnivorous?" **[179]**

232. Lee and DeVore, *Man the Hunter.* **[68]**

233. E.g., Washburn and Lancaster, "Evolution of Hunting"; Laughlin, "Hunting"; Pfeiffer, *Emergence of Man;* Isaac, "Activities of Early African Hominids," and "Food-Sharing Behavior"; C. L. Brace, "Biological Parameters and Pleistocene Hominid Life-Ways," in Bernstein and Smith, *Primate Ecology;* Isaac and Crader, "Were Early Hominids Carnivorous?" **[125, 166, 179, 185]**

234. Brace, "Biological Parameters," p. 264. **[233]**

235. F. Bourlière, "Observations on the Ecology of Some Large African Mammals," in Howell and Bourlière, *African Ecology.* **[204]**

236. Hayden, "Subsistence Adaptations of Hunter/Gatherers." **[181]**

237. Steward, *Theory of Culture Change;* J. Woodburn, "Stability and Flexibility in Hadza Residential Groupings," in Lee and DeVore, *Man the Hunter;* R. A. Gould, "Subsistence Behaviour Among the Western Desert Aborigines of Australia," *Oceania* 39(1969): 225–74; D. Damas, "The Copper Eskimos," in *Hunters and Gatherers Today,* ed. M. G. Bicchieri (New York: Holt, 1972); R. Harako, "The Cultural Ecology of Hunting Behavior Among Mbuti Pygmies in the Ituri Forest, Zaire," in Harding and Teleki, *Omnivorous Primates.* **[2, 68, 174]**

238. Isaac, "Activities of Early African Hominids"; Brace, "Biological Parameters"; Isaac and Crader, "Were Early Hominids Carnivorous?" **[179]**

239. Laughlin, "Hunting."

240. Washburn and Lancaster, "Evolution of Hunting."

241. A. J. Jelinek, "The Lower Paleolithic: Current Evidence and Interpretations," *Annual Review of Anthropology* 6(1977): 11–32.

242. Brace, "Biological Parameters," p. 285. Cf. Flannery, "Cultural Evolution of Civilizations"; Washburn, "Human Evolution." **[37, 165]**

243. See the similar arguments in A. Jolly, *The Evolution of Primate Behavior* (New York:

Macmillan, 1972); Washburn, "Human Evolution"; Washburn and Lancaster, "Evolution of Hunting"; Washburn and Moore, *Ape to Man;* Brace, "Biological Parameters"; P. J. Wilson, *Man, the Promising Primate: The Conditions of Human Evolution* (New Haven: Yale University Press, 1980). **[165, 166]**

244. A. Balikci, "The Netsilik Eskimos: Adaptive Processes," in Lee and DeVore, *Man the Hunter,* and *The Netsilik Eskimo* (Garden City, N.Y.: Natural History Press, 1970).

245. W. Suttles, "Coping with Abundance: Subsistence on the Northwest Coast," in Lee and DeVore, *Man the Hunter.* **[68]**

246. Hayden, "Subsistence Adaptations of Hunter/Gatherers." **[181]**

247. For more detailed discussions, see F. S. Hulse, "Technological Advance and Major Racial Stocks," *Human Biology* 27(1955): 184–92, "Race as an Evolutionary Episode," *American Anthropologist* 64(1962): 924–45, and "Group Selection and Sexual Selection in Human Evolution," in *Evolutionary Models and Studies in Human Diversity,* ed. R. J. Meier et al. (The Hague: Mouton, 1978).

248. Steward, *Theory of Culture Change.* **[2]**

249. H. Watanabe, "The Ainu," in *Hunters and Gatherers Today,* ed. M. G. Bicchieri (New York: Holt, 1972).

250. Balikci, "The Netsilik Eskimos," and *The Netsilik Eskimos.* **[244]**

251. Howell cited in Pfeiffer, *Emergence of Society;* H. de Lumley, "A Paleolithic Camp at Nice," *Scientific American* 220, 18(1969): 42–50. **[224]**

252. A. J. Ammerman, "Late Pleistocene Population Dynamics: An Alternative View," *Human Ecology* 3(1975): 219–33.

253. V. G. Childe, *Man Makes Himself* (New York: New American Library, 1951 [1936]).

254. L. R. Binford, "Post-Pleistocene Adaptations," in Binford and Binford, *New Perspectives in Archaeology* (Chicago: Aldine, 1968).

255. P. S. Martin, "Africa and Pleistocene Overkill," *Nature* 212(1966): 339–42, "Pleistocene Overkill," *Natural History* 76, 10(1967): 32–38, and "The Discovery of America," *Science* 179(1973): 969–74; P. S. Martin and H. E. Wright, eds., *Pleistocene Extinctions* (New Haven: Yale University Press, 1967); A. Long and P. S. Martin, "Death of American Ground Sloths," *Science* 186(1974): 638–40; J. E. Mosimann and P. S. Martin, "Simulating Overkill by Paleoindians," *American Scientist* 63(1975): 304–13.

256. For a review and critique, see D. Webster, "Late Pleistocene Extinction and Human Predation: A Critical Overview," in Harding and Teleki, *Omnivorous Primates.* **[174]**

257. Spencer, "A Theory of Population." **[27]**

258. R. Carneiro, "Agriculture and the Beginning of Civilization," *Ethnographische-Archäologische Forschungen* 4(1958): 22–27; Boserup, *Conditions of Agricultural Growth;* Cohen, *Food Crisis.* **[29]**

259. Cohen, *Food Crisis,* p. 285. **[29]**

260. See the discussion in J. E. Pfeiffer, *The Emergence of Society: A Pre-History of the Establishment* (New York: McGraw-Hill, 1977).

261. B. Hayden, "Research and Development in the Stone Age: Technological Transitions Among Hunter-Gatherers," *Current Anthropology* 22(1981): 519–48.

262. For an extensive review, see Pfeiffer, *Emergence of Society.* Also see T. W. Jacobsen, "17,000 Years of Greek Prehistory," *Scientific American* 234, 6(1976): 76–87; A. Marshack, "Implications of the Paleolithic Symbolic Evidence for the Origin of Language," *American Scientist* 64(1976): 136–45, and "Upper Paleolithic Symbol Systems of the Russian Pane: Cognitive and Comparative Analysis," *Current Anthropology* 20(1979): 271–313; P. E. L. Smith, "Stone-Age Man on the Nile," *Scientific American* 235, 2(1976): 30–38; N. Hammond, "The Earliest Maya," *Scientific American* 236, 3(1977): 116–33; A. M. T. Moore, "A Pre-Neolithic Farmers' Village on the Euphrates," *Scientific American* 241, 3(1979): 62–70; C. Niederberger,

"Early Sedentary Economy in the Basin of Mexico," *Science* 203, 2(1979): 131–142; F. Wendorf et al., "Use of Barley in the Egyptian Late Paleolithic," *Science* 205(1979): 1341–47; J. F. Jarrige and R. H. Meadow, "The Antecedents of Civilization in the Indus Valley," *Scientific American* 243, 2(1980): 122–33; J. Clutton-Brock, *Domesticated Animals from Early Times* (Austin: University of Texas Press, 1981). **[224]**

263. K. Polanyi et al., *Trade and Market in the Early Empires* (Glencoe, Ill.: Free Press, 1957); Sahlins, *Stone Age Economics;* Sabloff and Lamberg-Karlovsky, *Ancient Civilization.* **[9, 26]**

264. Pfeiffer, *Emergence of Society.* **[224]**

265. R. Carneiro, "Scale Analysis, Evolutionary Sequences and the Rating of Cultures," in Naroll and Cohen, *Handbook of Cultural Anthropology.* (New York: Natural History Press, 1970).

266. J. Harlan, "A Wild Wheat Harvest in Turkey," *Archaeology* 20(1967): 197–201.

267. Cf. Wright, "Recent Research on the State," and "An Explanation of the Origin of the State"; also Wright and Johnson, "Population, Exchange in Southwestern Iran."

268. For more detailed arguments along these lines, see Service, *Origins of the State,* and R. N. Cohen, "State Origins: A Reappraisal," in *The Early State,* ed. H. J. M. Claessen and P. Skalník (The Hague: Mouton, 1978). **[40]**

269. R. Millon, "Teotihuacán," *Scientific American* 216, 2(1967): 38–48.

270. Cohen, "State Origins," p. 37. **[268]**

VI. A General Theory of Politics

1. W. J. M. Mackenzie, *Politics and Social Science* (Baltimore: Penguin, 1967), p. 81.

2. H. J. Morgenthau, *Politics Among Nations: The Struggle for Power and Peace,* 4th ed. (New York: Knopf, 1967), p. 9.

3. R. A. Dahl, *Modern Political Analysis* (Englewood Cliffs, N.J.: Prentice-Hall, 1970 [1963]), p. 6.

4. J. M. Buchanan and G. Tullock, *The Calculus of Consent: Logical Foundations of Constitutional Democracy* (Ann Arbor: University of Michigan Press, 1962), p. 23; S. S. Wolin, *Politics and Vision: Continuity and Innovation in Western Political Thought* (Boston: Little, Brown, 1960), pp. 2–3, 10–11.

5. K. W. Deutsch, *The Nerves of Government: Models of Political Communication and Control* (New York: Free Press, 1966 [1963]), p. 124.

6. L. Tiger and R. Fox, *The Imperial Animal* (New York: Holt, 1971), p. 25.

7. For a more judicious and methodical attempt to relate ethological phenomena to human politics, see F. H. Willhoite, Jr., "Primates and Political Authority: A Biobehavioral Perspective," *American Political Science Review* 70(1976): 1110–26.

8. D. Easton, *A Systems Analysis of Political Life* (New York: Wiley, 1965), p. 21, *inter alia.*

9. Dahl, *Modern Political Analysis,* p. 8. **[3]**

10. For a fuller discussion of politics as cybernetics, see Deutsch, *Nerves of Government;* P. A. Corning, "Politics and the Evolutionary Process," in *Evolutionary Biology,* vol. VII, ed. T. Dobzhansky et al. (New York: Plenum, 1974); John D. Steinbruner, *The Cybernetic Theory of Decision: New Dimensions of Political Analysis* (Princeton: Princeton University Press, 1974). **[5]**

11. Dahl, *Modern Political Analysis,* p. 1. **[3]**

12. I. de Sola Pool, ed., *Contemporary Political Science: Toward Empirical Theory* (New York: McGraw-Hill, 1967), p. viii.

13. J. C. Charlesworth, ed., *Contemporary Political Analysis* (New York: Free Press, 1967), p. 7.

14. The parameters are spelled out in P. A. Corning, "The Biological Bases of Behavior and Their Implications for Political Theory," paper prepared for the annual meeting, American Political Science Association, 1969, "Evolutionary Indicators: Applying the Theory of Evolution to Political Science," paper prepared for the biennial meeting, International Political Science Association, 1970, "The Biological Bases of Behavior and Some Implications for Political Science, *World Politics* 23(1971): 321–70, "Politics and Evolutionary Process," "Human Nature Redivivus," in *Human Nature in Politics* (Nomos XVII), ed. J. R. Pennock and J. W. Chapman (New York: New York University Press, 1977).

15. Richard Smoke, "National Security Affairs," in *Handbook of Political Science,* vol. 8, ed. F. I. Greenstein and N. W. Polsby (Reading, Mass.: Addison-Wesley, 1975), p. 247.

16. D. Easton, *Systems Analysis of Political Life,* and *A Framework for Political Analysis* (Englewood Cliffs, N.J.: Prentice-Hall, 1965).

17. E.g., A. J. Gregor, "Political Science and the Uses of Functional Analysis," *American Political Science Review* 62(1968): 425–39; T. L. Thorson, *Biopolitics* (New York: Holt, 1970); J. P. O'Leary, *Systems Theory and Regional Integration: The "Market Model" of International Politics* (Washington, D.C.: University Press of America, 1978), *inter alia.*

18. Easton, *Systems Analysis of Political Life,* p. 29. **[16]**

19. Ibid., pp. 21, 22, 24.

20. Ibid., p. 24.

21. Ibid., p. 15.

22. In ibid., p. 368.

23. For elaboration, see W. T. Powers, "Feedback: Beyond Behaviorism," *Science* 179(1973): 351–56, *Behavior: The Control of Perception* (Chicago: Aldine, 1973), and "Quantitative Analysis of Purposive Systems: Some Spadework at the Foundations of Scientific Psychology," *Psychological Review* 85(1978): 417–35.

24. Deutsch, *Nerves of Government.* **[5]**

25. Steinbruner, *Cybernetic Theory of Decision.* **[10]**

26. Thorson, *Biopolitics,* p. 59. **[17]**

27. For a sampler of the literature in cybernetics that involves hard applications in systems engineering, biology, and psychology, see W. R. Ashby, *Design for a Brain* (New York: Wiley, 1952), and *An Introduction to Cybernetics* (New York: Wiley, 1966); R. M. Cyert and J. G. March, *The Behavioral Theory of the Firm* (Englewood Cliffs, N.J.: Prentice-Hall, 1963); M. J. Apter, *Cybernetics and Development* (Oxford: Pergamon, 1966); H. T. Milhorn, Jr., *The Application of Control Theory to Physiological Systems* (Philadelphia: Saunders, 1966); J. G. March and H. A. Simon, *Organizations* (New York: Wiley, 1958); J. Milsum, ed., *Positive Feedback; A General Systems Approach to Positive/Negative Feedback and Mutual Causality* (New York: Pergamon, 1968); J. Bowlby, "A Control Systems Approach to Attachment Behaviour," in *Attachment and Loss,* vol. I (New York: Basic Books, 1969); R. Rosen, *Dynamical Systems Theory in Biology* (New York: Wiley, 1970); R. L. Ackoff and F. E. Emery, *On Purposeful Systems* (Chicago: Aldine, 1972); M. A. Arbib, *The Metaphorical Brain: An Introduction to Cybernetics as Artificial Intelligence and Brain Theory* (New York: Wiley, 1972); G. J. Kliv, ed., *Trends in General Systems Theory* (New York: Wiley, 1972); R. Parkman, *The Cybernetic Society* (New York: Pergamon, 1972); E. Laszlo, "The Meaning and Significance of General System Theory," *Behavioral Science* 20(1975): 9–24; G. Pask, *The Cybernetics of Human Learning and Performance: A Guide to Theory and Research* (London: Hutchinson, 1975); R. Trappl et al., eds., *Progress in Cybernetics and Systems Research,* 6 vols. (Washington, D.C.: Hemisphere 1975); J. D. Sargent, "Biofeedback and Biocybernetics," in *Proceedings of the San Diego Biomedical Symposium,* ed. J. I. Martin (New York: Academic Press, 1976); F. H. George, *Cybernetics*

and the Environment (London: Elek, 1977); F. S. Hillier and G. Lieberman, *Operations Research*, 2d ed. (San Francisco: Holden-Day, 1977); Miller, *Living Systems* (New York: McGraw-Hill, 1978); Powers, "Quantitative Analysis of Purposive Systems"; F. Miles and E. Evarts, "Concepts of Motor Organization," *Annual Review of Psychology* 30(1979): 327–62; M. Rodin et al., "Systems Theory in Anthropology," *Current Anthropology* 19(1978): 747–62; H. A. Simon, "Information Processing Models of Cognition," *Annual Review of Psychology* 30(1979): 363–96, and *Models of Thought* (New Haven: Yale University Press, 1979). See also the journals *Biological Cybernetics* and IEEE *Transactions on Systems Analysis and Man.* **[23]**

28. In addition to such other recent converts as ethologist Konrad Lorenz and psychologists Roger Brown and Richard Herrnstein, Talcott Parsons has quietly shifted his position and now utilizes the cybernetic model, see *Societies: Evolutionary and Comparative Perspectives* (Englewood Cliffs, N.J.: Prentice-Hall, 1966).

29. R. Michels, *Political Parties*, trans. E. Paul and C. Paul (New York: Free Press, 1949 [1911]), p. 25.

30. G. Mosca, *The Ruling Class*, trans. H. D. Kahn (New York: McGraw-Hill, 1939 [1896]), p. 53.

31. H. Ziegler and T. H. Dye, "Editors' Note," *American Behavioral Scientist* 13(1969): 167.

32. G. Simmel, "The Number of Members as Determining the Sociological Form of the Group," *American Journal of Sociology* 8(1902): 1–46, 158–96.

33. A classic statement of the key role of information in evolutionary processes is E. Schrödinger, *What Is Life?* (New York: Cambridge University Press, 1944). A recent detailed and multilevel treatment is Miller, *Living Systems.* **[27]**

34. For an excellent brief review of social communications, see E. O. Wilson, *Sociobiology: The New Synthesis* (Cambridge, Mass.: Harvard University Press, 1975); also C. R. Darwin, *The Expression of the Emotions in Man and Animals* (Chicago: University of Chicago Press, 1965 [1873]); H. Frings and M. Frings, *Animal Communication*, 2d ed. (Norman, Okla.: University of Oklahoma Press, 1977 [1964]).

35. See K. von Frisch, *The Dance Language and Orientation of Bees*, trans. L. Chadwick (Cambridge, Mass.: Harvard University Press, 1967); J. L. Gould, "Honeybee Recruitment: The Dance-Language Controversy," *Science* 189(1975): 685–93, "The Dance-Language Controversy," *Quarterly Review of Biology* 51(1976): 211–44, "Behavioral Programming in Honeybees," *Behavioral and Brain Sciences* 4(1978): 572–73, and "Sun Compensation by Bees," *Science* 207(1980): 545–47; M. L. Brines and J. L. Gould, "Bees Have Rules," *Science* 206(1979): 571–73.

36. For primates, see especially J. Bastian, "Primate Signaling Systems and Human Languages," and P. Marler, "Communication in Monkeys and Apes," both in *Primate Behavior*, ed. I. DeVore (New York: Holt, 1965); H. Kummer, *Social Organization of Hamadryas Baboons; A Field Study* (New York: Karger, 1968); J. B. Lancaster, "Primate Communication Systems and the Emergence of Human Language," in *Primates*, ed. P. C. Jay (New York: Holt, 1968); J. van Lawick-Goodall, *In the Shadow of Man* (Boston: Houghton Mifflin, 1971); E. W. Menzell, Jr., "Communication About the Environment in a Group of Young Chimpanzees," *Folia Primatologica* 15(1971): 220–32; R. A. Hinde, ed., *Non-Verbal Communication* (London: Cambridge University Press, 1972), and *Biological Bases of Human Social Behavior* (New York: McGraw-Hill, 1974); M. von Cranach and I. Vine, *Social Communication and Movement: Studies of Interaction and Expression in Man and Chimpanzee* (New York: Academic Press, 1973); E. W. Menzel, Jr. and S. Halperin, "Purposive Behavior as a Basis for Objective Communication Between Chimpanzees," *Science* 189(1975): 652–54; Frings and Frings, *Animal Communication;* For social carnivores, see especially D. L. Mech, *The Wolf: The Ecology and Behavior of an Endangered Species* (Garden City, N.Y.: Natural History Press, 1970); Hinde, *Non-Verbal Com-*

munication; H. Kruuk, *The Spotted Hyena: A Study of Predation and Social Behavior* (Chicago: University of Chicago Press, 1972); G. B. Schaller, *The Serengeti Lion: A Study of Predator-Prey Relations* (Chicago: University of Chicago Press, 1972); R. L. Hall and H. S. Sharp, eds., *Wolf and Man: Evolution in Parallel* (New York: Academic Press, 1978). The literature on human communications is of course vast. A few of the landmarks are N. Wiener, *Cybernetics* (New York: Wiley, 1948); J. Ruesch and G. Bateson, *Communication: The Social Matrix of Psychiatry* (New York: W. W. Norton, 1951); W. Jackson, ed., *Communications Theory* (London: Butterworths, 1953); H. Quastler, ed., *Information Theory in Psychology: Problems and Methods* (Glencoe, Ill.: Free Press, 1955); L. Brillouin, *Science and Information Theory* (New York: Academic Press, 1956); C. Cherry, ed., *Information Theory* (New York: Academic Press, 1956); Deutsch, *Nerves of Government;* R. R. Fagen, *Politics and Communication* (Boston: Little, Brown 1966); C. R. Dechert, ed., *The Social Impact of Cybernetics* (Notre Dame, Ind.: University of Notre Dame Press, 1966); D. M. MacKay, *Information, Mechanism, and Meaning* (Cambridge, Mass.: MIT Press, 1969); S. Harnad et al., eds., *Origins and Evolution of Language and Speech* (New York: New York Academy of Sciences, 1976); Miller, *Living Systems.* **[5, 27, 34]**

37. For historical overviews in a world perspective, see N. Cohn, *The Pursuit of the Millennium: Revolutionary Millenarians and Mystical Anarchism of the Middle Ages* (New York: Oxford University Press, 1970) and E. Tuveson, *Millennium and Utopia: A Study in the Background of the Idea of Progress* (Berkeley: University of California Press, 1949). For a U.S. perspective, see M. Holloway, *Heavens on Earth: Utopian Communities in America, 1680–1880* (New York: Dover, 1966 [1951]); C. Nordhoff, *The Communistic Societies of the United States* (New York: Schocken, 1965 [1875]); W. Hinds, *American Communities and Co-Operative Colonies* (Philadelphia: Porcupine, 1974 [1908]); and R. S. Fogarty, *American Utopianism* (Itasca, Ill.: Peacock, 1977). Among the classic analyses, see L. Mumford, *The Story of Utopias* (New York: Boni and Liveright, 1923); M. Buber, *Paths in Utopia,* trans. R. F. C. Hull (London: Routledge & Kegan Paul, 1949); G. Negley and J. M. Patrick, *The Quest for Utopia* (New York: H. Schuman, 1952); and P. Goodman and P. Goodman, *Communitas: Means of Livelihood and Ways of Life,* 2d ed. (New York: Vintage, 1960). Two detailed sociological studies are H. F. Infield, *Utopia and Experiment: Essays in the Sociology of Cooperation* (New York: Praeger, 1955) and R. M. Kanter, *Commitment and Community: Communes and Utopias in Sociological Perspective* (Cambridge, Mass.: Harvard University Press, 1972).

38. Infield, *Utopia and Experiment.* **[37]**

39. See especially the bibliography in R. S. Fogarty, *Dictionary of American Communal and Utopian History* (Westport, Conn.: Greenwood, 1980).

40. K. Newman, "Incipient Bureaucracy: The Development of Hierarchies in Egalitarian Organizations," in *Hierarchy & Society,* ed. G. M. Britan and R. Cohen (Philadelphia: ISHI, 1980).

41. See W. Ouchi, *Theory Z* (Reading, Mass.: Addison-Wesley, 1981); E. Vogel, *Japan as Number 1* (Cambridge, Mass.: Harvard University Press, 1979); R. T. Pascale and A. G. Athos, *The Art of Japanese Management* (New York: Simon and Schuster, 1981).

42. As H. A. Simon, *Administrative Behavior* (New York: Macmillan, 1947), and *Models of Man: Social and Rational* (New York: Wiley, 1957), C. E. Lindblom, "The Science of 'Muddling Through,' " *Public Administration Review* 19(1959): 79–88, and others have long argued.

43. S. P. Huntington and J. I. Dominguez, "Political Development," in *Handbook of Political Science,* vol. III, ed. N. Polsby and F. I. Greenstein (Reading, Mass.: Addison-Wesley, 1975).

44. R. Naroll and L. von Bertalanffy, "The Principle of Allometry in Biology and the Social Sciences," *General Systems, Yearbook of the Society for the Advancement of General Systems Theory* 1(1956): 76–89.

45. For examples, see A. Etzioni, *A Comparative Analysis of Complex Organizations: On Power, Involvement, and Their Correlates* (New York: Free Press, 1961); S. N. Eisenstadt, "Social

Change, Differentiation and Evolution," *American Sociological Review* 29(1964): 375–86, and "Social Evolution," in *International Encyclopedia of the Social Sciences,* vol. V, ed. D. L. Sills (New York: Macmillan, 1968); Parsons, *Societies;* P. R. Lawrence and J. W. Lorsch, *Organization and Environment: Managing Differentiation and Integration* (Boston: Harvard Graduate School of Business Administration, 1967); P. M. Blau and R. A. Schoenherr, *The Structure of Organizations* (New York: Basic Books, 1971); J. E. Haas and T. E. Drabek, *Complex Organizations: A Sociological Perspective* (New York: Macmillan, 1973); R. H. Hall, *Organizations: Structure and Process,* 2d ed. (Englewood Cliffs, N.J.: Prentice-Hall, 1977). **[28]**

46. For a major attempt to sort out and reconcile these studies, see D. F. Gillespie and D. S. Mileti, "A Refined Model of Differentiation in Organizations," *Sociology and Social Research* 60(1976): 263–78.

47. J. Hage, "An Axiomatic Theory of Organizations," *Administrative Science Quarterly* 10(1965): 289–320.

48. Hall, *Organizations,* p. 135. **[45]**

49. H. Spencer, *Principles of Sociology,* vol. 1, p. 572.

50. For a comparison between Durkheim's and Spencer's sociology, see P. A. Corning, "Durkheim and Spencer," *British Journal of Sociology* 33(1982): 359–82.

51. See the reviews in Gillespie and Mileti, "Refined Model of Differentiation"; D. S. Mileti et al., "Size and Structure in Complex Organizations," *Social Forces* 56(1977): 208–17. **[46]**

52. P. M. Blau, "A Formal Theory of Differentiation in Organizations," *American Sociological Review* 35(1970): 201–18; Blau and Schoenherr, *Structure of Organizations.* **[45]**

53. Blau and Schoenherr, *Structure of Organizations,* p. 20. **[45]**

54. Mileti, "Size and Structure in Organizations." See also the various contributions of H. P. Hummon, "A Mathematical Theory of Differentiation in Organizations," *American Sociological Review* 86(1971): 297–303; G. E. Hendershot and T. F. James, "Size and Growth as Determinants of Administrative-Production Ratios in Organizations," *American Sociological Review* 37(1972): 149–53; S. R. Klatsky, "Relationship of Organizational Size to Complexity and Coordination," *Administrative Science Quarterly* 15(1970): 428–38; B. H. Mayhew et al., "System Size and Structural Differentiation in Formal Organizations: A Baseline Generator for Two Major Theoretical Propositions," *American Sociological Review* 37(1972): 629–33. **[51]**

55. E.g., F. Terrien and D. L. Mills, "The Effect of Changing Size upon the Internal Structure of Organizations," *American Sociological Review* 20(1955): 11–13 (428 local school districts); A. Hawley et al., "Population Size and Administration in Institutions of Higher Education," *American Sociological Review* 30(1965): 252–55 (97 colleges and universities); E. E. Raphael, "The Anderson-Warkov Hypothesis in Local Unions: A Comparative Study," *American Sociological Review* 32(1967): 768–76 (65 union locals); G. W. Childers et al., "System Size and Structural Differentiation in Military Organizations: Testing a Baseline Model of the Division of Labor," *American Journal of Sociology* 76(1971): 813–30 (37 military units); T. R. Anderson and S. Warkov, "Organizational Size and Functional Complexity: A Study of Administration in Hospitals," *American Sociological Review* 26(1961): 23–28 (49 hospitals); J. M. A. Woodward, *Industrial Organization: Theory and Practice* (London: Oxford University Press, 1965); and Lawrence and Lorsch, *Organization and Environment* (a total of 225 business firms). **[45]**

56. Childers, "System Size in Military Organizations." **[55]**

57. P. M. Blau, "Interdependence and Hierarchy in Organizations," *Social Science Research* 1(1972): 1–24.

58. Mileti, "Size and Structure in Organizations." See also the critique by M. W. Meyer, "Some Constraints in Analyzing Data on Organizational Structures: A Comment on Blau's Paper," *American Sociological Review* 36(1971): 294–97. **[57]**

59. Lawrence and Lorsch, *Organization and Environment.* See also C. A. Perrow, "A Framework for the Comparative Analysis of Organizations," *American Sociological Review* 32(1967):

194–208, and *Organizational Analysis: A Sociological View* (Belmont, Calif.: Wadsworth, 1970); Haas and Drabek, *Complex Organizations;* Hall, *Organizations;* M. Zey-Ferrell, *Dimensions of Organizations: Environment, Context, Structure, Process, and Performance* (Santa Monica, Calif.: Goodyear, 1979).

60. M. Crozier, *The Bureaucratic Phenomenon* (Chicago: University of Chicago Press, 1964).

61. For overviews, see Hass and Drabek, *Complex Organizations;* Hall, *Organizations;* Zey-Ferrell, *Dimensions of Organizations.* **[45, 59]**

62. E.g., Hawley, "Population Size"; Terrien and Mills, "Effect of Changing Size"; E. B. Haas et al., "The Size of the Supportive Component in Organizations: A Multiorganizational Analysis," *Social Forces* 42(1963): 9–17; Blau and Schoenherr, *Structure of Organizations.* **[55]**

63. Anderson and Warkov, "Organizational Size." **[55]**

64. Raphael, "Anderson-Warkov Hypothesis." **[55]**

65. G. Mosca, *The Ruling Class* (New York: McGraw-Hill, 1939 [1896]); Blau, "Formal Theory of Differentiation." See also Klatsky, "Relationship of Size to Complexity"; Blau, "Interdependence and Hierarchy"; Blau and Schoenherr, *Structure of Organizations;* Hendershot and James, "Size and Growth." **[45, 52, 54, 57]**

66. G. C. Theodoridis and L. Stark, "Information as a Quantitative Criterion of Biospheric Evolution," *Nature* 224(1969): 860–63.

67. Simmel, "Number of Members Determining Form of the Group." **[32]**

68. R. Thom, *Structural Stability and Morphogenesis: An Outline of a General Theory of Models* (Reading, Mass.: Benjamin, 1975); E. C. Zeeman, "Catastrophe Theory," *Scientific American* 234, 4(1976): 65–83; P. T. Saunders, *An Introduction to Catastrophe Theory* (New York: Cambridge University Press, 1980).

69. See especially the reviews in M. S. Olmsted, *The Small Group* (New York: Random House, 1959); E. J. Thomas and C. F. Fink, "Effects of Group Size," *Psychological Bulletin* 60(1963): 371–84; A. P. Hare and R. F. Bales, *Small Groups: Studies in Social Interaction* (New York: Knopf, 1965); A. F. Bales and E. F. Borgatta, "Size of Group as a Factor in the Interaction Profile," in *Small Groups;* D. Cartwright and A. Zander, *Group Dynamics: Research and Theory,* 3rd ed. (New York: Harper & Row, 1968); J. B. Kadane and G. H. Lewis, "The Distribution of Participation in Group Discussions—Empirical and Theoretical Reappraisal," *American Sociological Review* 34(1969): 710–23; B. A. Fisher, *Small Group Decision Making: Communication and the Group Process* (New York: McGraw-Hill, 1974); A. P. Hare, *Handbook of Small Group Research,* 2d ed. (New York: Free Press, 1976 [1962]); A. F. Zander, *Motives and Goals in Groups* (New York: Academic Press, 1971).

70. K. Krippendorff, "Communication and the Genesis of Structure," *General Systems* 16(1971): 171.

71. B. H. Mayhew et al., "Behavior of Interaction Systems Mathematical Models of Structure in Interaction Sequence," *General Systems* 16(1971): 13–29.

72. D. E. Broadbent, *Decision and Stress* (New York: Academic Press, 1971); P. H. Lindsay and D. A. Norman, *Human Information Processing: An Introduction to Psychology* (New York: Academic Press, 1972); G. A. Miller, "The Magical Number Seven, Plus or Minus Two: Some Limits to Our Capacity for Processing Information," *Psychological Review* 63(1956): 81–97; Quastler, *Information Theory.*

73. B. H. Mayhew and R. L. Levinger, "Size and the Density of Interaction in Human Aggregates," *American Journal of Sociology* 82(1976): 86–110.

74. C. E. Shannon, "A Mathematical Theory of Communication," *Bell System Technical Journal* 27(1948): 379–423, 623–56.

75. D. E. Apter, *Politics of Modernization* (Chicago: University of Chicago Press, 1965). For supporting evidence, see the crosscultural study by R. Wirsing, "Political Power and Information: A Cross-Cultural Study," *American Anthropologist* 75(1973): 153–70. There is also an

extensive literature on the role of communications in macro-level political development, see especially K. W. Deutsch, "Social Mobilization and Political Development," *American Political Science Review* 55(1961): 493–574, and *Nerves of Government;* L. W. Pye, ed., *Communication and Political Development* (Princeton: Princeton University Press, 1963); G. A. Almond and G. B. Powell, Jr., *Comparative Politics: A Developmental Approach* (Boston: Little, Brown 1966); Fagen, *Politics and Communication;* D. J. McCrone and C. F. Cnudde, "Towards a Communications Theory of Democratic Political Development: A Causal Model," *American Political Science Review* 61(1967): 72–79.

76. K. V. Flannery, "The Cultural Evolution of Civilizations," *Annual Review of Ecology and Systematics* 3(1972): 399–426 (actually derived from E. R. Service, *Primitive Social Organization: An Evolutionary Perspective* [New York: Random House, 1962]).

77. For example, E. R. Service, *Origins of the State and Civilization: The Process of Cultural Evolution* (New York: W. W. Norton, 1975), p. 303; M. Blute, "Sociocultural Evolutionism: An Untried Theory," *Behavioral Science* 24(1979): 46–59; M. Granovetter, "The Idea of 'Advancement' in Theories of Social Evolution and Development," *American Journal of Sociology* 85(1979): 489–515.

78. G. E. Lenski, *Human Societies: A Macrolevel Introduction to Sociology* (New York: McGraw-Hill, 1970) (after W. Goldschmidt, *Man's Way: A Preface to the Understanding of Human Society* [New York: Holt, 1959]).

79. Lenski, *Human Societies,* p. 130.

80. R. L. Carneiro, "The Chiefdom"; H. T. Wright and G. A. Johnson, "Population, Exchange, and Early State Formation in Southwestern Iran," *American Anthropologist* 77(1975): 267–89; see also H. T. Wright, "Recent Research on the Origin of the State," *Annual Review of Anthropology* 6(1977): 379–97, and "Toward an Explanation of the Origin of the State," in Cohen and Service, *Origins of the State.* (Philadelphia: ISHI, 1978).

81. R. Naroll, "Galton's Problem and HRAFLIB," *Behavior Science Research* 2(1976): 131.

82. Ibid.

83. Ibid.

84. H. E. Driver, "Geographical-Historical Versus Psycho-Functional Explanations of Kin Avoidance," *Current Anthropology* 7(1966): 131–82.

85. E. Durkheim, *Suicide,* trans. J. A. Spaulding and G. Simpson (Glencoe, Ill.: Free Press, 1951 [1897]).

86. R. Naroll, "A Preliminary Index of Social Development," *American Anthropologist* 58(1956): 702. The formula Naroll developed was: $\log P = 4 \log C = 6 \log (T/2)$, where $P =$ population size, $C =$ crafts specializations, and $T =$ number of team types.

87. Cf. Naroll, "Galton's Problem." **[81]**

88. R. L. Carneiro, "On the Relationship Between Size of Population and Complexity of Social Organization," *Southwestern Journal of Anthropology* 23(1967): 238.

89. G. K. Zipf, *Human Behaviour and the Principle of Least Effort: An Introduction to Human Ecology* (Cambridge, Mass.: Addison-Wesley, 1949), p. 376.

90. R. L. Carneiro, "Scale Analysis, Evolutionary Sequences, and the Rating of Cultures," in Naroll and Cohen, *Handbook of Cultural Anthropology.*

91. Wirsing, "Political Power." **[75]**

92. C. W. McNett, Jr., "A Settlement Pattern Scale of Cultural Complexity," in Naroll and Cohen, *Handbook of Cultural Anthropology,* "A Cross-Cultural Method for Predicting Nonmaterial Traits in Archeology," *Behavior Science Notes* 5(1970): 195–212, and "Factor Analysis of a Cross-Cultural Sample," *Behavior Science Notes* 8(1973): 233–57. **[90]**

93. A. Lomax and N. Berkowitz, "The Evolutionary Taxonomy of Culture," *Science* 177(1972): 228–39.

94. R. D. Schwartz and J. C. Miller, "Legal Evolution and Societal Complexity," in *Readings*

in *Social Evolution and Development,* ed. S. N. Eisenstadt (London: Pergamon, 1970); H. Wimberley, "Legal Evolution: One Further Step," *American Journal of Sociology* 79(1973): 78–83.

95. A. Tuden and C. Marshall, "Political Organization," *Ethnology* 11(1972): 436–64.

96. Carneiro, "Relationship Between Size and Complexity," and "Scale Analysis." **[88, 90]**

97. K. Otterbein, *The Evolution of War* (New Haven: HRAF Press, 1970).

98. R. Naroll, "What Have We Learned from Cross-Cultural Surveys?" *American Anthropologist* 72(1970): 1227–88.

99. B. M. Russett, *Trends in World Politics* (New York: Macmillan, 1965).

100. Almond and Powell, *Comparative Politics,* p. 300. **[75]**

101. D. R. Cameron, "The Expansion of the Public Economy," *American Political Science Review* 72(1978); 1243–61.

102. D. Black, *The Behavior of Law* (New York: Academic Press, 1976).

103. R. A. Dahl and E. R. Tufte, *Size and Democracy* (Stanford: Stanford University Press, 1973), p. 40.

104. J. Langrish et al., *Wealth from Knowledge: A Study of Innovation in Industry* (New York: Wiley, 1972). Other relevant works are H. G. Barnett, *Innovation: The Basis of Cultural Change* (New York: McGraw-Hill, 1953); F. Barth, ed., *The Role of the Entrepreneur in the Social Change in Northern Norway* (Bergen: Scandinavian University Books, 1972 [1963]); W. Goldschmidt, "The Operations of a Sebei Capitalist: A Contribution to Economic Anthropology," *Ethnology* 11(1972): 187–201; A. Strathern, "The Entrepreneurial Model of Social Change: From Norway to New Guinea," *Ethnology* 11(1972): 368–79; M. Weber, *Economy and Society: An Outline of Interpretive Sociology,* trans. E. Foschoff et al. (New York: Bedminster, 1968 [1922]).

105. See M. Gluckman, "The Kingdom of the Zulu of South Africa," in *African Political Systems,* ed. M. Fortes and E. E. Evans-Pritchard (London: Oxford University Press, 1940), and "The Rise of a Zulu Empire," *Scientific American* 202(1969): 157–68; D. R. Morris, *The Washing of Spears* (New York: Simon & Schuster, 1965).

106. R. L. Carneiro, "A Theory of the Origin of the State," *Science* 169(1970): 733–38.

107. R. A. Hackenberg, "Economic Alternatives in Arid Lands: A Case Study of the Pima and Papago Indians," *Ethnology* 1(1962): 186–95.

108. S. C. Oliver, "Ecology and Cultural Continuity as Contributing Factors in the Social Organization of the Plains Indians," in *Man in Adaptation: The Cultural Present,* ed. Y. A. Cohen (Chicago: Aldine, 1974 [1962]).

109. J. H. Steward, *Theory of Culture Change: The Methodology of Multilinear Evolution* (Urbana: University of Illinois Press, 1955).

110. See Aristotle's *The Politics,* book I. For more recent discussions, see especially V. G. Childe, *Man Makes Himself* (New York: New American Library, 1951 [1936]); K. Wittfogel, *Oriental Despotism: A Comparative Study of Total Power* (New Haven: Yale University Press, 1957); R. McC. Adams, *The Evolution of Urban Society: Early Mesopotamia and Prehispanic Mexico* (Chicago: Aldine, 1966); Carneiro, "Theory of Origin of the State"; Service, *Origins of the State;* Wright, "Recent Research on Origin of State"; H. J. M. Claessen and P. Skalník, eds., *The Early State* (The Hague: Mouton, 1978); Cohen and Service, *Origins of the State;* G. D. Jones and R. R. Kautz, eds., *The Transition to Statehood in the New World* (Cambridge: Cambridge University Press, 1981); C. S. Phillips, "The Origin of the State: Fortuitous or Evolutionary?" prepared for the annual meeting, American Political Science Association, 1981; F. H. Willhoite, Jr., "Political Origins and Legitimacy," unpublished, 1982. **[77, 80, 107]**

111. Cohen and Service, *Origins of the State.* **[80]**

112. T. Hobbes, *Leviathan: On the Matter, Forme and Power of a Commonwealth Ecclesiasticall and Civil* (New York: Collier, 1962 [1651]).

113. L. H. Morgan, *Ancient Society* (Cambridge, Mass.: Harvard University Press, 1964 [1877]).

114. M. H. Fried, *The Evolution of Political Society* (New York: Random House, 1967).

115. R. D. Alexander, *Darwinism and Human Affairs* (Seattle: University of Washington Press, 1979); F. H. Willhoite, Jr., "Reciprocity, Political Origins, and Legitimacy," prepared for the annual meeting, American Political Science Association, 1980, and "Political Origins and Legitimacy"; R. Pitt, "Warfare and Hominid Brain Evolution," *Journal of Theoretical Biology* 72(1978): 551–75; J. M. Strate, "The Sovereign as Protector: The Functional Priority of Defense," prepared for the annual meeting, American Political Science Association, 1981. For earlier versions of this approach, see A. Keith, *A New Theory of Human Evolution* (New York: Philosophical Library, 1949); R. Ardrey, *The Territorial Imperative* (New York: Atheneum, 1966); R. Bigelow, *The Dawn Warriors: Man's Evolution Toward Peace* (Boston: Little, Brown, 1969).

116. Willhoite, "Political Origins and Legitimacy," p. 26. **[116]**

117. Carneiro, "Theory of Origin of the State." **[107]**

118. Childe, *Man Makes Himself.* **[111]**

119. E.g., China. See J. Gernet, *Ancient China, From the Beginnings to the Empire,* trans. R. Rudorff (Berkeley: University of California Press, 1968).

120. R. McC. Adams, "The Origin of Cities," *Scientific American* 203, 3(1960): 153–68, and *Evolution of Urban Society;* S. C. Malik, *Indian Civilization: The Formative Period* (Simla: Indian Institute of Advanced Study, 1968); W. T. Sanders, "Hydraulic Agriculture, Economic Symbiosis and the Evolution of States in Central Mexico," in *Anthropological Archaeology in the Americas,* ed. B. J. Meggars (Washington, D.C.: Anthropological Society of Washington, 1968); Flannery, "Cultural Evolution of Civilizations"; E. Hunt and R. Hunt, "Irrigation, Conflict, and Politics" in *Irrigation's Impact on Society,* ed. T. E. Downing and McG. Gibson (Tucson: University of Arizona Press, 1974); R. C. Hunt and E. Hunt, "Canal Irrigation and Local Social Organization," *Current Anthropology* 17(1976): 389–411; Service, *Origins of the State.* **[76, 77]**

121. Gernet, *Ancient China;* O. Lattimore, *Inner Asian Frontiers of China* (Boston: Beacon Press, 1940). **[120]**

122. Carneiro, "Theory of Origin of the State," p. 734. **[107]**

123. Claessen and Skalnik, *Early State.* **[111]**

124. E. Boserup, *The Conditions of Agricultural Growth: The Economics of Agrarian Change Under Population Pressure* (Chicago: Aldine, 1965); D. E. Dumond, "Population Growth and Cultural Change," *Southwestern Journal of Anthropology* 21(1965): 302–24; C. Geertz, *Agricultural Involution: Process of Ecological Change in Indonesia* (Berkeley: University of California Press, 1963).

125. G. T. Hunt, *The Wars of the Iroquois: A Study in Intertribal Relations* (Madison: University of Wisconsin Press, 1940).

126. E. Brumfiel, "Regional Growth in the Eastern Valley of Mexico: A Test of the 'Population Pressure' Hypothesis," in *The Early Mesoamerican Village,* ed. K. V. Flannery (New York: Academic Press, 1976); R. Cohen, "Introduction" and "State Foundations: A Controlled Comparison," both in Cohen and Service, *Origins of the State,* and "State Origins: A Reappraisal," in Claessen and Skalnik, *Early State.*

127. Carneiro, "Theory of the Origin of State," and "The Chiefdom: Precursor of the State." **[80, 107]**

128. See E. P. Lanning, *Peru Before the Incas* (Englewood Cliffs, N.J.: Prentice-Hall, 1967); Sanders, "Hydraulic Agriculture"; Service, *Origins of the State;* P. Farb, *Man's Rise to Civilization: As Shown by the Indians of North America from Primeval Times to the Coming of the Industrial State* (New York: Dutton, 1968); Y. A. Cohen, *Man in Adaptation,* 3 vols, 2d ed. (Chicago: Aldine, 1974 [1968]); Wright and Johnson, "Population and Early State Formation";

Brumfiel, "Regional Growth in Mexico"; J. N. Hill, ed., *Explanation of Prehistoric Change* (Albuquerque: University of New Mexico Press, 1977); M. E. Odell, "Exchange and the Emergence of Unification in the Central Andes," *Anthropology* 1(1977): 50–64; J. E. Pfeiffer, *The Emergence of Society: A Pre-history of the Establishment* (New York: McGraw-Hill, 1977); Cohen and Service, *Origins of the State;* Jones and Kautz, *Transition to Statehood.* **[77, 80, 111, 121]**

129. See the cases cited in Service, *Origins of the State;* and the case studies assembled in Cohen and Service, *Origins of the State.* Also see Sander's study of Teotihuacán, "Hydraulic Agriculture." **[77, 80, 121]**

130. Service, *Origins of the State;* R. F. Stevensen, *Population and Political Systems in Tropical Africa* (New York: Columbia University Press, 1968). **[77]**

131. Adams, *Evolution of Urban Society.* **[121]**

132. W. T. Sanders and B. J. Price, *Mesoamerica: The Evolution of a Civilization* (New York: Random House, 1968); Service, *Origins of the State.* **[77]**

133. Adams, *Evolution of Urban Society.* **[121]**

134. Wright, "Research on the Origin of the State," and "An Explanation of the Origin of the State"; Cohen, "Introduction," "State Foundations," and "State Origins."

135. Cohen, "State Origins," p. 32. **[111]**

136. Cohen, "Introduction," and "State Foundations"; Service, *Origins of the State.* **[77, 80]**

137. Carneiro, "The Chiefdom," p. 63. **[80]**

138. See especially, S. N. Eisenstadt, *The Political Systems of Empires* (New York: Free Press, 1963), and "Breakdowns of Modernization," *Economic Development and Cultural Change* 12(1964): 345–67; R. G. Wesson, *The Imperial Order* (Berkeley: University of California Press, 1967); R. Taagepera, "Growth Curves of Empires," *General Systems* 13(1968): 171–75, "Size and Duration of Empires: Systematics of Size," *Social Science Research* 7(1978): 108–27, "Size and Duration of Empires: Growth-Decline Curves, 3000 to 600 B.C.," *Social Science Research* 7(1978): 180–96, "Size and Duration of Empires: Growth-Decline Curves, 600 B.C. to 600 A.D.," *Social Science History* 3(1979): 115–138, and "Growth-Decline Curves of Empires: Some Regularities," prepared for the annual meeting, International Studies Association, 1981.

139. M. Rostovtzeff, *The Social and Economic History of the Roman Empire* (Oxford: Clarendon Press, 1957); C. Clark, *Population Growth and Land Use* (New York: St. Martin's, 1967); J. Vogt, *The Decline of Rome* (New York: New American Library, 1967); S. Perowne, *Death of the Roman Republic: From 146 B.C. to Birth of the Roman Empire* (New York: Doubleday, 1968); R. Seager, *The Crisis of the Roman Republic, Studies in Political and Social History* (Cambridge, Mass.: Heffer, 1969); D. R. Dudley, *The Romans: 850 B.C.–A.D. 337* (New York: Knopf, 1970); K. D. White, *Aspects of Greek and Roman Life; Roman Farming* (Ithaca, N.Y.: Cornell University Press, 1970); P. A. Brunt, *Italian Manpower 225 B.C.–A.D. 14* (Oxford: Oxford University Press, 1971), and *Social Conflicts in the Roman Republic* (New York: Norton, 1971); M. I. Finley, *The Ancient Economy* (Berkeley: University of California Press, 1973); R. Duncan-Jones, *The Economy of the Roman Empire: Quantitative Studies* (Cambridge: Cambridge University Press, 1974); E. S. Gruen, *The Last Generation of the Roman Republic* (Berkeley: University of California Press, 1974); F. A. Hooper, *Roman Realities* (Detroit: Wayne State University Press, 1978).

140. P. A. Sorokin, *Social and Cultural Dynamics,* 4 vols. (New York: American Book Co., 1937), 3: 414–17.

141. A. H. M. Jones, "The Decline and Fall of the Roman Empire," *History* 40(1955): 226.

142. E.g., Sorokin, *Social and Cultural Dynamics;* Andreski, *Military Organization.* **[141]**

143. D. F. Doran and W. Parsons, "War and the Cycle of Relative Power," *American Political Science Review* 74(1980): 947–65.

144. See E. P. Eckholm, *Losing Ground: Environmental Stress and World Food Prospects* (New York: Norton, 1976).

145. Q. Wright, *A Study of War,* 2d ed. (Chicago: University of Chicago Press, 1965 [1942]); Sorokin, *Social and Cultural Dynamics;* P. A. Calvert, *A Study of Revolution* (Oxford: Clarendon Press, 1970); T. R. Gurr, "Persistence and Change in Political Systems, 1800–1971," *American Political Science Review* 58(1974): 1482–1504.

146. See especially, Sorokin, *Social and Cultural Dynamics;* Wright, *A Study of War;* Andreski, *Military Organization;* L. Richardson, *Statistics of Deadly Quarrels* (Pittsburgh: Boxwood, 1960); J. D. Carthy and F. J. Ebling, *The Natural History of Aggression* (New York: Academic Press, 1964); L. Bramson and G. W. Goethels, eds., *War* (New York: Basic Books, 1968); M. Fried et al., *War* (Garden City, N.Y.: Natural History Press, 1968); J. U. Nef, *War and Human Progress* (New York: Norton, 1968 [1950]); A. Storr, *Human Aggression;* J. D. Singer, *The Wages of War 1816–1965* (New York: Wiley, 1972); R. Rummel and R. Tauter, *Dimensions of Conflict Behavior* (Ann Arbor: Inter-University Consortium for Political Research, 1971); R. J. Rummel, *Understanding Conflict and War* (Beverly Hills: Sage, 1975); N. Choucri and R. North, *Nations in Conflict* (San Francisco: Freeman, 1975); M. Midlarsky, *On War* (New York: Free Press, 1975); M. Nettleship et al., eds., *War* (Paris: Mouton, 1976); T. R. Gurr, *Handbook of Political Conflict* (New York: Free Press, 1980); C. C. Brinton, *Anatomy of Revolution* (New York: Norton, 1938); J. N. Rosenau, ed., *International Aspects of Civil Strife* (Princeton: Princeton University Press, 1964); Calvert, *Study of Revolution;* T. R. Gurr, *Why Men Rebel* (Princeton: Princeton University Press, 1970); M. Stohr, ed., *The Politics of Terror* (New York: Dekker, 1979). **[141, 143, 147]**

147. W. H. Riker and P. C. Ordeshook: *An Introduction to Positive Political Theory* (Englewood Cliffs, N.J.: Prentice-Hall, 1973), p. 35.

148. G. S. Goh, "Stability in Models of Mutualism," *American Naturalist* 113(1979): 261–75.

149. M. Olson, Jr., *The Logic of Collective Action* (Cambridge, Mass.: Harvard University Press, 1965).

150. R. Axelrod and W. D. Hamilton, "The Evolution of Cooperation," *Science* 211(1981): 1390–96.

151. E. I. Altman, *Corporate Bankruptcy in America* (Lexington, Mass.: D. C. Heath, 1971).

152. Gurr, "Persistence and Change." **[147]**

153. Taagepera, "Growth Curves of Empires." **[139]**

154. Taagepera, "Size and Duration of Empires," and "Growth-Decline Curves"; see also Eisenstadt, *Political Systems of Empires,* and "Breakdowns of Modernization"; Wesson, *Imperial Order;* Service, *Origins of the State.* **[77, 139]**

155. E.g., J. Hicks, *A Theory of Economic History* (London: Oxford University Press, 1969); K. E. Boulding, *Ecodynamics: A New Theory of Societal Evolution* (Beverly Hills, Calif.: Sage, 1978); W. H. McNeill, *The Human Condition* (Princeton: Princeton University Press, 1980); D. C. North, *Structure and Change in Economic History* (New York: Norton, 1981).

156. R. Naroll, "Imperial Cycles and World Order," *Peace Research Society (International) Papers* 7(1967): 83–101.

157. R. L. Carneiro, "Political Expansion as an Expression of the Principle of Competitive Exclusion," in Cohen and Service, *Origins of the State,* p. 219. **[80]**

158. Lumsden and Wilson, *Genes, Mind and Culture,* pp. 354, 356–57, 360.

VII. Conclusion

1. H. Brandon, "A Talk with Walter Lippmann, at 80, About This 'Minor Dark Age,'" *New York Times Magazine,* September 14, 1969, pp. 25 ff.

Index

About the Author

Peter A. Corning is one of the pioneers in applying a biological perspective to the social sciences. In addition to a B.A. from Brown University and an interdisciplinary political science Ph.D. from New York University, Dr. Corning was the recipient of a two-year NIMH postdoctoral fellowship at the Institute for Behavioral Genetics in Colorado, where he studied evolutionary biology, ethology, psychology, and behavior genetics and conducted laboratory research in the genetics of aggression. He has also taught for eight years in the multidisciplinary Human Biology Program at Stanford University, lectured in the Political Science Department there, and held research appointments in Stanford's Behavior Genetics Laboratory and Engineering-Economic Systems Department.